D1210038

THE CHOCTAW OF OKLAHOMA

by
James C Milligan
Editor
Stacy C Shepherd

H. V. Chapman & Sons
Abilene, Texas

Copyright © 2003 by Choctaw Nation of Oklahoma with the Library of Congress, Washington, D.C. All rights reserved. No part of this book may be reproduced or utilized in any form or by any Means such as: electronic, mechanical, photocopying, recording, or otherwise without written permission of the Choctaw Nation of Oklahoma. For information regarding permission write to:

Choctaw Nation
Education Dept.
Drawer 1210
Durant, Oklahoma 74702
ISBN: 0-9710250-5-3

Table of Contents

Table of Contents

Dedication

To Kory, Kody, and Kylie

ACKNOWLEDGEMENTS

Many hard-working individuals contributed to the completion of this work. Their invaluable assistance and suggestions provided encouragement and support, and their collaboration over a composition period of more than three years was of immeasurable worth.

Foremost among supporters of the project was Chief Greg Pyle. Determined to teach the importance of Choctaw ancestral heritage to the children, he continues to search for programs that benefit them culturally, socially, and economically. A true advocate of Choctaw progress, his philosophy has been "to not just follow but to make a path and leave a trail." A proud leader and admirer of his people, the Chief has been behind the history since its conception.

Equally important was the work of the Council members who approved and maintained the history from the beginning. These dedicated men and women took the time and effort to give interviews and explanations of the labors and objectives of the tribe. They are all very proud of their Choctaw culture.

The volume owes its life to Joy Culbreath, Tribal Director of Higher Education. She has been involved in every aspect of the book since the project was first suggested several years ago. Working tirelessly with the tenacity of a schoolmarm to see the project to completion, her energy and enthusiasm kept the work on schedule. Often occupied with a myriad of other programs and activities, Joy was never too busy to answer questions or give advice and make suggestions. Her organizational ability was nothing short of phenomenal. In 2002, the Oklahoma State Regents recognized Mrs. Culbreath with a special award called the "Champion of Student Success" for her work in helping educate Choctaw students in southeastern Oklahoma. She stated that "We understand education is our way up; it is freedom for our people." Her support for the book has been a great part of this campaign.

She pulled together a team of dedicated advisors and assistants that worked on the project with equal enthusiasm. Their contributions proved invaluable. Wayne Coston, Sheila Harbin, Felicia Carnes, and Linda Tyler did the miscellaneous basic tasks while Language Director Richard Adams and instructors Hannah Bryan and Lillie Roberts freely gave of their time and expertise. Working intensely on correctness and accuracy, these highly competent and motivated Choctaw linguists unselfishly and patiently explained their language and culture to a Na Hullo (white man). Charley Jones and Bertram Bobb often joined them in many of the conferences on the project. Both Choctaw historian Jones and Chaplain Bobb willingly shared their extraordinary knowledge of the Choctaw culture. The suggestions given by these two distinguished Council members were greatly valued and respected.

Richard Adams deserves special credit. He is a fine example of his people. The Choctaw are proud, quiet, and polite and have great respect for each other and God. Growing up among the Choctaw as a boy in Golden, McCurtain County, I learned to love the Choctaw and their culture, and Richard reminded me of that time.

Numerous librarians and researchers helped gather materials and allowed access to primary sources. Most important of these was Librarian John R. Lovett at the Western History Collections at the University of Oklahoma. Dr. Lovett graciously gathered documents and microfilm and allowed free use of the materials. The Western History Collection has one of the largest collections of Choctaw papers and materials in the nation.

Other sites used extensively were the Oklahoma Historical Society Archives, the Southeastern Oklahoma State University Library, Robert L. Williams Library in Durant, and the Bryan County Heritage Association archives in Calera. These were all valuable sources of books and articles. A special note of appreciation goes to Monty Olsen at the Calera Archives of the Bryan County Heritage Association for his complete collection of the past issues of *Bishinik*. This was an amazing source of materials. The collections done by the heritage group, whose major interests are in genealogy, have resulted in wonderful collections of microfilm and documents. Another helpful source was the Atoka Library whose support through materials from the interlibrary system was greatly valued. Additionally, the Mississippi Choctaw Tribal Archives at Pearl River near Philadelphia was an important source of many materials. Director Deborah Boykin and her staff of Choctaw students were quite helpful and supportive.

The Archives and Manuscripts Division of the Oklahoma Historical Society deserves credit for the photographs and illustrations contained in the work. The tribe would like to express gratitude to the Society for permission to reproduce the pictures in this volume.

Stacy Shepherd deserves special credit. Stacy is a scholar, teacher, and editor without equal. A Choctaw lady proud of her culture, she made many contributions and editorial corrections. She worked a marvel as the editor of the book.

Finally, thanks to Joseph B. Crawford II, Keith Milligan, and Judy Allen. J. B. did the original artwork and computer graphics. He is truly a wonder with the computer and art. Keith helped with the proofreading, and Judy helped by making suggestions and providing photographs and materials gathered by the newspaper for use in the book.

Acknowledgements

Choctaw history is rich and colorful. The Choctaw Nation of Oklahoma is a great society, and their people have a proud heritage. As one tribesman stated: "We are survivors. No others have overcome so much tragedy building a Nation."

Chief Gregory E. Pyle

Introduction by Chief Greg Pyle

Choctaw Heritage Days at Tvshkahomma, our tribal Capitol, Trail of Tears Walks, songs in our native language, festivals of Choctaw arts and crafts, are ways to preserve our rich culture. The Tribal Council has been supportive of our many efforts to promote the Choctaw heritage and has been behind us in every way. It is extremely important that we teach each generation about the history of the Choctaw. The legacy of Choctaw history must be shared to keep it alive. Like the Choctaw Language Program that has increased in students with Internet classes broadcast all over the world, this volume is intended to teach others to appreciate the grandeur of our traditions.

Choctaw history is a story of adversity and achievement. The tribe has lived for five centuries among the whites including the Spanish, French, British, and Colonials. Learning to survive in the white world, the Choctaw became educated Christians but were still forced by treaties to remove their families to a foreign country. In 1830, the Treaty of Dancing Rabbit Creek, the first treaty signed under the federal policy established by the Indian Removal Act, forced our ancestors to remove to a wild, unsettled, virgin country in the middle of winter. The Choctaws walked over hundreds of miles on "a long, sad march" properly called a Trail of Tears. The event brought death and disillusion, but ultimately was overcome by determination and sacrifice. The trauma of removal and the construction of new homes and farms while plagued by floods, smallpox epidemics, and Plains Indians caused more death and destruction, but the Choctaw recovered again.

Establishing a new nation in Indian Territory, the Choctaw learned to cope with white settlement. They built schools, churches, and democratic governments. They established constitutions and passed laws to preserve order, established courts, jury trials, and were the first to enact prohibition law and organize a police force called the Lighthorsemen to enforce them. The tribe recovered to establish an orderly civilized nation in the wilderness. Then, the Civil War interrupted their progress. The Nation was set back by a generation but soon recovered once more. Native preachers and teachers who aimed at reestablishment of the Nation replaced the old missionaries, Kingsbury, Copeland, and Byington, and their work prepared the tribe for statehood in 1907. The Choctaw have served with other Oklahomans in every war fought since Independence and have distinguished themselves in modern wars.

The Nation has witnessed unprecedented financial recovery in recent years because of determined policies by the administration and the Council. This economic success has allowed great social and cultural progress for our people. The policies that we develop in the present will shape the future. Our history continues to be challenges and triumphs. A number of years ago the Choctaw Nation began to publish the legends and stories of the past in order to help preserve its heritage. This volume is dedicated to that movement.

The Tribal Council and I are determined to preserve our culture and national personality. Choctaw history is derived from both oral and written sources and much of the research for this work relies upon those sources, along with oral interviews of our people. We are grateful for our ancestral sacrifices that kept the Choctaw identity alive and are determined to continue in the future so there will always be a Choctaw history.

As we are proud of our ancestors, we are committed to making history so that generations in the future will speak with pride of our efforts. Returning sovereignty to the Nation has been a goal since the 1970s, and Choctaw social and economic programs, among the best in the country, have contributed to this objective. The growth of the tribe and the financial prosperity of its people are evidence of the great economic boom we are experiencing. The Choctaw people have seen major advances in health, education, welfare, housing, and employment, and we pledge to work harder in the future. The pride in being a Choctaw is back and must be passed on to our children. It is this reason this work is such an important part of our program to preserve the history of the Choctaw.

Assistant Chief Gary Batton

Foreword

BY ASSISTANT CHIEF GARY BATTON

The Choctaw people have a rich and proud history. Like many others civilizations, our past includes painful episodes as well as great ones. As Assistant Chief of the great Choctaw Nation of Oklahoma, it is my honor to play a part, along with the Chief and Tribal Council in helping to ensure that the future of this great nation is a bright one.

Our recent history is full of pride and promise. The Nation has implemented numerous programs to help individuals with health, education, and jobs.

The Choctaw Nation was the first tribe to build its own hospital with its own funding. Community health clinics have made health care more accessible than ever before for people living in remote areas.

As a tribe, we realize that the people we educate will lead this nation tomorrow. We strive to help improve people's lives, from infant to adult. The Choctaw Nation makes great effort to find scholarships and internships for Choctaw students, preparing them for successful lives in ways that could have only been a remote dream in years past. Jones Academy, originally founded by the Choctaw Nation in 1891, not only survived a time when many Indian schools were closed, but thrives today with elementary students from many tribes attending school in a beautiful new state-of-the-art classroom building.

Several successful business ventures have made employment opportunities available in rural areas where jobs have traditionally been scarce. When health care, day care, and educational services are also available in those areas, people's lives improve dramatically. The Nation also provides ways for workers to sharpen their skills for the workforce, giving them more employment opportunities.

Culture and tradition are greatly valued by the Choctaw people. The Choctaw Language department has produced curriculum, CDs, and definers. As of this writing, 88 Choctaw Language classes per day are being taught via interactive TV.

Thank you for your interest in both the history and the future of the Choctaw Nation of Oklahoma.

Tribal Council

Hap Ward - District 1

Mike Amos - District 2

Tribal Council

Kenny Bryant - District 3

Delton Cox - District 4

Tribal Council

Charlotte Jackson - District 5

Joe Coley - District 6

Tribal Council

Jack Austin - District 7

Perry Thompson - District 8

Tribal Council

Ted Dosh - District 9

Anthony Dillard - District 10

Tribal Council

Bob Pate - District 11

James Frazier - District 12

CHAPTA ACHVFFA

~ CHAPTER ONE ~

"THE PEOPLE OF CHAHTA"

Chapter One

Burial mound civilizations first appeared in the southeastern regions of North America about 1000 B.C. and developed in Mississippi among the Choctaw around 700 A.D. Most numerous of the Muskogean speaking tribes (Chickasaw, Creek, and Seminole), the Choctaw based an agricultural society upon the farming of corn supplemented by hunting for deer and wild game. Living in villages and cultivating food for themselves and for trade with the Chickasaw, their northern relatives, the tribe lived peaceful, rural lives with a culture similar to the Europeans who arrived in 1540.[1]

The tribe migrated from Siberia across the Bering Strait to Alaska over generations and then spread southeastward to America according to consensus hypotheses, a theory supported by tribal history and mythology. Choctaw verbal accounts concur that the tribe arrived in the Mississippi-Alabama country after traveling many years from a land a great distance away in the west following two mythical brothers, Chahta and Chikasah. The pair, one a wise, diplomatic prophet and the other a brave, fearless warrior, guided by a magical, Sacred Staff, called the Iti Fabussa, led the People, the Okla, on a march that lasted ages to their homeland in central Mississippi at Nvnih Waiya (Producing Hill). [2]

The Choctaw sometimes stopped in a place for a few weeks, a growing season, or an entire winter, remaining long enough to rest, harvest crops, or go on hunting trips for fresh meat, but ultimately the journey resumed eastward. The migration settled into a monotony of walking, eating, sleeping, and walking, but always they moved on, never leaving anyone behind, even carrying the bones of their ancestors with them. The family of the deceased temporarily left the migration to construct tall platforms to support the corpse and keep fires lit nearby to protect and guide the dead spirits until the body ripened sufficiently for preparation by the "Bone Pickers," a group of medicine men that used their long fingernails to cleanse the flesh from the bones of the skeletal remains. The family mourned each day until the priests arrived to host a final burial feast, and then the trek was resumed with the remains of the dead. Families sometimes took half their ancestral bones to a point at midday and returned to transport the other half in the afternoon as the journey lengthened into generations, but always they carried them regardless of the inconvenience.[3]

So many years on the march necessitated numerous social customs. One of the first sanctioned into a ceremonial rite was marriage. When a young man reached a mature enough level to take a wife, he made his selection, visited her family, and discreetly attracted the attention of the prospective bride by throwing to her some token of his intention, a piece of cloth, a pebble, or jewelry. If she responded, and he met the approval of the girl's mother, the relationship proceeded, but if she abruptly left or refused to acknowledge him, the courtship was over. When the romance went according to plan, the union was approved, and the girl's mother made all the arrangements for the nuptials.

The groom endured one last ordeal on the wedding day, the high point of the ceremony known as the "flight of the bride." The groom was taken to one location, the bride to another, a pole was erected approximately three hundred yards away at the farthest point, and at a given signal the bride was allowed to flee. If she succeeded in reaching the pole before the groom could catch her, she was released from her vows and the wedding was off. The custom allowed the bride a final chance to say no, but ordinarily she only ran fast enough that the groom caught her just before reaching the sanctuary of the pole. Should she change her mind and truly wished to call off the wedding, it was certainly possible to do so, and sometimes in the spirit of fun and as a test of his love, she made a seriously close race of the tradition, but under normal circumstances the bride allowed herself to be captured.

Once the ceremony was completed, a "shower" was given for the bride. She was seated on a blanket as friends and relatives piled gifts on and around her, but the presents were not for her. They were given to her aunts and close relatives who snatched them away so quickly that often they took along bits of hair or clothing. After a feast for families and friends, the couple began living together.

Upon reaching their lands in Mississippi, the newlyweds started a home by building a cabin near the bride's family. A few pieces of furniture were provided usually including a kettle for boiling deer, bear, or pork, a wooden bowl, and a Tafula Kitti, a hollowed-out section of a log used as a mortar for grinding corn. The grains of corn could be broken into three or four pieces, separated from the hulls, and boiled down into Tafula (from tanchi meaning corn and fuli meaning to stir), a soup enjoyed by the Choctaw that was offered as a courtesy to every visitor upon arrival and administered to the sick for medicinal purposes.

A young man always married a bride from an Iksa (clan) other than his own and lived and worked with her relations after the marriage. In the case of a broken marriage, either by separation or death, the woman kept the house and the children. A divorce was easy for either side. The man simply left and did not return, while the woman merely placed the man's possessions, his weapons, clothing, and eating bowl, outside the door, and he knew not to return.

Marriages were for older, more mature couples. A couple that married before reaching maturity was thought only capable of conceiving sickly, unhealthy children, thereby weakening the tribe as a whole. A girl had to be at least twenty years of age and a man normally twenty-five to thirty to be considered old enough for wedlock. Promiscuity among young people and teenage weddings were discouraged by the tribe, as was polygamy, although multiple wives were tolerated among the chiefs and more successful warriors. The first wife occasionally allowed her husband to take additional wives to alleviate housekeeping chores and cooking duties if he were a famed hunter and warrior or important chief. In some instances the first wife's sisters could be claimed if they reached marriage age without husbands or were widowed by circumstances. Should the groom's spouse die, he was expected to marry one of his wife's sisters or close relatives as a way of maintaining his support for the clan.[4]

The Choctaw were a moral people, although holding no strict notions of sexual morality. Theirs was a relatively chaste society whose family life was pure. In the case of adultery, the woman was subject to punishment by her husband, but if her family was more influential or stronger than his, she usually escaped. If not, she could be cast off by the husband or exposed publicly as the victim for all the men who chose to participate. Sexual deviation was frowned upon, although sodomy was common and not considered a punishable offense. Homosexuals were allowed to wear clothing like women but were held in great contempt by the tribe. Males took great pride in being men not women in Choctaw society. When the family had but one horse, the man rode while the woman walked and carried the child or bundle.[5]

Two unique customs accompanied marriage. The first mandated mothers-in-law never again looked sons-in-law in the eyes, often a practice that occasioned difficulty and embarrassment at social gatherings but was enforced through the power of tribal taboo. Mothers-in-law frequently walked with lowered heads and eyes on the ground to lessen even the chance of looking the man in the face. Another taboo attached to marriage involved the woman's use of her husband's name. Strictly forbidden to speak it aloud, she referred to the man by some other designation, calling him "the father of my children," or "my husband," or any similar reference, but never using his name as this would bring certain misfortune to him and the family.

A Choctaw was very reluctant to use his own name because it was considered unlucky and immodest. When a child was born, the mother separated herself from the father for the event, but as quickly as it was completed the family was reunited and the child given a name by its parents. Customarily, children were named for animals or some incident connected to their births and later in life given new names in recognition of a special skill or talent, or an event, personal achievement or characteristic. Accompanied by speeches and ceremonies, the bestowal of a new title was an important ceremonial rite. The word humma, red, was regularly added to a man's name as a mark of distinction while a great number of Choctaw war names used the phrase "abi" or "tubbee," meaning killer. At maturity the individual gave himself a secret name that was never told to anyone nor spoken aloud for should the identity be revealed it meant death and the loss of the soul to evil spirits. The name of a deceased person was never mentioned again if it could be avoided in any manner. The departed was spoken of simply as "the dead," or by some relationship to the living, to prevent complications with the afterworld should the spirits hear the person's name.

The Choctaw, a quiet, kind people, doted on their children. Youngsters were allowed to grow up completely unrestrained by any controls other than social pressures from older tribal members. Should a young person misbehave, cry excessively, or throw temper tantrums, the youth was simply avoided by everyone until the child changed his behavior. Never was a juvenile struck or disciplined by an adult, particularly by a mother. Although a woman did have some punitive power over a daughter, she risked reprimands herself for punishing a boy. Men did not have authority over their own children, except as teachers. Any discipline, should it be necessary, was administered by the child's maternal uncle. The son was not considered his father's heir. Inheritance was transferred from maternal uncle to nephew.

Both boys and girls were exempted from burdens or chores. Their primary duty was to exercise and play. Boys roamed the woods and streams from village to village unsupervised learning to shoot bows and arrows or blowguns at small birds and animals. They were taught to play stickball, to wrestle and run, and to hide their fears and pains. A sign of maturity was the ability to endure grief without showing weakness, and a young man had to submit to a severe beating by his peers without displaying physical reactions before being recognized as a warrior.

Within Choctaw society, twins were considered possessors of special powers. They were given preferential treatment, because it was believed they could do battle with evil. Horatio B. Cushman, a missionary's son, and his twin brother were called upon many times to participate in special rituals to combat worms in the cornfields.[6]

The Choctaw migration story accounted for their existence and their northern relatives, the Chickasaw. Called "the People," when asked by the Europeans "What people?" they replied simply, "the People of Chahta." Just as they were his descendants, the Chickasaw were believed to be the descendants of Chikasah.

As their migration progressed eastward, the tribe eventually encountered a great river, so wide that none could even see across it. Because such a large river had never been seen before, and neither its source nor terminus was known, it was given a special name, "Misha Sipokni," (Beyond Age). Once its crossing was accomplished, the Choctaw traveled on toward the east until reaching a large mound more than three hundred feet long and eighty feet above the tops of the trees around it leaning slightly toward a nearby stream, the Pearl River in Winston County, Mississippi. Their new home was filled with fresh springs, waters teeming with fish, woods abundant with game, buffalo, deer, black bears, and wild turkeys roaming the countryside, trees yielding many kinds of fruits, berries, and nuts, and, best of all, soil that was rich and fertile for farming.[7]

Since the winters were mild in the new land, there was no reason to build elaborate houses and cabins. Homes were simply built in a circular shape from bamboo cane stalks found along the streams. The walls were double rowed to keep out the wind, and roofs constructed of plant leaves laid over sloping frameworks that allowed the rain to run off onto the ground. A strong fence was constructed around the cabins for protection. Beds were built around the inside walls of the cabins by driving four stakes into the ground and a frame constructed by tying rawhide thongs to the stakes about three feet off the ground. Vines were used to lace over the frame and serve as support for the furs and hides used as bedding. An opening was left in each end of the cabin to allow the cool breezes to blow through during the summer months or to let out the smoke from the heating fires in winter. A small circular fire marked the center of the hut while cooking fires were built on the outside.

Hunters organized parties to hunt bears, deer, and panthers for food. Bears, valuable for skins for clothing and fat for use as grease, were hunted throughout the year but were trapped most successfully in their winter caves. The women gathered fruits, nuts, and berries, prepared the land for planting beans, squash, melons, pumpkins, and turnips, and made clothing and bedding from the animal skins brought in by the men. Bison hides were turned into mattresses or the hair removed and made into robes, while bearskins were made into moccasins and hunting pants. Deer, elk, and panther skins became shirts and dresses, softened even more by soaking them in a liquid made from green elm bark then chewed by the women until extremely pliant and flexible. Men boasted of the affection shown by their wives as evidenced by the softness of his clothing that she had processed by chewing until soft as the cloth obtained from white traders.

Clothing for women consisted of a blouse and short skirt made of animal hides tanned and softened by a mixture of deer brains. Later, women adopted blouses and skirts made of cotton materials, adding shawls in the winter. Normally, their only ornaments were wooden beads. The men ordinarily wore breechclouts, mostly going barefoot at home; as did the women, but when traveling they added moccasins, pants, shirts and turbans. In the winter they wore outer garments of furs with the lower ends of their leggings tucked into their moccasins. Both men and women wore their hair long and loose or plaited into braids.

Chapter One

In the Nineteenth Century, the Choctaw adopted the clothing of white settlers. The men wore blue serge suits and black hats like those worn by wealthier plantation owners. One of the last chiefs to wear traditional clothing, Coleman Cole, wore his hair shoulder length, a silk hat, and a hunting coat of many colors. The women wore loosely fitted dresses with the hemline just above the ankle with an apron over it. Both decorative and functional, dresses revealed the marriage status of the woman. An unmarried woman's dress opened in the back and a married one opened in the front to provide accessibility to nourishment for children. A kerchief or bonnet was worn over the head. The decorative white apron with contrasting trim and ruffles was considered part of the dress. Ceremonial dresses added certain symbols such as the circle and cross to symbolize the sun and stars. Believing that a person was bitten because he had invaded the space or territory of the snake and had not respected its home, the diamond-shaped trim symbolized respect for nature represented by the diamondback rattlesnake.

Women quickly learned to color the animal skins by making dyes from a variety of plants and trees around them. Indigo plants, pokeberries, and barks and nuts produced different shades that could be used as dyes. A bloodroot yielded yellow, wild indigo turned blue, pokeberries produced purple hues, and by mixing plants different colors were possible. Adding two parts pokeberries to one part bloodroot produced the distinctive "Choctaw red," a color greatly admired by the Choctaw.

By necessity women learned to fashion strong, useful baskets by peeling and soaking the outer skin of the bamboo cane found along the streams and rivers. Since they could be woven so tightly, the baskets were waterproof and provided innumerable uses for storing and carrying crops. In 1775, James Adair noted that the tribe also made clay pottery utensils, including many different utilitarian earthen pans, bowls, water pitchers, and dishes.[8]

The Choctaw homeland in Mississippi, western Alabama, and eastern Louisiana was a land of plenty. The ground was fertile, the corn grew high, and the People of Chahta enjoyed hundreds of years of peace and prosperity. Occasionally, clashes erupted with their neighbors, but disputes were ordinarily worked out by peaceful means. The tribe rarely resorted to actual warfare before the arrival of Europeans.

The basic unit of Choctaw society was the family, although not self-sustaining, but as part of the Iksa (clan). In its purest form an Iksa consisted of two or three hunting families, a warrior family, a family that worked with tools, a clubman or protector family, a watch family, and a runner family. These various groups served the Iksa in specific ways. The hunters supplied the food while the others provided their own particular skills for caring for the members and performed the necessary functions of life and order.

When they banded together for defensive purposes or merely for reasons of friendship, the organization was known as a moiety. The Choctaw used the term Tvmaha to identify them, a term later mistakenly used to denote towns, but it originally meant moieties living and working together in a particular place.[9]

Within this framework each band had a Mi̱ko who served as the voice of the Iksa when general councils were called for issues that required a general agreement by the tribe. Basically an extremely democratic people, the Choctaw held councils in times of grave danger or wars or when issues were of national importance and required tribal consensus, or for discussions of special events affecting the tribe's future. Only during a war was an individual, called a Hopaii (war leader), given absolute power.

Wars were seldom fought with other tribes but were considered patriotic occupations. Adopting a defensive stance and awaiting an attack, Choctaw warriors avoided invasions of an enemy territory from choice, but woe to the adversary who attributed this to cowardice. Once hostilities began, no braver combatants ever took the warpath. Like enraged animals they would gather to repel an invader with desperate, fearless courage. Strategy was commendable, but outwitting an opponent was considered the wiser method of skillful military action.

Preparations for a campaign began with a Hoyopahihla (war dance). A huge pile of brush and logs was set on fire after dusk, and the older warriors watched in somber approval as occasional kicks from one of the participants sent sparks flying into the dark sky as the flames mingled with the Hoyopa-taloah (war songs) and the Hoyopa-tas-suhah (war whoops). On the warpath the Choctaw traveled in small bands, walking one behind the other in a straight line. Each warrior stepped exactly in the tracks of the one in front while the last one in the rear disguised or covered the tracks, leaving little evidence of numbers or locations. Making these trips in absolute silence, the warriors communicated by predetermined, well-known hand or head signals. Verbal expression, used only when absolutely necessary, was by the use of a low imitative cry of some wild animal. A war party glided noiselessly through the forests, painted in many different manners, presenting a fierce appearance to an enemy.

There were great motives for warriors to perform valorous and perilous deeds in times of war. Chieftainships were bestowed on those who proved themselves by their skill and daring, and chiefs considered it a disgrace to be surpassed in battle by any of his warriors. The warriors regarded it equally dishonorable for them to achieve less than the chiefs. They did not wait for moments of heroism to come but sought out opportunities to display their bravery and daring, looking for the most dangerous times to distinguish themselves.

Retreats were another matter. Once deemed necessary, the band scattered quickly without regard for others; each individual helped himself. Survivors united again later at a predetermined spot, generally miles away. The Choctaw depended upon stealth, silence, and unexpected attacks to achieve victory, but when circumstances went wrong, or the element of surprise was lost, they resorted to other tactics. To fight an open battle giving the enemy equal chance was an unrealistic approach to war for a Choctaw. Conversely, it was considered evidence of a lack of military skill. The objective was to win the battle to protect Choctaw lands, not to "play fair."

Through the generations the lands owned in common by the Choctaw evolved into three distinct and separate districts, each with its own Mi̱ko. These districts were known as Ahe Apvt Okla, Okla Hannali, and Okla Falaya. The latter, Okla Falaya, meant "Long People," although the designation had two meanings. It originated from the fact the people wore their hair long and were extraordinarily tall, and that their country was a long strip along the banks of the Mississippi with the river located on their west side at their backs. Okla Hannali meant "Six Town," or moieties or "Six Iksa." They were the southern and eastern most of the three districts, located on the coast, bounded on the south by the Gulf of Mexico, on the east by the Creeks, and on the north by the Pearl and Tombigbee Rivers. Ahe Apvt Okla meant the "Potato-eating People," a name that recognized their habit of not storing their potato crop in the customary way. The Choctaw normally covered their potatoes after harvest in a stone cairn, but in the Ahe Apvt Okla district the people preserved them as "chips." After digging, the potatoes were washed, sliced into pieces, dried in bags, and stored until needed for food.[10]

Happy and content, the Choctaw were a spiritual people who attributed magical, supernatural powers to nature. Animals, fish, and the birds were all considered spirits. Scissor-tailed birds and chickens were considered to be beneficial to man and used their powers for good while owls were believed to possess powers that could be unfriendly or harmful to human and were feared and treated with awe and respect. Ishkitini, the horned owl, was believed to prowl at night and would attack men and animals given the opportunity by the darkness of night, and when it screeched, it meant sudden death, or murder. The screech owl, Ofunlo, predicted bad news, and if heard in the yard at night it forecast the death of the youngest child in the family within a short time. When the common owl, Opa, hooted near the house during the daytime, it meant that a family member or close relative would die before the changing of the next moon.

Chickens were considered news birds or watch birds. A rooster crowing at an unusual time forecast bad weather in the near future, crowing on the doorstep meant important news was on the way, and crowing at night meant

that a dispute among the women of the family or the neighborhood would soon erupt into serious trouble. The Biskinik, sapsucker, was known as a news bird. When one landed on a tree in the yard in the early morning, some "hasty" news would arrive before noon, and should one perch there late in the evening, the news would come before morning.

Considered a symbol of evil and greatly feared, the most hated and despised creature for the Choctaw was the snake. The Choctaw world was filled with copperheads, water moccasins, and coral snakes. Even the non-poisonous varieties were troublesome. The blacksnake was believed capable of locking its fangs into its own tail and scaring humans by rolling towards them like a hoop. Regardless of the type, the creatures were avoided and considered repulsive. Conversely, the rattlesnake held a sacred place in Choctaw culture, evidenced by the use of diamond shapes on their dresses and shirts as symbols of reverence for nature. Because they fed on the rodents and creatures that threatened the grain and storehouses, the diamondbacks were held in great respect.

Natural phenomena like thunder (Hiloha) and lightning (Mvlata) were another part of Choctaw mythology. In tribal stories, the two were believed responsible for the occurrence of dramatic thunderstorms. Comets and eclipses were other signs of disaster and chaos. The appearance of a comet was believed to be the signal for the beginning of a great war. A solar eclipse was said to be a black squirrel eating the sun and the tribe must make as much noise as possible to stop it. If one occurred, men, women, and children, old and young, stopped whatever they were doing and immediately began screaming, yelling, beating on drums, making as much noise as they could to scare away the squirrel and save the sun.

Each person had his own superstitions and "medicines." Every male had a special "medicine bag," containing a colored stone, a claw from some animal, a talon, a piece of fur or cloth, any small totem the person believed to be the symbol of his personal source of magic that kept him safe and strong. With him at all times for protection and good luck, the small pouch of secret "power" was generally buried with the individual without anyone ever knowing its contents.

Choctaw religion was dualistic with each person believing that he possessed a spirit and a soul. After death an inner spirit, called a Shilup, left the body immediately for the "Happy Hunting Land," while the Shilombish soul remained near the spot of death to watch over the body and the family during the funeral cry and feast. At night the family knew when the soul was around, since it could be heard as the voice of a fox or owl with no answering call. The family knew that it was the soul because the call of a real animal or bird would be answered. For the spirit to leave, the family boxed the belongings of the

deceased and put his bedding outside. Slowly, the Shilombish faded away as the funeral ceremony proceeded properly.

In the meantime, the Shilup made "the long journey home to the west" where all except murderers, men who abandoned pregnant wives, and those who gossiped about others could enter the "Happy Hunting Land" on the condition they passed the entrance test of crossing the Guardian Bridge. Those who could not negotiate it or were murderers and "bad people" or "bad spirits" could never enter paradise. They were forced to stay out in a world of darkness and gloom to watch all the happy spirits enjoying themselves in the sunshine all day.

The Happy Place was a nirvana of continual sunlight, beautiful green trees and plants, and wondrous fruits and nuts for food, a place with no storms or clouds, or extreme hot or cold weather, only cool, refreshing breezes that blew all day long. The people spent their time playing, feasting, and dancing, and there were no troubles and no illnesses. It was a place of delight where the people remained young, happy, and contented forever.

To enter paradise, the spirit had to first cross a peeled and very slippery sweet gum or pine foot-log that lay across a great canyon. Guardians protected the entrance into the "Good Place" by throwing stones and rocks as the spirit tried to walk over the "Bad Place," a damp, dark gorge filled with roaring waters, containing lifeless, floating fish and animals, and dead, decaying trees and plants. The spirits that dwelt there were always unhappy and sad, simply existing within sight of the "Good Place," but would never be allowed to attain it.[11]

The traditional Choctaw mourning "cry" for the departed lasted long after the age of the "bone pickers" into the removal period. The tribe considered interment in a foreign place or a cemetery equivalent to throwing the body away, and great efforts were made to insure the corpse was brought home for burial to allow mothers, wives, or other relatives to gather once a month at the grave for a "cry" until the completion of the final funeral for the deceased, normally six to twelve months after the death. The wife sometimes bobbed her hair during this time. It was believed that relatives and friends were not true and sincere unless the cries were done faithfully.[12]

All the tribes of the Muskogean speaking family have in common an emigration story of an early removal from some trans-Mississippi place to their homes in the southeastern United States. Probably, the Choctaw-Chickasaw tribes formed the vanguard of a great migration that spread over the entire southern portion of the continent. This dispersion caused their language to serve as the basis for all other southeastern tribes.

Numbering about 15,000 in 1650, the Choctaw increased through intermarriage to about 18,000 in 1800. Basically horticulturists, they prepared

their fields for planting in mid-winter and grew sufficient quantities to insure an annual surplus that was habitually sold to their neighbors, the Chickasaw. To insure good harvests on new fields, ceremonial dances preceded the cutting of underbrush and girdling of trees; the dried brush was burned and the ashes spread over the plots as fertilizer. Planting was done in the spring when the soil was turned and holes for the seeds were dug with the most primitive of plows, a stick, or sharpened pole hardened by charring over a fire. Men did the heavy labor of clearing and preparing the land while the women and children shared the other work. The most important crop, maize, or corn, was celebrated and enjoyed by the Choctaw with a great festival. The Green Corn Dance was held in early summer once the corn was gathered and stored for winter. Beans, squash, sunflowers, and gourds were planted in the same plots after the harvests. The tribe added peas, watermelons, sweet potatoes, and fruit trees to their fields in the Eighteenth Century.

Hunting, turtling, and fishing supplemented Choctaw diets. A favorite sport as well as a source of food, fishing was done in a number of ways. The fish were caught with traps or nets made of hoops covered with hides by communal drives in shallow water, or poisoned by buckeyes or crushed walnut hulls, a plant poison that stunned the fish, or simply shot with arrows or spears. One of the most prized tools after the arrival of the Europeans was the metal fishhook. Usually in the fall a hunt was organized to gather enough meat for the winter, and deer, one of the most valued game animals, were hunted by using deer calls and decoys made from the skin and antlers of a buck. Young boys hunted for turtles, alligators, rabbits, raccoons, turkeys, and quail. A favorite weapon for the boys was a blowgun, often over seven feet long. The meat could be sun-dried or smoked and dried over fires and stored for winter.

Another source of food was wild fruits, berries, and nuts. Women picked grapes, cherries, mulberries, persimmons, and plums. In the fall, they gathered hickory nuts, walnuts, and pecans.

Corn always remained the favorite food of the Choctaw, however. Green corn could be roasted on the cob or the kernels boiled with meat with some fermentation to make T<u>a</u>fula. The kernels could be ground after parching, or else boiled, dried and parched before grinding. For sifting and cleaning the ground corn, the Choctaw used baskets of plaited cane. Hominy, made by pounding the dried kernels to remove the husks and boiling the pieces (grits) for twelve to eighteen hours in water, was a mixture customarily kept in each house ready to eat at all time.[13]

The diet of the Choctaw produced an extraordinarily healthy person hampered by few diseases, but occasionally illness necessitated professional doctors. There were three distinct types of medical practitioners, the Alikchi,

the Apolumi, or conjurers, and the Isht ahullo, or witches.

The deeply religious Alikchi used spiritualism and knowledge of many different kinds of botanical medicines for cures for their patients. Truly skilled in treatments of wounds and diseases, they were trained by an apprenticeship system that began at an early age. It was believed that they possessed the powers of magic for good or evil, but ordinarily used their remedies only for good. Opinions of the Alikchi carried the power of life and death for the patient. If the medicine man declared a patient had no chance of recovery, the person could be put to death by strangulation to ease his misery.

Believed to have insights into the laws of nature, the Alikchi was a spiritual leader who could give skill and strength to a man, provide bravery to a warrior, and remove evil spirits and disease from the sick. Using the supernatural with herbal remedies and special treatments for illnesses, doctors treated the symptoms of disease while allowing nature to cure or kill, like most medical experts. Skillful in the use of medical treatments, the Alikchi made use of a variety of extracts from barks, leaves, and roots that were pulverized or mixed into medicines by the use of mortars and pestles from gum-tree wood that did not spilt easily. Some specific Choctaw remedies included:

- **Boneset**, a plant with flat clusters of white or bluish-purple flowers used as a tea to increase perspiration and break chills,
- **Rusty water**, made by allowing metal objects to stand in water and used as an iron tonic,
- **Broom weed**, brewed into a tea used for colds and a preventative against pneumonia,
- **Black root and ball willow**, a mixture used against measles and smallpox,
- **Sugar, soot, and spider webs**, combined into an application to stop bleeding,
- **Jerusalem oak or wormseed**, made into a candy and given to children against worms,
- **Wild Cherry**, made into wine as a pain reliever for girls and for purifying the blood,
- **Prickly ash bark**, powdered into a poultice or used in a tooth cavity to stop toothaches,
- **Pottage pea**, onion-like root used for diarrhea,
- **Ground ivy**, a poultice for treating sores,
- **Sycamore bark**, boiled and sweetened with sugar as cough syrup, and
- **Slippery elm bark**, boiled and combined with milk to soothe burn pains.

Choctaw doctors even had a remedy for skin cancer. Equal parts of honey, butter, the juice of the green vines and leaves of the pole bean were steamed together until the mixture reached a consistency that could be applied to the affected area as a salve. Persons using the cure had to refrain from the use of alcohol, fat meats, oils, and the drinking of any liquids other than water, buttermilk, or the liquid from boiled corn.

Depending upon a wide array of plants cures, Choctaw doctors identified nearly two hundred herbs and roots as possessing healing properties. From the root to the bark, tribal doctors drew on many botanical cures. Snakeroot was used to cure snakebites, willow bark to relieve pain and fever, and tobacco was considered a preventative for many illnesses, never a cause of them.

Tribal lore and trial-by-error yielded many kinds of medicines, and the Alikchi used many treatments and remedies including bloodletting, cold and warm baths, and cauterization. Cauterizing was done by fire, applying it directly to the lesions. Casts for broken bones were made from a paste of clay and wrapped in cloth kept damp with cold water to prevent swelling. Steams and sweat baths were prescribed for some fevers by medicine men. A hole was dug in the floor big enough to hold a large pot and over it was laid sticks to hold up a quilt, and a kettle containing water and medicinal herbs was then placed over a fire, the contents heated and placed over the hole, and the patient shut inside until the doctor permitted him to leave.

Certain remedies were prescribed for special symptoms. Readjustment of a patient's pillow was the solution for listlessness in the legs and thighs. The doctor merely reduced the height of the head end of the bed so the blood would flow less readily toward the feet. If a patient suffered much sickness in a particular place, the treatment was to move. It was not uncommon for a person to be directed to move several times over his farm by the doctor.

Bloodletting was another preventive remedy. The doctor made a punch from a piece of glass fastened on the end of a stick so that it could enter the flesh to a certain degree, then placed it over the affected area and drove it in with a mallet. The wide end of a cow horn was then clamped over the spot, and the doctor sucked as much of the air out then the hole was closed. When the horn was withdrawn, the doctor could make an inspection of the blood and diagnose the ailment. A wizard could abuse this practice by pretending to extract objects from the body of patients.

The all-powerful spirits of the Choctaw known as Kowi Anuka asha (the little people) assisted Choctaw doctors. Attaching themselves to an Alikchi as helpers in curing sickness, they taught the medicine men to identify and recognize herbs and plants that could be used for cures. Mischievous, and given to pranks, they loved to play with children, but could be terrifying if angered. Considered eternal by the Choctaw, they found another doctor soon after the death of the Alikchi.[14]

Not possessing the same quality of medicine as the Alikchi, the Ilaholbi medicine men were generally associated with the use of magic and trickery, relying upon superstition to predict future events, assure hunters of success, and impart bravery to warriors. They were the weather forecasters and rainmakers. Called Hattak Omba Ikbi (man rainmaker), the person strolled from village to village, observing the heavens, seemingly communicating with the other worlds, until finally specifying the day that he would make rain. Hailed as a great mystic power when successful, he simply blamed failures on another rainmaker living in some other village combating his spells and adjusted his calendar to another date.

The Isht ahullo were the wizards and witches who caused sickness and death by casting evil spells. Most feared by the tribe, their formidable powers were used for evil, and they sometimes sold their occult powers to cause death or injuries to enemies. They merely attributed failures of their magic to another nearby witch working against them, usually in the form of an old woman. Generally held in disfavor, they were driven out or killed when caught practicing their evil magic.[15]

The Choctaw world, a combination or realism and spiritualism, was thirteen months long, with each month of twenty-eight days beginning on the first night of the full moon. The year began with the first frost and lasted 364 days. The months were named for some action by the tribe or some natural event. They were:

1. **Hvshi Hoponi** - the month of cooking (*September*)
2. **Hvshi Hohchvfo iskitini** - month of little hunger (*October*)
3. **Hvshi Hohchvfo Chito** - month of big hunger (*November*)
4. **Hvshi Koi Chito** - big lion month (*December*)
5. **Hvshi Koịchush** - lion's little brother's month (*January*)
6. **Hvshi Watonlak** - month of the crane (*February*)
7. **Hvshi Mah li** - month of the winds (*March*)
8. **Hvshi Tekịhvshi** - month of the woman (*April*)
9. **Hvshi Bihi** - month of the mulberry (*May*)
10. **Hvshi Bissa** - month of the blackberry (*June*)
11. **Hvshi Kvfi** - the month of sassafras (*July*)
12. **Hvshi Takkon** - month of the peach (*August*)
13. **Hvshi Luak Mosholi** - month of the fires all out (*August-September*)

The year started with the first frosts in the month called the "cooking month" when the vegetables in Choctaw fields were preserved and stockpiled against the coming winter. Since there were no methods for canning, vegetables had to be dried or cooked in a manner that kept them edible for several months or made into breads that could be stored easily. The following months were related to the scarcity of the food supply in winter when much of the game was in hibernation. There was usually enough meat around to add a little flavor to the Tafula (cold corn), the mainstay of the Choctaw diet, but meals were less regular and farther between. The Crane Month, Hvshi Watonlak, was named for the white crane, commonly found in Mississippi that was considered a delicacy by the tribe. Everyone savored a number of crane squabs simmered in a pot with greens and crushed corn. The following month, the windy month, Hvshi Mah li, brought warm, southeasterly breezes from the Gulf, and the game began to return. Three months were Tofa (summer months) for gathering blackberries, mulberries, and peaches, because these fruits ripened during this time. The month, Hvshi Luak Mosholi, the time of the year the corn reached roasting ear size and could be gathered for the annual "Green Corn Dance," was the fun period. The ceremony sometimes lasted for two weeks with feasting, singing, and dancing to celebrate another good corn crop. The annual event was generally followed with an "owata chito" (a big hunting party) involving several families. The fires in their homes would remain cold for several weeks during this month "the fires were all out." The Choctaw spoke often of a hunt far away from their country across the Mississippi to the west for buffalo, and when the French heard the stories of these big hunts the term Ouachita, derived from owata (to hunt) and chito (big), was adopted for the region in the west.

The month, Hvshi Tekihvshi, month of the woman, was the time the Choctaw romanced his girl friends. The final two months, Hvshi Koi Chito and Hvshi Koichush, (wildcat and panther) were named in honor of the two big cats in Mississippi. During these months the cats' offspring were large enough to leave the den and make the mothers easier to hunt. As many as possible were killed at this time and the layers of lean meat stripped into thin pieces that were smoked and dried over hickory fires as jerky that lasted for many months.

The Choctaw method for counting time was by reference to the full or crescent moons; the years were counted by the killing of the vegetation in winters. Thus, for two years ago the Choctaw said: Hushuk (grass) illi (dead) tuklo (twice), literally, grass killed twice, or two killings of the grass ago. Their almanac was kept by the flight of the fowls, whose migrations announced the changes in the seasons.[16]

In their everyday life the tribe operated as a matrilineal society. Women held an honored and important position within the tribe, despite the appearance of being a system of unequal division of labor between the sexes, with the woman performing all the work while the men occupied themselves with hunting and fishing. This does not take into account the dangers of the male occupations. The women did most of the labor of the fields, made the clothing, and kept house, but the men were considered the protectors who provided the food, built the houses and tools, carried on government, and protected the family in times of crisis. In reality, women, and children, enjoyed freedom from arbitrary oppression by the men in their daily lives. The women were perceived as the "keepers of life," while the men were "keepers of death." The Choctaw realized the importance of women and gave them powers so that their position would not be considered inferior, but the exact opposite. As the "keepers of life" the women owned the home and fields and had complete charge of rearing the children. Additionally, ancestral lineage was determined through the mother's family.[17]

The one event that allowed women to participate equally with the men was the Choctaw stickball game, ishtaboli. Women played with just as much emotion as the men, organized their own teams, and often played women teams from other villages after the men. Their games were equally bloody if not more violent and lengthy. A game lasted until the score reached 100, which meant the time consumed could be hours, lasting from morning until night without a break.

In 1834, George Catlin compared the game to the Greek Olympics or contests at the Roman Forum. Providing the classic description of a contest that he witnessed near Skullyville in the Choctaw Nation involving an unusually high number of players, six or seven hundred players, with five or six times that many spectators, the artist painted the match, noting that games were played regularly between districts or counties, or even nations. Teams normally numbered twenty-five or thirty players each, and encamped with their supporters at the Hitoka (ball field) on the night before the game. Players with little or no experience would dress themselves in ballgame uniforms, a breechclout and the tail of some animal, a horse or raccoon, attached behind to the belt, and endeavored to represent an animal that was swift or a good fighter doing their best to attract the attention of leaders so that they might be chosen to play the next day. Leaders normally ranged in age from eighteen to thirty-five held meetings and discussed ways and strategies to win. Veterans sometimes were handicapped, recognizable by wounds suffered in a previous game, but the players were all "of splendid physique," according to Catlin.

Spectators and players slept out under the stars. Shortly after daylight on the morning of the event, the managers collected their teams and sent them to dress. When they were ready, each player charged onto the field trying his best to imitate the actions of the animal he represented. The playing field was usually about two hundred yards in length with goal posts, two poles lashed together, at each end. The objective of the game was to make a score by striking the goal post with a ball made from deerskin. Each player was equipped with two ball sticks called kapucha, manufactured from hickory saplings about thirty inches long, cut flat at one end and curved around to make a scoop-like hoop. The curved end was lashed to the handle with buckskin thongs, and the ends were used to lace the inside of the hoop.

Each team had a medicine man that painted his face, or wore appropriate costumes, and stood near the goal post during the play, singing, clapping, and otherwise performing certain maneuvers that would result in good luck for his team. Carrying a small hand drum or a cane flute, he conducted a dance before the game to insure success for the team. Just before the start of the game the players marched onto the field lead by a medicine man. As each team neared the goal posts, the players would break formation with shouts and turkey gobbles and gather around the posts hitting them with their sticks to "scare away the spirits of bad luck." Shouting, "Shukafa," literally "to peel off," the game was ready to begin. The players stationed themselves at appointed places from mid-field to the goals, and the ball was tossed into the air by those selected to do that duty to get the game underway.

Once play began, there were no rules. For months, even years, a Choctaw was told to be quiet, friendly, and courteous, to do nothing to attract attention, always to subordinate his feelings as an individual to the interests of his fellows and the tribe. During the stickball game, he was allowed to release his frustrations. Any violence, even murder, was forgiven during a ball game. The ball had to be carried or passed to the goal post without being touched by hand. A player who obtained the ball shouted for his teammates, and the result was a fight with the nearest opponent. Bloodshed and broken bones were common as players with the ball tried to run to the post and score or toss to their teammates who were closer to the goal.

Betting was heavy. Spectators often staked everything even the services of themselves and their families on the outcome. Separate tribes sometimes even wagered hunting lands. Catlin painted a scene in the game of a female fan "encouraging" a laggard contestant with a whip. The game was not for the weak or fainthearted. In some games men lost their lives.

The contests permitted the warriors to release tensions and settle disputes peacefully. Seldom did the tribe have to resort to force as a diplomatic policy. When war was the only choice, they fought defensively rather than offensively. Unfortunately, in 1540 opponents arrived that were not playing games, a foe known for cruelty and conquest the Spanish.[18]

CHAPTA TUKLO

~ CHAPTER TWO ~

"THE HATCHET SHALL BE FOREVER BURIED . . ."

Chapter Two

After establishing a burial mound civilization about 700 A.D., the Choctaw spread rapidly over central Mississippi, western Alabama, and eastern Louisiana. Tribal society was soon identified with major ceremonial centers characterized by temple mounds, council houses, and village life. By the time of the appearance of a new civilization from Europe, the Choctaw were in the final stages of mound culture.[19]

Their first encounter with the Europeans was the arrival of a Spanish army under the command of Hernando De Soto in the fall of 1540. After victories against the Inca in Peru, De Soto, a wealthy, aristocratic commander for Francisco Pizarro, lived a life of luxury and leisure, but privately longed to return to his former career of excitement, adventure, and conquest. Finally, King Charles I granted him permission to explore Florida. In 1539, De Soto gathered 550 men and 220 horses and sailed for Tampa Bay.

As the Spanish pushed north through Florida for God, glory, and gold, the Indians quickly learned to avoid them. De Soto's method of dealing with the Indians, enslavement of both the warriors and their leaders, had already proven successful in Peru. Keeping them in chains as assurances against retaliatory attacks, the Spanish forced the chiefs to serve as guides and advisors while their tribesmen were used as carriers and messengers. The Indians quickly learned to vanish until the invaders unhurriedly passed on to the next village.

Arriving in Alabama, the Spanish were, as usual, greeted warmly into the home of the Creek. The chief, borne on a litter covered with "white mantles," accompanied by sixty or seventy of his subjects, welcomed De Soto with feasting and dancing only to be shocked into disbelieving silence when placed under arrest. Once imprisoned the Creek were ruled through orders given to the chief. Learning that the tribe had no gold or silver, the Spanish forced him to supply carriers and women. Any who objected were placed in irons, including the chief. Held in chains for more than three months as the Spanish moved slowly into Choctaw country, the chief had been reduced to a state of tears by the time of his release.

According to Rodrigio Ranjel, De Soto's private secretary and chronicler, the Spanish intended the same treatment for the Choctaw. After meeting representatives of Chief Tushka Lusa (Black Warrior), the Spanish captain ordered a battle tactic that had served well in the past. Sounding the trumpets, the cavalry charged within feet of the Indian warriors, so frightening the tribesmen they quickly accepted two soldiers to discuss terms. On October 10, 1540, De Soto rode in to deal personally with the Choctaw chieftain.

Tushka Lusa, taller by more than a foot than any of the Spaniards, was proudly dressed in a long, feathered cape, and attended by his son and a number of the leading warriors, one who shaded him from the sun with a large, deerskin umbrella stretched over crossed sticks that resembled a battle standard.

Muscular and youthful in appearance, the great Miko greeted his visitors courteously, but remained seated, observing the men on horseback impassively as they approached his seat on a mound in the square at one end of the town. Finally, De Soto dismounted and walked over to him. What was said was never known, but the chief continued to sit calmly, "as though he had been a king," according to Ranjel.[20]

The two talked quietly as the afternoon passed peacefully with feasting and dancing. Only when Tushka Lusa announced that he was ready to leave did De Soto inform him that he was under arrest. The chief scoffed at the idea, but, surprisingly, did as he was told. He acquiesced again the next day when De Soto demanded carriers and women. Chief Tushka Lusa agreed to provide 400 carriers and 100 women on the condition the Spanish accompany him to Mabila, a small, palisaded town on the Gulf coast. Deciding to fight, Tushka Lusa had determined that the best possibility of defeating the Spanish cavalry was to engage them at the town, a Choctaw stronghold with a stockade surrounded by fifteen-eighteen-foot high walls. Secretly sending word ahead of their march, the chief instructed his people to cut down the fields around the town in preparation for battle. The trip, lasting six days, allowed the Choctaw ample time to get ready.[21]

Putting up a fierce resistance in the ensuing combat, the tribe almost defeated the Spanish before the invaders rallied to trap the Choctaw inside their own fortifications. Setting fire to the town, the conquistadors murdered and burned nearly all of the Choctaw warriors while losing only twenty-nine of their own. Spanish estimates put the number of Choctaw dead at 2,500 to 3,000, greatly exaggerated figures, but a very serious disaster for the tribe.

Wounded along with 148 of his men, De Soto remained in Choctaw country for more than a month resting his injured forces before moving on west of the Mississippi River. Harassed by daily attacks, the Spanish gradually exited the territory. De Soto later died of fever on the return trip in 1542. Buried in a tributary to prevent the Indians from finding his body, Luys de Moscoso de Alvarado led the Spaniards down the Mississippi, and eventually returned to Mexico in the fall of 1543.[22]

This first taste of European avarice and greed ironically resulted in another century of freedom and peace for the Choctaw. Since there was neither gold nor silver in their country, the Spanish quickly forgot about the tribe while their armies searched for riches elsewhere. Although claiming ownership by virtue of exploration, there would be little further direct contact for more than a hundred years.

The tribe numbered approximately 15,000 at the time of De Soto's arrival, living near the Pearl, Chickasawhay, and Pascagoula Rivers in Mississippi. They occupied about seventy towns, grouped into three political districts with one western district facing the Mississippi River, one along the Pascagoula and Chickasawhay Rivers, and the third eastern district with the most towns, including the largest called Koi Chito. From their villages they went out into the fields to farm corn, melons, beans, pumpkins, and potatoes, raising sufficient amounts for surpluses that were sold to the Chickasaw. The excess was stored in public houses for common use by everyone.[23]

The Choctaw, in effect, practiced a form of communism based upon the principle of tribal ownership of lands. Considering the idea of individual ownership of the earth as the height of egotism, the Choctaw believed that only the tribe could own land. Any person was permitted use of as much land as he desired, but no one could own it. It was even considered treasonous for an individual to take part in any actions that might be construed as giving away land. Their sharing of common property and lack of personal possessions kept class differences at a minimum and encouraged tribal cooperation. Since there was no private property, there was no accumulation of wealth, giving the tribe personal freedom and a communal economy.[24]

These very concepts, coupled with the neglect shown by the Spanish, invited other European nations into their country. In 1682, Robert Chevalier de La Salle (1643-1687) appeared at the mouth of the Mississippi River, unfurled the French flag and claimed the territory as Louisiana. The Choctaw were again confronted with European ambitions when Pierre Le Moyne, Sieur d'Iberville established a fort near Biloxi called Fort Maurepas in 1699. Accompanying him was Henri de Tonti, La Salle's chief lieutenant, who initiated contact with the Choctaw in 1702. The French founded Mobile the same year, followed by New Orleans in 1718. Soon French coureurs de bois (woods rangers) were living with the Choctaw and trading throughout their country.[25]

Over the next few years French Jesuits also tried several missionary efforts among the Choctaw, but met with little success. In 1726, Father Mathurin le Petit founded a Catholic mission in the Six Towns District, and another at Yazoo in 1729, but neither proved productive. One irate Choctaw convert returned to the mission after a short time to be "debaptized," because "the Na Hollo (white man) magic was ruining his deer hunting skills." After going through a ceremony of "debaptism," it was reported that the warrior had regained his shooting ability. In 1729, Michael Beaudouin, the Father's successor, established another mission near a village on the Chickasawhay River. Laboring for more than eighteen years among the tribe, often in danger for his life after the English began arriving in the lower Mississippi valley, Beaudouin continued the Catholic missionary efforts but had little success in conversions. The Jesuits persevered until their expulsion in 1764, but they convinced few Choctaw to convert and their missions quickly fell into ruin.[26]

Chapter Two

As the French worked to establish an empire along the Mississippi River, they inevitably encountered competition from the English and the Spanish. Seeking support from the Indians, the major powers were soon involved in intertribal relations and domestic quarrels between the nations, and generally allied with the tribes along geographic lines. The Choctaw and Natchez tribes along the lower river sided with the French while their kinsmen, the Chickasaw, and the Cherokee in the north joined the English, and the Seminole normally supported the Spanish in Florida. Naturally, the Europeans encouraged the tribes in their sporadic skirmishes, sometimes even helping them escalate into serious warfare.[27]

Over the next hundred years the European countries fought four world wars for domination of North America. The first began when Great Britain entered the War of the League of Augsburg in 1689. Lasting until 1697, it was known as King William's War in the colonies. In 1702, the War of the Spanish Succession began and lasted until 1713 as Queen Anne's War in America. Another short period of peace followed until the War of the Spanish Succession began in 1739, moving to America as King George's War that lasted until 1748. Finally, the Seven Years' War started in 1756. Different in that it began in the colonies two years earlier as the French and Indian War and moved to Europe, it lasted until 1763. During these wars the French governors of Louisiana purchased Choctaw support through a system of gifts and presents and medal honors to their chiefs and leaders. Being recognized as a Medal Chief was considered the highest honor that could be achieved by a Choctaw.

In 1690, King William's War began in the Mississippi country when a Choctaw-Chickasaw war started over the Chickasaw desires for English trade goods, especially guns. The Chickasaw, yearning for British approval, invited their neighbors to come for a friendly visit then turned on the surprised Choctaw and imprisoned them for trade to the English. They were later sold as slaves for labor camps in the West Indies.[28]

The capture of these five hundred Choctaw led to a war that cost more than eighteen hundred Choctaw and another eight hundred Chickasaw lives. In March 1702, the French finally arranged for peace at Mobile, and d'Iberville cemented an alliance with the Choctaw for his efforts. Chided about warfare with their Chickasaw kinsmen, the Choctaw explained that Chahta and Chikasah had argued and fought on their long journey before eventually going separate ways.

In 1704, fighting was renewed as Queen Anne's War in America. In the following year the Choctaw again asked for help from their French allies when English colonials led a combined force of 4,000 Chickasaw and Creek warriors against them. Unfortunately, the French proved incapable of protecting them, and in the fall the invaders laid waste to the Choctaw country. By 1708, Chickasaw superiority in English weaponry forced the Choctaw to sue for peace, but it was only a short respite. In 1711, the war resumed for another year until peace could be arranged again.[29]

Because of these setbacks, only three towns remained loyal to the French, but the French were able to convince the Choctaw to help them in wars against other tribes. In 1729, the two combined for an attack against the Natchez whom the French blamed for several injuries suffered at Mobile. More than 700 Choctaw joined the French in a campaign against the Natchez that resulted in virtual annihilation of the tribe. Some 147 survivors of the attack were captured and shipped off as slaves to Haiti while the remaining few went to live with the Creek and Chickasaw.

In 1736, the Chickasaw were convinced by the British to launch attacks against French traffic on the Mississippi from their stronghold at Chickasaw Bluffs (Memphis). The French governor, Jean Baptiste le Moyne, Sieur de Bienville, tried to counter by inviting the Choctaw under Chief Shulush Homma (Red Shoe) to join him in an offensive against the Chickasaw, but the Choctaw chief declined the offer. The French took the field anyway, and met with disastrous results. Failing to coordinate his forces while engaging a foe with superior firepower supplied by the British, Bienville doomed his campaign to defeat.

In the 1740s a peace party led by Red Shoe, whose wife, according to rumor, had been seduced by a Frenchman, developed within the Choctaw tribe advocating friendlier relations with the British. The group found enough support that violence threatened to erupt within the nation when a new French governor, Pierre-Francois de Rigaud, the Marquis de Vaudreuil-Cavagnal, arrived to exploit the situation. Able to defeat negotiations with the British, he caused such a rift within the tribe that civil war broke out between rival factions.

In 1748, on the eve of King George's War, a tribal council was finally called to debate the problem. When the Choctaw realized they were only exterminating each other, Red Shoe was killed in the interest of tribal harmony and unity. In 1750, peace was restored by the Treaty of Grandpre but at a very high cost. The Choctaw were virtually reduced to the status of being French protectorates. The death penalty was approved for any tribesman who killed a Frenchman or invited an Englishman into the Choctaw country.[30]

The Choctaw remained loyal to the French during these years, but their days were numbered. In 1754, the trade goods needed to keep the Choctaw loyal was such a source of embarrassment for Vaudreuil that he finally announced the French would no longer deliver presents to them. In 1759, a sign of growing French weakness was the insertion of British goods by the chief British agent to the southern tribes, Edmund Atkins.

By 1763, the world contests were over, and Great Britain was the victor. French power was completely broken by the Treaty of Paris. France ceded its claims to the New World to Britain and gave Florida to Spain. The Choctaw, forced then to deal with the British, met with the governors of the Carolinas and Virginia at Augusta in 1763. Two years later, John Stuart, Superintendent of Indian Affairs, arranged a peace treaty with the Choctaw at Mobile. In a message to the southern tribes, the representatives rather optimistically stated, "Our friendship will last as long as the sun shines, or the water flows."

While at the conference, however, a party of Creek attacked the Choctaw, killing ten of their people, and setting off a Choctaw-Creek War that lasted six years. During this conflict the Chickasaw sided with the Choctaw. As the two tribes met to smoke the peace calumet, the troubles between them began to settle.

When the Colonial Revolution erupted, the Choctaw remained largely neutral, but their history with the English and the French left them favorably inclined toward the Americans. The British tried to persuade the Choctaw to fight against the Patriots, but without success. One of the most bizarre efforts involved attempts to purchase Choctaw loyalty by distributing three thousand Jews' Harps among the tribe. The Choctaw preferred the mouth organ to other European musical instruments, but still they refused to join the Redcoats. Some served with the Americans, but most regarded it as a white man's war and stayed out of it. The tribe was more affected by the transfer of West Florida to Spain in 1781.

Anxious to block expansion of the Americans into the south, Spain signed a treaty with the Choctaw at Pensacola in 1784. An arrangement was made to exclude all but Spanish-licensed traders from their territories, a promise that particularly benefitted the Scotch traders, William Panton and John Forbes, who had established the trading firm of Panton, Leslie and Company in Pensacola only a year earlier. The tribe quickly learned the economic system of debts, but Spanish influence faded rapidly. Within a few years Spain transferred its claims to territory above the thirty-first parallel to the United States and its claims to Louisiana to Napoleon in 1800. Three years later, Bonaparte, needing money to go to war with Britain, sold it in turn to President Thomas Jefferson.[31]

In 1786, the Americans had gotten a foothold in the country by calling a conference of the southern tribes at Hopewell, South Carolina. Upon receiving an invitation to the meeting, Chief Franchimastabe, who resided in the Northwest District, turned to the Americans because the Spanish trading companies had failed to adequately supply the tribe. Considering his options, the Choctaw leader concluded that sending delegates to the conference was the best choice.

On December 26, the embarrassed Choctaw arrived late for the meeting. They explained that on their way through Creek country their horses were stolen and they were forced to finish the trip on foot. Having walked to Hopewell on the Keowie River, their clothing was so trail-worn that their wardrobes had to be replenished before negotiations could begin with American representatives, Benjamin Hawkins, Andrew Pickens, and Joseph Martin.

The Choctaw delegates included Yockonahoma, Yockehoopie, Mingohoopie, Tobocoh, Posshemastubie, and thirty-six lesser chiefs. John Pitchlynn, an adopted Englishman, served as the official interpreter. After much discussion, an agreement was reached and signed with X marks, since the Choctaw were illiterate at this time. Concluded on January 3, 1786, the Treaty of Hopewell contained a guarantee of Choctaw lands, recognition of American sovereignty and an agreement for American control of trade within the Choctaw Nation. The Choctaw further ceded three tracts of land, each six-mile square for establishing trading posts, but the location was to be decided on later.

It was the first of a long series of treaties with the United States. The final Article XI significantly provided: "The hatchet shall be forever buried, and the peace between the United States of America and friendship reestablished between the said states on the one part, and all the Choctaw Nation on the other part, shall be universal..."[32]

By 1798, the creation of the territory of Mississippi, and the growing white settlement around the Choctaw Nation, led to intense economic desires for Choctaw lands. In 1801, another treaty was negotiated at Fort Adams on the Mississippi River. This time the Choctaw ceded 2.6 million acres of hunting grounds along the Mississippi, from the thirty-first parallel to the Yazoo River. In addition, the tribe granted the United States the right to build a road through their country from Natchez northeastward to Nashville, Tennessee, the Natchez Trace. In return, the federal government paid the tribe $2,000 in merchandise and three sets of blacksmith tools, one for each district. Only one year later, on October 17, 1802, at Fort Confederation on the Tombigbee River, the tribe agreed to the survey of their eastern boundary, restricting them to the borders originally established with the British in 1763.

The Choctaw soon discovered a concerted effort by the Americans to trade them out of their homeland, a policy that gathered impetus during the Jefferson administration. One of the major reasons for the Louisiana Purchase was to secure a place for removal of the southern tribes, a place where tribes that did not want to adopt white ways would be safe from encroaching settlement. Since the American policy toward tribes was that occupying an area was not regarded as having sovereign rights and titles to that land, but having occupancy rights only, the federal government followed a rule of never giving titles to lands still in the possession of the Indians. The government would neither survey nor sell any lands until the Indian occupancy right had first been extinguished. This could be done only under the treaty-making clause of the American Constitution because the Indian tribes were regarded as independent nations.[33]

Jefferson's humanity was tempered considerably by his desire for land as seen by his schemes to convince the Indians along the Mississippi to cede their lands even before the Louisiana Purchase. As part of his efforts he arranged for the establishment of stores with liberal credit policies to attract the Indians with the intention of getting them into debt so they would be obligated to Washington. Knowing the tribes would accumulate heavy debts at the government store, known as a factory, Jefferson planned to liquidate them by land cessions. The factory system provided trade goods to the tribe at cost, since they were not intended to make a profit, only to force the Choctaw into a state of indebtedness.

In 1803, a Choctaw factory was opened on the site of an old French fort located at St. Stephens, chosen for the added advantage of being a buffer for trade from Panton, Leslie and Company from Mobile. Joseph Chambers, named to run the factory, was sent $10,000 worth of goods before he was even prepared to accept them. Later that same year Jefferson arranged another treaty at Hoe Buckintoopa. This time the Choctaw ceded 853,760 acres in southern Mississippi and Alabama for cloth, rifles, blankets, powder, lead, a saddle and blanket, and one silk handkerchief. Two years later, after George Strothers Gaines of Tennessee was appointed the American factor at St. Stephens, another treaty was arranged at Mount Dexter.

Despite paying taxes to the Spanish for bringing goods up the Tombigbee through Mobile, Gaines did a thriving business. The Choctaw, as expected, were turned into a debtor tribe bracketed by St. Stephens on the east and the Panton, Leslie Company on the south. John Forbes, a partner in the Panton, Leslie Company, personally lobbied Secretary of War Henry Dearborn for a treaty, promising to pressure the Choctaw to cede land if the government agreed to pay $55,000 owed to him by the tribe. The government naturally assumed the debt and agreed to pay the tribe $3,000 permanent annuity while the Choctaw ceded another 4,142,720 acres across their southern border.[34]

Relations with the tribe grew closer when a contingent of Choctaw warriors sided with the Americans as scouts for General "Mad" Anthony Wayne against the Northwest Indians, participating in the Battle of Fallen

Timbers in 1794. In 1808, when problems developed with Tecumseh and the Shawnee, the Choctaw again supported the Americans.

The quarrel grew out of a conference with Governor William Henry Harrison. Meeting the American leader for the first time, Tecumseh sat down on a bench very close beside the commander. Harrison grew increasingly annoyed as the chief continuously pushed closer as he talked, forcing Harrison to move until the two had reached the end of the bench. When Harrison finally protested, the Shawnee laughingly told the Governor that he had pushed him purposely to demonstrate how the Indian felt as the white man kept pressuring him to move over.

Added to the volatile mix was the voice of Tecumseh's brother, Tenskwatawa, the Prophet, who claimed to be the voice of the Great Red Father. Preaching a doctrine of throwing away their white trappings and returning to the old Indian ways, the Prophet urged the tribe to take up new songs and dances that would enable the Indian to drive out the whites forever.[35]

In 1811, Tecumseh, planning an Indian confederacy, recruited the Creek, causing a division within the tribe as their warriors argued loudly over the correct road to take. William McIntosh, Alexander Cornells, and Little Prince held hostilities in check, but a more vocal group called the Red Sticks led by Francis (Hillis Hadja), Peter McQueen, and William Weatherford advocated war.

Tecumseh then visited several Choctaw villages trying to persuade them to join his confederacy. Reaching Mokalusha, the principal village near modern Philadelphia, Tecumseh was received with honors and treated courteously as the Choctaw listened with sympathy to his words as he pleaded for intertribal peace, an end to treaties with the whites, and an alliance with the British against the Americans. Meetings were held at Chunky's Town near modern Meridian and at Moshulatubbee's Town on the Noxubee River, but everywhere Pushmataha, Chief of the Six Towns District, shadowed the Shawnee.

Following Tecumseh through the villages, Pushmataha spoke eloquently as he reminded the Choctaw of their unbroken friendship for the Americans. Declaring that the Choctaw had never shed the blood of white men in battle, the chief reasoned there was no cause to turn against them now. Joined by mixed bloods David Folsom and Peter Pitchlynn, Pushmataha pointed out the dangers of fighting against a stronger, more numerous people, but left the final decision for a later meeting. After consulting with a medicine man, advised by Pushmataha, a vote was taken concerning the wisdom of joining the Shawnee. The medicine man prudently discovered that the powers favored Pushmataha's side, and the Choctaw Council ordered Tecumseh to leave the nation.[36]

Chapter Two

In August 1813, the Red Stick Creeks, outnumbering the white settlers two to one, attacked Fort Mims on the Alabama River. Only thirty-six of more than 550 people escaped the slaughter. Andrew Jackson of Tennessee raised an army and attacked Talladaga, an upper Creek town, and the war was on.[37]

The three Choctaw district chiefs immediately raised an army of several hundred warriors to support the Americans. In one of the first campaigns Pushmataha, Moshulatubbee, Edmund Folsom, and John Pitchlynn joined the action against a Red Stick town in the western part of the Creek nation. Built at the beginning of the war, the site supposedly was located on Creek holy ground where, according to Creek medicine men, no whites could venture and live. Despite its supposed magical eminence, an army of Mississippi troops under General F. L. Claiborne, supported by 131 Choctaw forces, participated in the Battle of the Holy Ground in December 1813. The fighting turned into a rout, and the Americans put it to the sword.[38]

In 1814, the Choctaw joined Jackson for the decisive Battle of Horseshoe Bend on the Talapoosa River. On March 27, some 900 Creek warriors were attacked and defeated by Old Hickory's 2,000 forces. The Americans reported 557 were killed. At the head of his Choctaw warriors, Pushmataha next joined Jackson in the campaign into Florida and supported him later at the decisive Battle of New Orleans.

In 1814, peace negotiations were in progress at Ghent when the British decided to continue an operation that had been planned earlier, a raid on New Orleans. On December 2, Jackson arrived at the city fortifying it with two regular regiments, the Seventh and Forty-fourth, a thousand state militiamen, a battalion of three hundred city volunteers, a rifle company of sixty, a battalion of free blacks, primarily refugees from Santo Domingo, and twenty-eight Choctaw.

Despite Jackson's preparations, the British forces landed and moved without detection within a few miles of the town. On December 24, 1814, the Treaty of Ghent was signed ending the war, but the news did not reach America for another three weeks. By then another fight had already occurred. On January 15, 1815, Jackson's forces, barricaded behind cotton bales and logs, destroyed the British forces in the Battle of New Orleans. Just before the fighting began, Jackson sent Pierre "Peter" Gabriel Juzan with sixty Choctaw warriors into the swamp behind the British to attack at close range. Patrolling the edges of the slough, Juzan's men kept the British busy, killing more than fifty soldiers and wounding many more.

During the battle, Jackson reportedly asked Pushmataha if the fight was going well against the British for the Choctaw detachment. The chief responded with a Choctaw word, Hoke, "it is so," meaning things were all right. Jackson liked the word so much that he began using it as the American expression for O.K. Lasting only half an hour, the battle was total victory for the Americans. The British were forced to withdraw with 2,000 casualties, 289 dead, while the United States lost seventy-one, only thirty-one killed. News of the victory reached America at the same time as the Treaty of Ghent. The war was over, but so was the time of the Indian. The victory against the Creek proved no tribe could resist American advancement. The only alternative for the Indian leaders was to negotiate for the best terms possible for their tribes.

The treaty Jackson made with the Creek included a great cession of land in central Alabama that included an area between the Tombigbee and Black Warrior Rivers, long disputed with the Choctaw. Although staunch allies of Jackson, they found they had little choice but to relinquish their claims to the land and accept the eastern boundary between their country and the United States. In exchange they received $10,000 in goods and an annuity of $6,000 per year for twenty years.

As a wave of nationalism spread over the United States after the War of 1812, a major facet of that feeling involved making treaties of removal with the eastern Indian tribes. White settlement, creeping ever more closely toward the Mississippi River, caused federal authorities to endorse a serious effort to exchange lands in the west for Choctaw tribal lands in Mississippi.[39]

CHAPTA TUCHENA

~ CHAPTER THREE ~

"NONE OF THE CHOCTAW EVER DREW A BOW AGAINST THE

Chapter Three

UNITED STATES"

The people of the United States assumed an attitude of extreme chauvinistic arrogance after the Battle of New Orleans in 1815. A sense of national superiority that embraced justifications for American expansion swept over the nation, and the Southern states, already covetous of Indian lands, added removal of the eastern tribes to this ideology. The new philosophy, accompanied by a fever of evangelistic Protestantism, known as the Great Awakening, was soon aimed at the Choctaw, unresisting targets of both revivalism and jingoism.[40]

The tribe quickly accepted Euro-American culture as the deer grew scarce and cloth replaced buckskin for clothing. More dependent over time upon American trade goods and supplies in their daily lives, the Choctaw increasingly intermarried with the white traders and settlers moving into their country. The Durants, Folsoms, Pitchlynns, LeFlores, and McCurtains founded prominent family dynasties that gradually dominated Choctaw society. Serving as major agents of change within the tribe, their influence grew as the numbers of their mixed blood offspring enlarged proportionally during these years.[41]

In 1770, Louis Durant and the brothers, Louis and Michael LeFlore, French Canadians from Quebec, left on a trapping expedition down the Mississippi River. Exploring clear to the Gulf, the Frenchmen decided to settle among the Choctaw. Durant married a Choctaw wife, She Ni Yak, (A Rose Among Wild Flowers), fathered sons, Pierre, Charles, Lewis, and daughters, Margaret and Syllan, and was adopted into his wife's clan, the Hanak Iksa. In 1775, Durant purchased heifers and a bull in Mobile, imported them into the western Choctaw District along the Pearl River, and developed herding as a respected substitute for farming.

In 1803, the Durant family increased when Pierre married a Choctaw named Rachil, and their marriage produced seven sons and two daughters. When the Treaty of Dancing Rabbit Creek was signed, Pierre chose to keep his family in Mississippi, filed for land, and remained as a citizen until Chief Nitakechi visited the family a decade after the removal. The Durants, then numbering forty-eight, were convinced to remove to the West on December 30, 1844.

The Folsom family began with John Folsom, an Englishman of Scotch-Irish descent, who migrated to the Colonies and began a family in North Carolina. His son, Nathaniel Folsom, born in 1756, in Rowan County, moved to the village of Bok Tuklo (Two Creeks), in Mississippi, a town of about 400 Choctaw, after the Revolutionary War. Nathaniel and his brothers, Ebenezer and Edmond, settled in the Choctaw country in the 1770s, married full blood wives and founded large families. Nathaniel fathered twenty-four children with I-An-Ne-Cha and Ai-Ne-Chi-Hoyo, cousins of Chief Moshulatubbee. In 1803, Nathaniel moved the family to Pigeon Roost (Pachi a nusi), and opened a successful tavern on the Natchez Trace. He died in Indian Territory on October 9, 1833.

In 1791, his son, David, was born in Bok Tuklo. His mother was the full blood niece of Miko Puscus, the brother of Homastubbee, Moshulatubbee's father. Unfortunately, she contacted pneumonia during his birth and superstitious elders discussed killing the baby to drive out the evil spirits thought to be in possession of his body since a younger brother and sister had recently died of the disease, but David's grandmother stole him away and hid until the controversy ended peacefully. Sent to school in Tennessee, David only stayed six months before returning home to study. In 1813, after serving in the Creek War with Pushmataha, he married into another prominent mixed blood family when he wed Rhoda Nail, the daughter of Revolutionary War hero, Henry Nail, and his Choctaw wife. David sent his two younger brothers, McKee and Israel, to school in Cornwall, Connecticut, where Israel was the first to translate the Lord's Prayer into Choctaw.[42]

The Pitchlynn family began with the marriage of John Pitchlynn to mixed blood Rhoda Folsom. The son of Isaac Pitchlynn (Pitchland), a Scottish planter and friend of George Washington, who supposedly died while on a mission visiting the Choctaw, John was adopted into the tribe as an interpreter. He fathered three sons, James, John Jr., and Joseph, by his first wife and after her death in 1804, married her cousin Sophia, who bore him eight more children, the eldest being Peter Perkins Pitchlynn. Andrew Jackson once told Major Pitchlynn that the country in the west would belong to the Choctaw "as long as grass grows and water flows."

Sophia Folsom Pitchlynn, whose Choctaw name, "Lk-lo-ha-wah," meant "Loved but Lost," mothered her family plus three stepsons. Once while she was away, one of her stepsons, John Jr. (Jack), murdered her son, Silas, with a tomahawk, and to avenge his death according to Choctaw tradition she hired Jack killed. In May 1835, John Pitchlynn died while preparing to move to Indian Territory, but Sophia moved with her slaves to a plantation in the Choctaw Nation owned by son-in-law, Samuel Garland. She lived to be ninety-eight years old.[43]

In 1806, Pitchlynn's quarter-blood son, Peter Perkins Pitchhlynn, was born into wealth and tribal status in Noxubee County, Mississippi. Called Ha-tchoc-tuck-nee (Snapping Turtle) by his full blood friends, the Pitchlynn scion was told by his father that he was "wild, frolicsome, & fond of women, but yet strictly just and honorable and very liberal and too good to his friends just like his grandfather Ebenezer." After his first marriage to his second cousin, Rhoda Folsom, Pitchlynn established a plantation with slaves to work it near his father's home. Missionary Cyrus Kingsbury officiated at his wedding.

On August 5, 1826, the Choctaw drafted the first Tribal Constitution providing for three District Chiefs and a Council. Pitchlynn, only twenty years old at the time, was selected as Secretary of the National Council. Shortly, the first police force, the Lighthorsemen, was organized and Pitchlynn was appointed its head with the honorary title of "Colonel," a designation he proudly retained for the remainder of his life.[44]

Pitchlynn enrolled at Choctaw Academy in Kentucky, the first national Indian school but left after only a short time. Suggested by Choctaw agent William Ward, a native of Scott County, the school was founded by his friend, Colonel Richard "Dick" Mentor Johnson, a Revolutionary War hero credited with killing Tecumseh at the Battle of The Thames. Later elected Vice President of the United States, Johnson first located the school on a farm at Blue Springs, Scott County, before moving to White Sulphur Springs. The first Choctaw pupils, accompanied by Pitchlynn, arrived in October 1825.

The school opened officially on November 1, 1825. Objections by David Folsom that the first boys had all been from Moshulatubbee's district caused the leaders to send eighteen from each of the other two districts the next year to make a total of sixty-three. By 1830, there were eighty-nine Choctaw boys at the Academy. The instructors at the school, finding their Choctaw names too difficult to pronounce, assigned them names of prominent Americans. One of the most successful Academy graduates was Robert M. Jones who attended the school before it was closed in 1841. After removal, Jones operated plantations in Indian Territory that made him one of the richest plantation owners in the "Old South."

In 1828, the school adopted the Lancastrian system of education whereby older students taught the younger ones. Among the earliest student teachers were Choctaw students, William Trayhern, Pierre Juzan, and George Harkins, who also served as dormitory monitors. Another, Adam Nail, showed an aptitude for medicine and was allowed to study with the resident physician, Dr. H.T. Benedict. The boys studied reading, arithmetic, history, philosophy, algebra, surveying, blacksmithing, shoemaking, wagon making, and tailoring.

The Choctaw, in the meantime, instituted schools in their own homeland. By 1830, eleven schools had been established for the tribe. According to reports the school attendance was 260 boys.[45]

The LeFlores were descendants of Jean Baptiste LeFlau, a French soldier in Mobile about 1735. His son, Louis, was born in 1762, and married Rebecca and Nancy Cravat, nieces of Pushmataha. In 1801, Louis opened an inn on the Natchez Trace known as French Camps. During the War of 1812, he served as a major in the Battalion of Voluntary Choctaws. His children included Benjamin, Jack, Henry, Clarissa, Felice, Mary Ann, Forbis, and Greenwood. The young Forbis, turned over to his uncle in the Choctaw tradition, was taught the language and the culture of the tribe while his brothers went to white schools. In the fall of 1830, he was among the first to remove to Indian Territory. Leading a band of one hundred tribesmen, Forbis traveled up the Red River by flatboat to Doaksville.[46]

Greenwood LeFlore was born into the family in 1800. Developing a taste for the life of a wealthy planter, LeFlore built a plantation that boasted 15,000 acres of good cotton lands, 400 slaves, a steamboat, a sawmill, and a showplace mansion designed by James C. Harris, a famous Georgia architect. Known as "Malmaison" (House of Sorrow), the Southern manor was named in honor of a French chateau occupied by Josephine Bonaparte in the last years of her life. The two-story edifice, located atop a hill with landscaped views of the surrounding countryside, boasted fifteen rooms, six fireplaces, draped curtains, carpeted floors, and furniture imported from Paris. LeFlore's "palace in the wilderness" contained Benjamin West paintings framed in gold, a large library, and walls adorned with gifts presented to the family by the President of the United States. Greenwood personally financed the construction of a road over fourteen bridges across the rivers and streams to his estate at a cost of $75,000. Malmaison's greatest moment was the marriage of LeFlore's daughter, Rebecca, to Harris, who was given a plantation with one hundred slaves as a wedding gift. LeFlore was democratically elected chief at only twenty-two years of age.

The original McCurtain ancestors were Irish immigrants from Ulster. About 1753, the founder of the dynasty, Daniel McCurtain, arrived in America from County Down, Ireland, tracing his roots from a prominent family named McCartan. Settling in Mississippi where he married a full blood wife, he was licensed to trade with the Choctaw in 1765. His sons, Daniel and Thomas McCurtain, the eldest of ten mixed blood Irish and Choctaw children, set the family on the path to distinguished service to the tribe. Both were present at the signing of the Doak's Stand Treaty. Four of the sons, Canada, Samuel, Camper, and Cornelius, were students at the Choctaw Academy. Born in Mississippi in 1803, Cornelius removed to settle near Ft. Coffee and was the father of Jackson Frazier, Edmund, and Green McCurtain, all later chiefs.[47]

Missionaries arriving in the 1800s were equally liable for the rapidity of the white acculturation of the tribe. As the revivalistic Great Awakening spread over the frontier, Baptist, Presbyterian, and Methodist missionaries naturally sought out the Indians for conversion because the natives, perceived as living in darkness and sin, were deemed absolutely in need of evangelistic salvation. In 1762, an organization had been founded to work among the tribes called the American Society for Propagating the Gospel Among the Indians and Others in North America. In 1810, the equally influential American Board of Commissioners for Foreign Missions, an interdenominational association of Presbyterians and Congregationalists, was organized in Boston to evangelize particularly among the southeastern tribes. The American Board was immediately interested when Choctaw agent Silas Dinsmore informed the alliance that the tribe was "panting for instruction," and "earnestly requested" schools, more than religion, but the group knew that providing the tribe with schools would allow religious instruction at the same time.[48]

Although not particularly interested in changing their religious beliefs, the Choctaw were eager for education and accepted the missionaries on that basis. In 1818, the district chiefs expressed their gratitude to President James Monroe and the "Foreign Mission Society" for their efforts as the first missionaries arrived in the Nation. Only one year later the territory of Mississippi was granted statehood.[49]

The "Foreign Mission Society" had already made an impressive start towards distributing Christianity to the Indians. In May 1817, a school was founded in Cornwall, Litchfield County, Connecticut, aimed specifically at "educating youths of heathen nations." McKee Folsom, a member of the prestigious Folsom mixed bloods, enrolled in its second year of existence and was joined by his brother Israel in 1821. This was the same school attended by Cherokees Buck Watie, or Elias Boudinot, and John Ridge before it was disbanded in 1827. The two Cherokee later were major proponents of the removal policy for their tribe.[50]

In June 1818, Cyrus Kingsbury and Mr. and Mrs. Loring S. Williams arrived as the first missionaries to the Choctaw. Kingsbury (1786-1870), a native of Alstead, New Hampshire, graduated from Brown University then trained at Andover Theological Seminary where he was ordained in 1815. Known as Limping Wolf to the Choctaw, the missionary, lame from youth, supervised the construction of schoolhouses, storehouses, and cabins for his students at Elliot Mission, named for John Eliot, a Puritan missionary to the Algonquians in 1636. Located in the sparsely populated western district on the Yalobusha River, Adam Hodgson, a visitor from Liverpool, reported Elliot was a busy place for education in 1820. He stated: "In the morning at daylight, the boys were at agriculture and girls at domestic work. About 7 o'clock, they assembled for reading, singing, and prayer. Soon afterward for breakfast. After a time school opened with prayer and singing, a chapter on the Bible, and an examination on the chapter of the previous day. The children then proceeded to reading, writing, accounts, and English grammar. After school, boys returned to agriculture, the girls to sewing. After, they were free until the supper bell rang followed by a chapter of the Bible before their retirement to rooms in their log cabins."[51]

In 1820, Kingsbury established another mission, called Mayhew, on a site selected by John Pitchlynn and David Folsom. The missionary named the mission in honor of Thomas Mayhew, the first preacher to the Indians on Martha's Vineyard and founder of the earliest Puritan school for Indians in 1651. In 1821, Reverend Williams founded a mission at Newell on the Natchez Trace and Bethel a year later. By 1825, other missions had been established including Emmaus and Goshen in the Six Towns District.

The missionaries suffered greatly from the unaccustomed hot weather, fever, and dysentery, diseases and temperatures that the acclimated Choctaw scarcely noticed, but the faith and zeal of the evangelicals sustained them. More difficult for them as teachers was the emphasis placed on discipline for the students at the mission schools since the Choctaw had great concerns about any form of chastisement of their children. The most persistent problem for the early pedagogues was that Choctaw children were unused to discipline and never whipped by their parents while the missionary teachers were committed to corporal punishment. The most annoying issue for the missionary-teachers was that many of the Choctaw students, unable to cope even with criticism, often ran away and had to be brought back by their parents.

Learning the language so he could begin preaching, Dr. Kingsbury expressed great concern over the lax morals that he found among the tribesmen. Reporting that the greatest shock for him was the common practice of infanticide, the missionary exerted considerable pressure upon the tribe to persuade the Council to pass laws correcting the accepted societal practice that an unwanted child could be killed for any reason. In October 1822, Chief Aboha Kvllo Humma explained by letter to Kingsbury that rules had been enacted providing that a man could receive thirty-nine lashes for infanticide, introducing whiskey, and stealing hogs, cattle, or another man's wife. In 1821, the Lighthorsemen was created to enforce the new laws. The force took complete charge of the administration of criminal laws and the collection of debts within the Nation. The Lighthorsemen apprehended violators, tried their cases, and executed the sentences. There were no appeals.

In 1822, Cyrus Byington, the missionary scholar, joined Kingsbury. Born in 1793, in Stockbridge, Massachusetts, Byington had practiced law for five years before entering Andover Seminary to train as a Presbyterian minister. Licensed to preach in 1819, he was sent as a missionary to the Choctaw in November 1820. Making the trip to Mississippi by "ark" with twenty-three people, ten horses, a cow, and the household goods of several families, Byington arrived with seven other missionaries including Calvin Cushman, whose son, Horatio, later wrote one of the first histories of the tribe. Learning to speak the language, Byington's style of sermon delivery and his habit of blowing a loud cow horn to call the Choctaw in for services earned him an Indian name that meant "Sounding Horn."

Able to phonetically transpose Choctaw sounds into English words within a year of his arrival in Mississippi, the minister successfully authored a dictionary of more than 10,000 Choctaw words translated into English and 15,000 English words into Choctaw. Greatly aided by brothers, David and Israel Folsom, along with other educated Choctaw converts, Byington, as his own skills improved, supervised the translation of thousands of pages of English religious tracts and hymns into Choctaw while writing a number of books and tracts, including a Choctaw grammar. By the time of his death in 1868, he had a Choctaw dictionary, *A Dictionary of the Choctaw Language*, and a grammar.[52]

Another missionary sent by the American Board was Reverend Alfred E. Wright. A native of Columbia, Connecticut, Wright, born in 1788, was a graduate of Williams College in 1812. In 1819, he was ordained as a missionary in South Carolina and sent to Goshen in 1823. A student of medicine, Wright served as the "physician" of the missionaries. With the assistance of Israel Folsom as translator, Wright also completed a translation of part of the Gospel of St. Luke, and left with his wife for Utica, New York, to get it published in October 1831. He later moved to Indian Territory to create Wheelock Academy, named for the first president of Dartmouth College.

The "school teacher" of the Choctaw missionaries was Ebenezer Hotchkin. Born in 1803, in Richmond, Massachusetts, Hotchkin never attended college. Having only a common school education, he was nonetheless given an appointment as a teacher from the American Board and sent to Mississippi in 1828. In 1832, he receiving a license to preach and removed with the Choctaw to their new country. He continued working among them until his death in 1867.

All the mission institutions operated under the Lancastrian Plan whereby brighter students taught younger ones under the direction of an adult. Boys and girls were schooled in arithmetic and geography in separate classes while advanced classes studied the New Testament. The students stayed a full year with the missionaries, but were given a vacation of two or three months in the summer. By 1828, there were more than forty missionaries in Choctaw country.

The first lay preacher was David Folsom who united with the church along with his brothers, Isaac, Samuel, and John, in June 1829. Helping the missionaries with their translations, David and his brothers were responsible for ordering a large shipment of books from Boston that served as the nucleus of the first Choctaw library. Israel was the first translator of the Lord's Prayer.

When the missionaries were informed that the federal government intended to push for removal of the tribe, they reasoned there would be no armed resistance to the policy because it would be contrary to their religious training and traditions. Although many full bloods blamed the troubles that befell the tribe on them, for the most part, the mixed bloods realized the missionaries were correct. There was no other choice to removal, and the tribe must make the best of a difficult situation.[53]

The Choctaw Nation remained remarkably stable and dedicated to American customs during these years. District Chiefs Apuckshunnubbee, Homastubbee, and Pushmataha were all considered strong supporters of acceptance of the white culture as well, and each quietly maintained the political system and the boundaries of their respective political districts. Apuckshunnubbee was chief of the western district, Homastubbee was chief of the northeastern district until replaced by Moshulatubbee in 1809, and Pushmataha controlled the southeastern one.

The most loyal was the famed A-Push-ma-ta-ha whose name meant "no more in the bag." Born in 1764, on the Noxubbee River, two miles above Macon, the calmly dignified chief was wise in councils, an admired warrior, and eloquent orator. The one secret he always kept was his lineage, never revealing his parents or origins. Rumors circulated widely that his relatives were all killed by Creek, and accounted for his unending hatred of the tribe, according to some, but there was never confirmation of the stories. John Pitchlynn, who was only a few years younger than Pushmataha, stated that he had known him since childhood, but that he had no knowledge of Pushmataha's history. When questioned about his ancestry, Pushmataha would only respond, "Chacta sai Hoke" (I am a Choctaw).

The first occasion that brought the legendary chief into prominence was his mysterious appearance as a quiet, silent figure in the midst of a hunting party's camp. Nothing was said as it was considered impolite to question a stranger, but after a few days it was discovered that no one knew the young man. An old man was finally sent to learn the stranger's identity and where he was from, despite risking extremely bad etiquette. The old man, after talking with the mysterious newcomer, only reported that the young hunter refused to give his name. This prompted the others to begin calling him Hohchiffo Iksho (nameless) until something happened that they could learn his true name or give him one.

When the party reached bear country, they were all eager to be off and none wanted to take time to set up camp. This was left to those who came along to do the work. Besides only about half of them had rifles, mostly armed with bows and arrows. The nameless one only had a knife and a bow, and he was so skinny that few believed him capable of shooting such a bow as he carried. The others suggested that he should stay in camp. He was told that there would be plenty of time to do his share of hunting since the hunt was supposed to last for three or four moons, but he informed them immediately and calmly that he intended to hunt, not keep camp. That day many bear were killed, and in the evening the party sat around the fire and told stories of their adventures with the most daring coming from the nameless one. The boy told them that what he had done was nothing compared to what he intended to do before the hunt was over. The old men responded to this comment by giving him a new name. This time he was called Ishtalauata, which meant to brag or boast, but as time passed his reputation as a great hunter proved correct. It turned out that he was the most skilled one in the party, killing more bears and taking more meat and skins than even the most experienced of the hunters.

When spring arrived and the hunt was over, some forty or more of the party decided to extend the trip with a war party across the Mississippi for scalps. Volunteers were asked to come forward, and the first one to respond was Ishtalauata. The older, more experienced warriors only laughed, predicting the expedition would be a failure for allowing such a youngster along. The boy said nothing. As the others prepared to return home, he went to the older hunters and gave them his meat and skins, telling them that since he had neither home nor relatives they should divide the hunt equally among the less successful hunters.

Crossing the Mississippi on cane rafts, the warriors traveled many days before cautiously entering the Red River country. Taking care to leave no sign behind them, the party eventually reached the enemy camp safely, but they soon discovered they were outnumbered and were easily defeated. Only taking one scalp, the party separated and escaped, but the young Ishtalauata was left behind. Later, when the party reassembled, everyone was accounted for except him. Thinking that he had been killed, they admitted that he had not been treated very kindly, but just as they were packing to leave the young man quietly reappeared. Traveling several days before they felt safe again, the party finally stopped long enough to hold a feast and tell their war stories. When he was called upon to relate his experiences, the young man, holding aloft the trophies to prove his statements, told of taking three scalps from enemies killed by other Choctaw and one killed by him.

After much praise the warriors proposed that he should have a new war name, but he objected saying that when a name was given to him it must be from the deeds he had accomplished but told by someone else. The warriors returned home and held a great war dance, but the young man did not participate. He simply left quietly and was not heard from for several months.

His reputation as a warrior continued to spread through this time, because of his many battles with the Muskogee that supposedly stemmed from the fact his family had been killed by the tribe, leaving him an orphan. As his fame grew, he continued to try to find a suitable war name until finally consulting with an Ishtahullo, or high priest that always accompanied war parties. The Ishtahullo carried with him a leather bag containing thirteen stones of different colors, and when a man was deemed worthy of a war name, the priest would select one of the stones. As the man recounted his war stories, the stone would be the source of the new name. As the young man told each story, another stone was taken from the bag until all had been used, but the young man still refused to accept any suggestions for a name. After more raids and honors were bestowed upon the warrior, he returned to the priest and asked for a name a second time. He was told, "There are no more stones in the bag. I will give you a name that you greatly merit, the most distinguished name ever conferred upon a warrior. Your name will be Apushmataha, which means 'no more in the bag'." The young man, satisfied with the new title, responded, "Apushmataha. Finopa."

Pushmataha added more fame to his legend when he raised a large war party against the Osage in the western country. More than 320 warriors joined him in the most successful raid in Choctaw memory. Upon their return a three-day war dance celebrated the 890 scalps taken by the raiders. The old Chief Tuscona Hopaii offered to resign and permit Pushmataha to replace him, but Pushmataha refused. He was always called Chief ever after, and when the older leader died, Pushmataha was elected, without being consulted, by acclamation. He remained District Chief for the rest of his life.[54]

The handsome, six-foot two, robust, dignified warrior, famous for his eloquence as a speechmaker, was given the name "Waterfall" for his oratory skills. One of his greatest orations was in response to the speeches of Tecumseh, a recognized debater in his own right. Thinking the Choctaw would not be able to resist his logic, Tecumseh appeared before a general council of the Choctaw and Chickasaw tribes accompanied by thirty of his warriors. The great Shawnee chief spoke in Algonquin with his speeches translated by interpreters of the past relations between the tribes and the whites and repeatedly told the tribes of the many wrongs committed by the whites in the past. After a lengthy attack on the Americans, he concluded with an impassioned appeal to join with the Shawnee to drive the palefaces from their lands.

According to General Sam Dale, an eyewitness, Pushmataha rose as the Council finally quieted and calmly responded with the greatest speech he had ever heard. The Chief told the Council that he sympathized with the misfortunes suffered at the hands of the whites by the Shawnee but reminded his listeners this had not been the experience of the Choctaw. He pointed out that the whites had bought their skins, their corn, cotton, game, and baskets, and given them a fair exchange for their goods. Moreover, the whites had given the tribe cotton gins, taught their women spinning and weaving, helped in the production of crops, and taught the children to read and write from their books. "They have doctored our sick; they have clothed our suffering; they have fed our hungry," he added. "Where," he asked, "is the Chickasaw or Choctaw delegation who has ever gone to St. Stephens with a worthy cause and been sent away empty handed?"

The Chief told the Council that the Choctaw were bound in peace to the Great White Father in Washington by a sacred treaty and warned that the Great Spirit would punish those who would break this word. Finally, he advised his people to remember the consequences of war. It meant the death of many brave warriors, hunger and starvation for the children, and suffering and sadness for the women and old ones. He finished with an emotional appeal to side with him by throwing their tomahawks on his side of the council fires. The air resounded with the sound of hatchets cast in his favor.

Tecumseh, realizing the failure of his mission, spoke in Shawnee thinking the Choctaw could not understand him, "Pushmataha is a coward and the Choctaw and Chickasaw braves are squaws." Pushmataha, in fact capable of understanding the language, was enraged by the comment. He turned on the Shawnee, shouting:

"Halt, Tecumseh. Hear me. You have come here, as you have often gone elsewhere, with a purpose to involve peaceful people in unnecessary trouble with their neighbors . . . I know your history well. You are a disturber. You have ever been a troublemaker . . . You have made your choice; you have elected to fight with the British. The Americans have been our friends and we shall stand by them. We will furnish you safe conduct to the boundaries of this nation as properly befits the dignity of your office. Farewell, Tecumseh. You will see Pushmataha no more until we meet on the fateful warpath."[55]

Pushmataha, as a close observer of the white man, often tried to emulate him in public. Noting the treatment of wives by officers at St. Stephens while serving as a Lieutenant Colonel in the American army during the War of 1812, he determined to copy them as best he could. Since the custom every afternoon was for the officers to take a stroll along the heights overlooking the Tombigbee with their wives on their arms, Pushmataha immediately sent couriers home to fetch one of his wives. Thereafter, he could be seen each day walking with the equivalent pomp and ceremony of the other officers.

The same custom got him into trouble. When one of the enlisted men insulted his wife by poking fun at her, Pushmataha immediately sought out the man and proceeded to whip him with the broadside of his sword. Placed under arrest for the incident, Pushmataha explained that he had only given the man one or two blows to teach him some manners. General Claiborne corrected him by explaining that an officer did not strike a common soldier. Pushmataha responded, "Being only a common soldier was the reason he was hit with the side of the blade. Had you insulted her, General, I would have used the sharp edge." Claiborne persisted to tell Pushmataha the proper course in such circumstances was to bring the offender before a competent military authority for discipline. "The proper course," answered Pushmataha, "and the only safe one is not to insult my wife."

Pushmataha had difficulty accepting other white ways. Asked if he considered polygamy "a bad practice," the Chief, who had two wives, responded definitely not. He explained, "Is it not right that every woman should be married? How can that be, when there are more women than men, unless some men marry more than one?" On another occasion Pushmataha found a white soldier tied up and being punished for some indiscretion and inquired what the man had done to warrant such treatment. Told that it was punishment for being drunk, the astonished Chief could only state, "Is that all? Many good warriors get drunk!"[56]

General Jackson conferred the appointment of Brigadier General on Pushmataha as the commander of a brigade of 800 Choctaw warriors during the War of 1812. Knowing each other well, Jackson addressed him as "Brother Push" at the treaty talks at Doak's Stand in 1820, and although the two disagreed at times, the two signed a treaty. A perpetual school fund for the education of Choctaw youth was one of its provisions, and the Chief's comment on the treaty proved prophetic: "We have acquired from the United States her best remaining territory west of the Mississippi, and this treaty provided a perpetual fund for the education of our children. I predict that in a few generations its benefits will enable the Choctaw to fight in the white man's armies and to hold office in the white man's government."

In 1823, the Chief attended a Council near the residence of John Pitchlynn about eighty miles from Pushmataha's home. On July 3, the business was concluded and a banquet was held to celebrate American independence the following day. When the time came for the guests to depart, someone observed that Chief Pushmataha had no horse and Pitchlynn decided to give him one because the Chief was getting on in years. The gift was made on the condition that Pushmataha promised not to trade it for whiskey as he had acquired a reputation for drinking in his later years. The Chief happily rode away on a fine young pony, but not long afterward he arrived back at the Pitchlynn home on foot again. Asked what happened to the horse, he responded that he had lost it on a ball game. Angrily reminded that he had promised not to sell the animal, Pushmataha responded, "That was true, but I

was his daughter, Tioka, renown in her own right for support of her people. Selected as a tribal chieftain in 1801, Apuckshunnubbee advocated signing the early Choctaw treaties with the United States and influenced his followers to do the same. Described as a "large man, tall and bony, with a down look," the Chief "was of a superstitious and religious cast of mind." Called a "good Choctaw" by his people, he was a leader of deep thought and intellect who wielded supreme influence over the western district.

Living to be more than eighty years of age, his most famous moment was his death en route to visit President James Monroe in Washington in the early autumn of 1824. Since another treaty was needed to correct the error found in the Treaty of Doak's Stand when it was learned that the treaty lands given the tribe were already partially occupied by whites, the Choctaw were asked to visit Washington to make new arrangements. The Choctaw party invited to the Capital to discuss the problem was composed of the District Chiefs along with Nittahkachee, Talking Warrior, Red Fort, David Folsom, Captain Daniel McCurtain, John Pitchlynn, and Robert Cole, the son of a captive white man and Shumake, the sister of Apuckshunnubbee. The proposed route, along the Natchez Trace, was first to Nashville, then to Lexington, Kentucky, through Maysville, across the Ohio River to Chillicothe, then eastward over the National Highway.

On October 18, 1824, the party, traveling by stage, arrived in Maysville, Kentucky. The next day the *Maysville Eagle*, the local newspaper, reported that the "Medal Chief" had supped at an inn run by a Captain Langhorne and attempted to walk down to the river during the night. Losing his way, the Chief fell off an abutment on the road, hitting his head, receiving severe injuries. The unfortunate Apuckshunnubbee lingered for two days before succumbing to his illness. The townspeople arranged his funeral and buried him with full military honors. His nephew, Captain Cole, who succeeded the octogenarian leader, read his funeral oration in Choctaw. Chief Apuckshunnubbee was honored and respected for his judgment and wisdom by all who knew him. Celebrated as a famous warrior and orator, his influence was supreme over the entire nation.[58]

Whites continued to move into the Choctaw Mississippi country over the next several years, and the mixed blood leaders and families played a major part in bringing them in. Gradually, the mixed bloods came to identify their interests with the whites. Most were unconscious agents of white encroachment, men who came to believe that the adoption of European ways offered the best and only hope for the tribe. Unfortunately, it was not long before the Choctaw were displaced and the Trail of Tears became a reality.[59]

CHAPTA USHTA

~ CHAPTER FOUR ~

"THE TRAIL OF TEARS"

Chapter Four

The rich farmlands along the Tombigbee and Pearl River bottoms plus millions of acres of timber and hunting grounds bordered on the west by the Mississippi River proved an irresistible attraction for southern farmers in the 1800s. Colonial homesteaders drifting into the area soon inaugurated a concerted effort to take over the farms and plantations established by the Choctaw and replace them as the legitimate owners. For the next three decades American diplomacy was aimed at accomplishing this objective for the white voters of the United States.

The first success was the Treaty of Fort Adams. In 1800, the United States convinced the Choctaw Tribal Council to cede 1,641,920 acres bordered on the south by the Gulf of Mexico and the Mississippi River on the west as a buffer zone against the French after Spain returned all of Louisiana to Napoleon. The Choctaw Nation at the time was composed of three distinct political districts, Okla Hannali, or Six Towns, with Pushmataha as Chief, Ahe Apvt Okla, Potato eating People, under Moshulatubbee's leadership, and Okla Falaya, or Long or Separated People, with Apuckshunnubbee as Miko. Since all the acreage of the treaty came from the Okla Falaya district, Apuckshunnubbee strongly opposed the agreement and withdrew from the delegation, telling the other chiefs that he would never agree to a treaty giving up more Choctaw land, but the others, convinced by gifts, trade offers, and money, "touched the pen" to a treaty on December 17, 1801.

Less than two years passed before American negotiators returned for more land, and this time it was Pushmataha's turn to be unhappy. Despite objections from both Pushmataha and Chief Apuckshunnubbee, the Choctaw were persuaded to cede 853,760 acres from the Okla Hannali district. Although they refused to negotiate, Moshulatubbee agreed to sign a treaty and convinced enough others to "make their marks" to make a legal and binding compact. The Treaty of Hoe Buckintoopa was concluded on August 31, 1803.

Barely two years later the Americans, pressured by southern farm lobbyists, returned with more demands. The United States requested another 4,142,720 acres from the Okla Falaya and Okla Hannali districts, almost the entire Tombigbee River valley. Opposition came from Apuckshunnubbee and Pushmataha as usual, but with support, for once, from Moshulatubbee. Only a few Choctaw attended the conference near John Pitchlynn's home, but an agreement, the Treaty of Mount Dexter, was negotiated on November 16, 1805. The treaty acknowledged the Choctaw interpreter's support with an award of $2,500 for "losses and service" to the American government. The provision led to implications of bribery and wrongdoing on the part of Pitchlynn and his father, Isaac, who was still alive at this time despite having been reported dead for a number of years. Both were accused of impropriety, but apparently the money was a legitimate payment for work by the two men. Typically, authorities added a solemn pledge to the treaty that "this is the last time that the United States will ask the Choctaw Nation to give up any of its traditional homeland," a promise that lasted ten years.

In 1816, the Treaty of St. Stephens was signed as an agreement for the establishment of trading posts within the Nation, but the next major land cession was the Treaty of Doak's Stand in 1820. By then Secretary of War John C. Calhoun, very aware of the relationship between Chief Pushmataha and American negotiator, General Andrew Jackson, had made a decision to concentrate the policy of removal of all the southern tribes on the Choctaw. General Jackson's approach to the problem was an equal exchange of the land in the western United States for the Choctaw homelands in Mississippi. Specifically, he proposed to trade the "Quapaw Cession," approximately thirteen million acres between the Arkansas and Red Rivers from their sources to their confluence with the Mississippi, ceded by the Quapaw in 1818. Secretary Calhoun, in complete agreement with Jackson's assessment, ordered him to offer the Choctaw any or all of the Cession, just get them "the farthest south and the farthest west as possible."

Jackson asked for money from the government to pay Choctaw leaders for their signatures on a new treaty, but all Calhoun could get appropriated was $20,000. Already cognizant that he would have some trouble with Apuckshunnubbee, Jackson assumed that Moshulatubbee and Pushmataha would probably oppose any proposals that involved making the Choctaw leave their homeland, but he had an added, and powerful, advantage on his side, a strong ally within the tribe, John Pitchlynn. For more than a year Jackson tried to get the chiefs to meet with him before Pitchlynn's influence finally convinced them to attend a council at a trading post known as Doak's Stand on the first Monday of October 1820. Jackson, gleeful at the opportunity, laid in a twenty-day supply of beef along with corn and hundreds of gallons of liquor, planning on achieving an agreement in the customary American diplomatic way, by keeping the delegates drunk until they signed a treaty. He arrived from Washington to complete preparations for the appearance of the Choctaw on September 28.

On October 2, Moshulatubbee appeared with his delegation followed the next day by Apuckshunnubbee and Pushmataha, each with about eighty tribesmen. Jackson proposed food and whiskey before opening the formal conference, but Apuckshunnubbee and his people refused any rations. Explaining that they expected to oppose any future land deals, the Okla Falaya delegates stated that they did not want to feel indebted to the government for its hospitality.[60]

Jackson, without further hesitation, asked the Choctaw delegates to cede one-third of their land, some five million acres, in exchange for a tract in the West bordered by the Arkansas and Red Rivers, the "Quapaw Cession." Making the grant as attractive as possible, Jackson further offered financial and technical assistance for each emigrant and for the tribe in the form of weapons, domestic and farm implements, schools, subsistence, and annuities. The Choctaw, initially regarding the treaty proposals suspiciously, were encouraged by the missionaries, particularly Cyrus Kingsbury, who at first advised against signing anything. Only after personal consultation with Jackson was Kingsbury convinced of the wisdom of another treaty. Jackson told him candidly that an agreement was the only alternative to violence, stating directly that war would likely be waged against the Indians to force removal if his attempt at peaceful negotiations failed. Learning the truth, the missionary realized that supporting the treaty was the best and probably the only way of saving his beloved, adopted people.

The chiefs, also told the facts, finally realized there was little choice. Pushmataha, knowledgeable of the offered lands, as he often hunted the western country, soon acknowledged Jackson's predictions for the tribe's future. He understood that failure to accede to removal would likely result in extermination for the tribe. This sad, bitter conclusion, along with the American commissioner's continual warnings that not accepting a new treaty meant the end of American-Choctaw friendship, caused the Choctaw to reluctantly agree to the Treaty of Doak's Stand on October 18, 1820.

The Choctaw returned home dejected and suspicious. Jackson added offers of a blanket, an iron kettle, a rifle, a bullet mold, lead, powder, and enough corn to last a family a full year, but few were willing to take the final step of removal. They were tired of listening to American offers, and there was little faith in the government's promise that this was the last one. None doubted the federal negotiators would soon want more land.

There were immediate protests to the treaty, but, surprisingly, not from the Indians. An Arkansas delegation led by James Woodson Burns indignantly complained to Washington that the lands were already inhabited by white settlers and contained five of the largest populated counties and about one-third of the population in the entire territory. In 1820, a territorial census revealed a population of 999 pioneer-tough squatters and frontiersmen along with eighty-two slaves in Miller County, named for Governor James Miller. In 1824, a post office was established at Miller Courthouse to serve the growing numbers of settlers with John H. Fowler appointed as the first postmaster. While most of its settlers located on the north bank of the Red River near settlements called Pecan Point and Jonesborough, many of these former residents of Missouri, following in the wake of Moses and Stephen Austin, drifted across southeastern Indian Territory into southwestern Arkansas. By 1833, the population in Miller County had increased to 1,281, ninety-one of whom were slaves.

Chapter Four

Numerous complaints were sent into Washington from these white settlers who suddenly discovered the government had traded their lands out from under them. Accompanying their grievances were Arkansas newspaper editorials expressing additional opposition to the government's policy of giving away Miller County, the better part of Hempstead, and portions of Clark and Pulaski Counties. The editors argued bitterly that it was grossly unfair to ask 3,000 settlers to uproot themselves just to please the inhabitants of Mississippi.[61]

Calhoun, suddenly finding himself in a serious political dilemma, tried to avoid the problem by urging Agent William Ward to get the Choctaw moving, and when Ward failed to do it quickly enough, Calhoun replaced him with Edmund Folsom. Originally employed to guide emigrants west, Folsom had even less luck than his predecessor. The Choctaw seemed determined to stay in Mississippi despite the fact their homeland had been reduced to only 10,432,130 acres. As the situation increased in emotionalism, Calhoun reversed himself. In 1822, he announced a change in policy to allow time for boundary settlements to be worked out with Arkansas, hopefully also allowing enough time for the voters' tempers to cool down. At the same time, Calhoun, with the approval of Congress, appointed new commissioners to deal with the tribe, their mission now to convince the Choctaw to surrender part of their Arkansas cession for land farther west. In January 1823, Calhoun appointed General Thomas Hinds of Mississippi and William Woodward of Arkansas Territory to negotiate a new boundary with the Choctaw, but when they failed, Calhoun insisted the Choctaw send a delegation to Washington for personal discussions.

The date of the conference was set for June 25, 1824. Invitations asked the chiefs to bring a delegation of twelve with them to allow the sub-chiefs, war chiefs, and advisors to participate in the meetings, but the Choctaw did not even leave for Washington until September. They had only reached Maysville, Kentucky, before disaster struck. On September 23, Chief Apuckshunnubbee died of injuries sustained in an accident and was buried in the town. The commission, sad and discouraged, moved slowly on and finally arrived in Washington in November.

The delegation continued to be plagued by one problem after another. Housed in Tenneson's Hotel at government expense, President James Monroe's refusal to see the Choctaw commission forced the members to deal only with Calhoun. An ill and discouraged Chief Pushmataha wrote to the President, "I have been here many days, but have not talked with you and have been sick." On Christmas Eve, 1824, the Okla Hannali District Chief, revered by the tribe and whites alike, came down with the "croup" and died of his illness. Despite more than a dozen others with him, the delegation expenses included a bar bill for $2,149.50 and an additional tab for $349.75 for oysters and liquor prompting rumors that whiskey and high living were the real causes of Pushmataha's death, but regardless of the reason for his passing, the Choctaw had lost their most famous and prestigious leader.[62]

On January 20, 1825, a treaty was signed providing $6,000 per year perpetual annuity, an additional $6,000 per year for sixteen years for the Doak's Stand Treaty, a government waiver of all claims of debts owed by the Choctaw, and compensation to all Choctaw veterans of the War of 1812. The Choctaw promised evacuation of most of the Arkansas lands after a survey was run. Most important, the boundary of the Choctaw Nation was fixed at the 100th parallel for the western boundary, the south bank of the Red River for the southern, the Canadian to the Arkansas for the northern, and the eastern boundary would begin 100 paces west of Fort Smith and run due south to the Red.[63]

In 1825, John Quincy Adams succeeded Monroe as President, Calhoun moved up to Vice-President, and the new Secretary of War, James Barbour of Virginia and head of the newly created Office (Bureau) of Indian Affairs, Thomas L. McKenney, inherited the question of Indian removal. Displaying the same enthusiasm earlier shown by Calhoun, these officials supported the policy with equal fervor as the whites were already asking for more Choctaw lands and the Mississippi state officials were demanding action. Senator Thomas B. Reed was soon the most popular politician in the South loudly proposing that the Choctaw cede all their lands to the state of Mississippi and accept American citizenship or remove to the West. His policy, leading to threats and rumors of violence, made the older Choctaw less willing to resist, while new leaders, mostly mixed bloods favoring removal, like David Folsom and Greenwood LeFlore, moved into positions of tribal leadership.

In the fall of 1826, William Clark, Thomas Hinds, and John Coffee were appointed commissioners to meet with the Choctaw for yet another round of treaty talks. A committee of thirteen Choctaw listened to an offer of $1 million for the remainder of their lands in Mississippi plus finances for transportation to the west and land for those who wished to stay, but the Choctaw turned down the offer prompting McKenney, disappointed but determined, to arrange a personal visit through the Choctaw country. McKenney, the former Superintendent of Indian Affairs from 1816 to 1822, was one of the organizers of the New York Board for the Emigration, Preservation, and Improvement of the Aborigines of America. Preaching the doctrine of removal to all who would listen, he was received courteously everywhere but given only polite acknowledgments. Although failing to convince anyone, his visit, ironically, did improve relations. The Choctaw were much less suspicious and made an agreement with him to look over the country in the west.

A large party left in the late summer, returning in December, but while they were gone on their exploring expedition, Andrew Jackson was elected President, effectively ending any hope of moderation or patience toward removal. Until his election the policy had been one of choice. The commissioners had previously used threats, promises, bribery, any tactic available, but they had never resorted to outright force, always leaving the final option of removal to the Choctaw. Under Jackson's direction this policy changed. The Indians no longer had an alternative.[64]

Perceived as a trusted friend who had led the Indians into battle during the War of 1812, Jackson quickly revealed himself after the election of 1828. Astounding his former allies, Jackson revealed his true self by stating that money could be used to corrupt some of the chiefs into accepting removal. In May 1829, he instructed Secretary of War John Eaton to offer the Choctaw chiefs "rewards," because when they were brought into line "the rest would follow."

In December 1829, the removal issue was the first object of concern for the Tennessean in his annual message to Congress. The former Indian fighter stated, "I suggest, for your consideration, the propriety for setting apart an ample district west of the Mississippi, and without the limits of any State or Territory now formed, to be guaranteed to the Indian tribes as long as they shall occupy it. This emigration should be voluntary, for it would be as cruel as unjust to compel the aborigines to abandon the graves of their fathers and seek a home in a distant land. But they should be distinctly informed that, if they remain within the limits of the United States, they must be subject to their laws..."[65]

This simple solution, the same as had been previously suggested by Presidents George Washington, Thomas Jefferson, James Monroe and John Quincy Adams, resulted in quick action this time because of Jackson's personal prestige. In January 1830, the state of Mississippi passed legislation extending state laws over the Choctaw, revoking any privileges of the Indians and prescribing penalties of $1,000 and twelve months in prison for anyone presuming to serve as a tribal official or for failures to comply with the state statutes. Congress, responding with even more finality, passed the Indian Removal Act on May 28. After a long, bitter debate, the law authorized Jackson to begin the necessary steps toward securing an exchange of land with the tribes whether they wished to remove or not.[66]

The first treaty accomplished under the new policy was negotiated with the Choctaw. On July 30, 1829, Okla Hannali Chief David Folsom, informed by Secretary of War John H. Eaton that the Choctaw could not long survive if they remained in Mississippi, hurriedly called for a meeting with Okla Falaya Chief Greenwood LeFlore to discuss ways to deal with removal. At first opposed to the policy, the tribal leaders tried to beat the whites at their own game by organizing the tribe, writing a constitution, and proclaiming LeFlore Principal Chief, but the General Council rescinded these steps in October. Instead, the Council named Moshulatubbee Chief of the Ahe Apvt Okla, and Pushmataha's nephew, Nitakechi, Chief of Okla Hannali, and George W. Harkins, Apuckshunnubbee's nephew, Chief of Okla Falaya.

LeFlore, deposed as District Chief, then reversed his position and took action in favor of removal. In April 1830, he arranged to have himself designated as Chief at a Tribal Council friendly to his position, secured a vote in favor of emigration, and drafted a treaty of removal to send to Washington. Under the LeFlore treaty, each Choctaw family received 640 acres and each male 320 acres that could be sold to the state for cash. Each captain received a suit of clothes, a sword, and $50 annually for four years, and the tribe would be removed and sustained for one year and granted a perpetual annuity of $50,000. Given a copy of the treaty on May 6, President Jackson was pleased the Choctaw were willing to trade their land and move west but recommended rejection of the proposals feeling the price would establish a bad precedent for later treaties that he expected to make with other tribes. Jackson opposed acceptance of the LeFlore agreement on the grounds that its price was simply too high. Besides, both Moshulatubbee and Nitakechi attacked the treaty and the men who had drawn it up. The United States Senate, concerned primarily with President Jackson's stand, rejected the treaty and negotiations resumed once more.[67]

Jackson next invited the Choctaw to send delegates to discuss preliminary arrangements for a final treaty during his summer vacation in August in Franklin, Tennessee. The tribe dutifully debated the proposal for several months before finally deciding not to go. The Choctaw leaders explained that some were fearful for their lives should word be leaked that they were even discussing a final removal treaty. LeFlore, who by this time had secretly negotiated a deal that would allow him to stay in Mississippi on the condition he persuaded the tribe to move, wrote Jackson telling him to send "some good men" to explain the government's policy on removal. Although angry at the Choctaw refusal to meet him at Franklin, Jackson realized the opportunity for negotiation was still open and dispatched Secretary of War Eaton and John Coffee, a close personal friend, to meet with the tribe. The two quickly decided on a site in Noxubee County known to the Choctaw as Chukfi Ahihla Bok, Dancing Rabbit Creek, and sent invitations for a conference to meet on September 15, 1830.

By the time the Indians began arriving at the place, some of the worst elements of frontier society had learned of the meeting and set up shop. There were gamblers, prostitutes, outlaws, liquor dealers, all sorts of unscrupulous characters, but no missionaries. Using the excuse that the commissioners were negotiating a treaty not holding church services, none of the missionary groups were allowed to attend. Eaton even refused them permission to be on the grounds. He called them "improper" participants, but everyone was aware of the true reason since Kingsbury and Byington had openly opposed further discussions of removal.

On Saturday, September 18, 1830, the conference officially opened between the commissioners and more than 6,000 Choctaw tribesmen. John Coffee addressed the crowd in a paternalistic, bureaucratic manner with the astounding statement that the time for talking and negotiating was over. Counseling the tribesmen the time had come to sign a final treaty of removal, he remarked flatly that if the tribe did not want to negotiate on this basis they might as well all go home. As arguments broke out over his speech, the meeting was adjourned before tempers got out of control.

Three days passed before the meeting resumed and the American commissioners made any further proposals. Confident that the Choctaw would not dare refuse their offers, the American delegates proposed the Choctaw evacuate all their lands and emigrate to the west in return for money, farm and household goods, subsistence for one year, and payments for improvements on their Mississippi lands. After making the proposals, the two diplomats left the campgrounds to allow the Indians time to discuss their answer.

The next morning to the utter astonishment of the commissioners, the Choctaw informed them that the tribe had almost unanimously voted against the treaty. They were speechless to learn that the women had waved butcher knives at Killihota, the only one that had spoken in its favor. The Americans, thinking their mission was a failure, announced the conference was over but as they began to make arrangements to leave the next day, the resistance began to crumble among the more influential leaders. After more discussions, the entire tribe seemed to realize the inevitability of a treaty of removal and agreed to take part in serious talks for a final agreement.[68]

The policy started three decades earlier by Thomas Jefferson finally reached completion with the conclusion of the Treaty of Dancing Rabbit Creek on September 27, 1830. Sent onto Washington for ratification in December, the Choctaw secured a perpetual guarantee of their home in Indian Territory in return for all of their remaining 10,423,130 acres in Mississippi.

Twenty-two other items in the treaty related to general areas of agreement. The first group of articles, pertaining to removal, provided that the removals would take place over the next three years, that the government would pay all expenses of moving the Indians and their possessions, furnish all transportation facilities and supplies, and provide subsistence for one year after arrival in Indian Territory. The second series related to federal protection of the Indians in Indian Territory from invasions by both enemies and friends. It was agreed that no whites would be allowed without tribal permission, except for an Indian agent appointed by the President every four years, and all alcoholic beverages were banned from the nation.[69]

A third category listed the payments owed to the Choctaw. Annuities from the earlier treaties were guaranteed, including kettles, rifles, ammunition, and a year's supply of corn plus provisions for the first three years and an annuity of ten dollars per family for ten years for the acceptance of removal. Additionally, the treaty provided an annuity of $20,000 per year for twenty years, an annual payment of $2,500 to employ three teachers for schools, a donation of $10,000 to build a council house in the Nation, a church and schools, a gift of 2,100 blankets, 1,000 axes, and 400 looms.

Other important portions of the treaty concerned land to the Choctaw chiefs and provisions for those members of the tribe that wanted to remain in Mississippi. Each chief received four sections of land and $250 annually as long as he remained in office. Lesser leaders received smaller amounts of land and money. Those who wished to stay in Mississippi did so under Article 14 that provided any who remained must register within six months after ratification of the treaty. The clause added that each person was entitled to 640 acres, each child over ten, 320 acres, and each under ten, 160 acres, but failure to register resulted in complete loss of privileges. The Choctaw were warned, however, that choosing to remain in the state meant giving up their birthright and acceptance of the status of citizens of the state of Mississippi, subject to state laws.[70]

The tactics used by Jackson to achieve a final removal treaty should not have been a surprise. Having spent most of his life on the Tennessee border, Jackson held a typical frontier view of Indians. Considering them barriers to white settlement, "Old Hickory" believed that they should be moved west as Indians or allowed to remain as American citizens. Obsessed with forcing their removal during his presidency, it was no accident that he gave his personal attention to the removal process. Neither should it have startled the Indians to learn that Jackson refused to support Chief Justice John Marshall when the Supreme Court ruled that state laws passed over Indian tribes was unconstitutional in *Worcester v. Georgia* in 1832. A few years later the court reinforced the decision by legalizing an Indian tribe as a "separate, but dependent" nation, ruling that states cannot legislate laws over Indian nations, but Jackson still refused to enforce the decision, rendering it impossible to uphold. Tribal leaders reminded Jackson of his responsibilities and his debts to them, but he only answered that he was powerless in this situation and recommended the Indians accept their fate and proceed with the removals.

Chapter Four

According to Article 3 of the treaty, about one-third of the tribe was supposed to leave in 1831 with the remainder to follow in two stages over the next two years, but many decided to make the trip early to obtain their choice of lands in the new Choctaw Nation. By the end of November 1830, emigrants were gathering near Greenwood LeFlore's home in preparation for marching to Vicksburg, being ferried across the Mississippi, and traveling to Fort Gibson. In December, more than 400 leaders and high-ranking warriors who realized that they could sell their lands dearly to eager white settlers left early for Indian Territory knowing that if they waited a year or more the value of that land could be less. This proved correct, as two Choctaw captains, Ned Perry and Charles Hay, sold two-and-one-half sections in 1830 for $3,300, and two years later similar acreage sold for $500.

While some headed west, the majority took out their frustrations on their leaders. Elections in October resulted in George W. Harkins' defeat of Greenwood LeFlore, Joel H. Nail defeated Nitakechi, and Peter Pitchlynn defeated Moshulatubbee, but President Jackson refused to approve the new chiefs. They were deposed and the older ones reinstated to office.

Meanwhile, preparations for the first removal proceeded with a careful census conducted to determine the number of Indians to be removed. In February 1831, the census taken by William Armstrong reported a population of 17,963 Indians, 151 whites, and 521 slaves. Arrangements turned chaotic, however, when Lewis Cass was appointed Secretary of War in April. A political bureaucrat who knew little of the removal and had even less interest in it, Cass placed George Strothers Gaines in charge of the entire project with the imperious title of Superintendent of the Subsistence and Removal of Indians. At the same time Cass appointed Major Francis W. Armstrong, of Mobile, a personal enemy of Gaines, as the removal agent east of the Mississippi River. The animosity that existed between the two officials worsened into a feud that made preparations even harder.

In the first week of October 1831, after the hot weather subsided and the crops were all in, approximately 4,000 tribesmen gathered for the 550-mile trip to Indian Territory. Unfortunately, it began to rain, and kept on raining, and would not stop, turning into floods. The roads became impassible, but Gaines, determined to get the removals started despite the weather, sent the Indians out by wagon, horseback, and on foot for the Mississippi River. Those who lived in the north were directed to Memphis while all others headed for Vicksburg for transportation by steamboat up the Arkansas and the Ouachita Rivers. The state of Mississippi, meanwhile, urged the Choctaw to leave all their possessions, promising they would be reimbursed for them in the Indian Territory. The assurances were outrageous deceptions but were made by credible state officials and naively accepted by the Choctaw. The tribe left livestock, personal belongings, and all their property, expecting to be paid when they arrived in Indian Territory.

As the people were preparing to move, the newly created Bureau of Indian Affairs originated another idea. Announcing that special incentives would be given to any willing to walk to their new country, the bureau promised each Indian ten dollars in gold, a new rifle and three months supply of powder and ammunition, food along the way, and competent guides to their new homes. Approximately 300 agreed to accept the offer.

During the first week of October, camps began springing up around Memphis and Vicksburg as the tribe gathered for removal. As one Choctaw community prepared to leave, the women made a formal ceremony out of saying goodbye to their ancestral homes. A procession strolled through the woods surrounding their cabins, stroking the leaves of the oaks and elms in a silent farewell. Then, they began walking toward the gathering points.

Gaines did not have the steamboats ready, however, so further movements were halted for two weeks while he tried to find transportation. As the Choctaw waited in the cold rain, the townspeople grew increasingly uneasy and concerned with the numbers of Indians camped around their town. By November, food grew scarce and the situation worsened still more. Finally, Gaines hired five boats, the *Walter Scott*, the *Brandywine*, the *Reindeer*, the *Talma*, and the *Cleopatra*, and prepared to leave.

The travelers were divided into separate groups for easier transportation. The first was ferried across the Mississippi to Lake Providence, Louisiana, with plans of traveling through northern Louisiana and southern Arkansas to Indian Territory. A second party of two thousand was loaded on the *Walter Scott* and the *Reindeer* and carried upriver to the Arkansas River, onto Arkansas Post, and finally to Little Rock. The *Brandywine* left Memphis with a third group following the *Walter Scott*, while the *Talma* and the *Cleopatra* with another thousand traveled downstream to the mouth of the Red River, then toward the Ouachita River and Ecore a Fabre, which by this time was being called John Camden's Post and later Camden, Arkansas.

On December 5, the removal, started in an atmosphere of chaos and disorder, turned into disaster when a severe winter storm caught the agents and the Choctaw completely unprepared. A blizzard blanketed Mississippi and Arkansas that brought travel to almost a standstill. Six inches of snow fell and the thermometer dropped to below zero, and only averaged twelve degrees for the next week. Suffering and death joined the removal parties as the exhausted and freezing Choctaw were reduced to traveling barefoot and without clothes when they learned the agents had only rationed one blanket per family.

The Indians on the *Reindeer* and the *Walter Scott* plus those who debarked from Memphis on the *Brandywine*, a total of 2,500 Choctaws, were deposited at Captain Jacob Brown's Arkansas Post where they discovered there were only sixty tents for use in the whole place. Most of the Indians simply huddled together for what little warmth there was. Compounding the problem, there was little food. The Choctaw were forced to subsist on a handful of corn, one turnip, and two cups of heated water per day. Nothing could be done to help them. There were few blankets, no winter clothes or shoes, and the children went naked in zero-degree weather.

Alexis de Tocqueville, visiting in Memphis during this time, witnessed the tragedy of the Choctaw. He wrote that a ragged party of docile tribesmen passed through town despite freezing temperatures, ice clogging the river, and the ground frozen solid. Truly astonished, the European traveler was amazed that not a sound was heard from any of them. They possessed neither wagons nor tents for protection but not a cry or a whimper was uttered by anyone, only eerie silence from the entire band.

Officials tried to help by moving them in wagons by way of Washington, Hempstead County, to the Kiamichi River, but there were only forty wagons, and they were still 350 miles from Indian Territory. Complicating matters, the roads needed repairs from Arkansas Post to Little Rock. There were no supplies, nor money to purchase any, and Captain Brown, able to do nothing, could only try to keep the party moving. The wagons slowly headed west from Arkansas Post on January 13. Eventually they made Little Rock where they picked up a few supplies but more delays followed caused by washed out roads and wrecked bridges. Rain almost every day for the entire month of February made the region little more than a swamp. Moving slowly, fifteen miles a good day's march, the Choctaw trudged doggedly westward, because to stop was to die. In an interview with one of the Choctaw leaders, thought to be either George Harkins or Nitakechi, the *Arkansas Gazette* quoted the Chief as saying that the removal thus far had been a "Trail of Tears and Death." Picking up the phrase, the press made it analogous with the removal of all the tribes.

The fourth group that had gone up the Ouachita River found that no arrangements had been made for them either. The party, under Lieutenant L. T. Cross, was wondering what to do when word arrived that the band of 200 that had gone by way of Lake Providence, Louisiana, was in equally dire circumstances. Lieutenant Cross, going to their rescue, marched them to Monroe, Louisiana, where the *Cleopatra* was chartered to transport them to join his already starving groups. With over 1,100 Choctaws and no food, the exhausted officer hired wagons and horses on the credit promising twice the normal price for rations as the local farmers took advantage of their opportunity. Setting out for Fort Towson, over 165 miles away, he staggered on with them.

The old and the sick and the young walked as long as they could put one foot in front of the other. If they stopped, they died. The corpses had to be heaped in piles and burned or covered in shallow graves, because the ground was too frozen for burials. Conditions worsened when dysentery, diphtheria, and typhoid broke out among the weary, starving emigrants. Some of the white families living near the roads finally took pity on them letting them enter a small field of pumpkins. So hungry that they ate the pumpkins raw, the Choctaw still would not enter the fields along the roads without permission. They were starving, but they refused to steal or beg. Another sympathetic family let them into a winter turnip patch and not even a root remained when they left. Another granted them permission to burn the wooden fence around their home to provide a little warmth. Above all, they had to keep moving. Thousands died before the journey known as the "Long, Sad March" ended for the Choctaw.

In March 1832, five months after they had started, the first arrivals began staggering into Indian Territory. On April 30, Supply Agent Lieutenant J. R. Stephenson reported 3,749 Choctaw had been registered at four stations, Horse Prairie, a site settled by Reverend Alexander Talley and the 400 Choctaw who had voluntarily left Mississippi in 1830; Fort Towson; Old Miller Court House; and Eagletown on the Mountain Fork.[71]

The cost had been shamefully high. In April 1832, Gaines and the civilians, blamed for the debacle, were all discharged, and the task of removal turned over to the Army. Captain William Armstrong was appointed special agent for removal of the tribe as far as the Mississippi River, and his brother, Major Francis W. Armstrong, was named in the same capacity from the Mississippi to Indian Territory, but problems worsened in Mississippi as word of the first removals drifted back. Many Choctaw turned to whiskey and idleness as the War Department began preparations to renew the tragedy in August 1832.

In September, Captain William Scott Colquhoun reported in a preliminary survey that another 9,000 were ready to emigrate, and Armstrong, having learned nothing from the earlier fiasco, began the task of procurement of supplies. Announcing his decision to follow the same routes taken by the first parties, he ordered one-third sent to Memphis, while the others were told to cross the Mississippi at Vicksburg and proceed overland to Indian Territory. Amazingly, the government naively outfitted ninety-nine chiefs and leaders of the tribe with a new suit of clothes to wear as though on a parade. They were given beaver hats trimmed in silver bands, cockades, plumes, pantaloons, Irish linen shirts, sword belts and swords in bright scabbards. By October, these wondrous supplies had been dispersed and the removal was ready.

Chapter Four

The Army, efficiently prepared for everything except a catastrophe, was shocked when an epidemic of cholera swept down the Mississippi from the north bringing sickness and death. By the time the Indians reached Memphis, the disease had broken out along the river and was increasing in strength. Spread through contaminated water and food supplies, early physicians blamed the illness on a variety of sources including the climate, night air, evening mists, overindulgence in strong drink, and even the geological structures of the earth. Although its cause was unknown at the time, its presence caused hysteria among the Choctaw. Upon their arrival at Memphis in November, William Armstrong decided to split the group into two parties, one under his direction would be ferried across the river on the *Archimedes* and then conducted to Rock Row, seventy miles east of Little Rock; the other would board the *Helipolis* and proceed southwest to the White River and then on the river to Rock Row. Panic-stricken by the cholera, the Choctaw at first refused to board the boats, but eventually were persuaded to load up. The plight of Armstrong's party worsened as rain fell in a deluge, making the roads almost impossible. Incredibly, the Choctaw began to die of exhaustion and exposure just as they had the year before.

Colquhoun, on the *Helipolis*, grew so frustrated and upset with Armstrong that he attacked him. Asking Major Armstrong for more blankets because of the cold weather, Colquhoun, in an angry, drunken state, confronted Armstrong when he refused them. Giving the Major a verbal cursing, he drew his weapon and fired, narrowly missing Armstrong twice. Recovering quickly, Armstrong pistol-whipped the junior officer and had him thrown off the ship for insubordination. Colquhoun was subsequently dismissed from the Army because of the incident.

The other party fared equally badly. Hearing of the cholera at Vicksburg, they traveled around the area only to have the disease break out among them anyway while having to travel farther than their original route would have taken them. Major Armstrong, hastening them to Vicksburg, loaded them up and proceeded by steamboat to Rock Row, arriving there on November 12. Eventually, the emigrating Choctaw all arrived at Rock Row and proceeded overland to Little Rock. Following the Arkansas River to Fort Smith, three smaller groups of 600 each split off across southwestern Arkansas through Washington, Arkansas, to Fort Towson on the Red River. Major Armstrong reported the traveling was easier, since the roads were better and they had wagons, but it turned out they had only five wagons for every thousand people. The majority of them walked. Armstrong wrote, "Fortunately they are a people that will walk to the last, or I do not know how we could go on."

In mid-January, the agents began reporting that the various bands were starting to appear. From January through February 1833, a total of 5,538 arrived, but the Army emigration had been as big a failure as the earlier one. Although more Indians had been removed, even more had died of cholera and disease. Some seven hundred Choctaw did not stop, but continued on southwest to Texas to try their luck with the Mexican Government.[72]

Despite these fiascos, the authorities insisted on continuing the tragedy. By June 1833, agents were busily gathering supplies for a third fall removal that began when a small party left on foot for Memphis on October 1, 1833. Arriving there almost two weeks later, Armstrong hired the *Archimedes* to transport them across the river, but once the boat was loaded a broken shaft was discovered and could not leave. The Choctaw were unloaded and put on the *Thomas Yeatman*, but as the steamboat pulled up to its mooring, one of its boilers exploded, killing some of its hands. The Choctaw, now so frightened that they would not board anything, waited around for another three days before finally being persuaded to load up again. Finally underway, the party reached Rock Row on November 7, and then traveled by foot to Little Rock. Passing the town on November 21, the emigrants arrived in Indian Territory on December 10.

Indians continued to come through the early months of 1834 and 1835. Stragglers eventually brought the total to approximately 12,500, leaving another 6,000 in Mississippi. The cost of removal and subsistence was officially listed at $813,927, but items like removal agents' fees ran the total bill to $5,097,367.50. On the other hand, the government received $8,095,614.89 for the Choctaw land sold in Mississippi to white settlers. The difference was supposed to be paid to the Choctaw but was not done so. This became the "Net Proceeds" case that found its way to the National Courts for years. Eventually $2,981,247.39 was paid with the majority of it going to lawyers.[73]

Classic examples of bureaucratic waste, chaos, and inefficiency, the 1832 and 1833 removals were not as bad in some respects as those in 1831, but worse in others. The Army carried out the latter removals with better financial controls than the civilians but with equal incompetence. The Army, due to its organizational abilities, lost fewer lives than the civilians, but the result had been another "Trail of Tears" for the Choctaw tribe.[74]

Approximately 6,000 still remained in Mississippi when the War Department terminated its operations at the end of 1833. Agent William Ward forwarded his register roll under Article 14 of the treaty, but he submitted only sixty-nine heads of families, half of which were mixed bloods or intermarried citizens. Ward, who opposed the right of the Choctaw to remain in the state as citizens of Mississippi, drunkenly destroyed applications, deleted names from the register, and urged removal agents to whip any who refused to emigrate, and nothing was done to stop him. Dismissed in November 1833, he was released because, according to his superiors, the number of Choctaw remaining in the state was so few that he was no longer needed.

By 1833, more than 6,000 tribesmen had been removed and another thousand had moved themselves in parties of twenty to a hundred per trip, including a party of fifty slaves by Peter Pitchlynn. Emigrants continued to come for years. In 1838, a group of 177 emigrated on the *Erin* from Vicksburg through Little Rock, in 1844, 550 removed after learning they were not going to get land promised under Article 14, in 1845, some 1,200 moved; in 1846, another 1,000; in 1847, 1,623 in eight separate removal parties, and in the following years several hundred arrived in annual emigrations. By the end of the century, almost 25,000 had moved to new homes in Indian Territory.

Angry protests over the abuses of removal led to charges of fraud and profiteering that ultimately resulted in a federal investigation. In November 1841, Major Ethan Allen Hitchcock, ordered to Indian Territory by the War Department to look into complaints, arrived with the authority to investigate all charges and report his findings to the Congress. The Major found evidence of bribery, perjury, forgery, shortweights, and issues of spoiled meat and grain rations and reported that: "every conceivable subterfuge" had been used by "designing white men on ignorant Indians." Hitchcock concluded with the scathing indictment that a severely high death rate had resulted from the removals. The testimony set the population at removal at 18,963, but afterwards, the figure, including 804 whites and 2,349 slaves, was 13,666, a decline of 5,297, or twenty-seven percent. Along with over one hundred exhibits to support his opinions, Hitchcock detailed a lengthy list of charges, but his report was never introduced into Congress. Too many high-placed individuals and top government officials were involved in the affair, and the report disappeared from the official files with no trace ever found of it.[75]

Meanwhile, the Mississippi Choctaw were forgotten, and their pleas for justice went ignored for more than a score of years. In 1851, they were reported to be a landless people living in "deplorable" conditions, far worse off "than that of black slaves in the state." Their position continued to deteriorate through the Civil War. When the war ended, federal authorities again tried to get them to move but without success. The Mississippi Choctaw existed as sharecroppers and woodcutters, illiterate, disenfranchised, living a life of debt peonage until the years of the Dawes Commission when they were finally given some recognition as a people. Another round of removals took place as they were included in the division of the western lands, but most still avoided the Commission whenever possible. In 1944, a century after the removal, the Mississippi Indians were granted a reservation and a year later allowed to establish a government as the Mississippi Band of Choctaw. The tribe proudly proclaimed "Chahta Hapia Hoke," "We are Choctaw."[76]

Chapter Four

Nowhere was the spirit to defraud the Indians more evident than in Mississippi. Treaties were negotiated through violence and intimidation by the whites, land swindles publicly committed by speculators and unscrupulous state officials, and the Choctaw were transported to their new homes in Indian Territory in the middle of winter without supplies and forced to sleep in trees to avoid the frozen ground. They found only hardships and more hard work awaited them. Their first years were difficult and dangerous, and many more died before they reestablished themselves, but, working diligently and devoutly, the tribe within a decade was once more prosperous and successful.[77]

CHAPTA TAHLAPI

~ CHAPTER FIVE ~

"EDUCATE! OR WE PERISH!"

the Cross Timbers, a forest of scrub oak, hackberry, and elm from five to thirty miles in width that extended generally along the Ninety-eighth Meridian from the Arkansas to the Colorado in Texas.

In the summer of 1834, General Henry Leavenworth and Colonel Henry Dodge led a peace mission of eight companies of Dragoons into the American Southwest, locating the tribes in the Wichita Mountains. With the Leavenworth expedition were George Catlin and former North Carolina Governor Montfort Stokes, seventy-two-year-old head of a three-man commission charged with settling the tribes on their new homes in Indian Territory. Traveling in the dry, hot, southwest summer in heavy uniforms, the soldiers quickly grew ill from the extreme heat and high temperatures that often soared more than 107 degrees, although one of the Indians accompanying the expedition blamed the great numbers of sick and dying men on a spell that he had seen in the poison coming from the glasses worn by Stokes. General Leavenworth died of the less mysterious accident of having his horse fall with him, but in spite of setbacks and delays the Dragoons successfully met the Plains tribes and returned with a pledge for peace.

Bands of Kiowa, Comanche, and Kickapoo continued occasional raids against both the Choctaw and the Chickasaw, not to mention the white settlers in Texas, but the major accomplishment of the Leavenworth-Dodge expedition was the first treaty with the Plains Indians. In August 1835, the tribes agreed to peace at a great council at Camp Holmes. Chief Moshulatubbee, one of the negotiators in attendance, expressed much optimism for peace in the future, but it was a hopeless prospect. In 1838, William Armstrong, reporting thefts, murders, and problems from the Plains tribes were on the rise again, petitioned for a new military post on the Washita River. Armstrong pointed out correctly that Fort Towson was located too far east to protect against raids from the Plains tribes, adding that the Choctaw had never planted settlements in the western lands because of the wild tribes. Based upon the Agent's recommendations, Colonel Zachary Taylor was sent to select a site for the fort in the summer of 1841.[80]

The following year, Captain George A. H. Blake began construction of the post about two miles above the mouth of the Washita. Completed on April 23, 1843, the barracks and buildings, quarried out of shell-rock from the nearby hills, were occupied immediately by two companies of soldiers as a major station for protecting the eastern tribes. Supplies were received by boat coming up the Red River, and communications were maintained with Fort Gibson along a military road cleared by General Leavenworth in 1834.[81]

The fort brought relative peace to the region and the Choctaw quickly adjusted to their new home. Within a decade the tribe had resumed intensive cultivation of their cotton and corn crops and divided into two basic socioeconomic classes, mixed bloods and full bloods. The full bloods tended small tracts of three to ten acres, raised subsistence crops of corn and vegetables with a small surplus for barter purposes, and lived in simple log cabins with only the barest necessities for furniture. Conversely, the mixed bloods took up large sections of lowlands and river bottom lands as theirs for exploitation, secured permits to employ white laborers, or purchased slaves to cultivate large cotton farms. The wealthy mixed bloods patterned themselves after the slave owners of the South and built large plantations that were the showplaces of the Choctaw Nation. The system developed because Choctaw lands were owned in common. Each person could use all the land he wanted with the only rule being that a fence could come no closer than a "hog call" to another farm. This meant one-fourth of a mile, but unfenced lands could also be used by any who wanted them, insuring that all had sufficient land for grazing or farming.

There were obvious economic advantages for the mixed bloods. Since there were no taxes on the tribe for the land, other means of gathering money for the operation of the tribal government were used by the Council. A common way was to charge whites coming into the Nation. A white was subject to fees of fifty cents per head per year for grazing, and to cut hay was another fifty cents per ton. White traders were subject to pay one and one-half percent as royalties; lawyer, doctors, and editors were charged ten dollars per year. A royalty of twenty-five cents per ton was charged for coal, and citizens who operated farms were required to pay five dollars per year for each tenant farmer. Additionally, all laborers were required to pay two dollars and fifty cents per year.

Nonpayment of these fees was punishable by whippings, fines, or deportation. Other crimes were given similar penalties while murder brought the death penalty. The Choctaw had no jails for their violators. A convicted person's word was his bond. The accused agreed to appear at the court at the designated time even if he were given the death penalty. Normally, a period of thirty days between the trial and the execution of the sentence permitted sufficient time for appeals and for the accused to get his life in order. If a man refused to give his word, he was chained to a tree and the sentence carried out immediately. The sentence for murder was a firing squad because the Choctaw did not believe in hangings.[82]

The Choctaw continued to rely upon their white missionaries for guidance even after removal. Among the first to depart from Mississippi for Indian Territory had been Methodist missionary, Alexander Talley, who had conducted camp meetings that attracted large numbers of followers. Talley professed to have converted more than 1,300, including Greenwood LeFlore, by 1829, while the American Board could only claim 360 despite being at work since 1818. In December 1830, Talley brought LeFlore's emigrants to the region near "the ruins of Cantonment Towson" (Fort Towson), followed by another one hundred Choctaw in February. About half of them were Methodists who immediately began holding regular Saturday and Sunday services. Contributing another $400 in mission funds to cover the costs of providing corn at suitable points along the route for friends, Talley reported nearly five hundred Choctaw Methodists had settled eastward along Little River by June 1831. That same year he hired a full blood traveling preacher and two others as teachers for his school.

In 1831, Chief Moshulatubbee was not so friendly to Talley or the missionaries. Blaming them for the removals, the District Chief wrote to the Secretary of War demanding that Talley be "ordered out" of the Choctaw Nation. He later changed his mind when he learned the missionaries were not responsible as he had first thought, and Talley reported a reconciliation had occurred the following July. Moshulatubbee, a bitter foe of Christianity for a time, invited the preacher to visit his people, make the Christian "good talk," and "teach them the good way."

The first Presbyterian to arrive from Mississippi was Loring S. Williams who established a home at the crossing of the Mountain Fork River. Calling the place Bethabara, in honor of the Hebrew ford or crossing where John baptized Jesus, he organized the first church on the west side of the river on August 10, 1832. A village was soon in existence with fifty-six people that petitioned for a post office at a location they named Ossi Tvmaha (Eagletown). In 1834, the request was granted, and Reverend Williams was appointed as the first postmaster.

On December 9, 1832, Reverend Alfred Wright arrived to establish a mission between Fort Towson and the Mountain Fork that he named in honor of the first president of Dartmouth College, Eleazar Wheelock, who operated a school for Indians from 1754 to 1769 at Lebanon, Connecticut, Wright's hometown. The following year, Reverend Ebenezer Hotchkin arrived with his family. In 1835, Reverend R. D. Potts moved to the Nation at the same time as Byington and Kingsbury.

By 1835, there were five schools in existence. Williams was in charge at Bethabara with Eunice Clough of New Hampshire as the teacher until she transferred to Lukfata (White Clay) in 1835. Wheelock was founded by Wright in 1832, Clear Creek, eight miles west of Wheelock under Hotchkin in 1833, Bok Tuklo, (Two Rivers) under Henry R. Wilson, seven miles southeast of Wheelock in 1834, and Bethel, under Samuel Moulton, five miles southwest of Wheelock, in 1834. Some two thousand Choctaw immigrants were soon settled around the Wheelock mission.

For a few years the most important town in the Nation was the supply station at the Choctaw agency maintained by Major Francis W. Armstrong at

Skullyville, named for the Choctaw word iskvli (money). In 1833, a post office was established with him as postmaster. Southwest of the village was Charby Prairie, one of the famed Choctaw ball fields, where Catlin painted a picture of a game in 1834. The artist, astounded by the violence of the event, reported more than three thousand in attendance, an unusually high number, with the game lasting from nine in the morning until nightfall. Nearby lived Chief Moshulatubbee.[83]

Fort Towson soon surpassed Skullyville as the center of commerce for the Nation because of its location on the Red River. The fortification, originally named Cantonment Towson for Postmaster-general of the Army, Nathan Towson, had been founded near the mouth of the Kiamichi River in 1824 but was abandoned after only five years. Restored in 1831, the post was assigned the task of protecting the migrating tribes and white settlers in Arkansas Territory from attacks by the Plains tribes in the west. Located six miles from its earlier site, the garrison was called Camp Phoenix until reverting to its former designation as Fort Towson.

The village of Doaksville was located near the fort by the Doak brothers at the very beginning of the removal period. The Doaks, operators of a trading post at Doak Stand in Mississippi, loaded their goods on a boat and moved to Indian Territory as early as 1831. Josiah S. Doak navigated the Mississippi and the Red to near the mouth of the Kiamichi, carried his trade goods to a spot called the "Witch Holes," and set up a store about a mile from Fort Towson that in a short time grew into the largest town in the Choctaw Nation. A post office, the first in the entire territory, was established in 1832.

Other towns followed closely behind Doaksville. In 1841, Perryville was established on the Texas Road. Another settlement grew up at Boggy Depot at the intersection of the road to California and the highway used by Texas emigrants on the Clear Boggy River.

Other roads were soon cut to connect the villages to Fort Smith. In 1832, Agent Armstrong ordered a detail of soldiers to construct a wagon road from Fort Smith to the Red River for the emigrating Choctaw under the rights of the Dancing Rabbit Creek treaty to build roads. In March, Captain John Stuart and a detachment of forty troopers began the road blazed by Colonel Robert Bean, a famous woodsman of the region, and Jesse Chisholm, a mixed blood trader. Exchanging their rifles for axes and spades, the soldiers hacked a right-of-way from sixteen to twenty feet wide through briars and thickets, fell trees, and moved rocks and boulders from Fort Smith to Horse Prairie, twenty miles north of Fort Towson. Completed in July, the trail covered a distance of 147 miles. In 1838, another road was built within the Arkansas line that ran about forty miles south of Fort Smith then turned southwest to Fort Towson. Captain Joseph Bonnell of the Eighth Infantry reported that his command made the trip over this route in eight and one-half days, considerably faster than Stuart's road. In the summer of 1834, two companies of the Third Infantry also opened a path to the mouth of the Washita preparatory to the establishment of another fort.[84]

One of the first commanders at Fort Towson, Lieutenant Colonel J. H. Vose, was complimented by the new emigrants for maintaining a "highly moral condition of the troops," a status achieved when he banished alcohol from the post in 1834. Arriving one year later, Dr. Kingsbury was most impressed by the morality displayed by the soldiers when he found a flourishing society of temperance in existence with more than half the garrison enrolled as members. Quickly adding a Sunday school at the fort, Dr. Kingsbury proved quite popular with the men.[85]

Another vocal supporter of the growing temperance movement in the region was Peter Pitchlynn. In 1842, the mixed blood planter declared that the white man had brought the Indian many "good things, except for whiskey." As temperance grew in respect, the recognition of the degradation caused by alcohol led the Choctaw to attempt several campaigns to prevent both its sale and consumption within the Nation. In 1848, David G. Ball, founder of the *Choctaw Telegraph*, appointed David Folsom as his crusading temperance editor to publish articles against the use of alcohol, and the paper petitioned for the establishment of a "Division of the Sons of Temperance" in September 1849. The *Choctaw Intelligencer*, successor of the *Telegraph*, owned by L.D. Alsobrook and co-editor Jonathan Edwards Dwight, a Choctaw preacher educated at Dartmouth College, announced the organization of Chapter Fifty-one of the Sons of Temperance on June 14, 1850.[86]

The news for the region had been dispensed previously from Clarksville, Texas, through *The Northern Standard* by Editor Charles DeMorse, an aide to Sam Houston at San Jacinto. Established in 1842, the paper was quickly tied economically to the Choctaw Nation as DeMorse often ran advertisements for his close friend, Choctaw planter, Robert M. Jones. In 1843, the editor published an angry offer by Jones for a fifty-dollar reward for each of two mares that had been stolen from him and another two hundred dollars for the capture of the two white thieves from Texas that had committed the crime. The paper also publicized horse races for Jones. Although there was only one reference to a match within the Nation, over the St. Leger Course, near Major Pitman Colbert's home in 1844, the races held in Texas often took Jones, a frequent participant in the "sport of kings," to town. At one race "Choctaw Filly," a sorrel mare owned by Jones, ran in a match race against a Texas thoroughbred for a $600 entrance purse but Jones lost the contest, reported the paper.

Jones and a number of other mixed bloods established large, successful plantations along the Red River after the removal with a thriving cotton, corn, and tobacco trade through Doaksville from the Fort Towson Landing near the mouth of the Kiamichi. Doaksville was soon a small, prosperous center with blacksmith shops, stores, public houses (hotels), and several cotton gins. By 1842, Doaksville had five mercantile stores that carried sugar, coffee, and food, a resident physician, a blacksmith shop, a wagon maker, a wheelwright, a tavern, and a church. In 1847, an article in the *Indian Advocate*, published by the American Indian Mission Association in Louisville, Kentucky, reported Doaksville had grown from an abandoned post to a sizeable town with a population of 50 to 60 people, six stores, two saddle shops, one tailor, a blacksmith, cabinet maker, one shoe shop, a drug store, three physicians, a small log meeting house kept by Dr. Kingsbury, and a public house owned by David Folsom, one of the wealthiest slave owners around Doaksville. He had served as an officer in the Army under Jackson and was first Chief to be married under Mississippi state laws rather than tribal custom.

The even richer Jones, owner of one of the stores in Doaksville, along with several plantations farmed by hundreds of slaves, was the major political power in the region. His father, a Scotch-Irish Mississippi farmer and trader married to a full blood Choctaw wife, had assured Jones a prosperous future by giving him a good education at the Presbyterian Mission School and a legacy of $1800. At the age of nineteen Jones enrolled in the Choctaw Academy in Kentucky and graduated three years later as an honor student. Starting a farm with his inheritance, Jones accumulated full legal title to 2,000 acres of Mississippi cotton land within three years and held out against land grabbers after the Treaty of Dancing Rabbit Creek, keeping his plantation and slaves until he was assured a good price.

In 1834, he sold his holdings, kept 150 slaves, bought another 100, and transported his family to Indian Territory in style. Only twenty-six years old, Jones moved west in a convoy of fifty wagons with the male slaves leading the oxen and horses while the females and children all rode in comfort. He soon owned farms up and down the Red River and his neighbors were the Garlands, the Pitchlynns, LeFlores, and Harkins, all wealthy Choctaw planters in the region. By 1836, Jones had more than 3,000 acres planted in cotton with gins for each of his plantations. His agricultural estates expanded to include Rocky Comfort, ten thousand acres located southwest of Idabel, Kullichukchu (Maple Tree Springs), later called Kulli Inla (Strange Springs) and still later Shawneetown, a farm of seven thousand acres south of Rocky Comfort, Lake West, six thousand acres nine miles south of Boswell, and Hog Wallow, five thousand acres south of Bennington.

Jones was also the first owner of "chain stores" in Indian Territory. He maintained twenty-eight in all but only used whites to run them. White overseers were also used on his farms and plantations.

Because all his farms and stores were along the Red River and his second wife, Susan, daughter of wealthy Chickasaw planter, Pitman Colbert, suffered health ailments associated with the climate, Jones built a mansion for her at the most salubrious site that he could find. The beautiful, elegant Mrs. Jones selected a spot four miles southeast of Hugo on a hill covered with roses named "Rose Hill." Jones constructed a large, two-story, fifteen-room frame home with tall columns supporting the front porch. The first floor was finished in maple, walnut, and mahogany from Jefferson, Texas, and New Orleans and much of the furniture was imported from France. Boasting a large library, a prized collection of portraits of all the American presidents hanging in the hallway gallery, and a walk of native stones, lined with cedar trees, the manor was a showpiece of Southern architecture.[87]

Jones serviced his plantations with a fleet of privately owned steamboats on the Red River. In 1844, he named one for his daughter, the *Frances Jones*, and another was called the *Belle of Red River*. Navigation on the Red had been opened by Captain Henry Miller Shreve, who brought the first steamboat, the *Enterprise*, into the river and began clearing the Great Raft, more than one hundred miles of obstructions caused by large logs, stumps, and debris, in 1815. In 1833, Captain Shreve and the Army engineers brought in the snag boat, *Archimedes*, earlier used in the removals, to complete the task of freeing the river of rubble. Fort Towson Landing, six miles from Doaksville, was the most important stop on the river after 1838, but steamboat operations could be conducted to within sight of Fort Washita that opened in 1843.

A few years later another fort was established inside the Choctaw Nation. In 1850, Captain Randolph B. Marcy chose a site for Fort Arbuckle on the banks of the Canadian River, but it was moved south near the Washita River in 1851. Located on Wild Horse Creek, a branch of the Washita, the fort was occupied by troops supposed to keep peace with the Plains tribes, but it, too, proved inadequate to accomplish this duty. Later, it would be occupied by Confederate forces and then replaced by Fort Sill.[88]

In 1840, evidence of the tribe's recovery was the notification given to Superintendent Armstrong that the Choctaw wished to send no more boys to Choctaw Academy in Kentucky. Using the justification that the boys were returning home with little knowledge of their own people, the Choctaw announced their intention to establish a school in their own country but permitted the students to attend the Academy one more year on the condition that Peter Pitchlynn was named as its superintendent. In 1841, he arrived with authority to investigate the school but left after spending just fifty-five days, apparently considering the position merely a temporary solution until a school could be set up in the Nation. Already displeased with the Choctaw Academy, Pitchlynn accused the school of providing poor food and bad dormitory accommodations, using soiled table linens and tolerating insolent Negro waiters. After one of Johnson's slaves got into a fight with a Choctaw scholar over a cockfight, Pitchlynn, watching closely for the right excuse, pulled all the students out intending to destroy the school. Branding it "a nursery of violence and degradation," he left for Washington with plans for an academy in the Choctaw Nation. Finding the new Secretary of War, John Canfield Spencer, a New York Whig, receptive to the idea of a national academy, particularly since part of the plan was to name the school for him, Pitchlynn persuaded the Secretary to lend his assistance. Spencer was removed from office not long after the deal was struck, but Chiefs James Fletcher, James Gardner, and Johnson McKinney, determined that no more Choctaw students would be sent to Kentucky, proceeded to build Spencer Academy, a new school, in the Nation.[89]

In 1842, Pitchlynn, elected Speaker of the unicameral house, convinced the Council to appropriate $18,000, the first educational appropriation in American history, to establish Spencer Academy for boys and Wheelock for girls. These funds initiated a general awakening of support for education in the Nation. Even before removal, Choctaw elders had insisted upon money for education in their treaties, warning the children: "The whites are near us . . . unless you can speak their language, read and write as they do, they will be able to cheat you and trample on your rights." The Dancing Rabbit Creek treaty had provided funds over a period of twenty years for higher education of Choctaw men under Article XX, known as the "Forty Youth Fund" that provided "forty Choctaw youths" should "be kept at school." Serving as the financial basis for college educations for Choctaw students, the clause provided that three churches in each district should be used for schoolhouses and an appropriation of $2500 annually for twenty years for the support of three teachers.

In 1842, Charles Dickens commented on the Choctaw attitude toward education after meeting a group of Choctaw traveling on the Ohio River. Dickens stated that tribal members confessed to him they realized that unless the tribesmen assimilated themselves into American civilization, "they must be swept away before the strides of civilized society." By 1844, the annual expenditure for education in the Nation was $30,000.[90]

In 1840, Reverend E. R. Ames of the Methodist Episcopal Church organized a school system for the Choctaw chartering three seminaries of learning for males and females "to board, clothe, and teach books and useful manual labor." Suitable appropriations were secured from the annuities, and three schools were established, one for each district. Spencer Academy was located in the Apuckshunnubbee District and supervised by the Council, Nun-ne-wa-ya Academy in the Pushmataha District, and Fort Coffee in the Moshulatubbee District. The latter two received an annual appropriation of $12,000, and the Missionary Board of the Church made an appropriation of $2,000 annually.[91]

The Choctaw expected Spencer Academy to serve as the model for its school system. Its administrative board was composed of William Armstrong, Kingsbury, Pitchlynn, Jones, and Thompson McKinney until Chief George W. Harkins reduced the membership to Jones, McKinney, and Pitchlynn in 1844. Edmund McKinney, a Presbyterian missionary, was hired to head the school and arrived on December 8, 1843. McKinney was joined by two mixed bloods, Reuben Wright and Jonathan E. Dwight, and an assistant teacher, William Wilson, but the school was not ready for opening until the following February. By the end of the month, fifty-seven students had enrolled and were soon joined by another fifty-two. By August, the enrollment topped 109. Ninety-five were boarding students and the others "day scholars" from the area.

During classes, they studied English, since thirty-four of the original students neither spoke nor understood it, arithmetic, and Latin devoted to Caesar's Commentaries. Morning and evening prayers and Sunday sermons were included as part of the curriculum. The boys were then put to work three hours per day farming corn under the supervision of George C. Farquhar.

The missionaries were responsible for cultural mixing in every way except in the case of foods. Missionary enthusiasm waned when it came to liking Choctaw foods. The Choctaw griddlecakes of corn and potatoes were too dry and Tafula seemed tasteless, while the missionary dishes were just as distasteful to the students because they did not like fatty foods. The missionaries were also forced to eat pastries secretly. The students so disliked pies that they asked for them as they were being prepared just so they could throw them away rather than even smell them baking in the ovens.

The major problem was runaway boys, especially before the missionaries learned not to scold them. Choctaw students, reared in almost complete freedom, could not understand nor tolerate discipline, especially in public before the other boys. Some hated school rules and regulations so badly they even tried burning the dormitories down. Disappointed with the progress and hampered by constant arguments with Pitchlynn, McKinney resigned. In October 1845, James B. Ramsay, a thirty-one-year-old graduate of Princeton and a native of New York, replaced him, but shortly after his arrival, the school was hit by an epidemic. Taking the lives of several of the boys along with the young Superintendent's wife and infant son, Ramsay, in mournful despair, resigned and left the Nation in 1849. Replaced by Alexander Reid, a graduate of Princeton Theological Seminary, the school was revitalized with new teachers, including three of Reid's classmates at Princeton, and enrollment increased to 141.

Reid, Superintendent from 1849 to 1861, was responsible for recording "Steal Away to Jesus" and "Swing Low Sweet Chariot" sung by Uncle Wallace and Aunt Minerva, slaves of Britt Willis, who worked at the Academy in the 1850s. The old couple, composing the spirituals while resting in the middle of cotton rows, were brought from Hickory Flat, Mississippi, and leased out during the winters to Spencer Academy where Reid overheard them singing, "I'm a Rollin." On one of his visits to New York, he gave the songs to the Jubilee Singers from Fisk University at Newark, New Jersey, who popularized them.

In the summer of 1851, combining his teaching with evangelical work, Reid spoke fifty times, rode 1,500 miles, and preached to more than 3,000 people. In 1854, Reid remarried Miss F. K. Thompson, a missionary teacher at Wapanucka Institute. Remaining in the Choctaw Nation until 1856, Reid retired, but returned in 1859. Since most of the missionaries left when the Civil War started, the school was forced to close, although its buildings were used as hospitals for the Confederates and places of shelter for the refugees that arrived from the north. In 1864, Reid's second wife also died, suffering from childbirth complications.

In 1871, Reverend J. H. Colton reopened the school with thirty-two students, but three years later there were still only fifty enrollees. In 1876, John J. Read of Mississippi replaced Colton. He remained until 1881, but the school was in poor physical condition after years of neglected repairs. Finally, it was decided the most economical solution would be to simply move to a new location. The Council ordered the transfer to Nelson, about twenty miles west. New buildings, a two-story dormitory, and a classroom were built as "New Spencer." In 1882, its first superintendent, Oliver Porter Stark, a former Spencer teacher, assumed control but died two years later, replaced by Harve R. Schermerhorn. The new administrator put the students to work on his own farm, causing more controversy, and for a time, control of the school was passed back and forth between the Presbyterian Board and the Choctaw Council until finally the Council took over full authority in 1894. A Choctaw citizen, J. B. Jeter, was named Superintendent, but two years later a fire brought an end to the school. Disciplined by Jeter, three students poured coal oil on the stairway of the main building, burning it, along with five of their classmates. Reopened in the fall of 1898, New Spencer burned a second time, and the academy experiment was over in 1900.

The second institution established by the Choctaw was Fort Coffee Academy in the Moshulatubbee District in 1842. Taken over by Methodists in 1843, Reverend William H. Goode, appointed superintendent, opened the school the following year. The first boys, all full bloods, ranging in age from six to twenty, learned the first order of business was a bath and a haircut followed by a new suit of clothes and a new name. Located five miles away was the New Hope Seminary where young Choctaw ladies were later instructed in sewing, the kitchen, the dairy, laundry, and "housekeeping" along with "books." On July 2, 1843, the first classes were held with teacher Henry C. Benson in charge of six students in the morning classes at Fort Coffee.

The students came in shirts, pants, calico hunting shirts, but only a few wore shoes or moccasins; most were bare footed. None wore hats. They either were bareheaded or wore cotton handkerchiefs twisted into turbans, their hair worn long, sometimes braided. Upon arrival at the school each student was provided a suit of clothes, but one eight-year-old suddenly began to sob miserably when it was time for his first night. Upon questioning, it was learned that he was crying because he did not want to ruin his new clothes by sleeping in them on the ground. Shown a bed for the first time in his life, he was most happy to learn that he would neither have to sleep on the ground nor in his new suit.

The academy schedule began at five in the morning in the winter and at sunrise in the summer. An hour later, students were assembled in the chapel for worship, reading the scriptures, singing, and praying, and then sent directly to the dining room for breakfast followed by work in the fields or woods doing manual labor until eight-thirty. At nine classes began and lasted until noon. Afternoon sessions lasted until four followed a half-hour later by another round in the fields until almost sunset. The students were then free until nine in the evening when a bell sounded to signal lights out in half an hour. Saturdays were days of no classes, but the students spent their mornings cleaning the grounds with the afternoons free. Attendance at Sunday school was required at nine in the morning and again for one hour in the afternoon.

Benson later reported his accounts of life at Fort Coffee, including the story of one of the young students swimming near the mouth of the Canadian River about forty miles above the school, being seized by a giant catfish, pulled underwater, and carried off. Benson stated that when friends dragged the river, they pulled up both the fish and the six-year-old as the fish had taken the boy's whole head into its mouth and both had perished. Benson swore to the truth of the story, stating that while he was at the school no fish was ever caught in the nearby streams that weighed less than twelve pounds while most weighed in excess of fifty.

In 1846, New Hope Seminary opened about a mile from the agency at Skullyville for girls between the ages of eight and fourteen. Only one pupil per family was allowed to attend. Its first superintendent was Reverend W.

L. McAlister who conducted classes in reading, arithmetic, and geography. Among the texts used was Noah Webster's Dictionary. The students, taught not to laugh out loud or to speak Choctaw, were punished should they break the rules by having to take a teaspoon of red pepper.

Education was a difficult task at New Hope. In 1854, the session began with fifty-four students, but only forty-two completed the term on July 6. Seven had died, three of tuberculosis, two from typhoid fever, one from dropsy, and one of congestion of the brain. The school, suspended during the war like the others, was the first to reopen in 1871. A year later, New Hope accepted forty girls under the direction of Superintendent Reverend Edwin Ruthven Shapard of Tennessee. In 1875, he and trustees, Edmund and Houston McCurtain, formed a teacher's institute devoted to the improvement of teaching methods and procedures for the children. On September 13, it established a new working arrangement between the two schools whereby the girls sewed and made clothes for the boys, who, in turn, provided vegetables and firewood for New Hope. A considerable competition occurred weekly between the boys for delivery of the food to the girls' dormitories.

In 1880, New Hope reported an enrollment of fifty-one girls. In 1892, Thomas D. Ainsworth, the first administrator of Choctaw blood, was appointed superintendent. He reported an average attendance of eighty in 1894-95 with the health and studies of the girls ranked as "Good." His final report was 1896. The school was destroyed by fire on December 30.

Meanwhile, Reverend Alfred Wright had established a school for both boys and girls at Wheelock on December 9, 1832. Ten years later there were forty-eight students, mostly boys. In 1844, fifty-three were enrolled, but only three boarded at the school. In 1845, Harriett Mitchell reported there were 102 girls at the institution under her care. Later married to Wright, she helped publish forty-one volumes in the Choctaw language. At one point she copied the New Testament three times in long hand in preparation for publication of her husband's manuscript. Her instruction included five hours with "books," and another four in the afternoon with needlework and manual exercises. Subjects included English, geography, math, and the Bible.

In 1835,Wright added a boys school about five miles northeast of Wheelock named Norwalk for the home in Connecticut of its first superintendent, Jared Olmstead. The Reverend and his wife, Julia, labored for seven years at Norwalk using music to teach the boys English. The school established a reputation for instruction in music until Olmstead's unexpected death in 1843. Replaced by Charles C. Copeland of Vermont, the major problem was soon attendance. Although more than fifty young boys were enrolled, rarely more than twenty attended classes. In 1849, Copeland moved to a new station in northeast Bryan County called Mount Pleasant. In 1854, H.

V. Pitkin, his replacement, an ardent abolitionist, caused such controversy with his views on slavery that Norwalk lost its funding and ceased operations.

Built of native stone quarried nearby in 1842, the church at Wheelock was a monument to Choctaw religion and education. From 1832 until Wright's death in 1853, nearly 600 members were taken into the church, and Mrs. Wright continued the school for ten more years until her death. Surviving the years as a boarding school, Wheelock was supported as an institution for orphan Choctaw girls after 1875.[92]

Other schools opened by the American Board of Commissioners for Foreign Missions were all given Choctaw names, Chuahla (Cedar) Female Seminary, Kushak (cane or reed), and Iyanvbi (ironwood or witch hazel). Deriving its name from the vast pine forest in the region, Chuahla was located two miles west of Doaksville at the Pine Ridge Mission by Kingsbury in 1842. Opening its doors with seventeen scholars in 1844, its principal teacher was Miss Harriet Golding of Ware, Massachusetts, who spent ten years at the seminary for the Presbyterian Board before returning to her home because of poor health.

Kushak Seminary received its name from the "cane or reed" towns in Mississippi whose residents had settled around Good Water, the site of an American Board station ten miles southwest of Fort Towson near the mouth of the Kiamichi. In 1844, Ebenezer Hotchkin opened Kushak with teachers recruited from his home state of Massachusetts as the first female school in the Nation. Considered a girls boarding school until 1853, Hotchkin convinced the Choctaw Council to enlarge it later on as a higher grade "Young Ladies Seminary" equivalent to a high school level institution. Its first teachers included Harriet Mitchell, later Mrs. Wright, Miss Jennie Hollingsworth, Miss Clara Stanislaus, and Miss M. E. Denny. Appointed in 1858, George Ainslie served as its superintendent until the Civil War.

In 1835, Cyrus Byington moved his family by wagon more than five hundred miles from Mississippi to a new home he called Stockbridge in the southeast corner of the Choctaw Nation near the Arkansas line on Lapittah Bok (Buck Creek). "Sounding Horn" Byington soon started Lapittah Bok Aiitvnaha (Buck Creek Church) and a school, while one of his teachers, Mrs. N. W. Barnes, served as the head of a school at nearby Eagletown. Her students, including some of the wealthier Indians like Colonel David Folsom, who paid $300 a year for private tutoring, were taught writing, the scriptures, catechisms, and hymns.

Faced by many hardships and losses, Byington suffered personally at his mission. A smallpox epidemic swept the region in the latter part of the decade, causing numerous deaths within the tribe and the missionary's own family. In 1839, Rebecca, Byington's sister, visiting at Stockbridge, died with the disease. Only a year later Mrs. Barnes succumbed to illness, followed by Byington's eldest son, Edward, in 1840, and still later a younger son, Horatio, in 1846. Despite the fewer numbers in attendance caused by the sickness and death, Byington continued to serve, traveling to Mountain Fork, Eagletown, and White Clay, or Lukfata, a settlement west of Broken Bow started by Reverend Loring Williams. In September 1844, Byington established another mission school called Iyanvbi Female Seminary west of his Buck Creek Church. Serving as the superintendent, Byington prospered with the help of two teachers from the East, Lydia S. Hall and Harriet N. Keyes, and a Choctaw co-worker named Emily Dwight.

In 1842, Byington proudly reported that the rapid growth of the Nation had increased his preaching stations to nine and his circuit to more than thirty miles in width and sixty miles in length. In 1845, the missionary, assisted by Pliny Fisk, a licensed Choctaw preacher, held a camp meeting on the Boggy River that was attended by more than fifty people. Riding over the region, Byington observed that almost every farm had horses, hogs, and cattle, while those without livestock raised crops of beans and potatoes and fields of corn. Noting that Calvin H. Howell, a son-in-law of Pitchlynn, produced sixty-four bales of cotton from his gin that year and David Folsom owned a salt works and four other Choctaw tradesmen served Boggy Depot with a blacksmith shop, Byington reported that the Choctaw were recovering quickly from the removals and that the prosperity could be seen throughout the Nation.

On January 31, 1852, George Dana II arrived at Stockbridge from Belpre, Ohio, to claim the missionary's twenty-one-year-old daughter Lucy for his bride. The young man and his betrothed had not seen each other for more than four years. They were married by Reverend Kingsbury as Byington was away in the East getting a publisher for his books. Dana's first impressions of the region were favorable ones. He wrote: "The civilization the missionaries had established here was manifest. Here were improvements and conveniences with the dwellings, the Church School buildings-books, teachers, —all things necessary to educate the young and instruct the aged."[93]

Unfortunately, Byington, uncharacteristically Yankee, was a supporter of slavery, and got into trouble with the anti-slavery American Board of Commissioners. Calling all abolitionists "insufferable," the missionary lost the board's support for Stockbridge Mission in 1859. He only stayed two more years before returning to the East where he died the last day of the year, 1867. His mission was not reopened after the war, and Colonel Peter Pitchlynn moved his family into the buildings later taken over by his daughter.

In 1843, appropriations were made for the establishment of the Armstrong Academy in the Pushmataha District, and Baptist missionary, Reverend Ramsay D. Potts, was appointed at its first superintendent. In 1834, he had run a mission called Providence southeast of Hugo, not far from Jones' Rose Hill plantation. In 1844, when the Baptist Board of Foreign Missions gave up its work in the Choctaw Nation, Potts and his wife joined Isaac McCoy's American Indian Missionary Association, located in Louisville, Kentucky, and assumed the work of the Baptist mission. By 1845 all the paper work had been completed and Potts assumed supervision of Armstrong Academy, located three miles northeast of Bokchito. The nearest village at the time was Mayhew, the court ground for the Pushmataha District, located a few miles north of Boswell. In 1846, Chief Nitakechi's sons, Henry Graves and Captain Jackson, joined the Philadelphia Baptist Church that was established near Armstrong Academy as the "First Baptist Church of the Choctaw Nation."

On December 2, 1845, the school, with strict rules against speaking Choctaw, opened its doors with thirty-three pupils. The boys were put to work and soon had fifty acres planted and the fields enclosed with split rail fences. In July 1847, Reverend P. P. Brown, on an inspection tour for the American Indian Mission Association, attended examination exercises at the Academy with Robert M. Jones, George W. Harkins, and Chief Silas Fisher, and wrote favorably of his impressions of the school to the *Indian Advocate*. He noted that enrollment had steadily increased to fifty. Enrollment continued to climb until Potts retired and moved to Texas in 1853.

A lack of funds caused the school to gradually disintegrate. Although a new control, the Cumberland Presbyterian Board, revitalized the school for a time, the Civil War caused its end. Built before the fighting started, the new brick building was used as the National Capitol for the Choctaw during the war, a purpose that continued from 1863 to 1883 when Tvshkahomma was rebuilt. In 1884, Armstrong was reopened as an orphan school for boys, serving until it was destroyed by fire in 1921.[94]

Another missionary teacher among the Choctaw was John Harpole Carr of Wilson County, Tennessee, whose parents immigrated to Arkansas in 1833. Carr embraced religion at a Cumberland Presbyterian camp meeting and was licensed as a Methodist preacher in 1845. Joining the Indian Mission Conference, Carr traveled the Doaksville circuit over the southeastern Choctaw Nation, western Arkansas, and north Texas around Paris. In 1847, he was appointed to oversee construction of Bloomfield Academy, a boarding school for Chickasaw girls in southern Bryan County. In 1852, Carr selected the site for the school and began work as its first superintendent.[95]

The missionary teachers provided an excellent college preparatory core curriculum and the most promising Choctaw scholars were given money to continue their educations in eastern universities under the "Forty Youth Fund." Until 1842, these students were sent to the Choctaw Academy in Kentucky and then were divided among four colleges, Ohio University, Athens, Ohio; Jefferson College, (later Washington and Jefferson College), Cannonsburgh, Pennsylvania; Asbury University (now Depauw), Greencastle, Indiana; and Lafayette College, Eaton, Pennsylvania. In time the scholarship program was expanded to include other colleges, and women were allowed to participate. In 1848, five graduates of Spencer Academy, Allen Wright, Leonidas Garland, Joseph R. Hall, Lycurgus Pitchlynn, and William F. Howell, enrolled at Delaware College, Newark, Delaware, but when the school closed after only two years, its students transferred to Union College, where President Reverend Eliphalet Nott presided in Schenectady, New York. In 1852, Wright transferred to Union Theological Seminary in New York City to work on a higher degree. The Choctaw orphan, Kiliahote, (Let's go make a light), whose teacher in Indian Territory, Eunice Clough, had named him after Reverend Alfred Wright, was the first Indian in America to receive a master's degree.

Other Choctaw students who made reputations as scholars included Joseph P. Folsom, the only Choctaw to attend Dartmouth College before the Civil War. Graduated in 1855, Folsom was followed by Choctaw student, Albert Carney. Between 1850 and 1856, tribal students matriculated at Georgetown College, Kentucky, and three students at Centre College in Danville, Kentucky.

Women attended college at Southern Masonic Female College in Covington, Georgia, or the Virginia Female Institute at Staunton, Virginia, where Mary R. Pitchlynn, enrolled with her friends. Others studied in Fayetteville, Arkansas, and Edgewood Seminary in Pennsylvania, the alma mater for Jane "Jennie" Austin, who later married Chief Jackson McCurtain. From 1825 to 1906, the list of students educated under the Forty Youth Fund included 466 names as students enrolled in colleges in Kentucky, Tennessee, Virginia, and Texas. In 1879, Chief Isaac Garvin summarized the attitude of the Choctaw by urging the Council to promote schools with the words, "Then I say educate! Educate! Or we perish!"

Through education and hard work the tribe eventually recovered from the removals. Within a generation the Choctaw Nation had been converted from a wilderness to a prosperous country equal to the white states around it. The Choctaw toiled through the next several years to build roads, towns, and institutions that reflected their return of prosperity.[96]

In 1845, Reverend William Graham, a Methodist missionary impressed by meeting John Page, a full blood Choctaw preacher, made a tour through the Red River country reporting a number of observations that reflected the development, as well as the difficulty and lack of progress, being made by the tribe. Staying for a time with a friendly, mixed blood family living on the military road near Fort Towson, the Reverend noted that the family lived well, owning a profitable farm worked by twenty slaves. The owner's wife was "a clean lady," who kept a tidy house and the family consisted of two young daughters, one educated at a mission school by a "pious Massachusetts lady." Both girls were "easy and graceful in manners but plainly attired," according to Graham. This was the home of Peter Pitchlynn, and the Reverend conducted worship services each morning and evening during his stay at their comfortable, Southern style farm.

Moving on with his trip, the preacher encountered the other side of Choctaw culture. He met a party of men on their way to a ball game who were obviously drunk, but they only sat on their horses and watched for a time before riding away. He then passed through an Indian village, noting that the men wore buckskin leggings and moccasins with their heads covered by turbans. They all sat on blankets, no other furniture being used. Their women wore nothing except their moccasins and a string of large beads around their necks, although they kept large blankets drawn over them. Their children were completely naked, and the preacher noted that he gave them his "entire inattention."

Graham's observations illustrated the slow evolution of the Choctaw toward "civilized society." The mixed bloods were leading the way, but the full bloods were gradually learning to accept white Christianity. The Nation still had a long way to go, but great strides were being made.[97]

CHAPTA HANNALI

~ CHAPTER SIX ~

"ROADS OF RECOVERY"

Chapter Six

In 1819, Major Stephen Long, commander of an early exploration of the Louisiana Purchase, concluded that the American Southwest was "completely unfit for human habitation." His appraisal included the Indian Territory that was traded to the Five Civilized Tribes in the 1830s, but the Choctaw proved this supposition invalid by converting the unsettled wilderness into a prosperous democratic republic within a single generation. The full bloods cleared and tamed the land and established small subsistence farms in the woods and hills of the eastern half of their country while the more capitalistically ambitious mixed bloods created a society patterned after Southern plantation owners along the Red and Kiamichi Rivers. Recovering quickly from the trauma of removal, the Choctaw founded villages and towns, established churches and schools, and built trails and roads across their Nation. For more than a score of years, they lived proudly as free, wealthy farmers and planters.

From Removal to the Civil War, the official most responsible for the development of the Choctaw Nation through the establishment of peaceful relations with the United States and other tribes in Indian Territory was the Choctaw Indian agent. Part of the administrative structure of the Office of Indian Affairs, the Choctaw agents, all Southerners and Democrats, faced many major problems including the illegal trade of alcohol, arguments with the military since the Choctaw Nation was an occupied territory, and invasions from the Plains tribes who resented the encroachment of the tribe on lands they believed belonged to them. Each of the agents brought special solutions to these problems.

In 1825, the Choctaw agency was created under the supervision of the Arkansas Indian Agency but was separated when William McClellan was assigned as an agent to the Office of Indian Affairs. Born in 1779, the North Carolina native had served as an army officer with Jackson at the Battle of New Orleans. In 1827, he set up an agency eighteen miles west of Fort Smith near "New Hope Spring," two miles east of the later village of Skullyville. Agent McClellan erected buildings for an expected large Choctaw removal after the Treaty of Washington but was greatly surprised and disappointed when only eight arrived.[98]

From 1831 to 1855, there were separate agents for the Choctaw and Chickasaw, but one agent directed the affairs of the two tribes after this time. The first Choctaw agent after Dancing Rabbit Creek was Francis W. Armstrong. Born in Virginia in 1783, Armstrong resigned from the Army in 1817, campaigned for Jackson in the election of 1828, and was rewarded with an appointment as census taker for the Choctaw in 1831. Completing his task in two months, he was appointed Choctaw agent west of the Mississippi River, but by the time of his arrival in Indian Territory, the agency had depreciated and fallen into ruin. His first action was to request $600 to repair the roof of the agent's home. In April 1833, the Choctaw began arriving in large numbers, and he started letting contracts for homes for the chiefs, a council house, and a church and a schoolhouse for each district.

The first major problems for Armstrong were raids on the Choctaw farms and villages by the nomadic Plains tribes, particularly the Comanche. In 1835, Secretary of War Lewis Cass appointed Montfort Stokes, Mathew Arbuckle, and Armstrong to negotiate peace with these tribes. Their effort resulted in the Leavenworth-Dodge Dragoon expedition and a treaty at Fort Holmes in August, but Armstrong died on the way to the conference.

William Armstrong, a tall, light-complected, auburn-haired veteran of the Battle of New Orleans replaced his brother on September 8, 1835. Personally handpicked by Jackson to direct the earlier removals and given the title of Special Agent for the Choctaw, East of the Mississippi River, William immediately demonstrated his concern by trying to find doctors to accompany the Choctaw on their removals. Finding none, he joined the tribe in its ordeal to help as best he could. At one point, Armstrong's party, traveling with a company led by Moshulatubbee, struggled for seven days, floundering through waist-deep water to cross forty-two miles of swamps. On another occasion Agent Armstrong went into private debt to borrow 500 bushels of corn to feed his starving Choctaw. In 1833, Armstrong persuaded another 2,000 to make the trip, but rumors circulated that the government would pay ten dollars per person to make the trip by themselves, a rumor credited to white traders, and only half the original number moved with him.

Armstrong was poor, deeply in debt, owing $20,000, when first appointed as Choctaw agent, but he paid off all his debts within a few years and accumulated property worth more than $40,000, all on his agent's salary of $1,500 a year. Scandalous rumors circulated freely about him until his death in Doaksville in June 1847. Despite the stories and insinuations, David Folsom memorialized Armstrong as "an honest man" unlike other agents "who would run away with Indian money." As testimony to the admiration and respect for him, Armstrong Academy was named in his honor.

On July 10, 1847, Samuel M. Rutherford, a politician from Arkansas, was rewarded for his support of Martin Van Buren's successful bid for the presidency with the appointment as Armstrong's replacement. His biggest problem turned out to be the arrival of hundreds of Choctaw, many of whom suffered from sickness and disease, along with addictions to alcohol after living among the whites in Mississippi, compounded by numerous whiskey stops and traders along the Arkansas and Texas borders. The poor health of the Choctaw was exacerbated by epidemics of whooping cough, mumps, and measles plus the arrival of another 547 with cholera in 1849. The situation was so bad for a time that Fort Coffee Academy and New Hope Seminary were forced to close to give the students time to recover. Rutherford was replaced by President Zachary Taylor but obviously was not too upset by his dismissal.

On May 29, 1849, John Drennan succeeded him but was removed in less than two years when he proved to be a heavy gambler. William Wilson, a graduate of Washington College in Pennsylvania, who had lived in the Choctaw Nation for a number of years as principal of Spencer Academy, replaced him in 1851. Education was a major concern during his administration, and the Choctaw school system flourished under his guidance.

Upon his death Douglas Hancock Cooper was appointed as a reward for his support of New Hampshire Democrat Franklin Pierce. Cooper, son of a wealthy Southern physician and slave owner, was born in 1815, attended the University of Virginia, and returned to Mississippi as a planter and lawyer. His plantation, known as "Mon Clova," was located near Jefferson Davis' home, and the two neighbors visited often. In 1853, Cooper was appointed Choctaw agent when President Pierce named Davis his Secretary of War.

The agents performed their duties with varying degrees of success, but most provided the leadership skills necessary to achieve peace and harmony within the tribe. Equally importantly, they maintained cordial relations between the tribe and the occupation forces stationed at numerous military posts within the Choctaw Nation. Under the helpful eyes of the agents, the tribe established thriving communities and commercial centers.[99]

Along with the towns and villages the Choctaw founded educational systems that rivaled and often even surpassed nearby American states. No people ever applied so large a portion of its revenue to the purpose of learning. Based upon a national system of boarding schools for boys and girls, the Choctaw Council provided the buildings and approximately seventy-five percent of the funding necessary for the maintenance of the schools. The Choctaw leaders were determined to be prepared the next time the "White Tide" caught up with the tribe.

Beginning with the establishment of academies and seminaries, a network of local, "Neighborhood" and "Sabbath schools" was created and financed from accumulated treaty obligations. By 1838, more than a dozen of these local schools were in existence. The community's only obligation was to provide a site for the school. The tribe provided funds for everything else including teachers. Teachers' salaries compared favorably with nearby states, ranging from $500 for a school year of six months to $833.33 for ten months. Salaries of mission teachers remained comparatively low, but daily living costs and all expenses together with charges for travel and regular leaves-of-absence to the states were borne by the mission boards. The boards appointed the superintendents, teachers, and assistants that supervised the schools, while

Choctaw citizens appointed to the Board of Trustees by the General Council selected the pupils to attend the schools and inspected the teaching methods and quality of education provided in them. The schools particularly emphasized English and sewing and housekeeping skills for girls and farming and livestock raising skills for the boys.

Neighborhood schools and Saturday and Sunday schools were provided for any village that requested them. The first Neighborhood school in the Moshulatubbee District, consisting of Skullyville, Sugar Loaf, Gaines, Coal, and Sans Bois counties, was established at Skullyville and averaged around sixty pupils in attendance. Among its students were brothers Jack, Edmund, Greene, Dave, and Robert McCurtain, who lived about five miles away. Other Neighborhood schools included Lapittah Bok (Buck Creek), with Greene LeFlore as its first teacher, and Tiak Lukoli (Pine Grove), near Milton. These primitive, log schools were mostly furnished with split timbers for wooden benches and provided with simple chalkboard slates for materials but were always conducted by trained, professional teachers. They successfully transformed the Choctaw into literate, educated people.

A typical Neighborhood teacher was Tryphena Wall who conducted classes at Mayhew in 1841. A Choctaw born in Mississippi, the young student moved with her family to a new home on Clear Boggy River near a church called Mayhew after the old mission in Mississippi organized by Kingsbury in 1839. Based upon the missionary's personal recommendation, Miss Wall was hired by Agent William Armstrong to teach twenty-four students for a school term of ten months and Sunday school for their parents at the church. Since Miss Wall considered teaching English her first duty, language was the most practical and common subject taught by her despite having few books for her students. Other courses were given a lesser priority, but the use of English only in all the schools was enforced by a variety of penalties and procedures.

The Choctaw demonstrated their dedication to their educational system in many ways. Normally operated at capacity enrollments, the schools discouraged truancy and were always closely monitored by tribal elders. Since tribal members selflessly sacrificed the services of the students at home to send them to boarding schools, neither parents nor relatives ever missed commencement exercises. Although examinations lasted hours, sometimes twenty or more, hundreds of tribal leaders and friends commonly waited patiently for news of their students' progress or appearances at graduation ceremonies.

The Choctaw, understandably proud of their educations, sometimes displayed their scholarship at the expense of their audience. On one occasion, a white visitor, observing a Choctaw man dozing underneath a tree with his hat pulled down over his eyes, walked over to the person that he considered lazy and shiftless and kicked him awake. When the Choctaw opened his eyes, the intruder inquired, "You speak 'um English?" "Only when spoken correctly," replied the Choctaw graduate of a college in New York.[100]

One of the major arguments for an educated society was having the ability to deal with the whites the next time treaties were demanded by the federal government. In January 1837, the Treaty of Doaksville allowed the Chickasaw to join the tribe, but it proved a situation that neither liked, especially the Chickasaw who discovered they were a minority within the Choctaw tribe. In 1853, the two tribes were invited to send delegates to Washington to discuss separation of their nations along with other outstanding issues. Upon their arrival, delegates were given four separate propositions for discussions. The Americans wanted the tribes to cede any claims to the territory west of the 100th Meridian, and to lease back to the federal government the territory between the 98th and 100th that was occupied by the Plains tribes. Additionally, the Chickasaw wanted a separate nation, and the Choctaw wanted a settlement of the Net Proceeds claims.

Negotiations over the next three months resulted in the two tribes agreement to a treaty on June 22, 1855. In exchange for $800,000, three-fourths to the Choctaw and one-fourth to the Chickasaw, provisions were made to lease the country west of the 98th Meridian, afterwards known as the Leased District, an area neither tribe had ever occupied, for the settlement of Wichita and other tribes. The Choctaw and Chickasaw further agreed that both would have separate nations, but each could settle within the borders of either nation. The Chickasaw were given territory west of Island Bayou, west of Durant, between the Canadian and Red Rivers to the 98th Meridian. The tribes further pledged to make no future treaties nor sell lands without approval of the other. On November 16, 1855, the treaty was approved by the General Council and signed by Tandy Walker, President of the Senate, Kennedy McCurtain, Speaker of the House, George Washington Harkins, Chief of the Apuckshunnubbee District, Nicholas Cochanaur, Chief of the Pushmataha District, and Adam Christy, acting Chief of the Moshulatubbee District.[101]

The treaty had also recognized the validity of Choctaw removal claims. Federal authorities were directed to either reimburse those individuals defrauded or pay the tribe the net proceeds from the sale of the Mississippi lands, an issue that created a controversy in United States-Choctaw relations and caused problems for years. The subject was averted for the immediate moment by sending it to the United States Senate for adjudication. In March 1859, the Choctaw were awarded nearly $3 million, but Congress remained reluctant and delayed payment for more than two years. In March 1861, Congress finally appropriated $250,000 in cash and bonds, most of which was distributed among the delegates who had worked for the settlement. The Civil War interrupted further payments.

The Choctaw created a constitutional republic in the Nation in the meantime. In 1834, the first constitution in the state was written near Tvshkahomma. Placing executive power in the hands of the three district chiefs elected every four years, the charter contained a bill of rights for males over the age of sixteen. In 1842, a new constitution acknowledged representation for the Chickasaw and provided for the organization of a General Council composed of a House of Representatives and a Senate to offset the domination of the Council by the more populous Apuckshunnubbee District in the southeastern part of the Nation. In January 1850, a convention at Doaksville with Peter Pitchlynn as president adopted constitutional changes that provided for the organization of counties and county courts in the four districts. In 1857, Tandy Walker, elected president of a convention at Skullyville, drafted another constitution for the tribe with an article that abolished the District Chiefs for one "Governor" of the Nation, causing such a storm of protests that opponents held another convention in Blue County proclaiming yet another constitution at Doaksville. The situation degenerated into a virtual civil war within the tribe until finally, to ease the trouble, "Governor" Walker called for an election to "alter or amend" the existing constitutions. The result was a new convention on September 28, 1859. Elected as its president, George Hudson presided over the draft of a constitution known as the Doaksville Constitution that created the position of "Principal Chief."[102]

Displaying the national pride of the Choctaw at the same time, an act directed Chief Hudson to design a Great Seal for the Nation on October 16, 1860. Symbolizing the tradition and history of the tribe, the seal was inscribed with the words, "The Great Seal of the Choctaw Nation" around the edge and engraved in the center was a design of an unstrung bow with three arrows and pipe-hatchet blended together. The seal recognized the old custom of smoking the calumet in the council circle during deliberations of important matters. The pipe-hatchet with a pipe of red or black stone and a stem decorated with feathers and rare fur in the center of the seal was not considered an instrument of war but of purely ceremonial use. A calumet for a peace council was decorated with white feathers and those for war with red. The unstrung bow represented peace with preparedness for defense with three arrows at the ready to symbolize a united people and one arrow for each of the great chiefs, Apuckshunnubbee, Moshulatubbee, and Pushmataha.[103]

The removals continued during these years. In 1849, George S. Gaines, a longtime friend of the Choctaw, was requested to help move more tribal members, and small parties of four to five hundred got underway in the winter of 1850. Weather and cholera still plagued the emigrants, but the removals were less traumatic than a decade earlier. In December 1851, a party of twenty-five Catawba Indians, traveling from South Carolina, asked for permission to come into Choctaw country. In February 1852, nineteen survivors reached the Choctaw agency and appealed for admission to tribal membership. The following year William and Thomas Morrison, Betsy and Rebecca Heart, Philip Keggo and child, and Rosey, Betsey, Julian, Mary, Sopronia, and Sally Ayers were formally accepted into tribal membership.[104]

Tribal growth and prosperity prompted the Choctaw Council to develop a safe and practical transportation system across their Nation in these years. Keenly aware of the advantages of roads through their country from their experience in Mississippi with the famous thoroughfare built out of Tennessee to Natchez in 1802, the Natchez Trace, the tribe knew the benefits to be gained from the traffic brought by good highways. Beginning in the 1830s, traders from St. Louis developed a workable transportation and communication system over the very early trails across the Nation. Their trails allowed easy access to trade for the products from the Choctaw farms.

The movement to Texas caused even faster economic development in the Nation. For years the most widely used trail to the Lone Star Republic was the "Texas Road" that ran north and south through Choctaw country. Entering Indian Territory from the southwestern corner of Missouri, the road ran south to Cabin Creek, and Pryor, then generally followed the Grand River to the Three Forks near Union Mission then southward to Okay, where Sam Houston had operated a trading post before joining the migration himself. The road moved on past North Fork Town to Boggy Depot, Ft. Washita, and Colbert's Ferry. So many wagons traveled down the road that one observer claimed that his party had hardly been out of sight of a wagon since leaving Missouri. In 1845, more than a thousand wagons crossed into Texas in a period of less than six weeks.

The trail between Fort Smith and Clear Boggy River was generally called the Fort Smith-Boggy Depot Road. In 1842, the road was extended by Fort Washita, striking the Texas Road about a mile north of Stringtown where intermarried citizen, A.W. Georg, operated a farm for many years. The roads then merged toward Red River.[105]

In 1853, tribal leaders were greatly excited to learn of a large government expedition through their territory by a company of soldiers, surveyors, scientists, and frontiersmen as part of a railroad inspection known as the Pacific Railway Survey. Its leader was twenty-six-year-old, five foot-ten Lieutenant Amiel Weeks Whipple, who instructed his men to make scientific observations of the land along the way. The expedition proved an extremely valuable record of the plant and animal life, the availability of water, and the tribes in the Indian Territory.

Chapter Six

On July 16, 1853, the government crew, escorted by a contingent of fifty Dragoons, arrived at Camp 1 on the Ring plantation located near Skullyville in the Choctaw Nation. After three days of survey work, the camp was moved to the Choctaw agency where it remained for almost a week as Whipple attempted to learn as much as possible about the tribe as part of his scientific investigations for the survey project. He was informed during a visit with Agent Douglas H. Cooper there were between fifteen and twenty thousand Choctaw in the Nation and that they were making great advances in government and education. The Lieutenant was understandably impressed when shown a book of Choctaw laws and a copy of the *Choctaw Definer*, a newspaper printed in Choctaw and English.

On one evening visit Whipple was introduced to Choctaw District Chief Cornelius McCurtain. After discussing the possibility of a railroad through the Nation, McCurtain offered his best advise on the most suitable routes for its location. Whipple, later reporting his conversation, gave a favorable description of the Chief and his followers. He observed that a few of the Choctaw wore breechclouts with shirts and pants and others wore printed hunting shirts but all wore high crowned hats with silver bands, satin vests, moccasins, and wampum belts. The women all wore calico dresses, added Whipple.

Accompanying the Whipple expedition was German artist Heinrich Balduin Mollhausen who was employed by the Smithsonian Institution as a naturalist and painter for the party. Moved by the appearance of two Choctaw, the artist produced a graphic portrait of "Shang-bee and Alatakabee-Choctaws," along with a drawing of "Ring's Farm Camp" only nine miles west of Fort Smith. Later producing his own book of the survey trip to the Pacific entitled *Diary of my Journal*, the Prusian artist reported "blooming farms" in the Nation with "luxuriant crops, and a general prosperity that enables... these sons of Nature to aspire to higher culture..."[106]

An astute naturalist, Mollhausen linked the problem of alcohol encountered among the tribesmen to earlier tribal misfortunes. Learning that the whiskey trade had been one of the contributing causes of the removals, the painter warned the tribe to be on the watch in the future. He wrote that once the Indian was drunk and lost all his possessions, the whites could easily drive him away again as they had done in Mississippi.

Lieutenant Whipple took time to visit Fort Coffee Academy while he was in the area. Impressed by the large crowd of mixed bloods at the school for a Sunday meeting, he was surprised to learn that Choctaw laws prohibited racial intercourse between blacks and Indians, laws that were enforced by severe penalties. Whipple observed that he did not think this rule was followed to a great extent. The American explorer was more impressed by the fact that wherever he traveled he encountered friendly, courteous Choctaw, some who spoke no English but still treated the party graciously. This, he observed, was the major strength of the Choctaw character, their polite, quiet friendship for each other and outsiders alike.

His observations were echoed by the acting quartermaster of the expedition, Lieutenant David Sloan Stanley, who also kept a diary of the visits made by the party. Stanley was complimentary of the Choctaw progress as well, often mentioning "the fine, large farms and fine herds of cattle, sheep, and poultry" that existed among the Choctaw along Sans Bois Creek. Others in the survey party made similar statements about the prosperity and improvements of the tribe.[107]

Visitors particularly were struck by the productivity of the Choctaw farmers. Observing that most tribesmen had enclosed fields of corn, potatoes, peas, beans, pumpkins, and melons, they added that thousands of bushels of corn and bales of cotton were being produced as surpluses. This was true particularly in the southern portion of the Nation that had proven especially suitable for the production of cotton where hundreds of bales were being transported down the Red River to New Orleans. By 1842, a dozen gins were operating and more than a thousand bales were shipped during the year. When the price of cotton fell that year so low that only a marginal profit was made, the farmers quickly converted to corn and produced a record surplus of twenty thousand bushels the following year.

In the late 1850s, severe droughts caused a period of economic reversals for the tribal farmers, but they soon recovered and were producing enough corn to meet demands and make a profit. Despite especially severe weather problems in 1855, productivity increased to the point that it was impossible to find an idle farm hand during harvest time. By mutual consent the tribesmen helped each other once their own crops were gathered. As the decade ended, the Indian farmers combined their crops of cotton, corn, and potatoes with orchards of apples, peaches, and, plums, and better fenced their livestock for protection, resulting in dramatic increases in production.

Choctaw prosperity was reflected in their homes. Many boasted wooden floors, chimneys, and roofs fastened with the latest invention, nails, instead of "rib poles." By the end of the decade, the tribe had physically and culturally restored its former designation as one of the "Five Civilized Tribes."[108]

This growth was greatly aided by the construction of a modern stage road through the Nation in 1858. The first mail coach of the Butterfield Stage line crossed the 192 miles from Fort Smith to Colbert's Ferry on Red River as part of a national effort to establish an Overland Mail Stage Route to California. More commonly called the Butterfield Overland Mail, it was named for company president, John Butterfield, of New York, who invested more than a million dollars in teams, especially designed "celerity coaches," stage stops, and employees in his quest to build a line across the continent. The routes from two eastern terminals, Memphis and St. Louis, met at Fort Smith, crossed the Choctaw Nation to Preston, Texas, then west to El Paso, Fort Yuma, to San Francisco. The rates averaged $10 per letter and $200 per fare from St. Louis to California. The first trip required twenty-nine days, from September 19 to October 15, 1858. The route across the Choctaw Nation included stops between thirteen and nineteen miles apart.

On September 19, 1858, about 3:00 p.m., a brightly painted coach forded the Poteau River and crossed into the Choctaw Nation toward its first stop at Walker's Station near Skullyville where Tandy Walker operated a stopover. As his slaves cared for the horses, the passengers ate the innkeeper's meal of bacon, biscuits and gravy, mush, and coffee for seventy-five cents. Although not an official stop, the next station was located on Brazil Creek and operated by Washington McDaniel and Charles Jones as part of the mail route. Three miles to the southwest, the next stop was a trading post run by James Trayhern. The next station, Edwards' Store, later designated Red Oak when it acquired a post office in 1869, provided a meal for forty-five cents a serving. Next was William Holloway's stand at the northern end of the Sans Bois Mountains' pass where Holloway had operated a toll road for years. The fourth official stop was John Riddle's station near present Wilburton.

The Overland Stage wound westward to Mountain Station at the crest of Blue Mountain, then southward across Gaines Creek to Silas Pusley's home where passengers rested while attendants cared for the teams. Later, Pusley built a toll bridge across the creek to speed up travel through his farm. The next station was Caspar Blackburn's home seventeen miles down the road on Brushey Creek. Waddell's Station, probably named for one of Butterfield's employees, was sixteen miles farther southeast. Another stop was located at A. W. Geary's Station located fifteen miles away at a toll bridge over the North Boggy River near Stringtown, where a hotel and stable served the passengers and stock. The trip resumed for sixteen more miles to Boggy Depot where a small community soon sprang up to provide services for the travelers. By 1858, Boggy Depot contained shops, warehouses, an inn, a church, and a school.

The road proceeded to Nail's Crossing operated by J. H. Nail, seventeen miles farther on the east bank of the Blue River. Fourteen miles further the road crossed into Chickasaw country near the Island Bayou stream. Here, Fisher's Station, better known by its old name, Carriage Point, was only a quick change of horses. The final station was Colbert's Ferry operated by Benjamin F. Colbert in the 1850s. Passengers reported good hot meals and warm hospitality at the stop, and traffic across the ferry remained heavy even after the

Butterfield Stage route closed. Railroad officials surveyed for a bridge at this point after the Civil War. On the other side of Red River, the next division of the Butterfield Route took over. The entire journey across the Choctaw Nation took thirty hours of travel, but the route was a casualty of the war. In March of 1861, the southern route ended its runs and never reopened.[109]

The roads and trails across the Nation revealed a prosperous, economically progressive society. Unfortunately, that very prosperity brought problems. In 1849, David G. Ball, publisher of the *Choctaw Telegraph*, instructed his editor, David Folsom, to report in the July 19 issue on the killing of some whiskey dealers by the Lighthorsemen. The newspaper, revealing the existence of lawlessness within the Nation, acknowledged as well the law enforcement body, organized to combat the problem. Editor Folsom answered questions concerning the legality of these deaths without the benefit of trials or juries at the hands of a roving police force by quoting the Choctaw law of 1834 that persons killed under these circumstances committed crimes at their own risk and Lighthorsemen were protected against complaints for deaths committed in the line of duty. Folsom saw no reason for further inquiry into the matter.[110]

This was the general attitude of the tribe towards its beloved Lighthorsemen, a mounted police led by a captain under other commanding officers who dispensed justice for the tribe. A hard riding, hard fighting group carrying only rifles and revolvers, a few handfuls of parched corn, and Wak nipi passa (beef jerky) in their saddle bags, the Lighthorsemen ranged freely over the entire Nation.

The organization traced its roots in Mississippi to the Doak's Stand Treaty in 1820 that provided for a corps of thirty Lighthorsemen paid for by an annuity of $600 from the government. By 1822, provisions for law enforcement had been initiated by Mi̱ko Aboha Kvllo Humma, who boasted that: "his company of faithful warriors takes every man who steals and ties him to a tree and gives him thirty-nine lashes." The chief based his action upon a criminal code with laws against theft, the transportation and sale of liquor, adultery, and murder.

Punishments were also decreed by Choctaw statute. Whipping, the most common penalty, was done by a switch not longer than thirty inches of seasoned hickory and not larger than the smallest finger of a man's hand. The sentence was executed by the official standing not farther nor nearer than two feet to the victim and must not be done by raising the arm past a right angle when delivering blows. If the victim fainted during the punishment, as often happened, he was released and told to return at a later date for the completion of his lashing. His peers gave much praise to any man who could withstand the dreaded lashes without crying or fainting.

Chapter Six

The earliest organizers of the Lighthorsemen were mixed bloods. Greenwood LeFlore served as a captain in the northwest district, and Peter Pitchlynn and David Folsom raised companies in their districts. All three had been educated in white schools and knew the American law system. The general duty of the Lighthorsemen was riding the country, settling disputes, and arresting, judging, and executing punishment against violators.[111]

The most common crimes in the Nation were violations of the liquor laws. In 1826, the Council prohibited the importation of liquor and prescribed violations punishable by one hundred lashes on the bare back. The issue, a concern even before the Council met near Turnbull's Stand on the Kiamichi River to draft the first constitution in June 1834, was immediately inserted into the new law code. Section VII of Article VIII of the document forbade and limited the trespassing of whites into the Nation and declared that no person would be permitted to bring liquor into the country. Section VIII of the same article instructed the Lighthorsemen to enforce the laws and authorized them to destroy any "ardent spirits" within the Nation. The Choctaw amended and changed their constitutions numerous times after 1834, but the whiskey law always remained the same.

The problem of alcohol permeated all levels of Choctaw society. The young students attending schools, their parents, and their friends were plagued with the sickness of liquor. The master of Spencer Academy often criticized Peter Pitchlynn's son, Lycurgus, as a notorious liar and drunk while attending the school, and his father, who delivered frequent temperance speeches at meetings, rarely heeded his own advice. At a meeting of the "Eagletown Social and Intellectual Society" attended by the wealthy Pitchlynn and his educated neighbors, the participants debated two questions, both concerning the most preferable of life styles. The choice for Pitchlynn and his friends were the farmer versus hunter society and the sober versus drunkard life. After much discussion the members of the debating group decided in favor of the farmer, drunkard life, concluding the meeting with a stiff drink.

Another lengthy deliberation on the evils of alcohol at one meeting of the Choctaw Council resulted in a decision to prohibit all intoxicating liquors in the future, followed by the question of the proper dispensation of the current supply on hand. It occurred to the delegates that the reserves should be depleted immediately to help the campaign along. Therefore, a resolution was proposed and passed that the Council consume any and all that could be found in order to prevent drinking by the young people in the future. Two hours later the stores had been exhausted and the law was declared in effect.

The Lighthorsemen were ardent enthusiasts of temperance and worked hard to stop bootleggers in the Nation but served in many other capacities. On February 1, 1844, Reverend Edmund McKinney at Spencer

Academy, expressing his concern that the mixed blood children were being "insubordinate," and more important, prone to skip classes and run away, called upon the Lighthorsemen to round up those that had left and return them to school. There were much fewer truancy problems once the Lighthorsemen began checking attendance.

Lighthorsemen were the only law enforcement officials in the Nation until the Civil War. The Constitution of 1834 had set their number at eighteen, six for each district, elected by the voters in each district, and in 1838, the Council created a judicial system relieving the Lighthorsemen of their trial duty, leaving them more time for enforcement. The officers continued to serve as juries until their duties were reduced to arrest and execution only in 1850. The Choctaw boasted proudly that prisoners captured by the Lighthorsemen never tried to evade punishment. The accused always appeared on the day appointed for execution of the sentence, normally a whipping administered by the policemen, and once it was done the incident was never mentioned again.

One of the most famous Lighthorsemen was Peter Conser. Born in 1852, near Eagletown, the mixed blood officer became a farmer after the Civil War, then at the age of twenty-five, a Deputy Sheriff in Sugar Loaf County. Appointed Captain of the Lighthorsemen, Conser also served as both a Senator and a Representative on the Tribal Council and was a successful businessman, owning a farm, blacksmith shop, gristmill, and a sawmill.[112]

From 1834 to 1860, the Choctaw went through six phases of government. In 1834, the first constitution vested all power in a unicameral legislature whose laws could be vetoed by two of the three district chiefs. In 1837, a new constitution was adopted to permit Chickasaw as a fourth district. In 1842, an amendment provided for a bicameral legislature, and the withdrawal of the Chickasaw allowed a new constitution written and adopted at Skullyville in 1857. This one supplanted the District Chiefs with a "Governor." It prompted a counter constitution the next year by conservative Choctaw that almost erupted into civil war. Finally, a compromise constitution was adopted at Doaksville in1860 that remained in effect until 1907.

The Doaksville Constitution of 1860 provided three branches of government, legislative, executive, and judicial. The legislature was a bicameral General Council with a Senate of four members from each of the three districts, serving two-year terms, and a House of Representatives of eighteen to twenty members elected annually on the basis of one representative per thousand people. The executive power was vested in the Principal Chief with veto power over each bill and three District Chiefs of whom none could serve more than two consecutive two-year terms. Other officers included a National Secretary, Treasurer, Auditor, and Attorney who were elected for two-year terms. A national corps of Lighthorsemen operated under the Principal

Chief and the District Chiefs. Additionally, each county had a sheriff and a ranger for livestock and brand records. The judiciary was composed of a Supreme Court, Circuit Court, and County Courts.

These officials were charged with the duty of enforcing a criminal code that included a list of crimes and punishments. Killing a witch or wizard was a capital offense, and sixty lashes for accusing someone of the offense, thirty-nine lashes for arson, perjury carried a fine of ten to one hundred dollars and up to thirty-nine lashes for not paying it, rape was 100 lashes for the first offense and death for a second (1846). In 1850, the death penalty was imposed for murder. In 1853, violation of the Sabbath by ball games or horse racing carried a punishment of ten dollars; in 1858, grand larceny for property was twenty-five dollars, and second offense horse theft carried the death penalty by hanging. In 1858, the first kidnapping law was enacted with the penalty being the letter "T" branded into the forehead followed by 100 lashes. In 1860, sodomy was punishable by death by hanging. In 1866, the death penalty was changed to "shooting the convict until he is dead."

The Choctaw placed the most emphasis on law enforcement among the tribes. The Council supported the regular Lighthorsemen, special Lighthorsemen, sheriffs, and deputy sheriffs with large budget appropriations, and the Lighthorsemen rigidly enforced the Choctaw law. By doing so they preserved peace and prosperity until the beginning of the Civil War.

The Choctaw had made great strides toward recovery. The Removals had decimated the tribe, but within twenty years the Nation had recovered and established a successful, industrious society. Their farms and plantations were beautiful and productive, and the people were happy, contented, and educated. Then, within a period of five years the whole structure was destroyed. In 1860, the white man's war found the Choctaw again.[113]

CHAPTA UNTUKLO

~ CHAPTER SEVEN ~

"MANY HAVE BEEN SLAIN; FEW HAVE BEEN SAVED"

Chapter Seven

In 1860, Choctaw civilization was interrupted again. When Abraham Lincoln, the first Republican president, won the national election, South Carolina launched a movement of secession that ultimately led to war. Soon followed by more Southern states that formed the Confederate States of America, Lincoln was forced to use arms to preserve the Union. The division of the states, a perplexing problem for the Indian tribes, forced the Choctaw to choose sides, and their decision to break their old treaties and make new ones with the Confederacy dramatically altered tribal history.

The Choctaw chose the Southern side because of the influence of mixed blood plantation owners. The Choctaw generally were not slave owners. In February 1831, a census taken prior to removal revealed a total of 521 slaves in the entire nation, and the number had increased to only 600 by the census of 1839, but the numbers grew steadily. The institution flourished only among mixed bloods as a means of maintaining equality with the ruling white, Southern aristocracy. In 1860, the Choctaw owned 2,297 slaves, distributed among 385 owners, averaging about six slaves to each owner. Only the Cherokee held more, 2,504 owned by 384 persons.

As an institution, Choctaw slavery was less strenuous than the white system. Slaves were treated better and fed more healthily by their Choctaw masters. Normally, they served as cooks and servants in the "Big House" and seldom, if ever, punished. The slaves, reluctant critics of their Indian masters, later stated, "We went to Church all the time. We had both white and colored preachers. Master Frank wasn't a Christian but he would build a brush-arbor for us to have church under and we sho' would have big meetings I'll tell you." Still, laws passed before the war increased the power of the slaveholders and new edicts forbade teaching slaves to read or write or to sing without permission. One former Choctaw slave later said, "I'm glad that slave days is gone. Even if the master was good the slave was bad off."[114]

In 1836, a statute aimed at the missionary elements suspected of being leaders in local abolitionist movements within the Nation decreed that all persons who favored abolitionism must leave the Nation. In 1850, editors of *The Northern Standard*, a popular north Texas newspaper, railed against the missionaries branding them all as abolitionists, a charge that infuriated John P. Kingsbury, one of the editors of the *Choctaw Intelligencer*. The missionary's son responded angrily to the blanket indictment pointing out that while most preachers did oppose slavery, some, like his father and Byington, supported it. Most active of the abolitionists were the Presbyterians, sponsored by the American Board of Commissioners for Foreign Missions.

As the issue intensified, a number of missionary teachers were forced to leave the Nation. Music teacher, Horace W. Pitkin, was removed for his anti-slavery remarks in 1849. Another, Sue L. McBeth, a graduate of Steubenville

Female Seminary in Ohio, was allowed to teach at Goodwater until Texas ruffians finally forced her to leave in 1861. The lady, who had endured snakes crawling through the logs into her cabin and ticks that were characterized as having "amazing sticking power," proved incapable of coping with threats and intimidation from Texas slave owners.[115]

The missionary abolitionists caused a degree of real fear among the slaveholders. Perceived as rebel rousers, the missionaries were closely watched by tribal slave owners that were extremely wary of them. In 1860, Jubal B. Hancock wrote other slave owners expressing his concerns that the missionaries might be dangerous. He was especially fearful that they would use their positions to incite riots or rebellion among the slave populations. Actually, little danger existed, but the rumors persisted within the mixed blood factions.[116]

The leading slave owner was Robert M. Jones, the first Choctaw millionaire and richest man in Indian Territory. Jones owned 227 slaves by census and by his own admission, "between 250 and 300 head," that operated six cotton plantations in the Nation plus a sugar plantation in Louisiana. Practically single-handedly forcing secession upon the tribe, Jones outfitted the first company of Choctaw with guns and horses and then served as a delegate to the Confederate Congress in Richmond. Elected in October 1861, fifteen months passed before he swore his oath of office and claimed his seat in January 1863. Although his third wife that he married in 1861 was an educated, cultured, former teacher at the Armstrong Academy, Jones spoke only a little, broken English. His major action as a delegate on the floor of the House of Representatives was a memorial on behalf of his commercial firm, Jones and Thebo, asking compensation for the supplies furnished to the Choctaw volunteers. The recommendation, referred to committee and promptly forgotten, was followed by the only other bill sponsored by Jones, an appropriation to print 200 copies of the Report of the Commissioner of Indian Affairs. Although it was later distributed among the tribes, Jones realized the futility of remaining in Virginia, resigned his position, and returned home in 1864.[117]

The close economic ties to the South were another reason to support the Confederacy. Besides trade and commerce downriver to New Orleans, the mixed bloods pursued many financial interests in the slave states of Texas and Arkansas. Jones owned a mansion in Paris along with several other pieces of Texas real estate, and he and other affluent mixed bloods worked diligently to persuade the full bloods their interests would be best served by the Confederacy.[118]

The rapid withdrawal of federal forces from Indian Territory leaving the tribes to the mercy of the South at the beginning of the war was another selling point for Confederate sympathizers. The mixed bloods quickly pointed out that the forces stationed at Forts Washita, Arbuckle, and Cobb immediately abandoned the tribes to their fate when hostilities erupted in the east. In April 1861, Colonel William H. Emory, Commander of Indian Territory, ordered evacuation of the forts one day before Colonel William C. Young, commander of the Texas Eleventh Cavalry Volunteers, arrived at Fort Washita on May 1. Young, a forty-nine-year-old slave owner and the richest man in Cooke County, failed to prevent the federal retreat when Black Beaver, a Delaware scout, successfully avoided the Confederates and conducted the Union Army out of Indian Territory to Fort Leavenworth, Kansas. Southern sympathizers quickly seized upon the retreat as evidence that the North had no intentions of protecting the tribes during the coming crisis.[119]

Choctaw agent Douglas Hancock Cooper also used his influence to persuade the tribe to support the Confederacy. A hard drinking, plantation owner and lawyer from Mississippi who had served with Jefferson Davis in the Mexican War, Cooper learned that a secret society, the Knights of the Golden Circle, was actively encouraging Choctaw secession shortly before the outbreak of hostilities but refused to take any action against it. Conversely, he publicly supported the movement.[120]

Combined with pressure from Texas hotheads, loyalty to the Union was unthinkable. Principal Chief George Hudson called a meeting to discuss the tribe's position, but so many Texans showed up the loyalist Choctaw were outnumbered and not allowed to speak. Men like Peter Pitchlynn advised the tribe to adopt a policy of neutrality, but any serious opposition to the idea of secession was impossible. Considering its position, the tribe displayed great courage by even holding debates on the matter.

On February 7, 1861, a resolution passed the Choctaw General Council giving notice that: "In the event of a permanent dissolution of the American union . . . the Choctaw must follow the natural affections, education, institutions, and interests which bind us to the destiny of our Southern neighbors." By the summer of 1861, the Secessionists within the tribe had won. The Confederacy offered full rights of citizenship in the new government, full representation in its Congress, or the option of remaining independent under the protection of the Confederacy, and Chief Hudson issued a proclamation declaring the Choctaw Nation free and independent of the United States on June 14.[121]

In the spring of 1861, Jefferson Davis was authorized to appoint an agent to negotiate an alliance with the western tribes for the South. David Hubbard, recently named Commissioner of Indian Affairs for the Confederacy, was instructed to pursue the negotiations but was too ill to make the trip to Indian Territory. On March 16, Albert B. Pike, a known and respected native of New

England who lived in Arkansas, replaced him. A veteran of the Mexican War, poet, Mason, and newspaper editor, the tall, robust Pike was an attorney that often represented the tribes in civil actions before the Arkansas courts. In 1859, projecting the image of a tribal elder to the point of wearing shoulder length hair and fringed, buckskin jackets, Pike talked with Peter Pitchlynn about sponsoring him for honorary membership into the Choctaw tribe.[122]

Pike's primary mission was to convince the tribes to break their old treaties and make new ones with the Confederacy. Whenever possible, he was authorized to raise Indian armies for use in Indian Territory. In essence, his instructions were to keep all the tribes friendly to the Southern side in the coming war and to recruit Indian battalions as the opportunity arose.

In May, Pike traveled to Fort Smith to confer on the procedures for recruiting an army with Confederate General Benjamin McCulloch, a former Texas Ranger and veteran of the war for Texas independence and the Mexican War. Advised to proceed accordingly, Pike was commissioned to spend up to $100,000 to insure treaties with the Indian tribes and set out from Arkansas traveling in the comfort of a horse-drawn buggy. He was at the head of a long line of wagons loaded with food, wine, and provisions and trade goods for the tribes.

He met first with Chief John Ross and the Cherokee, but the full blood members of the tribe, remembering the disasters of their removal, refused to break their treaties. They insisted on maintaining a position of neutrality in the coming "War Between the States." Pike and McCulloch, disappointed but more determined than ever, moved to North Fork Town to talk with the Creek, Choctaw, and Chickasaw. The Creek finally agreed to join up, but their treaty resulted in a split within the tribe. The full blood faction led by eighty-year-old Chief Opothle Yahola decided to remain loyal.

As expected, the Confederate diplomat had little trouble with the Choctaw and Chickasaw, and there was no talk of splitting the tribe. Requiring little more than a personal visit, Pike easily convinced the Choctaw to join the Confederacy. Representatives Robert M. Jones, Allen Wright, Forbis LeFlore, Alfred Wade, Coleman Cole, James Riley, William B. Pitchlynn, McGee King, John P. Turnbull, William Bryant, and Sampson Folsom signed with him without delay. Only twelve tribesmen were credited with loyalty to the Union, serving in Kansas regiments.

The new Confederate-Choctaw treaty carefully delineated the boundaries of the Choctaw Nation and guaranteed the area for the tribe "as long as grass shall grow and water run." It provided that the border began one hundred paces east of old Fort Smith, where the western boundary of Arkansas crossed the Arkansas River. From there it ran south along the Arkansas state border to the Red River, where it turned west and followed the river to the 100th Meridian then ran north along the meridian to the Canadian River and along it to its junction with the Arkansas River, which it followed back to Fort Smith. In essence, the Confederacy replaced the United States as the protector of the Choctaw Nation.

The treaty promised perpetual peace and friendship for the Choctaw and made the tribe wards of the Confederacy with representation in the Confederate Congress. The Choctaw and Chickasaw were entitled to one delegate each with the legislator selected alternately beginning with the Choctaw. The Confederacy further promised an opportunity for Confederate statehood in the future for the Choctaw and Chickasaw, subject to proving their ability to maintain orderly government. Pike promised that a future convention of delegates could be elected to petition for tribal statehood in the Confederacy.

The Choctaw adopted a national flag during this alliance with the Confederacy. The flag was light blue in color bearing a red circle in the center edged in white. Containing a design similar to the national seal, a calumet, a bow, and three arrows representing the three political Choctaw national districts were depicted within the red circle.

Meanwhile, Pike and his entourage met with the Seminole. One faction of the tribe balked at the treaty and, as in the case of the Creek, loyally joined Opothle Yahola, but the tribe on the whole broke its former treaties and joined the Confederacy. The Cherokee were also more receptive to his proposals as conditions had changed by the time the Confederate diplomat returned to Tahlequah. In 1861, a victory by General Sterling Price at Wilson's Creek in southwest Missouri gave the southern rebels a chance for victory, and the Cherokee, eager to be on the winning side, were convinced to sign with Pike as the other tribes had already done.

Pike's treaties provided that the Confederacy assumed all responsibilities and obligations of their former treaties with the United States. In addition, the tribes were authorized to raise armies and were promised they would be furnished with arms to protect themselves but not used outside Indian Territory. After convincing all the tribes to join the Confederacy, Pike was rewarded with an appointment as Commander of the Department of Indian Territory and Brigadier General of all troops recruited within Indian Territory.[123]

The Confederate military had already authorized Choctaw Agent Douglas H. Cooper to organize a regiment. Born in 1815 in Wilkinson County, Mississippi, Cooper attended the University of Virginia from 1832 to 1834, returned home a planter and lawyer, was elected to the Mississippi legislature, and served under Colonel Jefferson Davis in the Battles of Buena Vista and Monterrey. Appointed to the rank of colonel in the Confederate Army, Cooper raised five rebel regiments among the Indians in May 1861. By November, he had more than 4,000 ready to fight. Among them were two companies mobilized and drilled at the Goodland Mission, southwest of Hugo. One was the Second Choctaw Regiment under Captain Ben Smallwood known as the "Company of Threes," because its membership included three brothers from the LeFlore family, three of the Spring family, and three each from other families in the vicinity. The other company was composed of full bloods. While awaiting orders, Colonel Cooper prepared his forces.

Drilling, whooping mounted charges, dismounting, taking cover, firing by squads, and cleaning rifles were training tactics accepted by the Indians with few complaints, but there were concerns with weaponry. Most were armed only with rifled muskets or old, often useless flintlocks or pistols and revolvers. A few were reduced to fighting with bows and arrows and tomahawks. Makeshift clothing or uniforms of un-dyed homespun cloth comprised the customary dress for the rank and file soldiers. The material, after months of wear without the proper laundering and care, yellowed to a distinctive butternut color. The families of the Confederate warriors supported them with garments and equipment whenever possible but most looked more like civilians armed with a few pieces of military equipment than soldiers in the field. As time passed, clothing and hats were normally pilfered from the losing side in a fight.[124]

The commanders of the Choctaw troops, more concerned with their fighting ability, generally overlooked their demeanor as soldiers. Seemingly impervious to criticism of dress and appearance, neglectful of camp duties, careless with equipment and routines, including furloughs and leaves, the Choctaw troops redeemed themselves in battle. They performed well in combat and were often commended by the officers.[125]

The health of the regiments, always an issue within the Nation, was a major concern of both officers and men. In the Indian Appropriation Act of 1856, an item was devoted to the payment of doctors in the Indian service, but these few physicians were usually employed only for the benefit of the white agents and their families. Due to the severe shortage of medical doctors and supplies, the Confederates were greatly pleased when Dr. Thomas J. Bond, a practicing physician at Boggy Depot in 1859, joined the Choctaw regiment as a surgeon. Dr. Bond, the first Choctaw to receive a medical degree, had recently completed his studies in Kentucky and returned to marry the daughter of Reverend Israel Folsom.[126]

Reverend Joseph Samuel Murrow, a Baptist preacher from Georgia, was another welcome recruit. The teacher-evangelist had arrived as a missionary to the Creek and then transferred to the Seminole. Serving with the Indian troops Murrow always set up a brush arbor at each new camp and preached every day, even in retreat when fleeing a hostile force. Baptizing over 200 Indian recruits, he joined the Choctaws after the war, helped found the town of Atoka, and organized the Baptist church there with six members in 1869.[127]

On June 14, Chief Hudson decreed that all residents between eighteen and forty-five were eligible for service in the military and was greatly pleased that the Choctaw responded quickly and volunteered for induction into the new regiment. By August 1, 1861, Colonel Cooper had completed organization of the Choctaw and Chickasaw Regiment of Mounted Rifles at the agency at Skullyville. Daniel N. McIntosh, youngest son of William McIntosh, was elected colonel of the First Creek Regiment that was raised within the tribe along with a battalion under Lieutenant Colonel Chilly McIntosh and a company under Captain James M.C. Smith. The Seminole also raised a battalion under Major John Jumper, and the Cherokee raised the First Cherokee Mounted Rifles under Colonel John Drew. Another regiment of Cherokee was organized as the Second Mounted Rifles composed of pro-slavery mixed bloods commanded by Colonel Stand Watie.[128]

Afterwards, Loyalist Creek and Seminole determined their best action was to leave the country in order to "stay out of the war." Believing that "it was no affair of the Indians," they rallied behind the leadership of Opothle Yahola, the elderly chief of the Creek, and Halleck Tustenuggee, the Seminole chief, and gathered their families near North Fork Town in preparation for the trip north to Kansas. In the fall of 1861, the Neutralists numbered over 4,000 including women, children, and slaves. The warriors numbered approximately 1,700.

On October 1, 1861, Colonel Cooper dispatched a communiqué to Chief Opothle Yahola in a futile effort to keep the peace, but the Loyalists ignored the message and headed north. Colonel William B. Sims, a wealthy Texan from Clarksville, was, by luck, on the road to Fort Smith with the Ninth Cavalry near North Fork Town when a courier from Cooper requested Sims to send 500 men under Lieutenant Colonel William Quayle. The Confederate Indians welcomed the Texans into camp with a staged war dance and were amused by the white reaction to "a ring filled with painted Indians." Cooper at the head of six companies of Mounted Rifles and the Ninth Texas Cavalry, about 1,400 men, took the field in pursuit of the Neutralists on November 15.

The first engagement of the Civil War in Indian Territory was between "Red Brothers." Cooper's forces followed the Loyalists until they crossed Red Fork on the Cimarron River, where, near dusk on November 19, a detachment of Quayle's cavalry overtook them at Round Mountain. As night began to fall, the opposing armies advanced to within sixty yards of each other. Dismounting and opening fire, the Choctaw and Chickasaw reinforced the Texans, but few casualties were suffered during the fight. The Loyalists slipped away undercover of darkness, and at daylight the following day the Confederates moved against the main camp of the Loyalists only to find it deserted.

Cooper called the skirmish "a short but sharp conflict" and reported the Loyalists' loss at 110, an exaggerated figure, while giving his own losses as six men dead, four wounded, and one missing. While also admitting to the loss of "many" of his own horses, he reported the capture of "the chief's buggy, 12 wagons, flour, sugar, coffee, salt, besides many cattle and ponies." The Battle of Round Mountain was over, but it was only the first engagement between the Indian forces.[129]

Further pursuit was delayed by orders from General McCulloch, fearful of an invasion by General John C. Fremont, to watch the Arkansas border, but once it was certain that this was only a rumor, Cooper returned to the escaping Creek. By November 29, his command numbered about 780 men, including 430 of the Choctaw-Chickasaw Regiment under Major Mitchell LeFlore, fifty men of the Choctaw Battalion under Captain Alfred Wade, and 300 Confederate Creek commanded by Daniel N. McIntosh. Passing through Tulsey Town, Confederate scouts reported that Colonel John Drew's Cherokee had found an encampment on Bird Creek at a place called Chusto Talasah on December 7. Unfortunately, the weather turned cold as they awaited the arrival of Cooper, and all but twenty-eight of Drew's troops deserted to join Opothle Yahola or go home.

On the morning of December 9, Cooper arrived to divide his forces into three detachments. The First Choctaw-Chickasaw Regiment was ordered to link up with the rear guard on the right wing, while the Ninth Cavalry and Drew's Cherokee took a position in the center of the line, and the First Regiment, Creek Mounted Volunteers, was posted on the left wing. At 2:00 p.m. he ordered his forces forward. Marching within one hundred paces of the Loyalists, the battle quickly turned into a line of engagements up and down the creek lasting for four hours. One of the major clashes involved the Choctaw-Chickasaw Regiment under Captain R. A.Young against a much larger Loyalist force until reinforced by Captain Lemuel M. Reynolds, Jackson McCurtain, and Joseph R. Hall. With their troops, the Confederates forced the Loyalists across the creek. In the end, as Captain P. Pitchlynn stated, the men adopted the tactics of fighting like Indians in hand-to-hand duels until once more Opothle Yahola broke off the fight as light faded.

During the night a blizzard blew in three inches of snow, forcing the exhausted Cooper, out of supplies, to return to Fort Gibson. Claiming another victory, he reported 1,100 men had been engaged and that he had lost fifteen dead and thirty-seven wounded while the Loyalists were estimated at 2,500 and had lost more than 500. The Cherokees more accurately reported a body count of twenty-seven dead.[130]

Colonel James McQueen McIntosh of the 2nd Arkansas Mounted Rifles arrived from Van Buren, replaced Cooper, and set out in pursuit of Opothle Yahola's forces with 1,380 troops. McIntosh, a graduate of West Point, class of 1849, had served in the First Cavalry at Fort Arbuckle and Fort Cobb from 1858 to 1860, and Fort Smith in 1861, before resigning to join the Confederacy. In August, the glory-seeking McIntosh had been at the fight at Wilson's Creek and was determined to have a victory that would make him famous. On Christmas Day, his scouts picked up the Creek trail. Locating their camp on Hominy Creek, McIntosh ordered a charge against Opothle Yahola's 1,700 men shortly before noon on December 26. The attack turned into a rout when a fierce sleet storm struck in the middle of the fight.

The engagement of Chustenahlah ("a shoal in the stream") was a complete victory for McIntosh. Reporting that he had only eight killed and thirty-two wounded, the Texas cavalry officer boasted: "My regiment killed 211."[131]

Cooper and his Indian brigades did not arrive until the next day. By then the weather had worsened to sleet and ice. Even the victorious Confederates were suffering. Spending a miserable week chasing stragglers into Kansas, Cooper returned to Fort Gibson on January 7, 1862. Angry with McIntosh for not waiting on his arrival before the attack, Cooper was infuriated at being given the job of cleaning up the remnants of the Creek forces. He claimed that a final and decisive battle could have been won and Opothle Yahola captured had McIntosh not been so eager to have a victory.[132]

The Creek chief and his followers were allowed to escape into Kansas, but army surgeons reported amputating hundreds of limbs. The Loyalists spent the winter in camps in Kansas as refugees, totally destitute, living on gifts supplied by civilians and many began to die. Within two months more than 240 were dead as was Chief Opothle Yahola in 1863. In summary, the first year of the war in Indian Territory had been a disaster for both sides. The Reverend Willis F. Folsom stated sadly at the end of the year that "Many have been slain this year; few have been saved."[133]

General Albert Pike arrived back in Indian Territory the following year to assume command. Hardly having time to establish his headquarters, Pike received orders from General Earl Van Dorn, the commander of the Trans-Mississippi District, to march his forces to northwestern Arkansas in support of Confederate troops defending Elkhorn Tavern against a federal invasion from Missouri under the command of General Samuel R. Curtis. Although his earlier treaties had assured the Choctaw and the other tribes that they would not be used outside Indian Territory, Pike dutifully led his forces eastward to the Battle of Pea Ridge in March 1862.[134]

Cooper had prepared to move in February, but the Indians refused to march until they were paid. It took another three days for Pike to get them ready to leave. A detachment of federal forces awaited them at Pea Ridge, south of Fayetteville, where never was fought a more strange battle with the Indians giving war whoops, Rebels were yelling, and Yankees singing "John Brown's Body." Pike, leading 1,000 men, encountered heavy fighting.

The battle was lost when General McCulloch was killed by a sharpshooter completely demoralizing the Confederates. Originally from Tennessee, the General had fought with Jackson in the Creek wars, joined the migration to Texas with Davy Crockett, fought with Sam Houston at San Jacinto, raised a company of Texas Rangers, and served as a major in the Mexican War with Zachary Taylor. A legend to his troops, the General was killed by Peter Pelican of the Thirty-sixth Illinois, although rumor said it was James Butler (Wild Bill) Hickok.

The General's death, along with Colonel McIntosh's, and the loss of a Confederate battery caused Pike to assume command and order the withdrawal of forces from Arkansas. Finding Cooper and the Choctaw Battalion, Pike learned they had missed the main battle. By the time of their arrival, the Confederates were already in retreat. Joining Colonel John Drew's Cherokee to cover the supply wagons, Pike was dismayed to learn that the Indians had resorted to scalping the dead as they reverted to their old habits in the middle of the heat of battle. Embarrassed by the charges, Pike immediately issued orders to prohibit such action in the future as "inhuman and barbarous."[135]

The battle proved the "Gettysburg" of the war in the West. Fought on March 7 and 8, 1862, the Confederacy in Indian Territory never recovered from the fight. Pike found that he no longer liked the horrors of war and withdrew to the Blue River east of Fort Washita on the Texas Road. Retreating to the west side of Nail's Crossing, Pike busied himself with the motions of war and refused to participate further.[136]

Setting his troops to work building a new post that he named Fort McCulloch, Pike gave a number of reasons for his decision to move so far south. He claimed that a large fortress erected at the Blue River would give his forces control of the major roads from Forts Smith, Gibson, and Washita. Should the Yankees attempt to follow their victory with an invasion of Texas, he argued, his position allowed control of the southern half of Indian Territory even though the federal army held the northern half. He claimed that by holding his location, Fort Washita could be used as a depot for an eventual recovery of the north.

Pike, a brilliant strategist but lackluster combatant, kept his men busy through the summer erecting defensive breastworks and fortifications along the river. He appealed to the local slave owners to supply labor, but when they refused to donate, he put his men to work digging in the hot, summer sun while he spent his own time reading history books, writing letters, and smoking his meerschaum pipe as his Indian troops silently watched in awe. Most of his letters dealt with trivial matters or requests that Fort McCulloch be designated as a supply depot, but his major concern was payment to the 3,035 troops in his command. Since no money was getting through federal lines, Pike and his quartermaster, Captain William Quesenbury, concocted a daring scheme to make their own money. After confiscating a printing press, Pike began issuing money printed on the backside of a roll of wallpaper, an ingenious plan that worked until he ran out of paper.

General Pike's inactivity quickly led to problems. By June 1862, General Thomas C. Hindman, commander of forces in Arkansas, ordered him home, a directive Pike refused to obey. Explaining that by moving his troops he ran the risk of being surrounded and cut off from possible retreat to Texas, Pike satisfied himself by simply refusing to do anything. The weeks passed, and Pike vented his frustrations on others, growing increasingly critical of his immediate superiors. When he printed up circulars attacking President Jeff Davis personally, an action that went too far, he was arrested by newly promoted General Cooper at Tishomingo and sent under guard to Arkansas to await a military trial. General Theophilus H. Holmes replaced him, but Pike slipped back to Fort Washita before his trial by way of Sherman, Texas. Arrested a second time, he was escorted out of Indian Territory and told not to come back. Pike, declaring that he had never wanted the "damned command" in the first place, retired to obscurity. In 1879, the destitute former Confederate officer, broken by the war, accepted a retirement salary of $1,800 per year from the Masons. He died in 1891.[137]

On March 13, 1862, the war was renewed when the Kansas refugees asked to be allowed to go home. Deciding to send two regiments with them for protection, a force of almost 6,000, called the Indian Expedition, pushed south toward the Arkansas River. The expedition, commanded by Colonel William Weer of the Tenth Kansas Infantry, was composed of one regiment of eight companies of Creek, Seminole, Cherokee, Delaware, Quapaw, Kickapoo, and Osage, and another of Kansas Volunteers.

In June, the Union invasion moved by way of Baxter Springs toward Tahlequah. Colonel Stand Watie's troops delayed the enemy advance by guerrilla attacks and a full battle at Locust Grove, but federal artillery finally forced Watie's retreat. Weer moved on to capture Fort Gibson and to arrest Cherokee Chief John Ross at Tahlequah. The old chief was allowed to move to Philadelphia to sit out the war in protective custody.

The Union Army appeared capable of driving the Confederates from Indian Territory when an unexpected turn of events saved the Rebels. On July

18, Weer's second in command, Colonel Frederick Saloman, placed Weer under arrest and ordered a retreat to Kansas. Salomon, accusing his superior officer of being a habitual drunk, took command, explaining that Weer had either planned treason or gone insane. Claiming that since the army was deep within enemy territory and completely out of supplies, the Union officer argued that he was saving his troops. Although Salomon had committed a clear case of mutiny, it meant little as Weer was later restored to command. The real results of the action were to save the Indian Territory for the Confederacy. The Indian expedition was a complete failure.

By the end of 1862, the defeat at Pea Ridge and the subsequent invasion by Union forces left the Confederates in a demoralized and confused state. Matters were further complicated by the arrest and removal of Chief of the Cherokees and his replacement by Stand Watie. Watie announced his own election when a Loyalist faction within the tribe attempted to repudiate the treaty with the Confederacy and elect a new chief. As the old factionalism resumed within the tribe, the Civil War worsened for the Indians.

In September 1862, the Rebels made an effort to mount a counter offensive by pushing into southwest Missouri. Cooper led his Indian forces and four regiments of Texas cavalry, totaling 8,000 troops and batteries of artillery, through Scott's Mill, Missouri, past Pineville to occupy Neosho, Granby, and Newtonia. The Federals quickly dispatched forces to meet them at Newtonia on September 30. The Union forces, attacking with infantry and artillery, outnumbered the Confederates until Choctaw forces under Lieutenant Colonel Simpson N. Folsom arrived as reinforcements. Surprising the federal army by riding through a cornfield, the Rebels fought fiercely, gaining the advantage. By nightfall Cooper had pushed the Yankees out of Newtonia in a retreat toward Sarcoxie, twelve miles south.

The engagement, fought all day, was a credit to the Choctaw brigades. Colonel Tandy Walker and his forces aided by Folsom and his men achieved a sizable victory, counting only twelve dead and sixty-three wounded, but the Federals soon regrouped. On October 4, three columns were sent against Cooper and the outnumbered Confederates had to fall back. A heavy rain allowed them to slip away in a retreat to Indian Territory. The encounter ended any hope of a Confederate invasion of Kansas and put the Southerners on the defensive for the remainder of the war.

Since it was the Yankees' turn again, plans were laid for a second invasion of Indian Territory. General James G. Blunt, a short, chubby medical doctor before the war, ordered the offensive in October and encountered Cooper at old Fort Wayne on October 22. Cooper had arrived on October 17, planning to move north to attack Fort Scott, Kansas. The two armies met with customary results and conflicting reports of victory. Blunt claimed that he lost four dead and fifteen wounded and reported 150 enemy soldiers killed and wounded. Cooper, conversely, reported being attacked by a superior force of 5,000 against his own 1,500 and losing only six dead while estimating seventy-five Federals killed.

In reality, Cooper acknowledged defeat and gave Indian Territory north of the Arkansas River to the Union Army. In December, he returned to Skullyville where he continued skirmishing forays against the Yankee forces, but fortunately, for the Confederates, the Federals did not try to consolidate their control. At the end of the year, Colonel William A. Phillips, a Scottish immigrant correspondent for the *New York Tribune* living in Kansas, attacked and burned Fort Davis, north of present Muskogee, as a show of force, and then returned to Fort Gibson. It was the only attack launched between October 1862 and April 1863.

In January 1863, General William Steele, commander of a regiment in the New Mexico Campaign of 1862, assumed control of all Confederate forces in Indian Territory in an effort to restore confidence in the southern army, but in the spring General Blunt arrived with supplies for Fort Gibson and ordered his forces across the Arkansas River and down the Texas Road again. In April, Colonel Phillips led a detachment south to Webbers Falls to attack Watie. Killing fourteen Rebels in another victory, Phillips lost only one man in the fight and returned to Fort Gibson that he renamed Fort Blunt in honor of the general.

In July, another excursion was ordered across the Arkansas River. The result was the Battle of Honey Springs in the Creek Nation twenty-five miles south of Fort Gibson on July 17, 1863. Blunt, in command of a force of about 3,000 men, confronted General Cooper with his four Indian regiments and one Texas cavalry troop, an army of approximate equal size. At midnight, July 15, Blunt left the fort arriving at the Confederate camp at 8:00 in the morning. Giving his men two hours of rest, he ordered an attack that caught the Confederates by surprise.

The largest engagement in Indian Territory, the fight involved more than 9,000 troops, including the First Kansas Colored Volunteer Infantry Regiment. The unit had earlier proven its battle fitness at Cabin Creek and the Honey Springs fight was an even greater victory. Well aware of the feeling of Southerners toward black troops, they knew no black prisoners were ever taken by the Confederates. The Unionists inflicted heavy casualties with their howitzers and allowed the black troopers to pour devastating rifle fire into the Rebels. Forced to withdraw, the Confederates deceived Blunt into thinking they were moving toward Fort Smith, and he broke off the fight to return to Fort Gibson.

As usual the two opposing officers gave different reports of their losses. The federal losses were seventeen dead and sixty wounded while the Confederate dead numbered one hundred fifty and seventy-seven prisoners. Cooper later reported losing 134 dead and forty-seven prisoners while killing over 200 Federalists. Blunt reported that he captured "1 piece of artillery, 1 stand of colors, 200 stands of arms, and 15 wagons" while Cooper, choosing to ignore most of the equipment, only admitted the loss of "an ambulance purposely thrown in the way of the enemy."[138]

The Honey Springs engagement signaled the end for the Confederates in Indian Territory. After the defeat, the Rebels fell back toward the Canadian River valley, concentrating their forces at Perryville on the Texas Road until August when another Union advance of 4,500 men forced them to retreat again. After forty-eight hours of marching, Blunt found the Confederates with their army split into three units, the largest force under Cooper and Watie. A sharp conflict between artillery and dismounted cavalry followed that forced the Confederates to retreat. As they were leaving, their rear guard was overtaken in a skirmish called the "Battle of Perryville" on August 25. After the fight the Union forces burned the village and all the supplies stored there. The Confederates retaliated by pouring a large quantity of salt into the village well before their "hasty" departure.[139]

The Confederates expected the Yankees to follow their victory with an attack on Boggy Depot, but the Unionists surprised them by turning on forces under Confederate General William L. Cabell at Fort Smith. Blunt sent Colonel William J. Cloud and the Second Kansas Cavalry against him in a successful attack six miles from Fort Smith on September 1. Blunt occupied Fort Smith later in the day as Steele was forced to fall back deep into the Choctaw Nation to Middle Boggy Creek.

In October, the Confederates reached a low point when Cooper and part of the army were ordered to Texas, leaving 999 white troops and 1,643 Indians. Conditions in Indian Territory were reported to be "a perfect wreck" by Major W. C. Schaumburg, a Confederate inspector, on a tour in 1863. Stating that the troops were poorly uniformed and unprotected against the coming winter and discipline was completely lacking, the major complained that at one post three captains admitted to being incompetent to drill the men. As for the troops under Cooper, the inspector informed his superiors that they were "poorly armed, and most officers failed to even keep reports."

By this time Cooper, already instrumental in the removal of Pike, had determined to replace General William F. Steele. Wanting the position for himself, Cooper began a campaign of complaints against Steele. Flooding Richmond with requests to give the position of superior rank to him, he was supported by the Choctaw Council with a resolution requesting a change in leadership. Steele, at the same time, counterattacked with accusations that Cooper avoided the "chain of command," falsified reports, and handled his troops in an unmilitary manner.

In December, Steele lost the battle. He was relieved of command, but Cooper lost, too. General Samuel B. Maxey was given command of the Department of Indian Territory. The appointment did little to improve conditions.[140]

In February 1864, Colonel William A. Phillips marched practically unmolested to Boggy Depot distributing copies of Lincoln's "Pardon and Amnesty Proclamation." Designed to bring the Southerners back as easily as possible, Lincoln required only a solemn oath of allegiance to the constitution to return to the Union. It was translated and distributed by Union forces, but the Southerners were not yet ready to give up.

Another setback for the Confederacy was the "Battle of the Middle Boggy" in the same month. Lieutenant Colonel John Jumper's Seminole Battalion, Captain Adam Nail's Company A of the First Choctaw-Chickasaw Cavalry and some detachments of the Twelfth Texas Regiment were attacked by Union forces, including three companies of the Fourteenth Kansas Cavalry under Major Charles Willette and a section of howitzers under Captain Solomon Kaufman. The poorly armed Confederates were badly mauled in the attack that lasted approximately thirty minutes. Word that a detachment from Boggy Depot was en route to reinforce the Confederates caused the federal forces to withdraw after butchering their prisoners by cutting their throats. The Southerners lost forty-nine dead.[141]

If matters were not bad enough, William Clarke Quantrill led his band of miscreants through the Nation in the spring of 1864. The former Missouri school teacher turned outlaw, gambler, and killer had formed an army after falling in with General Sterling Price at Wilson's Creek in 1861. Attracting a following of deserters, robbers, and murderers like Frank and Jesse James, Cole and Jim Younger, and "Bloody" Bill Anderson, Quantrill raided both sides, North and South, but his most famous escapade was the sacking of Lawrence, Kansas, in 1863.

Crossing into Indian Territory on the way south after the raid, the band captured and executed a Union patrol of twelve troopers near Perryville. After a short visit with Cooper, the guerrillas crossed Colbert's Ferry to safety in Texas, spending the winter of 1863-64 on the outskirts of Sherman. Quantrill's raiders began foraging in the area in February, killing a citizen of Grayson County, George N. Butt. When told of the attack, General Henry E. McCulloch ordered Quantrill placed under arrest to appear before him in Bonham. Although taken into custody, Quantrill managed an escape within hours, gathered his men, and fled north. The General ordered him captured dead or alive, but the bandit-officer and his army made it back across Colbert's Ferry. General McCulloch called off his pursuit at Red River and Quantrill moved to Boggy Depot, refitted his men, and returned to Missouri letting tempers cool in Texas. A year later he was killed in Kentucky.[142]

In the summer, General Maxey, hoping to improve matters, assigned Cooper the task of threatening Fort Smith. On July 26, 1864, after scouts discovered Union cavalry units near the town, Cooper sent Colonel Richard Gano with a Texas brigade and Colonels Simpson Folsom and Tandy Walker with a combined force of 1,500 to attack them. At dawn on July 27, the Sixth Kansas Cavalry, five miles south of Fort Smith, was surprised and surrounded. After stampeding their horses, Gano captured 127 federal prisoners and forced them to run ahead of his force to prevent their rescue. Losing only nine men, Colonel Gano captured 200 Sharps rifles, 400 six-shooters, horses, and camp equipment that his men needed desperately.

Encouraged by the victory at Massard Prairie, Cooper moved to Fort Smith on July 30. Approaching from the south, he expected an easy victory as the Union pickets were chased back inside their fortifications, but his initial momentum soon shifted. The Union forces, supported by artillery, rallied to push Cooper back just as daylight began to fade. Fearful of his position after dark, Cooper ordered a retreat back to Indian Territory.[143]

A month earlier, the Confederates had won a minor victory when the Kansas Colored Volunteer Infantry met General Stand Watie at Iron Bridge, Choctaw Nation. The engagement came from a Union decision to send a supply boat to Fort Gibson after heavy summer rains raised the Arkansas River enough for shallow draft boats to make the run. On June 15, 1864, the *J. R. Williams*, sent out with supplies guarded by Lieutenant Horace A.B. Cook and twenty-six men, was attacked by Confederate artillery overlooking the river five miles above the mouth of the Canadian at Pleasant Bluff. Cook and his troops, thinking they were helpless, off landed on a sandbar on the opposite shore and went for help. An army of 800 troops under the command of Colonel John Ritchie was located only ten miles away at Mackey's salt works, but by the time they returned Watie had already towed the boat across the river. The Union army could only watch and fire harmlessly as the Confederates unloaded the sternwheeler. The Rebels seized a priceless cargo of 150 barrels of flour, 16,000 pounds of bacon, and quantities of store goods, washtubs, kettles, coffee pots, plates, cups, and dippers. The fight was of little military significance, but its psychological impact was priceless. Some of Watie's men loaded what they could carry and left for home as their families had been starving for months.

Lieutenant Cook was blamed for the loss of the boat and its supplies, and his angry commander dispatched Colonel Samuel B. Crawford and his Kansas black troops to recover them. Told that the Yankees were on the way, Watie immediately decided to withdraw. On the evening of June 16, after burning the steamboat and the supplies that could not be packed away on horseback, Watie moved to Iron Bridge where another skirmish broke out, but he managed to escape with most of the supplies.[144]

Unfortunately, the victory was "too little and too late." The Union Armies continued to advance and forced more than 14,000 Confederate Indians to flee their homes in the north for refuge in the Choctaw Nation. They "were only too glad to escape with their lives," according to Watie, whose own wife and family had fled to Rusk County, Texas, to live with relatives.

The Choctaw suffered complete destitution from the war. Since nearly all the men were away in the army, little was done to cultivate crops or care for livestock. The refugees only worsened conditions. The poor, scattered throughout the Nation, were primarily concentrated at Boggy Depot, along the Jacks Fork and the Kiamichi and in Sugar Loaf and Wade Counties. More than 4,000 were in serious circumstances when General Maxey began a rationing system for the refugees. The principal point of distribution was Fort Towson under agents Basil LeFlore, John P. Kingsbury, and Mitchell McCurtain, but their efforts were greatly inadequate. A ration amounted to one and one-eighth pounds of flour and one and one-half pounds of beef, all the Choctaw had to spare. Refugee camps were located at Bonham and Sherman when newly elected Chief Peter Pitchlynn sent out appeals for support from Chahta Tvmaha, Choctaw Town, where the tribe had moved its council sessions from 1863 to 1883. The Texans responded but with too little to make a difference.

Desperately trying to feed the tribe, the Choctaw planted corn and vegetables, and usually had a little sugar and flour, but coffee and tea were considered luxuries. They experimented with coffee substitutes, parched wheat, roasted sweet potato peelings, and even dried okra, sometimes known as "Lincoln coffee," but nothing could replace the real product. As observer Joseph S. Murrow reported, "Portions of Indian Territory are all ruined and laid waste. All improvements are burned, stock all driven off or killed, and the entire western settlements are deserted."[145]

By then, the main commissary depot for the Confederates in Indian Territory was located at Boggy Depot. A cavalry post and hospital occupied by the Choctaw-Chickasaw Rifles under Captain J. William Wells, Adjutant General for Cooper, Boggy Depot served as the scene for a short-lived newspaper publication in 1863-64. William E. Rosser and Thomas White, two young soldiers attached to Company K, momentarily turned journalists to produce a handwritten newspaper that carried stories of interest to the men concerning their families and girl friends and any other news that culd be gathered, but their careers as reporters only lasted for a brief time as a diversion from the boredom of camp duty.[146]

In 1864, the various Indian units were consolidated with a battery of Texas volunteer artillery to form the Indian Division under Cooper. The unit consisted of Watie's First Indian Brigade, the Second Brigade of Colonel Tandy Walker, Colonel David N. McIntosh's Creek and Seminole Brigade, a "Reserve Squadon" under Captain George Washington, Chief of the Caddo, and the Texans under Lieutenant H. A. Routh.[147]

No amount of reorganization could stop the disintegration of the Southern cause. Defeats on the Middle Boggy River and Boggy Depot left Maxey with great problems with the Choctaw, especially as the Confederate paper money declined in purchasing power combined with the setbacks in military engagements. In July 1864, the General wrote to the Confederate Treasury agent in Houston, Peter W. Gray, pleading for help, but nothing could be done to correct the problem. By the beginning of 1865, Chief Pitchlynn was attacking the Confederate system as the Choctaw found themselves in dire economic straits. Their Confederate money was worthless, their crops, those that could be produced, could not be sold, and their military was losing the war.[148]

The problems caused the feud between Maxey and Cooper to erupt into open hostility. In February 1865, Cooper made a personal trip to Richmond to speak with his mentor, President Davis. On February 21, the Confederate commander-in-chief responded by naming Cooper Superintendent of Indian Affairs in Indian Territory and commander of all Confederate forces in the territory, but it was too late. In April, the war ended when Lee surrendered at Appomattox.

On April 24, 1865, Union forces under General Cyrus Bussey, unaware of the surrender, attacked a party of twenty Confederates moving north from Boggy Depot in an engagement that became known as the "Old Boggy Depot Skirmish." Three Rebels were killed and their mail dispatches captured, including a letter stating that Watie was expected to arrive soon to collect horses from forage trips into Texas. The mail showed that the Confederates had not received news that the war was over either.

The word reached Indian Territory in May, but Cooper refused to believe it until the following month when orders finally reached him to surrender his command. In June, Watie was the last general to turn in his arms. After confirmation of the war's end, Chief Pitchlynn requested the Indian armies not be surrendered as prisoners of war so that the tribes could make separate surrender terms.

On June 19, 1865, Chief Pitchlynn formally surrendered the Choctaw army at Doaksville. The war was over, and the tribes had lost. The Choctaw, along with the other Five Civilized Tribes, were ordered to send delegates to a conference in Fort Smith to sign new treaties with the United States, but even the Loyalists did not expect the harshness of the terms. The treaties were not completed for more than a year and tribal history changed again.[149]

CHAPTA UNTUHENA

~ CHAPTER EIGHT ~

"A CLAP OF THUNDER IN A CLEAR SKY"

Chapter Eight

No part of the South suffered more than Indian Territory during the War of the Rebellion. Indian soldiers died on both sides of the battles, massacres occurred among the civilian populations, property lay burned and destroyed, livestock was stolen or slaughtered, farms were neglected and abandoned, and armed bushwhackers roamed the countryside, problems that required immediate attention. Making matters worse, the war left more than one-third of the Choctaw people entirely destitute along with thousands of refugees from other tribes camped along the Red River. Added to the misery, the Choctaw learned that their official status no longer existed with the United States and new treaties must be negotiated with the federal government. The Choctaw quickly realized that reconstruction of their Nation would require years of adjustment and hard work.[150]

On September 1, 1865, Chief Peter Pitchlynn called for a council at Armstrong Academy, but the arrival of orders from the Department of Interior for the Five Civilized Tribes to meet with U.S. representatives at Fort Smith caused much confusion among the tribal leaders. The chief objected, but without much enthusiasm, since the federal government, victorious in war, was able to dictate terms and refused to tolerate excuses. The authorities demanded that the tribes send delegates without further delays, and the Choctaw, with no real choice, dispatched a twenty-one-member commission, headed by Chief Pitchlynn, accompanied by an escort of fifty-three men, to the talks in Arkansas.

Along with thousands of speculators, schemers, promoters, and con men, contingents from both Loyalist and Confederate sides filled the streets and saloons of Fort Smith anxiously anticipating great changes in the Indian Territory. They were not disappointed. At exactly 10:30 a.m. on Friday, September 8, 1865, Commissioner of Indian Affairs Dennis N. Cooley of Iowa stunned the first session of the Fort Smith Council with the opening pronouncement that the tribes no longer had treaties with the United States and must accept new ones dictated by the government. Ominously, the tribes were informed that Congress had decided upon a number of contemporaneous policies for them because they had broken their former treaties and made new ones with the Confederacy.

Federal negotiators insisted upon agreements to establish a centralized territorial government for Indian Territory, to relinquish surplus lands for the resettlement of Indians from other areas around the country, to grant freedmen the same legal rights and privileges of tribal members, and to permit the building of railroads through their nations. Even former supporters of the Union were astonished by the terms. On September 15, the late-arriving Choctaw delegates answered the demands with a resounding rejection of all points, especially on proposals concerning land concessions, but the federal authorities were in no mood for negotiations. Finally, realizing the futility of their arguments and recognizing the federal determination to accept nothing less than total capitulation, the Choctaw decided to take their appeals directly to Washington.[151]

A month later Chief Pitchlynn, National Treasurer, Allen Wright, Alfred Wade, John Page, James Riley, Robert M. Jones, Douglas H. Cooper, and his brother-in-law, John H. B. Latrobe, a Baltimore attorney, were appointed to present the Choctaw case to Washington. Insistent that the United States already had treaties with the tribe, the committee tried vainly to convince federal authorities of the legitimacy of their former treaties but the government refused to listen. The Choctaw were forced to comply with the federal demands and accept a joint treaty with the Chickasaw on April 28, 1866.

The agreements provided that the Choctaw cede the Leased District, the western third of their Nation, and adopt their former slaves as tribal members. It was provided that if the tribe agreed to these provisions, the federal government would pay $300,000 for tribal claims to the Leased District. If not, the money would be used to resettle the Choctaw freedmen. Another provision of the Treaty of 1866 granted a right-of-way for a north-south railroad and an east-west line through the Choctaw Nation.

Additionally, the treaty created a future territory for Indians to be called "Oklahoma," a combination of the words, Okla, meaning people, and Humma, meaning red, or Red People, a title of honor suggested by Allen Wright. All the Indian nations were to become part of this organization under a plan providing that "the U. S. Superintendent of Indian Affairs shall be the Executive of said Territory, with the title of Governor of the Territory of Oklahoma." Reverend Isaac McCoy, an early day Baptist missionary in the 1830s, had suggested the name "Aborginia" for an Indian area that would extend from the Platte River in Nebraska to the Red River and from Arkansas to Mexico, but this was defeated in favor of the Wright name.

Elected chief while in Washington, Reverend Wright presented the Treaty of 1866 to the Council on December 21. Surprisingly favorable to the tribe, the treaty turned out to be the most lenient to the tribe that had been the most loyal to the Confederate side. The explanation was the excellent representation the Choctaw received in Washington, although a future squabble was started when the attorneys' fees were paid in the amount of $100,000. Half of this amount was paid to the delegates, and Wright distributed $10,000 to each of the representatives, creating a tribal scandal.[152]

Once negotiations were completed, the Choctaw began the slow process of recovery. The first question was what to do with the former Choctaw slaves. At first the tribe refused to adopt them and asked that they be removed, but the federal government ignored this solution. Finally, on October 14, 1865, the liberated slaves were assimilated into the tribe by a law providing that those who wished to remain with their former masters must negotiate a labor contract mutually agreeable to both sides. A formal contract was negotiated and certified by a local judge whereby the employer assumed the responsibility of the care of the laborer. The employer was legally required to clothe the freedmen and their families, pay all their doctor bills, furnish them housing and fuel, and provide compensation for their labor with wages. There were eight levels of wages according to the kind of labor done by the freedmen that ranged from two to ten dollars per month.

The transition from slavery to freedom was a difficult procedure for many and old customs died slowly. Since previous monogamous behavior was practically nonexistent and many had never even been considered part of a family, there was much uncertainty among the freedmen. Finally, General John B. Sanborn was appointed Special Commissioner to guard the interests of freedmen. He decided that his first duty was to assure the former slaves that they were under his protection, because along with concerns about security, many thought they were to be removed to an area set aside exclusively for them while others were content to remain dependent upon their masters. In January 1866, Sanborn reported that cruel mistreatment was being imposed on many of the freedmen, but after a personal tour of the Nation on January 27, he modified his opinion. Expressing his belief that prejudices were rapidly passing away and treatment was much better than he had been led to believe, Sanborn generally approved the arrangements being made between the Choctaw and their former slaves.

Most of the Choctaw slave owners had adopted the approach taken by Robert M. Jones who opted to keep his slaves as laborers. In June 1864, the former staunch slaveholder returned to the Choctaw Nation to find his plantations in shambles. The army had confiscated all his horses and mules and depleted the goods and groceries in his stores, and he was forced to start over again. Jones financed an expedition into Texas for wild horses to be broken for farm use, diverted his former slaves to growing vegetables and potatoes to feed his family and workers, and, having managed to save his steamboats by hiding them, transported his goods and cotton that had been salvaged up the Mississippi to St. Louis without attracting any notice from outlaw elements and sold his stores for premium prices. His former slaves chose to stay with him when the war was over simply because they were better cared for by him. Jones kept them employed and recovered his fortune valued at $2 million when he died in 1882. His estate was given to his heirs, including his third wife, two stepdaughters, and a nephew, and the decision to adopt the freedman into tribal membership was not taken until after his death.

Chapter Eight

On April 28, 1866, the Choctaw and Chickasaw treaty allowed the federal government to hold from the Leased District $300,000, invested at five percent until the tribes passed laws granting citizenship to their former slaves. If these laws were passed within two years, according to federal authorities, three-fourths of the money would be paid to the Choctaw and one-fourth to the Chickasaw. If not, the money would be used to resettle the freedmen. The problem was that the tribes wanted them moved, while the slaves wanted to stay. Complicating the matter was the fact that the freedmen were neither Indian nor American citizens. Politically and socially, the former slaves were actually worse off in the Nation because they had no legal rights nor were allowed to go to the Indian schools. The Secretary of Interior reported that the tribes had given them voting rights but the blacks did not use them for fear of offending their former masters.

The Choctaw, hesitant for years about adopting their former slaves, finally began a change of policy when a school was opened for the freedmen at Boggy Depot in 1874. Others followed as the freedmen donated the schoolhouses, and the church mission boards furnished the teachers and books resulting in Tushkalusa Academy being built and maintained as a high school for blacks. Later, Oak Hill Mission was opened for a large black settlement near the Red River. In October 1875, a controversy developed when Chief Coleman Cole recommended citizenship and forty acres for each of their former slaves, but delays over the question continued for years until a law was passed on May 21, 1883. Adopted into the tribe with full citizenship and all the rights and privileges of Choctaw, the only exception was that the freedmen were given forty acres of land but not allowed to share in Tribal Trust Funds or the public domain of the Nation.

The end of the slave labor system necessitated the establishment of new economic patterns in the Nation. In 1866, the basis for a more complex financial system for the tribe was laid when Charles LeFlore was given permission to establish a toll bridge for ten years over the Clear Boggy at the intersection of the Fort Smith and Boggy Depot Roads. Fees from all except Choctaw citizens were set at twenty-five cents for four-wheeled vehicles drawn by horses, twelve and one-half cents for a man and a horse, and one cent for each additional animal. LeFlore's bridge proved a lucrative business as Boggy Depot grew into an important town after the war. Giles Thompson, a mixed blood, operated a salt works on Salt Creek three miles south of Boggy Depot. Thompson was so financially successful that bandits, rumored to be Jesse James and his gang, robbed him. Another business at the town was Captain G. B. Hester's bois d'arc apple seed mill. The enterprising Hester washed and cleaned the seeds for sale back east where timber was scarce to build Osage orange hedges. A flourmill, the only one within seventy-five miles, and a cotton gin also existed in Boggy Depot.

Chapter Eight

In December 1866, the Choctaw Council made more grants for businesses. James D. Davis was given permission to build a toll bridge over the Middle Boggy Creek, Jonathan Nail was allowed one over the Blue River, and George W. Riddle built one across the Fouchmaline on the Fort Smith Road. In the same month Greenwood Thompson was permitted to build a tollgate at the Narrows, known as Limestone Gap, on the road to North Fork Town. Similar grants were made to Wade H. Hampton, Jack McCurtain, Allen W. Carney, John Wilkin, and David A. Folsom.

Captain Peter Maytubby of the First Chickasaw and Choctaw Mounted Rifles started one of the most successful businesses after the war, a hotel and health resort at Maytubby Springs, located midway between Boggy Depot and Fort Washita west of the later town of Caddo. The hotel consisted of thirty rooms built in a T-shape with a huge parlor, a large dining room with six to seven tables, rocking chairs and straight-backed chairs with seats covered with rawhide, and a large organ for entertainment. Its featured attractions were oil springs with black mud and waters containing alum, salt, Sulphur, and magnesium located about one-half mile from the hotel. Famous for their "healing properties," the waters were called "God's Medicine" by the Choctaw. Captain Maytubby built a bathhouse with three rooms for bathtubs with piped in mineral waters.

Recognizing the economic value of the springs, Maytubby charged for rooms, meals, and, if the customers were too poor to afford his rates, he permitted camping on the grounds for fifty cents per week. The enterprising former Confederate, a deeply religious man, read the Bible every day, conducted evening prayer services, and offered thanks before every meal. Along with his close friend, Allen Wright, he often held services in the open under a brush arbor. Wright conducted the meetings in Choctaw and Maytubby translated into English. Built in 1866, Maytubby's business exploded after the appearance of the railroad in Caddo. Sophisticates from the town arrived by wagon, surrey, and horseback during the summer. Few vacancies existed after the word spread of the advantages of the health resort. The spa operated at its peak from 1875 to 1907.[153]

Another impetus toward recovery in the Nation was the development of the range cattle industry in Texas. Returning from the war, the Texans found thousands of "longhorns," identified by their "very long, sharp, pointed horns," running wild without brands over a diamond-shaped area from Austin to Galveston to Brownsville. The region was so overcrowded with cattle that an animal only worth two to three dollars in Texas brought forty to fifty dollars in Chicago. The problem was that the nearest railroad shipping point was in Missouri. The solution was the long drives to Sedalia.

Choctaw herds had multiplied rapidly at the same time on good grass, water, and mild winters in their new country. In the 1850s, travelers to California created a lucrative market for tribal beef and the livestock industry developed into a profitable business in the Nation. The tribe benefitted greatly from the migrant commerce and the drives that took place before the war. In the summer of 1854, Captain Randolph B. Marcy encountered a herd of more than a thousand longhorns at Boggy Creek being driven from Texas to Missouri. By 1859, the cost of a yoke of oxen was fifty dollars, cows ten dollars each, and horses twenty dollars, but the war interrupted the growth of the industry as cattle rustling became a widespread civilian and cavalry troop enterprise. Only after the restoration of peace was the raising of livestock resumed at an even greater rate.

The long drives were profitable business ventures after the war. One of the first successes was Upton Bushnell, an early entrepreneur, who went to Texas for a herd in the spring of 1866. Buying cattle in south Texas, he and his trail crew moved north to Clarksville and across the Choctaw Nation to the "line road," a route that ran just inside the Arkansas border, but the travel was so rough and difficult that the drovers realized they must move westward to a less populated and mountainous terrain in the future. They shifted west to the Texas Road, turning it into a "cattle highway" linking the Texas ranches to the northern railheads.

The principal routes through the Choctaw Nation were the East and West Shawnee Trails. The East Shawnee began at Colbert's Ferry, headed north through Boggy Depot, followed the Texas Road to Baxter Springs, Kansas, and terminated at Sedalia, the railhead. The later West Shawnee Trail forked at Boggy Depot and ran northwest to Abilene and other cattle towns in Kansas.

Problems encountered passing through Indian Territory caused the cattle trails to quickly move further west. The Texas longhorns carried a tick that killed the native cattle, the country was too hilly and forested, the region too thickly populated for a safe, quick drive, and the number of toll roads and gates made the eastern trails so expensive and annoying that the cowboys continuously moved their trails westward. Few profits were made the summer of 1865-1866, but as the drives moved westward revenues soared dramatically. In 1870, more than 300,000 steers went to market and twice that many the next year, restoring prosperity to Texas and Indian Territory. Over the next ten years in excess of three million head crossed the nations. So many crossed the Nation that the Choctaw Council imposed a tax of fifty cents per head on all cattle, horses, and mules passing through their country. In 1882, after the Chisolm and the Great Western or Dodge City trails were started, the transit tax was lowered to ten cents per head. The Council made up the lost revenue by instituting a charge for wintering stock or loitering on the trail by some of the Texans to take advantage of the open range.

In 1870, the number of cattlemen stopping in the Nation created such a serious concern that the Council prohibited its citizens from leasing portions of the public domain to non-citizens for grazing purposes. After 1880, when the measure failed to correct the situation, non-citizens in the Nation were allowed to maintain a herd for home consumption only. In 1888, more legislation prohibited the renting of pastures to non-citizens. Another law forbade Texas cattle in the territory except in November and December, but these regulations all proved inadequate to handle the problem.

Grazing on the open range proved to be a "boom and bust" industry. The cattle business suffered its greatest setback when extremely cold weather, deep snows, and severe freezes swept the region during the winter of 1874-75. The winter was so bad that the Red River froze bank to bank. By spring, more than fifteen percent of the Indian herds were gone. This disaster, followed by two years of drought, caused more trouble for the ranchers. They were forced to turn to more conservative practices and fences. The free range was ended forever.

The cowboy ethic entered the Choctaw culture in the score of years the range cattle industry had prospered. Many former hunters and farmers became pastoralists, and large-scale ranching was established in the Nation by 1880. Some tribesmen were soon recognized as wealthy cattlemen, including Joe Nail, of Caddo. Dealing in horses, mules, and cattle, Nail hired a crew of cowboys and a trail cook each spring and set out across Indian Territory with a chuck wagon loaded with food, supplies, and a safe full of silver and gold to purchase cattle because no one used paper money after the disasters of the Civil War. Buying steers from small ranchers and farmers, Nail covered the territory with stops that normally netted a herd of two to three thousand that his drovers pushed to markets in Kansas for a sizable profit.[154]

Several members of Allen Wright's family also ran lucrative ranching businesses, including his youngest son, J. B., who operated a highly successful ranch near Boggy Depot. Wright's cattle and horses ranged over the creek bottoms and prairies around Cherokee Springs, north of Coalgate. The two sons of Wright's sister, Kate, who died during the war, were adopted and reared by Wright, established profitable ranching businesses. The older boy, Robinson Telle, was sent to college in Tennessee but died there, while the younger, Alinton Telle, graduated from college at the age of twenty, studied law in Albany, was admitted to the bar, and returned to practice at Atoka. Adding ranching as his vocation, Telle was credited with bringing the first Hereford bulls into the area.

Capturing and breaking wild mustangs as riding horses was an integral part of ranching in these years. Herds of wild horses, descendants of strays from the Benard de la Harpe expedition into the eastern Choctaw Nation in 1719, ranged through the present counties of Pushmataha, Atoka, and Pittsburg, and every spring the Indian cowboys, many very adept at the profession, worked diligently catching and taming them. Fenced lots were constructed of brush and poles near a water hole or place the horses normally would run, and wings were built to create chutes to drive them in. Stories were told of the younger Choctaw boys who could run a horse down on foot and throw a lariat on it.

As cattle ranching expanded into a major industry, the use of brands and other identifying marks became necessary to differentiate the animals allowed to run freely on the Choctaw open range. Brands were usually simply the initials of the owner, as in the case of Wilson N. Jones' WJ brand, and each county had a ranger whose job was to check brands and take charge of stray livestock. Laws were soon passed that were designed to protect the rightful owners of animals. The Council passed statutes that required butchers to keep marks and brands of all cattle slaughtered by them on file monthly with the county clerk and another prohibited the skinning of dead animals on the range.

The Choctaw rangers had less trouble after barbed wire was invented in the 1870s, but Chief Jackson McCurtain grew concerned about that practice, worrying that "our whole country will soon be fenced up." His fears proved legitimate as the open range gradually disappeared over the next few years until becoming almost nonexistent by the time of Wilson Jones' election in 1890. Jones, representative of those Choctaw who had fenced in their ranges, had more than 17,000 acres under wire between the Boggy River and Caddo with a herd valued at more than $200,000.[155]

In the Census of 1867, the Choctaw listed 18,001 horses, mares, and colts, 820 mules, fifty-five jacks and jennies, 59,210 cattle, 51,424 hogs, and 5,970 sheep with the number of acres in cultivation ranging from one acre to 9,450 acres run by Wilson Jones. Former Chief Wright had forty-eight acres under fence with 205 head of cattle and forty-four hogs, and Henry Hotchkin, son of the missionary, used 100 acres, producing three bales of cotton, and 200 bushels of corn. A few years later, the Commissioner's Report, 1884, listed 20,000 horses, 5,000 mules, 170,000 cattle, 200,000 swine, and 12,000 sheep in the Choctaw Nation. Thus, farming and ranching were again profitable along the Red River by the 1890s.[156]

Unfortunately, another lucrative business in Indian Territory after the war was cattle rustling. In 1865 alone, a conservative estimate placed losses by the Five Civilized Tribes at 300,000 head valued at $4 million. Thieves could drive their stolen herds to Kansas, sell them at a low price to brokers for the northern markets, and answer few questions. By 1873, organized gangs specializing in the theft of livestock were so bothersome in the Nation that Chief William Bryant ordered a concentrated assault on them.

One band, the Lewis Terrell Gang, harassed LeFlore County with such increasing frequency that the population demanded action. In 1873, the outlaw band was finally eliminated by one of its own members. John Jenkins, hopeful of getting himself safely out of the gang, turned informant and told the authorities the location of the band's hideout. Surrounded by a large posse of Lighthorsemen, seven of the outlaws were captured after a short gunfight, escorted to a place near Cavanal Hill, the highest in the territory, 1,999 feet, near Poteau, and shot. A formal trial was not demanded by the gang members nor offered by the militia.

In the 1890s, an outlaw gang led by John Carpenter had to be driven from a hangout at the mouth of the Blue River. From his headquarters, the elusive Carpenter systematically conducted "thief runs" into the Nation and north Texas. Driving stolen herds along the Red River, his bandits crossed the Nation to the Washita River and then swung north to Kansas or west to New Mexico.

In these lawless years, some of the most notorious outlaws of the period visited the Nation. Belle Starr, living just north of the Canadian River, often rode through the territory or to her hideout at Robber's Cave in the Sans Bois Mountains. Just a mile south of the Red River on the Texas Road one of William Quantrill's men established a store after the war that was visited often by Frank and Jesse James, Cole Younger, and other former members of the Quantrill gang. Frank James often worked at Colbert's Ferry while hiding from the law.

On one occasion a posse from Sherman recruited men to go after an escaped outlaw from Texas discovered holed up on the Choctaw side of Red River. Catching up with the escapee in an abandoned house near Colbert's Ferry, the posse members called out for him to surrender but were answered with bullets. After a half day of exchanging gunfire with the outlaw, one of the band from the Ferry grew tired of the battle and angrily walked up to the door of the cabin demanding that the bandit give up or else. When the fugitive refused again the stranger kicked in the door, charged through with his guns blazing and shot him. After the incident, the sheriff's inquiry concerning the identity of the man who had arrested the bandit was met with evasive answers. Smart enough not to pursue the matter further until safely back in Texas, he was told that the hero had been Jesse James.

The children of W. J. B. Lloyd, a Presbyterian missionary among the Choctaw who resided at Bennington, told the story that one day three well-dressed men mounted on fine horses rode up to their home and asked to buy some chickens. Mrs. Lloyd agreed but told them they would have to catch them, causing the men to quickly draw their guns and shoot the chickens' heads off in a great display of marksmanship. Mrs. Lloyd grew concerned that these were not ordinary travelers because she had more than a thousand dollars in gold on hand that she was keeping for Wilson N. Jones, but nothing happened as the men paid for the chickens and rode away. Years later, Mrs. Lloyd's son, a witness to the incident, was in Paris, Texas, and met Frank James who happened to be in court there. Recognizing the man as one of the three riders that had visited his home, he asked the famous outlaw what would have taken place had he had known about the gold. James answered that nothing would have happened because he and his brother never bothered women or children.[157]

Railroads through the Nation were another economic advancement after the war but were accepted with mixed emotions by the Choctaw. Article VI of the Treaty of 1866 provided the United States the authority to build a north-south line and an east-west line, but opposition quickly developed to the projects, primarily by the full bloods. Aware that the roads would bring an increased white population into their country, they feared the railroads, while the intermarried citizens and mixed bloods generally supported their coming.

In March 1869, the Choctaw Council made an early attempt to begin a railroad through the Nation by granting a right-of-way and alternate sections of land for six miles on either side of the tracks running from east to west across the Nation to the "Thirty-fifth Parallel Railroad Company." The same agreement was made with the "Choctaw and Chickasaw Railroad Company" for a north-south line, but the projects were abandoned when the Secretary of the Interior ruled that surveys could not be made in Indian Territory. The decision was loudly praised by the full bloods, objecting to the railroads with unreasoning conservatism as secluded, rural people. They feared the trains as some kind of futuristic monsters. Reverend Murrow in Atoka told the story of one Choctaw who opposed the railroads because he believed the whites planned to distract the men during a ball game, load all the women on the "little houses on wheels," and run off with them to Texas or Missouri. "Then what will we do for women" asked the concerned Choctaw? Horror stories circulating around the construction of the railroads included one of a small girl reportedly crying hysterically because she had been told that the engine was a fire-breathing dragon that would chase her home and eat her. Another involved an old lady who sat all day waiting for the train to appear only to walk away muttering there could be no such thing after seeing the locomotive. Regardless of rumors or images, the rails were coming, and nothing could stop them.

The first was the Union Pacific Railway, Southern Branch, incorporated under the laws of Kansas, in September 1865. Among its original company stockholders were August Belmont, J. Pierpont Morgan, John D. Rockefeller and Levi P. Morton, who were supposed to receive alternate sections of land in a strip five miles wide through Kansas and Indian Territory, but the railroad had to be reorganized as the Missouri, Kansas and Texas Railroad Company, a consolidation of three other companies, to build to the border of Indian country in February 1870. Since it was agreed that the first railroad to build to the border would receive the grant to build south through Indian Territory, a race developed between the M-K-T, or the "Katy," from K-T to symbolize its "friendly, neighborly manner," according to its owners, and a railroad owned by James F. Jay of Detroit who bought the Kansas and Neosho Valley Railroad and reorganized it as the "Missouri River, Ft. Scott and Gulf Company."

The Katy pushed forward from Junction City to Chetopa, Kansas, but actually lost to the Jay line that reached Baxter Springs in April 1870. Although the Katy did not make it until June, Katy owners appealed to Secretary of Interior Jacob D. Cox on the grounds that the company had built closer to the exact spot where the road was supposed to enter Indian Territory, the Grand River Valley, and, for whatever reason, the Secretary agreed. He sent the Katy decision to the President who approved the grant.

On July 20, 1870, the Katy began construction, building one-half mile of track per day. In 1871, Route Engineer George M. Walker followed the Texas Road from Baxter Springs, Kansas, across Indian Territory southward through the Choctaw Nation to Colbert's Ferry. In 1871, the Katy laid 212 miles of track, another 247 miles in 1872, and reached the Red River in December. The Katy officials planned to build a terminus at "Red River City" but renamed it for George Denison, one of the railroad promoters. The route was completed, and the first passenger train crossed the Red River on December 25, 1872.

McAlester, Stringtown, Atoka, Caddo, and Durant were built about twelve miles apart, the distance from one rail station to another, along the tracks as the railroad pushed southward. A typical town along the route was "Durant's Station" that traced its origins to the removal of the family led by patriarch, Pierre Durant, from Mississippi in 1844. Beginning the trek to Indian Territory in the fall with forty-eight relatives on eight wagons marked with the family seal, the party boarded the steamship, *Erin*, and left Chickasaw Bluff on January 10, 1845. Traveling up the Mississippi and Arkansas Rivers, the company arrived at Fort Coffee in February. None of the family had died on the trip. After twelve days of fighting an ice and sleet storm, the family proceeded on to Horse Prairie, two miles south of present Hugo, and spread over the area as farmers. Pierre later moved to Pigeon Roost, two miles west of present Boswell and then to New Bennington where he remained until his death in 1855.

In April 1845, his son Fisher moved on west with his family to Carriage Point, three miles southwest of present Durant, where he operated a stage stop for the Butterfield line. Living until 1876, he fathered three sons, Dixon, Besant, and Jesse. In 1855, Dixon married a Chickasaw and remarried three more times when his other wives died. Ordained as a Presbyterian minister, he established the first general merchandise store on the site of a Katy water stop on his property. First called "Durant's Station," the name of town that grew in his pasture was gradually shortened to Durant. Dixon died at the age of ninety-seven on April 13, 1906.

Although the railroads attracted population and brought growth and progress, the Choctaw remained fairly evenly split in the debate over their advantages. The Katy had introduced tent cities, gamblers, booze peddlers, prostitutes, and criminals, while its monopoly status allowed it to charge triple prices for rates and fares, and equally importantly, its promoters believed in exploiting the land to make money, at the very least opening it to white settlers. The attitude of Robert S. Stephens, M-K-T General Manager, was typical of the philosophy of the railroaders. When charged with buying illegal ties from private individuals rather than the tribe, Stephens responded, "You can't stop us. We don't care who we buy ties from." The Katy never received the land grants that owners expected because the Choctaw Nation was not public domain, and Congress did not have the authority to make the land grants. The company was a success even without them.[158]

The Atlantic and Pacific Railroad, the first railroad approaching Indian Territory from the east, was awarded the east-west route. The A. and P. had grandiose plans to build from St. Louis to the Pacific, but, with a line constructed only to Seneca, Missouri, near the Indian Territory border, the company went into bankruptcy. Further construction was halted until the matter of land grants could be settled after building only thirty-five miles of track to Vinita, where a junction with the Katy was established on September 1, 1871.

The Panic of 1873 delayed further railroad construction for more than a decade. The problem was that the Treaties of 1866 allowed right-of-way only, not the millions of acres of public lands through Indian Territory builders thought was going to be opened. Since the Indian lands were not part of the public domain, Congress had to settle the matter. In 1877, a crucial decision from Federal Land Office Commissioner J. A. Williamson ruled that the Frisco Railroad had no land grant in Indian Territory "except as such grant might be acquired from the Indians." In 1880, the officials of the company met with Chief Jackson McCurtain who put the question to a vote of the Council and sent it to Washington for ratification. When it emerged as Senate Bill No. 60, so many changes had been added that the Indians did not recognize it. Further debate was emotional, but the final vote was thirty in favor to thirteen against;

almost half of the Senators did not even bother appearing for the vote. From this point on no Indian legislative approval was needed for bills concerning Indian Territory. Congress passed the railroad charters and the right-of-ways were subject to eminent domain. When Choctaw clerk Isham Walker pulled a copy of the Choctaw minutes from his pocket to show the Choctaw vote on the matter, the committee ridiculed him. Within two years railroad building resumed with full force.

The A. and P. Company, reorganized as the St. Louis and San Francisco Railroad Company, the Frisco, as it was called, built westward to Tulsa, across the Arkansas River, and pushed into Sapulpa in 1886. In 1882, it was authorized by an act of Congress to build a railroad through the Kiamichi Valley to Paris, Texas. Building south from Fort Smith, the line closely followed the route laid out by Captain John Stuart as a wagon road in 1832. Completed in 1887, one of the towns along its route was named Talihina, a Choctaw word for "iron road."[159]

The construction of the Frisco established a definite pattern for railway companies organized to build across the Choctaw Nation. The M-K-T had received a free right-of-way, but the Frisco and succeeding lines had to pay for them and the station sites. After the Katy, a company wanting to build through the Choctaw Nation had to receive special authorization from the Congress, file articles of incorporation with the Department of the Interior, and survey and map the route location, together with maps of desired stations. Right-of-ways were assessed at the rate of fifty dollars per mile and an annual rental of fifteen dollars a mile with the fees made part of the Choctaw national funds. By 1907, Indian Territory was crossed by 5,488 miles of track.

Coal mining, developed in the region by J. J. McAlester, an intermarried citizen, served as the inducement for many of these lines. Reared in rural Arkansas, McAlester had served in the Confederacy with General Ben McCulloch at Pea Ridge. Deciding to go to school after the war, he lived with a man named Weldon who had been a member of an engineering corps that had surveyed the Choctaw Nation and discovered coal deposits near the crossing of the Texas Road. McAlester found the memorandum books of the geologists and noted the coal in the region. Drawing a map of it, McAlester realized the location of the coalfields was the "Cross Roads" of the Texas Road and the California Trail. Taking a job with freighters to transport a sawmill to Fort Sill, McAlester took advantage of his employment to look over the area. Going to work for Reynold and Hannaford, a firm of post traders in Fort Smith, he convinced J. T. Hannaford to build a store not far from the outcropping on his map. In 1869, McAlester married a Chickasaw wife and picked a spot to build the store. The first day he sold $19 worth of merchandise, and two years later bought out his partners.

By driving a stake into the ground, McAlester, as provided by Choctaw law, claimed all the coal in a radius of one mile around it. Learning that the Katy planned to start building through the Nation, he drove a wagon with a load of coal to Parsons, Kansas, and persuaded the railroad officials to come by his store. A mine was opened in the vicinity of Krebs, and the industry was assured. In 1872, the tracks were laid directly to his store, and the town was named McAlester. His Oklahoma Mining Company claims were later sold to the Osage Coal and Mining Company. By 1887, Choctaw mines were producing more than 600,000 tons of coal per year.[160]

The Osage Company contract allowed anything for which the company paid a royalty of one cent per ton. When Principal Chief Coleman Cole learned this, he was so incensed that he ordered McAlester and his partners arrested and executed. The Lighthorsemen were dispatched to apprehend McAlester and partners, Tandy Walker, a relative of former Confederate officer, Tandy C. Walker, and two other men named Reams and Pusley; all were captured except Walker.

They were to be executed, but the captain of the Lighthorsemen, a friend and Masonic lodge brother of McAlester, released them, telling them to be back in time to carry out the sentence. McAlester, an intermarried white citizen not bound by Choctaw honor, got out of the country with no intention of returning to be shot. Two large, Irish railroad workers were paid to get him to the Creek Nation and safety. They all piled on a handcar and set out north, pumping as fast as possible, but got the car going so fast that it jumped the tracks, spilling them. Fortunately, no one was hurt, and they made their escape without further trouble. Meanwhile, Walker got fifty supporters and secretly surrounded Cole's house. Challenged by the former Confederates, Cole got the message. Meeting later with McAlester at Atoka, Cole showed him the papers for the coal sanctioned by the Council, and the two agreed to divide the coal royalties, half for the Nation and half for the mine owners. That ended the trouble.[161]

A number of mining entrepreneurs entered the business after McAlester opened the first shaft mines. Dr. Daniel Morris Hailey, a Louisiana native who had studied medicine at Tulane and served with Stonewall Jackson during the war, moved into the Nation after Appomattox as a schoolteacher and physician, married a Choctaw wife, and settled near the McAlester coal regions to get into the mining business. Operating a store, practicing medicine, and editing a newspaper, the former Confederate operated mines with financing from Jay Gould, a wealthy Eastern business entrepreneur. Hailey also organized an early telephone company, the South McAlester and Eufaula Company. Hailey left a town named in his honor, but his partner Gould and the Missouri Pacific Railroad soon dominated the mining industry.

Shafts were opened at Lehigh, Coalgate, Dow, Bache, Hartshorne, and Henryetta.

Opening the mines in the northwestern part of the Nation led to building more railroads. The construction of the next railroad, the Choctaw Coal and Railway Company, had its inception in a wild turkey hunt when a party of hunters from Minneapolis came to Indian Territory on a vacation in 1885. For a time the hunting of turkeys was an industry as early travelers noted that the wild flocks were "as thick as blackbirds" in the Choctaw Nation, so many that the engineers stopped the trains to let the passengers shoot them. The railroads further obliged their bored passengers by organizing target shooting of the birds while many farmers resorted to wholesale slaughters just to protect their game birds from them. One observer, S.V. Tucker, reported that he had encountered a flock of over 150 near Salt Springs on the way to Hugo. In 1875, so many were killed the Choctaw Council passed a law making it illegal for non-citizens to hunt them or to rent land for turkey hunting purposes.

Just as railroads were the source of the destruction of the turkey population, they decimated one of the last great flocks of pigeons in America at Ten Mile Creek in the Choctaw Nation. A short-lived occupation called "pigeoners" existed in the Nation as the flocks were so large, estimated in the millions, the birds could be killed with clubs, although they could fly up to sixty miles per hour. The pigeons were packed in barrels, shipped to markets in the eastern cities for food, and sold for fifty cents per dozen.[162]

On one of the turkey hunts in the 1870s, Edwin D. Chaddick, a businessman from Philadelphia, was intrigued with the coal mining efforts in the Nation. Introduced to Fritz Sittle, an intermarried Choctaw, he was shown coal deposits around McAlester, and Chaddick organized the Choctaw Coal & Railway Company in 1888. The first president, George R. Kirkbrile of Minneapolis, and a group called the Lehigh Valley Railroad, officials that were listed as directors, envisioned a transcontinental railroad through the region, but their charter only gave them the right to build from the eastern boundary to Fort Reno, a distance of 216 miles. Construction began with lines laid from Wister to McAlester to the M-K-T, and a line from Fort Reno to Yukon laid in 1889, but financial problems forced the company into receivership in 1891. Francis I. Gowen, a Philadelphia lawyer, reorganized the line as the Choctaw, Oklahoma & Gulf Railway with its headquarters located at "South" McAlester; a town founded a mile south by Chaddick after he became enemies with J. J. McAlester. In 1893, the Philadelphia owners again reorganized as the Choctaw, Oklahoma & Gulf with Henry Wood as general superintendent. Plans were made to build a line to Oklahoma City, which was done in 1895. In 1902, the main line, absorbed by the Rock Island Railroad, extended from

Memphis to Amarillo with a number of branch lines including one of 117 miles from Haileyville through Tishomingo to Ardmore.[163]

During the next two decades a number of other lines were constructed through the Nation. The Kansas City Southern, originally the Kansas City, Pittsburg and Gulf, locally known as the Splitlog, was completed across the northwestern corner of the Nation in 1900. Three others followed, the Fort Smith and Western, along with the Midland Valley in the north, and the Missouri, Oklahoma and Gulf, a north and south line. A number of branches were built from these, especially into the coalfields.

The first telegraph lines came with the roads. In 1859, the Choctaw General Council had granted Campbell LeFlore, a mixed blood, the first telegraph right-of-way, but while it was never built, others soon would be. By 1907, the companies were being taxed five dollars annually for every ten miles of line and three dollars and thirty cents a mile for damages of right-of-ways.

The mines and the railroads signaled the end of isolation for the Nation as the railroads started a land rush that quickly turned into a flood. Advertising the country as "B. I. T." (Beautiful Indian Territory) around the United States and in Europe, the M-K-T caused a tide of immigration into the Choctaw Nation. Going so far as to publicize the towns and villages as domed cities with climate-controlled temperatures, air-conditioned in the summers and heated in winters, Euro-Americans were lured to the Nations by the thousands. They had no legal rights unless they qualified as intermarried citizens, but their numbers never decreased as they secured permits as legal immigrants or entered as intruders, simply establishing permanent farms, ranches, and businesses despite efforts to stop them.

The coal mining industry was another major source of imported population. Agents recruited miners from the eastern coalfields and from Europe where miners were given steamship tickets that were deducted from their salaries in monthly payments. The miners were encouraged to send for their families after the companies learned the workers were more contented laborers when accompanied by wives and children, a process that supported the growth of villages and towns, but the immigrants, ironically, soon found themselves subjected to "debt slavery" after renting houses from the companies and purchasing food from company stores. In 1907, small, inexpensive, frame structures, constructed for about one hundred dollars, rented for one to two dollars per month with the rent deducted from the miners' paychecks. Food, clothing, and supplies were furnished through company-owned stores under similar arrangements.

Scotch, Irish, English, and Welch, all came to work in the mines. In 1874, the first Italians arrived at McAlester, and by 1883, there were 300 families in nearby Krebs. McAlester soon had a population of 8,144 with one in four foreign born, 900 from Italy, 250 from Lithuania, 275 from England, 50 from Poland, and 125 representing other European nationalities. By 1907, there were 10,000 Italians in the region. In 1875, Lithuanians arrived from Europe; in 1881, a large colony of French settled in Lehigh; and the Slovaks in 1883. Similar populations existed at Alderson, Hartshorne, and Coalgate, the miners having arrived with wives and children as permanent residents.

These Europeans brought different customs and cultures with them. The new immigrants largely ignored prohibition laws because their traditions of drinking beer and wine were ingrained within them. In many instances, the manufacture and sale of wines and stronger liquors supplemented family incomes from the mines that averaged two dollars and twenty-five cents an hour. By 1894, Dew M. Wisdom, United States Indian Agent at Union Agency, was complaining that the sale of "Choctaw Beer," a homebrew favorite, compounded from barley, hops, tobacco, berries, and alcohol, had developed into a worrisome issue within the mining towns.

A dangerous profession, the early mines were little more than hazardous deathtraps, and mining had the highest fatality rate of any major industry in the Nation. Plagued by explosions and fires in the early days, some 187 miners lost their lives between 1885 and 1906, all but twenty killed by explosions of gas and dust. Another 200 were killed in related accidents, including eighteen men lost and another twelve killed by a coal dust explosion that occurred during the rescue attempt at Savanna in April 1887. The greatest disaster was Mine No. 11 in Krebs at the Osage Coal and Mining Company where more than 300 miners were trapped underground by an explosion set off prematurely on January 7, 1892. The rescue effort lasted days but sixty-eight were lost.

Mine disasters were commonplace. In 1897, five were killed at Alderson. In 1901, six more died at McAlester No. 5, and another six were killed at Hartshorne when a cage fell while pulling the men up from the shaft. The accidents and deaths continued for generations. Miners were still being killed in 1930 when fifteen were lost at Lutie and nine at Haileyville in 1945. Losses placed the toll at more than 1,600 fatalities for producing 190 million tons of coal since 1873.

Mining was also a violent profession, subject to strikes and strikebreakers as evidenced by a struggle in 1894. In March, statistics showed huge profits, but the mining companies, claiming to be losing money by a market flooded with cheap coal, announced a shutdown of a few days each month and a wage cut to take effect April 1. The Atoka Coal and Mining Company and the Choctaw Coal and Railway Company then warned miners that any objections to the cuts would force the mines to shut down. A secret vote by the miners, nevertheless, approved a strike that spread to the mines at Krebs, Lehigh, and

Coalgate by April 26. The companies retaliated by hiring black miners from Texas protected by deputy marshals, and Agent Dew Wisdom, fearing violence, telegraphed the Commissioner of Indian Affairs for a company of soldiers to be sent to Alderson on May 11.

At this juncture, Chief Wilson N. Jones stepped in. Because tribal income had declined as the strike shut down the mines, officials composed a list of 200 strike leaders, revoked their residence permits, and declared them illegal intruders. Chief Jones forwarded the list to Wisdom who sent it on to Washington. Lieutenant Colonel John N. Andrews of Fort Leavenworth, Kansas, was dispatched by rail with companies of infantry to remove the striking intruders "peacefully if possible but by force if necessary" on May 22. Troops arrived first at Hartshorne and Alderson, while a cavalry troop from Fort Reno equipped with a Gatling gun was sent by way of Denison, Texas, on May 29. Meetings and discussions intensified immediately but only resulted in charges back and forth between the strikers and company representatives. As many of the miners began leaving, Governor J. S. Hogg of Texas, a hunting friend of Chief Jones, fired off orders not to let them into the Lone Star State.

In June, ejections began in earnest. Colonel Andrews arrested eighty-five miners at Alderson and Hartshorne, loaded them on railroad cars, shipped them to Wister, and then transferred them to the St. Louis and San Francisco Railroad for transport to Arkansas. Sensationalism set in when newspapers picked up the story in the eastern cities. Headlines embellished the stories to include articles of women and children being beaten and clubbed and "loaded into flat cars." On June 27, faced with such publicity, Chief Jones sent Wisdom a letter ordering all evictions stopped at once, although most of the evictions had been completed by this time.

Intending to help ease the mood of the eastern protestors, the troops were ordered back to Fort Leavenworth, but Jones reversed himself again when Choctaw Treasurer W. W. Wilson reported that four months of coal strikes and violence had emptied the National Treasury. In July, matters worsened when some of the companies tried to reopen at Krebs but were met by a mob of 500 men and women waving clubs and guns determined to stop the "reign of terror." With such an atmosphere the troops were sent back in. On July 14, thousands of strikers showed up at Kiowa to discuss returning to work, but while voting to continue the strike, support was obviously dwindling, especially since Wisdom continued rounding up people to be shipped to Arkansas. By July 25, the miners began returning to work as wages fell by twenty percent, but rents were reduced by ten percent to soften the blow. By August, the mines were running again.[164]

An industry associated with the arrival of the railroads was the lumber business. As all types of lumber were needed for building purposes, the

Choctaw Nation served as a major source of pine, oak, ash, walnut, hickory, cypress, cottonwood, and bois d' arc. The first important center of the enterprise was Stringtown, so called because the village seemed to "string out along the road through the hills." Pine logs were cut from the mountains to the east, hauled by wagon to mills in the small village, and loaded on trains for shipment. Soon twenty sawmills were in operation, but the growing numbers of logging businesses alarmed the Choctaw legislature. Fearful of the exploitation of their forests, the Council passed several laws to try to slow the process. In 1873, a law declared that only authorized agents of the Nation could legally sell timber or minerals to railroad companies. In 1878, another made the sale of timber to non-citizens illegal. A year later Chief Isaac Garvin proposed an additional bill stating that no further timber shipments would be allowed, but the law could not be passed. In 1882, Chief Jackson McCurtain claimed that non-citizens were stealing Choctaw lumber and asked for permission to collect for the stolen lumber, but that also proved an impossible task.

The earliest lumber mills were small operations until the Dierks Lumber and Coal Company came into the Nation with the Kansas City Southern Railroad in 1898. Armed with a contract to manufacture, sell, and ship Choctaw lumber along that line, the Dierks Company began large-scale operations after 1907. The exploitation of Choctaw timber began in earnest and lasted for generations.[165]

Beginning in the 1870s, census reports showed that the Nation was recovering quickly from the effects of the Civil War. The Census in 1872 reported a population of 16,000 that cultivated 27,082 acres out of a total of 6,688,000 acres. These farms produced 1,000 bushels of wheat, 2,115,195 bushels of corn, 50,000 bushels of potatoes, 250 bales of cotton, 5,940 head of cattle, 50,000 head of swine, and 6,000 head of sheep. A few years later the Commissioner's Report in 1884 estimated the livestock in the Nation at 20,000 horses, 5,000 mules, 170,000 head of cattle, 200,000 swine, and 12,000 sheep.

The Choctaw recovery was aided by the great influx of population resulting from a Choctaw permit law passed in 1867. Carrying a fee of only five dollars for admission of intermarried citizens into membership in the tribe, great numbers of immigrants began arriving until Chief Coleman Cole, who had suffered at the hands of white intruders in his old home in Mississippi, grew fearful of the growing white population and imposed a more drastic marriage law in 1875. His legislation prohibited marriages between whites and Indians without a license that cost twenty-five dollars and raised the permit tax to six dollars. Later the same license was raised to one hundred dollars, but the immigration never ceased or even slowed.[166]

Chapter Eight

In 1870, a report to the Secretary of the Interior, identifying the Choctaw boundaries and its population, remarked on the many accomplishments by the tribe since the Civil War, including a reference to Joseph P. Folsom who had just completed a compilation of tribal laws. Folsom was praised as a graduate of Dartmouth College, the school founded for the "Christian education" of Indians by Reverend Eleazar Wheelock at his home in Lebanon, Connecticut, in 1754. Originally named Moor's Indian Charity School to honor Joshua Moor, the donor of a house and two acres for the school, the school was renamed after a delegation to England raised 10,000 pounds in 1768. The money, under the control of an English board of trustees headed by the Earl of Dartmouth, was used to create a college in 1770. In 1838, a Choctaw student, Jonathan Edwards Dwight, was enrolled at Dartmouth. After graduation he became a preacher, editor, and co-editor of the *Choctaw Intelligencer* in 1850. From 1844 to 1893, twelve of the students at Dartmouth were listed as Choctaw. Enrolled in 1844, Folsom remained until 1850 at Moor's School and then entered Dartmouth, graduating in 1854. After so many years at college, it was reported that Folsom was "profound in Latin and Greek and thinks English nothing but a borrowed language." When he returned to the Choctaw Nation as an attorney, he served with the Council and in Washington, but his major effort was codifying the Choctaw laws. All the statutes were compiled and published in a printed volume entitled *Constitution and Laws of the Choctaw Nation and Treaties of 1855, 1856, and 1866*. In 1869, the volume was published in New York and remained the basic law book for the Nation until statehood.[167]

In 1870, Folsom was chosen as one of the delegates to the intertribal council in Okmulgee for the purpose of consolidating Indian Territory into one governmental system. Since the Civil War the goal of the federal government had been the establishment of a new political arrangement in the Indian Territory, a confederation of nations to serve as a single territorial government with the eventual objective being statehood. First proposed at Fort Smith in 1865, the plan was accepted in principle by the Treaties of 1866, and Ely S. Parker, a commissioner at Fort Smith, was appointed by President U. S. Grant to begin the creation of a general legislative council in 1869. Two years earlier, the Indians had made an effort themselves. In 1867, they had met at Okmulgee and adopted the Okmulgee Constitution proposing to set up a government for Indian Territory in December 1870. Folsom was one of twelve delegates to draft the document, the first constitution drawn up and considered for the territory, but it was lost in congressional discussion and never considered by Congress nor ratified by the tribes.

The group continued to meet for a number of years but not as a lawmaking body. The meetings of the delegates each year provided opportunities for discussion of common interests and problems. Its annual report presented a sound assessment of Choctaw progress as evidenced by Alex R. Durant, leader of the Choctaw delegation, at the fourth annual session of the General Council of the Indian Territory in Okmulgee in May 1873. The delegation of fifteen represented the most influential in the tribe, although only one, Mish-a-ma-tubbee, was full blood. The other members included Coleman Cole, Wilson N. Jones, Nelson McCoy, Alfred Shoner, John Garvin, David Roebuck, Jonas White, Harris Carnes, William Fry, Joseph P. Folsom, John McKinney, Campbell LeFlore, and McKee King.

Durant proudly reported to the meeting that the tribe cultivated 65,000 acres, raised cereals, planted gardens and trees, tobacco for home consumption, and shipped bales of cotton by steamboat to St. Louis and New Orleans. He added that the tribe was involved in raising stock and was improving native cattle by mixing pure breeds imported from the eastern states.

The Okmulgee Council continued to meet until 1878, but the Indians interpreted it as a threat to their independence and self-determination and fought hard to prevent its adoption. Rather, they preferred to send lobbyists to Washington to represent their opposition while the federal government viewed it as a way of creating a traditional territorial model for the Indians.

In April 1869, another effort was made by President Grant to create a territorial government with the appointment of a Board of Indian Commissioners to serve without pay to supervise expenditures of Indian appropriations and to share the direction of Indian affairs. Officially organized by Congress, this body of humanitarians and philanthropists, primarily wealthy business leaders, served as a sounding board for the Choctaw. Peter Pitchlynn, in Washington at the time working on the Net Proceed issue, for one, met with the board to request aid for the Choctaw school system. Later, in January 1872, Pitchlynn made an impassioned plea in a conference with the board to support the work of the missionaries among his people, especially concerning the temperance movement. The former chief stated, "It is the politicians who ruin us. I shall always remember with gratitude the American Board and the Presbyterian Board; they saved me."

Delegates and officials met with the board to voice their objections to the establishment of territorial governments through 1875, but as time passed the board took up the issue of allotments as a solution for the Indian problems causing the delegates to change their opinions of its work. When it announced its support for the Dawes Bill, the organization lost all credibility with the Indian delegates. In 1886, the board passed a resolution in its favor as the bill was being argued in Congress, and the Indian delegates turned completely against it.[168]

Chapter Eight

In 1879, the Choctaw again tried intertribal councils as a possible defense against white intrusions but achieved little success. On July 2, alarmed by the apparent growing popularity of the "Boomer Movement," delegates were called to Eufaula, Creek Nation, for a meeting with the Five Civilized Tribes and the Wichitas, Keechies, Caddoes, Delawares, and Ionies, to petition President Rutherford B. Hayes to stop the Boomer activities along the Kansas border. Choctaw Chief Isaac E. Garvin, elected President of the Council, appealed to the President to obtain a stiffer penal law from Congress against intruders into the Nations, including within the ceded lands but was given only promises. Another council was scheduled for May 1880, but before it was held, Secretary of the Interior, Carl Schurz, visited the Indian International Fair held in Muskogee in October 1879. All the tribes sent delegates for a rare opportunity for a face-to-face meeting with such an important federal official on their home ground, but to their utter disbelief and surprise, the Secretary told them to give up landholding in common and agree to accept allotments in severalty. He honestly confessed that the government would never be able to uphold the treaties that guaranteed the tribes protection against intruders. Tribal representatives, astounded that the top official in the federal government admitted that it neither could nor would stop the flood of immigration into their nations, received the news as "a clap of thunder from a clear sky."

In January 1880, the thirty-four delegates in attendance at the Eufaula Convention received some assurance when President Hayes issued a proclamation warning that intruders would be removed by military force if necessary, and, meeting again in May, they congratulated each other and went home thinking their campaign had been a success. They were celebrating their reprieve prematurely because at the same time David L. Payne assumed leadership of the Boomer Movement. Recognizing Payne as the "tool" of the railroads that wanted the Indian Territory opened to white settlement as quickly as possible, the tribes, almost in desperation, agreed to meet again in convention at Eufaula on October 20. Principal Chief Jackson F. McCurtain, Cherokee Chief Dennis Bushyhead, and Chickasaw Governor B. F. Overton were all in attendance as was former Chief Allen Wright. Agreeing to pool their defenses, the tribes arranged to pay the expenses of a "Committee of Prosecution" against Payne and the Boomers, with the Choctaw and Cherokee pledging $1,540 each and lesser amounts being donated by the other tribes.

On December 15, the Choctaw delegate, James Thompson, a former representative to the Okmulgee Convention, met with other members of the committee and decided to deal with the Boomers directly. Proceeding to Kansas to talk with Payne and his followers in person, the Indians, completely unimpressed by the seventy-five "Oklahomists," characterized them as "hungry, half-clad, backwoods white men," and Payne as a "man of little account who spent his time in the local saloons." Realizing there was little to be accomplished by discussions with the Boomers, the committee returned home and turned its focus on Payne's trial in Fort Smith before Judge Isaac Parker.

The "Hanging Judge" decided in favor of the Indians but without real results. Parker ruled that the Boomers had no right to homestead the Oklahoma Unassigned Lands, but there was no way to enforce his decisions. The Boomers were intruders and would be prosecuted until the law changed, according to Parker, but that was all that he could do. Payne was fined $1,000 and released, but since he had no money there was no further action. Although not immediately successful in opening the Oklahoma lands, the movement continued after Payne's death under the leadership of William L. Couch and ultimately succeeded in taking the country completely.[169]

A final political problem for the Nation after the war was the settlement of the Net Proceeds Claim. Peter Pitchlynn returned to Washington to lobby for its payment, but with him were the delegation of 1866 and their associates, John H. B. Latrobe and Douglas H. Cooper. They argued constantly over who would control these funds, and then Chief Coleman Cole entered the fray by accusing Pitchlynn of causing delays in the Net Proceeds payments because of exorbitant attorney fees over the years. In October 1874, Pitchlynn responded by beginning annual trips to Armstrong Academy to try to get the Council to settle his authority over the funds. Eventually, the claim was paid but not in Pitchlynn's lifetime. In 1881, dying penniless and in debt, he was buried in Washington near Pushmataha's grave.

In 1866, the United States Court of Claims had ruled against the tribe, but the Supreme Court overruled that court. Finally, after thirty years of effort, the Congress agreed to pay the claim as a kind of memorial to Pitchlynn for working on it since 1853. In 1886, Congress awarded $658,120, of which $250,000 had already been paid. In 1889, Congress funded the award, and Edmund McCurtain and Campbell LeFlore distributed the twenty percent voted to the original delegation. An amount of $85,000 went to sixteen people on the basis of "promises made at Tvshkahomma." Henry E. McKee, Pitchlynn's legal advisor, claimed thirty percent for attorneys' fees and fifty percent was paid to Choctaw heirs for suffering during the removal from a list established by Chief Coleman Cole in 1875.[170]

The economy of the Choctaw Nation had remained basically rural and agricultural after the war. Their farms and ranches ranged from log cabins on one-acre garden plots to many-storied homes on thousands of acres of fields and pastures. Before the railroads, there were few towns, mostly villages, and far distances between them, but the railroads brought population and change. The people were diverse in background and cultures, and new cities came into existence along the rail stops, as many of the former villages became ghost towns and moved to the new sites. Skullyville disappeared into Spiro, Doaksville became Fort Towson, Boggy Depot moved to Atoka, and Perryville was transferred to McAlester. These were signs that the Nation's independence was in jeopardy. The Choctaw had invited the whites in to bring progress not realizing they risked their entire domain.[171]

CHAPTA CHAKKALI

~ CHAPTER NINE ~

"PROGRESS IN EDUCATION AND RELIGION"

The rigors of frontier evangelism, old age, and sickness exacted a high price on the health of the early missionaries during the Civil War. In October 1868, Ebenezer Hotchkin died on a trip to New England. Only a few months later, on December 31, 1868, Cyrus Byington, who had stayed on through the war until poor health forced his departure immediately after its conclusion, died in Belpre, Ohio. Serving as a mission teacher since 1842, Reverend Charles C. Copeland died in 1869. Copeland was a replacement for Reverend A.G. Lansing who built a mission station in 1853 and then left in 1855. A student of the Choctaw language, Copeland produced several religious translations before founding a station at Bennington, named for a site near his home in Vermont. He left during the war in defense of his stand on slavery but returned to spend his last years at Wheelock. In 1870, Kingsbury, the venerable old Methodist missionary, died at the age of eighty-four at Boggy Depot after fifty-two years of service with his beloved people. The short, club-footed "Limping Wolf," was credited by Allen Wright, his Choctaw protégé, with "All the civilization, Social Improvement, and Progress in Education and Religion, of which the Choctaw can boast..." Their passing brought new religious pioneers to replace them. Representing many different religious denominations, native preachers and teachers taught by the masters before the war assumed a more important role in the religious leadership of the Nation during the years of reconstruction.[172]

Among the greatest of them was Reverend Willis F. Folsom, the mixed blood descendant of Nathaniel Folsom. In 1832, Willis and McKee removed to Eagletown, but Willis moved on to Pocola, converted to Christianity, and traveled to churches over the Southern Methodist circuit as an interpreter for other ministers. In 1858, he was ordained as a deacon at the 50th Session of the Indian Mission Conference at Skullyville. His ministry, stretching from Pocola to Pauls Valley, was covered by horseback until his death in 1894.[173]

Folsom and his colleagues worked under difficult circumstances, but their determination brought slow recovery to the Nation. In 1876, the Commissioner of Indian Affairs declared the condition of all the churches much improved after a decade of hard work and devotion. He reported that the Choctaw had more than 1,600 worshipping in twenty-four churches under the direction of nine missionaries.

Doing little missionary work prior to removal, Southern Baptists rivaled the Presbyterians and Methodists after the Civil War. One of the most energetic and faithful was Joseph Samuel Murrow. Born in 1835 in Jefferson County, Georgia, "Father" Murrow was educated as a teacher, baptized, and entered the ministry in 1854. Answering David Folsom's plea to the American Board of Commissioners for Foreign Missions to "do something for us," Murrow left

Mercer College before his senior year with an appointment as a missionary by the Baptist Association of Georgia. Sent first to the Creek in Indian Territory, he turned to the Choctaw after attending a meeting of over 300 at Brushy Creek Church in the Choctaw Nation in October 1858. At the meeting were Choctaw preachers Peter Folsom, William and Lewis Cass, and Simeon Hancock, but he and Reverend Robert Jasper Hogue were the only white ministers present.

In October 1859, Murrow, after the death of his first wife, married Clara Burns, the daughter of Reverend Willis Burns, another Baptist minister to the Choctaw at Skullyville. Named agent to the Seminole by Jefferson Davis, Murrow gathered supplies for the refugees during the Civil War. By 1865, he was caring for more than 3,000 Indians.

The Baptist preacher's favorite war story concerned his duties as a minister to the Confederates. Once paid $500 for officiating at the wedding of General Douglas H. Cooper's daughter, Father Murrow reported it was the most he ever received for performing a service. The problem was that it was Confederate money and actually worth about two dollars and fifty cents.[174]

After a short stay in Texas when the fighting ended, Murrow returned to the Choctaw Nation in 1867. Arriving at Boggy Depot, he found a thriving community of 300 but did not stay since Reverend Allen Wright was already there. He moved on to a small village consisting of a store, a blacksmith shop, and a court ground on the Middle Boggy River in Atoka County. Originally named Shappaway County by the Choctaw Council in 1850, five years later the village had been divided into two sections with the new county called Atoka, in honor of the oldest resident of the region, Rtoka, a member of the Tribal Council who lived twenty miles southeast of the small village. According to local legend, Rtoka was the man responsible for instructing a medicine man to place a good spell on the place, the explanation for the fact a tornado has never hit the town. At the time of Murrow's arrival, Atoka served as the site of an inn run by the widow Eliza Ann Juzan Flack and her three daughters, all Baptists. Mrs. Flack, the youngest daughter of Charles Juzan, was the granddaughter of Shanke, the sister of Pushmataha. Moving his family to the new mission, Murrow and his wife opened a school for the Indian children, and he convinced the government to authorize a post office at A-tok-ka, as it was spelled in 1868.

In July 1869, he organized the Rehoboth Mission Baptist Church with six members and employed James Williams, a Choctaw preacher, as a missionary to the surrounding counties at an annual salary of $100. Within three months there were seventy-seven members and a new church building. In 1877, W. J. Hemby established one of the earliest newspapers in the region, the *Atoka Independent*, a four-page edition printed in the Choctaw language with English translations, to keep the Choctaw informed of events in their Nation.

Remaining with the tribe for more than sixty years, the Masonic missionary founded the Baptist Academy for Indian Orphans north of Atoka in 1887. The school became the Murrow Orphans Home and the Baptist Indian University, later called Bacone College at Muskogee.[175]

Originally from Greene County, Reverend Robert J. Hogue was another Georgia missionary. In 1847, Hogue was ordained as a Baptist missionary and appointed to the Choctaw by the Domestic and Indian Mission Board of the Southern Baptist Convention. In 1858, he was dispatched to the Indian Territory with his family for a salary of $600 per year. His ministry in the Choctaw Nation lasted until his death at the age of eighty-six at Atoka in 1906.

One of the great Choctaw Baptist ministers was Peter Folsom. Born in Mississippi in 1814, Folsom converted to the Baptist Faith at the Choctaw Academy before moving to Indian Territory. After organizing an estimated 2,000 Baptist churches in the Nation, Folsom decided to return to the Choctaw in Mississippi. By 1889, old and tired, "Uncle Peter," as he was called, had converted more than 700 Mississippi Choctaw. Reverend Murrow later stated that Folsom had "organized more churches and ordained more preachers than any other minister in his Nation."[176]

William James Beard Lloyd, a missionary that arrived after the war, labored for more than forty years among the Choctaw. Born in South Carolina in 1834, Lloyd saw service in the Confederate Army at Pea Ridge before being licensed to preach. Moving to Bennington as a circuit-riding parson, he helped establish the first post office in the town in August 1873. There were soon four stores, a hotel, gin, gristmill, and several homes in the town. By 1893, Bennington was a distribution center for Oberlin, Mayhew, and Jackson.

Bennington merchants bartered with local Choctaw for venison, hams, pelts and hides, and cotton, and after collecting a supply, the goods were sent by wagon across the river to Caddo, sold, and more merchandise purchased to re-supply the "Red Store" in town. Chickens and eggs were the major money items for Bennington residents with fryers selling for ten cents each and eggs for two to five cents per dozen. Mastering the Choctaw language, Reverend Lloyd conducted Armstrong Academy for six years and later helped establish Oklahoma Presbyterian College at Durant.

Calvin J. Ralston, a minister from Virginia, served as an assistant in the field hospitals during the Civil War and then attended Union Theological Seminary. Preaching in Tennessee and Texas before moving to the Choctaw Nation, Ralston replaced Lloyd at Armstrong. At the time of his arrival, the school sheltered more than seventy orphan boys. Ralston's son was born at Armstrong but drowned in a pool at the age of four. In 1894, his parents gave the child's school fund of $200 to the Home Mission Committee to start a church and a school at Durant on condition that it was named Calvin Institute as a memorial for him. Reverend Ralston later moved to Caney and continued preaching among the Choctaw for many years.

From 1894 to 1896, Calvin Institute, located on Durant's Main Street, was headed by Reverend R. K. Moseley and members of a board that included W. J. B. Lloyd, J. J. Read, and C. J. Ralston until Mrs. Mary Semple Hotchkin and son Ebenezer took over. Born in luxury in 1877, the teacher from Ohio converted to missionary work and moved to Wheelock to teach. She transferred later to Bennington, Goodwater, Mayhew, and Caddo after marrying Henry Hotchkin, son of the elder Ebenezer. Always carrying her Bible, the lady missionary successfully ran the school until it was designated a co-educational school and supported by tribal funds. In 1900, William Brown Morrison was named president and served for eight years.

Thornton R. Sampson completed a brick building for the school, but the structure was moved to the northern edge of the city as dormitories for a new school called Durant College when Reverend Ebenezer Hotchkin became head of the institution. Born at Goodland in 1869, he attended Haskell Institute in Kansas, worked for a time as a cowhand in Pauls Valley, and retuned to college in Missouri before going to Fort Worth University in Texas. Trained in teaching and preaching, he eventually returned to the college at Durant that was purchased as a girl's school in 1907. Officially renamed the Oklahoma Presbyterian College for Indian Girls in 1910, Pauline Anderson Dennis, who lived in the dormitory from 1941 to 1942, recalled that OPC consisted of two buildings divided into the north and south buildings connected by a "breezeway" with the north building containing a gymnasium where the students skated and played basketball, a cafeteria, and dormitories for junior and seniors girls, while the south building had a swimming pool, auditorium, and dormitories for freshman and sophomores. On Sundays the students gathered at the gym for a devotional led by one of their numbers and boarded buses to the local Presbyterian Church for services. The same transportation took students back and forth to Southeastern State College for classes until the school was closed in 1963. The buildings were later remodeled as the Choctaw national headquarters.[177]

Although the characters and places changed, the methods and topics of religious instruction did not. One of the most popular social events continued to be summer camp revival services that lasted up to two weeks or longer. A brush arbor, constructed by driving eight to ten foot posts into the ground as support for a roof of branches and brush near the site of a log church, served as a central meeting place, and huge amounts of food, beef, pork, Ta̲fula, and coffee were consumed during the semi-formal gatherings. Smoking was allowed during the sermons since tobacco was thought to be conducive to receiving spiritual messages. Sometimes the meetings were united efforts as Baptists, Methodists, and Presbyterians joined together for worship and fellowship.

The revivals prompted the wearing of the latest fashions, or at least more than ordinary dress, by both men and women. The newness did not matter for most of the year, but worshippers wanted to look their best at meeting time. While the material value of clothing was never emphasized, camp meetings were the major social events of the year, and everyone wished to show off their finery. Beginning with the singing of spirituals and hymns in Choctaw and proceeding to the sermons, the men and women, seated on opposite sides throughout the meetings, conducted the services in an atmosphere of sincere, devout worship.

At full blood churches no one spoke other than the preacher, or his interpreter, if the pastor was white or unfamiliar with the language. There was no cooking or work on Sunday, the Lord's Day, nor were there any activities not associated with religion. Sunday afternoons were spent reading the Bible or in prayer or other religious work, and ball games and frivolity were frowned upon or completely eliminated. Most Choctaw went so far as to teach that it was sinful to even watch ball games on the Sabbath.

Another custom carried over to modern times was the Choctaw funeral cry. Often conducted after the worship period at summer camp meetings, sermons for the deceased were sometimes not preached for six to twelve months after death, allowing a time for relatives of the dead to periodically conduct crying sessions at the grave. Since the deceased were normally buried near the home, the family and friends had an opportunity to meet and sympathize until the funeral was performed with prayers, songs, a final cry and a communal meal. The cry allowed the living to handle the loss of a loved one rather than making death an obsession that continued for years. The early missionaries did not prohibit these ceremonies, but they were seen less frequently until finally disappearing over time.

Many of the issues for the missionaries remained the same. Before the war the belief in witches and evil spirits was found impossible to eradicate and persisted even among the highly educated members of the tribe. As early as 1834, the Council had prescribed the death penalty for anyone killing another person as a witch or wizard, but the Choctaw superstition endured into modern times. In 1899, Solomon Hotema, a full blood Presbyterian minister trained at Roanoke College, Virginia, discarded his education and murdered three people for practicing witchcraft against his family. Although considered a progressive leader who believed firmly in learning for his people, Reverend Hotema reverted to the tribal belief in witchcraft when three children in his family died from diphtheria. Blaming the tragedy on the work of witches, Hotema, returning to the law of lex taliones, "an eye for an eye," killed two women and a man in the community that he thought had caused the disease. Arrested for the deed, Hotema admitted that he had committed the murders, "because I love the Lord's work and because I love the people." Found guilty and sentenced to death by a federal court, his punishment was later converted to life imprisonment by President Theodore Roosevelt. In 1907, the former Choctaw minister died in prison in Atlanta.

Witchcraft continued as an accepted practice in Choctaw society. Reporting a modern experience with the phenomena, a highly educated college graduate stated that after having repeated nightmares a Choctaw doctor, consulted for a cure, informed the person that the frightening dreams were the result of the powers of wizardry being "willed" to the individual by a witch or a wizard. The doctor added that the dreams would end once a decision was made by the individual to accept or discard the magical powers. Accordingly, the person renounced the gift and the terrifying dreams disappeared completely.[178]

In 1876, Peter James Hudson reported alcoholism was another endless problem. Born near Eagletown in 1861, Hudson as a boy was taught by Rhoda Pitchlynn, known by her Choctaw name, Pashhuma (red haired woman). In 1867, he was so reluctant to give his name, as was the Choctaw custom, she had to guess it on his first day in school. Hudson once had the opportunity to observe a Temperance meeting when word went out that a battle would be fought against Oka Homi (Bitter Water), a Choctaw term for whiskey, at Big Lick Church near Hochatown, a full blood settlement of about twelve families at the time, named for the Hocha family who changed it to Bob, including a son, Joseph Bob. In October 1876, Hudson accompanied his father to the meeting, along with several people from the Eagletown area including Cornelius Homa, the son of John Homa, a Creek captured by Jackson and adopted into the tribe.

Hudson reported that these kinds of meetings were very common in the post-war years. The particular gathering he attended drew over five hundred tribesmen but no whites. Those who participated in the meeting marched in groups to the music of drums and flutes as soldiers in the fight with the evil brew. Other subjects were discussed during the course of several days of conferences including farming, schools, and tribal business, but whiskey continued to be the most important issue. Oka Homi was portrayed as one who took a person's money, brought suffering and misery to a person's family, and "left a man in a mud hole." By the end of the assembly everyone present had signed a pledge to never use whiskey again.[179]

The Roman Catholic Church was instrumental in the renewed missionary zeal after the war. Because of early contacts during the French period, their work should have given them a foothold among the Choctaw, but after Jesuit

Father Le Petit established a mission in the Eighteenth Century, the Catholics practically abandoned the tribe as "wild and lawless." In 1763, the Catholic mission closed when the French lost North America and Catholic missionaries appeared only occasionally until after the Civil War when Father Michael Smyth, an itinerant 36-year old Irish priest from County Cavan by way of Fort Smith, began making missionary rounds into the Nation.

In 1872, the Father established St. Patrick's Church in a small, wooden, single story building located next to the Katy railroad tracks at Atoka. Opened with proper pomp and ceremony, including a special letter addressed to the Choctaw from the Pope and a bell sent from Germany to adorn the building, the church failed to attract many Choctaw members. Father Mike's progress was evident by being forced to conduct services at an altar "made from dry goods boxes" donated by a local merchant. Despite the priest's every effort, including visiting the Atoka church dutifully once a month, the people simply refused to come. Early parishioner, John Hardin, editor of the *Atoka Vindicator*, was joined by some of the Irish section hands along with Chief Benjamin Franklin Smallwood and John Fisher of the Choctaw Nation but only one family ever joined the congregation. The church eventually was closed until Father Isidore Robot, a French Benedictine priest, arrived as the first residential pastor for Atoka.[180]

Born in 1837, in Tharoiseau, Burgundy, Father Robot became a missionary priest in 1862. Sent to Louisiana with authorization to work among the tribes in Indian Territory, Father Robot obtained permission to preach among the Choctaw at a meeting of the Tribal Council at Armstrong Academy in November 1875. He ran into difficulty when he tried to start a school, however, as a dispute developed over administrative controls. Since the authority to conduct schools fell under the jurisdiction of the Nation, the Council, determined to maintain complete control of its system, instructed Chief Coleman Cole to inform the priest that according to tribal law only Indians by blood or intermarried citizens could obtain permits to teach without prior approval. Robot's school lasted from January to June 1876. Thirty pupils, twenty Indian and ten white enrolled in its first term, but the priest decided not to reopen after the first term. Chief Smallwood showed interest in it later on and gave Father Robot much encouragement but it remained closed.

At first there was considerable opposition to the Catholics in Choctaw country by other denominations. The Tribal Council even passed legislation prohibiting the establishment of Catholic missions in the Nation, but Chief Thompson McKinney vetoed the proposal. Although the church continued to lag behind in recruitment of members, Father Robot successfully converted the Osage and Pottawatomie and found the other tribes patiently respectful of Catholic teachings. Some even recalled priests in Mississippi.

Robot successfully maintained the church in Atoka and started others in McAlester, Savanna, and Lehigh, towns with large numbers of immigrants from southeastern Europe. Despite disappointing numbers in converts, the Father sustained his work until his death in 1886. He was buried in McAlester.

Robot's mission was taken over by Bishop Theophile Meerschaert. Born in Belgium in 1847, he came to America to work as a missionary in Mississippi in 1871. Determined to send priests into other Nations after visiting the Pottawatomie Sacred Heart Abbey in 1891, he focused first on the town of Atoka and then Antlers. On October 6, 1892, he left a priest, Father Bernard Murphy, at Atoka with the advice that "This is a very bitter town and the few Catholics are rather lukewarm."

The dedicated Catholic bishop was eventually successful in his persistent efforts to spread religion and schools among the Choctaw. By 1916, there were nine Catholic schools operating in the Nation with an enrollment of 422 pupils. Bishop Meerschaert died in Oklahoma City in 1924.

The groundwork laid by these early priests bore results during the administration of Monsignor William Henry Ketcham. Born in Iowa in 1868, Ketcham and his family pioneered in Texas before taking part in the Land Run into Oklahoma. Ordained in 1892, Ketcham attended Jesuit College in Louisiana and did mission work at Eufaula, Sapulpa, Miami, and other northern cities until his transfer to Antlers in 1896. Within a year the hard-working priest mastered the Choctaw language and translated the prayer book and the catechism with the able assistance of Victor Locke, Ben Henderson, George Nelson, Bailey Spring, and Peter Hudson. Father Ketcham also translated several health pamphlets into Choctaw leading to better physical conditions for the tribe.

Later founding missions at Poteau, Cameron, Howe, Wister, Fanshawe, Talihina, Tushkahoma, and Albion, Antlers remained Ketcham's pride. He first lived in a room at the railroad section house in the town and said Mass on Sundays in the courthouse. Beginning with six baptized Catholics in Antlers, the Father worked diligently promoting Catholicism and baptized the first white convert in Antlers, Mary Berry, and the first Choctaw, Victor Locke, in 1899. He enrolled one hundred members, seventy-five of them full bloods, over the next four years later. In a note to the Bishop thanking him for help in the baptismal ceremonies, Father Ketcham remarked, "I hope the next time you come, I will be able to offer you something more delicate than possum."

He also started a school, St. Agnes Mission, in this time. In 1897, the school began with two boys, one Choctaw and one white, and twenty-five dollars for supplies. It was named for Agnes T. Grace, the daughter of philanthropist W.R. Grace of New York, who, along with Mother Mary Katherine Drexel, heiress to a Philadelphia banking fortune, gave the Father the money to build the school as a memoriam. When the bank he used in Paris failed that year, he lost the little money he had saved, but his dogged persistence paid off, aided by the timely arrival of the Sisters of St. Joseph from Muskogee to begin teaching duties. After visiting the Indian families, a kindergarten was started with six Choctaw girls, Lizzie Turnbull, Mary Freeny, Missie Adams, Maud Taafe, Clara Wooley, and Mary McClure attending at a cost of $110 per year from 1897 to 1898. In 1901, Ketcham was so involved with the school that he adopted one of the Choctaw orphans, a boy that he named Thomas Simpson Ketcham.

Later transferred to Washington, D.C., Ketcham never lost his interest in the Choctaw missions. His support never waned, and he visited them at least on an annual basis. He also took particular pride in helping with the establishment of the "Carter Sanitarium," the tuberculosis sanitarium at Talihina, named in honor of Congressman Charles D. Carter of Ardmore, who helped secure finances for the hospital. Ketcham died in Mississippi in 1921.

The Reverend Aloysius Hitta, a Benedictine priest, succeeded Ketcham at Antlers. He stayed until 1901. At the same time the Sisters of Divine Providence of San Antonio were given charge of St. Agnes. The sisters took control of sixty-six pupils, a number that increased to ninety boarding students in 1904. In 1905, the student body grew to 127 and continued to enlarge until ten teachers were needed to handle the work in 1934. The school was operated as a neighborhood school with the Sisters employed by the Choctaw Council and supervised by Choctaw trustees until the Atoka Agreement gave the federal government control as a "contract" school. In 1915, the contract ended when tribal funds were ruled unauthorized for private or mission schools, a ruling that also affected schools at Goodland, OPC, and Murray State School. Stopping the payment of twelve dollars and fifty cents per month for board and tuition for each pupil paid by the government out of "Educational Funds" of the Nation was a setback for Choctaw education for years.

As the Director of the Bureau of Catholic Indian Missions in Washington, D.C., Father Ketcham had kept the school alive as long as he lived, but the buildings, old and in disrepair, desperately needed renovation by 1924. The minimum estimates for repairs was $1,000, but appeals made for funds went unanswered until Meerschaert's successor, Bishop Francis C. Kelly, visited the school in 1929. The Bishop agreed to refinance the school and rebuild the mission buildings for the Sisters at a cost of $5,000. Housing seventy-five Choctaw students at the time, the school remained in operation until the Antlers tornado on April 12, 1945. The storm destroyed the entire school with only the building where the children had taken refuge to pray miraculously spared. Nothing was left. The Sisters returned to San Antonio, and the parish priest moved to Hugo. Antlers had no Catholic church until a new St. Agnes was constructed in 1947.

The Church did continue to have its supporters. Among the most important was Anselm J. Stroub. Born January 24, 1924, Stroub graduated from Oklahoma City schools, attended St. Gregory's High School, and went to junior college at Shawnee. After attending Notre Dame and South Dakota State College and the University of Nevada, he became the first Choctaw Catholic priest.[181]

A former slave, Charles W. Stewart, conducted important religious work for his people in these years as well. Taught to read and write by a former master's wife, and the Bible by Reverend Kingsbury personally, Stewart labored practically single-handedly to keep churches and schools alive for the Choctaw freedmen. His reward was the establishment of a separate presbytery for black churches in 1896. First called the Tuskaloosa and later Kiamichi Presbytery, it reported sixteen churches with four hundred members in 1916.

Stewart, a Presbyterian minister, settled among a large number of freedmen just west of where Valliant would be founded in 1902. He and Henry Crittenden, another former slave, led the movement for the establishment of a school for the freedmen by affiliating with the Presbyterian Board of Missions that required each black pastor to maintain a day school in each church for a few months of every year. In 1868, Stewart organized Oak Hill Church followed by the opening of Oak Hill School in 1876. Its first native teacher, J. Ross Shoals, taught school and Sunday school for the freedmen, and two years later, George Dallas built a small school near the church. In 1878, Dallas became the full-time teacher for weekday classes. A few years later the school moved approximately ten miles from Wheelock to an old log house originally owned by Chief Basil LeFlore.[182]

The freedmen eventually asked for a boarding school for their students. In 1886, the Presbyterian Board approved the request by sending Eliza Hartford, a white teacher from Ohio. In February, the lady opened the school with seven students. Riding horseback to the school while living in Crittenden's home, she and the students moved in after repairs were made to a house at the school. Families of students were required to furnish twelve bushels of corn per student as tuition. The following year the institution, officially named the Oak Hill Industrial School, added Priscilla Haymaker as a second teacher. A classroom was soon built to handle the twenty-four enrolled students and the old home served as the dormitory. In the fall of 1887, sixty students arrived, thirty-six of them were lodged in the old dormitory and the rest found homes with the local families. Another classroom and a dormitory were constructed the following year when Superintendent James McBride arrived from Indiana in October. Successfully appealing to his home state for funds, more buildings were erected until McBride's death in 1892. His wife assumed control and kept the school going until Reverend Edward Haymaker arrived in October. Serving for eleven years, he resigned in 1894. Haymaker stayed to arrange for acquisition of the land from the Choctaws as the process of allotting land was taking place and the freedmen were to share in it. Haymaker, arranging for two allotees to take land near the campus and then sell it to the school, obtained governmental approval of the arrangement in 1908. Within four years the school had title to 270 acres.

Closed for a time until Bertha Ahrens arrived to take charge, Reverend Robert Flickinger and his wife from Iowa took over in February 1905. Insisting on using the Bible as the daily text, there were ninety-six students by the end of the school term. In 1908, after a fire damaged the buildings and a new girls dormitory was needed, a fund-raising effort was organized that netted the necessary funds including a gift of $5,000 from David Elliott of Lafayette, Indiana, in 1910, as a memorial for his wife, Alice Lee Elliott. In 1912, officials renamed the school and Superintendent Flickinger retired the same day, replaced by William H. Carroll, the former principal of the school. Elliott remained a public school in the Valliant system until classified as a "separate" school in 1937.[183]

Opening each meeting with prayer, the Tribal Council allowed all religious denominations into the Nation. The churches reciprocated by fully restoring the Choctaw educational system within a decade after the war. Each district soon had a neighborhood school provided at the request of a local community that was only required to supply the building and equipment. Three citizens in each community, reduced to one in 1882, served as local trustees with their salaries set at two dollars per month to hire the teachers and support the system. In November 1881, a free textbook law was passed followed by the passage of attendance laws in 1884, providing fines of ten cents per day for parents allowing unexcused absences of pupils. Although English was compulsory while Choctaw was discouraged on school property, many of the teachers were Choctaw educated in the tribal schools. Paid two dollars per student per month, they were considered professionals, and a professional magazine was published for them entitled the *Choctaw School Journal*.

Boarding schools were also reopened after the war. In the fall of 1870, a contract was negotiated with the Methodist Episcopal Church South to provide $5,000 for New Hope and a similar arrangement was made with the Presbyterians for Spencer Academy. Both reopened in 1871. Students in these schools, ranging from ten to sixteen years old for girls and twelve to eighteen for boys, were required to be proficient in reading the Third Reader upon entrance. The schools continued until 1896 when Spencer was destroyed by fire with four boys burned to death and only a few months later another fire occurred at New Hope.

In 1885, Wheelock was designated a school for orphan girls. Continued into the 1950s, there were 127 girls attending the school with Reverend Roy Craig of Idabel as pastor for the 1950 school term. Another for boys was established at the old Armstrong Academy. Children from six to twelve, not necessarily orphans but who had lost one or both parents and needed a home, could be placed in these schools. They were allowed to stay until the girls were sixteen and the boys were eighteen.

In 1891, Jones Male Academy was founded for boys four miles northeast of Hartshorne. The school has been in continuous operation since opening for classes in 1892. Its first superintendent, Simon T. Dwight, a full blood, was followed by Mrs. Jack McCurtain, W. A. Durant, Wallace Butz, Sam L. Moseley, W. F. Aver, Edwin L. Chalcraft, H. P. Warren, and Joseph N. Kagey.

Tuskahoma Female Institute for girls was opened at the same time with Peter J. Hudson as superintendent. Educated at Spencer before graduating from Drury College, Springfield, Missouri, in 1887, Hudson attended Hartford Theological Seminary in Connecticut. Returning home as a Presbyterian missionary, he was selected as the first administrator of Tuskahoma. The problem was that he was a single man working in an all-girls school. It was quickly suggested that he get married. Hudson, told of a Choctaw family who had two daughters of marriage age, hired a buggy and went out to meet them. One appeared rather sickly and weak and the other strong and healthy, and he chose the sick one, Amanda Bohannon. On the same afternoon, shortly after being introduced to her, Hudson, at the time thirty-three years old, asked Miss Bohannon, nineteen, to marry him.

Two weeks later he returned to perform the ceremony but was told the wedding would have to wait. He had not asked permission of the father and the family in the proper manner. When the arrangements were finally worked out, the wedding was rescheduled for three weeks in the future allowing the bride's family sufficient time to arrange the customary feast and wedding ceremony. On August 16, 1892, the nuptials were performed with the proper etiquette and decorum. Amanda was placed at the head of one table with the women while Hudson was seated at another table with the men. Having never even been on a date, Hudson and the girl were married. Their first child, Helen Hudson, was born in the dormitory at Tvshkahomma. Hudson later served as Tribal Auditor and as an interpreter in Washington, 1907-1910, 1916-17, and 1920-26.[184]

Another lasting institution among the Choctaw was the "School with a Soul," Goodland Indian Orphanage. In addition to Bible study in the classroom, there was Sunday school worship, young people's societies, morning prayers, and bedtime prayer groups in the dormitories. Founded on Christian principles, its first administrators, John Lathrop in 1848 followed by Oliver Porter Stark in 1850, relied upon the basic, deeply spiritual Choctaw instinct to make the school a success.

Afflicted students were also supported by tribal funds for special schools. Several deaf children were sent to school in Illinois and blind children went to other special schools. The entire system was paid from annuities, income from invested funds, coal and mineral royalties, and taxes and fees paid by non-citizens. In 1874, Edmund McCurtain even got a livestock property tax passed to support schools in his district, the only tax bill ever attempted for the Choctaw Nation. It was never passed as a general tax but was indicative of Choctaw support for their educational system.[185]

The Choctaw quickly restored tribal institutions and government after the war. Prosperity soon returned to the Nation, but the greatest challenge was still ahead for the tribe. Their leaders had supported education and religion knowing that white settlement would eventually reach them again, and they intended to be prepared to cope with the white intrusion the next time. That long expected white encroachment was at hand.[186]

CHAPTA POKKOLI

~ CHAPTER TEN ~

"WE WANT TO PRESERVE THE INTEGRITY OF OUR RACE"

Chapter Ten

In 1879, Elias Cornelius Boudinot, a Cherokee mixed blood, created a national furor in an article published in the *Chicago Times* suggesting the opening of the Indian lands ceded by the Treaties of 1866 to white settlement. Once made, the proposal verbalized the majority opinion of Americans toward Indian Territory and there was little doubt of the ultimate outcome. A number of factors favored the white settlers while others supported the Indians, but those in favor of the whites greatly outweighed the other side.

The groups supporting white settlement included white farmers from nearby states, western politicians, railroad promoters, and merchants and businessmen. Young men with large families from Texas, Missouri, Arkansas, and Kansas saw Indian Territory as a vast land of free or cheap homesteads, and since they were voters, they could apply pressure on congressmen and senators in Washington for the necessary legislation to obtain it. The politicians had no choice. If legislators wanted to be elected from the West, they had to stand for opening Oklahoma to white settlement. Another major supporter of the "Boomer" movement, the railroads, had the money needed to promote the demand for towns and population and to advertise for white settlers. Finally, the merchants and businessmen who established towns along the railroad tracks backed the openings as a means of extending their trade into the territory for more profit. Collectively, these forces were formidable lobbyists for white settlement of the Oklahoma lands.

Opposed to opening Indian Territory were the Indians, both full bloods and mixed bloods, for a change. The full blood factions considered the proposal just another broken promise while the mixed bloods, holding privileged positions within the tribe, realized it meant the end of a profitable arrangement for them. And, in one of the few times the cowboys and Indians were on the same side. The cowmen, arguing that there was not enough grazing land to go around, adamantly opposed the fencing of good pasture or ruining it with plows and barbed wire. Allied against the land openings with the cattlemen and the tribesmen was a plethora of frontier characters, all with different and often disparate reasons, including missionaries, traders, and outlaws. The missionaries considered the taking of Indian lands as another example of white injustice against the tribes, while the traders and peddlers who carried their wares into Indian Territory feared the loss of their business. The outlaws and whiskey dealers objected over their use of the Indian Territory as a safe haven since the nearest justice was "Hanging Judge" Isaac Parker at Fort Smith. These groups opposed any kind of organized government in the nations but were greatly hampered by not being part of the legal voting public.

In 1879, the Boomers centered their activities on the Unassigned Lands in Indian Territory. Charles C. Carpenter, David L. Payne, W. L. Couch, and their followers worked tirelessly for the cause for ten long years until their battle ultimately proved successful. On March 2, 1889, the Springer Amendment, a rider attached to an Indian appropriation bill, allowed President Benjamin Harrison to open more than two million acres in the very "heart" of Oklahoma for white homesteads. This was the beginning of the end for the tribes.

In April, Oklahoma Territory was settled within hours by the first land run into the Nations. The Organic Act was then passed to add other western lands as they became available to the territory. The Jerome Commission, also known as the Cherokee Commission since its major objective was the Cherokee Outlet, was charged with the mission of handling future land transactions over the next decade. Headed by David H. Jerome and including Warren G. Sayre and Judge Alfred M. Wilson, the commission successfully concluded an agreement with the Cherokee and eventually persuaded all the western tribes to take allotments in severalty and open their excess lands to white settlers.

Thousands of white farmers legally swarmed into Oklahoma Territory by runs, public auctions, and lotteries, while thousands more moved illegally into Indian Territory. By 1894, there were 250,000 whites and 100,000 more a year later. At this juncture, a commission was appointed to deal with the Five Civilized Tribes in Indian Territory.[187]

Events reached this point as a result of a change in policy adopted by Eastern reformers after the publication of a pair of influential bestsellers. *Our Indian Wards* (1880) by George Manypenny, former Commissioner of Indian Affairs, recounted the sordid history of Indian-white relations, and *A Century of Dishonor* (1881) by Helen Hunt Jackson denounced the whole federal Indian policy and blamed the government for failing to formulate programs that educated and civilized the tribes. The works inspired the organization of two powerful reform societies by advocates of Indian rights searching for a more suitable solution to the Indian question. Jackson and her friend, Senator Henry L. Dawes of Massachusetts, organized the Boston Citizenship Association, while Herbert Welsh, a prominent artist and the son of John Welsh, the Minister to Great Britain for President Rutherford B. Hayes, founded the Indian Rights Association in Philadelphia.

Founded on December 4, 1882, the IRA was the most influential of the reform associations. In the 1880s, Welsh, as its first executive secretary, pleaded with Congress for legislation for education, Christianization, and assimilation of the Indians. He and other IRA members claimed that the tribes must undergo acculturation after destruction of their native cultures based on tribal organizations with systems of communal ownership of lands and argued that assimilation would be achieved only after tribal lands were exchanged for individual land ownership.

In 1883, delegates attended the Lake Mohonk Conferences in New York to discuss and encourage debate on this latest proposal of tribal allotment as a reform movement for governments, universities, churches, and reform groups. At the 1884 meeting a year later, Richard Pratt, head of the Carlisle Indian School, lent his voice to the reform proposal. Calling for immediate and compulsory allotment of lands in severalty, Pratt stated categorically that Indians would never improve their lot until the loss of their allotments to white settlers "reduced them to the necessity of working for a living."

On February 8, 1887, aroused by such inflammatory remarks, Congress passed the Dawes General Allotment Act providing for the first allotments of Indian land in severalty. Under the new law each head of family was given 160 acres, which could not be sold for a period of twenty years, and the President could negotiate for all surplus lands for white settlement. The Choctaw and the other Civilized Tribes mounted copious opposition to the law and were exempted from participation at the time, but it was a losing battle in the long run. Christian reformers, determined to extend the law to all Oklahoma tribes, renewed efforts to apply the law to Indian Territory.[188]

By 1890, major changes were needed in Indian Territory. Serious social and economic problems had developed from the continuous influx of white intruders into the Nations. Indian agents reported 15,000 non-citizens in 1881, 35,000 in 1884, 140,000 in 1890, and 150,000 in 1893, approximately three whites to one Indian, all living without permission in the Nation. Within this framework, Choctaw society had divided into four distinct groups: non-citizen whites and blacks, white tenant farmers and intermarried citizens, Indians, and freedmen, and intensely bitter rivalries existed between these groups.

Investigations further revealed the reality that whites and mixed bloods had taken control of large tracts of tribally owned lands, made improvements, and claimed the lands as their own. Sixty-one citizens controlled 1,237,000 out of a total of 3,040,000 million acres in the Choctaw Nation. Wilson N. Jones, for one, controlled more than 17,000 acres of rangelands. Understandably, the proposal for allotments in severalty gradually gained popularity in the tribe because of the widening economic and social gaps between wealthy mixed bloods and the poorer full bloods.

Violence during national elections was another glaring problem seized upon by the proponents of destruction of tribal entities. In September 1892, Wilson N. Jones, the candidate for the Progressive or Eagle Party, was charged with controlling the National Council and the election count by Jacob B. Jackson, leader of the National or Buzzard Party, and the two sides resorted to armed force. Jones was declared the winner of the election but was forced to call out the Lighthorsemen at Tvshkahomma to try to preserve the peace.

Threats and anger that had plagued the election resulted in murder only one day after it was over. An angry mob shot Sheriff Joe Hoklotubbee on his front porch, and the incident caused everyone to react to the violence. Taking matters very seriously, Chief Jones quickly dispatched a message to the Council condemning the deplorable, violent actions of the election and requesting calm. In October 1892, the Chief made a dramatic appeal to the tribe to stop the killing in a public message proclaiming that "Life must be protected and our laws enforced, or we perish as a nation."

It was already too late. Silon Lewis, the leader of the eighteen gunmen involved in the attack, was arrested, tried for murder, and given the death penalty at the Choctaw court at Red Oak and, according to Choctaw tradition, was then released and told to return for execution on November 4, 1894. The sixty-four-year-old farmer married the seventeen-year-old daughter of his white sharecropper, honeymooned in McAlester, and conducted business as usual until the Day of Atonement. Notified that his time was up, Lewis overruled advice from his white wife and family to flee the country, calmly saddled his horse and rode to Red Oak. Rejecting their pleas, Lewis commented, "White men would never understand, but I have to go."

Quietly keeping his rendezvous with death, Lewis walked serenely to the site with his friends and presented himself for termination. The execution went awry, however, when a nervous member of the firing squad placed the target over the right side of his chest and the bullet missed his heart. After several minutes of watching him suffer, a posse member mercifully placed a handkerchief over his mouth and nose and smothered him to death.[189]

Congress used the violence in the nations as an excuse for government intervention. On March 3, 1893, a proposal was passed that extended allotments to Indian Territory. The law allowed President Grover Cleveland to appoint a commission of three men to make arrangements with the Five Civilized Tribes to give up tribal titles and accept allotments. The duties of the commission were, in effect, to prepare the Indian Territory for statehood.

The President appointed Senator Henry Laurens Dawes as Chairman of the Commission along with Meredith H. Kidd of Indiana and Archibald S. McKennon of Arkansas as his colleagues. A congressman with thirty-six years experience in Washington, eighteen of them in the United States Senate, Dawes was seventy-seven years old with a long acquaintance with Indian affairs. Officially, the commission was designated the Commission to the Five Civilized Tribes but was more commonly called the Dawes Commission. On December 8, 1893, the first meeting was held in Washington, and then the commission moved to Muskogee to begin work.

Just the news of the establishment of the agency stimulated another run into Indian Territory. In 1894, Senator Henry M. Teller reported that the Indian court systems were being overwhelmed by the chaos generated by thousands of white intruders pouring into Indian Territory. By the end of the year, 250,000 non-citizens had crossed into the nations knowing that an opening was coming whether the tribes approved or not. The whites were determined to be in position to take advantage of the situation.

On January 24, 1894, the commission addressed the Tribal Council at Tvshkahomma but encountered opposition from several different fronts. Since some Choctaw did not even want to discuss allotments and refused to come to a meeting on the subject, the chief obligingly arranged for a guided tour of the Nation as a courtesy to the commissioners. Supposedly sent along for protection, in reality, the three appointed escorts were given orders to advise the people to have nothing to do with any proposals from the commissioners.

The commission adopted various campaign tactics to convert the Choctaw, but nothing seemed to work. On April 23, a formal, written proposal was sent to the Choctaw Council and the Council did not even bother to reply. In October, the commission had thousands of handbills printed for distribution and advertisements placed in local newspapers, but all were accepted without comment or acknowledgment. Finally, an intertribal conference with the other tribes led to the flat pronouncement that the tribes wished no further negotiations with the commission. In November, the members of the commission, realizing there was little else to do, returned to Washington to report conditions in the territory were intolerable and in need of immediate reform, but the tribes refused to admit the situation or even recognize the validity of the commission.

On May 7, 1895, Chief Jefferson Gardner announced his personal resistance to the government's propositions and agreed to a meeting of the tribes in Fort Smith to present a united front against the commission. About the same time Choctaw National Secretary Jacob B. Jackson, concerned that some Choctaw were beginning to discuss the proposals positively, in particular, Green McCurtain, who had publicly endorsed the allotment idea, declared that he was attending a conference in Fort Gibson to help organize opposition to the commission. Jackson stated that another meeting would be held in Antlers on May 29.

On October 29, after a lengthy correspondence between governmental representatives and a Choctaw committee headed by Olosachubbee, three members of the Dawes Commission traveled again to Tvshkahomma to present a verbal appeal to the Tribal Council. Written assurances arrived the next day from officials in Fort Smith pledging that the commission only intended the best for the tribe, but the Council still refused to accept any proposals. Instead, a bill passed the Council Senate with only one negative vote making it a capital offense to attempt any overthrow of the Choctaw government, to hold lands in severalty, or to betray Choctaw land by allowing any to fall under the control of a foreign power. The proposed law would be enforced by a prison term of six to twelve months and a fine from $1,000-10,000 for the first offense and death for the second. Although the House refused to pass the bill, the argument graphically illustrated the division within the tribe over the Dawes Commission.[190]

Actually, the debate was an academic one. Powerful pressure from proponents of allotment had already convinced several prominent leaders of the Tribal Council that it was time to accept the inevitable. Alex R. Durant, Wilson N. Jones, Peter Hudson, Wesley Anderson, Green McCurtain, Allen Wright, and his son, Dr. Eliphalet Nott Wright had reached the conclusion that coming to an arrangement with the commission was the best, if not the only, way for the Choctaw Nation.

Dr. Wright was a typical mixed blood supporter of the issue. The eldest son of Reverend Allen and Harriet Mitchell Wright was born near Armstrong Academy in 1858. His father named him for Eliphalet Nott, president of Union College of Schenectady, New York. In 1878, Wright enrolled at Union but grew interested in medicine and transferred to Albany Medical College where he graduated in 1884. Returning to Indian Territory, Dr. Wright opened a successful clinic and practice at Boggy Depot. After another year of postgraduate study in New York City, he opened an office in Atoka. Instrumental in getting a law to establish a board of medical examiners for the Nation when he learned there were doctors practicing medicine that had never even attended school, Wright helped organize the Indian Territory Medical Association in 1889. In 1903, he served as its president.

Another interest for Dr. Wright was the development of the oil industry in the Choctaw Nation. In 1884, along with his father, A. R. Durant, and J. F. McCurtain, he organized the Choctaw Oil and Refining Company. Serving as president of the company, Wright sank an oil well twelve miles west of Atoka in 1887. Drilling for 1,400 feet, the first test drill for oil in the state, the company found traces of gas and oil but did not make any big strikes.

In 1895, Dr. Wright ran for a seat in the Council House on a platform of coming to an agreement with the Dawes Commission. One year later, he was selected chairman of the Indian Territory Republican Convention at Muskogee and named as a delegate to the Republican National Convention to vote for William McKinley. As one of the authors of the platform for the "Tuskahoma Party" in the chief's election in the same year, Wright served as campaign manager for the party candidate, Green McCurtain.[191]

The opposition party, the National Party, better known as the Buzzards, split over Chief Gardner's refusal to deal forcibly with the commission after his election in 1894, but a branch of the party at Tvshkahomma changed its name to the Independent Party and nominated Gardner for election to a second anti-allotment term in the fall of 1895. In February 1896, an opposition branch composed mostly of full bloods met in Atoka and nominated the National

Secretary, Jacob B. Jackson. In March, the Progressive Party, popularly called the Hawks, called for an agreement with the commission and met at Talihina to nominate Gilbert Dukes. His political opponents met again in May, however, and nominated McCurtain as head of the Tuskahoma Party. In August, McCurtain received 1,405 of the votes cast in the election, Jackson tallied 1,195, Dukes won 613, and Gardner, 596.

Chief McCurtain's first action was to replace Jackson as national secretary with Solomon J. Homer. He then led a delegation to McAlester to meet with the Dawes Commission on November 11. After the meeting, the delegation returned to the General Council with the recommendation that the Choctaw enter into negotiations. The major reason for the advice was information that Congress had enlarged the authority and scope of the commission with permission to complete rolls of the Indians in the territory on June 10, 1896. The Curtis Act had been introduced and passed in the House at the same time.

After the national election in 1896, a new negotiator was also appointed for the Dawes Commission. Dawes had served as chairman since 1893, but the elderly ex-senator spent most of his time at home leaving the real work to Vice-Chairman Tams Bixby. Born in 1856, Bixby dropped out of school, worked as a baker, a newsman, hotelkeeper, and publisher before becoming an influential Minnesota politician as the chairman of his state Republican Party in 1884. Later serving as secretary to three governors, he was rewarded for his support with an appointment to the commission. On July 1, 1897, Bixby and Thomas B. Needles of Illinois, a United States Marshal in Muskogee, replaced Alexander Brooks Montgomery of Kentucky and Thomas Banks Cabaniss of Georgia, who had served since 1895. Dawes lent his name to the commission and wrote letters of advice from his home in Pittsfield, Massachusetts but otherwise left the work to Bixby, who was officially appointed chair after Senator Dawes' death.

The commission labored many long, hard years with controversy over almost every decision, not counting the many arguments within the committee. By 1900, Bixby's colleagues were even drafting complaints to Secretary of Interior Ethan Allen Hitchcock against him. Despite protests against the Chairman Bixby's "most insatiate lust of power," the work progressed, although sometimes much more slowly than anyone expected. The commission was still working away eight years later. On June 30, 1907, Bixby retired to serve as the publisher of the Muskogee *Phoenix* and the *Times Democrat*.[192]

Green McCurtain's elevation to the office of chief seemed to signal a change in attitude as breakthroughs were seen after the summer election. Chief McCurtain quickly organized a group to go to Washington to begin negotiations with the commission, and delegates were selected and given

$1,000 each for their services. The three sent to Washington received $3,500 each, and the Chief was given an expense account of $1,500. On April 1, 1897, less than a month after the next round of meetings had been arranged with the commission, Green McCurtain, J. S. Standley, N. B. Ainsworth, Ben Hampton, Wesley Anderson, Amos Henry, D. C. Garland, and Reverend Alexander S. Williams, a Methodist preacher until his death and burial east of Golden in 1925, signed the Atoka Agreement providing for the final allotment of Choctaw lands on April 23. The agreement added provisions allowing the Choctaw to reserve town sites and mineral rights and declaring that the tribal government would continue to operate until a specified time set by the federal government.

The agreement was made with Acting Commission Chairman General Frank Crawford Armstrong. Born in Skullyville, the son of F. W. Armstrong, he was the only native born member of the Dawes Commission. The agreement was ratified at a special session of the Choctaw Council by a vote of thirteen-six in the House and six-four in the Senate. After the Chickasaw signed the accord, all the other tribes made arrangements to take allotments as well.[193]

Procrastination by the tribes had already caused Congress to pass legislation to force allotment upon them. Sponsored by Senator Charles Curtis of Kansas, a law had been approved to permit termination of tribal ownership of land whether the Indians agreed or not. On June 28, 1898, the Curtis Act, virtually another Organic Act for Indian Territory, authorized the Dawes Commission to proceed with allotment as soon as rolls could be completed. The Curtis Act, purposely aimed at complete destruction of the Indian cultural and political integrity, provided that each Indian would receive an allotment of 160 acres that would be prohibited from sale during the allottee's lifetime, but any additional land could be disposed of after twenty-five years. The law then disbanded tribal governments, forbade Indian religion, and discouraged native arts and crafts.

Although the Curtis Act had not made provision for the appraisal or grading of the Indian lands, the Choctaw, while giving their permission for the division of their empire of almost twelve million acres, had retained the right of classification of their land before its allotment by the Atoka Agreement. When this survey was completed, the total amount of land to be divided for the Choctaw and Chickasaw tribes amounted to 11,653,151.71 acres. On December 5, 1902, the Dawes Commission set an arbitrary value on the land according to the different classes at prices that ranged from six dollars and fifty cents an acre for land in Class 1 to twenty-five cents per acre for Class 10. The size of the allotments ranged from 160.19 acres for all first class land to 4,165.12 for all in the tenth category. The Choctaw portion of this was

6,953,048 acres, and when rated according to physical features, each Choctaw was entitled to 320.39 acres with a value of $1,040. 28. Each Choctaw freedman was entitled to forty acres valued at $130.16. In 1903, a completed geological survey of the mineral lands showed 444,863.03 acres set aside as coal and asphalt deposits.[194]

The Choctaw school system was also taken over by the federal government under the Curtis Act. Soon after its passage John D. Benedict of Illinois, appointed as Federal Superintendent of Schools for the Five Tribes, opened an office in Muskogee and recommended the institution of summer normal school programs to raise the level of teacher preparation in the nations. In June 1900, the first Choctaw normal was conducted at Tuskahoma Institute with a fee of twelve dollars for board, lodging, and salaries of the normal instructors for a four-week school term. E. T. McArthur, the federal supervisor of the Choctaw schools, was in charge with Benjamin S. Coppock and Benedict as instructional aides. While little attention was given to methodology or teaching procedures, about one hundred teachers attended the entire four weeks, spending their time reviewing textbooks and preparing to take examinations for teaching certificates. In 1901, the next year's session was held at Jones Academy with seventy-three teachers the first day and one hundred at the end of the week. Most of their time was again spent drilling for certificate examinations since teachers receiving first grade certificates were those with the higher grades while the lower scorers were given second and third grade certificates or failed.

After 1902, more attention was devoted to pedagogy. A demonstration class of primary orphan boys was brought from Armstrong Academy and used to illustrate techniques of teaching and work. According to reports of the meeting, the teachers received better training than teachers in the public school systems in nearby Kansas. The institutes were continuously held at Jones Academy until 1907. By then, more than 270 were in annual attendance at the sessions.[195]

The Choctaw courts, in the meantime, had also been taken over by the federal government. In March 1895, two United States courts were created for the Indian Territory with full authority over all major offenses. The final case involving capital punishment with Choctaw jurisdiction resulted from the murder by William Going of his uncle near Eagletown in 1896. Tried and found guilty, the murderer was given the death sentence on August 6, 1897. The sentence was delayed when the condemned killer escaped jail for a time, but after his recapture, the execution was carried out on July 13, 1899.[196]

The most difficult task for the Dawes Commission turned out to be making up tribal rolls because full bloods did not understand nor desire to be registered while non-Indians tried to get enrolled to qualify for the land division. Complicated by the freedmen and Choctaw from Mississippi who were entitled to be listed on the rolls, years of work were consumed by the issue of who was Indian and who was not. Finally, the commission compiled a list of 7,087 Choctaw full bloods, 10,401 mixed bloods, for a total of 17,488, and 1,651 whites and 6,029 freedmen for a total number of 25,168 Choctaw, and 1,660 Mississippi Choctaw. The figures were gathered by hundreds of clerks and attorneys hired by the commission, including Charles H. Sawyer, a Connecticut lawyer, who accepted a position on the commission in 1900.[197]

The work of the commission progressed steadily until a Creek named Chitto Harjo, popularly known as Crazy Snake, because of his use of a coiled snake as the symbol of his movement, organized a protest against the allotments within the Creek Nation known as the "Snake Rebellion." Spreading the reaction to other tribes, Harjo's supporters insisted that the Dawes Commission had no authority to force the tribes to relinquish tribal lands let alone tribal sovereignty. Harjo personally recruited followers, primarily full bloods, from the other Five Civilized Tribes to form a "Snake Band" that embraced the "old ways" and opposed accepting allotments of any kind.

The Choctaw Snake Band, numbering about 600, elected Jacob B. Jackson as their leader at a meeting at Smithville. An educated, tribally prominent Choctaw who twice narrowly missed election to the position of chief, Jackson, trusted completely by the full blood faction of the tribe, created a "Snake Council," composed of J. C. Folsom, Saul Folsom, S. E. Coe, and Willis Jones at his store in Hochatown, where most of the activities of the Choctaw Snakes were planned and set in motion.

Jackson, an atypical full blood, was a college graduate, a Baptist, a Mason, a man of unquestionable integrity, and a teetotaler, who had distinguished himself among the whites. As a student at Roanoke College, Virginia, he had joined a literary society and been given an opportunity to deliver an address to the group in his Choctaw language but refused, although agreeing to make one in English. When he made his presentation, his audience was surprised as he spoke in Choctaw and then switched to English after a few minutes. His explanation for not making the address in Choctaw was obvious. No one would have understood it. Although it might be a beautiful language, it was necessary to present it to people who could understand it, according to Jackson.

The political debates over allotments grew more heated as the Tuskahoma Party nominated McCurtain for a second term while the Union Party selected Wilson N. Jones as its candidate in 1898. The National Party did not bother to nominate a candidate for chief, but the Snake Band numbering more than

2,000 reactivated the National Party two years later to nominate Jackson who had confirmed his control over the rebellion in 1897-98. Leading a group of followers to Mexico to discuss the possibility of relocating the Choctaw from the United States to lands across the Rio Grande, Jackson had achieved promises allowing self-government over a region to be called the "Choctaw Nation of Mexico" from the ruling Porfirio Diaz dictatorship.

In 1900, Jackson was the National Party candidate, Dr. Eliphalet N. Wright ran on the Union Party ticket, and McCurtain, limited by the Constitution of 1860 to two consecutive terms, turned control of the Tuskahoma Party over to Gilbert W. Dukes. When the Tuskahoma party claimed victory, the Nationals were so upset they refused to run a candidate or participate in the next election.

In 1902, the Tuskahoma Party abandoned Chief Dukes, however, and named McCurtain as its candidate. The chief was so angered by the insult of only serving for one term that he threw his support to the Progressive Party candidate, Thomas W. Hunter. As revenge for not being nominated for a second term, Dukes allied with Hunter and allowed him to take the chief's seat without counting the ballots. Voting, as customary, was on the third Wednesday in August, but Dukes ordered the votes locked in a shed, appointed Hunter to the position of Principal Chief, and called the Council into special session to confirm his actions.

Not surprisingly, both sides threatened violence. When Hunter took over the capital, his forces requested troops from Fort Reno to keep the peace and a company of black soldiers was sent, but Indian agent, J. Blair Schoenfelt, supporting McCurtain's side, also asked Washington for troops, resulting in more being sent in. Finally, a compromise was worked out whereby both sides agreed to allow the votes to be counted. In the last free election for the position of Principal Chief for more than half a century, McCurtain was confirmed as the winner with 1,645 votes to Hunter's 956.[198]

Meanwhile, in July 1902, a Supplemental Agreement was negotiated with the Choctaw and Chickasaw and ratified by the Tribal Council that set the method of determining the citizenship rolls, the status of the Chickasaw freedmen, and the rights of the Mississippi enrollees. It also made special provisions for leasing the coal and asphalt lands reserved from allotment, directing that payments be made equally to both tribes in a ration of three-fourths for the Choctaw to one-fourth for the Chickasaw. Afterwards, several large tracts of coal lands were sold or leased to mining companies operating in Oklahoma while another valuable property, 1,373,324 acres of timber land, was sold to large timber companies.

The issue that arose to cause the most trouble was the enrollment of the Mississippi Choctaw who could not be persuaded to remove because of old fears, an impasse graphically illustrated by Charles H. Sawyer in a series of articles in issues of *Twin Territories: The Indian Magazine*. The only periodical founded by an Indian, twenty-year-old Ora V. Eddleman, *Twin Territories* was published from 1898 to 1903 in Muskogee as an outlet for articles on Indian issues. In 1902, the magazine published Sawyer's work on the commission meetings in Mississippi. He reported that some Mississippi Choctaw had agreed to move, but most remained as frightened as their ancestors seventy-five years earlier.

In 1903, the commission, working diligently to protect the Choctaw whenever possible, successfully arranged cheap transportation with the railroads for the Mississippi Choctaw. In April, they were taken to Ardmore and then to Atoka where a land office was opened for them to file on their lands. Although speculators, real estate dealers, and attorneys lined up to take advantage of them again, most of these immigrants were successful in filing for land east and south of Atoka in the Bennington area.[199]

Persuading the Oklahoma Choctaw to accept their allotments proved an equally intricate, daunting task. In 1916, Lacy Pierce Bobo, later State Senator from Latimer County, reported that the typical response to the opening was the one at the Choctaw Land Office in Atoka. In April 1903, all the preparations were made for the swift selections of their 320 acres, but the Choctaw simply refused to come in. Despite provisions that specified the filings be done over a period of eighteen months, the time period expired with the Choctaw simply refusing to comply with the rules forcing the commission to proceed with the process on its own.

Bobo, an employee of the United States Interior Department, was appointed head of a party to enroll the Choctaw but only received complaints and threats to his overtures, sometimes even encountering violent responses from the "Snakes." One recalcitrant Choctaw near Antlers ordered the commission representatives off his farm with a shotgun. Upon the party's return to town, the Choctaw interpreter quit without bothering to collect his salary.

Meanwhile, Jacob Jackson and the Snakes pursued their campaign to remove the Choctaw Nation to Mexico. In early 1906, armed with petitions signed by more than 2,000 Choctaw, mostly full bloods, Jackson took his appeal to Washington for a personal appearance before Congress. His simple, eloquent plea was that:

"Surely, a race of people, desiring to preserve the integrity of that race, who love it by reason of its traditions and their common ancestors and blood, who are proud of the fact that they belong to it may be permitted to protect themselves, if in no other way, by emigration. Our educated people inform us that the white man come to this country to avoid conditions which to him were not as bad as the present conditions are to us; that he went across the great ocean and sought new homes in order to avoid things which were to him distasteful and wrong.

All we ask is that we may be permitted to exercise the same privilege. We do not ask any aid from the Government of the United States in so doing. We do ask that we may be permitted, in a proper way, by protecting our own, to dispose of that which the Government says is ours, and which has been given us over our protest against the distribution, to the end that another home may be furnished and another nation established.

Because the white man does not want the Indian anymore than we want him, and by carrying out the plan he will get the land that he wants-the Indian land. We will leave and trouble him no longer. We believe that the Great Father of all men created the Indian to fill a proper place in this world. That as an Indian he had certain rights, among which is a right to exist as a race, and that in the protection of that right it is our belief that we are fulfilling the purpose of the Divine Creator of mankind."[200]

In essence, Jackson argued that the full bloods were not ready to live as American citizens. He pointed out that they had voluntarily withdrawn from the white settled areas of their own country to live a more communal life in the mountains, that they were too poor to farm large sections of land, that they were at the mercy of unscrupulous whites who would take their lands away from them once allotment was done, that they did not know enough English or white laws to protect themselves, and that they did not want the whites around to take advantage of them. He concluded with the sad declaration, "We do not know what to do. We are helpless. We want to preserve the integrity of our race."[201]

Jackson proposed that the federal government purchase the land instead of allotting it and allow the Choctaw to use the proceeds to buy land in Mexico. Not even bothering to respond politely, the incredulous congressmen ridiculed Jackson as merely an ignorant Indian and sent him on his way.

Some tribal members took an equally pernicious view of his proposals. Jackson returned to his home with little support from his own people, took an allotment near Hochatown, and lived out his remaining years quietly. The *Atoka Indian Citizen* editorialized that "Jackson has despaired of ever being elected governor in this nation, and now he wants to lead his followers to Old Mexico where they can grapple with smallpox, starvation, and him as governor. Of the three disorders we would prefer to be affected with the two first at one and the same time, than the last one alone."[202]

Five companies of militia were called out to stop the revolt with warrants issued for the leader of the Snake Rebellion, Chitto Harjo, in McIntosh County. Harjo was shot by the posse of deputies sent to arrest him for threats and intimidations against his people for filing on claims. He was fired on without

warning and wounded in the hip. Charles Coker, his lieutenant, managed to help him escape by killing two deputies before being shot to death. Harjo, helped by a Choctaw friend, Daniel Bob, took refuge with Charles Babb, about four miles south of Smithville, where he lived until his death in 1911. After the elimination of their leaders, the Snakes were told that they would be given individual allotments whether they wanted them or not. They finally resigned themselves to the inevitable.[203]

The date set for the end of Choctaw sovereignty was March 4, 1906. Supposedly, protection for the allotments had been accomplished by then because no land could be sold legally before this time, while the McCumber Amendment, passed on April 25, 1906, restricted the entire allotment of full bloods for twenty-five years. These efforts proved grossly ineffective, however. In 1908, Oklahoma politicians, greedily craving more taxable lands, persuaded Congress to enact a law declaring all unrestricted lands eligible for tax purposes, effectively canceling all restraints on the sale and taxation of land allotted to members of the Five Civilized Tribes of less than one-half Indian blood. The same law removed restrictions upon the death of the allottee except in certain cases such as large estates inherited by full bloods that required approval before being sold by probate courts.

A further abuse arose when all matters of guardianship of minors and administration of estates were removed from the jurisdiction of the Choctaw courts and turned over to the federal courts. Federal policy ruled that no Choctaw parents could act for their own children unless first approved as competent by the courts, and if parents were ruled incompetent, a guardian should be appointed. The decree left the individual Indian little option and opened the gates for the whites grafters. For years the country was known as the "Land of Guardians," because unscrupulous whites besieged an Indian that lay near death or his heirs requesting appointments as guardians. In 1908, Chief McCurtain said, "It makes me sad indeed when I consider that the helpless among our people seem to be regarded as legitimate objects of prey, and we are made the subject of the most shameful robberies."[204]

The imbroglio caused many to sell their allotments for a fraction of their value while others were willed away to whites for lifetime monthly pensions of ten or twenty dollars, and the court-appointed guardians leased the allotments of their minor charges for scandalous prices. One discovered to have 177 minors in his charge boasted of making $50,000 in a few months. Legislation in the 1920s attempted to stop the abuse by extending the restrictions, but the damage had already been done. By 1973, nine of every ten allotments had been lost, and few Choctaw had their original allotment.

As the Dawes Commission neared the end of its work, the discussion arose anew of the possibility of single or double statehood for Indian Territory,

a question that had been debated by citizens of both Oklahoma and Indian Territories since 1890. In the summer of 1905, the proponents of double statehood had their closest opportunity when leaders of the Five Civilized Tribes attempted to create a separate state for their former nations.

Two years earlier, Chief McCurtain had met with executives of the Five Civilized Tribes at Eufaula and agreed to call a constitutional convention, but the meeting was postponed until the national political situation settled down. Theodore Roosevelt, who had served out the term of assassinated President William McKinley, ran on his own in 1904, but when he made no mention of Oklahoma statehood during the campaign, the Indian leaders proceeded to call for a convention to meet in Muskogee in 1905.[205]

On August 21, the convention for separate statehood for Indian Territory opened with Charles N. Haskell, a railroad promoter, asked to serve as its chairman by Chief McCurtain and Chief John F. Brown of the Seminole Nation. Haskell declined in favor of Pleasant Porter, Chief of the Creek, and Alexander Posey, as secretary, to give the appearance of the convention being an Indian movement, but Haskell agreed to serve as vice-chairman. Held in the Hinton Theater, the meeting was attended by more than sixty delegates from Indian Territory.

The President of Henry Kendall College, Reverend A. Grant Evans, provided the invocation beginning the sessions. Other prominent leaders at the meeting were William C. Rogers, Chief of the Cherokee, and William H. Murray, representing the Chickasaw. Green's son, D. C. McCurtain, was elected temporary chair for the nomination of officers. Chairman Porter succeeded him and Haskell was elected vice-chair. Robert L. Owen, another representative at the convention, reported that Solomon J. Homer, a full blood Choctaw graduate from Harvard, made one of the best speeches that he had ever heard delivered on the subject of single statehood for Indian Territory. After the proposals were all concluded, two weeks of adjournment followed to allow a committee to draw up a constitution for the proposed state of Sequoyah.

Reconvened on September 6, delegates presented the convention with a prepared constitution for a new state of forty-eight counties with Fort Gibson selected as the site for the state capitol. Reverend Evans also presented a proposed state seal from copy drawn by Charles H. Sawyer. Adopted by the convention, it served as a pattern for the later state constitution seal suggested by Choctaw delegate, Gabe E. Parker.

Haskell, Murray, and others carried the Sequoyah Constitution to Washington, while a nationwide election certified it for ratification, but there was never any real chance for its adoption. President Roosevelt and the Republican-dominated Congress, knowing that the new state would be a

stronghold for the Democratic Party, wanted single statehood for Oklahoma and Indian Territory. In reality, the effort at double statehood only delayed passage of the Enabling Act in 1906 providing for admission of Oklahoma as the 46th state in the Union.[206]

The Choctaw Republic ended in 1907, but the tribe, in danger of losing its identity, struggled to remain independent. Determined to return to a status of self-determination, Choctaw leaders sought every available means to keep local sovereignty alive. Appointed by Washington, the tribal chiefs fought long and hard to maintain tribal integrity. They had been defeated, but not destroyed.[207]

CHAPTA AUAH ACHVFFA

~ CHAPTER ELEVEN ~

"THE REMOVAL CHIEFS OF THE CHOCTAW"

Alfred Wade

Tandy Walker

Basil LeFlore

George Hudson

Chapter Eleven

In Mississippi, the Choctaw Nation consisted of three separate political divisions each governed by a District Chief, a system carried to Indian Territory where it existed until 1860. The Choctaw then turned to a governmental arrangement with a single executive called a "Principal Chief." The administrative title continued until 1983. It was ultimately replaced by the designation Mi̲ko, "Chief."

Western District Chief, Apuckshunubbee, served from 1802 until his accidental death en route to Washington in 1824. Robert Cole replaced him to discuss making another treaty after Doak's Stand but only served a year and a half. His nephew, Greenwood LeFlore, succeeded him and signed the Treaty of Dancing Rabbit Creek in 1830. In 1809, the middle division Chief was Moshulatubbee, who succeeded his father, Mi̲ko Homastubbee, in one of the few cases of father-son heredity in the tribe, but Moshulatubbee resigned the office when David Folsom took over by election in April 1826. Folsom remained chief until he emigrated to Doaksville in March 1830. He died on September 27, 1847.

Pushmataha, the celebrated leader of the southwestern division, was buried in Washington. Succeeded by his nephew, Oklahoma, who did not serve long, the United States government recognized General Humming Bird as Pushmataha's legitimate successor. Having served with General Anthony Wayne in the Indian wars in Ohio, Humming Bird was a hero of the early Republic and was awarded a silver medal with a picture of George Washington shaking hands with an Indian in 1794. He remained chief until succeeded by another of Pushmataha's nephews, Nitakechi, in 1828.

In 1826, the western division elected Greenwood LeFlore for a four-year term to succeed Cole. The southwest district selected Samuel Garland as their chief for a four- year term at the same time but both Nitakechi and Humming Bird refused to acknowledge him. In the spring of 1830, LeFlore called for a council to talk of removal, and Folsom and Sam Garland resigned their offices as District Chiefs on the grounds they were elected to oppose removal. At this point, LeFlore prepared the Treaty of Dancing Rabbit Creek, and Folsom and Garland signed it but only as common warriors rather than chiefs. As a result the United States Senate refused to ratify it. In September 1830, federal authorities recognized LeFlore, Moshulatubbee, and Nitakechi as chiefs to make the treaty legitimate. While on an inspection tour of the Choctaw Nation in the West, LeFlore's nephew, George Washington Harkins, was elected to succeed him.

In 1830, an attempt was made to name Joel H. Nail as the successor to Moshulatubbee, but Secretary of War John H. Eaton refused to accept it. On January 16, 1831, the Chief offered to resign in favor of his nephew, Peter Pitchlynn, but again the United States refused to accept the arrangement. As the immigration continued on through 1833, the only recognized leader from 1830 to 1834 was southwest District Chief, Nitakechi.

Without consulting LeFlore, Nitakechi and Moshulatubbee, while still in Mississippi, agreed to separate the Choctaw Nation in the West into three geographic-political divisions. One was the Moshulatubbee, or First District, located between the Arkansas and Canadian Rivers on the north, by the Winding Stair Mountains on the south, and by the state of Arkansas on the east. The Second District, first called the Red River District, then Okla Falaya, and later the Apuckshunubbee District, was situated east of the Kiamichi River, south of Winding Stair Mountain, and extended north from the Red River. The Third District, or Pushmataha District, was west of the Kiamichi, north of Red River, and south of the Canadian, with the western limit being the United States-Mexican border. The purpose of this agreement was to allow the transfer of people in Mississippi to the same territory as they were at home, but removal problems resulted in the destruction of the clans as the Choctaw scattered over the entire Nation. The chiefs made it to their designated districts as planned, but their people did not.

In October 1834, Moshulatubbee took charge of the First District, Captain Thomas LeFlore, the first cousin of Greenwood, assumed charge of the Second or Apuckshunnubbee District for four years, and Nitakechi, the Third District. Thomas, the son of Michael LeFlore, lived near Wheelock until his death in 1850. In 1836, Moshulatubbee died of smallpox, and Joseph Kincaid was selected to fill out his unexpired term. Kincaid's brother Robert had been a student at Choctaw Academy and removed to near Shady Point.

The site selected for the first capital of the new Nation by the chiefs was a mile and a half west of Tvshkahomma at a location called Nvnih Waiya, named to honor the beloved mound in Mississippi. Built according to Article XX of the Dancing Rabbit Creek Treaty that provided for a Council House at a conveniently located central point for the entire nation, a house for each chief was also constructed along with a church for each of the three districts.

In 1834, Nitakechi was elected chief of the Third or Pushmataha District for another four-year term. He was followed by Pierre Juzan, Jr., the son of Frenchman, Pierre "Peter" Gabriel Juzan, a student at Catholic Academy in New Orleans, who was married to a niece of Pushmataha and a sister to Oklahoma. Captain Pierre had led a force of Choctaw against the British in the Battle of New Orleans in 1815. Given the problem of stopping the British attack coming by way of the swamp, the weakest sector of the American lines, Juzan and sixty warriors had held it against an overwhelming number of British forces. Attacking from the rear and harassing the English from the sides, the Choctaw warriors kept the British nervous and ineffective in the battle, killing and wounding more than fifty of the "Redcoats." Moving his family to Hugo and then south of Bennington on the Red River during Removal, Pierre, Jr. died in office in 1841. Isaac Folsom completed his unexpired term and won a full four years on his own in 1842.

In the election of 1838, John McKinney, a lawyer and tribal officer, took over as Chief of the First (Moshulatubbee) District for a four-year term. Upon his death McKinney was buried about a mile east of Howe on the Fort Smith-Fort Towson Military Road. Elected chief of the Second (Apuckshunnubbee) District in 1838, James Fletcher lived on Rock Creek near Spencerville. On one occasion when he was absent from a Council meeting, he was represented as chief by full blood William Winans, a Methodist preacher who lived south of Stanley on the old military road.

In 1842, Nathaniel Folsom, Jr. was elected Chief of the First (Moshulatubbee) District. Thomas LeFlore was elected in the Second (Apuckshunnubbee) District and succeeded himself in 1846. Nitakechi was elected chief of the Third (Pushmataha) District but died in office of acute pleurisy on a visit to his brother's funeral in Lauderdale County, Mississippi, on November 22, 1845. Nitakechi, (meaning "hold the day") was the last to have the Choctaw name as his son took the name, Henry Groves. Silas D. Fisher, the son of Joseph Fisher, a white settler who lived in present Bryan County, succeeded Nitakechi.

In 1846, Peter Folsom, the son of Daniel Folsom, was elected Chief of the First (Moshulatubbee) District. Peter, a former student at the Choctaw Academy, represented the tribe as a member of Peter P. Pitchlynn's delegation in Washington to discuss the Net Proceeds Claims in 1853. In 1861, he served as President of the Choctaw Senate and as the First District Trustee, 1863-64. He died in 1885.

In 1850, the Choctaw governmental system was reorganized and the capital moved to Doaksville. In that year, Cornelius McCurtain was elected Chief of the First (Moshulatubbee) District for four years. Born in Mississippi in 1803, he moved to Indian Territory to settle near Fort Coffee in 1833. The father of three later chiefs, Jackson, Edmund, and Green, the elder McCurtain served as a member of the Council in 1844, 1846, and 1855. David McCoy succeeded him and served until 1857.

George Washington Harkins was elected Chief of the Second (Apuckshunnubbee) District in 1850. A former student at the Choctaw Academy and the nephew of Greenwood LeFlore, Harkins had been elected in Mississippi but had not been recognized in 1830. In 1846, he was elected as a member of the Council and later moved up to the position of chief. In 1854, he was elected again, staying until the Skullyville Constitution was adopted in 1857.

In 1850, George Folsom, son of David Folsom, was elected chief of the Third (Pushmataha) District. Educated and ordained as a Cumberland Presbyterian preacher in Georgia, Folsom served until 1854. Previously, he had worked as one of a nine-member Board of Trustees for the tribal neighborhood school system. Nicholas Cochanaur succeeded him, serving until 1857.

In 1857, a new constitution was adopted at Skullyville that abolished the positions of District Chiefs and replaced them with a "Governor" for the Nation. In October, Alfred Wade was elected Governor, but matters were complicated when a Council meeting in May at Doaksville refused to accept him. Born in Mississippi and educated at Choctaw Academy, Alfred, the son of John Wade, emigrated with his family, including six brothers, Henry, Alex, Jerry Ellis, Cunningham, and Kennedy, to Indian Territory, settling east of Talihina in LeFlore County. Sworn in for two years at Boggy Depot, he resigned the office because of the controversy over the Skullyville Constitution. In 1858, the majority of the Nation wanted to restore the system of District Chiefs and Wade abdicated in favor of Tandy Walker, Chairman of the Constitutional Convention. Wade died in 1868.[208]

Walker, a resident of Skullyville and former member of the Choctaw Council at Fort Towson in 1855, called on the people to vote on whether to accept the Skullyville Constitution, the Doaksville Constitution, or to make a completely new one. Although his term was already ended, Walker held elections for the next convention in August 1859. The following year a majority voted to hold a new convention at Doaksville.

Many Choctaw families had settled in the Skullyville area with the Walkers, including the McLeans, Folsoms, Wards, and McCurtains. Skullyville, so named because the annuity payments were made there, dated from the time Major Francis W. Armstrong ordered an agency building erected about fifteen miles west of Fort Smith in 1832. The town had served for years as the capital of the Moshulatubbee District, and the chief had lived there with 500 of his neighbors until his death from smallpox. Just southwest of the town was Charby Prairie, one of the great Choctaw ball fields where Catlin painted the game that lasted all day and was attended by more than 3,000 people in 1834.[209]

In August 1859, Basil LeFlore was elected chief and took office in October but only served for one year to preside over the transfer of power to the new constitution. The son of Louis LeFlore and Nancy Cravatt, Basil had three brothers, Greenwood, William, and Ben, five sisters, and two half-brothers, Forbis and Jackson. After a time as a student at Choctaw Academy, Basil immigrated to Indian Territory and established a home east of Fort Towson near Clear Creek. A first cousin of Thomas LeFlore, Basil acted as his private secretary, since LeFlore lacked a formal education when Thomas was chief of the Second District from 1834 to 1838 and 1842 to 1850. Basil also served as the secretary and treasurer of the Second District from 1834 to 1857. When Alfred Wade requested reports from the officials from each district, Basil was the only one who bothered to respond with his report. In 1866, he was elected treasurer of the Nation serving two-year terms until 1871 when he was elected auditor where he served until 1885. Basil later moved to near Goodland where he died.

In 1859, Lewis Cass was elected District Chief of the First (Moshulatubbee) District as one of three sub-chiefs and was succeeded by Reuben Perry, 1860-62. In the same year, the uneducated full blood, Hot-abi ("To look for and Kill") from near Pickens, in McCurtain County, was elected District Chief of the Second (Apuckshunnubbee) District. Ahulitubbee ("To catch him and kill him") succeeded him. The uneducated chief lived near Wheelock and was the father of Henry Clay, an educated attorney, whose son, Abner, attended Roanoke College in Virginia. In 1859, Isaac Achukmatubbee was elected as the Third District (Pushmataha) Chief. In 1860, William Lucas followed him. Lucas lived near Armstrong Academy and died in 1875. Isaac Folsom was district chief of the Third District in 1861.

The office of District Chief was restored in 1860. An incomplete list of the men who have held this position included in the First District, Kenney McCurtain, 1859; Olasichubbi, 1877; William M. Anderson, 1888-1890; James Bond, 1891-93; Jackson Kamplelubbi, 1893-96; and Sam Hicks, 1896. The Second District Chiefs were Captain Nanomuntubbi, 1874-1880, a good orator who lived and died four miles east of old Spencer Academy on the Choctaw-Pushmataha line; James Wright, 1881, who served in Nanomuntubbi's absence; Thomas H. Byington, Chief Pro Tempore in 1881; Felekatubbi, who lived and died near Bethel, 1886-1888; Philip Noah, who lived near Mt. Zion in McCurtain County, 1888-1890; Alex H. Reid, a slender, tall man who lived in Red River County (McCurtain), 1890-94; Stephen Ontahubbi, 1895-96; Gooding Nelson, Sam Taylor, who lived north of Smithville; Imayubbi, who lived three miles north of Mt. Zion; and Cosum Wade. The Third District (Pushmataha) Chiefs were George Folsom, 1860; Harris Franklin, 1880; Stephen Hobart, 1888-1890; Mack McGould, 1891-1894; and Abel Foster, 1895.[210]

George Hudson was the first Principal Chief under the Doaksville Constitution adopted in January 1860. Hudson, a Mississippi native, was born in 1808 and briefly attended the Mayhew Mission School before removal. His white father died sometime before 1831, and his full blood mother was registered on the removal rolls as Widow Hudson, but she perished en route to Indian Territory in one of the first removal parties that left by way of Memphis.

In March 1832, Hudson made it to the Mountain Fork River and settled on a farm near Bethabara Mission. Earning a reputation as a good orator, he practiced law before the tribal courts and served on the Tribal Council from 1844-1846, 1849-50, and 1855. In 1846, he ran for chief but was defeated in a three-man race by Thomas LeFlore. LeFlore received 300 votes, Hudson, 242, and Joel Nail, 171, but Hudson used his position as the chairman of the Doaksville Convention as a springboard to the office of Principal Chief in 1860.

Peter Pitchlynn, in Washington trying to get a settlement of the Net Proceeds Claims when the Civil War broke out, hurried home to urge Chief Hudson to remain neutral, and the chief agreed until Southern sympathizers led by Robert M. Jones attacked him verbally and publicly for opposing slavery and secession. Discarding a neutrality proclamation drafted for him by Pitchlynn, Hudson gave into pressure. He was practically forced into making a treaty with Albert Pike at Eufaula on July 12, 1861. In reality, Hudson had no other choice since the tribal majority overwhelmingly supported the secessionist movement.

Once committed, Hudson issued a proclamation for all Choctaw men between the ages of eighteen and forty-five to enlist in either the volunteer or reserve militia. He was gratified by the response from his tribesmen, but the war brought disaster to the Choctaw Nation. Cattle rustling, robbery, and murder were commonplace, and Chief Hudson, utterly powerless to stop the anarchy and lawlessness, received the blame for the entire mess. In October 1862, Hudson, disillusioned and depressed, returned to his home on Mountain Fork where he died in 1865.

His successor was Samuel Garland, a direct descendant of Major James Garland, a Scottish soldier in the British army. With no particular love for the English when he was shipped to the colonies, Major Garland deserted during the War of the American Revolution and moved to the Choctaw country for safety in 1779. Often acting as a spy for the Rebel Army, Major Garland served as a liaison between the colonists and the Choctaw. Adopted into the tribe, he married the sister of one of Chief Pushmataha's wives, a Choctaw full blood named Hushi Yukpa (Happy Bird). Rewarded for his services with money and contacts with the new United States government, he founded a trading post at Garlandsville, the oldest town in Jasper County, Mississippi. He later signed the Treaty of Doak's Stand but died before the removal period. His son, John, assumed control of the trading post.

John Garland, Pushmataha's nephew, replaced the old chief after his death in 1824, although the Okla Hannali General Council had earlier chosen another nephew to head the district but then removed him from office. Garland not long after met with Greenwood LeFlore, Chief of the Okla Falaya district, and David Folsom, Chief of the Ahe Apvt Okla district, on the banks of the Noxubbee River, where the three, along with their sub-chiefs, drafted the first written constitution of the Choctaw Nation. Although never adopted, it was the first document to propose election of a principal chief to serve as a spokesman for the three district chiefs.

In the spring of 1828, Greenwood LeFlore, supported by Garland and Folsom for Principal Chief, spoke in favor of adoption of the constitution at another Council, but it was considered unacceptable by the majority of the tribe and was defeated in the Okla Hannali and Ahe Apvt Okla districts. Two of the chiefs were quickly replaced, Folsom by Moshulatubbee and Garland by Nitakechi. Garland, despite being deposed by election, wielded great influence throughout the tribe from his trading post and was primarily responsible for allowing Jackson's representatives to set up a meeting place at Dancing Rabbit Creek leading to the final removal. He was living at the family home in Garlandsville when it was designated as the gathering place for the 1,900 emigrating Six-Town Choctaw in 1832.

In December 1803, his eldest son, Samuel, was born at Garlandsville, as were Samuel's brothers John, Silas, and James and his sisters, Nancy and Lucy Garland. Samuel, a student at the Choctaw Academy, later moved to Noxubee County to marry Mary Pitchlynn, born in 1811, the younger sister of Peter. They had one son Crockett.

Sam Garland, a successful Southern plantation owner, amassed a small fortune in cotton and slaves in Mississippi. In 1831, Chief Moshulatubbee appointed him to lead one of the removal parties to the Choctaw Nation by way of the southern route. He and his companions moved up the Red River to the Ouachita to Ecore a Fabre (Camden, Arkansas) and then walked the remainder of the way. In late 1832, Garland returned to his family in Mississippi, farmed cotton for the next four years, and purchased another twenty slaves before selling his plantation for cash in preparation for removal to the Choctaw Nation. In 1836, he and brother-in-law, Peter Pitchlynn, who had traded his own farm for fifty slaves, moved west to the Mountain Fork to make a new home. Settling on a site approximately three miles east and one-half mile north of present Tom, Oklahoma, Garland returned to Mississippi to visit the elderly patriarch, John Pitchlynn, on his deathbed. Named the executor of Pitchlynn's estate, Garland took control of the inheritance and removed his mother-in-law and her possessions to the Choctaw Nation, where he built a grand Southern mansion on 600 acres in the rich, Red River bottoms.

Garland established his own village with a trading post on the Doaksville road in order to secure food and clothing for his family and slaves. The route ran from Fulton's Landing on the Red River through Rocky Comfort, now

Foreman, Arkansas, westward to Doaksville, Indian Territory. He fared well at his new location. By 1850, Garland farmed more than 1,000 acres, owned more than fifty slaves, and ran a cotton gin for his farms.

In 1853, Garland joined Pitchlynn as an advocate of the Net Proceeds Claim in Washington. In 1855, he, Israel Folsom, Dixon W. Lewis, and Pitchlynn worked out a treaty that would have brought the tribe $200,000 in gold had the Civil War not broken out. Appropriated by Congress in 1861, the gold was en route to Indian Territory when the Choctaw decided to join the Confederacy. The shipment was stopped at St. Louis where it was stored for a time before being returned to Washington. Thirty-six years later, a settlement of $2,981,247 was paid for the Net Proceeds Claims and Garland was entitled to a share for his work in behalf of the tribe. In 1889, the Garland heirs received $43,943.20 as part of the settlement.

Returning as a member of the Council in 1861-62, Garland served in the convention that wrote the Constitution of 1860, the charter that created the office of Principal Chief, a position much like the one his father had conceived more than thirty years earlier. In August 1862, he defeated Hudson in the campaign for Principal Chief, but his administration was just as difficult as that of his predecessor because of the war. Armed bands of whites rustled the Choctaw cattle, drove off their horse herds, and committed innumerable atrocities and criminal actions against the tribe. Chief Garland, without troops to preserve order or to control the numbers of intruders coming into the Nation, was powerless to stop them. Making matters worse, all federal annuities were stopped, which meant the schools and churches had to be closed down. These financial problems were further exacerbated by thousands of refugees pouring into the Nation from the North, pushing Choctaw resources to the straining point. In October 1864, after two years of service, Garland relinquished the chieftainship to Pitchlynn.

After the Treaty of 1866 was signed on May 5, Garland returned home to find his slaves gone, except for a few that had been treated well and chose to remain with him. Garland served the Nation again as a member of the Council in 1865, 1867, and 1869, but his health began to fail. Never able to recoup his losses after the war, the devout Presbyterian and Mason died near Tom on May 20, 1870.

His mother-in-law, Sophia Folsom Pitchlynn, died only a few months later on December 18, 1871. The Garland plantation was taken over by her grandson, David Crockett Garland. Restoring the trading post near the family home, Garland applied for a post office charter that was granted officially on December 29, 1894. Named the Janis post office in memory of his first child, a beautiful daughter christened Janis who died at the age of four, the post office continued in existence until 1917.

The little village boasted a cotton gin, blacksmith shop, a gristmill, and a horse market. Garland, who developed a taste for cigars, liquor, and racehorses, turned the Janis horse market into one of the busiest in the Nation. Buyers from Arkansas, Louisiana, and Texas were attracted to the sales for plow horses, quarter horses, and even Arabians and Choctaw ponies. Years later Crockett was sent by Chief Green McCurtain to meet with representatives of the Dawes Commission to begin the discussions that ultimately led to the allocation of Choctaw tribal lands.[211]

Peter Perkins Pitchlynn, surpassed in fame only by Pushmataha and Moshulatubbee, was the next Principal Chief. The eldest son of interpreter John Pitchlynn and his second wife, Sophia Folsom, the mixed blood daughter of Nathaniel Folsom, Peter had seven brothers and sisters and three older half-brothers, James, John, Jr., and Joseph C. Pitchlynn. Born on January 30, 1806, Peter grew up in wealth and affluence at his father's trading post on the Noxubee River. Only a quarter Choctaw, Peter preferred the name, Ha-tchoc-tuck-nee (Snapping Turtle), in the company of his full blood friends. Although he only received two years of education at any place he attended as a young man, he was appointed head of the first Lighthorsemen organized after the Doak's Stand Treaty in 1820, using the title of "Colonel" that he received for his service the rest of his life. Pitchlynn's position in the tribe was illustrated when Reverend Cyrus Kingsbury officiated at his wedding to Rhoda Folsom. Given a home and acreage near the Pitchlynn family plantation, along with a number of slaves to work it, the couple lived a life of prestige and prosperity.

On August 5, 1826, a constitutional assembly drafted the first Choctaw constitution that provided a decentralized government with a weak executive of three district chiefs elected to four-year terms, a national council, and an important law that prohibited selling tribal lands. Only twenty years old at the time, the privileged Southern scion served as secretary of the Council but was somewhat embarrassed by his poor education and decided the experience illustrated his need to go to school. In January 1826, he started to Transylvania University in Kentucky to study law but changed his mind and enrolled at Choctaw Academy. After a short stay, he entered the University of Nashville (later George Peabody College) but only stayed until 1828. Returning to Choctaw Academy, he soon changed into the Academy's most bitter and loudest critic, often denouncing the food as poor and cheap, consisting of "fat bacon, corn bread, and coffee, served by insolent, filthy Negroes."

In 1828, Pitchlynn was appointed as a member of the party of forty-one Choctaw sent on an inspection tour of the western lands prior to talks of a final removal treaty and then was assigned to lead a group west after the Dancing Rabbit Creek Treaty. In October 1831, Pitchlynn, without his own family, started for Memphis at the head of a party of four hundred. Thirty days later the band loaded its ponies on flatboats and boarded the *Brandywine* for a trip to the mouth of the White River. Progress was slowed by low waters, and on December 28, the travelers were forced to stop, stranded near the mouth of the Arkansas River along with 2,000 others in the middle of winter without provisions. The Pitchlynn party was forced to remain until January when the *Reindeer* arrived to take them aboard and head upriver to Fort Smith. Only ninety miles short of their destination, the boat stopped again and his party was put off once more as one of the worst blizzards in Arkansas history blew in. On February 20, 1832, Pitchlynn and his people were finally deposited at Fort Smith, most of them deciding to settle southwest of the town around Skullyville.

The following year Pitchlynn brought his own family to New Hope. In the summer of 1834, he moved with thirty slaves to a plantation near Eagletown on the east side of Mountain Fork. The same year he met George Catlin, the New England artist on a tour of the Choctaw Nation, who was so impressed with his handsome mixed blood looks that Catlin asked him to sit for a portrait.

In 1841, the owners of the Choctaw Academy, hoping to keep it alive, appointed Pitchlynn as superintendent, but he would only agree to accept the position for two years, secretly planning to destroy the school in order to start one in the Choctaw Nation. Intending to use tribal funds for a national school rather than the Kentucky academy, Pitchlynn found an excuse to close the school when one of the Choctaw pupils got into a scuffle with Johnson's slaves over a chicken fight. Pulling all the Choctaw students out, he declared the Academy "a nursery of violence and degradation."

His special project was Spencer Academy. In 1844, Pitchlynn used his influence as a member of the first Choctaw Board of Trustees to establish the school. He hoped for the appointment as its superintendent but it was not offered to him, although one of the buildings was named in his honor as a way of soothing his feelings. In January 1844, the other members of the board, Robert M. Jones, Thompson McKinney, and Agent William Armstrong, did approve his choice of Edmund McKinney, a Presbyterian missionary, as the Academy's first administrator.

The same year Pitchlynn's first wife died and was buried at Wheelock. Afterwards, his personality seemed to change. He grew habitually late about paying his bills, never paying them until dunned at least twice, and more than once he appeared in public drunk, all the while continuously preaching his hatred of liquor and praising the temperance movements among his people. He customarily carried brass knuckles and a brace of dueling pistols everywhere he went, and he took up with a widow named Carolyn Eckloff Lombardi who moved in with him and bore him five children before he eventually married her in 1869.

Pitchlynn's children by his first wife included Lycurgus (called Posh), Melvina, Loren, Peter P. Jr., and Rhoda. Most of the Pitchlynn brood led successful lives, one being Posh, who after a problem with alcoholism, was the grandfather of William F. Semple, an attorney and later chief from Tulsa. Two other Pitchlynn descendants did not fare quite as well. In 1858, Loren and Peter P. Jr., were convicted of killing a white man in Van Buren, Arkansas, and sent to the penitentiary at Little Rock for three years. Immediately after his release from prison, Peter P. Jr., got into serious trouble again when he killed another man, Lorenzo Harris, his aunt's husband.

Taking a turn as a member of the Choctaw Council, Peter Pitchlynn served in 1849, 1850, and returned again in 1860. In 1853, his most public project was to begin working as the head of the Choctaw delegation to Washington for an agreement to pay the "Net Proceeds Claim," the difference between what was paid to the tribe for the tribal lands in Mississippi and what was received from their sale by the state of Mississippi.

In 1861, he returned to the Nation to talk with Chief Hudson about remaining loyal or at least neutral in the coming war so the Net Proceeds could be paid, but Texas Confederates, learning of his return, surrounded the family home and threatened bodily harm unless he changed his attitude as an abolitionist. Pitchlynn was forced to go along. When the Council met on the subject, Robert M. Jones arose to state that anyone who opposed secession should be hanged, and Chief Hudson discarded his Pitchlynn-prepared speech to state that the Choctaw planned to make a treaty with the Confederacy.

Meanwhile, a consortium of white businessmen arranged to try collecting the Choctaw gold being held "in escrow" in St. Louis by purchasing "rights" to it from the tribe. In 1862, Sampson Folsom, acting for his deceased father Israel, sold the "rights" to the gold to a syndicate of Missouri partners for $60,000, but when representatives went to collect their treasure, they learned the gold had been moved to Memphis. In 1863, Pitchlynn and Garland sold the rights to another white pool for $80,000, but this bunch was also refused access to the gold. Charges and countercharges were flung around in the newspapers for months with nothing coming from any of the complaints and both claimants ultimately lost their investments. In reality, the Choctaw collected more than $140,000 in funds that were used to finance the Choctaw war effort without being out a cent.

In 1864, Pitchlynn and three other candidates filed for the position of chief. The former Southern gentleman was elected to a second term with 294 votes over Franceway Battiest, 284 votes, and Jerry Wade, 265. Pitchlynn was declared chief primarily because the South was losing the war. The Choctaw felt that he was probably the only person with the contacts and prestige to save them.

Chapter Eleven

By now the Choctaw Nation had serious economic troubles as destitute, hungry, and homeless Indians flocked into the country after the Confederate defeat at Perryville, and Pitchlynn, whose loyalty for the South had quickly dissipated, conferred with other tribal leaders to concoct a bold and rather devious plan to bring an end to it. In May 1865, he and leaders of the other tribes met at Camp Napoleon on the Washita River for a conference to discuss resuming relations with the United States. Setting the craftily conceived strategy in motion, Pitchlynn simply declared the war was over and promised perpetual peace and friendship for the Union. Calling for a conference to meet later at Armstrong Academy to discuss specific issues, the Choctaw planned to just ignore the war and the peace.

The scheme was naturally doomed to failure. Federal authorities learned of the ruse and sent orders that a conference would be held at Fort Smith, and the Choctaw must be there or else. Pitchlynn capitulated and agree to attend the conference but was shocked when American Commissioner D. N. Cooley informed the delegation that the tribe had forfeited its former treaty rights by making new ones with the Confederacy, that the tribe must cede territory for the settlement of friendly Indians outside Indian Territory, and that it must form a territorial government.

The Choctaw delegates, horrified by the demands, immediately withdrew from the conference and proceeded directly to Washington to make an appeal. Pitchlynn, Robert M. Jones, Allen Wright, Alfred Wade, James Riley, and John Page traveled to the Nation's capital to talk personally with officials in the Department of the Interior. Accompanying them was former General Douglas H. Cooper who stopped in Baltimore to pick up his brother-in-law, John H. B. Latrobe, to represent them in Washington. Latrobe, son of the architect of the Capitol building, was a well-known attorney in Maryland with a reputation for success as the lawyer for the Baltimore and Ohio Railroad.

In the end, the impressive entourage was forced to accept the Treaties of 1866, but, in reality, the Choctaw got off lightly when compared to other tribes. Forced to relinquish the Leased District, the tribe was given $300,000 in return with the understanding that their former slaves would be integrated into the tribe or the money would be used to pay for a new home for them. Additionally, the tribe agreed to allow a north-south railroad and an east-west line through their country and to accept a territorial form of government for the "Territory of Oklahoma," the name suggested by Allen Wright. All totaled, the Choctaw did not receive as harsh a punishment as might have been expected.

Pitchlynn returned to private affairs but remained a controversial figure for the rest of his life. In October 1874, Chief Coleman Cole accused him of purposely causing delays in the Net Proceeds payments because of exorbitant attorneys fees for himself and Douglas Cooper and others through the years.

In retaliation, Pitchlynn personally attended every regularly scheduled session of the Council at Armstrong Academy to prevent any erosion of his control over the Net Proceeds Claims until 1880. As the years passed and the claims went unpaid, the elderly Pitchlynn grew financially poorer, ultimately losing everything. He died penniless and in debt at the age of seventy-five at his home in Washington on January 17, 1881. Shortly after his death and partially in tribute to him, the Claims were paid. In 1886, Congress awarded $658,120, of which $250,000 had already been paid.

Two months after his death, friends petitioned to have Pitchlynn buried in the Congressional Cemetery in Washington. When permission was granted the former chief, a regular attendant of the Lutheran Church and prominent member of the Masonic Order, was buried in a grave located not far from Pushmataha. Inscribed on his monument were the words: "Chief and Delegate of the Choctaw Nation for whose advancement many years of his life were devoted—Choctaw Brave."[212]

In 1866, five major candidates, including Allen Wright, and three lesser ones filed for election. He received 552 votes, Jerry Wade, 367, Coleman Nelson, 265, Peter Folsom, 199, Samuel Garland, 80, David Harkins, 1, J. P. Folsom, unknown, and Wilson Jones, 1. Elected chief primarily for his part in the negotiations of the Treaties of 1866, Wright persuaded the Council to ratify the deal shortly after it was presented to them while Pitchlynn took a turn on the Council. Wright served two terms as chief. In 1868, he ran again against Franceway Battiest, receiving 1221 votes to 501 for Battiest, and served until 1870.

Wright, seven-eighths blood Choctaw, was named Kiliahote (Let's Go Make a Light) at birth in Attala County, Mississippi, in November 1826. His parents neither spoke nor understood English. In 1832, the family, including two brothers and one sister, who later became the mother of Alinton Telle, a lawyer in Atoka, moved to one of the western prongs of the Pearl River, but his mother died in June. In October 1833, his family made the removal overland by packhorses. Not joining other migrants, the small party arrived in present McCurtain County in March 1834. Kiliahote was seven years old at the time. Making inquiry of their Uncle Billy Fry who had migrated in 1832, and his sister Sally, who had removed a few months before in January 1834, they joined their relatives living on Lukfata Creek.

Their problems were just beginning. After enduring months of hardships and exposure, having to swim their horses across streams, and building rafts for themselves, the family was forced to depend on the mercy of others to survive the winter. Since they arrived too late to be given promised provisions for traveling alone, the family was forced to survive with little help until provisions were issued the next fall.

Wright had never seen a book or a school before the trip, but passing through Arkansas he was intrigued by the small white houses with children playing around them. Told that these were schools where the white man obtained knowledge, the fascinated youngster asked to be sent to one on arrival in their new home. His eldest brother Willis was allowed to attend school with Mr. Daniel Folsom, but despite Kiliahote's pleading, he was not permitted to go until the spring of 1834. Enrolled in a neighborhood school about a mile south of Skelton Depot (just west of present Broken Bow) in Boktuklo County, he was taught in Choctaw by Joseph Dukes. The following year, his teacher, Eunice Clough (later Mrs. Noah Wall) from New Hampshire, named him Allen Wright in honor of her friend at Wheelock, Reverend Alfred Wright. In 1839, Kiliahote's father died, and the young man, at the age of thirteen, went to live with an uncle who agreed to let him attend school.

In 1840, Wright, hardly able to read or write English, entered Pine Ridge near Doaksville where Reverend Cyrus Kingsbury, recently arrived from Mayhew, Mississippi, was his instructor. Wright studied with the celebrated teacher until entering Spencer Academy in 1844. Staying for four years, Wright called the Academy his turning point toward Christianity. He credited his transformation to the influence of visiting Reverend Anson Gleason, the old Choctaw missionary from Mississippi who taught the Choctaw from 1823 to 1832. Full of his former magnetism, Reverend Gleason preached eloquently at Spencer convincing many of the young students, including Wright, to devote their lives to religion. In April 1846, the young scholar united with the church at Wheelock.

Deciding to major in Theology in college, Wright and four friends traveled east with intentions of entering Princeton on a scholarship from the Nation. Going by way of Washington, D.C., they met several senators and congressmen and President Polk, and more importantly, Peter P. Pithlynn. In September 1848, "Colonel" Pitchlynn advised Wright to enter Delaware College at Newark, Delaware, because liquor was freely drunk at Princeton, and Wright was warned that he should not be around it. When Delaware College closed in 1850, Wright moved to Schenectady, New York, to matriculate at Union College. The president of the Union, Dr. Eliphalet Nott, made such a lasting impression upon Wright that he later named one of his sons for him. Graduating with an A.B. Degree and a membership in Delta Phi Greek Fraternity after two years, Wright entered Union Theological Seminary in New York City. In 1855, Wright completed his advanced course work and was the first Indian to receive a Master of Arts Degree.

Ordained and appointed as an honorary member of the American Board of Commissioners of Foreign Missions, Wright returned to Indian Territory as an instructor and superintendent at Armstrong Academy for the 1856 term. His preaching appointments were at five outlying stations. On February 11, 1857, he married Harriet Newell Mitchell, a missionary teacher from Dayton, Ohio. Born in 1834, she was the daughter of James Henry and Martha Skinner Mitchell. Her father, a lineal descendant of Elder Brewster, the fourth signer of the "Mayflower Compact" of 1620, was a civil engineer by profession, having laid out the original town site of Dayton. Her parents disowned her for the marriage but her descendants quipped that: "A Pilgrim married an Indian." Bearing eight children, Eliphalet Nott, Frank, Mary, Annie, Clara, Kate, Allen, Jr., and James Brooks, Mrs. Wright lived until 1894.

All her children enjoyed distinguished careers of their own. Eliphalet Nott Wright attended medical school and established a family practice at Atoka. Another son, Frank Hall Wright, was born at Boggy Depot, attended Spencer, and then Union College, as had his father. When he graduated, he married Addie Lilienthal of Saratago, New York, and returned to do missionary work with the Comanche and Apache at Fort Sill and later in Ontario, Canada, where he died in 1922. A third son Allen, born October 6, 1867, attended neighborhood schools at Boggy Depot and graduated from Kemper Military College in Missouri in 1889 and then went to Union College in New York where he graduated with a Bachelor of Arts Degree in the Class of 1893. Returning to Indian Territory, he read law in Atoka before moving to McAlester to enter the office of General Solicitor of the Choctaw, Oklahoma & Gulf Railroad. In 1895, he was admitted to the bar. Two years later he was appointed United States Commissioner at McAlester. Socially, he belonged to the Elks Lodge; politically, he was a Republican; and religiously, an Episcopalian.

In 1856, Reverend Wright began his service with the tribe as a member of the Council as part of the effort to unite the three Choctaw District Chiefs into one executive with the Skullyville Constitution in 1857. The new constitution placed executive power into the hands of a single "Governor" with Boggy Depot designated as the new capital, but this action only caused more consternation among the tribe. After much debate a new constitution was written, aided by Wright, and submitted for approval at the Doaksville Convention in 1860. Approved by a majority vote, the constitution provided for a "Principal Chief" as the major executive officer. In 1863, the capital was moved to Chahta Tvmaha, (Choctaw Town) or Armstrong Academy where it remained for the next twenty years. In 1885, Wright was one of those who worked to get the capital permanently established at Tvshkahomma.

In 1858, Reverend Wright moved to Boggy Depot to establish a farm. Spending his days at his large, two-story, Southern frame home as overseer of his slaves that tended two farms and a cattle ranch, he also took charge of the Presbyterian Church and its missions within a fifty-mile radius. An indefatigable worker, Wright served as the regional preacher, sermonizing against the evils of alcohol and the open saloons that had developed across the Red River in Texas. Carrying on his worldly affairs with his ministerial duties, Wright found occasion to participate in public affairs at the same time. In 1859, he was raised to the position of Tribal Treasurer. Elected to the Tribal House of Representatives in 1861, Wright was appointed a delegate to the Intertribal Council at North Fork Town that signed a treaty with Albert Pike and the Confederacy in June. In 1862, Wright enlisted as a private in Captain Wilkin's company of Choctaw Infantry and then transferred to Company F of the Choctaw Mounted Rifles as a chaplain. At the end of the war, Wright accompanied Pitchlynn and others to the Fort Smith conference. In October 1865, he was selected to go to Washington as a delegate to the peace treaty negotiations and signed the Treaty of 1866 for the tribe. In April, he suggested the name, Oklahoma, for the new Indian Territory, explaining that Okla meant people and humma meant red. The phrase meant Red People.[213]

Wright stated in his inaugural address as Principal Chief that he accepted the office as a preacher with no desire other than to govern "to do good." He added, "Unavoidable necessity as well as self-preservation had forced the Choctaw to take up arms against the Government of the United States. This was the second time in our history that the bright future prospect for the Choctaws, in the rapid march to civilization-progress of education, and wide spread religion among them have been impeded and paralyzed by direct and indirect acts of the United States." Expressing his disgust that this educational progress had been made "retrograde" by not less than forty years, Wright predicted sadly that it would require many years to catch up again. The Principal Chief-Minister added that "matters had been made worse" by the country being overrun by lawlessness brought about by the war. Suggesting that an entire "peace keeping force" was needed to restore order, he promised to see that "Law knows no friend and it shall know no different nationalization under our jurisdiction." Wright concluded that if he "erred" as chief, it would be the fault "of the head and not of the heart."[214]

Chief Wright blamed the drunkenness, thievery, and murder after the Civil War on "transients" passing through from other states and his solution was a proclamation requiring non-citizens to obtain permits to remain in the Nation. Only a few years later he suggested an additional bill requiring permits for salesmen within the Nation. Wright argued that a law was necessary that required a seller must post up to $1,000 in bond money to obey the laws and pay any taxes on his goods into the treasury. It was further required that any non-citizen artisans or mechanics (carpenters, wagon makers, and others) must obtain permits costing twenty-five dollars with a two dollar processing fee plus another five dollars for people employed by these businessmen. In 1867, the bill was passed and signed into law by Chief Wright.

As the crime rate continued to climb through the years, Chief Wright recommended other laws to the Council to combat the more serious social problems in the Nation. On his suggestion the Council prohibited the bearing of firearms in public places and social gatherings except by peace officers. Taking the commission of crimes more seriously, Wright also made punishments more severe. Only one of the laws sponsored by the chief made the first offense of highway robbery punishable by death by hanging. Concerned that "this crime will soon be as common as horse stealing," Chief Wright asked, "Who can endure such a thing in our midst?"

The penalty for robbery had previously been death but not by hanging. Only two crimes, sodomy and second offense horse theft, were considered heinous enough to deserve a punishment so degrading as hanging. In 1891, Silas Peters was executed for horse stealing as the single criminal ever given such a sentence by the Choctaw courts. Capital punishment for crimes of murder, treason, and second offense rape was normally performed by firing squads composed, preferably, of friends and acquaintances or legal authorities. Minor offenses were punishable by fines or lashes, thirty-nine to one hundred "well laid on the bare back."

Wright's major contribution was the restoration of peace to the Nation. In 1876, he ran for the office of chief again but was defeated by Coleman Cole. He continued to serve his people for many years, nevertheless, attending Council sessions and offering his advice and opinions on subjects of consequence to the tribe. From 1880 to 1884, he also served as superintendent of schools for the tribe.

In later years, Wright acted as translator of numerous religious tracts and editor of a Choctaw dictionary. Erudite in Latin and Greek, Wright translated scriptures and the Psalms of David from Hebrew into Choctaw without having to resort to the medium of English. Wright's other literary works included publishing a Choctaw definer for use in academies and schools under the title *Chahta Lekiskon*, translating and editing the "Choctaw Department" in the Atoka *Indian Champion*, serving as editor of the *Indian Champion* in 1885, and drafting and translating various treaties and laws of the Choctaws. One of the greatest tributes paid to Wright was his employment by the Chickasaw to translate their statutes, enacted in English, into the Choctaw language under the title *Chikasha Okla Kvnstitushvn Micha Nan Vlhpisa*, for use by the non-English speaking elements within their tribe. Reverend John Edwards, a Presbyterian missionary, stated, "No other Choctaw whom I ever met could give such clear explanations of difficult points in the grammar of the Choctaw language."

In 1880, Wright was invited to attend the World's Presbyterian Assembly in Philadelphia. A member of the Masonic Lodge, Wright was a charter member of the first lodge formed after the Civil War. He died at Boggy Depot on December 2, 1885.

Chief Wright's administration marked a transitional period from violence to peace in the Choctaw Nation. The tribe struggled to return to the level of culture and civilization enjoyed before the Civil War. Another long, difficult battle followed but just as before, the tribe once more restored its churches, schools, and laws. Within a decade, the recovery was complete.[215]

CHAPTA AUAH TUKLO

~ CHAPTER TWELVE ~

"NO 'COUNT WHITE MAN COME TO OUR COUNTRY"

Samuel Garland

Peter P. Pitchlynn

Allen Wright

William Bryant

Coleman Cole

Isaac Garvin

Gov. Jackson McCurtain

Edmund McCurtain

Captain Tompson McKinney

Chapter Twelve

The chiefs given the responsibility for meeting the challenges of reconstruction of the Choctaw Nation included William Bryant (1870-74), Coleman Cole (1874-78), Isaac Garvin (1878-80), Jackson McCurtain (1880-84), Edmund McCurtain (1884-86), and Thompson McKinney (1886-88). They enabled the tribe to resume societal progress, but their abilities were severely tested by the increasing emigration of whites into their country.

In 1870, William J. Bryant, a mixed blood, was elected Principal Chief. A student at the Choctaw Academy in his youth, Bryant emigrated after the general removal to Octavia in Red River County. In 1840, he moved to the region around Wilburton and served as the postmaster at Pleasant Ridge before settling his family at Tvshkahomma. In 1844, he was elected to a seat on the General Council and then served as a delegate to the convention in North Fork Town in 1861. Four years later he served as a Supreme Judge of the Second District.

In August 1872, Chief Bryant was opposed for a second term by Turner B. Turnbull, another former student at the Choctaw Academy. Turnbull's career included service as a judge from Blue County in 1853 and District Chief of the Third (Pushmataha) District in 1863. Bryant won with a large majority and served until 1874.

The most important event of his administration was the building of the M-K-T Railroad through the Nation, and his election to a second term was considered a mandate for the construction of more railroads in the future. A member of the Masonic Lodge, he was buried east of Tvshkahomma, north of the Frisco Railroad.[216]

In 1874, Coleman Cole was elected by a victory over Joel Everidge. Cole had little formal education but possessed an inordinate amount of native shrewdness that made him a strong, positive leader. On August 2, 1876, the most controversial chief in the entire reconstruction period was elected for a second term in a three-man contest with Allen Wright and William Bryant. Cole gave his last messages to the General Council in October 1878.

Born in Mississippi about 1800, he was the son of Robert Cole and his full blood wife, Sallie. His grandfather was a white man named Roscoe Cole and his grandmother was a Choctaw full blood named Sho-ma-ka, whose family belonged to a tribe known as Shvkchi Humma that was attacked and virtually eliminated by Chickasaw shortly before the Revolutionary War. Only 200 women and children survived the massacre, among them Sho-ma-ka and her family of four daughters and a son who had been deserted by Cole. After the few survivors joined the Choctaw, Sho-ma-ka served as a cook for a Choctaw contingent of Andrew Jackson's army during the Creek Wars.

Her nephews were Captain Atoka and Greenwood and Forbis LeFlore. One of her daughters married a Frenchman named Louis Cravatt, and they had two daughters, Nancy and Rebecca. Louis LeFlore married Nancy Cravatt and Greenwood was their son. Louis married Rebecca after Nancy's death and their children included Forbis LeFlore. Alive in 1838, Sho-ma-ka lived to the estimated age of 120 according to testimony before the United States Courts.

In 1824, her son, Robert, replaced Chief Apuckshunnubbee as the representative to Washington and signed the Treaty of 1825. Cole, illiterate and forced to sign the treaties by "making his mark," met General Lafayette, the French Revolutionary War hero, during his visit. Greatly impressed by the widely traveled and educated Frenchman, Cole insisted that his children receive an education and sent them to Elliot Mission School. Serving as District Chief in Mississippi for two years, Cole turned the chieftainship over to his nephew, Greenwood Leflore.

His son, Coleman Cole, did not remove immediately to Indian Territory. He decided to stay in Mississippi as a registered citizen so he could care for his grandmother who was too old to make the trip. Since she only spoke broken English, not enough to care for herself if left alone, Cole delayed his own removal until after her death. At the same time, he lost his wife and two children to disease and the family home when his bid for citizenship was turned down. In 1845, the deeply saddened Cole moved to a lonely farm twenty miles northeast of present Antlers in Cedar County, Pushmataha District.

A deeply religious man who never drank nor used foul language, Cole was a dedicated and devoted member of the Cumberland Presbyterian Church. An extremely humble, unpretentious Christian, he lived in a small, one-room cabin with other huts built around the place as the need arose for them. Scattered about with no particular plan or design, the ramshackle buildings were spread over the entire farm. One shack served as a kitchen, another as a guesthouse, employee quarters, a corncrib, smokehouse, potato house, or whatever suited the chief's purposes. Usually dining in the yard, he fed his dogs directly from the family table. The eccentric Cole refused to have any furniture in his house, making his bed on a simple pallet on the floor. Only after reaching high public office was a second story added to his home with the upstairs used as a dining room for state occasions.

Cole's erratic behavior extended to his personal grooming. He scorned fine clothes, content with wearing old, traditional garments. Generally, he wore coarse brogans, pants, a calico shirt, a hunting shirt without vests or ties with a bandana or turban around his head and a red sash around the waist. Accepted as the typical Choctaw attire before the Civil War, Chief Cole continued the style during his lifetime. Along with wearing his hair long and cut with a bobbed shape from right to left, Cole added a silk top hat, called a "Beegum." His costume choice sometimes made him look ridiculous, but he paid little, if any, attention to critical slurs or comments about his appearance or his outfits.[217]

Cole's behavior was equally capricious. In the spring of 1876, he rode over thirty miles to Doaksville, the nearest post office to his home on Big Cedar, but only took time to ask for mail and greet one of the men at the store, Captain Nanamentubbee, before climbing back aboard his horse and starting for home without another word. Others sometimes found him peculiar, but the aberrant chief refused to be insulted or change his habits.[218]

In 1874, Cole was elected chief with the major issue of the campaign being the expected payment of the Net Proceeds Claims. Since the Claims were supposed to be paid in a few months, Cole told the Court of Claims shortly after the election to make up rolls of those entitled to participate in the disbursement of the payments. Unfortunately, once the rolls were completed, Cole got involved into a serious argument with Peter Pitchlynn over who should receive the Claims. He finally dispatched a request to President U.S. Grant for soldiers to protect the funds, an action that proved unnecessary as the appropriations for the funds were delayed anyway, but the affair escalated into a lifelong dispute with Pitchlynn.

The following year the contentious chief got involved in still another political dispute, this time over an attempted transfer of the Choctaw capitol to Atoka. Local residents argued the city, one of the fastest growing settlements on the Katy tracks, would be more accessible and attractive than Tvshkahomma and initiated a movement to transfer the government to their town, but Cole vetoed the idea. At the same time, he moved to the city to establish an office for his role as chief but only opened on Mondays and Thursdays of each week and completely avoided business the rest of the time. The Choctaw accepted his approach to his duties and his idiosyncratic behavior without complaint. They realized that Cole's intentions were only to help them.

Having suffered personally at the hands of whites in Mississippi, Cole grew increasingly fearful of the white tide streaming into the Nation. Trying to get a hold on the number of intruders already in the Choctaw republic, he issued a proclamation for all whites to appear before the Council to prove their status as intermarried citizens. At the same time, he raised the marriage fee to twenty-five dollars for anyone wanting to marry a Choctaw, and when this amount seemed too little to make a difference in the numbers of white-Indian marriages, he increased the fee to one hundred dollars.

Equally alarmed by "worthless characters," as he called them, coming into the Nation and marrying Choctaw wives to take advantage of the status of intermarried citizens to avoid paying fees to the tribe for doing business, Cole imposed a license for white traders and increased it in 1875. Later, he successfully passed a marriage law requiring anyone wanting to obtain a license from a Choctaw court to swear that they did not already have a wife because some unscrupulous whites were marrying Choctaw women and then abandoning them.[219]

Chief Cole had a special objection to white "exploiters" of Choctaw timber and coal reserves. In 1875, a major scandal arose when he challenged J. J. McAlester, Dr. D. M. Hailey, Robert Reams, and Tandy Walker, the nephew of Colonel Tandy Walker, over mining operations near McAlester's store. Upon learning the businessmen had sent a wagon load of coal to Parsons, Kansas, without telling anyone about it, the Chief grew so angry over the tribe being cheated out of its royalty payments that he ordered Captain Olasechubbee of the Lighthorsemen to arrest the entire lot, clear a spot of ground, and shoot the whole gang immediately. The Captain, a friend of McAlester, did as he was told and made the arrests but also arranged for McAlester and his associates to avoid the death sentence. Accepting an invitation to dine with the prisoners, he allowed the capitalist entrepreneurs to escape. They commandeered a railroad handcar and made a dash for the Creek Nation where they remained as fugitives until Cole left office.

In 1878, Cole established a home on the Kiamichi River about three miles from Stanley in Pushmataha County. He made another run for the chief's office two years later but was defeated by Jackson McCurtain. Completely honest and straightforward in his dealings, Chief Cole had no knowledge of artful politics but used his good judgment and his integrity for the benefit of his people regardless of the consequences. He passed away in 1886. He left one son, Logan, by his second wife Abbie. He lies in an unmarked grave in a farm field in Pushmataha County.[220]

In 1878, Judge Isaac Levi Garvin, a prominent jurist from Red River County, was elected Principal Chief. Born April 27, 1832, in Mississippi, he made the removal at the age of two with his father Henry, a white man. Settling near Wheelock, his family located approximately one mile south of the town later named in his honor.

Educated at Norwalk and Spencer Academies, Garvin studied law to become an attorney and served as a judge and presiding officer of the Choctaw Nation Supreme Court. His wife, Melvina, the daughter of Captain Miashambi, was a sister to Peter Hudson's mother. Hudson later reported that Garvin once visited his house, but both his parents were gone at the time. The children did not know him and did not let him in. They thought he was a white man, and Hudson's sister remarked in Choctaw, "No 'count white man come to our country," completely unaware that Garvin understood and spoke the language fluently. The Hudsons were greatly embarrassed to later learn that he had known what was said about him.

Garvin and Melvina had one daughter Francis who married a Dr. Shi and moved to the Chickasaw Nation, but the Judge did not live to see his grandchildren. On February 20, 1880, Garvin was the first Principal Chief to die in office. The community that had grown up around his farm home continued to thrive and use his name but was moved about a mile northwest by the Choctaw and Arkansas (later Frisco) Railroad in 1902.[221]

President of the Senate Jackson Frazier McCurtain completed Garvin's term according to constitutional statute. Sworn into office in October, he won the position in his own right by election over A. R. Durant in 1880. McCurtain was elected to a second term in 1882.

Jack was the son of former Chief Cornelius McCurtain and Mahayia Nelson Belvin and the brother of Edmund and Green, both later Principal Chiefs. Born on March 4, 1830, in Mississippi, he made the removal with his family at the age of three. Enrolling in Spencer Academy at fourteen, he remained a little more than two years but did not like school and did not return. All his brothers attended school at Fort Coffee.

In 1850, McCurtain began a public career as the elected representative to the Choctaw Council from Sugar Loaf County. He served until enlisting in the Confederate army on June 22, 1861. Less than a month passed before he was elected Captain of Company G of the First Choctaw and Chickasaw Mounted Rifles under Commander Douglas H. Cooper. He was promoted a year later to the rank of Lieutenant Colonel of the Second Choctaw Battalion. His regiment participated in several campaigns in northern Indian Territory including the Battle of Honey Springs in July 1863, and the Battle of Poison Springs, Arkansas, with General Sterling Price on April 18, 1864. Earning a reputation as a faithful, efficient officer absolutely without fear in the middle of a battle, McCurtain served until the formal surrender. In 1866, he returned to his home in the "Narrows," three miles northeast of Red Oak. McCurtain was again elected to the Council as a senator for Sugar Loaf County by unanimous vote because of his military record in August 1866. He served until succeeding to office of chief upon the death of Chief Garvin.

McCurtain's first wife, Marie Riley, was the sister of Judge James Riley of the First District, a delegate to the treaty negotiations after the war. The couple made a home for many years at Red Oak where McCurtain lived when he was elected chief, but while still in office he moved the family about ten miles north of Hugo. In 1883, Chief McCurtain personally selected the site of the capital building at Tvshkahomma, naming the surrounding geological formations north of the location that he so enjoyed viewing, the "Potato Hills." Moving there while the Council House was being built, he transferred the Council meetings from Chahta Tvmaha in 1884.

When McCurtain's wife died unexpectedly, he assumed responsibility for raising two daughters, but after one died young, and the other, Sophie, married Lewis Garvin, he married the elegant and charming Jane Frances Austin. One of the most public "First Ladies," Jane, born in 1842, was the daughter of a wealthy, progressive couple, Lewis and Millie Austin, who sent her to Wheelock Female Seminary at the age of eleven. Receiving a scholarship to Eldgeworths Seminary in Pittsburg, she studied for three years in Pennsylvania, until the Civil War threatened, and she was forced to return home. In 1861, she took a teaching job, but the school was soon forced to close. Married to McCurtain after the war, she bore him ten children while also acting as his private secretary and political advisor. Mrs. McCurtain, a keen observer of social and cultural events within the Nation, kept her husband apprised of affairs and remained deeply loyal to him until his death.[222]

On October 3, 1883, Chief McCurtain made his fourth appearance before the General Council at Armstrong Academy to present a number of audacious, bold recommendations for improvements in schools and royalty collections and plans to curtail some of the lawlessness inside the Nation, but only a few of his suggestions were adopted. Most were too controversial for the conservative Council.

One was his proposal to reduce the number of neighborhood schools. He argued that so many had been established without sufficient funds to run them that the entire school system was threatened. He wanted four each in Blue and Kiamitia Counties, three each in Sans Bois, Skullyville, Atoka, and Red River Counties, and two in each of the remaining counties but recommended that none be operated with less than twenty scholars. His plan meant forty schools would be operated by the tribe with an appropriation of $12,800 for teacher salaries of forty dollars per month for an eight-month session or $14,400 for a nine-month term. He further recommended that Armstrong Academy be again utilized as an orphan school for boys and Spencer Academy for girls with fifty children assigned to each, and the number of students at the New Spencer and New Hope Seminaries increased to one hundred each.

Jackson quickly pointed out that royalty payments on timber, coal, and other minerals were sufficient for financing these projects as well as pay for the construction of a new capital at Tvshkahomma. He reported that revenues from these sources amounted to $28,165.62 for the fiscal year that ended July 31, 1883, while other national collections, including taxes on licensed traders and royalties from each of the three districts, increased revenues for the year to $38,196.75.

Chief McCurtain's major concern, like his predecessors, was the increasing number of white intruders coming into the Nation. There seemed to be no way for the tribe to stop the continual migration into the Nation or even slow it down. Expressing great dissatisfaction with the existing permission laws, Jack asked for help in at least getting compliance with the current rules. He added that more laws were needed to strengthen the present statutes, pointing out that non-citizens living under permits were not required to work the roads the same as citizens, a system that he argued should be changed or the whites made subject to fines and penalties. Otherwise, McCurtain felt that non-citizens would pay little attention to the Choctaw road law, a condition that could greatly affect the tribe.

Plagued by white intruders who caused continual violence, McCurtain witnessed problems in some counties so out of control that keeping the peace seemed impossible. His primary worry was the robbery and murder in Atoka and Jacks Fork Counties in the Pushmataha District, in Towson and Boktuklo Counties, and in the Red River County of Apuckshunnubbee. He sought solutions for the chaos in these areas, but his efforts saw little success.

Boktuklo was the worst because finding suitable peace officers was almost unachievable. Those that could be employed were so intimidated by the outlaws they were afraid to carry out their duties. Within a few months a man and his wife had been killed in their sick bed at home, and a few days later two more persons were murdered. Another man, Inowatubbee, who attended the Council session the previous May for Eastman Willis, went to Boktuklo County on a visit and was arrested and killed by the sheriff. Stating that he had replaced the sheriff, McCurtain added that the successor had only caused more trouble when he killed two prisoners in his charge. McCurtain asked, "How can the laws be enforced when even the officers participate in murdering people?"

Blaming the problem on the courts that refused to convict the criminals and the jurors and witnesses who were either intimidated by the outlaw elements or were part of the gangs, McCurtain recommended the establishment of a large militia to suppress the violence, but his suggestion went unheeded. As a result the numbers of intruders continued to rise in his term, and there were no workable solutions.

So many were migrating into the Nation by the end of McCurtain's term that he asked for federal troops to assist in the removal of whites from Arkansas that were overrunning the northeastern sections of the Nation. Troops were sent in, but it was already too late. The whites merely moved back in as soon as the soldiers left. McCurtain continued to rely upon the Lighthorsemen as a police force, but the sheer numbers of whites and outlaws in the region rendered them incapable of keeping the peace. Even federal marshals sent out from Fort Smith under the direction of Judge Parker were incapable of controlling the intruders. One of the rumors concerning

McCurtain's move to Hugo was that the intruders were threatening his life for causing them problems.[223]

An incident mentioned by McCurtain in his speech as an example of the violence running rampant through the Nation was the attempted holdup of the M-K-T "Flyer" in the spring of 1883. The raid occurred when the Christie Gang tried to rob the "Flyer" as it stopped for water at the Reynolds Tank about five miles north of Limestone Gap. Living nearby was Captain Charles Leflore, a member of the Lighthorsemen, who was warned of the planned holdup by an informer. Going into action, Leflore secretly stationed twenty-five Lighthorsemen around the tank shortly before the train arrived. The bandits, thinking everything was safe, began to occupy the places where they had planned to stage the robbery only found armed deputies waiting on them. Under orders not to fire until the captain gave the order, the Lighthorsemen allowed the outlaws to come within a few feet of their hiding places. When the signal rang out, the outlaws were stunned by the opening blasts but recovered quickly as the train came into sight. The engineer, on the alert, stopped his train and waited for the shooting to end before moving forward. Among the wounded was a recent recruit who was hit in the eye by a splinter from the wooden tank when a bullet smashed into it. The highly excited young deputy yelled, "Captain, we have them. They are shooting at us with bows and arrows." Captain Leflore had only two men wounded, but five of the outlaws were killed. Placing those captured in a baggage car on the Katy Flyer, the prisoners were escorted to town and turned over to authorities. The Lighthorsemen had won this particular exchange, but most times they were not so lucky.[224]

In 1885, McCurtain, noted for his support for his people, especially the poor and orphans, was paid a great tribute for his honest love for them. Buried in the old Tvshkahomma cemetery, the inscription on his monument read: "In the other world he lives in bliss. If there is none he made the best of this."

After his death, Jane Austin McCurtain took a more active, public part in Choctaw politics. Chiefs and lawmakers alike visited her home to enjoy her hospitality and seek her advice on tribal matters. Slowly, a tradition developed for incoming political leaders to pay a courtesy call upon the lady who had known and welcomed every chief from 1860 until her death. In 1894, she was named superintendent of the recently built Jones Academy, a position she kept until the Atoka Agreement turned selection of teachers and administrators of Choctaw schools over to federal authorities. In 1898, Mrs. McCurtain moved back home. When the United States government ruled that Choctaw personnel should be terminated as employees, she turned her attention to helping the Tuskahoma Female Seminary, built a short walk from her home.

Serving as custodian for the Council House for a number of years after statehood, she pestered the chiefs and officials in Washington for appropriated funds and managed to keep the structure together until her death. In 1924, she died at the age of eighty-two and was buried near her husband.[225]

In October 1884, Jackson's younger brother Edmund was elected to the office of Principal Chief after a campaign against Joseph P. Folsom. Born near Fort Coffee in Sugar Loaf County on July 29, 1842, Edmund was the first native-born chief and the third member of the McCurtain family elected to the office. He completed only one term.

Edmund attended local neighborhood schools until the age of nineteen when he enlisted in his brother's command as a lieutenant. Serving through the entire campaign, he returned from the war to establish a home in Sans Bois County. Married to Susan King in 1862, he fathered three children before his wife's unexpected death. He then married Jane McCurtain's sister, Harriet Austin, by whom he had another child before her death two years later. A third marriage ended in divorce before McCurtain married Israel LeFlore's daughter Clarissa.

In 1866, he started a political career as an elected County Judge, a position he served for four years. He then became a District Trustee for five years, holding the post of Trustee until his appointment as Superintendent of Public Schools.

McCurtain, a champion of education throughout his career, caused a furor by his proposal for a tax on livestock to support the Nation's school system in May 1875. Serving as a District Trustee for the Moshulatubbee District, he grew tired of the annual problems with school finances caused by customarily late payments, sometimes as long as fifteen months, from the federal government, a circumstance that resulted in continuous difficulties for the Tribal Council. Arguing that the Council should petition the federal authorities for immediate payment of funds, McCurtain proposed a temporary tax to allow the schools to conduct ten-month school terms. Since no taxes of any kind had ever been passed by the Council, the idea revealed just how far McCurtain was willing to go to aid the school system.

Already an opponent of J. J. McAlester on the grounds the Arkansas mine owner enjoyed an unfair mining monopoly, McCurtain also began loudly demanding the intermarried Arkansas coal miner pay more in royalties thereby providing funds for tribal educational programs. In June 1875, Chief McCurtain publicly protested McAlester's control of the mining regions in a letter to the editor of the *Atoka Vindicator*. He complained that McAlester and R. S. Stevens, the manager of the Osage Coal Mining Company of McAlester, were not paying the tribe its rightful share of the company's coal sales and proposed drastic actions to collect revenues. Proclaiming that both Stevens and McAlester deserved punishment for exploiting the Nation, he suggested the tribe tear up the railroad tracks into the city where they "ran things." McCurtain was willing to aggressively pursue every avenue to force the mine owners to more equitable terms for support of the school system.[226]

On October 9, 1884, McCurtain referred to himself in his inaugural address at T*vs*hkahomma as the "Principal Chief of the whole Choctaw people and not of any party." He added that he favored "whatever tends to Christianize, civilize, educate and otherwise builds up the Choctaw Nation." Although a former Confederate rebel, he worked hard to maintain that commitment throughout his term of office.[227]

The major issue settled in his administration, to the surprise of many, was the dispensation of the freedmen, a controversy that had plagued the Nation since the end of the war. On November 6, 1880, a resolution was passed that provided for the registration of freedmen in the Choctaw Nation, an action that allowed all freedmen citizenship in the Nation. The chief then informed the federal government that the tribe had complied with the proposition of 1866. On June 1, 1885, McCurtain established a commissioner for proper identification and registration for compliance with the proclamation and issued notices that all former slaves should appear either at Skullyville, Doaksville, or Goodland within sixty days. The chief warned those who did not comply with the registration process would be considered intruders subject to removal.[228]

On October 21, 1886, McCurtain declined a run for a second term and gave his retirement message to the General Council. He threw his support to a friend, Thompson McKinney, and returned to his 300-acre farm at Sans Bois where he owned a herd of more than 500 cows as a partner in the "7XR Ranch," with his brother Green and a close friend from McAlester, N. B. "Dime" Ainsworth. In 1887, McCurtain was appointed United States Marshal for the Choctaw Nation. A year later he was elected senator from Sans Bois County but died unexpectedly two years later in Skullyville on his way home from a meeting of the General Council. He was buried there on November 15, 1890.

His friend, "Dime" Ainsworth also had a reputation for helping the needy as the Tribal National Attorney, National Auditor, and Commissioner. Known for being a "big hearted" individual, Ainsworth spent lavishly and boasted of making and spending two fortunes in his lifetime.[229]

While the McCurtains loudly fixed the blame for the violence and disorder in the Nation on the white tide of intrusion, the brothers completely ignored the fact that their own family shared some of the responsibility for the lawlessness loose in the country. In 1874, the murder of a younger sibling Robert caused the McCurtains to contribute greatly to the turmoil they railed against as chiefs. The youth had started courting Tandy Walker's daughter but was not considered worthy of the girl and told to stay away from her. One day in August Robert rode up to the Walker home despite warnings from her family and demanded to talk with her. Before he reached the door, Henderson Walker, Tandy's son and the girl's brother, burst from the house onto the porch with a gun and ordered Robert off the place. When the rash McCurtain defiantly kept coming, Walker shot him. Managing to remount, McCurtain rode off a few hundred feet before collapsing dead in the yard. Walker, realizing what he had done, immediately left town and purposely stayed away for more than two years. When he did make his reappearance, Jackson and Green McCurtain heard of it and set out after the young Walker. The brothers eventually caught up with him and Green shot him to death.

Fortunately, cooler heads calmed the affair before it exploded into a blood feud, but the episode seemed indicative of the moral condition of Skullyville. The town had declined rapidly after the Civil War. Its stores and residences were burned or otherwise destroyed, and the people, growing tired of the trouble and crime, slowly moved away. When the railroad passed by, the villagers relocated about a mile west to Spiro, a new town.[230]

In 1886, Thompson McKinney won the election for Principal Chief. McKinney, who lived on Eagle Fork about three miles west of the town of Smithville, was probably born in 1847, but no records exist of his birth or his education. A younger brother studied at a neighborhood school and then attended Spencer, so Thompson possibly did as well, paving the way for him. In 1877, he served as a member of the Choctaw Council and a term as National Secretary before his election as chief through the support of Edmund McCurtain. He served only one term because his political career was destroyed by a robbery in the summer of 1887.

Hiring his brother William, a minister educated at Yale College, to carry several thousand dollars of tribal school funds to Paris, Texas, McKinney placed the money in saddlebags and started William on the long trip but along the way William was ambushed and robbed by two men. Released unhurt, he hurried to Paris to report what happened, but tribal members, not believing his story, accused him of being an accomplice in the robbery. Since Chief McKinney had selected his brother to carry out the mission, he was implicated as well. Nothing was ever proven, but William was forced by rumors and innuendos to withdraw from his church and Thompson decided not to run again.

Years later, after Belle Starr's death on February 3, 1889, an account of the robbery was found in her handwriting. Admitting to dressing as a man, Starr claimed credit with a partner for committing the holdup of William Thompson. This news exonerated the McKinney brothers, but it was too late to restore their careers. Chief McKinney died the same year at his home in

Wilburton. He left three minor children, Alexander, born in 1880, Baxter, 1882, and Louisa, 1886. The Reverend Jackson James of Boiling Springs, appointed as their guardian, placed them in the Murrow Orphan Home in Atoka.

The Choctaw chiefs faced many difficult, trying problems, but they generally accomplished their major goal of restoring prosperity in the Nation. Perhaps, too well, because the renewed wealth quickly attracted the attention of white "intruders" that migrated into the Nation by the thousands. The next chiefs had their hands full keeping the Nation together.[231]

CHAPTA AUAH TUCHENA

~ CHAPTER THIRTEEN ~

"GONE BUT NOT FORGOTTEN"

Ben Smallwood
1888 - 1890

Wilson N. Jones
1890 -1894

Jefferson Gardner
1894 - 1896

Green McCurtain
1896 - 1900, 1902 - 1910

Chapter Thirteen

In 1889, the establishment of Oklahoma Territory inaugurated a similar movement in Indian Territory. From 1888 to 1907, the chiefs of the Choctaw Republic were forced to deal with the difficult tasks of opening the Nation to white settlement and preparing for statehood whether they supported the movements or not. Chiefs Ben F. Smallwood (1888-90), Wilson N. Jones (1890-94), Jefferson Gardner (1894-96), Green McCurtain (1896-1900), Gilbert Dukes (1900-1902), and Green McCurtain (1902-1907) accepted the challenges of the job without any illusions of its seriousness or consequences.

In August 1888, the McCurtain brothers, leaders of the Progressive Party, suffered a temporary setback in their campaign for conversion to statehood when Benjamin Franklin Smallwood of the rival National Party defeated their party candidate, Wilson N. Jones. An opponent of any negotiations concerning changes in the Choctaw Nation, Smallwood was a determined fighter against the factions of the tribe that supported the movement.

Born in 1829, the son of William Smallwood of Mississippi, Ben traced his family roots to his grandfather, Elijah Smallwood, an English migrant married to a Choctaw wife. Their son William attended the Choctaw Academy, returned to Mississippi, married Mary LeFlore, a sister of Thomas LeFlore, and enlisted in the militia during the Creek wars in 1814. After the wars he opened a rest and food stand on the Robinson Road, a mail route that ran from Columbus to Canton, Mississippi. William closed the stand when Robinson Road was reduced to a minor trail by the construction of the Natchez Trace. William and Mary Smallwood had six children, including Benjamin, who, along with his brothers, enrolled in the Choctaw Academy just as removal was beginning. In the 1830s the family moved to the Kiamichi River area and William turned to farming for a living. In 1863, he served a term in the Choctaw Council.

Ben went to school at Shawneetown on the Red River and attended Spencer Academy before joining his father as a farmer and rancher in 1847. In 1849, he married Annie Burney, a Chickasaw who died during the Civil War, and he remarried Abbie James. After completing an enlistment as a Captain in the Second Choctaw Regiment, Smallwood returned to ranching. In 1862, he opened a mercantile store and a year later moved to Lehigh where his fortunes soared by trading goods from his store for livestock. Over time Smallwood prospered into one of the wealthiest men in the Nation.

Starting a political career as a cattle ranger for Kiamitia County, Smallwood was elected to the Council as a representative from 1847 to 1887. Serving four terms as Speaker, he was a conservative leader and even opposed granting a right-of-way to the Frisco Railroad in 1881. In 1886, he ran for chief on a platform advocating a complete stop to white immigration into the Nation but was defeated by Thompson McKinney. In 1888, he ran again and won, but his opponent, Wilson N. Jones, and the Progressive Party carried both houses of the Council by a large majority. Angered and disappointed by the returns, Smallwood took the oath of office at the Roebuck Hotel in Tvshkahomma rather than the National Capitol.

In 1888, the lingering feud between Chief Smallwood and the Council escalated into open warfare over the Net Proceeds Claims. When Washington made a payment for disbursement to the tribe, the dispute erupted into public accusations and counter charges when Chief Smallwood called a special session of the Council to distribute the money without an audit by the Net Proceeds Commission. Because he was paid $5,500 for doing it in this manner, his political opponents immediately charged him with corruption for committing a fraudulent act. The argument lasted into the next election and Progressives used the honesty issue to insure the election of Smallwood's opponent, Wilson N. Jones, but Smallwood was defeated by the slim margin of only two hundred votes.

He retired to his home in Coal County. He had accomplished little in his two-year administration as a result of the continuous political partisanship. He died in 1891. Reverend Joseph S. Murrow, helped by Chief Smallwood to establish the site of the Tishomingo cemetery, conducted the funeral.[232]

In 1888, Wilson Nathaniel Jones had been defeated for Principal Chief by Smallwood but won the office two years later. In 1892, he was elected to a second term after a bitter contest with Jacob B. Jackson. Jones was one of the richest men in the country at the time of his election.

Wilson was the youngest son of mixed blood Captain Nathaniel Jones whose father had immigrated into Mississippi from Virginia and married into the Battiest family. In 1833, the family removed to Little River in Red River County. Nathaniel later served as an annuity captain in charge of payments to the tribe and as a member of the Choctaw Council at the first Council meeting at Nvnih Waiya.

Born in Mississippi in 1827, Wilson was given little education beyond reading and simple arithmetic and could barely write his name. In 1849, he started a family with Susan Pickens and fathered two children, but both died in childhood, soon followed by his wife. He was remarried to Louisa LeFlore, the daughter of Thomas LeFlore, in Towson County, and had four more children but only Annie Bell and William W. "Willie" Jones lived to maturity. A family plagued by personal tragedy, Jones' daughter died in her senior year while away at college and Willie turned bad. In 1864, after Louisa died, Wilson had an affair with Martha L. Risener, the daughter of George Risener of Tennessee, a union that resulted in the birth of a boy, Jackson Nelson Jones, but the elder Jones never acknowledged him except as "my good friend," not as his son. In 1876, he married a third time to Belle Heaston Curtis, a white widow from Arkansas, and two more children were born, but they also died in childhood.[233]

Jones sold his farm for $500 after the Civil War, moved to Shawnee Creek in Blue County, and opened a mercantile store three miles west of Cade, a village near Caddo, the largest town in the region. Accepting livestock in trade for goods, he went into ranching and began raising cattle, along with horses and pigs. In 1867, Jones, who only spoke broken English, entered into a partnership with James Myers, a Kansas businessman, who contributed $400 to the stock. Within four years the two entrepreneurs had more than a thousand head of cattle, and Myers agreed to drive them to market at Ft. Scott, Kansas. Jones never saw him again. Myers disappeared completely with the money, and Jones lost his entire investment. Suffering his losses without complaint, he started over by collecting on debts owed the store, especially from W. W. Hampton who made 300 head of cattle available for Jones to begin another herd.

In 1872, Jones moved his general store to Caddo, a principal shipping point on the Katy Railroad, but naively turned it over to another partner to run, again with disastrous results. Making matters worse, Jones was held responsible for the business failures of two other men, B. J. Hampton and L. A. Morris, after lending them five thousand dollars along with his name and credit to purchase stock to start another business in town. Recovering once more, he was soon in operation again. Trusting yet another partner that once more absconded with the profits, Jones was left with more than $20,000 in debts owed to merchants in St. Louis.

Finally turning against any more white business partners, Jones mostly hired full bloods and blacks to work on his ranch and businesses after his earlier experiences. He only tolerated whites as employees in his cotton gin. Starting over once more, Jones soon recovered his financial fortunes. By 1890, he was in charge of 17,600 acres between Caddo and Boggy River with 550 acres under cultivation. The rest was fenced as pasture for his ranch herd numbered at more than 5,000 head and another 300 horses. Recognized as the "Cattle King" of Indian Territory, Jones owned stores, a cotton gin, and several mines as the uncontested richest man in the Nation.

As befitted his economic station as a rich cattleman, Jones constructed a huge, two-story frame home for himself and his family on Shawnee Creek. Built with two wings, the house contained a number of rooms with fireplaces in each, and one room, used both as a ballroom and a courtroom, measured thirty feet in length. A wide veranda around the house overlooked large cedars and fruit trees. Particularly proud of his fruit crops, Jones claimed to have the most bounteous apple orchards in the territory. Growing ever wealthier, he expanded his business into Texas and purchased a second home in Sherman.[234]

Chapter Thirteen

In 1883, his personal troubles resumed when his son "Willie" returned from school in Missouri to take over as the ranch foreman. A typically spoiled, rich child, Willie grew into an abusive bully who liked to drink and carouse the nightspots of Caddo, the center of the bootleg liquor trade from the crossover into Texas near the mouth of the Blue River. Unfortunately, Willie turned surly, tough, and mean when he got drunk. On September 18, 1885, while strolling down Main Street one afternoon after a day of hard drinking with a friend, Madison Bouton, who had arrived from New York in 1870 and married Christiana, the daughter of Israel Folsom, Willie suddenly pulled his six-shooter and shot Bouton to death simply for amusement. Totally unconcerned by what he had just done, Willie calmly mounted his pony and rode back to the ranch trusting that his father's wealth and position would protect him. Willie knew, correctly, that nothing would ever be done about the murder. The authorities even refused to bring charges against him.

Not long after, Alex Powell, another intermarried citizen, moved into competition with Jones for use of the open range and opened a small store in town. Keeping a little bell on the outside for his customers at night, the unsuspecting Powell was shot down as he stepped out to answer when it rang one evening late after closing time. Two bullets smashed into his body, but he lived long enough to identify his assailants as Willie and Steve Belvin, a hand at the ranch and later sheriff of Jackson County. Wilson again silenced the deathbed identification of the killers and no charges were ever filed against his son or Belvin. Willie soon had a reputation as a drunk and a killer, a very dangerous man to be around.

On January 26, 1888, he and three friends, Tuck and Chris Bench and Josh Crowder, the sheriff of Jackson County, were on a spree when one of them suggested a trip across the Red River to Garrett's Bluff, a "honky-tonk" that sold liquor to customers on both sides of the stream. After Tuck returned from Texas with a fresh supply of liquor, the drinking turned deadly when a fight broke out that ended with him pulling his pistol and shooting Willie to death. Sheriff Crowder, drunk as well, did not interfere. The men left Willie on a sandbar on the Choctaw side of the river and went home to sober up. When his faculties returned, Tuck, realizing the severity of his action, fled the country, and did not return until after Chief Jones' death.

A feud between Jones and Sheriff Crowder did develop over the murder but nothing ever came of it. Jones hired Green McCurtain to prosecute Crowder and Chris Bench and the attorney filed a complaint in the courthouse north of Boswell, but the defendants retained William A. Durant to negotiate their release. Durant got bonds posted for the two, and the trial was never held. Years later, Crowder was waylaid and killed by blacks in McCurtain County. His murderers were captured and convicted at Atoka and sent to the penitentiary, but there was never any indication Jones had any hand in the matter.[235]

A man with a remarkable capacity for accepting adversity, Chief Jones concealed his grief by returning to politics. In 1884, he served as a Pushmataha District Trustee and three years was elected Treasurer and Chief in 1890. A close friend, Dr. Leroy Long, who arrived in Caddo from Louisville Medical College to work with Dr. J. S. Fulton and married a Choctaw wife, Martha Downing, said that Jones often used business to cover his personal misfortunes. Dr. Long stated that Jones once gave him the best economic advice that he ever received. Jones, who thought the physician should not work as hard as he did, advised Long to get a farm and start raising cattle, "because they grow while you sleep."[236]

In 1892, Jones won a second term after a bitter contest with Jacob Battiest Jackson, a full blood born in Mississippi in 1848. Removed to Indian Territory, Jackson served in the Confederate army as a private under Captain Coleman E. Nelson of the First Regiment of Choctaw Mounted Rifles and attended King's College in Bristol, Tennessee, after the war. Receiving a law degree at Roanoke College in Salem, Virginia, Jackson returned to Indian Territory to set up a successful practice at Skullyville. In 1876, he was elected senator. In 1889, he won election as National Secretary, an office that inspired him to run for chief a few years later. Establishing a political reputation as a supporter of schools by helping found a "new" Spencer Academy and as a determined, vocal opponent of Choctaw allotments, Jackson ran unsuccessfully for the position for years. In 1894, he was again defeated by Jefferson Gardner and by Gilbert W. Dukes in 1900.

Both parties resorted to violence during the controversial campaign of 1892. Jones, after much strife, was finally declared the winner by only seven votes out of 3,402. One of the consequences of the election was the shooting of Joe Haklotubbe in Hartshorne by political enemies that led to widespread turmoil throughout the Nation. Leaders of both factions gathered at McAlester supposedly to fight it out, but Indian Agent, Leo Bennett, threatened to abolish the whole tribal government and eventually talked the opposing sides into putting up their weapons.

The violence was almost ignited again in Antlers when Chief Jones assembled a militia to arrest a political opponent who had taken refuge in the home of Victor M. Locke. The so-called Jones-Locke affair resulted in the windows being shot out of the Baptist church and the Masonic Lodge, but luckily no one was hurt seriously. With supporters equally armed on both sides, it appeared a battle might break out until tempers cooled with the arrival of troops from Fort Reno to preserve order. Unfortunately, the whole tragic business only provided more ammunition to support the arguments for allotments by proponents of the Dawes Commission.[237]

Jones' most notable accomplishment was the establishment of two boarding schools for the Nation, one for boys called Jones Academy and one for girls called Tvshkahomma Female Institute. This made five in all, including Wheelock Seminary and Armstrong Academy, set aside as orphans' homes and Tuscaloosa Institute, a school for freedmen.

Established four miles east of Hartshorne in 1891, Jones Academy provided residential care for students in a campus setting of 540 acres. The campus expanded until its buildings consisted of a gymnasium, dormitories, Spurlock Hall, foster grandparents building, a plant management building, employee cottages, student activity center, swine barn, museum, maintenance buildings, and storage buildings. Playgrounds included three softball fields, two outside basketball or tennis courts, and an eighteen-hole miniature golf course.

In 1952, Jones Academy discontinued its academic program when its children entered public schools through the Johnson O'Malley Act, 1934, authorizing the Secretary of Interior to enter into contracts with the states for the education of Indians. Approximately sixty boys enrolled in the schools at Hartshorne. In 1955, Jones was designated as a co-educational school when fifty-five girls were transferred to Jones Academy when Wheelock school closed its doors. In 1962, the Agnes J. Spurlock Hall was built and named for the lady who served as principal from 1955 to 1964. In April 1985, the Choctaw Nation contracted the operation of the school under Public Law 93-638, and Jones became a tribally controlled grant school under P. L. 100-297 in October 1988.

On February 12, 2,000, Council Members agreed to provide funding to begin an academic program for Jones Academy again after forty-eight years. Brad Spears served as administrator and former administrator, Assistant Chief Mike Bailey, announced there were 200 students at Jones. In February, a $66,000 grant was received from the Bureau of Indian Affairs for improvements of the gymnasium at Jones.[238]

Chief Jones left his name on one other lasting monument. Acquainted with the medical staff in Sherman as the Texas doctors traveled through the Nation giving medical help during his administration, Jones was convinced by them to transfer much of his banking business to their city. Later, he purchased the home of Texas Supreme Court Judge Thomas J. Brown at the site of the later Grayson County State Bank. In 1898, Chief Jones, spending his retirement years as a resident of Sherman, ran again in an unsuccessful campaign for chief on the Union ticket. He passed away in Sherman three years later. The seventy-four-year-old former chief was shipped back to Caddo and transported fifteen miles east to his home for burial beside his beloved Willie. The tombstone marker read simply: "Gone But Not Forgotten."

At the time of his death, the bulk of the Jones fortune, an estimated $250,000, was bequeathed to his grandson, Nat. Wilson Nathan "Nat" Jones was Willie's son from his marriage to Amelia McCauley, a beautiful Chickasaw girl, in Atoka in 1887. Nat was named the beneficiary of the Jones riches, but his life proved as controversial and violent as his father's. The will, drawn up on September 13, 1900, witnessed by Sherman businessmen, F. A. Batsell and P. R. Markham, provided that Nat would receive his inheritance in increments of $10,000 at the age of twenty-one, $25,000 at twenty-five, and the remainder at thirty, with the stipulation that if he died before the age of thirty, the money would be used to build a Wilson N. Jones Memorial Hospital in Sherman. The young man received the first two payments, but before he reached his thirtieth birthday he fell to his death from the ninth floor of an Oklahoma City hotel. Relatives contested the will for years based on speculation that the Wilson heir had been killed, but the Texas Courts ruled that the estate, valued at $140,000 in 1917, could be used to create the hospital.[239]

In August 1894, Jefferson Gardner of Eagletown defeated National Party nominee, Jacob Jackson, to succeed Jones. Born near Wheelock on July 12, 1847, Gardner and his brothers, Jerry and James, were sons of Noel and Hannah Gardner, both mixed blood natives of Mississippi. Gardner's father, a former student at Choctaw Academy, served for a time as an interpreter for the early missionaries. Jefferson was placed in the Norfolk School in Towson County at an early age and then enrolled at Spencer Academy in the fall of 1855. He stayed for two years. In 1862, he married Lucy James and fathered a daughter Alzira. When his first wife died, Gardner moved to Eagletown, married Lucy Christy, daughter of Joseph Christy, and after her death, married her sister Julia. Starting a farm and ranch along the Mountain Fork River, Gardner built a home a short distance from the largest cypress tree in Indian Territory. In 1878, he started a mercantile business and a cotton gin in Eagletown to supplement his income and was later appointed postmaster. A successful storeowner, he soon opened others at Alikchi and Sulphur Springs.

In 1864, the balding, five-foot six-inch, mixed blood began his political career with an appointment as County Clerk of Eagle County. A year later he served as District Clerk. In 1873, he was elected to serve Eagle and Wolf Counties in the Tribal Senate. Although earning a reputation as a man of few words, ten years later he was elected Treasurer of the Nation. In 1888, he was elected as Circuit Judge of the Second Judicial District, a position he held until his election as Chief.

In 1890, Gardner was alarmed by the news that the Choctaw composed only about one-fourth of the total population of the Nation. Greatly disturbed because most whites were growing insistent about allotments in severalty, Gardner summed up the feelings of many of his people when he stated, "Therefore, with all candor and courtesy to the Dawes Commission I am opposed to a change, knowing that our people are not prepared for it and that a consent will never be given..." Actually, most leaders saw the end coming, and the Chief, if honest with himself, probably did, too.

In 1896, Gardner withdrew to his Mountain Fork home and assumed a passive attitude toward the possibility of allotments. He flatly refused to meet with any commission representatives and declined to furnish any papers or documents or copies of tribal rolls to it. He had decided to try to stop the allotment movement by simply ignoring it.

In 1896, tribal elections turned into another bitter affair when forces opposed to acceptance of allotments divided into three parties, each with a candidate, thereby automatically giving the election to the side of proponents. Gardner ran for a second term against Jacob B. Jackson and Gilbert W. Dukes while the Progressive candidae, Green McCurtain, ran on a platform of coming to terms with the Dawes Commission. When McCurtain won, Gardner accepted his replacement graciously, called a special session of the General Council to arrange for the taking of tribal rolls, and made plans to meet with the commission representatives.

Gardner found that he had stayed too long in politics. His stores had been neglected and suffered financially, and he was finally forced out of business. He retired to the postmaster's job in Eagletown. In 1906, Gardner attended a court session in Antlers but contracted pneumonia. On the way home by train, he stopped at Idabel where he died on April 6. He was taken to the Joe Christy Burying Ground, three miles south of Eagletown, for burial.[240]

Political parties were virtually unknown in the Choctaw Nation until the debate over opening the Indian Territory to white settlement and acceptance of allotments in severalty reached the national tribal election of 1892. They developed when the discussions over the issues caused a severe separation within the tribe that lead to political polarization. Those opposed to the proposals of the Dawes Commission were recognized as the National Party and were followers of full blood Jacob B. Jackson while those favoring the proposals were called Progressives and led by Green McCurtain.

Green organized the party to support Wilson N. Jones for Chief and had supported Jefferson Gardner in 1894, but McCurtain became a supporter of allotments while Gardner did not. Their dispute caused a split within the Progressive Party. Green was in Washington when the Dawes Commission legislation for the Five Tribes was before Congress in 1893, and his followers, who advocated coming to an agreement with the Commission, organized a new party called the Tuskahoma Party to run him for Chief in 1896. The other parties were the Independent National Party that supported Gardner and his passive resistance approach to allotment, the old Progressive Party that supported Gilbert W. Dukes, and the conservative Full Bood National Party under Jackson that advocated having nothing to do wth the Dawes Commission. When McCurtain was elected, the Choctaw prepared for acceptance of allotments in severalty.

The McCurtain dynasty was started by Green's father Cornelius and continued by his two older brothers, all previous Principal Chiefs. Born at Skullyville on November 28, 1848, Green went to the local neighborhood schools before entering politics at the age of twenty-four. In 1872, he served one term as sheriff of Skullyville County, three terms in the National Council, 1874-1880, four years as the trustee of schools, 1880-84, treasurer in 1888, and senator for two years in 1893.

The large, balding, six-feet-two, 220-pound McCurtain was married twice. His first wife, a white lady, was the mother of his son, David Cornelius "D. C." who was born in 1873. D. C. was educated at Roanoke College, Virginia, and Kemper Military School in Missouri. Studying law at Missouri State University and George Washington College in Washington, D.C., he returned to Indian Territory as a judge. Serving for a time as mayor of McAlester, he later opened a law practice at Poteau. Green's second wife was the daughter of John Spring of Tvshkahomma. Their children included Alice Scott, Lena Moore, and Bertha and Cora Pebworth.[241]

In 1896, Green moved from conference to conference with intentions of making the tribe the first to come to an agreement with the Dawes Commission. On April 23, 1897, his efforts were successfully completed with the negotiation and ratification of the Atoka Agreement by a tribal vote. Only a few months later the Curtis Act, 1898, authorized the commission to proceed with its campaign whether the tribe approved or not. Green was elected for another term at the same time, but the main issue in the campaign was the liquidation of tribal government within eight years, a topic that caused considerable opposition to the proposals of the Dawes Commission. In 1900, McCurtain, ineligible to run for a third consecutive term, threw his support to Gilbert W. Dukes, who pledged to continue his olicies as the candidate for the Tvshkahomma party.[242]

Gilbert Wesley Dukes was the descendant of William Dukes, a white man of French-English ancestry, who moved to Mississippi and married Nancy Wade, a sister of John Wade, one of the signers of the Dancing Rabbit Creek Treaty and the aunt of later Governor Alfred Wade. William's son was Joseph Dukes. Born in Mississippi, Joseph married Nancy Collins, the mixed blood daughter of Charles Collins, a white man, and Mary Bell, a full blood. Serving as an interpreter and friend of Reverend Cyrus Byington at Mayhew Mission, Joseph, a Presbyterian minister, removed his family to a farm near Fort Towson in Boktuklo County. Working for the next twenty-five years as a teacher and translator for Reverend Alfred Wright, Joseph was buried at Wheelock in 1861. His wife Nancy moved the family to Wade Settlement near present Talihina to live close to her son Gilbert. She lived until 1875.

Gilbert, the tenth member of Joseph and Nancy's twelve children, was born at Lukfata, Boktuklo County, on November 21, 1849. Educated at Spencer Academy, he read law, joined the Confederate army at the age of fourteen, served with Jackson McCurtain's regiment, and returned to the law as an attorney before the Choctaw tribal courts after the war. In 1870, Dukes moved from Wheelock to Wade Settlement where he farmed 500 acres east of Talihina. Married to Angeline Wade, Governor Alfred Wade's daughter, the couple had two children, Henry and Joseph. After the death of Angeline, Dukes married Isabel, the daughter of Horace Woods, a white farmer from Massachusetts. Dukes' five children with Isabel were Edwin, D. H., Josephine, Minerva, and Leatta.

The six-feet-four, 250-pound attorney often tried cases at the Tobucksy Indian Courthouse located at North McAlester where he achieved a reputation as an eloquent speaker in both English and Choctaw. His political career included terms as sheriff of Wade County, as a legislator in the House and the Senate, as a judge on the Supreme Court from 1885 to 1889, and as a Circuit Judge of the Second District from 1889 to 1895. In 1897, he helped frame the Atoka agreement, the major issue in his 1900 campaign for Chief. Advocating support for the agreement, Dukes further committed to the settlement of tribal affairs and the leasing of mineral lands for the support of tribal education. Jacob B. Jackson, the perennial leader of the National Party, was his greatest political opponent, while Dr. E. N. Wright, Allen's son, was the third candidate in the race as the standard bearer for the Union Party.

In January 1901, Dukes, who preferred the title "Governor," promptly called the Council into special session to introduce legislation for the establishment of a committee to work out a speedy agreement with the Dawes Commission. The Council supported him by appointing him head of the proposed committee. Breakthroughs followed on the heels of the arrangement until severe political problems developed for Dukes when Green McCurtain announced his intention to recapture the job for the Tuskahoma Party in the fall of 1902. Dukes angrily bolted the party to support Thomas W. Hunter, a County Judge from Hugo, of the Union Party. The campaign quickly degenerated into one of the most violent contests yet as McCurtain and Dukes began attacking each other although Hunter was McCurtain's opponent.

Before the votes were counted, troops had to be called into Tvshkahomma.

Dukes, on the morning of the vote canvass, walked into the Capitol with Hunter, and turned over everything to him as his successor. Major Hackett, the United States marshal, who supported them, took possession of the grounds, proclaimed Hunter the chief, and proceeded to organize a Council with the supporters of McCurtain barred from entering the building. At this juncture, Indian Agent J. Blair Shoenfelt, present in the yard, attempted to settle the argument but was unable to do so since the federal marshal claimed to have jurisdiction in the matter. Therefore, Shoenfelt sent a message to Washington, D.C. asking for troops as the standoff continued until the final day provided by the constitution to count the votes. Soldiers, composed of black troops commanded by white officers, marched to the Capitol, consulted with the marshal and the Indian agent, disarmed all the occupants, and took command of the building. As the two factions fought outside the building, the counting of the votes continued inside. The soldiers refused to admit anyone until dark when Green McCurtain was declared Principal Chief of the Nation, but troops had to keep monitoring the peace until Dukes finally stepped down.[243]

Dukes and McCurtain, once close political allies, became bitter personal and professional enemies. McCurtain's animosity was clearly evident in his response to a remark on one occasion that Dukes was an impressive attorney who could convince any Choctaw jury that no white man ever told the truth. Irked into anger by the statement, McCurtain sarcastically responded that Dukes was so anti-white, "Because a white man stole his last bottle of whiskey."[244]

In 1910, Dukes was a candidate for the Republican Party for the office of Lieutenant Governor. His party, suffering from the statehood stigma of "carpetbag government," lost the race by an overwhelming majority. Dukes only received 94,621 votes to J. J. McAlester's 118,544.

In 1911, Dukes presided over the final session of the Choctaw Council Senate. In one of its last actions, the Council appointed him a delegate to represent the tribe in discussions about tribal health problems in Washington. A successful mission, Dukes and the delegation convinced Congress to set aside four sections of un-allotted lands north of Talihina and $50,000 of tribal funds for construction of an Indian Hospital.

Dukes, an elder in the Presbyterian Church, a Mason, and a member of the Odd Fellows and the Knights of Pythias, passed away on December 26, 1919. He was buried at the Post Oak Presbyterian Cemetery on the south side of the Kiamichi River about twelve miles southeast of Talihina.[245]

In 1904, another election was held with McCurtain as the incumbent candidate opposed by N. J. Folsom, a district judge, W. H. Harrison, an attorney, Adam Joe, a district chief, G.W. Choate, a senator, L. H. Perkins, a representative, S. H. Mackey, a county judge, Joe Anderson, a sheriff, and Gilbert Arpelar, a ranger. The results were the same as two years earlier. McCurtain served until Wesley Anderson of Tvshkahomma was elected in August 1906, but Anderson was not confirmed because tribal government was supposed to end on March 4, 1906.

McCurtain, the only man elected to alternative terms, and the last elected chief until modern times, served until his death at Kinta in Haskell County on December 28, 1910. It was said that McCurtain was "first an Indian and then a Democrat but there came a time when he believed the Democratic delegation in Congress was unfriendly to his people and he became and died a Republican."

On April 26, 1906, legislation was passed providing for "the final disposition of the Affairs of the Five Civilized Tribes in Indian Territory and for other purposes." The Choctaw, included in this law, saw the powers of the Chief and the Council dismantled and taken over by the federal government. The Chief only held office at the pleasure of the American president and served until removed from office or death. Another democratic election for the position would not be held until 1971.[246]

CHAPTA AUAH USHTA

~ CHAPTER FOURTEEN ~

"WE MUST REMEMBER THE PAST…"

Gilbert Dukes
Chief of the Choctaw Nation, February 1901.
1900-1902

Gov. Green McCurtain,
Victor Locke, Jr., Peter Hudson,
and Dr. E. N. Wright.
Photo By G. Buck Wash. D.C.

William F. Semple
Principal Chief,
1912 - 1922

William H. Harrison
Principal Chief
1922-1929

Ben Dwight
1930 - 1936

Wm. A. Durant
1937 - 1948

Harry J. W. Belvin
1948 - 1975

C. David Gardner
1975 - 1978

Hollis Roberts
Chief
1978 - 1997

Greg Pyle
Chief
1997 -

Choctaw Nation of Oklahoma

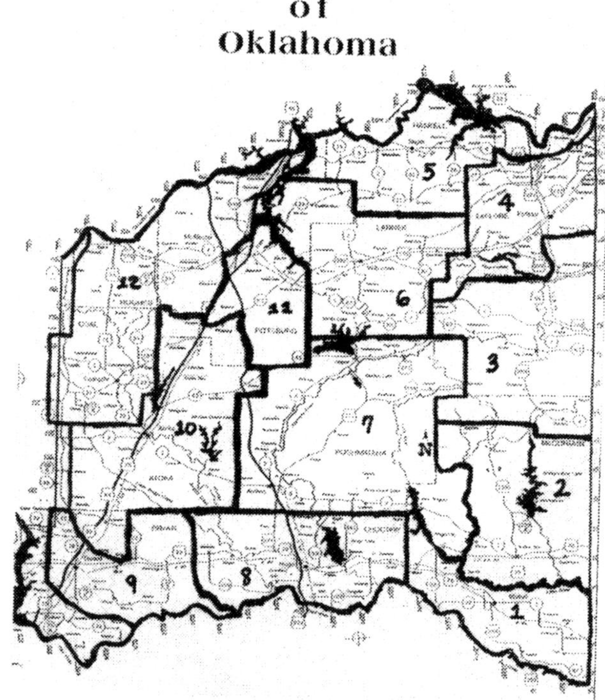

Chapter Fourteen

In 1906, elective government ended for the Choctaw, but the office of Principal Chief continued as an appointive position until 1970. Green McCurtain remained in office by appointment to preside over the dismantling of tribal government while serving at the same time as an agent for the tribe in formal negotiations with Washington. The staunch Baptist mixed blood continued as chief until his death in 1910. His successors were chosen at the pleasure of the United States President. They included Victor M. Locke, Jr., 1911-18, William F. Semple, 1918-22, William H. Harrison, 1922-29, Ben Dwight, 1930-37, William A. Durant, 1937-48, and Harry J. W. Belvin, 1948-1975. In 1970, Belvin was chosen chief in the first election since statehood. C. David Gardner replaced him in 1975. Three years later Gardner's untimely death brought Hollis E. Roberts (1978-1997) into office. In 1997, Gregory E. Pyle replaced Roberts.

In February 1911, President William H. Taft appointed Victor M. Locke, Jr. to succeed McCurtain. Locke, a Republican and Spanish-American War veteran, served until 1917.

Born at Doaksville in 1876, "Dickie" Locke was the son of Tennessee immigrant, Victor "Uncle Dick" Locke Sr. and Susan Priscilla McKinney Locke of Antlers. Uncle Dick was an ex-Confederate cavalryman who migrated to the Choctaw Nation in 1866 after some trouble with reconstruction authorities in his home state, married a Choctaw wife, and reared five boys, James "Shub" S., Victor, Jr., Ben D., Jesse "Babe" N., and Edwin "Alex," and one girl, C. E. "Dolly." He later stated that his children were all Republicans and Catholics but added that he could never be a Republican because he was a Southern Democrat and could never be a Catholic because of the confessional. He said, "I am not going to confess to anyone; they have got to prove it on me." He died in 1929.

Sent to school at White Church six miles east of Antlers, Dickie and his sister later attended St. Agnes Academy in Antlers. Entering Jones Institute at Paris, Texas, Locke transferred to Austin College in Sherman in 1893. Another year was spent at Drury College in Springfield, Missouri. In 1898, he enlisted in the army for the Spanish-American War but never engaged in combat service.

In 1904, Locke, a Catholic by faith and Republican by affiliation, began his political career as a delegate representing Indian Territory at the Republican National Convention. A supporter of Theodore Roosevelt, Locke campaigned for the former Rough Rider for president. In 1908, he organized Company L of the Oklahoma National Guard and was given the rank of major by Governor Lee Cruce in 1915. In 1913, he married a widow, Mrs. Vivia Nail Robertson, the daughter of J. H. Nail, a prominent Choctaw citizen. They had one daughter, Rose Banatima (Bunny), before divorcing. In 1910, President William Howard Taft appointed him Principal Chief. He served until 1917.

One of the most serious problems for Locke and the tribe in early statehood was a concerted effort by federal authorities to sell tribal assets at bargain prices to wealthy white citizens. In 1912, the surface areas of tribal coal deposits, amounting to 444,052 acres of coal and asphalt lands, were sold to private interests, followed by another sale of 64,415 acres in 1918. The proceeds from these sales, along with the earnings from the sale of 1.3 million acres of timber lands, totaling $19,775,463, were distributed per capita to the Choctaw with each enrollee entitled to $300 beginning in 1916. The following year a payment of $100 was made and in 1918, $200, in 1919, $140, in 1920, $100, in 1921, $50, in 1924, $25, and in 1925, $10 was paid. These payments, increased by trust funds from other sources, allowed a total payment of $1070 to each Choctaw in 1920.

Locke later served a term in the Oklahoma Legislature and then was appointed superintendent to the Five Civilized Tribes with headquarters in Muskogee in 1921. By then the allotments were completed but the county probate courts were flooded with estate and guardianship cases, and Locke, a confessed "poor politician," attempted to administer the agency with honesty and fairness only to encounter immense opposition from corrupt officials. Surrounded by crooked politicians, oil companies seeking favorable leases, white guardians determined to squander the fortunes of their clients, and immoral auto dealers and furniture salesmen seeking opportunities to sell their wares, Locke was overwhelmed. He was replaced in June 1923.

In September 1927, Locke's personal life suffered when he was charged with the murder of Abner Battiest, a twenty-two-year-old Choctaw. He was convicted of murder but appealed his conviction and received a ten-year sentence. One year later the appeal was dismissed, but Governor W. J. Holloway of Hugo granted him a full pardon on December 29, 1930. In 1931, Locke married Sudie McAlester Barnes, the daughter of wealthy mine owner, J. J. McAlester.

Locke's particular service to the tribe was as its official spokesman in Washington giving testimony before many different congressional committees on Indian affairs. Chief Locke worked particularly hard to accomplish educational goals for the Choctaw people with the ultimate objective of preparing for the time that his people could handle their own financial affairs. He died March 1, 1943, and was buried in the family cemetery in Antlers.[247]

In 1917, Locke and other Choctaw warriors had joined Oklahomans as volunteers for service in World War I. In 1918, Democratic President Woodrow Wilson appointed William Finley Semple, an attorney from Durant, as the next Principal Chief. The Choctaw contributed their lives and property to the war effort and established a record for sacrifice that proved their worth as Americans. One of their rewards was full, unrestricted citizenship in 1924.

Semple was born March 16, 1883, at Caddo, I. T., the son of Charles Alexander Semple and Minnie Pitchlynn, a descendant of the John Pitchlynn family. A student at Jones Academy as a young man, Semple graduated with a degree in law from Washington and Lee University at Lexington, Virginia, in 1907. Returning to Bryan County, he set up a law practice in Durant, specializing in land titles. His political career began with his election to the House of Representatives during the second session of the state legislature. Later appointed as District Attorney for the Choctaw Nation, he also served on a Council for the Bureau of Indian Affairs.

In 1918, Semple's administration witnessed a growing awareness of Choctaw culture when the Board of Missions of the Methodist Episcopal Church, South, established a mission school near Smithville in McCurtain County. The school was named Folsom Training School in honor of Reverend Willis F. Folsom, a Methodist minister, who removed from Mississippi to Eagletown in 1825 and then moved to Skullyville as a preacher in 1852. In November 1920, Reverend Walter B. Hubbell of Conway, Arkansas, arrived to find only a basement had been built for the school, although the year before Preacher E. A. Townsend and his wife had taught twelve Indian and white students. In 1921, the boarding school opened with dormitories for its pupils from sixth grade through high school. By 1923, the student body of Choctaw, Chickasaw, Creek, Seminole, and Kiowa students numbered more than 250 with one-fourth being white. In 1924, one year of college was added with tuition for one semester set at twenty-five dollars and board at eighteen dollars per month. For those unable to afford these prices, there were work programs for care of the campus, serving meals, doing laundry, or working on the 300-acre farm.

The Folsom Training School operated under a severe set of rules that emphasized discipline for all students. Scholars worked five hours per week without pay from the school, shared all the chores, and endured a strict dress code with no students allowed to wear silk, and girls were not allowed to wear lipstick, rouge, or short dresses. All skirts had to be a minimum of three inches below the knee. Surprisingly, the school did allow movies in the auditorium, literary societies, glee clubs, and athletics.

In 1924, Sealey Chapel was added with Reverend C. E. Nisbett as pastor. Among its early contributors was Johnson Bobb, a Choctaw preacher. By 1930, the school included a two-story administration building, a three-story dormitory for girls, and a comparable one for boys, a superintendent's home, a faculty house, cottages for married students, a variety store, drug store, power plant, woodworking plant, and barns. In 1932, the entire operation, valued at more than $200,000, went into decline after a fire destroyed the girls' dorm. The Depression caused serious economic problems that eventually forced the closure of the campus. Its facilities were turned over to the Civilian Conservation Corps (CCC) for three years and eventually torn down.

While the position of Principal Chief carried considerable prestige, there was little in the way of monetary recompense, and Semple worked diligently to keep costs at a minimum. In 1919, his expenses for the month of January, one of the highest of his term in office, amounted to $242.46. The expenditure was unusually high because of two business trips to Washington for testimony on the sale of Choctaw coal and asphalt lands. The trips were itemized at a cost of forty-five dollars and ninety-three cents each with additional amounts for subsistence, meals and lodging, necessitating the costly figure. Most of Chief Semple's monthly expenses ranged only from fifty to seventy dollars.

Semple also made several trips around southeastern Oklahoma for discussions with other Choctaw leaders about issues. On December 18, 1919, former Chief Locke called a caucus meeting at Hugo with other Choctaw leaders in the area that led to an invitation to Semple, who forwarded it to Superintendent Gabe E. Parker in Muskogee. An agreement was made to enlarge the meeting into a general session to include all Choctaw in the county as a means of keeping the tribe informed of recent tribal matters.

Semple held the position of Chief until 1922. William H. Harrison of Poteau replaced him by appointment from Republican President Warren G. Harding. Married to Clara Petty, who died in 1966, Chief Semple passed away in 1969. Both were buried in Tulsa.[248]

In 1876, William Harrison, the mixed blood son of Mitchell and Louisa Harrison, was born near Tamaha, Choctaw Nation. William's early education was at Spencer Academy and Henry Kendall College in Muskogee. In 1902, he began work toward a law degree at Centre College, Danville, Kentucky. After graduation he established a private practice in Poteau, was appointed District Attorney for the tribe, was authorized to practice law before the United States Supreme Court, and served for a time as a postmaster. In 1908, he married Minnette Roberts, the daughter of Dr. C. S. Roberts of Lee's Summit, Missouri.

Harrison labored long hours as an attorney to protect Choctaw traditions and rights by personally lobbying many different members of Congress to prevent the passage of a bill introduced to allow Congress to reopen the citizenship rolls of the Choctaw and Chickasaw. He continued to be an advocate for his people until his death at the age of fifty-three on September 25, 1929. His funeral was held at the Presbyterian Church in Poteau.

Chief Harrison and other Choctaw leaders tried many efforts, admittedly weak, to keep their status as a tribe alive during these years. In July 1922, delegates participated in a convention called at Albion in LeFlore County to review tribal affairs and to protest the long delay in the settlement of the

Atoka and Supplemental Agreements by the Indian Office. After sixteen years without a settlement, Dr. E. N. Wright was elected the chair of a Committee of Five Choctaw to work for a solution. The committee met at Wright's home after the convention to conduct a study of tribal affairs and set a program of procedure. An accounting of all tribal funds expended by the Indian Bureau for the Choctaw was sought along with a petition demanding a settlement of claims. Pressure was further applied for the government to either purchase tribal coal and asphalt properties at the minimum valuation set in 1910 or allow the tribe to dispose of these properties in cooperation with the Interior Department.

Since these matters involved millions of dollars of tribal funds and all Choctaw were owners of the properties, the committee publicly called for a General Council to meet for discussions. Since a council had not met in more than two decades, Wright and the Choctaw Committee pushed hard for one. Conventions were held, memorials sent to Washington, and interviews were conducted in the state capital, but all met with little success. Finally, the Choctaw leaders concluded that the Indians must make themselves into a political force, a political entity to be reckoned with on both the state and national levels. In 1926, the group entered congressional elections that year with the formation of a nonpartisan organization of Indians called the "Tuskahoma League" dedicated to involving Indians of all tribes in the use of the ballot as a means of getting politicians elected that would be more sympathetic to Indian issues.

Increasingly more personally involved in politics, Dr. Wright agreed to serve as a Republican state committeeman from Coal County in 1927. Picking the winning side, he was an early supporter of Charles Curtis for president and then backed the Hoover-Curtis ticket in the campaign of 1928. Wright applied for the position of chief after the election but was not appointed. The appointment went to Ben H. Dwight of Durant, 1930-1936.

Appointed by President Herbert Hoover, Dwight was continued in office by Franklin Roosevelt. Born on November 24, 1890, near Mayhew, Choctaw Nation, he was the son of a prominent Choctaw, Simon Timothy Dwight, a full blood, and Mary Jane Hunter. His father, a former Supervisor of Public Instruction for the Choctaw, instilled the need for an education in young Dwight, and his uncle, an influential sheriff of Jackson County, who served one term as a county judge, fascinated him with stories involving a law career.

The former judge's narrations of the "old days" kept the boy enthralled with anecdotes about the Choctaw courts, particularly their punishments by whippings, varying from thirty-nine to one hundred lashes on the bare back. Judge Dwight told Ben that he had seen grown men faint and cry from the whippings as they were done by several men including the sheriff and his deputies, with each man administering ten lashes then passing the whip to the next officer who gave ten more. The result was that men often collapsed from the whippings, but the former Choctaw attorney and judge reminded his nephew that no women were ever whipped or executed under Choctaw tribal law.[249]

Dwight attended Jones Academy, Armstrong Academy, and Caddo Public Schools. In 1908, he graduated from Honey Grove, Texas, High School. In 1913, he received a Bachelor of Arts degree from Columbia University, did postgraduate work at the University of Michigan and the University of Oklahoma, and completed work for a Bachelor of Law Degree at Leland Stanford University at Palo Alto, California. In 1916, he married Eileen Perkins, daughter of Thomas J. Perkins, in Durant. Volunteering for the army in 1917, Dwight served in World War I at Fort Sam Houston, Texas, as part of the Intelligence Department. He engaged in multitudinous occupations after the war, including serving as an automobile distributor, working in the furniture business, being employed in the production department of a movie studio in Hollywood, California, and trying a stint as an oil and gas entrepreneur. His public career began as an attorney in Durant when he was hired as City Attorney and later as Assistant District Attorney for Bryan County.

The Indian political movement continued to attract attention with more people beginning to question the policy of allotment and acculturation of the past. In 1928, an organization known as the Institute for Government Research, the Brookings Institution, began a full-scale investigation of the conditions of the tribes through research by intellectuals and historians including Lewis Meriam of the University of Chicago and Dr. Edward Everett Dale of the University of Oklahoma. Based on the groundwork of Secretary of Interior Hubert Work, the need for a change of direction was reported in an 872-page essay that revealed poverty, disease, suffering, and discontent among all the tribes. The Brookings group recommended "generous" help and expenditures over a long period for improved social circumstances of "shocking" housing and living conditions among the tribes. After receiving the report, Charles J. Rhodes, Commissioner of Indian Affairs for President Hoover, added his voice to the cry for changes in policies. Congress refused all his suggestions at the time, but the Indian Bureau started a new program consistent with the conclusions and recommendations of the institute.

In 1933, the radical departure started in the Hoover administration was extended by Franklin Roosevelt's New Deal program. Senator Elmer Thomas, a pro-New Dealer from Oklahoma, suggested Gabe Parker of Tulsa for the office of Commissioner of Indian Affairs to continue the program, but Roosevelt wanted John Collier of California in the position. A fifty-one-year-old Georgian who had studied at Columbia and the College de France, Paris, Collier had worked at State Teachers' College in San Francisco and with the Pueblos in New Mexico in 1923. As secretary of an organization known as the American Indian Defense Association, Collier argued that past policy based on the General Allotment Act of 1887 was a disaster. Intended to make Indians landholders, Christians, and capitalist farmers, Collier argued that the policy had resulted in the exact opposite, with the effect of degrading the Indians. As head of the Bureau of Indian Affairs, he called for a new and different philosophy and an altogether fresh direction. After taking office Collier consulted with Indian leaders, asked for suggestions for change, and sent out questionnaires to the tribes for recommendations. Eventually, he developed a three-pronged mission for the tribes, including economic habitation of the tribes on their own land, reorganization of the tribes with the goal of management of their own affairs, and civil and cultural opportunities for the tribes.

Senator Burton K. Wheeler of Montana and Edgar Howard of Nebraska, Chairman of the House Committee on Indian Affairs, pushed these goals into law as the Indian Reorganization Act, more commonly known as the Wheeler-Howard Act. Endorsed by President Roosevelt as a "New Deal" for the American Indian, surprisingly, it was opposed by many private interests and several tribes. In 1934, Collier arrived in Oklahoma to discover that most state newspapers, particularly *The Daily Oklahoman*, attacked it, as did many Indian leaders. *The Oklahoman's* objections were purely political, rejecting the plan outright as a Democratic proposal, and more outrageous, a Roosevelt New Deal proposal. The Oklahoma City paper stated that the "Indians do not like a white man coming fifteen hundred miles to tell us what to do." More seriously, Senator Thomas opposed the bill and successfully inserted an amendment that excluded Oklahoma tribes.

On June 18, 1934, the Wheeler-Howard Act was passed without Oklahoma participation, but a major media campaign had already started to change state attitudes. Choctaw leaders had organized meetings throughout the Choctaw and Chickasaw Nations and in Oklahoma, Tulsa, and Muskogee Counties to support passage of the law. On June 5, 1934, 168 delegates held a meeting on the matter several weeks before its passage at Goodland Indian School near Hugo. For three days the Goodland Convention openly discussed the bill and tribal affairs before passing resolutions for approval of the Act.

The Goodland representatives took advantage of their opportunity to organize an advisory council for tribal affairs. Composed of eleven delegates, the Advisory Council was formally established and passed a number of resolutions of interest to the tribe. The Council approved the selection of the Principal Chief appointed recently by the President, made recommendations for the purchase of land for landless members of the tribe, and suggested that historic places be marked and the old Council House at Tvshkahomma restored as a monument to Choctaw history. The Choctaw Advisory Council further called for a special session to meet in October 1934, followed by annual meetings in the future. The councils continued to meet through 1946, and their recommendations were considered by the Department of the Interior and the Congress but had no legitimate status.

The Wheeler-Howard Act prohibited further allotments, authorized $2 million per year for acquisition of Indian lands, permitted the organization of tribal governments with control of tribal funds, authorized tribal corporations for management of properties, and established a $10 million revolving fund for use by the tribes. Unfortunately, Oklahoma was not included in these laws until Senator Thomas moved up to chair the Senate Indian Affairs Committee. In 1935, bills for the Oklahoma tribes were introduced as the Indian Welfare Bill, or the Thomas-Rogers Bill, co-authored by Will Rogers of the House Indian Affairs Committee. The bill divided the Indians into two degrees. The first were half bloods or more who would have their property held in trust, and the second degree, those with less than one-half Indian blood, had all restrictions removed as rapidly as could be done. A commission was established to meet every four years to determine competency of second degrees.

A controversial section of the measure, Part Eight, placed first degrees under the Secretary of the Interior in matters involving estates, determination of heirs, approval of wills, and portioning of lands, funds, or other restricted properties. Most important, the bill provided that "no guardian . . . could be appointed by the courts of the State of Oklahoma for Indians of one-half or more except by petition approved by the Secretary of the Interior." Senator Thomas introduced the bill with approval from Secretary Harold Ickes, but a vote killed the amendments on February 26, 1935. Shortly afterwards, Chief Dwight wrote Senator Thomas a ringing endorsement, suggesting the bill be rewritten without the objectionable Section, a compromise that allowed the bill to pass in 1936. FDR called it a "Newer New Deal" for Oklahoma Indians and proclaimed the act the first step toward ending the policy of termination of Oklahoma tribes.

Representing the tribe in protection of tribal property rights in Washington on numerous occasions during his tenure, Chief Dwight also accomplished the prosecution of the Leased District claims for two-and one-half million acres from the 98th to the 100th Meridian taken from the tribe in 1866. Aided by the National Attorney for the Choctaw, Grady Lewis, provisions were made for the payment of $10 million as compensation for the claims. Oklahoma Senator William B. Pine sponsored a bill to make the payments but President Hoover vetoed the remuneration, and the case became a source of argument in the Court of Claims in 1939.

National Attorney Lewis, from LeFlore County, attended Jones Academy, Bokchito High School, Southeastern Oklahoma State University, and the University of Oklahoma, graduating with a law degree in 1920. Setting up a law practice with William F. Semple and Judge Jesse Hatchett in Durant, he later moved to Antlers and then to Sapulpa where he served one term as state representative from Creek County, 1929-30. During the Hoover administration, Lewis was appointed to the position of Choctaw National Attorney with offices in Muskogee and Washington, D.C. In World War II, he served as the provost marshal for London with the rank of major under General William S. Key.

In 1936, Dwight took over the position of attorney for the Choctaw Nation. In 1946, the Congress passed legislation for the Indian Claims Commission that gave the tribe a new day in the prosecution of its claims. In 1951, Dwight and Lewis obtained a judgment in the Court of Claims for $3.5 million. Although awarded less than half the original amount, the decision was a victory for all tribes because the Choctaw Leased District Claims was the first decision rendered in favor of an Indian tribe in the history of the Indian Claims Commission.

In 1935 and 1936, Dwight, Lewis, and George Dewey Peck served as the publishers of the *Tushkahomman*, an Indian newspaper, first at Oklahoma City then at Stroud. While focusing on national issues and events, the journal's articles supported the efforts of John Collier and the Indian New Deal. The paper aimed at a national Indian audience and included works by Choctaw writers Czarina Conlan, Muriel Wright, and Todd Downing.

In 1942, former Chief Dwight was selected as an Administrative Assistant by Governor Robert S. Kerr. He continued to work as an aide for Kerr after the Ada attorney was elected to the United States Senate. Dwight remained in Washington until shortly before his death on July 18, 1953. He was buried in Memorial Cemetery, Oklahoma City.[250]

With the presidency firmly in the hands of the Democratic Party after 1933, the next presidential appointee for Principal Chief was a staunch Democrat, William Alexander Durant. Born on March 18, 1866, in Bennington, Chief Durant was the son of Sylvester, a Presbyterian minister, farmer-stockman, and Martha Robinson Hutchinsons Durant. His father had served as a major under Colonel Douglas H. Cooper during the Civil War, and his mother was a Scotch-Irish widow from Tennessee with four children who had arrived in Indian Territory with her brother and met Sylvester Durant. William Durant's brothers and sisters were Pierre "Bud" Durant and Mrs. Fred (Zarina) Thompson. His paternal half-sisters were Cassie Crowder and Isabel

Jones, and his maternal half-sisters were Mary and Elizabeth Isabell Durant, Sarah Powell, and his half-brother was James Hutchinsons.

William's education began at Bennington and continued in Durant. In 1881, after the death of his parents, he resided with William and Mary Gardner of Bennington. In 1886, he entered the teaching profession after earning a Bachelor of Arts degree at Arkansas College, Batesville. He returned home to Durant to teach, but his cousin and brother-in-law, Dixon Durant, the founder of the town, refused him a position on the faculty of Durant Indian School until William went over his head to the County Superintendent to have pressure applied to approve his employment. After a time as a teacher, William was appointed superintendent of Jones Academy. He subsequently abandoned the education field for a more lucrative law career.

In 1892, he married Ida May Corber, a Kansas girl that he met when she came to visit relatives in Durant. They were parents of two sons, William E. L. "Spot" and James Gordon Durant. A successful farmer and rancher, Durant's political career included positions as Inspector of Academies, Royalty Collector, Special District Judge, and Indian Trustee for the school in Durant. Making an agreement for the Indian Presbytery to provide two teachers for a school session at Double Springs near the later location of the town of Mead, Durant helped start Calvin Institute that grew into Oklahoma Presbyterian College at Durant. In 1890, he was elected to the Choctaw House of Representatives and a year later Speaker of the House.

In 1906, he served in the Constitutional Convention as Sergeant-at-arms. On Statehood Day, November 16, 1907, Durant took part in the ceremony that united Oklahoma and Indian Territories into the forty-sixth state. Mrs. Leo Bennett, a mixed blood Cherokee from Muskogee, played the part of Miss Indian Territory, and Durant "gave away the bride" to C. G. Jones, former mayor of Oklahoma City, representing Mr. Oklahoma Territory. Some in the crowd gathered at Guthrie laughingly shouted that it was a shotgun wedding.

Winning election to the House of Representatives as the first Representative from Bryan County for the first six legislatures of the new state of Oklahoma, Durant served as Speaker for the Third Legislature with his primary success being the establishment of Southeastern State College. Durant worked hard to achieve a teacher's college for the city of Durant with the support of Jesse Mercer Hatchett, Bryan County's first State Senator, intermarried citizen, and former Chief Semple's law colleague. Senator Hatchett watched legislation in his chamber while Durant pushed for the selection of Durant as the site of a new college in the House.

Governor Martin E. Trapp appointed Representative Durant, after eleven years in the House, as Secretary of the Oklahoma School Land Commission.

Leaving the land office after six years, Durant served as Chief Clerk of the House of Representatives in the first legislature of William H. Murray's term. Subsequently employed by the Tax Commission in Murray's administration, Durant was employed as a gas agent when Ernest W. Marland was elected governor.

Appointed Principal Chief on January 15, 1937, Durant resumed efforts to make a deal with the Secretary of Interior over tribal coal lands. Discussions lasted through the years until Representative William Stigler secured legislation that enabled the tribe to enter into a contract with the government to purchase its coal and asphalt lands in 1944. Three years later an agreement was reached that included the Chickasaw whereby the government purchased the residue of the lands with the federal authorities agreeing to pay $8.5 million for 370,000 acres of coal and asphalt. Of this amount, the purchase price was $3.5 million. The remainder was for losses sustained under the supervision of the Indian Office for the previous forty-six years. In June 1948, Congress approved by the sale resulting in money being appropriated a year later with per capita payments of $350 to enrollees and their descendants in 1950.

Durant was a Mason, Elk, Presbyterian Sunday School teacher, and a member of the Order of Knights of Pythias. He remained in the office until his death at the age of eighty-two in Tvshkahomma on August 1, 1948. His funeral service was held there and he was buried in Durant.[251]

In August 1948, Harry James Watson "Jimmy" Belvin was appointed by President Harry S. Truman to succeed Durant. Although the position had been stripped of all powers other than signing legal documents for the tribe when he assumed office, the system was totally changed by the end of his term. He served as Principal Chief until 1975.

Born in Boswell on December 11, 1900, the son of Watson J. and Mabel Powers Belvin, Jimmy attended school in Boswell and entered Southeastern State College, graduating with a Bachelor of Science Degree in Education. On December 21, 1922, he married Lucille Brightwell and the couple had one child, Louise Belvin Frazier. Majoring in history and English, Belvin returned to college to obtain a Master's Degree in Education at the University of Oklahoma and taught in the classrooms of Bryan and Choctaw Counties for fifteen years. In 1941, he was elected Bryan County Superintendent of Public Instruction and held the office until 1952. Belvin next ran successfully for the Oklahoma legislature and served six years in the House and four in the State Senate.

Appointed Principal Chief in 1948, Belvin remained in office for the next twenty-seven years. In 1949, he convinced Washington to let the Choctaw conduct an election for chief and was elected and approved by the President.

Receiving many honors during his tenure, Belvin was an active member of the National Congress of American Indians, the American Indian Institute, the Choctaw-Chickasaw Confederation, and the Oklahoma Indian Club. Nicknamed "the Little Warrior," the flamboyant Belvin was always ready to fight, even with fists if necessary, for his beliefs or to make a point.

Learning that the Choctaw had no official status as an organized tribe, Belvin made efforts to get this condition changed as quickly as possible. Realizing that a tribal structure would be needed to make any forward steps, he established Councils in each county of the former Choctaw Nation and drafted a constitution that was approved at meetings of the tribe in each of those counties. Providing for the democratic election of officers to serve one term each, these councils enabled the Chief to meet his people and get to know them in the 1950s. At the same time the tribe was given a platform to air grievances against the chief or the federal government, the first such opportunity since statehood. Despite having only one person as his staff, a part-time secretary, Belvin kept direct contact with the tribe for his entire term. Eleven Choctaw councils were established, and Belvin met once each quarter with each of them. The meetings allowed the councils to conduct business with the chief while a general meeting was held each Labor Day in Tvshkahomma to inform the tribe of important issues.

The 2,500 visitors at the fourteenth Choctaw-Chickasaw Labor Day festival witnessed a serious turn in the annual business meeting when the question was raised of the tribe's handling of its own affairs and electing its own chief, known as the "Choctaw self-rule Plan." The short, fiery Belvin pointed out that the issue had been delayed for more than fifty-five years, despite an act passed in 1960 that set the termination date for August 1969. Stating that while the Choctaw could abolish the office of Principal Chief as the federal government wanted, Belvin, strongly opposed to any proposals for the dissolution of tribal leadership, advised other approaches and worked diligently to get the law repealed that would have terminated the tribe. In 1970, Belvin, with help from Speaker Carl Albert of Bugtussle, finally ended the policy of termination, and elections were held again for Chief. Five years later, President Gerald Ford proclaimed the passage of Public Law 93-638, the Indian Self-Determination and Education Assistance Act, praised as "milestone" legislation because it assured Indian participation in federal services.

Chief "Jimmy" Belvin inaugurated numerous programs during his long term in office, but there were some he considered most important. These were:

- Public housing, 1,300 low-rent units at a cost of $22 million
- Community health programs

- Choctaw arts and craft programs
- The founding of the Choctaw Nation Enterprises, Inc., a nonprofit organization for the construction business
- An industrial park on tribal lands two miles west of Talihina and $310,000 to develop industry
- Renovation of the Choctaw Council House and grounds at Tvshkahomma
- Organization of the Choctaw Nation Historical Society
- Building three Indian clinics
- Procuring an Adult Indian Education Program through the Bureau of Indian Affairs, particularly the Choctaw Bilingual Project headed by Pierce Martin and Randy Jacobs at Battiest, Broken Bow, Smithville, and Wright City in July 1970
- The establishment of the Choctaw Museum in the Council House
- Convincing the Indian Health Service to reduce the one-half degree Indian blood requirement to one-fourth
- Influencing the Bureau of Indian Affairs to allow investment of tribal funds in buildings and grounds at the Broken Bow "Y" east of Idabel as a perpetual Arts and Craft Center
- A Choctaw cultural center on a two-acre site in Hugo
- A 2,600 acre ranch on tribal lands at the Choctaw Council House established with the BIA and the Office of Native American Programs
- The granting of 2,000 Indian scholarships.[252]

In August 1971, Belvin became the first elected chief since statehood. A Labor Day Festival at Tvshkahomma four years later celebrated his twenty-six years in office, but the following year he was ousted by C. David Gardner. Chief Belvin, an elder in the Presbyterian Church, died in Bryan Memorial Hospital on September 19, 1986. He was buried in Highland Cemetery, Durant.

In 1971, C. David Gardner had spearheaded the opposition to Chief Belvin's continuation in office and won the election but was disqualified because the age requirement was thirty-five, and he was only thirty-one. He filed suit against Belvin, but the courts dismissed the case. In 1975, the frustrated Gardner started working for the next campaign.

A descendant of former Chief Jefferson Gardner, 1894-96, a great-uncle who had opposed the Dawes Commission, Gardner spoke highly of his ancestors during the campaign. Advocating a two-party governmental system for the tribe, he campaigned hard against Chief Belvin, also a distant relative, but eight candidates entered the primary election on August 9, 1975. The top five with the highest number of votes included Gardner, 1,412 votes; Calvin

Beams, 864; Tom Coleman, 725; Dub Victor, 463; and Robert Anderson, 347. Gardner won the runoff election with 2,049 votes to 1,329 for Beams. Not allowed to take the office as chief four years earlier, he was elected to serve a full term. In August 1975, the highlight of the annual Choctaw Labor Day Festival at the Choctaw Capitol was the ceremonial swearing in of the newly elected chief by District Judge Sam Sullivan of Durant.

The oath was purely a ceremonial one. Although scheduled for Labor Day, United States Senator Henry Bellmon administered the official oath of office at Southeastern Oklahoma State University on Tuesday evening, August 26, 1975. According to Bureau of Indian Affairs rules, a tribe could not be without a Principal Chief over a certain length of time, and if a new chief was not sworn in within this period, the BIA and the outgoing chief had the authority to appoint a new one, even if an election had been held previously. Since the term of "Jimmy" Belvin had expired, Gardner did not want to take a chance and maneuvered to have the oath completed early.[253]

Born April 22, 1940, at Boswell, Clark David Gardner, the son of a Cumberland Presbyterian minister and his wife, Reverend Critten A. and Ida Mae Jones Gardner, attended schools at Boswell until the age of thirteen when the family moved to Sulphur. Gardner graduated Sulphur High School and then entered East Central State University at Ada. Earning a Bachelor's degree, he transferred to Southwestern State University for a Master's degree and later did postgraduate work at the University of Oklahoma. In 1958, he married Carol Jean Parker. They were parents of three sons and a daughter. After serving in the United States Navy from 1958 to 1963, Gardner taught at the University of Oklahoma and Southwestern State University.

On December 1, 1976, Chief Gardner presented "A Brief Talk on Choctaw History" that was published in *Hello Choctaw*, the newspaper that he founded in Durant. The chief attributed the recent tribal successes to the continued support of the Choctaw people for Christian religion. Saying that Christianity played an important part in Choctaw daily life, because it remained a "simple thing" to them, Gardner pointed out that religion was shown not by the cars they drive, the houses they live in, the clothes they wear, but in "the very simplicity of their worship for a higher Power, Chitokaka." Chief Gardner concluded with the advice: "We must remember the past history of your people and my people that has brought us together in this one place to give thanks to this one God for the blessings that are ours, for the future that belongs to our children, and for the heritage that makes us strong and steadfast."[254]

Upon learning the Choctaw Board of Directors had acquired a grant of $150,000 from the Economic Development Administration for the second phase of the Choctaw Capitol restoration, Chief Gardner said, "We feel there is a great future for the Choctaw Nation." The money was used to repair the upstairs portion of the Council House and to develop a recreational vehicle park west of the Council House. This was the beginning of an economic revival of the Nation.

Chief Gardner followed his successes with the establishment of the Choctaw National Headquarters in the buildings formerly known as the Oklahoma Presbyterian College in Durant. Transferred to private hands in 1963, the buildings, neglected and unused by the new owners, had deteriorated into a condition of complete dilapidation by the time the Red River Valley Historical Society acquired title to the property ten years later with plans for its renovation as a museum. Unable to raise sufficient donations to save the buildings, the history association made an arrangement with Chief Gardner to turn the property over to the tribe as a national headquarters in return for a lease in the north basement for a museum.

Another major project in Gardner's administration was the Choctaw Manpower Program. On October 1, 1976, it began Fiscal Year 1977 with federally assisted funds in the amount of $732,510 and was given an additional $289,648 to be expended on jobs under the Emergency Jobs Program in February 1977. By the end of the month, the Choctaw Manpower enterprise had served 252 persons with emphasis on veterans, household heads, and school dropouts. Skill training areas included cosmetology, heavy equipment operations, welding, truck driving, mechanics and electronics.

The organization of the Choctaw-Chickasaw Alliance, a union supported by leaders of both tribes, was another success for the young chief. The undertaking was an effort by the two tribes to work together to bring about positive changes based on cooperation.

Finally, Gardner worked to reverse a trend that he felt greatly threatened the tribe. Keenly concerned that the Choctaw language was dying, he gained permission to reprint a Choctaw dictionary by Cyrus Byington and provided it for sale in paperback form to the tribe in an effort to return to the correct spelling and use of the language. The project greatly aided the revival of interest in the Choctaw language and culture.

Gardner oversaw a number of innovative improvements for the tribe including the establishment of *Hello Choctaw*, later renamed *Bishinik*, a monthly newspaper published by the tribe devoted to Choctaw culture. He also supported a Community Health Representative Training Center at Talihina, an Extended Health Care Facility at Antlers, and a community building at Idabel.

Unfortunately, Chief Gardner died in the Durant hospital after a losing battle with cancer on January 13, 1978. Gardner, a Presbyterian, was buried with private graveside services held in Sulphur.

On April 15, 1978, a special election caused by his death brought Hollis Earl Roberts into office. Roberts defeated Charles E. Brown by 339 votes. He received 1,668 votes to Brown's 1,329.

Born on May 9, 1943, in Hochatown, the son of Darrel E. and Laura Beam Roberts, Hollis grew up in Holly Creek, a rural village a few miles north of Idabel. Completing the eighth grade at the country elementary school, he rode the bus to Idabel High School where he graduated in 1961. Married to Helen R. Rodriguez, Roberts established a home in Hugo where the couple had three children. Serving a term in the state legislature before running for Principal Chief, Roberts served as Tribal Chief from 1978 until 1997.

Gardner had announced that he intended to "take it slow and easy" in making changes but stressed the fact that a new tribal constitution was needed and should be drawn up by the people. In 1983, Roberts took this goal to its logical end with the adoption of a modern constitution with major political changes including the division of the Nation into twelve districts, each with a Council representative, the reduction of the number of Council members from fifteen to twelve, and the elimination of the three "at-large" Council seats. The counties were Atoka, Bryan, Choctaw, Coal, Haskell, Hughes, Latimer, LeFlore, McCurtain, Pittsburg, and Pushmataha. Other changes were the elimination of the term "Principal Chief," providing that the title should be simply "Chief," and a provision giving authority to the Chief to appoint an Assistant Chief to serve in his place should the need arise.[255]

At the same time Chief Roberts continued the efforts begun by Gardner and Belvin to expand tribal economic ventures. In December 1987, his plan to initiate work programs to earn money to go directly back into projects for the people began with the Choctaw Bingo Parlor. The facility generated sufficient funds to finance other enterprises. Money was provided to start the Choctaw Finishing Company and the Choctaw Travel Plaza, and to finance special programs, such as the purchase of medicines not provided by the Indian Health Services, and Head Start Centers in Bennington, Durant, McAlester, Bethel, Wright City, Broken Bow, Idabel, Poteau, Antlers, Hugo, and Atoka. In addition, scholarships were initiated for future teachers, rodeo enthusiasts, and participants in the Miss Choctaw Nation pageant.

The pride in the revitalized Choctaw Nation could be seen in its return to more traditional cultural values in music and dance. One of the leaders of the movement was Reverend D. Eugene Wilson of the United Presbyterian Church near Idabel. Recruiting a company of dancers and developing a repertory of Choctaw native dances, the group, supported by the Mississippi Choctaw and singer Tony Bell of Bogue Chitto, presented its first public appearance at the Owa Chito Festival at Beaver's Bend, north of Broken Bow in 1974. Another organization of Choctaw dancers was led by Buster Ned of Mannsville, who as a boy had played in one of the last stickball games at the Yellow Hills dance grounds until modern times.

The troupes performed a variety of cultural dances, including the Stomp Dance, done by men and women dancing in costumes in celebration of victories in war and successes in hunts. Other dances were the Walk Dance, Tick Dance, Yelling Dance, Goose Dance, Wedding Dance, Turtle Dance, Raccoon Dance, and the Snake Dance. The movements of the people or the animals that were imitated during the performances were done as honors and were greatly appreciated by audiences.

In the midst of the economic success and progress, Roberts was suddenly arrested, removed from office, and imprisoned for sexual harassment in 1997. On June 9, Assistant Chief Greg Pyle was sworn into office as his replacement. Two years later, Pyle was elected for a four-year term.[256]

Chief Gregory Eli Pyle was born April 25, 1949, in Ft. Bragg, California, the son of Alvin Pyle of Paris, Texas, and Juanita Wilmouth of Hugo. The family, including his two brothers and a sister, traveled alternately between California and Oklahoma until moving permanently to Hugo in 1966. Growing up on a ranch six miles north of the city, Pyle graduated from Hugo High School in May of 1967. After attending college at Murray State College in Tishomingo, he graduated from Southeastern Oklahoma State University in Durant with a Bachelor of Science in Business and a minor in Psychology in July 1972. In September 1971, he was married to Pat Baker, and the couple had two children, a daughter, Andrea, and son, Eric.

In 1975, Chief Pyle began his service for the tribe with his election by popular vote to the Agriculture Board to oversee the Choctaw Nation Ranch at Tvshkahomma. While remaining a part-time rancher, he was appointed as a full time general agent with the Farm Bureau Mutual Insurance Company. In 1982, he was hired as Personnel Officer for the tribe, and then was appointed to represent the Choctaw on the Arkansas Riverbed Board to determine ownership for the Choctaw, Chickasaw, and Cherokee. A year later he testified before Congress for the Riverbed case, which was won by the tribes. The same year he was appointed as the Tribal Program Monitor to oversee and assure contract compliance of all federally funded programs undertaken by the tribe.

In 1983, he was appointed as Assistant Chief, a position he held for fourteen years. Much of his time was spent in Washington representing the Choctaw on behalf of congressional legislation affecting Indian tribes. He was then appointed by Secretary of Interior Manuel Lujan to serve on a task force to reorganize the Bureau of Indian Affairs. In 1985, he was appointed by Secretary Bruce Babbit to head a number of subcommittees on the force. In 1994, Assistant Chief Pyle was appointed to the Intertribal Council of the Five

Civilized Tribes. In the same year he was called to testify before Congress in support of the appointment of Michael Trujillo as Director of the National Health Service Director. In 1996, he was appointed President of the Oklahoma area Health Board and as a member of the National Health Board. In 1997, he was appointed to the Board of Directors of the Landmark Bank in Durant and the Durant Chamber of Commerce. Chief Pyle, elected to a full term in 1999, was selected as a Distinguished Alumni by Southeastern Oklahoma State University in October 2000. Two years later he was named a member of the Board of the First United Bank & Trust.

He continued to closely monitor all Congressional actions to insure the Choctaw had a direct influence upon all legislation affecting the tribe. Since he had worked closely with the Bureau of Indian Affairs and the Indian Health Service in his fourteen years as Assistant Chief, Pyle believed strongly that this relationship should be continued to maintain current programs for the tribe and search for additional service-oriented ones in the future. His integrity in dealing with officials on the federal, state, and local level resulted in unprecedented cooperation in delivering vital services to his people.

Under his leadership, the tribe added clinics in Hugo, McAlester, Broken Bow, Poteau, and Durant, and built its own hospital, a 140,000 square-foot Health Care Center in Talihina that opened in 1999. Another priority for Chief Pyle was education. After he took office the number of scholarships grew from 500 to 1,300, based on his philosophy and advice to the young to "Do Not Follow Where the Path Leads-Go Instead Where There is No Path and Leave a Trail."

A supporter of cultural programs that promoted the Choctaw heritage, Chief Pyle participated in placing a memorial on the grave of Choctaw Chief Peter Pitchlynn, flying the Choctaw flag on the State Capitol in Oklahoma City, and walking in Commemorative Walks at Eagletown and Wheelock. Backing projects that emphasized teaching the language and cultural richness of the Choctaw to the young were a source of great pride for Chief Pyle.[257]

The Constitution of 1983 established another administrative officer for the tribe. Section 2 provided for "an Assistant Chief who shall assist the Chief and perform all duties assigned to him by the Chief." Section 7 further stated: "The Assistant Chief shall be appointed by the Chief with the advice and consent of the Tribal Council and may be removed at the discretion of the Chief." Chief Pyle selected Michael Lynn Bailey for this position in 1997.

Born March 2, 1960, Bailey's education after high school began at the Kiamichi Area Vo-Tech in Hugo. Enrolling at Southeastern Oklahoma State University, he received a Bachelor of Science in Education and next attended East Central University, Ada, where he earned a Master of Education Degree in Educational Administration. He was employed as a coach and teacher in Whitesboro, Texas, from 1981 to 1982 and as a teacher at Leonard High School, Leonard, Texas, from 1981 to 1984. From 1984-85, he served as Facility Director for Jones Academy and as Director of Jones Academy until his appointment as Assistant Chief. Bailey was named Executive Director of Education responsible for all educational programs of the Choctaw Nation from 1993 through 1996.

Assistant Chief Bailey promoted better jobs and opportunities for the tribe and southeastern Oklahoma in order to improve the quality of life in the region. In 1999, Bailey was listed in Who's Who Among Top Executives Internationally; in 2000, he was appointed to the National Advisory Council of the United States Small Business Administration by the President; in 2001, he was selected as one of Oklahoma's CareerTech Champions; and, in 2002, he was awarded the American Indian Business of the Year Award from the American Indian Chamber of Commerce in Texas.

Choctaw leaders have come from varied backgrounds and careers, but they have all had a commitment of care for their people in common. In every instance they worked tirelessly to improve the health, wealth, and status of the Choctaw Nation.[258]

CHAPTA AUAH TAHLAPI

~ CHAPTER FIFTEEN ~

"THE CHOCTAW WAR CRY IN FOREIGN LANDS"

Chapter Fifteen

The United States has experienced a war in every generation since Independence, and Choctaw warriors have always fought alongside American soldiers. Fulfilling a prophecy by Pushmataha that the Choctaw "War Cry" would be heard in many foreign lands, tribesmen volunteered for service in the Spanish-American War in 1898, World War I in 1917, World War II in 1941, and in wars around the world since 1945. The Choctaw soldiers were distinguished in them all.

Knowing little of the causes of the Spanish American War, nor, like their white comrades, caring very much, the Choctaw willingly volunteered to fight in the American army in 1898. Few Indians, or whites, had ever heard of Cuba or knew that they were going there to fight, but they joined the army in response to a fevered propaganda campaign against Spain by the United States press. Enlisting eagerly, as they had always done in the past, many joined the U. S. Volunteers known as the Rough Riders under Lieutenant Colonel Theodore Roosevelt. Among those serving in Troop M under Captain Robert H. Bruce of Mineola, Texas, and Lieutenant Ode C. Nichols of Durant, were Peter "Bud" Maytubby, Jr. of Caddo, Indian Territory, and a number of other Choctaw Americans. Later, Principal Chief Victor Locke, Jr. was another Choctaw volunteer that contributed greatly to the victory over Spain.

The tribal pride displayed during the Spanish American War was magnified when the United States entered the war in Europe in 1917. Despite the indignities of having their language attacked as "strange" and "obsolete" and insults from their white neighbors who treated them as second-class citizens, the Choctaw ignored the prejudices that Indians were not American citizens and hurriedly joined the Army to be part of the "crusade for democracy" proclaimed by President Woodrow Wilson. More than 17,000 Indians, including Choctaw tribesmen, registered with the Selective Service without being required to do so by law, and 8,000 Indian soldiers went to war in 1917.

Among the Choctaw "Doughboys" were sixteen members of the 142nd Infantry and two members of the 141st Infantry who earned immortality as "Code Talkers." Ranging in age from nineteen to thirty-three, the original eight Code Talkers included Solomon Bond Louis, born at Hochatown in 1898 and then moved to Bennington; Ben Carterby, a full blood born in 1892 who lived at (Bismarck) Wright City; Mitchell Bobb, a full blood born in 1895 at Smithville; Robert Taylor, born in 1895 in Bokchito, McCurtain County; Calvin Wilson, born in 1895 near Eagletown; Pete Maytubby, Broken Bow; James (Jimpson) M. Edwards, born in 1898 at Golden; and Jeff Nelson, Goodwater. The others were Tobias William Frazier, born in 1892; Benjamin W. Hampton of Bennington; Albert Billy, a full blood born at Howe in 1885; Walter Veach, born in 1884; Joseph Davenport; George Davenport; Noel Johnson; and Otis

Leader. The two members of the 143rd Infantry were Victor Brown, born at Goodwater in 1896, and Joseph Oklahombi, born in McCurtain County in 1894.

On October 1, 1917, the 142nd was organized as regular infantry and given training at Camp Bowie near Fort Worth as part of the Thirty-sixth Division. Transferred to France for action, General John J. "Blackjack" Pershing, the American military commander, opposed their proposed use as British and French replacements and insisted that his forces be given responsibility for a separate piece of the battle line. He ordered additional training that continued until the Germans initiated a major offensive in August 1918. Keenly aware that his troops were needed for the campaign, Pershing lobbied successfully for their assignment to the front lines, and Field Marshal Ferdinand Foch, the Allied Commander, ordered the Thirty-Sixth Division moved to the western front on October 6, 1918. Although the American forces were late in entering the war that had raged since 1914, their participation provided the margin of victory as the war played out to its bitter end.

Within days the Thirty-Sixth was engaged in a major battle. Attacking the Germans in the trenches, the Americans were soon involved in crossing "No Man's Land" in the open with only artillery fire as cover. Noticing German communications lines lying openly on the ground, the Americans decided that they had been left behind purposely so they would be used and the messages could be intercepted. In one of the first actions of the 142nd at St. Etienne, runners were sent out with fake coordinates of an American supply depot to test the theory that the Germans were monitoring telephone communications. Within thirty minutes the Germans had begun shelling the location given by the captured prisoners proving that the Germans, able to intercept and decipher every word, knew exactly what the Americans were doing and when they were going to do it. Colonel A. W. Bloor, commander of the 142nd, quickly sought a plan to turn the strategy against the Germans.

Determined to devise a code that would confuse them, Colonel Bloor soon found the answer. Captain E. W. Horner, a company commander, walking through the area happened to overhear Solomon Louis and Mitchell Bobb talking in Choctaw and remembered that the regiment contained a company of Indians that spoke more than twenty-six different languages, only four that had ever been written down. The American officer realized that it would be highly unlikely the Germans would be able to understand them. After listening a few minutes, he asked Corporal Louis how many Choctaw there were in Company E and was told there were eight that could speak the language fluently and that two, Ben Carterby and Peter Maytubby, were at headquarters. The Captain told Louis and Bobb that he was giving them a message to transmit in Choctaw and called headquarters with a communiqué that PFC Bobb sent over the field telephone to Ben Carterby.

The first message was an immediate and complete success. Bloor quickly placed a Choctaw Code Talker in each of the field headquarters to transmit information in Choctaw for translation into English. The system worked to perfection. The original eight were shifted around until there was at least one Choctaw-speaking soldier in each company that not only translated radio messages but also wrote field orders to be carried by runners to the company commanders. The language that had been outlawed by the American schools system and compared to "cursing" by some white preachers and teachers was used to save thousands of lives.[259]

Bloor witnessed the effectiveness of the Code Talkers after ordering a withdrawal of two companies of the Second Battalion. On the night of October 26, both were moved without mishap from Chufilly to Chardeny. Communications improved immediately, and over the next few days, American assaults caught the enemy by complete surprise. The German intelligence officers could neither decipher the messages being sent by the Americans nor break the code since there was none to break. A German officer later admitted the Choctaw language completely baffled his intelligence officials because the obscurity of the language made it impossible for them to understand.

Eighteen men were recruited to transmit messages and devise a system of communication for the Code Talkers. Since the Indian vocabulary did not have sufficient military terms to cover all the orders and the Choctaw language did not permit verbatim conversions, the Code Talkers utilized a strategy of literal translations. Choctaw phrases for "Big Gun" indicated artillery, "Little Gun shoot fast" meant machine guns, and the battalions were indicated by one, two, and three "grains of corn." Within twenty-four hours after the Code Talkers began their work, a significant change could be seen in the tide of battle. The achievements were sufficient to encourage a training program for future Code Talkers, but the war was over in a few months. The armistice was signed on November 11, 1918.

One of the distinguished Choctaw warriors in World War I was Joseph Oklahombi (people killer). Born in 1892 north of Bismarck, the German-named town that was changed to Wright City in honor of William Wright, the first man killed from McCurtain County during the war when he drowned after the steamship "Tuscania" was sunk by a German U-boat. Oklahombi lived quietly in the Kiamichi Mountains with only a few neighbors around him, a large percentage of them bilingual, full blood descendants of the Removalists. A Dierks sawmill and pine forests surrounded the company town when Oklahombi walked from his home to enlist at Idabel, the county seat. After basic training, the young Choctaw was sent to France.

Not long afterwards he and some friends, cut off from the rest of their company, encountered a machine gun nest with about fifty trench mortars in use. Crossing "No Man's Land" numerous times, the Choctaw warrior assisted his wounded friends and carried information back to headquarters about the enemy. Oklahombi was cited for bravery for moving about 200 yards over open ground against artillery and machine gun fire, rushing a machine gun nest and capturing one of the guns. Turning the weapon on the enemy, the Americans held the Germans down with blistering fire for four days until their surrender.

On another occasion, Oklahombi confronted a German troop having a meal and resting in a cemetery. Enclosed by high walls with only one gate, Oklahombi covered the gate with blistering fire. A true marksman, Oklahombi killed the Germans by the dozens, seventy-nine according to some reports, until the whole force surrendered.

Ben Carterby later told one of Oklahombi's adventures with prisoners. According to his account, a French detention camp officer spotted Oklahombi coming with two German prisoners, but when he arrived there was only one. When the officer realized this, he asked, "Where's the other one?" Oklahombi, somewhat bewildered by the inquiry, answered, "I kill him." And, before the astonished officer could recover, added, "Want me to go back and kill him some more?"

The Choctaw hero was always very reluctant to talk of his experiences after the war. Finally refusing to even speak English in public, the modest Oklahombi, honored at a reception at Southeastern State College, only spoke in his own Choctaw language. In 1992, his medals were placed on display in the 45th Infantry Museum in Oklahoma City. His son, Jonah, a veteran of World War II, accepted the medals before his death in 1993.

An Oklahombi colleague was Tobias William Frazier from Rattan. Frazier's major action involved helping break through the Hindenberg Line, the strong defensive line maintained by the Germans from Belgium to within fifty miles of Paris. The Allies tried time and again to penetrate the line, but every time they "went over the top," the Germans were prepared for them and beat them back. Obviously, the Germans had tapped into American communications lines and knew what the Americans were going to do and when. This was the point that the Choctaw Code Talkers were brought into use, and Frazier, already wounded and sent to the hospital, was called back to use his linguistic talents as Pershing planned an assault on the Germans at Metz. The armistice was signed before the attack took place, but Frazier was awarded the Purple Heart for his earlier actions.

Albert Billy, a native of Poteau, was another of the first Code Talkers instrumental in successfully confusing the Germans with Choctaw messages.

Billy was asked the nationality of the soldiers on the phones by a German officer after one of the battles, and surprised the inquirer with a rather cryptic response. He answered simply, "They were only Americans."

Choctaw hero Victor Brown suffered a mustard gas attack and sustained a broken nose and head injuries in the Meuse-Argonne offensive. Wounded and given a citation for bravery by President Wilson, the quiet, modest Brown seldom talked of his war experiences but was always proud that his fellow Choctaws had "fooled" the Germans. He stated later that he had been very excited to see Paris since he was of French descent. His mother was the daughter of a French trader to the Choctaw. Brown was an orphan looked after by Gabe Parker who sent him to Armstrong Academy and then to Haskell Institute in Lawrence, Kansas. Brown later attended Southeastern State College in Durant.

Solomon Bond Louis, a Choctaw full blood, was another of the first Code Talkers. Underage when he enlisted, Louis, from Bryan County, attended Armstrong Academy before joining the army with his school friends. Receiving his basic training at Fort Sill, he was sent to Fort Worth and attached to the all-Indian company of the Thirty-sixth Division. Louis, at field headquarters, communicated with James Edwards from the front lines to keep the American commanders informed on German movements.

Another was Walter Veach, Commander of Company H, a unit organized at Durant as part of the Oklahoma National Guard. Company H put down the Crazy Snake revolt and then patrolled the border between the United States and Mexico prior to entrance into World War I. The company's job was to stop the raids by Mexican bandit-revolutionary general, Pancho Villa. In 1917, the company was merged with the Texas 36th Division and sent to Europe. There, Company E, an all-Indian company, was formed from eleven Oklahoma tribes. Receiving recognition for using the Indian languages as a code to confuse the Germans, the company played an important role in obtaining the publicity necessary to obtain American citizenship for Indians in 1924.

Code Talker Ben Carterby, born in 1892 at Battiest, the son of Ebon and Taboll Carterby, preferred, like most combat veterans, to remember his humble beginnings rather than his war experiences. Recalling that his grandparents had removed from Mississippi to locate the Carterby home place in the woods of the Ouachita Mountains, the quiet hero chose to talk about the simple pleasures of life rather than the violence of war. Often reminiscing about his family, he recalled there was always plenty to eat. The country was filled with deer and wild game and the creeks and river full of fish. The five acres owned by the Carterbys enabled them to raise enough corn to live on along with a large vegetable garden. In his later years he liked to remember the times passed gathering onions, tying them together, and hanging them in the house for use. He recalled that his family and most of his neighbors raised a few cattle, hogs, and ponies. The animals were allowed to roam freely, taking care of themselves. They were not fed or watered and sometimes went wild making it difficult to herd them in for spring branding, but their owners were never out any expense on their care. He recalled that his mother made all the family clothing with a spinning wheel and a weaver. She wove all the material at home, making shirts, pants, and dresses, all sewn from heavy materials that lasted a long time and was warm in the winter.

These were the memories of a soldier. Carterby embraced the unpretentious, quiet existence of an ordinary man in private life. Determined not to remember the war and the fighting, he purposely avoided discussions and nostalgic memories of the frightening experiences of war, a common thread among all veterans.

Otis W. Leader, another hero of World War I, was born near Citra in Hughes County, on November 5, 1882. He entered the army at the age of thirty-five, one of the oldest men in the service. He had attended Oklahoma Presbyterian College and Texas A&M playing baseball and football in his youth. Upon his arrival in France, Leader was selected to pose as the model representative of the newly arrived American soldiers by a French artist commissioned to paint portraits of the Allied army by the French government. His portrait and statue are in Paris and London.

Winning the French Croix de Guerre twice, a Purple Heart, and Battle Stars for Sommerviller, Ansauville, Picardy, Cantigny, Second Marne, St. Mihiel, Meuse-Argonne, Mouson-Sedan, and Coblenz Bridgehead, Leader was called one of the "war's greatest fighting machines" by General Pershing. Placed in Company B, 2nd Machine gun Battalion, 16th Infantry, 1st Division after enlistment, Leader was among the first contingent to arrive in France where his division trained with the French "Blue Devils." On the night of November 2, 1917, Leader's company drew the first relief assignment, moving into the trenches at Bathlemont. The following day his company defended the flank in the first engagement of Americans in combat of World War I.

On May 28, 1918, Leader was wounded and gassed during the American offensive at Cantigny but rejoined his division near Soissons in July. In the next battle, he crawled through a ravine to attack a machine gun nest. Getting within sixty feet of the enemy, Leader picked up a rifle and fought with the infantry after his own machine gun crew had all been killed. Attacking the German positions, Leader captured two machine guns and eighteen enemy soldiers manning them. On October 1, 1918, he was wounded again and hospitalized at Vichy. He was still in the hospital when the armistice was signed on November 11.

Returning to Oklahoma, Leader quietly married Minnie Lee and moved to Scipio in Pittsburg County, where he worked with the Highway Department for twenty-five years before retiring to Lehigh. In 1955, the Oklahoma House of Representatives praised Leader as the Outstanding Soldier of World War I. He was buried at Coalgate in 1961.

Another veteran of World War I was Clifton L. Richards. Born in McAlester in 1886, he lived there until joining the service, serving as a sergeant in the Ambulance Corps until 1919. After the war he went into the petroleum tanker car business transporting oil across the nation and later entered the oil production business. Becoming wealthy, the businessman-philanthropist known as "Mr. Shoes" for his support of the Assistance League of Tulsa funded many charitable organizations in the city. He died at the age of 102 on October 17, 1998.

Another elder veteran of World War I was George Hudson of Eagletown. Born in 1897, the Choctaw warrior was honorably discharged and returned home to a quiet, peaceful life. He died at the age of ninety-eight in 1995.[260]

A veteran who served with Company I, 357th Infantry, was Ben Green Foreman, son of Ben and Leatha Foreman. The Choctaw soldier, named for Green McCurtain, was born in 1891, on a ranch near Enterprise, I. T. In 1905, he married Daisy Landrum and settled down to farming allotted land near Chickasha until the United States entered the war. Foreman leased out his farm, enlisted in the army, took basic training at Camp Travis in San Antonio, and went to France. Gassed in a battle in the Argonne Forest, he returned to his farm and later served as Deputy Sheriff of Grady County from 1935 until his retirement in 1943. Foreman suffered a fatal heart attack only a few months after returning to private life.[261]

The Thirty-sixth Division lost twenty-three officers and 1,450 men dead, thirty-five officers and 427 men gassed, and another eighty were listed as missing. Despite the high losses, the Thirty-sixth was awarded numerous citations and medals for bravery. The Division received three Medals of Honor, twenty-nine Distinguished Service Crosses, one Distinguished Service Medal, and several French awards. The Division was further credited with capturing a large number of enemy weaponry including three pieces of heavy artillery, six pieces of light artillery, four howitzers, seventeen trench mortars, two hundred seventy-seven machine guns, and large quantities of rifles and small arms.

The first full blood American Indian to receive an officer's commission was Charles Watson McGilberry, an original enrollee whose Choctaw name, Immayitchie, meant "in the race." Born in 1893, the officer was the son of Abel and Kittie McCurtain McGilberry of Boggy Depot and a grandson of Edmund McCurtain. McGilberry graduated from college with a Bachelor's

Degree at Ada and then enrolled in graduate study at Merserburg Academy in Philadelphia in preparation for entrance into Harvard. On May 18, 1917, he was commissioned into the U.S. Army Company I, 3rd Battalion, 79th Infantry. Donning war paint and carrying a tomahawk, McGilberry was called "Chief" by his men as a symbol of their respect. The young soldier was the first commissioned officer of any tribe. After the war he returned to more peaceful pursuits, enrolling at the University of Oklahoma for a Master of Science in Education. He served as a teacher in many one-room schools in the state from 1918 until joining the BIA as a teacher from 1931 to 1953. He died in 1960.

Serving overseas with other Indian soldiers, Choctaw warriors encountered many different lifestyles and cultures and were treated with respect and honor by their comrades. Learning skills that could be useful in peacetime, the Choctaw understood that assimilation could be achieved with the general population. In September 1986, the first official recognition of the Code Talkers was allowed when Chief Hollis Roberts presented medals to their group. In November 1989, France presented the "Chevalier de l'order National du Merite" medal to the combat veterans in recognition of their service.[262]

The "Code Talkers" worked so well that the system was revived with many different tribes used as communications liaisons in World War II. The Choctaw and Comanche were used in Europe while the Marines relied upon Navajo soldiers in the Pacific. Ironically, the Comanche, Navajo, and Choctaw were trained to transmit information in their native languages that had been forbidden in the schools in the years prior to the war.

The Germans made preparations for the second war. So fearful of the use of Indians as communicators, Nazi agents posed as writers and anthropologists on the reservations to subvert the Indians and to learn their languages, but their efforts were of no avail. Nazi propaganda minister Joseph Goebbels naively predicted the Indians would revolt rather than fight Germany, because the swastika was similar to an Indian mystic, a bird symbolically depicting good luck, but the Fascist leaders grossly miscalculated Indian allegiance to the United States. All their attempts failed miserably. Conversely, the Nazi tricks may have even encouraged the Indians to fight Hitler and Mussolini, who they derogatorily referred to as "He who smells his moustache" and "Gourd Chin."

More than 4,000 American Indians, including the six sons of Houston S. Terrell of Sans Bois, Oklahoma, joined the military after Pearl Harbor. Commissioner John Collier lobbied for an all-Indian division administered by the Bureau of Indian Affairs when Congress authorized the first peacetime draft law in September 1940, but nothing came of the suggestion. In 1941, *Ex Parte Green* ruled that Indians were required to register for the draft, and the BIA announced that it had registered 7,500 Indians in March 1941. By the end of the war, more than 25,000 had served: 21,767 in the Army, 1,910 in the Navy, 874 in the Marines, and 121 in the Coast Guard, along with several hundred women who served as nurses and in the WACS and WAVES.

The Army 45th "Thunderbird" Division had the highest proportion of Indian soldiers of any division, more than 2,000 from Oklahoma and New Mexico. Indian soldiers also served in the 4th and 88th Divisions, Oklahoma National Guard, the 19th and 180th Infantry Regiments, and the 147th Field Artillery Regiment.[263]

Preston Christopher Moore served two hitches in the United States Navy, once in 1918-1922 and again in1943-45. Moore, the son of Christopher and Tennessee Holson Moore was born on December 5, 1900, at Redden. After his service, Moore was employed at the Navy Ammunition Depot in Savanna.

One of the most decorated Choctaw warriors of World War II was Schlicht Billy, the son of Williamson and Lucinda Thompson Billy. Born in rural Pittsburg County northwest of McAlester, he was the first child delivered by a German doctor, Otto Schlicht, who insisted that the boy be named after him. Starting school at Jones Academy, the full blood from the Tannehill community went to Chilocco Indian School. In 1940, he completed high school and enlisted in the military at eighteen years old.[264]

In October 1940, Billy was assigned to the 180th Regiment, 45th Infantry Division. He trained at Fort Sill with Company K, "The Choctaw Platoon." Others in the company were Schlicht's brother, Loy, Elner Martin, Rayson J. Billey, Louis Wade, Loyal Conn, Gilbert White, Emmanuel Gage, Ben Filmore, and Jesse Wall. Although never out of Oklahoma previously, Billy's regiment was sent to Camp Barkley near Abilene, Texas, then to Fort Devines, Massachusetts, and onto Hampton Roads, Virginia, for transfer to Africa for the "Torch" campaign. He recalled that the voyage across the Atlantic was by convoy that stretched as far as the eye could see. The trip lasted twenty-two days causing most of the troops to get seasick, but the ships were placed on alert only once during the entire crossing. Warnings to prepare to abandon ship were given when a German submarine was sighted, but the American transports dropped explosives and the orders were rescinded when there were no further signs of attack. The convoy continued without further mishap to land at Oran on the North African coast.

When the Americans ran into the same problem of intercepted messages that occurred in World War I, the Choctaw soldier and his friend, Davis Pickens, revived the Code Talkers by using their language to transmit accurate details of German movements. Since Billy and the other Choctaw soldiers were high school graduates, they had been placed in company headquarters, a spot perfect for communications with each other. Billy, mostly talking to Pickens, often conversed in Choctaw when using the field radios to coordinate his company's military maneuvers. Pickens, a machine gunner, was usually in a position to do the most damage to the enemy, and the two could give exact details and locations without fear of the Germans intercepting their conversations.

Serving in North Africa as a platoon sergeant, Billy later saw action in Sicily, Salerno, and Italy. After thirty-eight days of action in Sicily, he and his troops went to Salerno, below Naples, on an "end run" on Rome. His company spent four months at Anzio before "breaking out" for Rome in May 1944. Taking Anzio required 120 days of intense fighting because the Germans had been digging in for years and were prepared for an invasion. Billy stated, "It was hard fighting, because the Germans were ready. They had Big Guns, some so large they required 155 men to operate and fire." Besides, the territory was relatively open terrain, almost level, and the situation was made worse for the Americans by the rain. "Rain, rain, and more rain, and no place to go," he said. "We drove them back to within fifteen miles of Rome, where both sides had been asked by the Pope to declare the Vatican a safe haven. We all honored it," he added.

After Rome, Billy and his men returned to Anzio in preparation for the invasion of France. Calling the campaign "the easiest action" of the entire campaign, his unit invaded Monte Carlo, Lyon, and the Rhone Valley with the fighting continuing to Nancy, France. The Germans fought harder as the Allies pushed them closer to their home ground. Billy reported that his company went through 511 days of combat.

Given a battlefield commission, Billy was placed in charge of the First Platoon, Company F, Fox Company, 180th Infantry Division. Second Lieutenant Billy explained that he had been with his platoon for over a year, but every time a new officer was assigned to the unit the officer was soon either wounded or killed, and he had to take over until another was assigned. This happened so often that headquarters decided to let him take over permanently. Billy received a commission, although at first he thought it was a furlough. Called to headquarters without being told anything, the commander sent a jeep for him, and he thought that he was going to get to go home because he had been in combat so long. Instead, he was outfitted with an officer's uniform and sent back to the front lines, but not to his old unit. He was assigned to F Company where he knew no one. When he arrived at the location of his new squad, he was forced to crawl around to look the place over without being able to stand up because the area was under constant fire from snipers, artillery, and tanks.

He was sent with his "new" troop to the Alsace-Lorraine area where the 101st was surrounded at Liege, Belgium. Sent to occupy the Maginot Line, he stated, "It was the first time we had a warm place to sleep." His unit, sent on forward, met heavier resistance as the American army crossed the river into Germany as the German forces fought even harder.

On March 17, 1945, Billy led his outfit in an attack on the Siegfried Line, a line of reinforced "pillboxes," placed to support and defend each other, linked together by head-tall trenches in a heavily wooded area. The pillboxes were six feet thick and grenades could not penetrate them. Their only vulnerable spots were the ventilation shafts on top of each one. Billy's platoon was given the job of taking the first ones. The Germans fought ferociously with artillery and machine gun fire. After only a short advance, Billy's men were pinned down. Several were badly wounded, but Billy reorganized the platoon and led the men forward pushing to within fifty yards of the enemy. Running through the machine gun fire, Lieutenant Billy threw a smoke grenade down the ventilation shaft into the pillbox, and the Germans came out with their hands raised in surrender. By evening, Billy and his men held seven pillboxes, but with the place overrun by the Americans, the Germans turned their own guns on it. Artillery fire was poured on top of the Americans, and Billy was hit. Receiving a spinal injury that paralyzed one side of his body, his men carried him out of the woods to a hospital in Nancy and then to Bordeaux. He would receive numerous medals for his actions, but it was two years before he was physically able to return to Oklahoma.

For gallantry in action, Lieutenant Billy, wounded four times, received the Purple Heart, American Defense Service Ribbon, and the European African Middle Eastern Theater Medal with a cluster of five Bronze Stars. Unfortunately, his brother Loy never made it back. Billy lived at Blanco, Pittsburg County, until his death in 1994.[265]

Rayson J. Billey, a corporal in the "Choctaw Platoon" under Sergeant Schlicht Billy, served as the model for the character Willie in a Pulitzer-prize winning comic strip about the war entitled "Willie and Joe" by cartoonist Bill Mauldin who served with him. Mauldin reported in his book, *The Brass Ring*, that Billey's mother was notified by the War Department that Billey had been killed in 1943. After the publication of the book in 1969, Mauldin saw Billey again, and exclaimed, "You're dead!" and Billey responded, "Yes, I know. I read it in your book."

Billey's proudest moment of the war was the capture of an entire airport with only four men. Assigned to lead a mission to eliminate sentries around the field, Billey led his platoon up a steep plateau during a night assault against the Bascaria Airport, located seventy miles north of Naples. He and his men killed fifteen guards, using only their knives. Early the next morning American troops arrived to complete the attack and captured a garrison of pilots, fifty panzers, twenty-two Messerschmitts, and a large number of German and Italian troops, all without the loss of a single man.

Billey received twenty-two medals for his bravery in this engagement and other combat experiences. His decorations included a Silver Star, Purple Heart, American Defense Service Ribbon, a European African Middle Eastern Theater Medal with a cluster of five Bronze stars, and the French Croix de Guerre. Wounded three times and reported missing in action twice, Billey died at Keota in 1989.[266]

Many other Choctaw served in World War II with distinction. Among them was Roy McClish of Lancaster, California. Born at Blanco, Oklahoma, on September 10, 1915, Roy, at three years old, and his brother Buster were sent to Morrow Indian Orphanage at Bacone College. At fifteen he and Buster joined the Oklahoma National Guard, serving with Headquarters Company, 180th Infantry, 45th Infantry Regiment, and later with Company I, of the 45th Division. McClish attended the Gulfcrest Military Academy and then moved to California to work as a tractor driver. In September 1941, he was mobilized into service and assigned to the Presidio at Monterrey. He was transferred next to Camp Phillips, California, until the war broke out.[267]

He was assigned to the 30th Field Artillery, 26th Brigade, and sent to North Africa. After volunteering for jump training as a paratrooper at Fort Benning, Georgia, McClish was returned to the United States and assigned to Special Forces as a parachutist. He served with the 101st Airborne, 45th Division and the 3rd Division, participating in several battles including the Battle of the Bulge. His decorations included the American Defense Medal, a Purple Heart, a Bronze Star, Paratrooper Wings, Glider Wings, and Combat Infantryman's Badge. He was discharged from service in 1949, but because his health had deteriorated, he became disabled in 1964. He had been separated from his brother in 1945, but the two men were reunited in 1975.[268]

Choctaw soldiers served in all branches of the military during the war. In 1941, Floyd Thompson enlisted in the Air Force after graduation from Goodland, trained at Shephard Air Force Base in Texas, and was sent to England as part of the 8th Air Force under the command of General Ira C. Eaker of Durant. The mixed blood Thompson flew twenty-five missions over Germany, went on leave, and returned to fly more. General Eaker decorated him with the Air Medal with two oak-leaf clusters and the Distinguished Flying Cross with three oak-leaf clusters.[269]

On a later mission his plane was shot down, and he was captured near Kiel, Germany. Spending the next fourteen months as a prisoner of war, he almost starved to death but miraculously survived the POW camp. After being liberated by the American army, he was sent home to a hospital in Florida for leg problems that had developed from flying at high altitudes. Thompson was grounded permanently after more physical problems and eye surgery. He returned to Goodland to teach woodworking and shop. Soon married, he had two daughters, Patsy of Ada and Cathy of Arkansas, and an adopted son who was killed in action in the Vietnam War. Thompson died at the age of fifty-eight and was buried in Del City. He was later inducted into the Goodland Hall of Fame.[270]

Veteran Bertram Bobb was born in Smithville on March 30, 1924. The son of Reverend Johnson W. and Mary Estelle Edwards Bobb, he was reared in southeastern Oklahoma where his father, a strong advocate of the gospel, known for his fiery messages, taught him Christianity. His father, the presiding Elder of the Choctaw Indian Methodist Mission for the Choctaw Nation, had a powerful influence upon his children. Bertram and his sister, Evangeline, often traveled with their father to camp meetings where Bertram worked the concession stands with assistance from his friends, Dave Kaniatobe, Pete Noah, and Gordon Wilson.

As a young boy, Bertram liked to listen to the radio fights and always remembered hearing the second Joe Louis vs. Max Schmeling fight that lasted two minutes. After attending Jones Academy, Bobb went to the Horace Mann Elementary School in Hugo, 1936-37, and to Goodland, 1937-42, where he played guard on the football team. The game that he remembered most was the victory over Coalgate ending its twenty-one-game winning streak.

In 1942, Bobb enlisted at the age of seventeen in the American military after Pearl Harbor. Inducted into the United States Navy in the same division with actor Henry Fonda, he was stationed at Ford Island Naval Air Station in Oahu where his duty was in Visual Communications as a Signalman. When he was discharged after three years, he was eligible for forty-eight credits under the G.I. Bill of Rights, and he used all of his hours at Chillocothe Business College, Missouri, and Murray State College in Tishomingo. In 1952, Bobb graduated from Northeastern at Tahlequah with a Bachelor's Degree in Business Administration, attended the University of Tulsa Graduate School, and transferred to the Dallas Theological Seminary.

While at Murray he played football for Coach "Bois d'Arc" Beames against men like Bob Fenimore and Neil Armstrong, who later played at Oklahoma State. Fenimore won the Heisman Trophy and Armstrong played in the National Football League and later coached the Chicago Bears. Bobb, having developed his boxing skills in the Navy, continued to box in college. One of his fights was against Golden Gloves Champion Alvin Williams, a Caddo Indian, who later fought Floyd Patterson in Madison Square Garden.

Reverend Bobb served for many years on the Choctaw Tribal Council and was named Chaplain of the Tribal Council and the Inter-Tribal Council of the Five Civilized Tribes. He was most proud of the Bertram Bobb Christian Camp for Youth. The camps were held in four sessions of six days each in the mountains near Ringold. His family including his wife, the former Mary Ann

Greenwood, three sons, and two grandchildren, supported his work. Bobb, a noted singer, recorded numerous renditions of Choctaw hymns. He believed completely in Psalm 33:12, "Blessed is the Nation whose God is the Lord..."[271]

In May 1988, Choctaw veteran Cortez A. Nicewarner died at the age of sixty-nine at Mineola, Texas. Born in 1918 at McAlester, he was in the Oklahoma National Guard when World War II broke out. Placed on active duty, he saw combat in the Sicilian and Italian campaigns with the rank of Sergeant. He received the combat infantry badge, the American Defense Service Ribbon, two Purple Hearts with Oak Leaf Cluster, a Bronze Star, EAME Theater Ribbon, and a Silver Star for his service.

On December 2, 1992, veteran Jesse Wickson died at age seventy-seven at Tahlequah. Born in 1915 at Soper, the son of Simm and Leona Gibson Wickson, he joined the Army in 1942. On June 6, 1944, he participated in the D-day invasion of Normandy with the 276th Infantry. Awarded three Bronze Stars and the Distinguished Unit Badge, Wickson returned to work for the railroad following his discharge.

Veteran James Millard Thomas, born September 9, 1900, north of Mead, was an original enrollee with the lucky number of 711. After working for a time in the oil fields of west Texas, he completed studies at the Southwest Baptist Seminary in Fort Worth and was ordained as a Baptist minister in 1932. He went to work as the Director of Student Air Mechanical School at Wright-Patterson Air Force Base in Ohio during World War II. Later, he worked at Liberal, Kansas, and then was transferred to the new Tinker AFB where he remained until his retirement in 1962. He was buried at Silo on December 21, 1991.

Wesley Samuels was a Choctaw veteran from Smithville. Born in 1923 to Jerry Harris and Rosie Nell Mayabb Samuels, he was stationed in Italy with the 505 Parachute Infantry of the 82nd Airborne Division in 1944. Samuels, a platoon sergeant, was in Rome when given orders to load his men, their parachutes, ammunition, and all the equipment that they could carry onto airplanes. Later that night of June 5, the men were dressed in combat gear, their faces blackened, and flown to Normandy. At 4:00 a.m., General James "Slim Jim" M. Gavin in the lead plane announced they were over the drop zone and bailed out. The general always jumped first.

Each of the men, loaded with more than 400 pounds of equipment, jumped after him. Leaving a trail of white silk, the Germans spotted them and opened fire. Making matters worse, the planes had actually missed the chosen drop zone and men were scattered over a forty-mile area, most of them behind enemy lines in a bivouac zone. Lost and alone in the dark, the Americans mistakenly shot each other, thinking they had run into Germans. One of the planes was also hit by "friendly fire."

Many of the German soldiers had lived in the United States before the war and were able to penetrate the American lines causing more chaos. As the two armies began to find each other, hand-to-hand combat often raged along the battle lines. When the Americans encountered bunkers that had to be penetrated, they approached with as much caution as possible to get close enough to throw grenades through the small openings left by the Germans for weapons. German tanks guarded mountains, rocks, hedges, and other parts of the landscape, but the Americans fought on, holding the Germans at bay long enough for the ships to get the invading armies unloaded on the Normandy beaches.

After a frightful battle with German forces, St. Mere-Eglise was the first town liberated on the western front. Many of the Americans had parachuted into the town directly into the waiting guns of the Germans, but the Third Battalion, 505 Parachute Infantry finally captured it several hours before the beach landings.

The 82nd destroyed sixty-two German tanks, knocked out forty-four anti-tank and artillery guns, and engaged five different enemy divisions in thirty-three days of combat that cost many American lives before being pulled out for a rest. From the time of the African invasion through Germany, the 82nd Division was in the front lines for 316 days, suffering 19,586 casualties. The Germans called them "butchers with big pockets," a phrase they took as a compliment.

Samuels was in the first group of Americans that went into Berlin. He was one of nine paratroopers selected to make an exhibition jump for Truman, Churchill, and Stalin at Potsdam. The "Big Three" were watching from the grandstands as Samuels landed, and he was honored to shake hands with them all. He received battle stars for Africa, Sicily, Italy, France, Holland, Belgium, and Germany and then returned to Oklahoma and retired in McAlester. Serving for several years as a member of the Tribal Council, he died in 1998.

Reverend Eli L. Samuels, born in Honobia, the son of Laymon and Ancey White Samuels, was another Choctaw veteran. Attending Honobia Elementary School and Dwight Mission in Vian, Samuels graduated from Sallisaw High School. In October 1942, he was inducted into the army. Samuels served with Company K, 194th Glider Infantry, of the 82nd Airborne.

One day after D-day, June 7, Samuels was wounded but returned to action in Holland on September 17, 1944. Participating in the Battle of the Bulge, he was wounded again on October 2, 1944. For his service, Samuels received the Silver Star, Bronze Star, EAME Service Ribbon with four Bronze Service Stars and one Bronze Arrowhead, two Purple Hearts, and a number of combat badges and stars. Samuels returned to attend Bacone College and Cook Christian Training School in Tempe, Arizona. In 1954, he was ordained into the ministry. Upon returning to the Choctaw Presbytery, the later Choctaw Parish,

Samuels served as the pastor for several communities and churches in southern Oklahoma.

Veteran Paul Henry Perkins, born on April 20, 1922, in Caney to Noah and Jincy Perkins, was drafted into the United States Army during the war. Participating in campaigns in North African, Italy, and France, he earned the Silver Star for his efforts. Perkins and his wife, Tillie Cole Perkins, had seven children and lived in California where he worked with heavy machinery until his retirement. When his wife died, Perkins moved home to Atoka.

Guy Whitfield, born in 1921 in Valliant, joined the Navy and was trained as a diesel mechanic on submarines during World War II. Participating in combat in both the Atlantic and the Pacific, he retired after twenty-one years in the service and moved to California. In 1962, the former sailor went to work for General Motors for another twenty years until his second retirement. He and his wife raised three children, and when his first wife died he returned to Idabel, remarried and moved to Gilmer, Texas, where he died in January 2000.

Choctaw soldier, Buster Dean Ned, was born at Simpson to Frank and Elizabeth Ned in 1924. In December 1942, one year after Pearl Harbor, he joined the Air Force and served in all theaters of the war. He transferred to the Marines after the war and served in Korea, Vietnam, and the Cuban invasion. Discharged after thirty years of military service, Ned died in 1992.

In 1994, Seaman First Class Marvin K. Campbell died of illnesses received from his service aboard the "U.S.S. Shangri La" in the forward thrust during the first atomic bomb test conducted on the South Pacific island of Bikini. The young sailor absorbed more radiation than a person should in a lifetime and contracted a rare heart and lung disease. His brother Delbert coincidentally serving on the "U.S.S. Blue Ridge" during the same time and place experienced four other tests conducted on the island of Enewietok.[272]

One of the most unusual events of World War II involved Charles (Bob) E. Boerner, Jr. and his father, Charles. Born in Durant in 1922, Bob graduated from St. Joseph Military School in 1940, devoted thirty years to service in the Army, and served with the Air Force from 1949 to 1972. His tours of duty included England, France, Germany, and Korea. Trained in bomb disposal, Boerner was involved in four major campaigns with the 67th Fighter Bomber Squadron in the Battles of Normandy and the Bulge in World War II. He later served with the 18th Fighter Bomber Wing during the Korean War.

The unusual story of this great-nephew of Will Durant occurred when his father, Charles E. Boerner, a soldier at the same time, learned where he was and joined him in World War II. By analysis of the number coding on postcards sent home, Mrs. Boerner discovered that her son's outfit was serving near his father's position and telegraphed the news to the two soldiers. In 1945, the men linked up in Antwerp. The two bunked together for the next two years of service. Boerner's last military campaign was as an Air Force advisor to the Air National Guard in Burlington from 1968 to 1972.[273]

Indian soldiers were fierce combatants. Realistic warriors, they knew that war meant killing and death. They did not give quarter nor expect mercy from their opponents and were aggressive and offensive in their thinking on combat. Although many never made their Indian identity a matter of record, those known Indians were awarded seventy-one Air Medals, thirty-four Distinguished Flying Crosses, fifty-one Silver Stars, forty-seven Bronze Stars, and two Medals of Honor. Five hundred and fifty Indian soldiers were killed in action and more than seven hundred wounded in battle in World War II.

Many did not return. In 1995, the "Choctaw War Memorial" was dedicated at Tvshkahomma with the names of one hundred Choctaw soldiers killed in action in foreign wars. Inscribed on a nine-foot slab of gray granite were the names of the original Code Talkers and the names of Choctaw veterans killed in action in World War I and II, Korea, and Vietnam.

The names of Calvin Bryant and Jacob Walley were listed for World War I. Veterans added to the list included Albert Billy, Mitchell Bobb, Nicholas E. Brown, Victor Brown, Calvin Bryant, Ben Carterby, Simeon Cusher, Joseph Davenport, James Edwards, Tobias Frazier, Ben Hampton, Noel Johnson, Otis Leader, Solomon Louis, Pete Maytubby, Jeff Nelson, Joseph Oklahombi, Leo Perry, Robert Taylor, Walter Veach, Jacob Walley, and Calvin Wilson.

For World War II, forty-five names were originally honored. They were Eugene Zephray Anderson, Woodrow Anderson, William Stanley Beard, Orville O. Black, George Brown, George R. Choate, Jr., Jonathan Coleman, Billie Joe Dukes, Benjamin Clay Freeney, Dewey Foster, Leonard Clark Goode, Bruce O. Gooding,, Wilburn R. Harkins, Tommy P. Hattensty, Clinton Lee Hulsey, Jack Franklin Irvin, Billie Boyd Jack, Woodrow W. James, Hanson H. Jones, J. Campbell LeFlore, Eltus C. Lewis, Ballard McCurley, Porter M. McCurtain, Alexander J. McKinney, LeRoy McNoel, Murray C. Mills, Hershel H. Nolen, Andrew Perry, Edgar O. Oakes, Jr., Robert Eugene Parrish, Frank M. Pittman, Andrew Perry, Jack Pebworth, Clarence Pulliam, John D. Sherred, William Edward Swink, Jr., Claude Stockton, Benjamin Tom, Henry T. Wall, Omagene Whitfield, Raymond Warren Williams, Joshua Wilson, Moses Winship, and Woodrow Wooley. Added to the list were Odell Bascom, James Calhoun Beck, Ray Bohanon, Buster Ray Burns, Hakin Christy, John Carney, Tandy Christy, Aaron Cusher, Robert Clay Florence, Kenneth Merle Folsom, Joe Ginn, Fred Hoklotubbee, R. G. King, G. W. Maxwell, Walter Dana McClure, Daniel McKenzie, Edgar O. Oakes, Jr., Johnnie Ott, Robert Eugene Parrish, Jack Pebworth, Walter Tobe Percer, Jonathan Perry, Davis Pickens, Walter A. Porter, William Clark Pratt, Jr., John Stallby, John Stevens, Turner Brashears Turnbull, and Eastman G. Ward, Jr.

The list continued for the Korean War. The names included Morris Amos, Tony Burris, Elam Frazier, Joe Calvin Green, Charles Kaniatobe, Jim McClure, Buster McCurtain, Isaac McCurtain, and Willie Rasha. Added later were William Arnold Bryant, Jr., Preston Franklin, Timothy Ontaiyabbi, and Leonard Sanders Watson.

The memorial also listed the names of Choctaw soldiers that died in Vietnam. They were Dean Edward Armstrong, James Scott Brown, Clyde Carter, Jr., Gilmore Christy, Forbis Pipkin Durant, Jr., Josh C. Noah, James LeRoy Russell, Roy Arnold Womack, and Michael Gene Warnick. Listed later were Edward Baker, Wallace Going, Joshua Hickman, Gatlin J. Howell, Clifford Curtis Johnson, Howard Lee Jones, Talton Lee Mackey, Marvin Noah, Charles D. Roberts, Frederick W. Sanders, Ernest Taylor, and Turner L. Thompson.[274]

The Choctaw Nation was the first Indian tribe designated as a World War II Commemorative Community. In 1995, the Department of Defense presented a Certificate of Designation and a commemorative flag in recognition for the honors given to veterans by the tribe. In March, a new Community Center was dedicated in McAlester with the event featuring the installation of a time capsule containing World War II memorabilia.[275]

Additional names could be listed. Killed in action were Paul B. Blanche, Osborne L. Blanche, Ray Bohanon, Jack LeFlore Brown, Aaron Cusher, Walter D. McClure, Grady Roberts, Dan Roebuck, John Stevens, Lewis L. Wade, and Aaron Watkins. Purple Hearts were awarded to Wilson Grimes, James R. Hattensty, Jack Hickman, B. Impson, Kern W. Jones, Luther King, Edmond Hoyt Massey (also awarded a Silver Star), Sam McCann, Isaac McCurtain, Rex Riddle, Solomon Roberts, Jesse B. Thompson, and Ersha H. Wallace. Choctaw POWs were Chauncy Calvin and Osborne L. Blanche, Jr.

One of the distinguished examples of a Choctaw officer was Lieutenant Colonel Edward Ernest McClish. A graduate of Bacone and Haskell Institute, he received a commission in the army in 1931. On active duty for the next ten years, he was shipped to the Philippines with the rank of captain to command scouting operations in 1941. After the Japanese invasion, he was promoted to colonel to mobilize a resistance force and move his headquarters to Mindanao. In April 1942, Japanese forces learned of his base and launched efforts to destroy him, but his ragged army eluded capture for three full weeks. For the entire summer, McClish countered the enemy, attacking, falling back, and attacking again. In September, he raised volunteers and linked with another army unit commanded by Colonel Fertig of the U.S. Army Corps of Engineers. Together, the commanders organized forces in three of the four Philippine provinces and harassed the Japanese with guerrilla attacks for the remainder of the war. By January 1945, the two had directed more than 350 engagements against the Japanese, killed an estimated three thousand, and wounded another six hundred.[276]

On Armistice Day, November 11, 1999, Chief Pyle, Major General LeRoy Sisco, and First Sergeant David McNerney honored Choctaw veterans including McClish at a service at the Tvshkahomma monument. Telling a large crowd of the many accomplishments of the soldiers, Chief Pyle displayed the medals of SFC Tony K. Burris, another Choctaw hero that had been killed in battle.

In 1950, Burris, from Blanchard in Grady County, entered the service with Company L, 38th Infantry Regiment, 2nd Infantry Division, and was sent to Korea. In February 1951, he was wounded in the leg and evacuated to Japan for recovery but was back in Korea and on the front lines again by April. He wrote home to his family that his feet and hands were frostbitten by the cold weather, but he proudly added that his group was called the "Fighting Vagabonds" by the other soldiers because the regiment had seen more combat than any other since January 1951. His last letter to his family arrived on September 12, 1951.

On October 8 and 9, Sergeant Burris was engaged in battle near Mundung-Ni, Korea. Leaving a sheltered position, he led his men in assaults against strongly fortified enemy posts time and again. Killing fifteen soldiers and destroying bases without mercy, Burris was wounded on the second day by machine-gun fire. Hit twice before being mortally wounded after throwing his last grenade at the enemy, his action inspired his men to secure Hill 607, a strategic position in the fight for "Heartbreak Ridge."

He was posthumously awarded the Purple Heart, the Silver Star, and the Medal of Honor. Awarded by the President in the name of Congress, the Medal of Honor is the highest decoration presented to an individual who distinguishes himself "conspicuously by gallantry and intrepidity at the risk of his life above and beyond the call of duty."

During the memorial ceremomy General Sisco of Choctaw descent, told the audience there were only 149 Medals of Honor winners alive in 1999. Sergeant McNerney then reminded the audience that the Indians volunteered at the ratio of ten percent of their population for World War II. He pointed out that there would have been no need for the establishment of a Selective Service system had the rest of America volunteered at a similar average.[277]

Jones Academy also listed its fallen heroes. Students who lost their lives in wars include Calvin Bryant, Henry McClure, David McGee, and Nathan Plunkett in World War I. Plunkett, although not a Choctaw, was given the honor because his father was a resident employee at Jones. The Jones Academy names for World War II include Woodrow James, Henry Nolatubbi, Leroy McNoel, Tandy Christy, John Carney, Loy Billy, Owen Mombi, Otis Yarbough, Davis Pickens, Walter McClure, Andrew Perry, Eugene Anderson, J. D. Sherrod, Odell M. Bascom, Jack Carlyle Hickman, Buster McCurtain, Clarence Pulliam, Porter

McCurtain, Andrew Brokeshoulder, Ray Bohanon, George Brown, John Floyd Wall, Charles Imotachey, and Melvin S. Arnett. The heroes of Korea include Morris Amor, Otto V. Brown, Jim McClure, and Isaac McCurtain. Vietnam veterans of Jones Academy were Henry Jennints and Johnson Ingram.[278]

The greatest memorials for the departed heroes were the memories kept by loved ones. They remained alive in the minds of their families and friends who continued to miss them after their deaths, especially by their fathers and mothers. One example was Ida May Merry Whitfield, an original enrollee, who served as the Golden postmaster after the death of her husband, Clinton O.C. Whitfield, in 1941, until her retirement in 1972. Affectionately known as Miss Whitfield, she was born on June 12, 1898, to J. L. and Bessie Durant Merry and attended Indian boarding schools until her marriage in 1915. The mother of two boys and two girls, Miss Whitfield lost her youngest son, Omagene, who was killed in the Pacific in World War II, and was carried in her thoughts for the remainder of her life. Her other son Lewis ran a grocery store at Golden until his retirement. Mrs. Whitfield died in Golden at the age of ninety-four in February 1993.[279]

Both men and women have carried the Choctaw war cry with the American flag. Choctaws have served in every branch of the military in Europe, Korea, Vietnam, the Middle East, and the Persian Gulf. T/Sgt. William H. Williamson of Bethany was a veteran of three wars in three separate branches of the military. Sergeant Williamson, born in 1922, in McAlester, the son of M/Sgt. Owen Williamson, USMC, served in the 45th Division, E Company, 179th Infantry Regiment from 1940-45, receiving the EAME Service Ribbon, two Bronze Stars, the American Defense Service Ribbon, and a Purple Heart for honors as a member of a machine gun crew in combat in North Africa, Sicily, and Salerno during World War II. In 1945, he transferred to the Marines and saw service with the Corps in Peking until 1947, when he enlisted in the Army Air Corps to serve in the Korean conflict with the 176th Fighter Interceptor Squadron. In this capacity he received the Bronze Clasp with Four Loops. In 1969, Williamson retired but served during the Vietnam War at Tinker Air Force Base until 1976. He died in 1991.

Another veteran of World War II who served in Korea was Chief A. Lewis. A native of Ti Valley, the son of Sullivan Lewis, an original enrollee, and Alice Goad Lewis, he was born in 1917. The Choctaw soldier, a commissioned officer, began his career as a flight instructor training pilots for World War II, receiving several presidential citations. During the Korean conflict, he flew a total of fifty-five night combat missions as a member of the 452nd Bomb Wing. Awarded a pair of Chinese Air Force Wings and the Distinguished Flying Cross for his work, Lewis ended his military career with the rank of captain in 1964. He continued to fly as a helicopter pilot in the oil service industry after his retirement. He died in 1995.

Veteran Bill Cornelius of Oklahoma City remembered the Korean conflict as "the forgotten war." In August 2002, the former member of the 5th Air Force Advanced that gathered top-secret reconnaissance for Air Force Intelligence, stated in a ceremony honoring veterans that: "We're all buddies in combat."[280]

Choctaw soldiers in Vietnam included Specialist Four Robert Lynn Gardner. Born December 8, 1941, in Anadarko to Watson and Arzie (Richardson) Gardner, he joined the army at the age of twenty-four in Oklahoma City in 1966. Receiving basic training at Fort Bliss, Gardner volunteered for airborne service in Advanced Infantry Training and was given jungle and survival training for Vietnam combat with three additional weeks at Fort Benning, Georgia, for Airborne Jump School. Assigned to the 101st Airborne Division at Fort Campbell, Kentucky, after a year he was sent to Vietnam to the 173rd Airborne Brigade. In 1967, he landed in Ben Hoa, Vietnam. Given two more weeks of jungle school, he was assigned as a gunner for machine guns.

After three months he was assigned as a medic with the 173rd. Called the "Gypsies of Vietnam" because they were always moving, his outfit was similar to a Mash outfit in Korea. Sometimes his unit saw as many as 225 casualties per day. Because the whole medical company was air mobile, the men were also called "Sky Soldiers." The 173rd was created just for Vietnam, and once it was over the unit was deleted. In March 1968, Gardner left Vietnam reassigned to William Beaumont Army Hospital in Texas. Hollis Roberts later selected him as Assistant Chief.

President Bill Clinton posthumously honored Austin Nubby, a former Marlow resident for "selfless devotion" to his country during the Vietnam War. Nubby attended Marlow schools until the sixth grade and transferred to Sequoyah Indian School in Tahlequah. After college at Louisiana State University and UCLA on athletic scholarships for football, basketball, and track, he entered the military and trained as a paratrooper. Serving with the Special Forces, he was decorated as a Green Beret for his action in Vietnam and later as a communications specialist during Desert Storm.[281]

A highly decorated Vietnam veteran was Wayne "Windy" Ward of Pocola, the son of Sherman and Kathrine Anderson Ward. During his tenure in the service, he received the National Defense Service Medal, Vietnam Campaign Medal, Combat Action Medal, a Vietnam Service Medal with one star, RVN Cross of Gallantry with Palm and Frame, and Rifle and Pistol Badges. After returning home, Ward traveled the world as a member of the "Straight As an Arrow" team playing professional fast-pitch softball. The veteran died at the age of fifty-two in October 1999.

Grover Murray, born in Bennington in 1931 to Arthur and Louella Jones Murray, retired to a quiet life in Boswell as a rancher and captain at the McLoud Correctional Center after a military career with duty in Korea and Vietnam. Those who knew him were generally unaware that the former Marine was a Silver Star winner for his service in Vietnam. He had earned the medal for his direction and rescue of downed helicopter pilots near Chu Lai, Vietnam. During the rescue he was with the 1st Reconnaissance Battalion, 1st Marine Division in charge of a platoon which was dispersed in a helicopter landing zone with elements of an infantry platoon awaiting evacuation. The unit came under heavy fire, and recognizing the danger, Lieutenant Murray signaled the pilots to take off while he directed fire against the enemy.

During the departure one aircraft was hit with machine gun fire, causing it to crash and catch on fire. Murray, at great risk from heavy fire, crossed seventy-five meters of open rice paddy to get the survivors out of the helicopter and returned through heavy fire to free the pilots from the burning wreckage shortly before it exploded. Once the action was over, Murray was presented a citation that read, "Lt. Murray with resolute calmness and professional skill, moved throughout the landing zone, continually exposing himself in order to direct the loading of the last troops and only at the last possible moment did he board an aircraft."[282]

Choctaw soldiers in other conflicts include Kevin W. Corley, Gilbert Dearman, and Kevin Isom. Corley, who joined the Marines in 1987, served in Panama, Korea, the Philippines, and the Middle East. Corley, a sniper with the 3rd Battalion, 2nd Marine Division, was stationed on the USS Raleigh in the Persian Gulf in 1991. SPC Gilbert Dearman, serving in the Army, was part of Operation Desert Storm. The twenty-three-year-old Choctaw was a graduate of John Jay High School, San Antonio. Former Daisy resident, SPC Kevin R. Isom was an electronic and hydraulic engineer in Saudi Arabia, maintaining guns and hydraulic systems on American tanks.[283]

Joe L. Campbell was eight when he began work dragging heavy cotton sacks through rows in the hot Oklahoma sun for his father's cotton gin located near Bennington. In his teenage years he added thrashing peanuts with a team of horses, raising hogs for shows at the county fairs, and tending chickens for eggs and poultry, but the son of a Scottish father and Choctaw mother was not destined for farming. Campbell enrolled in college and majored in business administration and was commissioned through the Air Force ROTC at Baylor University in Waco.

Joining the Air Force where his older brother was a flight engineer in the Army Air Corps in World War II, he went on active duty as a Second Lieutenant in 1960. As yet unaware of his Choctaw heritage, the military only recognized him as a white, male Caucasian, but his wife's interest in genealogy changed matters. Researching the family history, she learned that his great-grandmother was listed on the Choctaw rolls. Proud of the Indian heritage, Campbell and his family were soon registered as Choctaw tribal members. When Campbell became commander of the 403rd Tactical Airlift Wing at Keesler Air Force Base, Mississippi, he was one of only two Indians in the armed forces to reach the one star status at the time. The other was a Cherokee, Rear Admiral William L. Vincent.

As commander of the 403rd, Campbell was responsible for coordinating support for United Nations humanitarian efforts in Somalia and Sarajevo. His wing was also the only unit used to organize, equip, train, and perform all hurricane weather reconnaissance in support of the Department of Commerce. Campbell, a Brigadier General, logged more than 7,500 flying hours in various aircraft.[284]

Others who have contributed to the military include Corporal Chris Duschel, Poteau; Lance Corporal Bryan Groves, Muskogee; Paul Robertson, U.S. Navy, Hartshorne; PFC Harvey Ted Williams with the 44th EVAC Hospital in Desert Storm; and Sgt. Joe Nowlin from California. These men have all made fine soldiers, as well as Nowlin's brother, PFC Alan Nowlin; Staff Sergeant Timothy Nelson, Talihina; Sgt. Charles E. Riley, National Guard, Coleman; Lance Corporal Paul B. McMichael, Caddo; and Lyndon Paul Comp, Bennington.

Each Veteran's Day the Choctaw soldier proudly salutes his, and in recent years, her, country's flag that he and she have served so bravely. Among the women who have gone into the armed services was former councilperson Lu Bauer, who was the first United States Medical Corps officer to give birth while still on active duty. The Community Center in Coalgate was named in her honor. Recent recruits include April Sherrill, a 1993 graduate of Union High School in Tulsa and Rhema Bible Training Center in 1995. Sherrill entered training in the United States Air Force in San Antonio.[285]

Another Choctaw soldier was Captain Evi R. Hill who served in Bosnia where she was assigned as a company commander of twenty-five personnel in September 2000 to remain on duty until March 2001. A member of the United States Army since July 1996, Hill had previous assignments at Fort Jackson, South Carolina, Camp Red Cloud, Korea, and Fort Campbell, Kentucky. A graduate of Cache High School and Cameron University, Evi was the daughter of Larry Rowland, Milburn, and Jackie Harmon Rowland of Cache.

In 2003, Staff Sergeant Michael Harley of Idabel was deployed to Kuwait in support of "Operation Enduring Freedom" for Iraq. Assigned to the Third Infantry Division based in Fort Benning, Georgia, Harley had previously served in several countries in the Middle East. He earned five Army commendation medals and thirteen achievement medals in the process.

Another Choctaw in Kuwait was Corporal Brian D. Barcus of Palmer, Texas. Serving with the 15the Marine Expeditionary Unit, Barcus left Camp Pendleton, California, on the U.S.S. Rushmore destined for the Iraqi operation. He underwent training and was certified as "Special Operations Capable" for service in the campaign.

Choctaw warriors have never disgraced their tribe. Always serving bravely without complaint, the tributes to Choctaw veterans continue to be given both in private and public ceremonies. Taking their war cry around the world, Choctaw soldiers have been models of the American fighting man and inspirations for their people.[286]

CHAPTA AUAH HANNALI

~ CHAPTER SIXTEEN ~

"FOR THE GREATEST GOOD OF THE CHOCTAW NATION"

Chapter Sixteen

In 1983, the Choctaw Tribal Constitution placed the legislative authority of the Nation into the hands of a Council composed of twelve elected members, each represented one of the twelve districts in the ten and one-half counties in southeastern Oklahoma comprising the Choctaw Nation. Because the Choctaw traditionally looked to their tribal representatives for leadership, qualification for membership on the Council required that a candidate must have resided in the district for at least one year preceding the election and must remain a resident during the term of office to insure each member has a thorough knowledge of his or her district and its needs. Tribal Council members continue to receive information once in office through regularly scheduled council meetings. The Council members are strong men and women deeply committed to working with the tribe to achieve the ultimate goals of self-sufficiency and economic independence.

The Tribal Council roots were based in Chief David Gardner's term. Just getting the tribe organized again proved an extremely difficult task, and the Chief relied upon the County Council system of the Constitution of 1860 to help in this work. In 1976, Gardner asked county officials to support him and provide information for his administration in an appearance before members of the Pittsburg Council composed of President Wanda Byington, Vice-President Pat Fisher, Secretary-Treasurer Beatrice Zerbe, and Chaplain Israel Fisher.

The following year, Gardner established an Executive-Administrative Cabinet in an advisory capacity with the objective of drafting a new constitution to obtain a system of "one Choctaw, one vote." The organization's major work was to start the process of getting tribal members registered and accustomed to voting in elections again. The cabinet consisted of Robert Loyce Walker of Bethany, Chairman, aided by Hazel Anderson Webb of Smithville, Harvey York of Marlow, and Edwin Alexander Anderson and Charles Eastman Brown of Oklahoma City. Attorney L. V. Watkins, brother of Congressman Wes Watkins, and Program Director Emory Spears assisted in legal matters.[287]

Unfortunately, Chief Gardner, diagnosed with terminal cancer, died the following year, but Spears was approved to continue the administrative operations of the tribe until an election could be held in March 1978. Sixteen candidates filed for the position of Principal Chief including Robert Anderson, Frank R. Belvin, Charles E. Brown, Ellis Carnes, Jr., Dean Davey, Jr., Wyndle David, John Epperson, Randolph Jacob, Edward Leroy John, Lewis B. Logan, John T. Olive, Joe Thomas Packnett, Gabe Paxton, Albert Perry, Jr., Hollis E. Roberts, Minnie J. Thomas Voyles, and Roy Allen Willis. On March 25, the election primary gave Hollis E. Roberts 731 votes, Charles E. Brown 647, and Roy A. Willis 555. The others divided the remaining ballots out of 3,546 votes cast.[288]

On April 15, 1978, Roberts, a member of the state legislature from Hugo, received 1,668 votes to Brown's 1,329 in the runoff. Brown charged irregularities in the election, but nothing came of the accusations; Roberts was sworn in on May 1. His salary was set at $7,500 plus another fifteen to twenty thousand dollars per year for administering federal funds and programs.[289]

In 1978, a General Council was formed of members from the twelve districts of the Nation. In these meetings each county council was allowed four votes with the officers acting as representatives of the Choctaws in their area. Chairman of the sessions was Leroy John of Coalgate. The Council set up a Resolutions Committee with President John appointing Delton Cox, Randy Jacob, and Charles McIntyre to participate in the job of taking county resolutions, putting them into proper form, and passing them along to the Chief.[290]

Cox, chairman of a By-Laws Committee, soon reported progress toward the draft of a proposed, new constitution. A plan was completed within the year for provisions for a Chief, no longer to be designated "Principal Chief," a Tribal Council, and a Supreme Court. The Nation was divided into twelve districts, and legislative authority was placed in the hands of the Tribal Council consisting of fifteen members. The designated districts were District 1, McCurtain County south; District 2, McCurtain County north; District 3, LeFlore County south; District 4, LeFlore north; District 5, Haskell County; District 6, Latimer; District 7, Pushmataha; District 8, Choctaw; District 9, Bryan; District 10, Atoka; District 11, Pittsburg; and District 12, Coal and part of Hughes County south of the Canadian River. Each district was eligible for one Council member plus three "At-large" seats for the Choctaw outside the borders of the Nation.

The proposed constitution provided that the term of each office was four years. Additionally, the Council would select a speaker, secretary, and other officers when needed from its membership. Article IX, Sec. 10, provided the Council with its greatest power, the ability to override a veto by the Chief.[291]

On May 17, 1979, the Constitution won confirmation by a margin of only 302 votes. The tribe sent out a total of 5,897 ballots to registered Choctaw voters, and 1,528 of those returned voted yes for approval while 1,226 voted no. Chief Roberts immediately set a special election for the position of Chief and fifteen Council members for July 28, 1979. Tribal candidates for the Council were required to be twenty-one years of age, a member of the Choctaw tribe, one-fourth Choctaw by blood, never been convicted of a felony, and a resident of the Council district for more than one year. The At-large Council members were subject to the same requirements except they must have resided outside the Choctaw Nation for more than one year prior to filing for office. Labor Day, September 8, was set as the date for swearing in officers at Tvshkahomma.[292]

Filing for the office of Chief was Roberts of Hugo and Wyndle D. David of Sawyer, the owner-operator of a trucking business and a lumber mill. Roberts was elected for a four-year term with 2,013 votes to David's 1,205 votes. Other candidates in the race were Roy Willis, Wright City, who received 343 votes, Robert "Bob" Impson, Antlers, who polled 245 votes, and Leroy John, Coalgate, who garnered 72 votes. In the meantime, a United States District judge ruled the new constitution valid, legally replacing the old one of 1860.[293]

Winning elections in the Council races were Randy Jacob, Broken Bow, District 1; Lem J. Ludlow, Smithville, District 2; Malcolm Delos Wade, Talihina, District 3; Rubin White, Poteau, District 4; and William C. Martin, Lequire, District 5. A runoff was necessary in District 6, while Bertram Edward Bobb, Antlers, was elected in District 7. Another runoff race was necessary between Edna Belvin, Boswell, and Julius L. Bowen, Hugo, in District 8. Ted Gary Dosh, Bennington, was elected in District 9; Jasper Scott, of Atoka, in District 10; and Harriet Wright James, McAlester, in District 11. Since no candidate had filed for District 12, Chief Roberts announced that a Council member would be appointed in September.

Elected At-large members were Harvey York of Marlow, Buster Ned of Mannsville, and Dan Crossley from Oklahoma City. York, Chairman of the Southwest Choctaws, Inc., had served on the Marlow police force for a number of years. Ned had done much as a member of a committee active around Ardmore dedicated to the preservation of the Choctaw-Chickasaw heritage and as the sponsor of an album of Choctaw-Chickasaw dance songs. A former serviceman in two wars, Ned wore his hair long and braided as an expression of his pride in his Indian heritage. Crossley was the owner of a popular restaurant in Oklahoma City.

The voting had been close in all the contested elections. District 4 results showed White with 106 votes to Carl Walker Logan, 33 votes; District 7, Bobb, 135 votes to Dovie Underwood, 119; District 8 was Edna Belvin, 206 to Julius Bowen, 160, and Dosie Whisenhunt, 96; District 9 was Dosh, 186, and Atchman Arkansas, 141; and District 10, Jasper Scott with 93 votes to G.E. "Peno" Wilson, 44.[294]

On Saturday, September 8, 1979, the first duly elected and legally constituted General Council of the Choctaw Nation since 1904 met for its organizational meeting with thirteen members present. Two more would be added later to complete the list of fifteen after a special election was called to elect members to represent Coal-Hughes Counties and Latimer County.

Former County Tax Assessor Rubin White, Poteau, representing the South LeFlore District, was chosen as the first speaker of the new Council. Other officers elected at the inaugural meeting were Randy Jacob, Broken Bow, parliamentarian, and Harriet James, McAlester, secretary. Speaker White optimistically declared that the Council should "Let bygones, be bygones" and called on his fellow Council members to work for the "betterment of the Choctaw tribe." They responded by voting themselves a salary of $100 per month, a stipend of $100 per meeting day, and mileage at the federal scale of seventeen cents per mile for travel to Council functions. In other actions, the Council named Brock Wall as sergeant-at-arms. Wall, the ranch foreman at Tvshkahomma for the Choctaw Agri-Enterprises, Inc., was given a stipend of thirty-five dollars per meeting to set up the chairs and tables. Reverend Bertram Edward Bobb, the Pushmataha County Council member, was appointed chaplain.

Chief Roberts nominated three men by letter in the meantime for the new Choctaw Nation Supreme Court. Quickly confirmed by Council vote were Eugene Curtis, Wilburton, Charley Jones, Idabel, and Judge Joe Taylor, Durant. The only attorney was Taylor, but that was the only one required by the Constitution. Serving at the time as Bryan County District Judge, Taylor's primary function was to correlate tribal court actions with existing state and federal laws. Curtis was an administrative assistant assigned to Indian education with the Kiamichi Area Vo-Tech, and Jones was a health technician for the Indian Health Service with an outstanding reputation as a tribal historian.

Chief Roberts also recommended an Assistant Chief, allowed by the Constitution, by letter to the Council. He chose Robert L. Gardner, Durant, the son of Watson J. Gardner of Bokchito, grandson of Wellington (William) Gardner, and the great-grandson of Greenwood Gardner. At the age of thirty-two, Gardner had gone to work for the tribe four years earlier as Deputy Director of Health and Social Services, Health Planner, and had later served as Coordinator of Economic and Community Development. The Council obliged the Chief by giving its approval of all the appointments.

A major question for Speaker White was the issue of tribal lands in Pittsburg County. A debate had developed over the ownership of the lands on which the state penitentiary was located at McAlester. After researching the problem, it was learned that the state of Oklahoma had acquired title to 1,566.04 acres used for the penitentiary in a condemnation suit in 1909, and that these lands had been paid for as the "Coal and Asphalt Lands," an amount of $8.5 million. This money had subsequently been distributed in per capita payments of $350 in 1949, and $161 to the Choctaw and $171 to the Chickasaw in 1952. This settled the debate.[295]

In December 1979, the Council finally decreed a special election for the vacant seats for Districts 6 and 12. A special election board composed of Sam Farmer of Durant, Warren Sherred, Finley, Ola Maye Draper, Wilburton, and

Edwin A. Wall of Albion was selected to oversee the election. On Saturday, December 22, 1979, Mrs. Lillian Sullivan, Wilburton, was elected for District 6 and Edward Leroy John for District 12. John squeezed by Lula B. Bauer, an author from Coalgate of a book on the Choctaw, by only four votes. He received forty-two ballots while Bauer garnered thirty-eight. In District 6, Mrs. Sullivan won with seventy-six votes and her opponent, Victor Roebuck, of Tvshkahomma, received twenty-four. This brought the Council to full strength for the January meeting of 1980.

The County Councils all held elections at the same time. The Choctaw Nation County Council members and officers for 1979-1980 were Jasper Scott, Bunnie Burchfield, Wilson Jones, and Clark Bohanon representing Atoka County, and Frances Farrell, Ruth Morris, Waynoka Trobak, and Robert Sanders for Bryan County. Other delegates were Edna Belvin, Dosie Whisenhunt, Kathy Allen, and Simon Belvin of Choctaw County, and Edward Leroy John, W. R. Jones, Virginia Johns, and Ray Carney, Coal County. William Martin, John Lewis, Christine Barnett, and Abe Wallen represented Haskell County; Lillian Sullivan, Ola Maye Draper, Delton Cox, and Anna Belle Ott represented Latimer; Dale Cox, R. L. Owens, Joe A. Randall, and Bob Sockly, LeFlore North; William James, Malcolm Wade, Henryetta Imhese, and Nathan Benton, LeFlore South; Randy Jacob, Charley R. Harley, Diane Jacob, and John McKinney, McCurtain South; Hewey Jefferson, Joseph Lewis, Laura Lewis, and Laura Carney, McCurtain North; Wanda Byington, Jimmie Sams, Paul Wesley, and Osborne Kenieutubbe, Sr., Pittsburg; and Emerson Wade, Floyd Peters, Alice A. Ward, and Bertram Bobb, Pushmataha.[296]

In October 1979, Ron Scott profiled one of the Tribal Council members as the subject of "Ronnie's Veterans" in *Bishinik*. He was Jasper J. Scott of Atoka. Born on August 15, 1920, the son of Samson and Margaret (Crowder) Scott, the future Choctaw Council member attended a Catholic school in Antlers and Lone Pine School in Atoka County. At eighteen, he joined the Civilian Conservation Corps (CCC) at Pueblo, Colorado. Two weeks later he was made supervisor of a crew building log homes in the region. Scott attended night school at the same time and earned a diploma through the CCC program. On November 13, 1943, Scott was inducted into the Army at Tulsa, given some initiation at Fort Sill, and transferred to the Mojave Desert in California for Basic Training with 468 other members of the 440th Automatic Weapons Battalion. After six months, he made the training team, rated as a marksman in air-cooled 50-caliber machine guns and M-1 rifles. The team was next sent to Needles, California, for two and a-half months before transfer to Blackstone, Virginia, for more training with automatic weapons. Scott, a Master Machine Gunner, was sent to New York for chemical warfare training in preparation for being sent overseas.

In the winter of 1944, the 440th landed in Liverpool, England, where still more training in weapons was ordered for Scott. While there, the Normandy invasion occurred, and his outfit was sent to France. Scott's battalion won and lost battles at St. Lowe five times before successfully defeating and capturing thousands of Germans between St. Lowe and Paris. He participated in five major battles during the war but was finally hospitalized from lacerations received from a German soldier who attacked him from behind, cutting his face, head, and stomach. He received several medals for his service including a Good Conduct Medal with four Hash marks, a unit citation, five bronze stars, and one Silver Star. Settling in Atoka in 1951, the Choctaw warrior married Savannah Williams and was the father of seven sons and two daughters. In 1964, he was ordained as a Cumberland Presbyterian minister.[297]

In October 1979, Council member Malcolm Delos Wade was the honored guest at a ceremony recalling his career as an athlete and football star at Henderson State College in Arkansas where he graduated in 1914. Wade was presented with a "game ball" and acclaimed with his portrait hung in a place of honor. The Talihina councilman fondly remembered his playing days as a three-sport letterman in football, baseball, and track at Henderson where he had enrolled right out of the eighth grade. Since Talihina only went through eight grades at the time, Wade was recruited straight from elementary school as a sixteen-year-old freshman sports star. Wade and his older brother Dennis were enlisted as runners because the Talihina team had swept the county track meet in Poteau earlier, and the Henderson coaches heard about them. Wade had never seen a football game before enrolling at Henderson but joined the team and led them to "Arkansas collegiate championship" in 1912 and 1913. "We never lost a conference game," he recalled, despite playing teams like Vanderbilt, Mississippi State, and Arkansas University. "Vandy beat us, 33-0, however," he said.

Wade added, "There were only fifteen men on the traveling squad, and we played without pads. Most of us, including me, didn't even wear helmets." Playing end at 140 pounds, he stated that the biggest man on the team only weighed 155 pounds. Turning into a semi-professional athlete, Wade had a short career as a minor league baseball pitcher, playing for the Talihina Indians. After sports, Wade took work in highway construction, truck driving, and law enforcement.

Wade remembered the Chautauquas (oratorical and musical presentations) as the "big events" of his youth in Talihina along with a movie when a company was in town. The operators would set up a tent and show a movie by virtue of a hand-operated motion picture machine. He added, "My dad was strict, however. He didn't believe in things like that or dancing. The church was the main thing in most of our lives." Wade stated, "Everyone went to church or weekly prayer meetings. There was no smoking or drinking. The boys did not even go swimming with the girls. Even at college, we weren't around girls except at heavily chaperoned receptions." Wade met his wife, an Italian whose family name was Cenotto, when she arrived by train for a visit in Talihina. "We started for the OU-Arkansas football game, but never got there," he said, deciding instead to get married on the way. He was twenty-one and she was sixteen.[298]

On September 4, William C. Martin was sworn in for Council District 5 for an inaugural term of two years as the first Council members had drawn lots for two or four year terms to get the election process underway. Born on March 16, 1926 in Lequire, the son of William and Charolette Folsom Martin, he was married to the former Robbie Ford. The father of six children stated that he had been "raised poor but proud" and grew interested in tribal government from his own personal experiences with restrictions placed on the allotted lands of his parents. Determined to change a system that had made it impossible for his parents to borrow money to stock their farm or buy equipment to operate because of restrictions, Martin had decided that he must work to improve the plight of his people, and the Tribal Council provided the best means of doing it. In 1965, he had gotten involved in the Mutual Help Housing Program, and the first Mutual Help Homes were constructed in Haskell County six years later. In 1975, Martin was named chairman of the Haskell County Council and served as a member of the Advisory Board to the Chief. In 1987, in his eighth year on the Council, he objected to the establishment of the Tribal Bingo operation as an ordained Baptist minister on religious philosophy.[299]

By the end of August 1979, the fully organized Council had initiated meetings, beginning in September on the second Saturday of each month in the cafeteria of the Choctaw Capitol complex. Most of the first year sessions were "hit or miss" operations as the Council members struggled to gain a working knowledge of the many federal programs being administered by the tribe. They "felt their way" into government and made mistakes and sometimes were annoyed with each other and the Chief on issues, "But, for the most part, when the question came down to requiring an answer, our Council tried to come up with a decision that would be for the greatest good of the Choctaw Nation," said Len F. Green, editor of *Bishinik*.[300]

By this time the Council had evolved to the establishment of standing committees for programs. The Finance and Budget Committee was composed of Chairman Bertram Bobb with members Buster Ned and Harriet James. Randy Jacob chaired the Rules and Regulations Committee with memberships held by Dan Crossley and Ted Dosh. The Social Services Committee was chaired by William Martin with Dosh and Edna Belvin as members. The

Industrial Development Committee was composed of Randy Jacob, chair, and Leroy John and Bertram Bobb as members. There was also a National Resources Board chaired by Rubin White with Jasper Scott and Delos Wade as members. Ted Dosh chaired the Hospital and Clinic Committee with Lillian Sullivan, Rubin White, William Martin, and Lem Ludlow as members. Finally, the Labor Day Activities Committee was chaired by Dosh and composed of Leroy John and Buster Ned.[301]

On December 12, 1980, Council member Harriet James dropped a bombshell on the Council with the announcement that the two Choctaw owned corporations, Choctaw Nation Enterprises, Inc. and Choctaw Agri-Enterprises, Inc., were operating illegally according to the Oklahoma Secretary of State. The Choctaw Nation Enterprises, Inc. had responsibility for owning, renting, and maintaining IHS Indian Health Clinics in Broken Bow, Hugo, and McAlester, and a garment factory at Stigler leased to Mountain Industries of Tulsa. Choctaw Agri-Enterprises, Inc. had responsibility for operating cattle, haying, and ranching operations on more than 3,000 acres around the Capitol. James had been informed that the corporation charter of Choctaw Nation Enterprises, Inc. had been suspended for failure to pay franchise taxes for the previous year on March 9, 1979, and Choctaw Agri-Enterprises, Inc. had been suspended in 1976 for failure to pay franchise taxes for 1975. Moreover, as far as anyone could tell, Choctaw Nation Enterprises, Inc. had been operating without a board of directors for three to five years. Donald Moon, BIA office director, told the Council the solution was to reactivate the two corporations by paying the back taxes plus penalties or the tribe could take over operations. A committee was set up to study the best solution and Judge Joe Taylor approved the action.[302]

District 11, Pittsburg County Council member Harriet Allea Wright O'Leary James was a direct descendant of Chief Allen Wright. Her father was J. B. Wright of McAlester. The widow was a retired educator with a Bachelor's Degree in Business from Oklahoma College for Women and a Master's Degree from Oklahoma University. She had served as a teacher and supervisor in positions from elementary to the college level. In 1974, she served as Director of Title IV-A Indian Education Programs for the McAlester Public Schools, K-12. Mrs. James was a member of the First Presbyterian Church of McAlester and served on several boards for the Choctaws, among them, a position on the Board for Goodland Presbyterian Children's Home in Hugo. In 1983, she was the second woman candidate for Chief and placed third in a field of five.[303]

She was among those members that had to run for a second term for Tribal Council membership on July 25, 1981. Not all were running. Those campaigning for a second term with Mrs. James were Bryan County Council member, Ted Dosh; Coal County Council member, Edward Leroy John; Haskell

County Council member, William Martin; South LeFlore Council member, M. Delos Wade; North LeFlore Council member, Rubin White; and the At-large seat holder, Dan Crossley of Oklahoma City. The other members were slated to serve until 1983.[304]

There were a number of issues before the Council at election time. One was the announcement by Hugo Tribal Attorney Lon Kile that the 10th Circuit Court of Appeals in Denver, Colorado, had handed down its decision concerning the tribal constitution. In 1977, eight Choctaw including three members of the Council, Randy Jacob, Jasper Scott, and Leroy John, filed a suit to declare the 1860 Constitution a viable document, but the court had ruled that the Constitution of 1860 was no longer an effective government document and added that the 1979 one was not properly adopted either according to court guidelines. On the other hand, the court ruled that tribal government should continue until such time as a final ruling was made, setting the stage for another revision of the Constitution.

In February 1981, Harvey York was selected to replace Rubin White as the new Tribal Council chairman. A number of complaints had been lodged against White for not controlling some Council members who tended to dominate discussions of issues and interrupt other members who had the floor. It was thought York would allow more democratic debates.[305]

In 1981, a number of excellent candidates placed themselves before the tribe for consideration for office. Filing for Tribal Council District 3, South LeFlore County, against incumbent Malcolm Wade was Leslie A. James, son of Levicy and Allen James. Born in 1921 in Ludlow, James attended Ludow Schools, Jones Academy, and Whitesboro and had served in World War II and Korea. Married and the father of six, he had worked as a Licensed Practical Nurse at the Indian Hospital until his retirement in October 1981. Serving as vice-chairman of the Talihina Low Rent Housing Authority, he was the vice-commander of American Legion Post 86, and a member of the Board of Directors of the Eastern Oklahoma Historical Society and the National Oklahoma Kidney Foundation.

Dale Cox was a candidate for District 4, North LeFlore County. A lifelong resident of the district, Cox, born on August 19, 1929, was the one-quarter mixed blood son of J. C. and Ora Ida White Cox. He and wife, Juanita, were parents of four children, all of whom completed college and were employed as schoolteachers. His sons were vocational-agriculture teachers in Haworth and Allen and his two daughters taught in Spiro. The owner and operator of the Spiro Feed and Farm Supply, Cox had served as Supervisor of the Choctaw Housing Authority from 1974-1975. Serving as chair of the LeFlore County Council for four years, he had been a member of the Constitutional Commission for the Nation in 1978-79.

Filing for District 9 against incumbent Ted Dosh was Emerson Wade. Born in Boswell, Wade, one-half blood, was the father of three and a graduate of Antlers High School. Employed by the Nation in the On-the-Job Training program and CETA for three years, he had served as chair of the Pushmataha Tribal Council in 1979.

District 11, Pittsburg County, had two candidates vying for Council member James' seat. They were Eugene "Bud" Allen and William J. Frye. Allen, one-half blood, born in 1922 at Tvshkahomma, was a former student at Jones Academy and Haskell Institute. A World War II veteran and holder of a Purple Heart, he and his wife Margaret were the parents of two children. William J. Frye was born in 1939, the son of Edmond Thomas Frye, a full blood, and Eliza Pickens Frye, one-half Choctaw-Chickasaw. Frye's family included his wife Ruth Ann, a son, and a daughter. Having grown up in Ti Valley and the Blanco communities, Frye graduated from Pittsburg High School, Bacone College, and Northeastern Oklahoma State University with a Bachelor's Degree in American Indian Studies and Sociology. The bilingual Frye, after twenty years in the Navy, was acting director of the Choctaw Manpower Program from June 1975 to 1978. Having served with the Talking Leaves Job Corps Center in Tahlequah, he was employed at Jones Academy, working with elementary grade students.

The District 12 incumbent was Edward Leroy John of Coalgate. Born in Bentley, in 1939, the Air Force veteran was a gospel singer, piano player, Coal Creek Cumberland Presbyterian, and a member of several singing groups. He was the only Choctaw to graduate from the Program of Alternate Studies, a course of study for the gospel ministry of the Cumberland Presbyterian Church, Bethal College, Tennessee.

A candidate filing against incumbent John was Cecil Flowers, Jr. Born in 1935, near Centrahoma, Flowers was an Air Force veteran. He and his wife and five children lived in Coalgate. He was a silversmith with a diploma from the Arizona School of Jewelers Arts. Flowers grew interested in state politics while living in Arizona, working for the election of a governor and two senators. For twenty years he had worked as a glazier before his employment at the Ada Indian Hospital in the maintenance department. He served as chair of the Coalgate Parents Committee on Indian Education.

The At-large Seat Number 3 candidate was Robert Anderson, Mustang. At age forty-three, Anderson had more than seventeen years of professional management experience in Indian affairs. Employed as a Management Consultant under a contract sponsored by the Administration for Native Americans, Anderson cited health care, housing, education, and the opportunity for economic independence as major goals for the tribe. He was particularly interested in stressing tribal enrollment.

The third man in the race was Cecil E. James. Born in Sardis, he and his wife, Ruth, were parents of three children. James had attended Jones Academy and Chilocco Indian School and received degrees from Murray State College and Southeastern Oklahoma State University. With thirty-four years experience as an educator, James was an Education Specialist/Federal Programs with the B.I.A. Among his affiliations were the Choctaw Bi-Lingual Advisory Board, American Legion, Jones Academy/Chilocco Alumni Associations, and the Choctaw Nation Historical Society.

The incumbent At-large Seat 3 candidate was Daniel W. Crossley of Oklahoma City. At age fifty-eight, the five-sixteenth Choctaw was the son of Lee C. and Becky (Perry) Crossley. The father of two children and three stepchildren, Crossley had attended schools in Ada and Stonewall, served in the Navy during World War II, and worked as an ironworker in Local 48, serving as president of the local from 1968 to 1972, and vice president in 1981. He was a member of the Oklahoma City Council for Choctaws, the Intertribal Council for the Five Civilized Tribes, Masons, Shriners, Elks, Moose Lodge, V.F.W., and the Eastern Star.

Sometimes called "Taco Dan," Crossley, the owner of "Dan's Indian Tacos" in Oklahoma City, settled in the state capital after World War II. In 1974, he turned his recipe for tacos into a business by opening his own restaurant. Crossley had been given a gold medallion and citation at the 1980 Oklahoma State Fair for "serving the most unique and enticing food at the state fair." He had served on the Tribal Council and on the Intertribal Council for sixteen years.[306]

On July 25, 1981, tribal elections were held for four-year terms on the Council. The results were District 3, Leslie A. James, 91 votes to Malcolm Wade, 48; District 9, Ted Dosh, 122 votes over Emerson Wade, 70; District 11, Harriet James, 131, E. Allen, 79, William Frye, 44; District 12, Leroy John, 36, and C. Flowers, 27. The At-large Seat 3 candidate results were: Robert Anderson, 479, Cecil James, 338, and Daniel Crossley, 106. Other successful candidates who drew no opponents were Dale Cox, District 4, and William Martin, District 5.[307]

In October 1981, a new controversy arose over salaries and expenses paid to the Council members. Charges were made that the members were receiving inflated amounts of money at the expense of the tribe, and the rumors escalated until the Council members allowed expense amounts to be published in the October issue of the newspaper. Each member publicly revealed the amount received in salary and expenses in 1980 and 1981. Lowest amounts were paid to District 6 Council member Lillian Sullivan who received $2,343.85 in 1980 and $3,935.82 in 1981 for a total of $6,279.67, while the highest was McCurtain County Council member Randy Jacob who received $4,159.45 in

1980 and $6,649.48 for FY1981 for a total of $10,808.93. The other thirteen members ranged between these two for a total expenditure of $128,621.35, an amount that included salaries of $36,300, session stipends of $45,800, committee stipends of $12,223, travel of $29,052.20, and communications of $4,946.15. To those who criticized the amount as an exorbitant amount of money, the Council pointed to Randy Jacob who had arrived late for one of the sessions because his car had broken down on the way. The McCurtain Council member had worn out his automobile making the necessary visits to Tvshkahomma for Council meetings.[308]

The At-large seats were eliminated to reduce the number of members to twelve by 1983. Running for office that year were District 1, William Amos, Ryman Hodges Battiest, and Randy Jacob; District 2, Billy Paul Baker, Lem Ludlow, and Hazel Webb; and District 3, Leslie James and Malcolm Wade, Jr. In District 4, C. Dale Cox was unopposed for election to another term. District 5 had Dolores Christie Holloway, William Martin, and William T. Martlatt; District 6 saw Randle Durant challenge Lillian Sullivan; District 7 candidates were Reverend Bobb and Dovie Lois Underwood; District 8 had Edna Belvin, Daniel C. Hampton, and Curtis Wilson James as candidates; District 9 had Ted Dosh and William Harris; District 10 had Ronald C. Scott, Clayburn D. Simpson, and Thomas Sneed as candidates; District 11 included M. Alberson and William Frye as candidates; and the District 12 candidates were Lula B. Hopkins Bauer, Chester Estep, and E. Leroy John.

The same year, Wyndle David, defeated again by Hollis Roberts for Chief with a vote of 2,594 to 2,310, filed a protest of the election. Alleging nineteen violations of voting rules during the September 17 runoff, David took the election results to court but the Election Commission denied the request to overturn the election by a five to one vote. Chief Roberts was sworn in on October 15, 1983.

In February 1984, the Council listed its membership as: District 1, Ryman Battiest, Wright City; 2, Billy Paul Baker, Bethel; 3, Malcolm Wade, Jr.; 4, Dale Cox, Spiro; 5, William Martin, Lequire; 6, Randle Durant, Talihina; 7, Bertram Bobb, Antlers; 8, Wilson James, Hugo; 9, Ted Dosh, Bennington; 10, Ronald Scott, Atoka; 11, William Frye, Blanco; and 12, Lu Bauer, Coalgate.[309]

In September 1984, the Council elected officers for the next session. Dale Cox was named as speaker, Bertram Bobb as chaplain, and Randle Durant as secretary. The appointments by Speaker Cox included Theresa Blaine as recording secretary, Brock Wall as sergeant-at-arms, and Bob Rabon as parliamentarian completed the staff. The Council had hardly gotten organized when District 11 Council member William Frye stunned the others with the announcement that he was resigning his position effective October 1.

Explaining that "after a lot of prayer," he had decided to devote more time to his family and church and stated that his decision was final.[310]

By constitutional statute, an election to select a replacement had to be set in sixty days. In November, Speaker Cox and the Council set the date to fill the Pittsburg seat for January 12, 1985. Filing for the position was former Council member Harriet Wright O'Leary James and Dena Cantrell. Cantrell won with 159 votes to James' 86 votes.[311]

Born in the Talihina Indian Hospital on December 4, 1949, Cantrell, the daughter of Carl and Lucille Jameson of Crowder, was a life resident of the Ash Creek community outside McAlester. Married to Dennis Cantrell, Dena, the mother of two, was registered as fifteen/thirty-second Choctaw. She was the granddaughter of Jefferson Lee Hancock and Annie Ensharkle, both original enrollees. A graduate of East Central State University with a degree in Sociology, she worked for the Choctaw Nation Housing and Social Services Program.[312]

Tribal positions remained unchanged after elections on August 17, 1985. District 4, North LeFlore County, Dale Cox won with 155 votes over Neil S. Davis, 83 votes; District 6, Latimer County, Randle Durant, 207 votes over Jack W. Sparks, 68; District 7, Pushmataha County, Bertram Bobb won unopposed; District 9, Bryan County, Ted Dosh won unopposed; in District 10, Atoka County, Ronald Scott, 64 votes over Levi Jones, 50 votes; and District 12, Coal County, Lula B. Bauer, 91 votes over Chester L. Estep, 23 votes.[313]

In 1985, Dale Cox was chosen to serve another term as speaker, Bertram Bobb, the Pushmataha Council member-minister, was elected to another term as chaplain, and South McCurtain representative Ryman Battiest of Wright City was elected to the office of secretary. Born on December 10, 1939, educated in Wright City and the Sequoyah Vocation School in Tahlequah, Battiest had served eight years in the National Guard. Battiest, a full blood, and his wife, Mary Jane Wade, a three-quarters Choctaw, had two sons. He was an employee of Weyerhauser in Valliant. He had served on the Industrial Development Committee, Health Committee, and the Planning Committee for the Council.[314]

Another member, Malcolm D. Wade, Jr., was born in Talihina, on March 3, 1921, the son of Malcolm D. and Lucy Wade. His great-grandfather was Alfred Wade who had been the "Governor" of the Choctaw Nation in 1857. His grandfather was Judge Cyrus B. Wade, who had been elected to numerous offices in the tribal government, including the Council. His father, Malcolm, Sr., was a special officer of the United States Indian Service tracking "moonshiners" through the eastern Oklahoma Mountains and later was one of the original Tribal Council members.

Malcolm, Jr. held a Bachelor of Science Degree in Business from

Oklahoma City University where he had received a football scholarship as a halfback. A World War II veteran, he had earned a Bronze Star and a Purple Heart. He retired as a colonel after thirty-six years in the military in 1981. He was married to the former Mary Louise Honea and the father of three children.[315]

On July 11, 1987, Chief Roberts was elected to a fourth term with 3,484 ballots, or 64.3 percent of the vote. Other candidates filing for the position had been Wyndle David who received 729 votes, and Jim Thorpe, 1,204 votes. Six Tribal Council seats had also been up for election. The North McCurtain seat held by Billy Paul Baker was retained with 145 votes over Lem J. Ludlow with 103 votes. Ryman Battiest was elected for the other McCurtain seat with 420 votes over his opponent Randolph Jacob, who received 190 votes. In Pittsburg County, Dena Cantrell was elected with 401 votes over Harriet James with 153 votes, while newcomer Perry Thompson won the Choctaw County seat with 406 votes over his opponent Emerson Wade with 249 votes.

On August 1, 1987, runoff elections were necessary for two council seats because election rules mandated that a candidate must receive more than fifty percent of the votes or a runoff election must be held between the two candidates with the most votes. In South LeFlore County, Malcolm Wade and Leslie James were forced into a runoff when Wade got 131 votes, James got 162 votes, and Clifford Steelman got 71. Haskell County also needed a runoff when candidate William Martin received 89 votes, John Lewis, 65 votes, and the third candidate, Bobby Mayfield, got 50 votes.[316]

On August 1, 1987, runoff voters ousted William Martin from District 5. John C. Lewis replaced him in Haskell County. In South LeFlore County, Leslie James replaced Wade.[317]

In 1987, the Council received the announcement by Council member Randle Durant and Chief Roberts of an agreement with representatives of Investment Resources, Inc., a firm in Minneapolis, to a pledge of $1.8 million for the construction of a 2,000-seat gaming hall south of Durant on Highway 69-75. The contract provided the tribe sixty percent of the proceeds and the IRI forty percent for seven years. The arrangement allowed the construction of the Choctaw Bingo Parlor, and the hall was paid off early from its receipts.[318]

In September 1988, Tribal Council officers were selected and committee appointments made by Speaker Dale Cox. Brock Wall was appointed to continue as sergeant-at-arms, Bob Rabon as parliamentarian, and Teresa Jefferson as recording secretary. The committee membership included Bertram Bobb, Lu Bauer, and Ted Dosh, Finance and Budget Committee; Billy Paul Baker, Bauer, and Dena Cantrell, Rules and Regulations Committee; Cantrell, Leslie James, and John Lewis, Social Services Committee; Ron

Scott, Baker, and Lewis, Natural Resources; Bobb, Ryman Battiest, and Randle Durant, Industrial Development; Durant, Bauer, and Battiest, Health Committee; Durant, Bobb, Dosh, and Battiest, Labor Day Activities; Baker, Scott, and Perry Thompson, Education Committee; Dosh, Battiest, and James, Planning Committee; Scott, Cantrell, and Thompson, Election Committee; and James, Thompson, and Lewis, Ethics Committee.

One of the Council's major actions was the approval of a lease agreement for the tribally owned nursing home in Antlers. The home was leased to Dr. Bob Mitchell for seven years at $95,000 per year.[319]

In 1989, the Council approved plans for a unit of the Choctaw firefighters. On March 11, Tom Lowery, Tribal Forestry Director, explained that the program to train Choctaw firefighters could be done with no cost to the tribe as the United States Forestry Service provided the funding with the only requirement being that the firefighters would be on call anywhere they were needed for fire control. The distribution point would be Talihina, and the Council heartily approved the project.[320]

In 1989, elections were needed for seats in Districts 4, 6, 7, 9, 10, and 12. Before they could be held, a former member passed away. Reverend Jasper Scott died on April 18, 1989. His seat was up for election, too.[321]

In June, Dale Cox and Ruben L. Owens filed for the District 4 seat; Bertram Bobb and Dovie Shilling for District 7; Ted Dosh and Frank Watson, District 9; and Ron Scott and Esias J. Johnson, District 10. Randle Durant, 6, and Lu Bauer, 12, drew no opponents. The results were: Dosh elected with 259 votes to 132 for Watson; Dale Cox, 204 votes to Owens' 86; Bobb, 124 votes to 91 for Dovie Underwood; and E. J. Johnson won the Atoka County seat with 89 votes compared to Scott's 86.[322]

On September 8, 1990, the first order of business was the election of officers. Bertram Bobb of Pushmataha County, one of the few original members of the Council still in office since its inception in 1979, defeated Ryman Battiest for the position of speaker. Honored by the selection, Bobb was helped by Randle Durant, Latimer County Councilman, as secretary, and Haskell County Representative John Lewis as chaplain. Speaker Bobb then appointed Warren G. Sherred, Finley, as sergeant-at-arms and Teresa Jefferson as recording secretary.[323]

In September, Lu Bauer resigned her seat as Council member for Coal and Hughes County after being employed by the Indian Health Service. The community center in Coalgate was later named in honor of the former U.S. Navy Medical Corps officer. Born at the Lawton Indian Health Services Hospital, her grandmother, Dora Wade, had removed to Indian Territory, received an allotment, and lived in Atoka County until the 1950s. Educated at Nix (Caney) and Sequoyah High School in Tahlequah, Mrs. Bauer attended Southeastern and graduated from San Deigo State University in California. She was married to Martin J. Bauer, a Marine. A special election for District 12 to replace her was set for February 1991.

In other business, Council member Leslie James seconded the motion by Durant to amend the proposed Tribal Trust Budget to include increases in payments for the judicial and legislative branches of the tribal government. An increase for Council meetings was raised from $12,000 per year to $30,000, and salaries from $27 to $50,000 per year, but Chief Roberts later vetoed this proposal.[324]

In March 1991, Council members voted to override the veto. Those voting in favor were Battiest, Thompson, Baker, Cox, James, Cantrell, Lewis, Durant, Bobb, and James Frazier. The vote allowed members to receive an increase of twenty dollars per month, a stipend of seventy-five dollars per committee meeting, and a yearly stipend increase of ten dollars per meeting through 1995. The base salary for members was set at $40,000 per year.[325]

In other actions, Durant proudly reported that the increase in value of tribal properties was gathering steam. In 1980, the Nation had a net worth of $17 million and the net worth in 1991 was $32,349,411.88. The amount of cash on hand was $10 million. The tribe was gaining momentum.[326]

In June 1991, Clyde Raymond Jessie, Bokchito, Floyd G. Anderson, Talihina, and John Lewis, Stigler, filed for election against Chief Roberts. Both McCurtain County seats were up for election in the Tribal Council elections, and Billy Paul Baker drew two opponents, Willard Grant Wilson, Bethel, and Lem J. Ludlow, Smithville. South McCurtain County chose between incumbent Ryman Battiest and Charley George Jones, Idabel, and in Pittsburg County incumbent Dena Cantrell drew Wesley Samuel of McAlester as her opponent. Southern LeFlore incumbent Leslie James was running against Norma Austin of Talihina, and in Haskell County William C. Martin of McCurtain was running against Charlotte F. Jackson of Keota. Perry Thompson, the Choctaw County incumbent, did not draw an opponent.[327]

The results were another landslide for Chief Roberts, who won by carrying 74.2 percent, or 4,870 votes. Second place, John Lewis, received 762 votes, Anderson, 637, and Clyde R. Jessie, 436. The Tribal Council elections were closer. In South McCurtain Jones defeated Battiest, 351 to 342; in Pittsburg, Cantrell lost seat 11 to Wesley Samuels, 355 to 299; in Haskell County, Charlotte Jackson won with 195 votes over William Martin with 138; and South LeFlore kept Leslie James with 236 votes over Austin with 172. A runoff was needed for District 2 between Lem Ludlow with 96 votes, Billy Paul Baker, 86 votes, and Willard G. Grant, the third candidate in the race, who received 83 votes. The runoff was held on August 3, 1991.[328]

In September, six tribal officers took the oath of office during the Labor

Day ceremonies in the recently completed Tvshkahomma amphitheater. Head Tribal Judge James Wolfe of Hugo performed the inauguration for Council members Charley Jones in District 1, Billy Paul Baker for District 2, Leslie James, District 3, Charlotte Jackson, District 5, Perry Thompson, District 8, and Wesley Samuels, District 11. Latimer County Council member Randle Durant was elected speaker for the year at the regular session of the Council, taking the gavel from Bertram Bobb, who was elected chaplain. Charley Jones was elected secretary.[329]

On May 12, 1992, North LeFlore County District 4 Council member Dale Cox died and was buried in Spiro. He had served as speaker and on numerous boards, including the Choctaw Housing Board and the Hospital Board and was a member of the Lavaca Beagle Club in Arkansas, the Spiro Schools Athletic Boosters Club, and the Spiro Roundup Club. The Community Center in Poteau was named in his honor.[330]

On July 11, 1992, a special election for his replacement elevated Lois Wanda Jean White Burton into office. Sworn in by Tribal Judge Juanita Jefferson, Mrs. Burton was born at Reichert, the middle child of five children of Sampson G. White, an original enrollee. Her mother Edith Johnson White died in the sanitarium in Talihina. Lois was six at the time, and the family moved in with their grandparents, L. B. and Angeline White. They set the example for her and taught her to "have compassion and treat all people fairly." Having to walk to school, Lois became sick in the third grade, and she and a brother were sent to Goodland for a year. They returned home to attend school at Reichert and high school in LeFlore. She married Eardman Burton, who worked for the Army Corps of Engineers at Wister Dam, and the couple raised two daughters. Mrs. Burton went to work for Head Start in its initial year while continuing her own education; she received a Bachelor of Arts Degree in Education from Southeastern and later did postgraduate work in math and reading. She was the "1992 Teacher of the Year" at Shady Point where she had taught first grade for sixteen years. A member of the Oklahoma Education Association, she was a member of Delta Chapter of the Alpha Delta Kappa Sorority of Women Educators. Residing in Wister with her family, Lois served as a Sunday school teacher for the Church of the Nazarene.[331]

In May 1992, Speaker Durant and his wife Margaret traveled to Ireland to represent the tribe in the annual walk that had begun a few years earlier to mark the ceremony of the gift to Ireland during the Great Famine in 1847. Making President Mary Robinson of Ireland an honorary chief of the tribe, Durant set the stage for a visit to the Choctaw Nation for the Irish head of state.[332]

Only a few months later, Council member Charley Jones served as the official delegate of the Choctaw tribe to a meeting of Native Americans and the Occitan people of France. Jones was the guest of Occitania and Paris from July

11-27, 1992. Sharing his stories on Choctaw culture, Jones spoke the language and sang Choctaw hymns as part of a group representing one of seven tribes exchanging history and culture.[333]

Tribal leaders are rightfully proud of the people involved in the various housing programs and their accomplishments. In 1992, they saluted longtime Choctaw Housing Commissioner C. Wilson James for his years of working for improved living conditions for his people by renaming the Hugo Housing Authority building in his honor. Born February 10, 1919, in Hugo and educated at Goodland Indian School, James and his wife, Willie Lee Hyatt, were parents of four children. The former sheriff of Choctaw County, 1970-72, he worked as a paper mill employee until retirement in 1990. A member of the Council from 1983 to 1987, James was credited with the concept of the annual Choctaw children's Christmas party at the Cultural Center in Hugo. James and other volunteers began the tradition for hundreds of Choctaw children in District 8 to enjoy meeting Santa and receiving treats each December. He died at the age of seventy-five on March 4, 1994.[334]

In May 1993, elections again were held for Tribal Council. Lois Burton was elected without an opponent for District 4; District 6, Randle Durant faced Douglas Glenn Dry; District 7, Bertram Bobb opposed Floyd Gene Davis, Dovie Lois Shilling Underwood, and Lee Roy Webster; District 9 incumbent Ted Dosh faced Lorene Emma Sanders Blaine; District 10, Esias James Johnson was opposed by Ronald Curtis Scott; and District 12, James Mitchell Frazier drew Johnson J. Ott as an opponent. Election board members were Edmond Jones, Edna Loftin, and Alma Mason.[335]

Incumbents were kept in all contested seats. In July 1993, the election results were: District 6, Durant, 282 votes, Dry, 116; District 9, Dosh, 438, Lorene Blaine, 160; District 10, Johnson, 125 votes, Scott, 94; and District 12, Frazier, 168 votes, Ott, 42 votes. Pushmataha County required a runoff with Bobb receiving 48.84 percent of the vote. In the Antlers precincts, he received 66 votes, Webster, 42, Davis, 4, Ben, 2, and Underwood, 30. The final results were Bobb, 148 votes, Davis, 17, Ben, 16, Underwood, 49, and Webster, 73. Bobb would go on to win the runoff on July 17 with a tally of 237 votes to Webster's 143.[336]

In March 1994, the Tribal Council was composed of Charley Jones, 1; Billy Paul Baker, 2; Leslie James, 3; Lois Burton, 4; Charlotte Jackson, 5; Randle Durant, 6; Bertram Bobb, 7; Perry Thompson, 8; Ted Dosh, 9; E. J. Johnson, 10; Wesley Samuels, 11; and James Frazier, 12. On September 10, 1994, Randle Durant was elected speaker, Charley Jones continued as secretary, and Reverend Bobb was chosen as chaplain. Speaker Durant then appointed Sam McBride as sergeant-at-arms and Marsha Lloyd as recording secretary. During the meeting Council members praised the expanded space at the Capitol for visitors along with the Choctaw War Memorial.[337]

On July 8, 1995, races for Council seats for Districts 1, 2, 3, 5, 8, and 11 were scheduled along with tribal elections for the position of Chief between candidates Roberts and Douglas G. Dry. District 11 had three candidates including Bob Pate, Julie Rose, and incumbent Wesley Samuels. District 3 had five persons, Juanita Jefferson, Bobbie R. Carnutt, Floyd Anderson, and Bobby N. Ludlow, in the race including incumbent Leslie James. In District 1, Charley Jones drew no opponent nor did Charlotte Jackson in District 5 or Perry Thompson in District 8.

Roberts won the Chief's race with 13,342 votes to Dry's 1,583. In the Council races: District 11, Samuels received 334 votes, Pate, 438, and Rose tallied 191 votes; and in District 3, Leslie James received 295 votes to 173 for Jefferson, Carnutt, 25, Anderson, 67, and Ludlow, 148. Runoffs were necessary in both races and were scheduled for July 29. Pate won his election with 506 votes to Samuels' 287 ballots, and the runoff in District 3 was won by James with 285 votes to Jefferson's 249.

Tribal candidate Douglas Dry and two other activists were arrested while passing out political literature at the following Labor Day Festival before the inauguration of Chief Roberts. Dry, Juanita McConnell, and Rosie Burlison sued in Muskogee federal court claiming that tribal law enforcement authorities violated their rights, including free speech, the right to assemble and due process. The case was appealed to the U.S. Circuit Court in Denver, but the court ruled against the three in December 2000. The court stated that District Judge Michael Burrage was correct by originally ruling that tribal authorities have sovereign immunity from being sued in the federal courts.[338]

Resuming its work, the Council approved two new programs over the next couple of years. In January 1996, Joy Culbreath was placed in charge of $985,205 in grant funds for a program entitled "Indian Adult Education." Funded by a grant for five years from the Department of Education, the program provided finances for GED classes, career exploration, tutoring, financial aid assistance, and visiting potential employers in business and industry. The following year Wilma Rogers and Beverly Akin, the grant writers, were commended by the Council for winning a Community Development Block Grant for $750,000 from the Department of Housing & Urban Development for construction of a restaurant and motel to be located at the Choctaw Plaza south of Durant.[339]

Business could not have been better when disaster struck. A federal jury found Chief Roberts guilty of three counts of sexual abuse of two former employees at the tribal headquarters in Durant. Forced to resign the office of Chief, he was replaced by Assistant Chief Gregory E. Pyle on June 6, 1997. Sworn in by Chief Justice James Wolfe, Pyle thanked the Council for its support of the constitutional system and remarked, "We are going to look forward and keep the Choctaw Nation's momentum going as it has in the past." These strong, confident words restored the tribe's solid foundations and the Tribal Council returned to business. On June 14, Pyle, with approval of the Council, appointed Mike Bailey, Director of Jones Academy since 1984, as Assistant Chief.[340]

In July 1997, Tribal Council elections were a bit more exciting with a runoff election necessary for District 7, Pushmataha County, between incumbent Bertram Bobb and newcomer Glenn Dale Johnson of Antlers. In the general election, Reverend Bobb received 311 votes and Johnson, 283, but the third candidate, Lee Roy Webster, got 66 votes, forcing a runoff on August 2. Other elections kept incumbents in District 6, Randle Durant, 284 votes to Larry Don Coley's 92; in District 9, Ted Dosh received 573 votes to Emma Lorene Sanders Blaine, 263; and District 10 saw E. J. Johnson get 254 votes to Bobby Gene Bulison, Jr., 42 votes. Glenn Johnson won the runoff in August by twenty-two votes against Bertram Bobb.[341]

In September 1997, Speaker Durant returned to his position as head of the Council with Charlotte Jackson selected as secretary and Charley Jones named chaplain. The Council voted to make Reverend Bobb the official Chaplain of the Choctaw Nation as a reward for his many years of service on the Council.[342]

The following year the Council underwent another change of administration. On September 12, 1998, Bob Pate was elected speaker, Charlotte Jackson retained her position as secretary and Charley Jones was returned as chaplain. A year later, Pate was retained as speaker, Jackson was chosen by acclamation as secretary, and James Frazier was voted a term as chaplain. At the same time, Pate was voted president of the Choctaw Nation Enterprises Board along with Ted Dosh, vice-president, and Frazier, secretary. The speaker then appointed Marsha Lloyd as recording secretary, Fred Bobb as sergeant-at-arms, and Bob Rabon, parliamentarian.[343]

In May 1999, Leslie James announced his retirement at an appreciation dinner held in his honor in Talihina. A proud United States Army veteran, James often stated that his greatest moment was winning a medal that was pinned on him in the field by General George Patton immediately following the Battle of the Bulge. Few knew the details of the event, however, and he allowed the story to be told during the evening.

He had been on the edge of the battlefield, safely dug into a foxhole with the fighting going on in front of him and just across the field was the German army, firing heavily to keep the Americans pinned down. Between the two enemies the field was covered with dead bodies and wounded men. James left his place of safety to pull his wounded friends to safety through heavy fire time and again. His reward was a Silver Star.

Leslie served on the Council from 1981-83 and again from 1987-1999. Chief Pyle applauded his support for the new hospital at Talihina and the Hospitality House for family members. Kenny Bryant of Talihina was appointed to complete James' term.[344]

Tribal elections were held again on July 10, 1999. The candidates for Chief were Pyle, Larry G. Finch, Douglas G. Dry, and Glenn D. Johnson. In the Tribal Council elections, District 1 candidate Charley Jones drew opposition from Cinderella Taylor Deramus and Herbert Jessie; in District 2, Billy Paul Baker received a challenge from Jeffrey Jefferson and Faith Jacob-Parra; in District 3, Kenny Bryant was opposed by Bob Ludlow; in District 5, Charlotte Jackson was unopposed; District 8 drew Kenneth Winship and Adeline Frazier as opponents for incumbent Perry Thompson; and incumbent Bob Pate faced William Frye in District 11.

The most interesting work of the Council in session was the discussion for the future of Wheelock Mission. A federal grant had been received to begin restoring the buildings of the venerated school. This proved the most popular action taken during the meeting.[345]

In 1999, election results tallied from Choctaw voters gave Chief Pyle 17,864 votes, Johnson, 1,942, Dry, 1,393, and Finch, 1,075. The Tribal Council results were as follows: Jones, 472, Deramus, 123, and Jessie, 202, District 1; Baker, 470, Parra, 255, and Jefferson, 82, District 2; Bryant, 848, Ludlow, 282, District 3; Thompson, 762, Kenneth E. Winship, 599, and Adeline Frazier Hudson, 159, District 8; and Bob Pate, 1,144, Frye, 406, District 11.

The Council voted unanimously to retain Pate as speaker. James Frazier was selected as secretary, and the new chaplain was Kenny Bryant. Reporting a growth in tribal membership at the same time, *Bishinik* set membership at 118,128. In September 2000, Kenny Bryant was elected to serve a term as speaker, Charlotte Jackson retained her position as secretary, and Randle Durant was elected to serve a term as chaplain.[346]

In 2001, Lois Burton announced her retirement. Serving since replacing Speaker Cox, she recalled that it was the last day of her school year when Councilman Cox had passed away, and she was encouraged by her friends to run for the office. She told them that she did not know much about tribal affairs, but Rubin White told her that she could learn, knowing that she would work hard for her people, which was the most important prerequisite for the job. During her term in office she helped cut the ribbon for the Pocola Smoke Shop, rename the Poteau Community Center in honor of Dale Cox, and the new health clinic in honor of Rubin White. The tribe also received the deed to the Skullyville Cemetery and placed a chain-link fence around it. A commemorative walk was held there in the spring of 1993.

Elections in six districts were set for July 14, 2001. Along with District 4, Burton's seat, elections were required for District 6, 7, 9, 10, and 11. The first to file for Distict 4 was Delton Ray Cox, and no one filed against him. Candidates filing for District 6 were Randle Durant and Janie Pearl Emmert. In District 7, incumbent Glen Dale Johnson faced Frederick Bertram Bobb, Jack Clarkson Austin, and Darrell D. Nichols. District 9 incumbent Ted Dosh was elected when no candidate filed against him, but District 10 saw a plethora of candidates. Running against incumbent Esia James Johnson was Rayson Roy Nicholas, Johnnie Burleson, Clayburn Simpson, Charles Samuel Carroll, and Ronad C. Scott. District 11 incumbent, James M. Frazier, was unopposed for election.

On May 5, 2001, Frazier participated in the commemorative walk at Eagletown with Chief Pyleand Speaker Kenny Bryant. Calling the walk "a great privilege" to follow the footsteps of the Choctaw of 1831 and 1832, Bryant said, "I felt the spirit and encouragement of our ancestors." Chief Pyle, another participant in the walk, added that the walks were "one of the ways to preserve the Choctaw culture and heritage." He stated, "We should all teach our children about our history, our culture and our language."

On Saturday, July 14, 2001, elections were held in Districts 4, 6, 7, 9, 10, and 11. The press announced that four of the six members had been elected, one replaced, and one race needed a runoff in August. In District 7, JackAustin of Clayton unseated incumbent Johnson, who had served since 1997. Johnson received 382 votes, Frederick Bertram Bobb totaled 72 votes, and Darrell D. Nichols got 41 votes to Austin's 735 votes, a victory of 59.8 percent. In other races, Randle Durant defeated Emmert 385 votes to 226 for District 6. A runoff was necessary in District 10 where E. J. Johnson got 279 votes and faced Johnnie Burleson, 264 votes. On August 4, Johnson won with 501 votes, 53.4 percent, to 437 votes, 46.6 percent, for Burleson.[347]

Glenn Johnson of Snow was born in the Talihina hospital, and his daughter, Marissa, was born there shortly before the new hospital opened in 1999. Encouraged to go to college to make a better life, Johnson graduated from the University of Oklahoma with a degree in Business Administration in December 1986. He attended Officer Candidate School with the United States Marine Corps and returned to Oklahoma after a three-year hitch. In 1990, he was promoted to 1st Lieutenant, serving as a Logistics and Safety Officer at the Marine Corps Air Guard Combat Center in Twenty-nine Palms, California. By 1998, Johnson had been promoted from captain to major in the Marine Reserves. After serving on active duty, he received an MBA from National University.[348]

Council members are typical representations of their districts. They are hardworking, tireless individuals who spend long hours in the service of their people. Their dedication is unrivaled and unquestioned. They are valuable members of their districts.

In October 1992, Charley Jones Day was proclaimed by the mayor of Idabel to celebrate the work of the Tribal Council member for District 1 since 1991. A full blood Choctaw who speaks, reads, and writes the Choctaw language, Charley was born in Honobia, LeFlore County, on September 23, 1917. His parents were Robinson and Caroline McGee Jones. Charley's mother died during the flu epidemic of 1917. He was only seventeen months old. His two brothers and three sisters were separated and raised by aunts, grandmothers, community Choctaw families, and non-Indian mountain folk of southeastern Oklahoma. Charley lived with his totally blind grandmother until age nine when he was taken to Idabel to Aunt Silsainey Jones Johnson. He enrolled at Herndon Elementary School, but did not fare too well since he could not speak a word of English. Sent to Goodland Indian Orphanage boarding school near Hugo, he learned the "Three Rs," but it was an educational policy for an Indian not to speak the Indian language and students were punished when caught speaking Choctaw. Charley learned the white man's language. He later attended Bacone College at Muskogee. Enrolling in a business school in Paris, Texas, he was employed by the St. Louis, San Francisco Railway, Department of Interior, Branch of Land Operation, Bureau of Indian Affairs. When the U.S. Public Health Service took over the Choctaw Nation services, Charley transferred to the Branch of Indian Health for more than twenty years.

He worked for the Choctaw during Chief Jimmy Belvin's administration as the councilman for McCurtain County. He was instrumental in obtaining the first Indian Health Clinic in Idabel that later was moved to Broken Bow. He also worked with the Indian Health Service in establishing the sanitation program for existing Indian homes. This Public Law 86-121 led to the construction of Mutual Help Indian Homes. He married Louellen Hudspeth of Haworth. They have two children, four grandsons, and six great-grandchildren.

In 1975, Charley renewed interest in tribal affairs after the United States Congress passed the Self-Determination Act allowing the tribes to reorganize and elect their own leaders again. He served as secretary for the Tribal Council and has earned a reputation as the historian for his people.

An advisor on tribal events and people, Jones attends tribal functions the year round and happily shares his pride and knowledge of the Choctaw heritage. He likes telling stories of Choctaw history and displaying his museum-quality items that help preserve the Choctaw heritage, and he insists on the correct use and spelling of the Choctaw language. His goal is to see the language restored to its proper place in Choctaw culture. On January 24, 1991, the McCurtain County Historical Society awarded its Distinguished Service Award to Jones for helping preserve the Choctaw culture and heritage. He remarked proudly, "The Choctaw have gone from beadwork to Ph. Ds. We're revitalized. We're a proud people again."[349]

Billy Paul Baker represented District 2 on the Council until 2003. Born on November 9, 1944, at the Talihina Indian Hospital, the son of Samis and Ida Wesley Baker of Battiest, his father was an original enrollee and his grandfather, Elias Wesley, was a Choctaw judge nicknamed the "whipping judge." His ancestors had the first store in Eagletown near the big cypress tree when they first arrived from Mississippi over the Trail of Tears. Baker, a full blood, was reared on his father's restricted land. In 1918, some of the land was donated for the Bethel Hill Methodist Church and services are still held there. Appointed to the Council on October 28, 1982, and elected in 1983, the former log-skidder operator for Weyerhauser served as the chairman of the International Woodworkers of America Local Union #515. He resigned from the Council in March 2003.

In 2003, Mike Amos of Broken Bow was appointed to the Council seat vacated by Baker. Amos is full blood Choctaw, and the son of Bill and Louise Amos and has strong ties to McCurtain County. Mike and his wife Vicky have three children, Dayla, Nikki, and Andrew, all full blood Choctaw, and live in Broken Bow. Mike and Vicky work with Myrtlewood Baptist Church west of town where Mike serves as treasurer and van driver and Vicky teaches nursery and kindergarten children. Amos called his appointment to the Tribal Council "one of the most important challenges" of his life and promised to work to improve education, health, and housing services for District 2. "The tribe has been able to earn the money to provide college scholarships to Choctaws and I feel that now we need to work on encouraging more students to go to college," he stated. Also committed to health care for the Choctaw, he pointed out that McCurtain County has a large population of Choctaw and could benefit from a larger medical clinic with more doctors and health professionals. Another issue for Amos has been the encouragement of the Choctaw heritage. His daughter Dayla, a former princess, and her sister Nikki participate in Choctaw social dances, and he hopes to see his son join them. He encourages his children to "Learn our history, dances and language." He will continue to dedicate himself to serve his district from his position on the council. [350]

In 2001, District Three Council member Kenny Bryant was elected speaker of the Tribal Council. In tribute to the growth of the Nation, he stated at the annual Labor Day Festival: "We want to see the Choctaw Nation prosper, and with the help of God we will continue to do so." Quoting Romans 8:31, Bryant declared, "If God is for us, then who can be against us?" Secretary Charlotte Jackson and Chaplain Jack Austin supported Bryant.

In November 2001, Speaker Bryant paid tribute to Veteran's Day at ceremonies in Tvshkahomma. Remembering the day that he received a letter that began, "Greetings, you have been selected to serve the United States Army," he said that he never forgot that day or the day that he returned from overseas. He remarked, "When I hit the ground I kissed that old blacktop. I was so glad to be back in my own country."

District 4 Council member Delton Ray Cox has a long relation with the tribal government. Delton was born in 1943 four miles southeast of Summerfield, Oklahoma, the youngest son of John and Ora White Cox. He had seven brothers and three sisters. His mother was one-half Choctaw and one of the original enrollees. Delton is the youngest grandson of Livingston B. (Buck) White and Angeline Mitchell White who were the grandparents of three other Choctaw councilpersons who have represented the Fourth District on the Tribal Council: Rubin White, Dale Cox, and Lois Burton. Rubin White served as speaker of the Tribal Council, and Delton's brother, Dale, served as speaker until his death in 1992.

Public service is not new to this family. Delton's grandfather, Buck White, was a Methodist minister, and his great-grandfather, Jerry White, held elective offices in old Sugarloaf County, Moshulatubbee District, including the office of sheriff in 1874. He was one of the leaders of the "Snake" movement who opposed allotments until his death in 1904.

Delton was raised in LeFlore County as was his mother, grandfather, and great-grandfather. He attended school at Summerfield for three years, Spiro for five years, and returned to Summerfield. He graduated from LeFlore High School in 1961.

Delton's mother had only a fourth grade education, but wanted one of her children to attend college. As the youngest son, he knew that he had to find a way to go. In August 1961, he borrowed $300 to start to college at Eastern Oklahoma A&M in Wilburton. He later received a Bureau of Indian Affairs scholarship that paid most of his expenses. At Eastern, he was elected vice-president of the Indian club as a freshman and president as a sophomore. In 1962, he enlisted in the Marine Corps Reserve to fulfill his military obligation. In 1963, he graduated from Eastern and moved to Durant to attend Southeastern State College. He graduated from Southeastern in 1965. In 1970, he was selected to be in the Pennsylvania State University American Indian Leadership Program. He received a M. Ed. from Penn State in 1971, but stayed for another year to complete all the requirements for a Ph. D. except for his thesis dissertation when his funds ran out. He graduated from Mississippi State in 1978 with an Education Specialist degree. He also completed forty-two more graduate hours at Northeastern State,

Oklahoma State, and the University of Oklahoma. He was certified as a school superintendent, secondary principal, and social studies and business teacher.

Delton spent thirty-two years working in the field of education as a teacher, coach, counselor, education planner, and administrator. He worked twenty-six of those years with the Bureau of Indian Affairs, three years with the Cherokee Nation, one year with the Mississippi Band of Choctaw, and three years in Oklahoma public schools. He worked in six different boarding schools and was the administrator of the three largest Indian boarding schools still in operation in Oklahoma: Jones Academy, Tahlequah Sequoyah, and Riverside Indian School at Anadarko. After retiring from the Bureau of Indian Affairs in 1997, he returned to LeFlore County. Delton decided he could not stay retired and accepted a job as a social studies teacher at Spiro. In December 1997, Chief Greg Pyle asked him to come work for him as the Choctaw Nation Tribal Treasurer. Delton served as Treasurer until 2001 when Lois Burton retired as the Fourth District Council person and he ran unopposed for the position on the Council.

Mr. Cox had a long interest in Choctaw affairs and constitutional government. When he was working at Jones Academy, he served on the Latimer County Council of Choctaws as an officer from 1976-79 when the Choctaw Nation was not operating under a constitution. He was appointed by Chief David Gardner to serve as a member of the Choctaw Nation Planning Commission that developed a strategic plan for the tribe. He was a member of the committee that developed the 1979 Choctaw Constitution under Chief Hollis Roberts. He was a neutral member of the Choctaw Nation Reformation Committee that was responsible for the 1983 Choctaw Constitution.

Delton married Deloris Thompson from the Tucker Community at Philadelphia, Mississippi, in January 1970. After moving to Oklahoma in 1973, she graduated from Eastern State and Bacone College, and became a licensed Radiologic Technologist. They have two grown sons and two granddaughters. Their oldest son, Nate, graduated from Connors State and Northeastern State in 1994 and was commissioned as an officer in the Army Reserve. Nate's daughter was born in Tulsa in 2002. Delton's son, Daniel, graduated from Northeastern State and then Oklahoma City University with a M.B.A. in Finance, and completed a Master's in Accounting at the University of New Mexico. Daniel's daughter was born in 1997.

Charlotte Jackson of Keota serves as District 5 Council member. She is the granddaughter of original enrollees Ben and Lorena Martin Jackson and the daughter of Martha Jane Jackson and Dock Moore. Charlotte is the mother of Patricia E. Jones and Kevin W. Jackson. She has four grandchildren, Jeremy, Matthew, and Shasta Jones, the children of Pat and Darrell Jones and Kyle Jackson, son of Kevin and Tammy Garland Jackson. She has one sister, Betty

Wiedemann. Charlotte was elected secretary of the Council and has held the position since September 1997.

Stating that her family lived "way out in the country" when she was growing up, she was sent to the Sequoyah Indian Boarding School at the age of six because there was no transportation to any schools in her area. She returned home after three years to attend Keota and then went to Chilocco for two years. Always interested in nursing, she learned nursing care from her mother. "My mother used to set up with sick people, and I was always going with her to assist," she said. In 1966, she attended school for her LPN degree and worked as a Community Health Representative in LeFlore and Haskell Counties.

In 1990, she was recognized in a presentation ceremony in Tulsa as CHR of the Year. She was honored because: "Her devotion and love of her people are true and sincere." Charlotte still does home visits to check on her people, making sure they are following their doctors' orders, taking their medications, and have sufficient medicines. Elevated to the Council in 1991, she was especially proud of the new clinic in Poteau. Health and education remain important goals for her work on the Council.[351]

Randle Durant has served as Latimer County District 6 Council member since 1983. Born in humble beginnings at Bennington on December 27, 1921, his father was a victim of tuberculosis, called consumption then. He was unable to work and the family suffered financially. Durant remembered that at the age of six the family was so poor all they had to eat for one ten-day period was cornmeal mush. He and his brother and sister took the door off the cellar and propped up one end of it with a punching stick from the wash pot to catch small birds to add a little meat to the meals. When the birds landed under the trap, they pulled the clothesline tied to the stick to drop the door on them. After about a week his great-grandfather arrived with some fresh beans and turnips for them to eat.

In 1933, he went home on summer vacation after finishing his first year at Goodland to visit his mother, brother, and sister, all living in a two-room log cabin with his great-grandfather, George Orum. There were so many people that some of them slept outside in a wagon, and the family cooked outside in an old tub. Conditions worsened when the Depression hit. Durant remembered that the mosquitoes were so bad and were more threatening because there were no screen doors or nets to prevent them from biting everyone. He was bitten and became very ill with chills and fever. His mother treated him with Three 6s and Black Draught, but neither helped. She recalled that his father had used a Choctaw doctor at Unger, about fifteen miles from his grandfather's cabin, and the following morning she awakened him at 6:00 a.m., packed two biscuits, and a slice of cooked salt pork in a brown paper bag and sent him to the doctor. It took him fifteen hours to walk the fifteen miles because he was so weak, but he reached the doctor's home about 9:00 p.m., long after dark. Explaining that he was sick, he told the doctor who he was and why he was there and added that he had no money. "No iskvli needed," stated the man.

Putting him into bed, the doctor covered him with quilts and brought in a black pot about two gallons in size and built a fire in it. He then left for about half an hour and returned with an armload of plants with stems about a foot long covered with leaves. When the fire in the pot burned down to coals, the doctor placed the plants on them, causing a white-greenish smoke that smelled terribly bad. Next, he wrapped the pot with two "gunny-sacks" and an old cotton sack and placed it beside his bed. The doctor put more covers over him and continued the process through the night. Durant finally went to sleep around midnight saturated with perspiration from the smoke and the heat.

The following morning he was fed a piece of boiled squirrel and broth and told to stay in bed. More roots and bark were gathered, boiled into a drink in a crock jar, and given to Durant four times during the rest of the day. A glass of the concoction tasted as badly as the plants smelled. On the second day the doctor ordered Durant out of bed, gave him a quart of the medicine, and sent him home. Durant never had chills or fever again, even during World War II.

He attended school at Goodland Presbyterian Children's Home southwest of Hugo. Durant recalled that the school had been established in 1848 and contained the oldest continuously used church in Oklahoma. In its early days the men and women did not drink from the same cup nor did they enter the church through the same door nor sit together once inside. In the bell tower hangs the same iron bell given the church in 1888 by Choctaw minister John Turnbull, and on its grounds is the Oliver Porter Stark Memorial Chapel.

Among his classmates at Goodland was Jimmy Belvin. Both were from very poor families. Bertram Bobb and Charley Jones also went to Goodland. He recalled that the students had "only six books and we had to pass them around to have class." Durant played on the football team at Goodland and went undefeated for two years. He was also president of the Future Homemakers of America and an Eagle Scout. His favorite job at Goodland was working in the kitchen with Aunt Susie and Uncle Bud. In 1940, Durant graduated with eighteen classmates and then spent two years at a Catholic school near Ardmore. Finally, he caught a train to town, joined the Navy, and served through World War II and Korea. Sent to San Diego where his first breakfast consisted of grapefruit, cereal, and cornbread, he wondered what he had gotten into.

Durant visited thirty-seven different countries and graduated every school offered during his years in the service. Promoted to the rank of Chief Petty Officer before reaching the age of twenty-one, the youngest in the Navy at the time, Durant received medals for his service including a Presidential Unit Citation, Good Conduct Badge, citations for the American and Pacific Theaters, and a citation for saving a man's life at Port Hueneme, California.

Durant went to work after his service for the government on Indian reservations in Arizona. He met and married Margaret Hoopes and raised five children. He worked for the IHS on the Gila Indian Reservation as a Food Service Supervisor. When he retired, he went to work as the Equal Opportunity Employment officer and Civil Defense Supervisor working with the Elderly Nutrition Program, the Commodity Program, and WIC for eight and a half years.

Returning to Talihina, he attended County Council meetings and was struck by the arguments among the members. There were about sixty of them who only argued about solutions but took little action. Deciding to run for the Tribal Council, he found that the tribe had a budget of approximately $60,000, but half of that was wasted, according to Durant. A Council member for more than twenty years, Durant helped make the office into a paid position.

Durant talked Chief Roberts into taking over the Indian Hospital at Talihina after convincing the Chief that it was in extremely poor condition. The modern budget for the hospital is more than $22 million. In addition, there are four clinics, more than 400 employees in the health system, and a worldwide health advisory program. Durant has also seen improvements in education in the recent years. The Council appropriated more than $3.5 million for higher education in 2000.

Durant discussed improvements in job opportunities as well. The tribe has more than 4,000 employees in its various business interests, and Durant proudly pointed out that he suggested the tribe raise its own cattle and feed. When the operation began, the Nation owned 300 cows; currently, there are 1,500 cattle and 150 buffalo along with 60 longhorns. The tribe now owns five ranches and raises wheat, soybeans, alfalfa, oats, hay, and pecan orchards.

The tribe also made money from the Bingo halls. Starting with no money, the Council borrowed the necessary funds in Minneapolis and had eight years to repay the loan. It was paid in seven. There are bingo halls in McAlester, Pocola, Durant, and Idabel that net a total of $11 million annually. He admitted there was one setback. The Arrowhead resort was purchased for $2 million but lost money despite being enlarged and renovated by the Nation. It was used for meetings but was eventually sold and the money put into trust.

Council member Durant has served on various boards for the tribe including service as bingo commissioner, president of Choctaw Nation

Enterprises, Inc., and police commissioner. For more than ten years he has served as branch president of the Church of Jesus Christ of Latter Day Saints in Talihina.[352]

In 2001, Jack Austin, Sr., from Clayton replaced Johnson as District 7 Council member. Jack's parents were Sam and Margaret Austin. His father was full blood Choctaw and his mother was one-half blood. They lived in Valliant. Jack is proud to be a descendant of Thomas LeFlore who served as chief of Apuckshunnubbee District from 1834-38 and 1842-50. Born in 1933, Jack graduated from Valliant High School and attended Tyler (Texas) Junior College and Southeastern State College in Durant on a football scholarship. He left college and entered the military. He served in the U.S. Army for six years and was stationed in Hawaii from 1955 to 1957. After serving in the military he began working for the Indian Health Service. This office provides Choctaw families throughout the Choctaw Nation with safe water supplies and sanitary waste disposal systems. He worked thirty-two years with this and other programs that improved the health status of Choctaw families.

He is married to Norma Sockey, and they are parents of four children. Elected as the Council representative, Austin took over as chaplain for his first term. His district includes the site of Tvshkahomma. Present improvements include work at the capitol. Great developments include an elevator for the tribal museum and paved roads for the capitol. Renovation of the Wright City Senior Citizens building has been completed, and work to enlarge the Antlers Senior Citizens building is currently in process. Jack strongly supports education, senior citizens programs, improving health care services, housing, and other programs that benefit the Choctaw people.[353]

Perry Thompson represents District 8 on the Council. Elected in 1987, Perry was the forty-two-year old son of Joseph Ward and Josephine Thompson. He was seven-eighths blood Choctaw. A lifelong resident of Hugo where he attended school, Perry went to work for Babcock's Home and Auto Store after graduation. Nine years later, he accepted employment with the Burlington Northern Railroad and worked for the railroad for fourteen years. Perry and his wife Gail have three children.

Joseph Perry Thompson, his grandfather, served in the Choctaw legislature in 1904. One reason Thompson had first run for a seat on the Tribal Council was to "follow in his grandfather's footsteps." In 1997, Perry received a chair that had belonged to his grandfather as a gift that symbolized his commitment to his ancestor's efforts.[354]

In 1979, Ted Gary Dosh of Bennington was first elected as the District 9 Council member. Dosh continues to maintain an excellent attendance record as the only original member still on the Council. Born in Bennington in March 1945, Dosh was reared in Bryan County. Dosh, the quarter blood son of Eddie and Marie Minyard Dosh, is a descendant of Chief Nicholas Cochanaur. A Star Farmer in FFA at Bennington High School, Dosh attended Southeastern. Serving six years in the Army Reserves, Dosh has been active in his community as a coach for Little League, a member of the Board of Directors of the Bryan County Soil Conservation District, and as president of the Bennington Alumni Association. He was married to Carolyn Steward on June 11, 1965, and is the father of two sons. He was Bryan County District 3 Commissioner from 1983 to 1990.

Dosh remembers the time when the Nation did not have money to meet its payroll for fifteen employees. He has seen the number of employees grow to more than four thousand and finances are on a sound, progressive basis. Among his accomplishments has been the Choctaw Community Center for Bryan County. Ted has helped establish a hotel, gaming arena, convention center, elderly living center, a child development center, and two travel plazas in his home county. At the same time he has enjoyed his service as chair of the Health and Labor Day Committees. Dosh stated that: "The most rewarding part of my years as Council member has been seeing the Choctaw Nation's Food Program helping so many needy Choctaws." [355]

In 1987, Esias J. "Boat" Johnson won the Atoka County District 10 Council seat. He earned his nickname as a young man when his father took him swimming in the Blue River. His father simply pitched him into the river and told the youngster to learn to swim. Someone watching said, "Look at that little kid swim. He can float like a boat." That was his name from then on.

Attending Jones Academy through the eighth grade, he recalled that Bertram Bobb was there at the same time as was E. T. Dunlop, later Chancellor of Higher Education, who was boys' counselor and Ora Padgett was superintendent. "Punishment was rough," Johnson remembered. Caught swimming without permission, Dunlop gave him three licks with a paddle, and the youngster had to lower his pants for the whipping. He learned to not get caught again.

During the Depression he worked in forestry and agriculture with the Civilian Conservation Corps (CCC) in Broken Bow. He and the other young men helped build cabins and roads and small dams in Beavers Bend State Park. "It was pick and hammer days then," said Johnson. Moving to Hugo, Boat joined the army and received his GED while in Japan serving in the military. Serving in the 270th Field Artillery in 1942-45, he traveled to England, Scotland, France, and Germany during his military career and enlisted for three more years before returning to Oklahoma. In his early twenties he met his wife Marie while attending church at Lane. They have four daughters and four sons.

Working for highway maintenance until his retirement in 1988, Johnson became a Council member in 1989. During his tenure a beautiful community center was built to house the Atoka County Head Start Program and serve as the site for the Senior Citizens Nutrition Meals program.[356]

Robert L. "Bob" Pate of Krebs represents District 11. Born in Tvshkahomma on April 22, 1941, Bob was the youngest of seven children, four brothers and three sisters, of Kenneth Ike and Rena Mae (Harvey) Pate. Bob was educated in Latimer County. He completed eight years of elementary at Degnan, near Wilburton, and attended Wilburton High School. He was very active in sports. He participated in track and field, excelled in football and basketball, and was scouted by the Red Sox as a baseball player. He also participated in the Future Farmers of America (FFA) in high school and raised show calves and pigs as school projects, winning numerous ribbons with his animals.

Graduating from Wilburton High in 1959, Bob enrolled at Eastern Oklahoma A&M (EOSC) for two years, moved to Tulsa, and graduated from the Spartan Aeronautical School with a Certificate of Instrumentation as an electrical gyro-technician. He worked for a time at the Aero-Commander Wiley Post Airport in Oklahoma City and then transferred to Wichita, Kansas, to work for the Sperry Gyro-Scope Company.

His career was interrupted by a stint in the U.S. Army from 1963 to 1965. Enrolled in the Personnel Specialist School at Fort Polk, Louisiana, he completed the six-month course in two weeks and was assigned a permanent duty station at Fort Bliss, El Paso, Texas. Serving with the School Support Command as a personnel specialist, Pate supervised thirty-seven civilian and military personnel. He moved to McAlester after his military service to work at the U.S. Naval Ammunition Depot located at Savanna. Four years later, he began a career with the McAlester post office. In 1985, he transferred to Wilburton and retired from the postal service in 1992. Bob and his wife Terry live in Krebs. He is the father of three sons, Robert, Rick, and Rodger. His pride is his grandchildren, Isabelle Ashton Pate and Priscilla Sue Pate.

In July 1995, Bob was encouraged by his friends to run for the Choctaw Council. In 1998, he was elected speaker and was re-elected in 1999. Traveling throughout the United States and abroad as a representative for the tribe, Pate has earned a reputation as a compassionate and caring man who believes in the adage: "Together we can make a difference."

James Frazier of Coalgate represents District 12 on the Council. Born June 28, 1953, James is the son of E. M. and Clovis L. (Belvin) Frazier. His family originally lived in the Bennington area. His grandfather, Roger S. Frazier, was a Cumberland Presbyterian preacher, and his mother was the niece of Jimmy Belvin. His father found work at the McAlester ammunition plant, and James attended Savanna through the seventh grade. He attended Kiowa High School and graduated in 1971. Married with two daughters, James has his first grandson.

Frazier worked for a time as a certified water lab technician for the Department of Corrections at Mack Alford. A member of the Native American Youth Movement, he soon organized an all-Indian inmate crew at the prison. Frazier took an interest in their progress and was gratified the night he received a phone call from a former crewmember from California. Frazier proudly advised the young man about the possibility of going to school and getting certified as a technician.

Driving racing cars was Frazier's passion. He got interested in driving stock and factory stock cars as a family sport with his son-in-law. He began building his own cars and at one time owned four racers. "Running sixty to seventy miles per hour on a dirt track was sometimes dangerous, and I was involved in wrecks, but racing was always fun," he stated. He added that he raced twenty-three straight Saturday nights in a row to win the 2000 championship.

Appointed to replace Lu Bauer in 1989, Frazier has supported programs to help the young and the elderly during his tenure on the Council. Frazier believes that a Council member must be available to their people. He stated, "It's a twenty-four-seven job. I've had the phone ring at 12:00 at night, but you have to be willing to work for your people. I enjoy it." James credited this approach to the job as the reason that he has drawn only one opponent since his election in 1991. He said, "We have monthly meetings, and I don't try to hide anything from anyone. The meetings are run according to schedule, and people can say anything they want. I have great people in my district."

The Council members are dedicated, diligent servants. Their contributions to their districts, often done quietly and without fanfares, are honestly aimed at improving the economic and social status of the tribe. They take great pride in helping the people of the Choctaw Nation.[357]

CHAPTA AUAH UNTUKLO

~ CHAPTER SEVENTEEN ~

"FROM A TRAIL OF TEARS TO A ROAD OF PROGRESS"

Chapter Seventeen

The Choctaw are survivors of ill fortune and tragedy on a road of progress toward civilization for more than five centuries. An unprecedented era of improved economic prosperity has greatly accelerated this movement in recent years. More social changes have occurred in the past quarter century than in the previous hundred years as resourceful, aggressive Tribal Chiefs and Council members have actively sought and expanded business ventures and tribal opportunities. A rejuvenated financial status has renewed pride in the Choctaw heritage and economic growth strengthened respect for Choctaw culture, language, and traditions. The current fiscal success has encouraged young people to remember their ancestors and the sacrifices made for them. They base their faith in the future on their respect for the past.

In 1986, the first major economic success for the Nation was a loan arranged with a Minnesota firm for construction of the Choctaw Bingo Palace, a hall covering 28,000 square-feet of space, south of Durant. Opened in December 1987, the mortgage on the building was paid within seven years, providing a clear title, and revenues to fund other operations. Resources from the Bingo operations financed the first Choctaw Travel Plaza and Smoke Shop located directly west of the Bingo Palace on U.S. Highway 69-75. The Travel Plaza provided tourists, travelers, and truckers with tobacco products, gasoline and fuel, gifts, and food at tax-free prices. In 1996, the first facility outgrew its capacity and Travel Plaza and Smoke Shop # Two was opened across the highway along with a convenience store and a Burger King restaurant. A $500,000 U.S. Department of Housing and Urban Development (HUD) Community Development Block Grant and $1million in tribal funds funded the second 9,275-square-foot Travel Plaza. The project created more than 110 new jobs. The businesses generated a net profit of $100,000 a month in the first months and produced an average of $1.5 million in gross sales per month by 2000.[358]

In March 1986, the Arrowhead Lodge and Resort located on Lake Eufaula at Canadian, Oklahoma, was purchased from the State and renovated as a motel-convention park. Used as a meeting place and Powwow center, the resort boasted spacious rooms, cabins, and lake recreations for tourists. Another Bingo Center was placed at the Lodge until it was sold.

In March 1993, another high-stakes Bingo Parlor was located at the McCurtain Village Shopping Center in Idabel. The opening was held up for a time by federal "red tape" over placing the property in Tribal Trust Status, but the operation provided additional funds when the legalities were cleared away to support a variety of social and economic programs. The tribe began offering such diverse services as paying heating and cooling bills, supporting children's Christmas parties, college scholarships, and the EDH (Eyeglasses, Dentures and Hearing Aid Program). Bingo also funded tribal buses, an airplane, and medicines. In 1994, a bingo operation was authorized at Pocola followed by another at McAlester. The facilities featured off-track horse racing and electronic gaming besides the Travel Plazas and provided employment for more than two hundred people. The increased revenue allowed economic aid for the needy to purchase glasses, wheelchairs, air conditioners, and two buses for out-of-state patrons, the elderly, and youth activities. Twelve shuttle buses for the twelve districts of the Nation were later purchased for use by Choctaw senior citizens.[359]

A short time later Jim Hummingbird, the BIA area credit officer, hand-delivered a check for $100,000 from the BIA Economic Development Assistance Grant to begin construction of another facility south of Hugo on Highway 271 near Grant. After purchasing one hundred acres of land for construction of the site, the opening of the Hugo Travel Plaza drew a crowd of 2,000 to celebrate its beginning. On May 31, 1996, another Travel Plaza and Smoke Shop was opened at Pocola followed by others in McAlester and Garvin. In July 2000, Chief Greg Pyle and Assistant Chief Mike Bailey, accompanied by Speaker Bob Pate and Council members, Ted Dosh, Billy Paul Baker, Charley Jones, Randle Durant, Glenn Johnson, and James Frazier, presided over the grand opening of the Broken Bow Travel Plaza. Cutting the ribbon on the Travel Plaza/Smoke Shop, the Chief explained that each of the shops provided full time employment for a minimum of thirty-one employees. Economic expansion continued with construction of a Travel Plaza in Stringtown and another 4,000-square-foot Travel Mart in Atoka in 2003. E. J. Johnson, District 10 Council member, credited another fifty jobs to the new facilities.

The increased economic energy brought rapid employment expansion. In 1975, the tribe employed seventy-four people; in 1990, the number had increased to more than 1,400. The net worth for the same time increased from $2.6 million in 1975 to $35 million in 1993. As the spirit of growth spread, the number of Choctaw grew accordingly. In 1975, the voting membership was less than 5,000 persons but the number was more than 24,000 and the number holding Certificate Degree of Indian Blood (CDIB) cards more than 77,000 in 1993. The improving economic status quickly attracted the attention of others.[360]

In 1990, Chief Roberts was asked to lead a commemorative "Great Famine Walk" in Ireland to remember the tragic death of more than 600 men, women, and children who had perished in a single night while crossing the Mayo Mountains in search of food in 1847. The Choctaw were asked to lead the first walk of the Nineties in recognition of the generosity shown by the tribe for its contribution of $170, according to the *Arkansas Intelligencer*, collected at a Tribal Council meeting for the Irish Famine victims in recognition of its own "Trail of Tears" only sixteen years previously.

On May 26, 1990, Greg and Patti Pyle, Earlene Noah, and Judy Allen accompanied Chief Roberts on the human rights march to fight world hunger. The participants made the twelve-mile hike from Doolough to Louisburgh in County May over the route of the Irish victims to commemorate both the deaths of the Irish and the Choctaw on the Trail of Tears. On November 2, 1990, the Choctaw were again recognized for the 1847 donation by special ceremonies held in Manchester, England.

In 1992, members of the Action from Ireland (AfrI) organization returned the favor by staging a walk from Broken Bow to Mississippi. Twenty-two walkers from twenty-two to seventy-nine in age aimed to raise $71,000, the amount thought to represent the $710 rather than the reported $170. The walkers required four weeks to complete the trek of more than five hundred miles.

Earlier, Council Speaker Randle Durant and his wife Margaret participated in another walk in Ireland and met President Mary Robinson. Durant made the Irish president an honorary chief, a gesture so greatly valued by President Robinson that she decided to visit the Choctaw Nation. More than 500 Choctaw greeted the gracious executive upon her arrival in Durant on May 23, 1995. After a tour of the Choctaw Nation headquarters, she addressed the Nation to extend appreciation for the generosity of the Choctaw to her ancestors a century and a half earlier. Greeting the crowd in Choctaw, President Robinson said, "Chahta i̱ yakni vla li kvt na sv yukpa," meaning, "I am glad to have come to Choctaw country." She added that "I know that both the Choctaw people and the Irish people remember the past . . . I was very pleased to go and see the work that WIC was doing, to visit the clinic and see the good work that is going on there, to hear the children singing and to know that they, too, like me, are learning the Choctaw language. We'll learn together and see what progress we make."

President Robinson also made reference to the Oklahoma City bombing during the course of her address. Calling the incident another form of tragedy that plagued the modern world, she praised the Choctaw Council that had made a donation of $15,000 to help the families of the victims of the Oklahoma City disaster. She stated that she realized the emotional effect the bombing had on all Oklahomans and Americans.

President Robinson was presented a number of symbolic gifts to remember her visit. She was given a red and white traditional dress made especially for her, silver medallions featuring the Great Seal of the Choctaw Nation, and a book to help with her language lessons.[361]

The interest generated by the commemorative walks resulted in a symbolic "Trail of Tears" walk in 1992. The next year a walk was conducted from Horatio, Arkansas, to Eagletown in honor of the ancestral trek, and the event became an annual affair. Tribal members gathered at Eagletown each spring to remind their people of the great event in their history.[362]

The WIC Program praised by President Robinson was the Women, Infants and Children Program, a supplemental feeding program for mothers and children. The requirements for participation in WIC include being pregnant or breastfeeding and at nutritional risk, aged from birth to five years old at nutritional risk, and meet income eligibility guidelines. The WIC Program provided milk, cheese, peanut butter, beans, juice, eggs, and cereal, along with carrots and tuna, and other foods high in iron, protein, calcium, and vitamins. The federally funded USDA program served all counties in the Choctaw Nation with clinic sites located at Antlers, Atoka, Bethel, Boswell, Broken Bow, Coalgate, Durant, Hugo, Idabel, McAlester, Poteau, Stigler, Talihina, and Wilburton.

In May 2002, the Choctaw Management/Services Enterprise opened an overseas warehouse distribution center in Durant to house offices and goods that supply WIC sites in foreign countries. In December 2000, CMSE was awarded the contract to implement the Women, Infants and Children Program overseas. The WIC program has long been a mainstay to many junior military families assigned in the United States but was not available once those families were assigned overseas. CMSE recognized the extreme importance of this quality of life program in maintaining military readiness and improving family health and quickly moved to gain making this program a reality for eight pilot communities. CMSE demonstrated exceptional performance and a dedication to the military and DOD civilian community that is not often seen by an outside contractor. In just two short months, CMSE quickly assessed the requirements of the WIC stateside program using the Choctaw Nation WIC program as a model and began implementation within the eight pilot site communities.

From the initiation of the contract, CMSE developed an aggressive implementation schedule for the proposed sixty-seven sites at forty-five installations in eleven countries. They have constructed a dedicated automation network to track program participants through the eligibility process, track issued food drafts from each WIC Overseas site and complete that tracking with an audit of the drafts through the reconciliation and banking system. Upon the initiation of the CMSE contract, there was no Policy and Procedure Manual, a significant deliverable of another company, to guide the program. CMSE consulted with the Choctaw WIC Program to gather information and then quickly moved in a matter of days to write and publish an interim manual. The manual was an integral key in getting the WIC Overseas program implemented and functional quickly and remained in use until September 30, 2001.

With the help of the Choctaw program, CMSE created a full turnkey operation, which involved the establishment of a worldwide logistics network including over 400 line items from the most simple office supplies to the more sophisticated medical equipment. Further complicating the establishment of the logistics network were the varied voltages, electric and foreign shipping requirements, and Status of Forces Agreement regulations and procedures of eleven different foreign countries. These challenges have all been systematically solved to the degree that deliveries are now routine.

Another of the many social services provided by the tribe is the Children and Family Services Program, or the Indian Child Welfare Program. Divided into three projects, family violence, family preservation, and Indian child welfare, a variety of programs were offered to strengthen the family and avoid placement of children outside the home.

The Indian Child Welfare Program offers services to prevent abuse and neglect along with foster care and adoption services that utilize fifty-one tribal foster homes within the Nation. On an average, adoption placed two children each year with Indian parents, but the program also handles out-of-state adoptions, counseling services for families, and family advocacy in court proceedings to families that are active state child welfare cases. Highly qualified caseworkers cover the entire ten and one-half counties to unite families and prevent the separation of any children from birth to age eighteen from their families. Offices are in Durant, Hugo, and McAlester.

The Family Preservation Program promotes family strength. Parenting skills, crisis intervention, and identification of community resources and home-based services are among the services offered by the program. The Family Violence Program is an information and referral program for Choctaw women and children who are victims of domestic violence. The staff assists with finding shelters, setting up households, and providing counseling for those in need.

The Nutrition and Supportive Service Program provides information, transportation, and arts and crafts for Indian senior citizens. Offering one meal per week for those fifty-five and older at local community centers in Antlers, Atoka, Bethel, Broken Bow, Coalgate, Durant, Hugo, McAlester, Poteau, Stigler, Talihina, and Wilburton. The center at Talihina provides five meals per week and arranges meals for Indian visitors to the hospital. In February 2000, Wright City was added to the list of towns getting weekly lunches at their Choctaw Community Centers.

The Social Services Program processes the BIA assistance grant payments as a secondary resource for the needy that are at least one-quarter degree Indian of a federally recognized tribe. The individual must reside within the Choctaw Nation and meet eligibility requirements for income resources. Contracting with the BIA to provide assistance to individuals who are disabled or unable to find employment, the amount of assistance is determined by need and can be cash assistance or ongoing help. One-time emergency disaster assistance is also available under the program for a major loss of a home as a result of a natural or man-made disaster if the family is not protected by insurance.

Burial assistance was also made available to persons of at least one-quarter degree Indian blood. Contact and application must be done prior to burial and agreement made with the persons making funeral arrangements, the funeral home, and the agency. Costs of the services are limited, but another tribal service provided through this program is tribal burial assistance for Choctaw by blood. Eligibility is based upon family income and blood quantum, with an exception for original enrollees born before 1906.

The Welfare to Work Program is designed to put people to work by placing individuals on welfare into a work environment to learn the necessary skills for developing a work history. Applicants referred to the program by the Department of Human Services must be current recipients of Temporary Assistance to Needy Families (TANF) and live within the ten and one-half counties of the Choctaw Nation.

Other important service programs are the Vocational Rehabilitation and Disability Employment Programs. The Vocational Rehabilitation Program offers services that assist disabled Indians to obtain vocational training and employment. Eligibility requirements are that the applicants must have a CDIB card, live within the ten and one-half county Nation, and have a documental physical or mental disability that results in a hindrance to employment. The program provides counseling, guidance, job training, employment placement, and assistance to benefit individuals with disabilities in employment.

In 1997, the Choctaw Nation was the only tribe awarded a Department of Education grant for the Disability Employment Program. People with disabilities are given on-the-job training as the program creates an opportunity to send participants to a job and pay their salary up to 499 hours. The job developer for the program helps participants with job searching skills, writing resumes, and preparing for employment.

The Low Income Home Energy Assistance Program (LIHEAP) assists Indian households with payments for home heating and cooling bills. Outreach efforts are conducted throughout the Choctaw Nation to include eligible households within the program. The elderly and disabled are particularly sought to receive help.

Other social service programs include day cares, head start programs, and child-care assistance. The Child Care Assistance Program attempts to increase the availability and quality of child services. The objectives of the program are to enable Indian families to maintain and achieve self-sufficiency through employment and training to increase earning power to have a positive effect on the family. The program permits Indian parents to choose from a range of care providers, including day care centers, family child care providers, sectarian organizations, relatives, and neighbors. Emphasis is placed on parental choice in decisions regarding the type and location of care providers. To qualify the child must live with a parent or legal guardian that have membership in a federally recognized tribe, reside in the Nation, and both parents be employed or in school. Eligibility is dependent upon family size and income. Approximately 850 children ranging in age from birth through twelve are on the program with 200 care providers.

The Choctaw Nation Day Care provides care for infants six weeks to twelve years of age, including transportation to take and pick up children from school. Children are provided with a learning environment and experiences to help them develop socially and physically. The overall goal is to develop social competence among the children. Day Care centers are located in Bennington, Coalgate, Durant, Idabel, Stigler, Talihina, and Wright City.[363]

There are fourteen Tribal Head Starts located in Antlers, Atoka, Bennington, Bethel, Broken Bow, Coalgate, Durant, Hugo, Idabel, McAlester, Poteau, Stigler, Wilburton, and Wright City. In October 2000, Chief Pyle chatted with children at the newly opened Bennington Child Development Center, the first of three, as others soon opened in Coalgate and Stigler. Funded by a $2.2 million grant in Child Care and Development and tribal funds, the facility contained a head start and day care program and included a storm shelter, playground, and amphitheater. Children aged three to compulsory school age whose family fall within approved income guidelines of the U.S. Department of Health and Human Services Administration were eligible to participate along with children with special needs. At least ten percent of enrollment was for special needs children.

Chief Pyle stated, "The tribe is successful at many businesses, but the real reason we have these businesses is to make money for our children." His sentiments were repeated by others who stated, "The educational success of children is well worth the investment. Young people are truly the destiny of the tribe."[364]

In February 1984, the U.S. Department of Agriculture started the Food Distribution Program with commodities given to approximately 150 Indians. The program has expanded to the entire Nation and currently serves approximately 6,200 members monthly. Requirements for participation are applications accompanied by the last four check stubs to show weekly salaries. Households are not allowed both food stamps and commodities. In 2000, the tribe announced an improvement in the Food Distribution Program in southeastern Oklahoma with the beginning of commodity provisions for McAlester and Durant. The two "Little Dixie" cities had previously been exempt from the program because rules mandated that persons living in towns with populations of more than 10,000 were ineligible to receive food distribution. On March 2, tribal officials successfully obtained a waiver for the two towns after two years of diligent work. Participants lined up for sixty-six food items totaling eighty pounds of food per person. Items distributed were canned goods of fruits, vegetables, juices, canned meats along with frozen ground beef and chicken, flour, cornmeal, cheese, potatoes, oatmeal, butter, baking mixes, peanut butter, and macaroni and cheese. [365]

On March 10, 1997, CM/SE was chartered to provide revenue to support new and ongoing social service programs of the Nation, to provide jobs for members of the Nation and other Native American groups, and to contribute materially to the economic development of southeast Oklahoma. CM/SE is a qualified Native American enterprise certified by the Small Business Administration under Section (8a) operating as a small and disadvantaged business.

A four-member board of directors chaired by Assistant Chief Mike Bailey is responsible for establishing CM/SE policy and approving contracts. CM/SE has compiled an extraordinary record of growth, literally starting from nothing to reach its present size of more than 1,700 employees and 620 subcontractors in just four years. CM/SE's explosive growth is mainly attributable to outstanding performance in managing a number of government contracts. CM/SE has full-time employees at more than 215 separate sites throughout the United States and twelve foreign countries, including Belgium, Cuba, Great Britain, Germany, Iceland, Italy, Japan (including Okinawa), Portugal (the Azores), Singapore, South Korea, Spain, and Turkey.

CM/SE staffs physicians, physician assistants, anesthesiologists, surgeons, nurses, nurse anesthetists, social workers, dental personnel, dietitians, nutritionists, and a variety of other medical personnel. CM/SE also staffs multi-faceted facilities managers, files managers, data entry clerks, mail clerks, librarians, library technicians, and related support personnel.

In the Information Management/Information Technology arena, CM/SE provides the full spectrum of IM/IT services. These include conception, design, implementation, and conclusion for all aspects of systems implementation, including hardware, software, networking, and communications.

CM/SE clients are the Department of Defense, the United States Army, the United States Air Force, the United States Navy, the new Department of Homeland Security, and Anteon Corporation. In 1997, the CM/SE started with two contract employees to the Air Force in San Antonio. In 1998, CM/SE was selected as the contractor for a task force contract with the Immigration and Naturalization Service. Annual revenues exceeded $64 million, proving support for new and ongoing social service programs and employment for tribal members. Along with the gaming efforts, this program was the primary source of revenues for scholarships and senior projects.

CM/SE specializes in fulfilling unusual or scarce personnel requirements. It staffs health, mental, and dental health services at military and federal facilities worldwide. Staffs are located in Japan, Korea, Cuba, Guam, Singapore, Hawaii, Great Britain, Spain, Belgium, Germany, Portugal, Turkey, and throughout the United States. In 2002, the program received a multi-million dollar contract with the IHS to provide general dentists at Indian dental clinics nationwide. The five-year contract worth $2.7-$6.3 million the first year covers staffing of approximately one hundred dentists throughout the United States. Enterprise provides "good-paying jobs." "And all income from the enterprise comes back to the tribe, and we spend the money in southeastern Oklahoma," according to Chief Pyle.[366]

These services are available to persons with a Certificate of Degree of Indian Blood (CDIB) card through the Tribal Membership Program and Voter Registration. The card enables individuals to apply for tribal membership and entitles them to participate in tribal elections at the age of eighteen. There are no blood quantum requirements for obtaining a card or tribal membership as long as the person can connect to a direct descendant of a Dawes Commission enrollee. Members living inside the Nation are given the option of voting by mail or in person while those members living outside the boundaries are mailed ballots that must be returned to the Election Board.

CDIB cardholders are eligible for health and medical services at Indian Health Service (IHS) facilities located throughout the United States. The Talihina Indian Hospital has been a special source of assistance for the tribe since it opened its doors as a two-story, wooden building in 1917. The sixty-bed facility was financed from $50,000 in Choctaw-Chickasaw Trust funds for tuberculosis patients. Dr. W. E. Van Cleve, the first hospital superintendent, served for more than forty years. On October 5, 1938, the next building opened as the most modern hospital in the Indian Health Service at the time. With a 225-bed capacity, 75 for general use and 150 for tuberculosis patients, the hospital cost $1.2 million and was named the Carter Hospital in honor of Congressman Charles D. Carter of Ardmore who secured legislation for its construction.

On November 4, 1938, Ramona Faith Maggard from Octavia was the first baby born at the hospital. Growing up in Smithville, she married Melvin Edgel Phillips and lived on her mother's allotment on Eagle Fork Creek. Since her birth more than 15,000 children have been born in the Talihina facility. The first patient to have surgery at the hospital was Roosevelt Moore who had an appendix operation. Renamed the Choctaw-Chickasaw Sanitarium, and still later the Public Health Service Hospital, it catered primarily to tuberculosis patients until 1964 when the TB patients began to be phased out for more general health and surgery.

In 1985, the hospital became a tribal project as the Choctaw National Indian Hospital but continued to decline in services despite $5 million per year to cover operational expenses. The third floor was closed, it no longer provided surgery, and there was no O. B. on duty that could deliver babies. In 1997, Chief Pyle announced these problems would be corrected, an obstetrician placed on staff, and the Council had approved plans for the construction of a new hospital to replace the sixty-year-old sanitarium. The hospital has since expanded with more than 200 employees, including a sixty-five-member nursing staff. On October 25, 1999, Dr. Jeanolivia Grant delivered Austin Smittle as the first baby born at the new Choctaw Health Center. He was the son of Tina and Kevin Smittle from Heavener.

In 2001, the Choctaw Nation Health Services Authority announced an expansion of services by offering cardiac imaging studies at the new hospital. A full-service mobile cardiology unit equipped to perform heart ultrasounds called Mobile Cardiac Imaging provided "a new level of excellence for Choctaw patients." MCI goes to the hospital twice a month, and both an internal medicine doctor and a cardiologist see the test results to determine the best course of treatment for the patients.

A similar program resulted from an agreement with the University of Texas Southwestern Medical Center at Dallas to provide on-site patient care and research on memory loss and aging. The services include clinical evaluation, diagnosis and treatment of memory-related problems, and lectures for staff, patients, and families. The objective was research toward eliminating the problems of Alzheimer's disease. In February 2001, the first meeting was held with the UT group. "Available and accessible quality health care for our Choctaw people is my primary goal," stated Chief Pyle.[367]

New tribal clinics are another source of pride for the Choctaw. The clinics at Broken Bow, Hugo, and McAlester provide a full range of medical, pharmaceutical, laboratory, and x-ray services, medical records, and social services. In 1993, a facility was located at Poteau named in honor of Rubin Louis White (1914-1993), the former North LeFlore County Council speaker. The facility was a Joint Venture Demonstration Project with the Indian Health Service (IHS) and the Choctaw Nation whereby the tribe built the clinic and leased it to the IHS for twenty years without cost, and the IHS agreed to equip, supply, and maintain it. The construction costs ran $1.3 million with the BIA funding $250,000 and another $700,000 from a CDBG, Community Development Block Grant.[368]

On January 16, 1996, another clinic was formally opened in Durant in cooperation with Chickasaw Governor Bill Anoatubby. The following August, the Broken Bow Clinic proudly announced the arrival of two Choctaw doctors Michael West II and Hampton Aderro III to their clinic.[369]

The Nation also provides a number of treatment and abuse centers. In 1996, the Women & Children's Residential Program known as Project Chi̱ Hullo Li (a phrase meaning I Care for You) opened at Talihina. The program is a culturally sensitive residential treatment program for Indian women between the ages of eighteen and thirty-five who suffer from alcohol, marijuana, methamphetamine, inhalants, or other drugs and are parents of up to two children between the ages of one and ten. The six-month intensive treatment program was designed to decrease the use of alcohol and drugs, improve the social functioning of the individual, and provide care for the women and their children. In 1999, Chi̱ Hullo Li received a $1 million grant called Welfare to Work to expand its services. The substance abuse treatment included a place for residence for the clients and their young children with grants designed to help get these women back to work by training them for jobs, teaching them to dress, conduct interviews, write resumes, and generally provide confidence in themselves and their work skills. The grant funds from the Department of Labor were "designed to make the women in the program more independent," said Chief Pyle.[370]

The Choctaw Housing Authority operated two other drug elimination programs, Project McRoad in Broken Bow and Project Enhancement in Durant, with funds from a grant from the U.S. Department of Housing and Urban Development are designed to reduce drugs and drug-related crimes in federally funded housing. The purpose of the funding was to provide security, prevention, and intervention programs for the residents of the Housing Authority.

The tribe also operates the Choctaw Nation Recovery Center as a specialized treatment center to change the lives of chemically dependent individuals and their families. Treating chemical dependency as a curable illness, the Center provides a supportive atmosphere for the individual and the family. Admission is for males and females aged eighteen or older with a CDIB card in good physical health, and diagnosed as having a primary problem with alcohol, drugs, or other substances.

In 1999, Chief Pyle announced another health grant for the Choctaw Telemedicine Program by Oklahoma Governor Frank Keating and State Director Charles Rainbolt of the US Department of Agriculture Rural Development. The Choctaw Nation Health Services Authority had submitted the application for funds to further OneNet services for rural access to the system and for direct medical eye care services and medical training from connections wit Northeastern State University of Optometry in Tahlequah and Oklahoma State University College of Osteopathic Medicine in Tulsa. After receiving the award of $195,812 in Oklahoma City, Chief Pyle stated, "Obtaining this grant will enable the Choctaw Nation to further improve health care for Native Americans. By implementing stateof the art technologies in networking, telemedicine will not nly allow referral services to overlap with our own primary care services but will provide the means for extensive health educatin to be offered in community centers, local schools, and other potential locations."[371]

Another landmark partnership agreement was announced with the University of Oklahoma Health Services Center to combat an emerging diabetes epidemic that was ravaging the health of Choctaw Indian children. In August 2000, officials met at the Oklahoma Children's Hospital to sign a contract establishing pediatric diabetes care by Oklahoma University doctors at heath clinics in the Choctaw Nation. The agreement allowed specialists from the university to work with almost 20,000 Choctaw children suffering from type-2 diabetes. This disease that led to kidney failure, blindness, and complications such as heart attacks and strokes was once found only in adults but had become more prevalent in Indians than any other group. Choctaw Executive Health Director Gary Batton explained, "About 23 percent of Choctaws have diabetes, and we're trying to see why it is on the increase and what can be done." Dr. Kenneth C. Copeland and a team of doctors and psychologists from the university began to address this question with the start of a new study of the disease. The team planned visits to the Choctaw clinics and worked with diabetes specialists from the tribe in an effort to develop treatment plans for the disease. Copeland stated that the disease had begun to increase in children approximately ten years before and was directly related to obesity. Copeland suspected the increase in junk food was a cause of the problem and hoped the partnership with the Choctaw would launch future joint research projects to explore exact causes of the disease with the ultimate goal of completely eliminating the disease.[372]

In November 1997, the Choctaw Nation created a Diabetes Treatment Center in Antlers to improve the lives of American Indians with the disease and provide chronic diabetes care to patients from referrals by physicians. The Center gives the most advanced care to tribal members and others approved by the tribal administration. The first person to receive an Insulin Pump from the Center was patient Candace Gordon.

In June 2002, the Nation and REACH 2010 invited young people between nine and thirteen to attend a Youth Wellness Camp at Tuskahoma. The camps for children from Bryan, Choctaw, McCurtain, and Pushmataha counties and for LeFlore, Haskell, Pittsburg, Hughes, Coal, and Atoka counties were offered to provide diabetes prevention and education classes. Presentations were given on diabetes, nutrition, insulin pumps, and obesity along with talks on sexual abuse prevention, fire safety, and drug abuse prevention. The children participated in nature walks, cultural dances, and physical fitness events.

Another innovational program in health care was seen when the Choctaw Nation Health Care Center in Talihina announced the opening of a new "Drive Through Pharmacy." The new approach was started on February 14, 2000. Patients simply phoned in prescriptions and then picked them up the following day. Later, pharmacy supplies and medicines were made available through the mail to Choctaw tribal members anywhere in the United States at a greatly reduced price through the center.[373]

Dianne Hammack, spokesperson for the Indian Health Services, said the amount of money spent on Indian health care was poor when compared to other Americans but that the tribe did not have immediate monetary retrenchment problems. Hammack pointed out that the average Medicare patient gets $3,100 per year while Oklahoma Indians receive a fraction of that amount, approximately $851 annually. Since federal money was the major factor in how much the tribes can spend, the Choctaw have an annual health system budget of $37 million. All but $2 million of this amount comes from the Indian Health agency with the remainder coming from Medicare and private insurance reimbursements.

Choctaw Executive Director of Health Gary Batton praised the tribe's 465-employee health system as financially "healthy." He stated that its clinics receive good management because "You have to strategically plan. This is a business." The disturbing problem for Choctaw health was that Oklahoma receives less funding per capita than other states despite the fact Oklahoma has a quarter of the nation's Indian population. The average amount spent on Indian patients is $1,351 per year by the IHS, which represents $500 more than what was spent on Oklahoma tribal members. Batton suggested congressional funding for Indian health needs must be improved.

Another program aimed at better health for the tribe is the Choctaw Nation Office of Environmental Health (CNEH), a program to provide better sanitation facilities that include water and wastewater. The funding for the program from the U.S. Indian Health Service is designated for use on water wells, septic tanks, community water, and community sewer connections. Eligibility requirements are based on IHS guidelines: the home must be located within the Choctaw Nation, be the primary residence of the applicant, applicants must possess a CDIB, and provide proof of land ownership. The CNEH Program cannot serve a Mutual Help (Indian) home, but older homes with substandard water or sewer systems are eligible for services and some qualify for plumbing work inside the home. If the home is a mobile home, it must be at least forty feet long; equipped with a thermostatically controlled heating system, skirted, have tie-downs, and the wheels and trailer hitch removed before services can be installed.

In 1998, Chief Pyle announced that the Choctaw Nation and the city of Broken Bow had joined forces to provide community wastewater disposal facilities for families in the Burke and Collier Addition in the city. Ten Indian homes were connected to the new sewage system after the old septic tank and drain field systems had failed and allowed wastewater to flow into adjacent creeks and drainage ways. The total cost of the project, $225,375, was funded by a CDBG of $187,375 from the Oklahoma Department of Commerce and the Choctaw Nation participating through the IHS Office of Environmental Health with a check for $37,620. McCurtain County Tribal Council members Billy Paul Baker and Charley Jones accompanied the Chief to the ceremonial presentation of the funds.

Another health program is the Eyeglasses, Dentures and Hearing Aid Program (EDH) that provides health devices for tribal members over the age of fifty-five with physical limitations. EDH provides canes, crutches, commode boosters and chairs, wheelchairs, bath and shower chairs, and walkers for the elderly who live within the Nation's borders.

The Choctaw Nation Emergency Medical Services (EMS) participates in both youth and senior citizen programs. The EMS gives lessons on CPR (cardiopulmonary resuscitation), performs drug and alcohol tests for prospective employees, and makes life safer for Choctaws by giving classes, seminars, and in-service training on topics including blood pressure, blood sugar screening, and first aid techniques. Staff members provide courses on babysitting, home chemical safety, nutrition, exercise, and sexually transmitted diseases. Talks and lectures are given for schools, head starts, and nursing homes.

In 1969, the Nation inaugurated the Community Health Representative Program (CHR). Designed for those Indians residing within the Nation, the staff provides a variety of health services to CDIB members without income guidelines. With at least one-half of the staff fluent in the Choctaw language, CHR takes vital signs, monitors glucose for diabetes, educates clients on hypertension and cholesterol dieting, provides patient education, maternal and child health, counseling on drugs and alcohol, makes patient assessments, monitors blood pressure, assists with youth day camps, and provides flu shots along with other health services during October and November.[374]

Major accomplishments have been made possible in recent years because the Nation has adopted several loan policies that allow Indians to purchase homes. Projects that insure adequate, modern housing for all tribal members are more service programs of great pride for the Choctaw Nation. Especially successful was the Choctaw Nation Credit and Loan Department. Better known as the Southeastern Oklahoma Indian Credit Association, the program allows small business loans, agriculture, and housing loans that can be used for either home purchases or improvements for Indians who cannot borrow from other lending associations.

A number of programs are available through the Housing Authority of the Choctaw Nation based in Hugo. The Housing Authority includes a program called Affordable Rental Housing with units available in Talihina, Caney, Red Oak, Bokoshe, Quinton, and Wright City. Requirements for participation are current income guidelines, tribal membership, and passing an OSBI background check.

In July 1998, Chief Pyle signed a Housing Preservation Grant agreement with the USDA Rural Development Agency for $191,487 to rehabilitate twenty-five paid off mutual help homes in Choctaw and McCurtain Counties, the only counties eligible under their status as an "Enterprise Community." The Choctaw Housing award was the second largest in the nation due to its excellently written proposal. The Choctaw Housing Authority put $100,000 and another $100,000 in-kind contributions toward the program to assist in renovation of paid-off mutual help homes in the two counties.

The Housing Authority's Family Investment Centers in Broken Bow and Poteau educate and provide employment opportunities for housing participants. Its two drug programs, "Project Choice" in Atoka and "Project McRoad" in Broken Bow, were in effect from 1996 to 1998. The latter housed participants with drug and alcohol abuse counselors, and contracts with law enforcement agencies for safety patrols. The Authority's goal had been to provide safe, decent, and sanitary housing at affordable prices for the Choctaw people. Projects Choice and McRoad were closed out and "Project Horizon II" opened in Poteau until 2003.

The Home Finance Department includes a Choctaw Homebuyers Advantage Program (CHAP) in which Choctaw tribal members can reside outside the Choctaw Nation boundaries within the state and purchase a home with one to three percent down payment. The Choctaw Nation Indian Home Corporation in partnerships with other lending institutions and private mortgage insurance companies, including First American Mortgage Corporation, PMI, Freddie Mac, and Washington Mutual, serve more tribal members in Oklahoma and other states including Texas, Washington, Oregon, Arkansas, Arizona, New Mexico, and California.

There is also a Revolving Loan Fund whereby the applicant must possess a CDIB card and the home site must be located within the ten and one-half county service area. Income limits are eighty percent of the national median income level and loans provide up to 100% of the national median with approval from the Loan Fund Committee to purchase, refinance mutual help homes, and construct homes. The loans have a fixed interest rate, a maximum thirty years' amortization, and require one to three percent down payment. Another program is Down Payment/Closing Cost Assistance. Applicants must possess a CDIB, live within the Nation, and income guidelines are eighty percent of the national median income with preference given to the fifty percent national median income levels. A minimum down payment of one percent of the sale price is required and credit guidelines must be met. Section 184 provides aid for CDIB applicants with no set income guidelines for purchase, construction, and rehabilitation of home sites. The loan has a fixed rate with a thirty-year maximum amortization for low-income families with no down payment.

The Maintenance, Modernization, and Rehabilitation Program has three sections. Its programs includes the ALC Assistance Program for tribal members sixty-two or older that reside in the Choctaw Nation; the Non-Mutual Help Renovation Program for tribal members sixty-two or older, or physically disabled who reside within the Nation and own their own homes; and the Paid-Off Mutual Help Program for tribal members who are permanent residents of the unit. Applicants must have proof of land ownership, and the unit must be a paid-off unit from the Mutual Help Program of the Choctaw Housing Authority.

The Mutual Help Development Program provides home ownership for applicants that must possess a CDIB, meet current income guidelines set by HUD, be a legal resident of the Choctaw Nation, and own land free of encumbrances. The net family assets cannot exceed $20,000, and family income cannot be less than $5,000. There is also a Rental Assistance Program. The applicant must meet income guidelines of HUD, possess a CDIB, and the unit must pass housing quality standards.

The BIA Housing Improvement Program was designed to provide Indian families with safer, more sanitary homes. The requirements for qualifying for the BIA/HIP Program are that the applicants live within the Choctaw Nation, possess a CDIB card, with preference given to the elderly (fifty-five and over) and the disabled. The applicant must possess a clear warranty deed, furnish proof of income, furnish proof of limited financial resources, and must not have received funds from the BIA/HIP.

There is also a tribally funded Housing Improvement Program. To qualify for the tribal HIP program, the applicant must be a tribal member with a CDIB card, a permanent resident of the home, live within the Choctaw Nation, and be low income based on HUD guidelines. The applicant's home must be the primary home, the applicant must prove land ownership, and be sixty-two years of age. A three-member committee appointed by the executive director of housing reviews all applications.

The Choctaw Nation Modular Housing Program provides tribal members with an opportunity to own a modular home at an affordable payment. The manufacturing facility of the Housing Authority of the Choctaw Nation produces homes that are available to Indians whose household incomes are eighty percent below the national median. A family of four on a small income can qualify for a modular home and financing can be arranged through tribal housing and loan programs. The purpose of the program is to provide quality homes to low and moderate income Indians.

In October 2000, plans for more housing options were announced when the Choctaw Nation Housing Authority received zoning approval of its twenty acres located on Choctaw Road in Durant for building housing units for tribal members sixty-two and older on the property. Proposals include a $750,000 project that would begin with ten one-bedroom, twenty-five-foot by twenty-eight-foot facilities and then increase the number of dwellings to fifty.

In November 2001, Idabel was set as the site for the first "Independent Living Community" of ten homes on a beautiful location with lots of pine trees and privacy. A new concept for Choctaw elders, the homes were developed for those still capable of living independently in a safe, affordable environment. Since many elderly Choctaws live in rural, isolated areas, the community provides the opportunity for contact with others of their age. The Choctaw Housing Authority maintains the yards and housing units. The one-bedroom homes feature full kitchen and bath and utility rooms. Future communities are planned in Talihina, Durant, Hartshorne, Poteau, and Hugo.

In June 2001, Chief Pyle announced a $25 million mortgage program for tribal members as the Choctaw Housing Authority joined First Mortgage, PMI Mortgage Insurance Company and Fannie Mae in adoption of Fannie Mae's Desktop Originator automated mortgage loan system to provide tribal members access to mortgage financing options. The advantage of the program was that it made instant loan recommendations. Data from applications could be entered into computers for decisions within minutes instead of weeks or months. The first tribe in the country to utilize the new software, Choctaw tribal members around the nation have access to the most innovative, cost effective, and streamlined mortgage processing available.

The program is available for tribal members in all fifty states and allows low down payments in combination with credit flexibility for borrowers who have had previous credit problems. The Choctaw Nation earmarked tribal funds for a risk-sharing agreement with PMI Insurance Company, the provider of mortgage insurance on the loans. PMI and Fannie Mae agreed to set aside the $25 million for the Choctaw Nation under a pilot program that allowed borrowers to make as little as one percent down payments and the remaining amount and closing costs could be provided by the Choctaw Homebuyers Advantage Program.

In June 2002, Russell Sossamon was elected chairman of the National American Indian Housing Council in San Diego. Serving as director of the Choctaw Nation Housing Authority since 1997, he had served two years on the board of directors of the national council. He acts as president of the Southern Plains Indian Housing Association, a member of Fannie Mae's Southwest Regional Advisory Board.[375]

The Choctaw Nation operates a number of real estate programs. These are the Real Estate Appraisal Program, the Real Property Management Program, the Land Titles and Records Program, the Historic Preservation Program, the Transportation Program, and the Native American Graves Protection and Repatriation Act (NAGPRA).

The Appraisal Program provides appraisals for the Choctaw Nation Real Property Management Program for right-of-ways, easements, condemnations, and surface damages; the Choctaw Nation Agriculture Program; the Southeastern Oklahoma Indian Credit Association (mortgage loan appraisals); the Office of the Solicitor Tulsa Office; and the Choctaw Nation Industrial Development Committee.

The Real Property Management Program is responsble for the planning, organization, and direction within the framework of existing laws and regulations established by Congress, the Department of the Interior, BIA, and the Area Director for the utilization, development, and protection of Trust and Restricted lands. Concerned with all types of land transactions, the program provides income verification, title status reports, information for Quiet Title and Partition suits for the regional solicitor, and securing and furnishing data on presumptive heirs and inventory of estate for probate to the solicitor and private attorney. The program assists oil and gas workers with information on heirs for securing leases and assists individuals with the preparation of wills, allotments, and ancestry records. The office's multi-faceted duties include checking each truck stop for environmental contamination, inspection of the new water tower at the Capitol, and developing feasible land programs.

The Land Titles and Records Program receives, examines, and records documents relating to trusts and restricted lands of the Five Civilized Tribes. Area courthouses are routinely researched for records of property, maps, heirs, and title information. The staff microfilms title documents, provides certified copies of title documents, responds to inquiries on title matters involving lands with the Choctaw Nation, prepares and maintains legal descriptions for mapping purposes, and conducts field trips to county, state, and federal offices for land records. The department traces the ownership of a tract of land through the years, through each allottee to determine if it is still restricted, and puts purchased tribal lands in trust. It has built a record of tribally owned property and restricted lands and examined all records and documents that affect titles to trusts or restricted lands of the Five Civilized Tribes.

Another goal for Chief Pyle, Assistant Chief Bailey, and the Council has been providing opportunities for education for the Choctaw. Programs have been developed to provide education from the Day Care-Head Start programs to adult education and range from Higher Education Grants and Scholarships to the Indian Adult Education and the WIA Program.

In 1978, the Head Start Program was launched to provide services in education, health, parental involvement, social services, and family literacy for economically disadvantaged families with children between three and compulsory school age. Funds are provided from the Administration for Children and Families Agency of the Department of Health and Human Services.

In 1984, the Choctaw Nation contracted a higher education program from the BIA to disburse funds appropriated by Congress for educational grants and scholarships to aid Choctaw students attending an accredited college and working toward an associate or higher degree. Each spring staff members canvass all sixty-four schools in the Nation, although scholarships are not limited to the Choctaw boundaries. Any students within the United States are eligible and must carry twelve hours per semester while maintaining a 2.0 grade point average. All students are also eligible for a one-time payment for a post-high school clothing allowance. Any degree of Choctaw blood that has a CDIB may apply for this assistance after completing one full semester with passing grades at any institution of higher learning. In 2002, the tribe contributed more than four million dollars to the scholarship program that assisted more than three thousand students.[376]

The Indian Adult Education Program provides educational and employment opportunities for Indian adults by giving those who did not graduate from high school a place to acquire basic educational skills. At least four classes are going on at all times, normally each lasting three months, in Choctaw Community Centers and local education facilities that give tutoring, financial aid, and help to obtain a GED degree. Receiving the certificates enables the students to work for higher degrees on the college level. The eligibility requirements are a CDIB card, be at least sixteen years old, and reside within the Choctaw Nation. In September 1998, the Adult Education Program held its annual graduation handing out diplomas to 131 students who passed GED tests in 1997 and 1998.

Chapter Seventeen

The Work Force Investment Act (WIA) established programs to prepare Choctaw youth and unskilled adults for entry into the labor force and to provide job training for the economically disadvantaged or other serious barriers to employment. These persons are provided special training to help them obtain employment. Programs include classroom training and "on the job training," but time on the program is limited. The employment programs within the WIA are Work Experience and Summer Youth. In 2002, more than one thousand young adults between the ages of fourteen and twenty-one participated in the Summer Youth Program.

The Upward Bound Program provides high school students an opportunity to prepare for college. The students experience college-level course work, laboratory work, tutoring, career exploration, academic skill enrichment, financial aid, scholarship assistance, and numerous field trips to make their high school-college work enjoyable. The program annually recruits eligible students for participation in a six-week summer academic program at Eastern Oklahoma State College. During the academic year Upward Bound staff counsel and guide the students.

Students must meet eligibility requirements to participate in Upward Bound. Two-thirds of the participants must be from low-income and first generation families (neither parent has a four-year college degree), all students must demonstrate academic need and strong interest for successfully completing high school and college, and all selected students must be enrolled in grades 9-12 in schools in Atoka, Bryan, Pushmataha, Latimer, McCurtain, and Pittsburg Counties. The Upward Bound Program is federally funded annually through the U. S. Department of Education for fifty students ages thirteen to nineteen that are eighth grade graduates and have academic potential. By the time the student completes four summers with Upward Bound, it is possible to obtain fifteen college credits at no cost to the parents.

A similar program is the Upward Bound Math/Science Program. The eligibility requirements are the same as Upward Bound for students that have shown an aptitude and desire careers in math, science, and engineering. Forty students are allowed to enroll each year.

The Vocational Development Program assists Indians to obtain educational training in courses approved by the BIA in accredited colleges or at Oklahoma State Tech. Training is also offered in the cosmetology fields and the LPN program at all Kiamichi Area Vo-Techs. The program has provided services since 1986 to students with one-quarter or more Indian blood living in the boundaries of the Choctaw Nation. The staff also offers a Relocation Assistance Program to help applicants relocate to start new jobs.

According to Sec. 273.12 of the Federal Register and Public Law 99-228, Indian students, members of a tribe or descendants of a tribal member, from age three through grade twelve, except those who are enrolled in Bureau or sectarian operated schools, are eligible for special programs and services provided by the United States through the BIA. This is because of their status as Indians. On October 1, 1984, the Choctaw Nation under the jurisdiction of the BIA, Muskogee Area Office, contracted the Johnson O'Malley Program (JOM) for the tribe. It was the responsibility of the Nation as the prime contractor for the program to administer JOM funds for the operation of supplemental programs for the education of eligible Indian students. The JOM Program currently serves more than 8,233 students in approximately seventy schools.

In August 1997, the Tribal Council's commitment to education was seen when Chief Pyle announced the Council's approval of additional funds for a Choctaw Nation Boys and Girls Club in Broken Bow. Amounting to $175,000 for construction of a new gymnasium, the funds were used for a new basketball court and weight workout rooms. There was also a club in Talihina, complete with a gym, pool, ping-pong tables, and weight rooms to promote education for Choctaw youth.[377]

The educational capstone experience continues to be Jones Academy in Hartshorne. The Academy has provided outstanding residential care for elementary and secondary school age children since its establishment in 1891. Given the opportunity to grow academically and culturally, students receive twenty-four hour supervision and guidance at the Academy. Eligibility requirements are that each student is at least one-quarter Indian blood or a member of a federally recognized tribe and has met the criteria for placement in the boarding school. In 2002, almost 200 children lived at the Academy. A full academic school is being built at Jones beginning in August 2003. There will be a complete K-12 academic school within six years.

Students and staff are kept busy with programs and activities including the training and caring for registered Quarter horses, youth athletics, arts and crafts, and cultural events. The Academy annually hosts all-Indian rodeos, and Jones students have been named finalists in the "National Take Pride in America Contest." In December 2000, Chief Pyle and Assistant Chief Bailey donated their Christmas fund money to the students of Jones Academy. The young people were given a check for $2,500 to be spent on gifts for the students. The two executives have continued this donation each year.

In July 2001, Chief Pyle and U.S. Representative Wes Watkins, Bennington, led grand opening ceremonies for a $1 million library addition to the Academy campus. The structure, along with a storm shelter fund for $125,000 from the BIA, was financed through Academy carryover funds, Choctaw Nation business revenues, and private donations of $100,000 from Nebraskan philanthropist, Kenneth Burton.[378]

In 2000, Chief Pyle began an innovative program in education with the announcement of the Choctaw Language Internet Program. The language would be brought into students' homes over the Internet using video streaming. Students are able to see and hear the teacher, read what is typed to them, and view Power Point slides. Students living anywhere in the world with Internet access receive live, interactive teaching on their computer. The Nation had started the program three years earlier with community classes utilizing local teachers. Chief Pyle stated that teachers fluent in Choctaw would be used as instructors. There had been a pilot program of distance learning using satellite transmission, but the cost of satellite time was excessive. On February 22, the Language Program welcomed students to the first class, and the pilot program expanded rapidly to offer beginning and intermediate Choctaw over the internet to students across the world.

In August 2001, the OneNet program, the pilot telecommunications plan, made the language available to four public schools in Bryan County via H.323 two-way video over the internet. Both teachers and students see and hear each other almost as if they are in the same room. In August 2002, the program expanded to include twenty-seven public schools in the ten and one-half counties of the Nation. The fall of 2003 marked the addition of Intermediate Choctaw for our public schools and the addition of college level classes to be taught to a number of higher education institutions, including Carl Albert Junior College, Eastern Oklahoma State College, and Southeastern Oklahoma State University. The community classes, Internet classes, OneNet classes, and higher education courses compliment each other and support the goal of preservation of the Choctaw language.

Lillian Vaughn, a full blood Mississippi Choctaw teacher of a sixteen-week Choctaw language class at the Ardmore Public Library, called the renewed interest in the language by nineteen of her students "the revival of a God-given language." The students, ranging in age from twenty to senior citizens, wanted to learn the language correctly and wanted to understand the Choctaw hymns and read the Choctaw Bible. They were all determined to keep the language alive. One of the students, Rubye McMillan, the daughter of a Chickasaw mother and Choctaw father, echoed the feeling of many who have taken pride in the rekindled interest in the language: "Everyone has their own language—English, German, Chickasaw, Choctaw, Seminole Band—I wish I had learned it when I was younger."[379]

Reverend Bertram Bobb, famous for his renditions of Choctaw hymns, also lamented the past trend toward less use of the language. Bobb argued that young people enjoy the musical productions in Choctaw but do not know the language well enough to fully appreciate the traditional hymns.[380]

In October 2000, the Choctaw pride in their language was evident with the publication of *Pashofa Pole*, the first of a series of books produced by the Nation printed in English and then translated into Choctaw. Joy Culbreath directed the publication of the book by author Mary M. Frye. The series of children's books were translated by Henry Willis from McClain, Oklahoma, and illustrated by Choctaw artist Norma Howard from Haskell County. A fifth and final volume was completed in 2003.[381]

In November 2001, the Nation launched a program in conjunction with the Department of Human Services and school districts within the Nation to share the cost of having a social worker in each of the Council districts. Under the agreement the school systems each contribute $8,142 per social worker, matched by the tribe, and the DHS contributes $16,284. Called the School Based Social Work, the program is designed to help at-risk students and families. The social workers help reduce and prevent involvement by the courts and the Department of Human Services' Child Protective Services division. Contracts were signed with DHS State Director Howard Hendrick and tribal officials led by Assistant Chief Bailey.

Choctaw plans for the future include restoration of Wheelock Academy. One of five sites on the Preservation Oklahoma's 2002 list of Most Endangered Historic Properties in the state, the site had been placed on the list of the "Most Endangered Historic Places in America" in 2001. The forty acres of unallotted land with seven remaining buildings are being restored to their former golden years of Choctaw education.[382]

In March 2001, the Choctaw Nation received the "Business of the Year" award from the Durant Chamber of Commerce, an acknowledgment accepted by District 9 Council member Ted Dosh. The award represented the continuing goal of the tribe to develop and expand businesses across the Choctaw Nation. Tribal efforts to provide full employment for southeastern Oklahoma, with preference for the tribe, have been aggressively pursued since the 1970s.[383]

Deeply committed to economic development with the twofold objective of providing jobs and supplementing tribal programs and services, the Nation began with the opening of the Choctaw Bingo Palace, the purchase of the Arrowhead Resort, and the construction of Choctaw Travel and Smoke Shops. In 1990, the Nation purchased a shopping center containing thirty-seven tenants including a Dairy Queen, Piggly Wiggly Supermarket, Subway Sandwich Shop, a Dollar General Store, and a Smoke Shop in Idabel. These enterprises served as a springboard for the expansion of the tribe into many other varied industries as a means of providing more jobs. The Smoke Shop alone had provided ten full time jobs, and many more were needed.

In 1997, Chief Pyle and Assistant Chief Bailey with Council members and other dignitaries officially celebrated the purchase of a 700-acre Industrial

Park at Hugo. On August 15, Randle Durant, Lois Burton, Charley Jones, James Frazier, Charlotte Jackson, Bob Pate, Leslie James, Billy Paul Baker, Perry Thompson, Ted Dosh, and the Chief cut the ribbon to the 40,000-square foot building that was part of the purchase. Announcing that it would be working with Little Dixie Community Action Agency, KEDDO, Hugo Industrial Authority, and the Choctaw County Industrial Authority to develop the park, the Nation increased its effort to create jobs. One of the first businesses there was the Trailer Manufacturing Plant.[384]

A few years later, the Choctaw Nation Housing Authority announced the opening in Stigler of another factory to build modular homes for low-income tribal members. The Stigler plant was located in another 40,000-square foot facility with a payroll similar to the first modular factory. The first, an 18,000-square foot building with thirteen employees and a payroll of about $600,000 per year, had been opened in Coalgate in 1999. The Coalgate facility produced twenty-four homes per year that ranged from one-bedroom homes of 750 square feet to three-bedroom houses of 1,250 square feet. The price for one of the modular home included a home site, land development, and delivery and setup.[385]

In March 1996, Admiral John Lockard stated, "The Choctaw Nation Finishing Company is the first participant in the Mentor/Protege Program. It is a great success story. The partnership between the Choctaw Nation and the U.S. Defense Systems is one of tangible results. The Navy continues to look forward to continuing our partnership with Texas Instruments and Choctaw Nation." The Naval officer was referring to the Choctaw Finishing Company being designated as the subcontractor with TI since 1989 to construct and apply chemical finishes to parts of missiles and bombs used by the Department of Defense. Some of its jobs included construction of shipping and storage containers for the Joint Stand-Off Weapon (J-SOW), a bomb that drops "bomblets" in enemy territory, and manufacturing the Paveway air foils system. The Chief quipped that the bow and arrow were the first "Joint Stand Off Weapons." The Choctaw Finishing Company later branched out to manufacture stock trailers and parts for prefabricating metal buildings.[386]

A few months later the company was awarded a purchase order from TI to build "All Up Round Containers" for the High Speed Anti-Radar Missile (HARM) program. The work on the HARM containers was contracted for twelve months at a benefit of $459,916 for the tribe. The HARM missile targets enemy radar to protect friendly aircraft. The project increased employment opportunities for another forty staff members at the Hugo facility. This was the second award as the company had earlier received orders for the Paveway Guidance Section Containers.

Since the containers have a removable plate that allows the missile to be re-programmed for targets without being moved, their size makes it necessary for more workspace for manufacturing. Tribal employees manufacture the parts in one building and assemble them in another. The Choctaw Nation Finishing Company proved it could produce a quality product and maintain an excellent delivery record.[387]

In April 2000, business was booming for the Choctaw Manufacturing & Development Corporation (CDMC) when it shipped its first contract quantity of Stinger Missle containers to the U.S. Army Redstone Arsenal. It was the first shipment on a three-year contract awarded to the company in December 1999.

The following May, CMDC received a contract from the Battelle Memorial Institute for the first article production of ten InStreem Water and Wastewater treatment units. The units were in development by Battelle research scientists and after an international search, CMDC was selected as a manufacturing partner. The InStreem unit utilizes proprietary technology developed by the company to treat water and wastewater in streams and estuaries as well as swine and poultry wastewater treatment. Battelle, based in Columbus, Ohio, is recognized as a world leader in research and development technologies for government and commercial applications.

In January 2000, CMDC received the largest one-time order in its history. It was contracted to supply 7,000 shipping and storage containers to support the Paveway laser-guided bomb programs from Raytheon Missle Systems Company, Inc. The company also placed orders for ninety-three aluminum Joint Standoff Weapons (JSOW) shipping and storage containers.

Chief Pyle and the Council had founded the Choctaw Manufacturing & Development Corporation in December 1998. Assistant Chief Bailey served as chairman of the CMDC management committee. It operates facilities in Hugo and Atoka and a "Tool Crib" inside the Raytheon Manufacturing Facility in Sherman, Texas.[388]

In 2001, Chief Pyle was honored by the U.S. Department of Defense as its speaker at its annual Mentor/Protege Conference. The tribe had been a part of the program since an agreement had been made with the Navy partnering one of the tribal manufacturing companies with Raytheon/Texas Instruments so the tribe could share the expertise of the large company. Benefiting from the Mentor/Protege program, the tribe was fully capable of competing for and executing contracts without outside assistance, the exact result the program was supposed to produce. The tribe has continued to be a vital supplier of containers and components to Raytheon and continues to support the J-SOW and Paveway projects.

The Nation soon expanded as a contractor to the Army and Air Force for contracts for the Stinger Missile containers for the Army Redstone Arsenal and other aluminum shipping and storage containers. One of these containers was for weapon systems being sold to the Republic of South Korea. A large aluminum container, the CMDC built it efficiently because of the large vertical milling machine that was acquired through the Mentor/Protege program. The Nation also manufactures aircraft valves for the U.S. Air Force, a wing rack assembly for the U.S. Army, and adaptor kits to attach weapons to aircraft.

In October 2001, the Chief announced a ten-year contract with an estimated nominal gross value from $55 to $125 million for the Choctaw Manufacturing and Development Corporation, a prime contract from the U.S. Army, Communications and Electronics Command (CECOM) in Fort Monmouth, New Jersey, for the design and manufacture of the Army Space Heater (ASH). The ASH allows remote or manual temperature controlled heating to meet environmental needs of personnel and equipment in shelters, vans, and enclosed areas for the military. The ASH will allow the unit to provide clean, filtered air in chemically or biologically contaminated environments.

In 1999, the tribal business of CMDC assumed operations of the Choctaw Nation Finishing Company in Hugo that had been manufacturing Department of Defense goods since 1988. In January 2001, the rapid expansion of CMDC by more than forty percent allowed the tribe to purchase the Choctaw Nation Business Park in McAlester to expand the Hugo-based plant to produce the ASH at the McAlester facility. Covering twenty-four and one-half acres, the facility provided 150,000 feet of workspace and opened in the summer of 2001. Employing more than forty people by 2002, Chief Pyle stated, "It is thrilling to have watched this business grow and become so fruitful over the past few years." Expecting sixty jobs to be available at the end of the year, Chief Pyle predicted that: "This is only the beginning. This is a $55 million contract that could grow to $128 million."[389]

In 2001, the Choctaw Nation confirmed that a seven-year compact had been signed with the state of Oklahoma to allow the tribe to continue the pari-mutual wagering at off-track betting sites in four locations. In 1997, the tribe opened its first simulcast site in Pocola under the authority of a compact with the state followed by sites at four additional locations and provided simulcast signals from Choctaw Racing Services to eight other locations in the United States. Soon after the Pocola opening, however, a nearby live track, Blue Ribbon Downs, disputed the right of the tribe to broadcast signals to Pocola, arguing that the business interfered with gaming activities offered at the racetrack. The tribe and the track officials immediately began negotiations to resolve the problem.

In 2000, Choctaw leaders and representatives rallied in Oklahoma City in support of the Choctaw off-track betting compact. More than one thousand people crowded the hallways of the Capitol building visiting with state senators and representatives to back the simulcast racing business. The result was a compact signed by Blue Ribbon Downs and the tribe to close the off-track betting facility at Pocola in return for a seven-year compact with the state to allow the Choctaw Racing Services to continue to operate in all other locations. Governor Frank Keating signed the compact with the Joint State-Tribal Relations Committee composed of legislators from both state houses and chaired by Terry Matlock and vice-chair Jeff Rabon.[390]

The newest enterprises developed by Chief Pyle and the Council includes the Choctaw Inn and the Three Arrows Restaurants. Located directly west of the Choctaw Bingo Palace in Durant, the 34,500-square foot complex was constructed to provide overnight facilities for guests at the Bingo Parlor. Funded by a $750,000 U.S. Department of Housing and Urban Development Grant, the Inn featured a fully supplied restaurant that offers home cooked meals along with Pashofa and Indian tacos. Known as the Three Arrows Grill and Restaurant, symbolic honors for Apuckshunnubbee, Moshulatubbee, and Pushmataha, the inn contains the restaurant, rooms, a gaming room, and a gift shop, providing jobs for fifty-three full-time employees. On March 29, 2000, a second Three Arrows Grill was opened temporarily at McAlester, soon followed by a third at Stringtown. The restaurants provide home-style food for travelers and guests.[391]

In October 2000, Chief Pyle signed a compact with the state affecting economic development and opportunities in the future. In a move designed to clear up a water rights issue, state and tribal leaders met and agreed to be partners while defining where an ever-replenishing supply of southeastern Oklahoma water should go, an issue that was relevant as several large metropolitan centers expressed desires to purchase the water. The Oklahoma City area had an interest because half its water comes from Atoka and McGee Creek lakes. The agreement allows the various sides to be equal partners in future development of the water resources. The meeting resulted in a signed compact establishing a course of action for the state and the Choctaw and Chickasaw tribes to unite existing state water law with Indian water rights claims. The agreement laid the "groundwork through which the tribes and state could work together for economic development in southeastern Oklahoma," said Governor Keating. Chief Pyle agreed that negotiating a compact was the most logical solution. He stated, "While the tribes hold firm to our water rights claims, we recognize that the existence of two conflicting systems could impede economic development opportunities of potential benefit to all peoples."

Because of their treaties with the United States, the Choctaw and Chickasaw tribes claim ownership to the Kiamichi River basin, an area that begins at the Arkansas line and covers parts of six southeastern counties. The basin contains some of the best, unpolluted waters in America, and federal studies have shown that approximately half a trillion gallons of water flow over the spillway at Lake Hugo annually into the Red River. This became an issue when cities in western Oklahoma and north Texas began running out of pure water. In 1991, this water was offered for sale to Texas for $373 million over 100 years by the state but the tribes were left out. Threatening lawsuits and staking their claims to the water, the tribes prevented the sale of the water resulting in further meetings to work out a solution.

On January 12, 2002, news headlines read, "Water sale to Texas dries up." Negotiations with the Lone Star State fell apart over wide differences involving the value of the Kiamichi waters. Leaders of the tribe and Governor Keating placed the value of the commodity over the next century at $339 million, approximately double the offered price of $174 million. An agreement had been worked out to give one-half of the amounts to the state, 37.5 percent to the Choctaw and 12.5 percent to the Chickasaw, but halting the negotiations left the issue to the future.

Similar water arguments over approximately 7,700 acres along the Arkansas River from Sallisaw to Fort Smith have been another source of contention for decades. In 1970, the United States Supreme Court ruled that the Cherokee, who claim ownership of half this land, and the Choctaw and Chickasaw, the other half, owned the river bed and its banks from Muskogee to Fort Smith, but no settlement was ever made. In 1989, the tribes sued in the U.S. Court of Federal Claims prompting a Bureau of Land Management survey. In 1997, after the survey was completed, the federal government filed suit on behalf of the tribes against defendants and landholders along the river to establish a clear title to the area. In 1999, a judge dismissed the case, but tribal officials have asked for a $50 million settlement rather than refile the case and continue the debate. The sides were told to reach an agreement or the case would return to court. In November 2002, the United States Senate approved a settlement of $40 million.[392]

The increased economic development of the tribe has allowed a wide range of other programs. In 1995, a Family Investment Center was started in Broken Bow in a 7,500-square foot facility located east of town that brought services to the tribal members and eliminated long distances the Choctaw had previously traveled to obtain aid. The center provided assistance in education grants, a service that had previously resulted in the graduation of more Choctaw students than any other tribe, employment assistance, and transportation to tribal members. Secondary services provided at the center are personal welfare counseling, youth education, leadership counseling, and health care. The requirements for participation are that applicants must live in an Indian home, Affordable Rental Housing, or receive Rental Assistance in the

Choctaw Nation and have a CDIB card. Funded by a grant in the amount of $1 million to build two of the centers, a second Family Investment Center was established in Poteau.[393]

In 1993, the Transportation Improvement Program was created to develop the Choctaw Nation by improving roads across the Nation through BIA Indian Reservation Road Funds of the Intermodal Surface Transportation Efficiency Act. The function of the program has been to inventory existing roads, find roads and bridges that need building or improving, submit prioritized lists of roads that the Bureau considers for funding, and then survey the road, obtain an engineer's estimate, and take bids on the project.

Work has been done under the program on the Honobia road. The 14.2 miles of Highway 271 going to Honobia was resurfaced and new signs erected for the public. Another six miles of the Unger Road running north and south from Highway 70 to Highway 109 was improved, and the Pine Creek Road project was another road boosted by $360,000 in Reservation Roads Funds. This was a special congressional appropriation in addition to the original roads money. The project serves those traveling north of Valliant around the White Sands community. Another road completed with "set aside monies" from Congress was the Chief Pushmataha Road from Boswell to east of Lane. Other roads that have been worked on are the Goodland road projects, a two-year job, which included paving eight miles of dirt road that leads directly to Goodland Indian School and a prominent Indian cemetery. Completed road projects through the Bureau of Indian Affairs Reservation Road Funds include Highway 271 in 1987 to widen and resurface roads for the Labor Day Festival traffic to the Council Grounds at Tvshkahomma.[394]

In 1996, a bridge completed under the program was dedicated as the Hollis E. Roberts Bridge over Little River between Cloudy and Pickens. This project required two years of cooperative work between the tribe and Pushmataha County commissioners. The project replaced the old, low water crossing of wooden planks hardly wide enough for one vehicle with a new bridge that spanned 700 feet and accommodated two lanes of traffic.[395]

The 2000 Balance Sheet clearly illustrated the economic growth of the tribe. In 1990, total assets for the tribe were $50,380,214, including cash in the bank, cash in interest accounts, federal and state and other funds, inventory, prepaid expenses, notes receivable, investment in trust, equipment, buildings, and land. Total liabilities for the year were $3,730,631, total revenue for 1990 was $30,554, 972, total expenditures were $26,024,880, and the fund balance at the end of the year amounted to $46,649,583. These amounts increased approximately $10 million per year. In 1995, the amount increased by $50 million followed by another $10 million per year through 2000. The figures for 1999 were total assets, $192,533,712; total liabilities, $17,114,213; total revenues for 1999 were $239,625,301; total expenditures, $226,009,561; and the fund balance at the end of the year was $175,419,499.[396]

The exceptional economic strength of the tribe enabled the Council to sponsor a number of worthwhile community service programs in southeastern Oklahoma through contributions in money and manpower. A major service for the tribe has been the publication of a monthly newspaper free to tribal members. In 1976, the newspaper printed 9,000 copies as *Hello Choctaw* during Chief Gardner's administration under Editor Will T. Nelson followed by Len F. Green and Jon Bonds. On June 1, 1978, the paper was renamed to honor an ancient Choctaw legend, a Bishinik, or small, speckled yellow-billed scissor-tailed species of woodpecker that, according to Choctaw legend, was one of two birds, the other being a Folichik, a scissor-tailed flycatcher, to escape the Great Flood by flying as high as they could and perching upside-down upon the sky. The two birds became scissor-tailed when the waters separated their tails. Because of their bravery, God blessed the birds and made Bishinik a special friend to the Choctaw as a news bird who lived around them and let them know whenever anyone was approaching or warn warriors of enemies. During the hours of darkness, Bishinik would tap out a warning. *Bishinik* was selected for the newspaper because the Oklahoma City Council of Choctaws copyrighted the name *Hello Choctaw*, and Chief Roberts wanted the name changed and the paper published within the Nation. Editor Len Green, Assistant Chief Robert L. Gardner, and Associate Editor Ruth Morris selected the new name, but a controversy arose over its correct spelling. Some argued that Biskinik was the correct version, but the new spelling, Bishinik, was accepted as proper for the paper.

In 1981, Editor Jon Bonds was forced to announce that the May issue would be the last one for a time due to the announcement by the Administration for American Indians (ANA) that funds for the paper would be eliminated by Reaganomics, the Ronald Reagan economic policies. ANA, the federal agency that funded the paper, was affected by the administration policies, as were all areas of federal funding, but the paper resumed when finances for operational support of the paper were secured from Revenue Sharing Funds in August 1981. The change put the paper on a sound financial basis with a more stable publishing foundation. In May 2001, Editor Judy Allen reported that the newspaper "served 125,650 Choctaws around the world."[397]

Another program, the Cultural Resources Department, has been given the mission of preservation and protection of ancestral remains, sacred lands, and sacred objects under the Native American Grave Protection and Repatriation Act (NAGPRA) of 1990. On October 13, 2001, the first remains of a Choctaw warrior were reburied in a ceremony at the newly designated burial grounds at

Tvshkahomma. The remains were accidentally unearthed in 1939, sent to the University of Oklahoma for study, and stored at Woolaroc Museum for over fifty years. After learning of the remains, tribal officials began the process of recovering them and returning them to Choctaw land. Going to Mississippi to learn the burial ceremony, officials recreated the ceremony to bury the warrior, a man in his forties who had fought with Pushmataha for General Jackson, participated in the Trail of Tears removal, and been buried near Fort Coffee in 1839.

Another effort involved the Choctaw Firefighters, a program under the head of the Choctaw Nation Forestry Division, Tom Lowery, who manages tribal timberlands and protects over 54,000 acres of tribal land from fire, trespassing, and theft. Assistant Director Kendall Carpenter oversees the Choctaw Firefighters, who were used in the Swift Creek fire near Lake City, Florida. They were also used to mop up around Scottsmore, Florida, in 1998. The men in the Firefighters on the trip were Andy Whitener, Frank Jefferson, Dallas Turner, Willard Warley, Kendall Carpenter, Fred Locke, Floyd Choate, Raymond Ludlow, David Linton, Jason Kennedy, Marty James, Tony Ashalintubbi, L. MataHaya, Cole DeRose, Huey Jefferson, Steven Staples, Richard Bohannon, Calvin Ward, and Victor Baker.

The Choctaw Firefighters have been used throughout the United States. In the summer of 2002, the Firefighters participated in the Arizona fires that destroyed hundreds of acres of ponderosa pines on Bureau of Indian Affairs lands near Show Low. The firemen included Tony Anderson, Richard Bohanon, Keith Gammel, Robert Palmer, Silas LeFlore, Thomas Stewart, John Roebuck, Jonah Young, Walter Blevins, Steven Baxter, Alfred Noah, Theodore Roebuck, Michael Jocoway, Jason Kennedy, and Jeff Smith.

The Choctaw Nation also conducts its own Law Enforcement Program. Covering the ten-and-one-half counties in southeastern Oklahoma, tribal officers provide security on tribally owned, restricted, and allotted lands within tribal jurisdictional boundaries. To be a tribal officer, the participant must be CLEET certified and have completed the basic Academy Police Training Program. The department has grown rapidly since the first law enforcement officer was hired in 1991. In less than seven years the department has increased from two to twenty officers. The department works with county, city, state, and federal agencies and has full jurisdiction when an Indian commits a crime on Indian land. Grants have enabled the Indian officers to purchase weapons, body armor, and five new Ford Crown Victorias for police work. All officers have their own field offices in assigned areas where they submit reports by e-mail to headquarters in Durant at the Choctaw Nation Complex.

In 1992, the tribe collaborated on another program for the protection of the Nation by joining the Intertribal Bison Cooperation (ITBC) through the purchase of an original herd of five animals from the State of Oklahoma. The tribe has sold only twelve bulls since the original purchase with the proceeds used to purchase more females to go back into the herd. As of September 2000, the Choctaw owned 144 buffalo pastured on 2,600 acres on the Tvshkahomma grounds with the goal of the program being 200 animals with a pasture range of 5,000 acres. Funding through ITBC, the tribe has installed new fences and purchased handling equipment and buses that make a tour of the buffalo herd each year at the Labor Day Festival.

Other activities involving tribal participation have ranged from a $500 check to Sheriff Bill Sturch of Bryan County to upgrade departmental computers to a $1000 check to Community Health Promotions Director Gladys Haikey for use in sponsoring the Annual Oklahoma Indian All-State Basketball Games. Started three years earlier, the annual games are for both senior boys and girls selected by a panel of coaches from throughout the state. Eligibility is limited to American Indians with CDIB cards. Other sponsors of the games are Southwestern Bell, Conoco, Inc., Great Plains Coca Cola, and Four Winds, Inc.[398]

In 2001, the tribe again provided community assistance by helping alleviate the damages caused by the January "deep freezes" that hit Oklahoma during the Christmas-New Year holidays. An unprecedented ice storm destroyed trees and power lines across southeastern Oklahoma that created chaos for thousands across the state. Cities as large as McAlester were without electricity as power lines were downed over the region. Dispatching trucks loaded with candles, lamp oil, Coleman fuel, food, blankets, bottled water, and batteries to be distributed to families in need, the Nation volunteered to help clear roadways and streets. "Thanks to several four-wheel drive vehicles, we were even able to check on people in remote areas," stated Chief Pyle.[399]

The tribe willingly helped again after the terrorist attacks on the twin towers of the World Trade Center and the Pentagon on September 11, 2001. Spokesperson Judy Allen reported that the tribe diverted all profits from the fuel sales at the tribe's nine travel plazas for one week through September 28 for disaster relief to New York and Washington. In addition, gaming centers at Durant, McAlester, Pocola, Idabel, Stringtown, and Hugo offered games with the proceeds going toward relief. Finally, the Tribal Council voted to donate an additional $20,000 to the cause with the goal being $50,000. On October 11, 2001, Chief Pyle announced that the tribe had raised $71,773.89.

Chief Pyle added his personal encouragement to the nation to combat terrorism when he supported Oklahomans to vote in the election on September 25 on the Right to Work, SQ 695, issue. While he neither supported nor opposed the issue, the Chief asked the people to go out to vote because "we, as

Choctaw, will be sending a message that we intend to move forward as a free people, making choices that will affect our daily lives."[400]

Recent economic prosperity has instilled a new pride in the Choctaw people seen by the participation in the Red Earth celebration that was inaugurated for Native Americans in Oklahoma City in 1987. In 1998, Choctaw artist Norma Howard displayed her award winning paintings of Choctaw life, as did Dave Jones with his hand made pipes, and George Willis, a nationally acclaimed silversmith and jewelry maker. Chief Pyle and Assistant Chief Bailey also attended with a number of Choctaw Council members.

An example of Choctaw pride was the formation of the Choctaw Nation of Oklahoma Color Guard for the purpose of honoring Choctaw veterans. Volunteer members are provided uniforms, boots, headgear, flags, pistol belts, and rifles to perform at Choctaw ceremonies. On May 2, 1998, members Alto Battiest, Sampson Moore, James Owens, Bill Blankenship, George Robinson, Dennis Baptiste, Audie Gibson, Melvin Tom, Terry Cole, Herbert Jessie, Terry Loman, Eugene Bohanon, Nellie Hunter, Shirley Mantreno, Ron Scott, John Townson, David Jones, and John Burleson performed as the Color Guard at the Skullyville Cemetery. The previous year the Color Guard had participated in forty-nine different events, including one in Washington, D.C. and another in Bakersfield, California. Sixteen of these functions were funerals for Choctaw veterans.

In 2000, Choctaw pride was shown when Chief Pyle attended the annual Rose Bowl Parade in Pasadena to symbolize the Tribe's "Road to Progress." Along with Chief Perry Beaver of the Creeks and Chief Jerry Haney of the Seminoles, the Choctaw Chief began the millennium at the Tournament of Roses on national television.[401]

Gaming has been the economic boom of the tribe, but Chief Pyle and the Choctaw Council are pointing their people toward other more lasting industries. Since the Choctaw opened the first bingo hall in 1987, others have followed in McAlester, Pocola, Idabel, and Broken Bow with expanded electronic pull-tab machines and off-track betting, but the Choctaw leadership realized the future rests with other endeavors. "We try to use the gaming funds as seed money for other businesses," explained Chief Pyle. The tribe has opened travel plazas and large truck stops that sell fuel, snacks, fast food, and tobacco products in seven southeastern Oklahoma towns. In 2003, the tribe opened its eleventh and twelfth travel plaza at Stringtown and Poteau. "These are money-makers employing up to thirty people in each one," stated the Chief. Originally funded with federal grants, the profits have been turned back into starting other businesses and services like the $27 million hospital in Talihina.

The Choctaw have embarked on a plan to open new businesses throughout their Nation. The tribe owns manufacturing plants in Hugo and McAlester that build machines to purify water and build parts for the military, and Choctaw workers earn from ten to sixteen dollars per hour on the average. The tribe plans to employ upwards of 200 people at these plants within two years, and with the growth of these and other enterprises, the tribe is already less dependent on the gaming industry. While the gaming profits continue to grow, they make up less than half of the present tribal earnings. The businesses have allowed the tribe to compete and contribute at the same time.

In 1999, the Nation took a great stride by starting the Choctaw Nation Construction Company. The construction crews save the tribe money by eliminating the middleman and doing its own repairs, maintenance, and construction jobs. The projects are also completed more quickly. The Three Arrows Hotel, McAlester Bingo Parlor, and the Child Development Centers in Bennington, Coalgate, and Stigler are among the accomplishments of the company.[402]

Another program that helps economic development has been the creation of the Agiculture Department that gives technical assistance for conservation of soil, plant, and water resources on tribal lands. Since anyone on Tribal Trust or Restricted Land can seek assistance to develop their land resources, many agriculture-related businesses, farms, and ranches are aided by the department.[403]

The finances for the Choctaw Nation programs are derived from several major sources of federal funding, including USDA, the Department of Agriculture, DOL., the Department of Labor, DHHS, the Department of Heath and Human Services, HUD, Housing and Urban Development, CDBG, Community Development Block Grants, BIA, Bureau of Indian Affairs, and IHS, Indian Health Services. The tribe also has a Tribal Trust Fund of monies invested for the tribe with the BIA as custodian. These funds are kept in several different banks selected to pay the most interest to the tribe.

Tribal Trust Funds are used for a variety of tribal services. Trust Funds pay the costs of tribal elections. The funds pay salaries of Election Board members, workers at each ballot box, and postage for mailing ballots. Burial assistance isanother use for these funds. Choctaw original enrollees and full bloods are automatically eligible to receive an assistance of $300 paid directly to the funeral home; quarter bloods or more residing within the Choctaw Nation are entitled to $200. Additionally, the funds support the ranch, the Capitol buildings and grounds, heavy machinery, all lands held in trust, including the Bingo and Travel Plazas and the shopping centers. In 1991, the tribe had $7.6 million in Tribal Funds and a total of $35 million in land, buildings, and equipment. The amount has tripled in the past decade.

The General Fund is another source of revenue for the tribe. Monies go into the General Fund from tribal businesses including bingo receipts, leases on property owned by the tribe, profits from the garment factory, the nursing home, and taxes on the sale of fuels and tobacco products. In 1991, the fund amounted to $2,905,570.69 and has increased greatly in the past ten years.

The Tribal Council has approved a plethora of purchases from the General Fund. In 1991, two forty-eight-seat buses and a six-passenger Cessna 421 airplane were purchased from the General Fund. The plane and the buses were purchased to allow tribal leaders quicker travel time on business trips.

The General Fund also provides Christmas funds for parties for Choctaw children in each district. The children are given old-fashioned Christmas sacks filled with fruit, nuts, and candy or toys. The purpose is to assure a gift for every child at Christmas time. The same fund pays for medicines at the Choctaw Nation Health Services and scholarships for Choctaw students. Its varied purposes include support for EDH, the Eyeglasses, Dentures and Hearing Aids program, and the Student Clothing Allowance.

There are a number of Matching Food Distribution Funds. Matching funds make up twenty-five percent of the total budget. The USDA required them for funding for the commodity program.

Another fund for the tribe is the Arkansas Riverbed Fund. This is interest accumulated from a federal settlement along with the Cherokee and Chickasaw tribes in 1976. In 1991, the amount was $174,368.91.

The tribe is funded by a number of federal funds in addition to these monies. The USDA funds two programs, Women, Infants and Children (WIC) and Food Distribution, the commodity program. USDA also supports food for the Head Start centers and Title IV-Nutrition and Supportive Service Program. The USDA provides service to more than 8,000 participants through its efforts; the commodity program alone serves more than 6,000.

The DDHS provides money for Head Start, the Nutrition and Supportive Services, which also received a supplement from the Tribal General Fund, the Low Income Home Energy Assistance Program, LIHEAP, and the Talihina Recovery Center for the rehabilitation of chemically dependent persons and families.

An equally impressive number of tribal programs are supported by BIA funds. Included under the BIA banner are the Tribal Membership and CDIB Department, Forestry Department, the Law Enforcement Program, the Agriculture Program, Higher Education, Vocational Development and Relocation Assistance Program, Credit, Real Property, the Johnson O'Malley Program, Indian Child Welfare, Social Services, Housing Improvement, Appraisals, Adult Education, and Youth Work Learn Programs.

The IHS also funds several programs for the tribe. The two major operations are the hospital at Talihina and the health centers, but IHS also funds the Community Health Representative Program (CHR) and the Emergency Medical Services Program (EMS).

Additionally, the DOL funds the WIA, the Workforce Investment Act; HUD finances several programs under the Housing Authority of the Choctaw Nation; and the CDBG have funded programs such as the Hospitality House near the Talihina hospital, installed water and sewer facilities at the Capitol grounds, renovated the nursing home, helped build community centers, and provided help for building the Choctaw Travel Plazas. CDBG are grants to the tribe that do not have to be repaid.

These various funds and grants have placed the tribe on a sound financial basis. The value of the Choctaw Nation has increased to more than $100 million. A similar population growth has occurred at the same time. The census reported a population of 128,258 in 2000. The future of the tribe looks bright as its economic expansion continues into the Twenty-first Century. In 2001, the Tribal Council approved matching funds for a $750,000 grant from HUD for travel plazas in Wilburton, Poteau, Stringtown, and Atoka and continued to look for other ways to extend tribal prosperity.[404]

In May 2002, the financial statement for 2001 was reported to the tribe. The figures showed Total Assets at $258,462,363 and Total Liabilities at $23,275,594. Revenues were reported to be $366,699,468 and expenditures were listed at $321,794,603. The Fund Balance amounted to $235,186,769.[405]

These funds are directed from the Finance Department that has grown from a few money managers to fifty-six computer technicians keeping track of a multi-million dollar enterprise. In 1997, a new addition to the Headquarters building was needed to house the growing number of financial caretakers. The office controls accounting, accounts payable-receivable, payroll, purchasing, and insurance. The growth of the tribe has been at a rate of $10 million per year. Finances were exclusively federal money when the department first started, but by the 1990s sixty-five percent of Choctaw revenues were from its own businesses.

The employees of the Choctaw Nation all need tools, from paper to forklifts, and the Purchasing Department is responsible for getting them. The department controls all purchases through requisition forms, bids for the best prices, delivery, and billing for each item. Everything must be checked when it arrives to make sure of its condition, and equipment must be tagged with metal plates bearing the name of the Choctaw Nation. The Property/Purchasing Department also has charge of the Nation's extensive telephone system and the furnishing of the hospital in Talihina.[406]

The constant growing personnel of the Nation is tracked as well. More than 5,000 employees work for the Nation and all new personnel must undergo drug testing and fill out insurance forms. All Native American applicants for employment are given top priority for job opportunities.

The Choctaw Nation has developed into a viable economic force in southeastern Oklahoma. Its leaders have committed funds and energy to the continued improvement of Choctaw society. Their efforts have resulted in a new pride and respect for their people.[407]

Endnotes

I. Chapta Achvffa The People of Chahta

[1] Clara Sue Kidwell and Charles Roberts, *The Choctaws: A Critical Bibliography* (Bloomington: Indiana University Press, 1980), p. 1; Muriel H. Wright, "Historic Spots In the Vicinity of Tuskahoma," *The Chronicles of Oklahoma* Vol. IX (March 1931), p. 30; Joseph B. Thoburn, "The Tropical and Subtropical Origin of Mound Builder Cultures," *The Chronicles of Oklahoma* XVI (March 1938), p. 108; Anna Lewis, "Nunih Waiya," *The Chronicles of Oklahoma* XVI (June 1938), p. 215; Lonnie E. Underhill and John H. Battle, "Classification of Oklahoma Indian Tribes: Language Stocks, Population, and Locations," *The Chronicles of Oklahoma* XLVIII (Summer, 1970), p. 205; Muriel H. Wright Collection, Western History Collection, University Of Oklahoma, Norman.

[2] *Bishinik*, October 1979; John R. Swanton, *The Indians of the Southeastern United States*, Bureau of American Ethnology, Bulletin 137 (Washington: Gantt Printing Office, 1946), p. 777; Clyda Reeves Franks, "Oklahoma's Distant Past," *Oklahoma* (Fall/Winter, 1999-00), p.34; Henry Clyde Shetrone, *The Mound Builders* (New York: D. Appleton and Co., 1930), p. 383; Jesse O. McKee, *The Choctaws* (New York: Chelsea House Publishers, 1989), p. 7.

[3] *Bishinik*, November 1979; R. A. Lafferty, *Okla Hannali* (New York: Doubleday & Co., Inc. 1972), p. 1.

[4] *Bishinik*, December 1980; John R. Swanton, (ed.), "The Choctaw Indians In The Middle of the Nineteenth Century by John Edwards," *The Chronicles of Oklahoma* X (September 1932), p. 418; Carolyn Keller Reeves, (ed.), *The Choctaw Before Removal* (Jackson: University Press of Mississippi, 1985), p. 40; Jack Gregory and Rennard Strickland, *Choctaw Spirit Tales* (Muskogee: Indian Heritage Association, 1972), p. 1.

[5] Swanton, "*The Choctaw Indians In the Middle of the Nineteenth Century by John Edwards*," p. 410.

[6] Reeves, "*The Choctaws Before Removal*," p. 44; *Bishinik*, August 1994.

[7] *Bishinik*, January 1980.

[8] *Bishinik*, Feb.1980, March 1993, Feb.1994; Edward Davis, "Early Life Among the Five Civilized Tribes," *The Chronicles of Oklahoma* XV (1937), p. 95; Lewis, "Nunih Waiya," p. 215; Marshall Gettys, "Historic Choctaw Pottery in the State Museum of History," *The Chronicles of Oklahoma* LXVII (Winter, 1989-90), p. 417.

[9] *Bishinik*, April 1980, March 1996; Henry S. Halbert, "Nanih Waiya, the Sacred Mound of the Choctaw," *Publications of the Mississippi Historical Society*, 2 (1898); Henry S. Halbert, "A Choctaw Migration Legend," *The American Antiquarian and Oriental Journal* 16 (1894), p. 215; Reeves, *The Choctaw Before Removal*, p. 8; Richard White, *The Roots of Dependency: Subsistence, Environment, and Social Change Among the Choctaws, Pawnees, and Navajos* (Lincoln: University of Nebraska Press, 1983), p. 38.

[10] *Bishinik*, Nov. 1980, January 1993.

[11] *Bishinik*, June 1979, Sept. 1980, November 1995.

[12] Emma Ervin Christian, "Memories of My Childhood Days In The Choctaw Nation," *The Chronicles of Oklahoma* Vol. IX (June 1931), p.162.

[13] Colin F. Taylor and William C. Sturtevant, *The Native Americans* (New York: Salamander Books Ltd., 1996), p. 30; Peter J. Hudson, "Choctaw Indian Dishes," *The Chronicles of Oklahoma* XVII (September 1939), p. 333; Novella Goodman Martin, *Choctaw Little Folk* (San Antonio, Texas: The Naylor Company, 1970); John Howard Blitz, *Ancient Chiefdoms of the Tombigbee* (Tuscaloosa: The University of Alabama Press, 1993), p. 71.

[14] *Bishinik*, March 1993; Dorothy Milligan (ed.), *The Indian Way: The Choctaws* (Durant, Oklahoma: Title IV, Office of Indian Education, 1977), p. 54; Jules B. Billard (ed.), *The World of the American Indian* (Washington, D.C.: National Geographic Society, 1974), p. 139; Edward Davis, "Early Life Among the Five Civilized Tribes," p. 79; Virginia R. Allen, "Medical Practices and Health In The Choctaw Nation, 1831-1885," *The Chronicles of Oklahoma* XLVIII (Spring, 1970), p. 63; *Hello Choctaw*, February 1, 1978; John H. Peterson, Jr., *A Choctaw Source Book* (New York: Garland Publishing Inc, 1985), p. 157; Betty Jeanne Ward Poulin, *Choctaw Heritage* (Heavener, Ok.: Choctaw Heritage, 1981), p. 69; Arlene LeMaster, (trans.), *Eastern Oklahoma Indians and Pioneers: Choctaw Nation, Indian Territory* (3 vols., Poteau: Family Heritage Resources, 1992-93), I, p. 18.

[15] John R. Swanton, *Source Material for the Social and Ceremonial Life of the Choctaw Indians*, Bureau of American Ethnology, Bulletin 103 (Washington D.C.: U.S. Government Printing Office, 1931), p. 227; Horatio Bardwell Cushman, *History of the Choctaw, Chickasaw, and Natchez Indians* (Norman: University of Oklahoma Press, 1999) reprint, p. 199; Reeves, *The Choctaw Before Removal*, p. 81.

[16] *Bishinik*, March 1981, Feb. 1994; Muriel H. Wright, "Some Geographic Names of French Origin In Oklahoma," *The Chronicles of Oklahoma* VII (June 1929), p. 193.

[17] Angie Debo, *The Rise and Fall of the Choctaw Republic* (Norman: University of Oklahoma Press, 1934), p.17; John R. Swanton, Source *Material for the Social and Ceremonial Life of the Choctaw Indians*, p. 120.

[18] Billard (ed.), *The World of the American Indian*, p. 142: Marvin C. Ross, *George Catlin* (Norman: University of Oklahoma Press, 1979), p. 221; *The Indians Time Life Books*, p. 94; Emma Ervin Christian, "Memories of My Childhood In The Choctaw Nation," *The Chronicles of Oklahoma* XI (September 1933), p. 1036; Frances Densmore, *Choctaw Music* (New York: De Capo Press, 1972), p. 117.

II. Chapta Tuklo The Hatchet Shall Be Forever Buried...

[19] Alvin M. Josephy, Jr., *The Indian Heritage of America* (Boston: Houghton Mifflin Company, 1968), p. 107; Shetrone, *The Mound Builders*, p. 384.

[20] *Bishinik*, September 1991; Edward Gaylord Bourne, (ed.), *Narrative of the Career of Hernando de Soto*, (New York: Allerton, 1922, 2 vols.), p. 120; J. Leitch Wright, Jr., *The Only Land They Knew: The Tragic Story of the American Indians in the Old South* (New York: The Free Press, 1981), p. 35; Patricia Galloway, *Choctaw Genesis* (Lincoln, Nebraska: University of Nebraska Press, 1995), p. 209; Henry E. Chambers, *Mississippi Valley Beginnings* (New York: G. P. Putnam's Sons, 1922), p. 32.

[21] *Bishinik*, August 1991; Carolyn Keller Reeves, (ed.), *The Choctaw Before Removal*, p. 57.

[22] *Bishinik*, February 1979, March 1979; Bourne, *Narrative of the Career of Hernando de Soto*, p. 70; Charles Hudson and Carmen Chaves Tesser (eds.) *The Forgotten Centuries: Indians and Europeans in the American South, 1521-1704* (Athens: The University of Georgia Press, 1994), p. 87; Jerald T. Milanich and Susan Milbrath (eds.), *First Encounters: Spanish Explorations in the Caribbean and the United States, 1492-1570* (Gainesville: University of Florida Press, 1989) p. 97.

[23] R.S. Cotterill, *The Southern Indians: The Story of the Civilized Tribes Before Removal* (Norman: University of Oklahoma Press, 1954), p. 6.

[24] *Ibid*, p. 13; Reeves, *The Choctaw Before Removal*, p. 95.

[25] Clara Sue Kidwell, *Choctaws and Missionaries in Mississippi, 1818-1918* (Norman: University of Oklahoma Press, 1995), p. 6; Charles Wayne Goss, "*The French and the Choctaw Indians, 1700-1763*," Unpublished Ph.D. dissertation, Texas Tech University, Lubbock, 1977, p. 10; Jean-Baptiste Benard de la Harpe, *The Historical Journal of the Establishment of the French in Louisiana* Trans. Joan Cain and Virginia Koenig. (Lafayette: University of Southwest Louisiana, 1971).

[26] *Catholic Encyclopedia*, Vol. III (New York: Robert Appleton Company, 1908)

[27] R. M. Underhill, *Red Man's America* (Chicago: The University of Chicago Press, 1953), p. 48; France, Archives des Colonies, Archives Nationales, Paris, Serie C 13c, volume 1: folios 362-374. *Memoir of Bienville* (1725).

[28] George E. Hyde, *Indians of the Woodlands* (Norman: University of Oklahoma Press, 1962), p. 204.

[29] Thomas Naire, *Naire's Muskogean Journals: The 1708 Expedition to the Mississippi River* (Jackson: University Press of Mississippi, 1988), p. 20; Cotterill, *The Southern Indian*, p. 18; Kidwell, *Choctaws and Missionaries in Mississippi*, p. 19.

[30] Angie Debo, *A History of the Indians of the United States* (Norman: University of Oklahoma Press, 1970), p. 75; Frederick W. Hodge, *Handbook of American Indians North of Mexico,* Bureau of American Ethnology, Bulletin 30 (Washington: Smithsonian Institution, 1912), Part I, p. 380; Goss, "The French and the Choctaw Indians," p. 105; Pearl Vivian Guyton, *Our Mississippi* (Austin, Texas: The Steck Company, 1952), p. 48; Patricia Galloway, "Ougoula Tchetoka, Ackia, and Bienville's First Chickasaw War: Whose Strategy and Tactics?" *The Journal of Chickasaw History* Vol. 2 (1996), p. 3.

[31] Clark Wissler, *Indians of the United States* (Garden City: Doubleday and Co., Inc., 1941), p. 50; Kidwell, *Choctaws and Missionaries in Mississippi*, p. 14; J. Leitch Wright, Jr., *The Only Land They Knew*, p. 229.

[32] Charles J. Kappler, (ed.), *Indian Treaties, 1778-1883* (New York: Interland Publishing Inc., 1973), II, p. 12; Papers of Panton, Leslie and Co., Western History Collection, University of Oklahoma. Microfilm, 26 rolls, C-50.

[33] Joseph Stanley Clark, "The Eastern Boundary of Oklahoma," *Chronicles of Oklahoma* XI (December 1933), p. 1085; Kidwell, *Choctaws and Missionaries in Mississippi*, p. 20.

[34] Kappler, (ed.), *Indian Treaties*, II; Kidwell, *Choctaws and Missionaries in Mississippi*, p. 22.

[35] Arthur H. Hall, "The Red Stick War," *Chronicles of Oklahoma* XII (September 1934), p. 272.

[36] R. David Edmunds, *Tecumseh and the Quest for Indian Leadership* (Boston: Little, Brown and Company, 1984), p.148.

[37] Hall, "The Red Stick War," p. 280.

[38] Angie Debo, *The Road to Disappearance* (Norman: University of Oklahoma Press, 1941), p. 19; Hall, "The Red Stick War," p. 284.

[39] Debo, *The Road to Disappearance*, p. 112; Kidwell, *Choctaws and Missionaries in Mississippi*, p. 23; Kappler, (ed.), *Indian Treaties*, II; *Bishinik*, December 1999.

III. Chapta Tuchena None Of The Choctaw Ever Drew A Bow Against the United States

[40] Kidwell, *Choctaws and Missionaries in Mississippi*, p. 15.

[41] *Ibid*, p. 17; George H. Shirk, "Malmaison Today," *The Chronicles of Oklahoma* XLII (Spring, 1964), p. 74.

[42] Czarina C. Conlan, "David Folsom," *The Chronicles of Oklahoma* IV (December 1926), p. 342; Phil D. Brewer, "Rev. Willis F. Folsom, a Biographical Sketch with Excerpts from his Diary," *The Chronicles of Oklahoma* IV (March 1926), p. 57; George William Stevenson, "The Hymnody of the Choctaw Indian of Oklahoma." Unpublished doctoral dissertation to the School of Church Music, The Southern Baptist Theological Seminary, Louisville, Kentucky, 1977. p. 28; Randle Durant, "Randle Durant Writes History of Our Region and His Family," *Bryan County Heritage Quarterly* (November 1998), p. 28; Randle Durant, *Footsteps of the Durant Choctaws* (Durant, Ok: Private printing, 1980), p. 8; Randle Durant, *"Footsteps" of a Durant Choctaw* (Talihina, Ok: Private printing, 2002), p. 6; William Philip Pipkin, "Some of My Choctaw Kinfolks," Unpublished manuscript, comp. Lila Douglas Swink, Goodland, Ok: Choctaw County Genealogical Society, 1992, p. f-3; James C. Milligan, L. David Norris, and Ann Vanmeter, *Durant, 1872-1990* (Durant: Bryan County Heritage Association, 1990), p. 9.

[43] P.P. Pitchlynn to Nephew W.B. Pitchlynn, Sept. 5, 1874, Herbert Otho Boggs Collection, B-59, Folder 1, Western History Collection, University of Oklahoma, Norman, Oklahoma; *Bishinik*, September 1995; Charles E. Brown and Will T. Nelson, (eds.), *Choctaw Social and Ceremonial Life* (Oklahoma City: Oklahoma Choctaw Council, Inc., 1983), p. 3; Pipkin, "Some of My Choctaw Kinfolks," p. 30.

[44] W. David Baird, *Peter Pitchlynn: Chief of the Choctaw* (Norman: University of Oklahoma Press, 1972), p. 26; William Philip Pipkin, "Some of My Choctaw Kinfolks," p. f-5.

[45] Carolyn Thomas Foreman, "The Choctaw Academy," *The Chronicles of Oklahoma* VI (December 1928), p. 452; Carolyn Thomas Foreman, "The Choctaw Academy," *The Chronicles of Oklahoma* X (March 1932), p. 114; Carolyn Thomas Foreman, "The Choctaw Academy," *The Chronicles of Oklahoma* IX (September 1931), p. 408; Marjorie Hall Young, "Stars in A Dark Night: The Education of Indian Youth at Choctaw Academy," *The Chronicles of Oklahoma* LXXV (Fall, 1997), p. 286; Ethel McMillan, "First National Indian School: The Choctaw Academy," *The Chronicles of Oklahoma* XXVIII (Spring, 1950), p. 60.

[46] *Kidwell, Choctaws and Missionaries in Mississippi*, p. 20; Mrs. A. E. Perry, "Colonel Forbis LeFlore, Pioneer and Statesman," *The Chronicles of Oklahoma* VI (March 1928), p. 76; Jonathan Daniels, *The Devil's Backbone: The Story of the Natchez Trace* (New York: McGraw-Hill Book Co., Inc., 1962), p. 9.

[47] Mrs. Lee J. Langley, "Malmaison, Palace in a Wilderness, Home of General LeFlore," *The Chronicles of Oklahoma* V (December 1927), p. 373; Samuel J. Wells and Roseanna Tubby, *After Removal: The Choctaw In Mississippi* (Jackson: University Press of Mississippi, 1986), p. 62; John Bartlett Meserve, "The McCurtains," *The Chronicles of Oklahoma* XIII (September 1935), p. 301; *Hello Choctaw*, May 1, 1978.

[48] Kidwell, *Choctaws and Missionaries in Mississippi*, p. 25.

[49] Pushmataha and Moshulatubbee to the President, Oct. 20, 1818, Letters to the Secretary of War-Received, Microfilm Series 271, Record Group 75, National Archives, Washington, D.C.

[50] Carolyn Thomas Foreman, "The Foreign Mission School at Cornwall, Connecticut," *The Chronicles of Oklahoma* VII (September 1929), p. 246.

[51] Arminta Scott Spalding, "From the Natchez Trace to Oklahoma: Development of Christian Civilization Among the Choctaws, 1800-1860," *The Chronicles of Oklahoma* XLV (Spring, 1967), p. 12; W. B. Morrison, "The Choctaw Mission of the American Board of Commissioners For Foreign Missions," *The Chronicles of Oklahoma* IV (June 1926), p. 172; Edward Davis, "Early Advancement Among the Five Civilized Tribes," *The Chronicles of Oklahoma*, XIV (June 1936), p. 171.

[52] Cyrus Byington to Sophia Byington, Oct. 25, 1847, Byington typescripts, Research Library, Oklahoma Historical Society, Oklahoma City; Louis Coleman, "Cyrus Byington: Missionary to the Choctaws," *The Chronicles of Oklahoma* LXII (Winter, 1984-85), p. 367; Louis Coleman, *Cyrus Byington: Missionary and Choctaw Linguist* (Kearney, Nebraska: Morris Publishing, 1996), p. 23; Courtney Ann Vaughn, "Jobe's

Legacy: Cyrus Byington, Missionary to the Choctaws In Indian Territory," *Red River Valley Historical Review* III (Fall, 1978), p. 6; Bessie Kate Lewis, "A History of Education Among the Choctaw and Chickasaw Indians of Oklahoma." Unpublished Master's Thesis, Austin: University of Texas, 1927, p. 23; Cyrus Byington, *An English and Choctaw Definer; For the Choctaw Academies and Schools* (New York: S. W. Benedict, 1852).

[53] Morrison, "The Choctaw Mission of the American Board of Commissioners for Foreign Missions," p. 176.

[54] Anna Lewis, *Chief Pushmataha: American Patriot* (New York: Exposition Press, 1959), p. 19; Czarina C. Conlan Collection, "Notes on the Choctaws and Pushmataha," Box C43, Folder 3, Western History Collection, University of Oklahoma, Norman, Oklahoma.

[55] *Bishinik*, 1980, November 1987, November 1992; Arrell Morgan Gibson, "America's Exiles," *The Chronicles of Oklahoma* LIV (Spring, 1976), p. 4.

[56] *Bishinik*, November 1987; Kenny and Clyda Franks, "Thomas L. McKenney's Portraits of Oklahoma Indians," *Oklahoma* 4 (Spring/Summer, 1999), p. 16.

[57] *Washington Gazette*, January 22, 1825; Draper Collection, Frontier War Papers, "Indian Biography: Pushmataha," Mss. U10, 6 reels, Western History Collection, University of Oklahoma, Norman; Conlan Collection, Notes on Choctaws, Box C43, Folder 3, University of Oklahoma, Norman.

[58] *Bishinik*, February 1979, March 1979, August 1993; Maxine W. Barker, *The Third Arrow: A Story of Moshulatubbee, Choctaw Chief* (Carrollton, Miss.: Pioneer Publishing Company, 1997), p. 46; Pipkin, "My Choctaw Kinfolks,"p. m-1.

[59] *Bishinik*, October 1987.

IV. Chapta Ushta The Trail of Tears

[60] *Bishinik*, October 1978; Arthur H. DeRosier, Jr., "Negotiations for The Removal of the Choctaw: U.S. Policies of 1820 and 1830," *The Chronicles of Oklahoma* XXXVIII (Spring, 1960), p. 86; Samuel J. Wells, "Rum, Skins, and Powder: A Choctaw Interpreter and the Treaty of Mount Dexter," *The Chronicles of Oklahoma* LXI (Winter, 1983-84), p. 427.

[61] H. Glenn Jordan, "Choctaw Colonization in Oklahoma," in Arrell Morgan Gibson (ed.), *America's Exiles: Indian Colonization in Oklahoma* (Oklahoma City, Ok:

Oklahoma Historical Society, 1976), p. 17; Ed Bearss and Arrell M. Gibson, *Fort Smith* (Norman: University of Oklahoma Press, 1969), p. 43; Rex W. Strickland, "Miller County, Arkansas Territory, The Frontier That Men Forgot," *The Chronicles of Oklahoma* XVIII (March 1940), p. 34; Rex W. Strickland, "Establishment of "Old" Miller County, Arkansas Territory," *The Chronicles of Oklahoma* XVIII (June 1940), p. 157; Rex W. Strickland, "Miller County, Arkansas Territory: The Frontier that Men Forgot, Chapter III," *The Chronicles of Oklahoma* XIX (March 1941), p. 37; James Taylor Carson, *Searching for The Bright Path: The Mississippi Choctaws From Prehistory to Removal* (Lincoln: University of Nebraska Press, 1999), p. 89; Duane Gage, "Oklahoma: A Resettlement Area for Indians," *The Chronicles of Oklahoma* XLVII (Autumn, 1969), p. 290.

[62] Jerry G. Hayes, "Liquor in the Indian Territory," Th*e Chronicles of Oklahoma* LXIX (Fall, 1991), p. 298; Grant Foreman, *Indian and Pioneers: The Story of the American Southwest Before 1830* (Norman: University of Oklahoma Press, 1936), p. 157; Elmo Howell, "President Jackson and William Faulkner's Choctaws," *The Chronicles of Oklahoma* XLV (Autumn, 1967), p. 255.

[63] Charles J. Kappler, *Laws and Treaties*, II, Treaty of 1825.

[64] Angie Debo, *A History of the Indians of the United States*, p. 113; *Bishinik*, October 1978.

[65] John Bartlett Meserve, "The Indian Removal Message of President Jackson," *The Chronicles of Oklahoma*, XIII (March 1935), p. 65; Rex Syndergarrd, "The Final Move of the Choctaws," *The Chronicles of Oklahoma* LII (Summer, 1974), p. 214; Duane Gage, "Oklahoma: A Resettlement Area for Indians," p. 293.

[66] Meserve, "The Indian Removal Message of President Jackson," p. 66; *Bishinik*, October 1987; Sarah Sue Goldsmith, "Choctaw, Like Most Eastern Tribes, Had Little Control Over Own Destiny," *Advocate Magazine*, (Baton Rouge, La.), June 2, 1996; Ronald N. Satz, *American Indian Policy in the Jacksonian Era* (Lincoln: University of Nebraska Press, 1975), p. 6; Francis Paul Prucha, *American Indian Policy in the Formative Years: The Indian Trade and Intercourse Acts 1790-1834* (Lincoln: University of Nebraska Press, 1962).

[67] *Bishinik*, October 1978; Arthur H. DeRosier, Jr., *The Removal of the Choctaw Indians* (New York: Harper and Row, Publishers, 1970), p. 114.

[68] Daniels, Th*e Devil's Backbone: The Story of the Natchez Trace*, p. 227; DeRosier, *The Removal of the Choctaw Indians*, p. 124; Czarina C. Conlan, "Site of Dancing Rabbit Creek Preserved," *The Chronicles of Oklahoma* VII (Sept., 1929), p. 323.

[69] Grant Foreman, "A Century of Prohibition," *The Chronicles of Oklahoma* XII (June 1934), p. 135; Peterson, *A Choctaw Source Book*, p.157; H. Glenn Jordan, "Choctaw Colonization in Oklahoma," *The Chronicles of Oklahoma* LIV (Spring, 1976), p. 22.

[70] Kappler, *Laws and Treaties*, II, Treaty of Dancing Rabbit Creek; DeRosier, *The Removal of the Choctaw*, p. 128; Edward Davis, "The Mississippi Choctaws," *The Chronicles of Oklahoma*, X (June 1932), p. 57.

[71] DeRosier, *The Removal of the Choctaw*, p. 147; Gibson, (ed.), *America's Exiles*, p. 27; Grant Foreman, *The Removal: The Emigration of the Five Civilized Tribes of Indians* (Norman: University of Oklahoma Press, 1932), p. 96; Grant Foreman, *The Five Civilized Tribes* (Norman: University of Oklahoma Press, 1934), p. 24; Muriel H. Wright, "The Removal of the Choctaws to The Indian Territory," *The Chronicles of Oklahoma* VI (June 1928), p. 126; Peter Farb, *Man's Rise to Civilization As Shown by The Indians of North America From Primeval Time to The Coming of The Industrial State* (New York: E. P. Dutton & Co., Inc., 1968), p. 253; Peter Nabokov, *Native American Testimony* (New York: Viking Penguin, USA, Inc., 1978), p. 151; Arrell Morgan Gibson, "America's Exiles," *The Chronicles of Oklahoma* LIV (Spring, 1976), p. 10; *Bishinik*, April 1999; Henry E. Fritz, "Humanitarian Rhetoric and Andrew Jackson's Indian Removal Policy," *The Chronicles of Oklahoma* LXXIX (Spring, 2001), p. 62; Betty C. Wiltshire, *Register of Choctaw Emigrants to the West* (Carrollton, Ms.: Olde Times Publishing Co., 1993), p. 3; *Arkansas Gazette*, February 9, 1831, November 28, 1831, December 14, 1831; Arkansa*s Advocate*, December 7, 1831; Alexis de Tocqueville, *Democracy in America*, ed. by J. P. Mayer, trans. By George Lawrence (Garden City, N. Y.: Anchor Books, 1969), p. 324.

[72] DeRosier, *The Removal of the Choctaw*, p. 158; Peter E. Beau to Lewis Cass, Feb. 27, 1833, Choctaw Agency, 1824-1833, Letters Received, MSS, Records of the Bureau of Indian Affairs, National Archives; Gibson, (ed.), *America' Exiles*, p. 30; *Bishinik*, December 1987, March 1995; *Arkansas Gazette*, November 14, 1832, November 21, 1832, November 28, 1832, January 9, 1833; Philip A. and Beatrice J. Kalisch, "Indian Territory Forts: Charnel Houses of the Frontier, 1839-1865," *The Chronicles of Oklahoma* L (Spring, 1972), p. 75.

[73] DeRosier, *The Removal of the Choctaw*, p.163; *Arkansas Gazette*, May 22, 1833, July 3, 1833, October 16, 1833; Dorothy Arnote West, *Pushmataha County: The Early Years* (Antlers, Ok: Dorothy Arnote West, 2002), p. 10.

[74] Michael Kelleher, "The Removal of the Southeastern Indians: Historians Respond to the 1960s and the Trail of Tears," *The Chronicles of Oklahoma* LXXVIII (Fall, 2000), p. 351; *Arkansas Gazette*, November 13, 1833.

[75] Gibson, (ed.), *America's Exiles*, p. 31; *Bishinik*, November 1987; Michael F. Doran, "Population Statistics of Nineteenth Century Indian Territory," *The Chronicles of Oklahoma* LIII (Winter, 1975-76), p. 498; Mary Elizabeth Young, *Redskins, Ruffleshirts, and Rednecks* (Norman: University of Oklahoma Press, 1961), p. 51; Grant Foreman, (ed.), *A Traveler in Indian Territory: The Journal of Ethan Allen Hitchcock, late Major General in the United States Army* (Cedar Rapids: The Torch Press, 1934), p. 11.

[76] Samuel J. Wells and Roseanna Tubby, *After Removal: The Choctaw in Mississippi*, p. 24.

[77] Wright, "The Removal of the Choctaws to Indian Territory," p. 124; James E. Winston, "The Lost Commission: A Study in Mississippi History," *The Mississippi Valley Historical Review* V (Sept., 1918), p. 184; *Arkansas Gazette*, May 9, 1838.

V. Chapta Tahlapi   Educate! Or we perish!

[78] Milton D. Rafferty and John C. Catau, *The Ouachita Mountains* (Norman: University of Oklahoma Press, 1991), p. 21; Anna Lewis, "Nunih Waiya," p. 219; Morrison, "The Choctaw Mission of the American Board of Commissioners for Foreign Missions," p. 180; *Bishinik*, August 1997; Kiamichi is a French word for a species of bird known as the horned screamer.

[79] Peter James Hudson, "A Story of Choctaw Chiefs," *The Chronicles of Oklahoma* XVII (March 1929), p. 8-16.

[80] Grant Foreman, *The Five Civilized Tribes*, p. 26; Grant Foreman, *Advancing the Frontier* (Norman: University of Oklahoma Press, 1933), p. 127; Gaston L. Litton, "The Negotiations Leading To The Chickasaw-Choctaw Agreement, January 17, 1837," *The Chronicles of Oklahoma* XVII (December 1939), p. 419; W. C. Riggs, "Bits of Interesting History," *The Chronicles of Oklahoma* VII (March 1929), p. 148; Arrell M. Gibson, *The Chickasaws* (Norman: University of Oklahoma Press, 1971), p. 222; Muriel H. Wright, "Brief Outline of the Choctaws and the Chickasaw Nations in the Indian Territory," *The Chronicles of Oklahoma* VII (December 1929), p. 398; William Omer Foster, "The Career of Montfort Stokes in Oklahoma," *The Chronicles of Oklahoma* XVIII (March 1940), p. 38; Brad Agnew, "The Dodge-Leavenworth Expedition of 1834," *The Chronicles of Oklahoma* LIII (Fall, 1975), p. 376; Carl L. Davis and LeRoy H. Fischer, "Dragoon Life In Indian Territory, 1833-1846," *The Chronicles of Oklahoma* XLVIII (Spring, 1970), p. 15; David La Vere, *Contrary Neighbors: Southern Plains Removed Indians in Indian Territory* (Norman: University of Oklahoma Press, 2000), p. 78.

[81] Samuel Y. Allgood, "Historic Spots and Actions In the Washita Valley Up to 1870," *The Chronicles of Oklahoma* V (June 1927), p. 228; W. B. Morrison, "Fort Washita," *The Chronicles of Oklahoma* V (June 1927), p. 252; W. B. Morrison, "A Visit To Old Fort Washita," *The Chronicles of Oklahoma* VII (June 1929), p. 175; James D. Morrison, "Travis G. Wright and the Leavenworth Expedition," *The Chronicles of Oklahoma* XXV (Spring, 1947), p. 7; George H. Shirk, "Mail Call at Fort Washita," *The Chronicles of Oklahoma* XXXIII (Spring, 1955), p. 116.

[82] G.A. Crossett, "A Vanishing Race," *The Chronicles of Oklahoma* IV (June 1926), p. 104- 08; Laura Baum Graebner, "Agriculture Among The Five Civilized Tribes, 1840-1906," *Red River Valley Historical Review III* (Winter, 1978), p. 46; Muriel H. Wright, "American Corn Dishes," *The Chronicles of Oklahoma* XXXVI (Summer, 1958), p. 160.

[83] Muriel H. Wright, "Old Boggy Depot," *The Chronicles of Oklahoma* V (March 1927), p. 4; Angie Debo, "The Choctaw People Before 1865," p. 10, in Walter Scott Ferguson Collection, Box 47, Folder 4, Western History Collection, University of Oklahoma, Norman; W. B. Morrison, "The Saga of Skullyville," *The Chronicles of Oklahoma* XVI (June 1938), p.237; Muriel H. Wright, "Tewah Hokay," *The Chronicles of Oklahoma* XXXIII (Winter, 1955), p. 43; Walter N. Vernon, "Methodist Pioneers Along the Great Bend of Red River," *Red River Valley Historical Review* VI (Winter, 1981), p. 53; Foreman, (ed.), *A Traveler in Indian Territory: The Journal of Ethan Allen Hitchcock,* 1934), p. 186; Marcia Haag and Henry Willis, *Choctaw Language & Culture: Chahta Anumpa* (Norman: University of Oklahoma Press, 2001), p. 310.

[84] Edward C. Shoemaker, "Fort Towson: An Early Communications Route to Oklahoma," *Red River Valley Historical Review* VII (Summer, 1982), p. 25; Henry C. Benson, "Life Among the Choctaw Indians," *The Chronicles of Oklahoma* IV (June 1926), p. 158; Carolyn Thomas Foreman, "Report of Captain John Stuart on the Construction of the Road From Fort Smith to Horse Prairie on Red River," *The Chronicles of Oklahoma* V (September 1927), p. 334; William P. Corbett, "Rifles and Ruts: Army Road Builders in Indian Territory," *The Chronicles of Oklahoma* LX (Fall, 1982), p. 300; Marlynn Ann Fleck-O'Keefe, *Fort Towson Indian Territory: A Link to the West (*Fort Towson: Lakeside Publications, 1997), p. 58.

[85] W. B. Morrison, "Fort Towson," *The Chronicles of Oklahoma* VIII (March 1930), p. 227.

[86] Jerry G. Hayes, "Liquor in the Indian Territory," *The Chronicles of Oklahoma* LXIX (Fall, 1991), p. 302; Marcia Haag and Henry Willis, *Choctaw Language & Culture*, p. 313.

[87] Muriel H. Wright, "Early River Navigation in Oklahoma," *The Chronicles of Oklahoma* VIII (March 1930), p. 82; Theda Perdue, *Nations Remembered: An Oral History of the Chickasaw, Choctaws, Creeks, and Seminoles in Oklahoma, 1865-1907* (Norman: University of Oklahoma Press, 1993), p. 45; James D. Morrison, (ed.), "Notes From The Northern Standard, 1842-1849," *The Chronicles of Oklahoma* XIX (September 1941), p. 273; Grant Foreman, "Notes From the Indian Advocate," *The Chronicles of Oklahoma* XIV (March 1936), p. 71; Phil D. Brewer, "Rev. Willis F. Folsom, A Biographical Sketch with Excerpts from His Diary," p. 59; Colonel Charles DeMorse, "Indians For The Confederacy," *The Chronicles of Oklahoma* L (Winter, 1972-73), p. 478; *Bishinik*, April 1979.

[88] Carolyn Thomas Foreman, "Journal of a Tour in the Indian Territory," *The Chronicles of Oklahoma* X (June 1932), p. 219; Emma Estill Harbour, "A Brief History of the Red River Country since 1803," *The Chronicles of Oklahoma* XVI (March 1938), p. 79; Norman W. Caldwell, "The Red River Raft," *The Chronicles of Oklahoma* XIX (September 1941), p. 259.

[89] *Foreman, The Five Civilized Tribes*, p. 57; Evelyn Crady Adams, "Kentucky's Choctaw Academy, 1819-1842: A Commercial Enterprise," *The Filson Club History Quarterly* XXVI (1952), p. 35; Alice Read Rouse, "Colonel Dick Johnson's Choctaw Academy: A Forgotten Educational Experiment," *Ohio Archeological and Historical Quarterly* XXV (January 1916), p. 88.

[90] James D. Morrison, "Schools for the Choctaws," Durant, Oklahoma: Choctaw Bilingual Program, 1975; Baird, *Peter Pitchlynn: Chief of the Choctaws*, p. 61; W. David Baird, "Peter Pitchlynn and the Reconstruction of the Choctaw Republic, 1834-1850," in H. Glenn Jordan and Thomas M. Holm, (eds.) *Indian Leaders: Oklahoma's First Statesmen* (Oklahoma City: Oklahoma Historical Society, 1979), p. 20; Nabokov, *Native American Testimony*, p. 215; Gary C. Stein, "Indian Removal As Seen By European Travelers," *The Chronicles of Oklahoma* LI (Winter, 1973-74), p. 406; Thomas Brown, "The Miscegenation of Richard Mentor Johnson as an Issue in the National Election Campaign of 1835-1836," *Civil War History* 39 (March 1993), p. 6.

[91] Benson, "Life Among the Choctaw," p. 159.

[92] Britt Willis, "Personal Reminiscence of the Days of Indian Territory by Britt Willis," Czarina Conlan Collection, M928, C43-F3, Western History Collection, University of Oklahoma, Norman; *The Daily Oklahoman*, Dec. 29, 1999; W. David Baird, "Spencer Academy, Choctaw Nation," *The Chronicles of Oklahoma* XLV (Spring, 1967), p. 43; Allen Wright, "Wheelock Seminary," *The Chronicles of Oklahoma* I (Oct., 1921), p. 120; Morrison, "Schools For the Choctaws," p. 165; J. Y. Bryce, "About Some of Our First Schools in Choctaw Nation," The *Chronicles of Oklahoma* VI (September 1928), p. 358; Henry C. Benson, *Life Between the Choctaw Indians and Sketches of*

the Southwest (New York: Johnson Reprint Corporation, 1970), p. 193; Allen Wright, "Wheelock Seminary," *The Chronicles of Oklahoma* I (January 1921), p. 118; Emma Ervin Christian, "Memories of My Childhood Days In the Choctaw Nation," p. 157; Carolyn Thomas Foreman, "New Hope Seminary," *The Chronicles of Oklahoma* XXII (Autumn, 1944), p. 299; Lona Eaton Miller, "Wheelock Mission," *The Chronicles of Oklahoma* XXIX (Autumn, 1951), p. 319; Keith L. Bryant, Jr., "The Choctaw Nation in 1843: A Missionary's View," *The Chronicles of Oklahoma* XLIV (Autumn, 1966), p. 319; Justin D. Murphy, "Wheelock Female Seminary, 1842-1861," *The Chronicles of Oklahoma* LXIX (Spring, 1991), p. 59; Christopher J. Huggard, "Culture Mixing: Everyday Life on Missions Among the Choctaws," *The Chronicles of Oklahoma* LXX (Winter, 1992-93), p. 444; H. Glenn Jordan and Thomas M. Holm, (eds.), *Indian Leaders: Oklahoma's First Statesmen*, p. 21.

[93] Morrison, "Schools For the Choctaws," p. 224; Vaughn, "Job's Legacy," p. 18; Peter Hudson, "Recollections of Peter Hudson," *The Chronicles of Oklahoma* X (December 1932), p. 504; Anna Lewis, (ed.), "Letters Regarding Choctaw Missions and Missionaries," *The Chronicles of Oklahoma* XVII (September 1939), p. 284; Louis Coleman, "Twenty-five Days to the Choctaw Nation," *The Chronicles of Oklahoma* LXIX (Winter, 1986-87), p. 10; Coleman, *Cyrus Byington*, p. 69.

[94] Morrison, "Schools for the Choctaws," p. 242; W.B. Morrison, "Old Philadelphia Baptist Church," *The Chronicles of Oklahoma* XIII (September 1935), p. 266.

[95] Susan J. Carr, "Bloomfield Academy and Its Founder," *The Chronicles of Oklahoma* II (December 1924), p. 368.

[96] Morrison, "Schools for the Choctaws," p. 335.

[97] Rev. William Graham, A.M., "Lost Among the Choctaws During a Tour of the Indian Territory, 1845," *The Chronicles of Oklahoma* L (Summer, 1972), p. 229; Donald L. Parman, "Wholly Occupied With My Special Work: Reverend William Graham's Stay at Fort Coffee and New Hope, 1845-1847," *The Chronicles of Oklahoma* LXXVI (Fall, 1998), p. 265.

VI. Chapta Hannali Roads of Recovery

[98] Ben Collins Pickett, "William L. McClellan, Choctaw Agent, West," *The Chronicles of Oklahoma* XXXIX (Spring, 1961), p. 47.

[99] Cheryl Haun Morris, "Choctaw and Chickasaw Indian Agents, 1831-1874," *The Chronicles of Oklahoma* L (Winter, 1972-73), p. 428; LeRoy H. Fischer, "United States Indian Agents to The Five Civilized Tribes," *The Chronicles of Oklahoma* L (Winter, 1972-73), p. 411.

[100] Frank E. Parke and J. W. LeFlore, "Some of Our Choctaw Neighborhood Schools," *The Chronicles of Oklahoma* IV (June 1926), p. 152; Ethel McMillan, "Women Teachers in Oklahoma, 1820-1860," *The Chronicles of Oklahoma* XXVII (Spring, 1949), p. 12; William H. Hiemstra, "Presbyterian Mission Schools Among the Choctaws and Chickasaws, 1845-1861," *The Chronicles of Oklahoma* XXVII (Spring, 1949), p. 35; Muriel H. Wright, "Tryphena," *The Chronicles of Oklahoma* IX (June 1931), p. 183.

[101] Muriel H. Wright, "Brief Outline of the Choctaw and the Chickasaw Nations in the Indian Territory, 1820-1860," p. 409; Muriel H. Wright, *A Guide to the Indian Tribes of Oklahoma* (Norman: University of Oklahoma Press, 1951), p. 108.

[102] W. David Baird, *The Choctaw People* (Phoenix: Indian Tribal Series, 1973), p. 49.

[103] *Bishinik*, February 1998; Muriel H. Wright, "Official Seals of the Five Civilized Tribes," *The Chronicles of Oklahoma* XVIII (Sept. 1940), 369; Muriel H. Wright, "The Great Seal of the Choctaw Nation," *The Chronicles of Oklahoma* XXXIII (Winter, 1955), p. 431; Muriel H. Wright, "Seals of the Five Civilized Tribes," *The Chronicles of Oklahoma* XL (Autumn, 1962), p. 217; Lu Celia Wise, *Indian Cultures of Oklahoma* (Oklahoma City: State Department of Education, 1978), p. 70.

[104] Foreman, *The Five Civilized Tribes*, p. 76; Grant Foreman, *The Last Trek of the Indians* (Chicago: The University of Chicago Press, 1945), p. 319; Douglas Summers Brown, *The Catawba Indians: The People of the River* (Columbia: University of South Carolina Press, 1966), p. 319.

[105] Archie P. McDonald, "The Texas Road," *Red River Valley Historical Review* VI (Summer, 1981), p.57; Muriel H. Wright, "Historic Places on the Old Stage Line from Fort Smith to Red River," *The Chronicles of Oklahoma* XI (June 1933), p. 801.

[106] O. B. Jacobson and Jeanne d'Ucel, "Early Oklahoma Artists," *The Chronicles of Oklahoma* XXXI (Summer, 1953), p. 129; Francis R. Stoddard, "Amiel Weeks Whipple," *The Chronicles of Oklahoma* XXVIII (Autumn, 1950), p. 229; Muriel H. Wright and George H. Shirk, "The Journal of Lieutenant A.W. Whipple," *The Chronicles of Oklahoma* XXVIII (Autumn, 1950), p. 239; Muriel H. Wright and George H. Shirk, "Artist Mollhausen in Oklahoma, 1853," *The Chronicles of Oklahoma* XXXI (Winter, 1953-54), p. 400.

[107] David E. Conrad, "Whipple's Pacific Railroad Survey in The Indian Territory," *Red River Valley Historical Review* (Winter, 1974), p. 398; Lona Shawner, "Stanley Explores Oklahoma," *The Chronicles of Oklahoma* XXII (Autumn, 1944), p. 261; Gary C. Stein, "A Fearful Drunkenness: The Liquor Trade to the Western Indians as Seen

by European Travellers in America, 1800-1860," *Red River Valley Historical Review* I (Summer, 1974), p. 117.

[108] Norman Arthur Graebner, "Pioneer Indian Agriculture in Oklahoma," *The Chronicles of Oklahoma* XXIII (Autumn, 1945), p. 248.

[109] Wright, "Historic Places on the Old Stage Line From Fort Smith to the Red River," p. 804; J. H. Crosby, "The Butterfield Overland and Pony Express," *Prairie Lore* 13 (July 1976), p. 43; James C. Milligan, *Oklahoma* (Durant, Oklahoma: Mesa Publishing, 1985), p.117; Vernon H. Brown, "Committee Report Butterfield Overland Mail," *The Chronicles of Oklahoma* XXXVI (Winter, 1958-59), p. 447; Grant Foreman, "The California Overland Mail Route Through Oklahoma," *The Chronicles of Oklahoma* IX (September 1931), p. 312; Vernon H. Brown, "American Airlines Along the Butterfield Mail Route," *The Chronicles of Oklahoma* XXXIII (Spring, 1955), p. 10; Muriel H. Wright, "The Butterfield Overland Mail One Hundred Years Ago," *The Chronicles of Oklahoma* XXXV (Spring, 1957), p. 65; Susan Peterson, "The Butterfield Overland Mail in Indian Territory, 1858-1861," *Red River Valley Historical Review* VI (Summer, 1981), p. 77; Thomas J. Bond to Peter Pitchlynn, Sept. 18,1858, Peter P. Pitchlynn Collection Western History Collection, Box 3, Folder 33, University of Oklahoma, Norman; Betty Jeanne Ward Poulin, *Choctaw Heritage* (Heavener, Ok.: Choctaw Heritage, 1981), p. 21.

[110] James D. Morrison, "News for the Choctaws," *The Chronicles of Oklahoma* XXVII (Summer, 1949), p. 213; *The Durant Daily Democrat*, July 23, 2001.

[111] Bobby L. Blackburn, "Oklahoma Law Enforcement Since 1803," Doctor of Philosophy Dissertation, Oklahoma State University, Stillwater, Ok, 1976, p. 46; W. A. Carter, *McCurtain County and Southeast Oklahoma: History, Biography Statistics* (Idabel, Ok: Tribune Publishing, 19230, p. 274.

[112] Jerry G. Hayes, "Ardent Spirits Among the Chickasaws and Choctaws, 1816-1856," *The Chronicles of Oklahoma* LXIX (Fall, 1991), p. 300; Carolyn Thomas Foreman, "The Light-Horse In the Indian Territory," *The Chronicles of Oklahoma* XXXIV (Spring, 1956), p. 27; Arthur T. Burton, *Black, Red and Deadly: Black and Indian Gunfighters of the Indian Territory* (Austin: Eakin Press, 1991), p. 127.

[113] Oliver Knight, "Fifty Years of Choctaw Law," *The Chronicles of Oklahoma* XXXI (Spring, 1953)), p. 83; W. Julian Fessler, "The Work of the Early Choctaw Legislature," *The Chronicles of Oklahoma* VI (March 1928), p. 61.

VII. Chapta Untuklo Many Have Been Slain; Few Have Been Saved

[114] Carolyn Thomas Foreman, *Oklahoma Imprints, 1835-1907* (Norman: University of Oklahoma Press, 1936), p. 40; Edward L. Byrd, Jr., "The Old South As A Modern

Myth," *Red River Valley Historical Review* I (Spring, 1974), p. 60; Monroe Billington, "Black Slavery in Indian Territory: The Ex-Slave Narratives," *The Chronicles of Oklahoma* LX (Spring, 1962), p. 64.

[115] Anna Lewis, "Diary of a Missionary to the Choctaws, 1860-1861," *The Chronicles of Oklahoma* XVII (December 1939), p. 430; C. Calvin Smith, "The Oppressed Oppressors: Negro Slavery Among the Choctaw Indians of Oklahoma," *Red River Valley Historical Review* II (Summer, 1975), p. 249; James D. Morrison, "Note on Abolitionism in the Choctaw Nation," *The Chronicles of Oklahoma* XXXVIII (Spring, 1960), p. 79.

[116] Jubal B. Hancock to Peter P. Pitchlynn, Sept. 16, 1860, Peter P. Pitchlynn Collection, Box 3, Folder 82.

[117] Michael L. Bruce, "Our Best Men Are Fast Leaving Us: The Life and Times of Robert M. Jones," *The Chronicles of Oklahoma* LXVI (Fall, 1988), p. 296; Milton D. Rafferty and John C. Catau, *The Ouachita Mountains*, p. 23; Ohland Morton, "Confederate Government Relations With The Five Civilized Tribes," *The Chronicles of Oklahoma* XXXI (Summer, 1953), p. 200; T. Paul Wilson, "Delegates of the Five Civilized Tribes to the Confederate Congress," *The Chronicles of Oklahoma* LIII (Fall, 1975), p. 364; LeRoy H. Fischer, "A Civil War Experience of Some Arkansas Women in Indian Territory by Francena Lavinia (Martin) Sutton," *The Chronicles of Oklahoma* LVII (Summer, 1979), p. 162.

[118] James D. Morrison, "Problems In the Industrial Progress and Development of the Choctaw Nation, 1865-1907," *The Chronicles of Oklahoma* XXXII (Spring, 1954), p. 71.

[119] Prince to A. Montgomery, June 7, 1860, William Hemsley Emory Papers, Western Americana Collection, Beinecke Rare Book and Manuscript Library, Yale University, New Haven; Prince to D.B. Sackett, April 3, 1861, Emory Papers; Samuel Y. Allgood, "Historic Spots and Actions In The Washita Valley Up to 1870," p. 228; James C. Milligan and L. David Norris, "William H. Emory and Fort Arbuckle," *The Chronicles of Oklahoma* LXIX (Fall, 1991), p. 280; L. David Norris, James C. Milligan, and Odie B. Faulk, *William H. Emory: Soldier, Scientist* (Tucson: The University of Arizona Press, 1998), p. 203; W. B. Morrison, "A Visit to Old Fort Washita," p. 177.

[120] Muriel H. Wright, "General Douglas H. Cooper, C.S.A.," *The Chronicles of Oklahoma* XXXII (Summer, 1954), p. 156.

[121] Smith, "Oppressed Oppressors," p. 253; Dean Trickett, "The Civil War In The Indian Territory," *The Chronicles of Oklahoma* XVII (September 1939), p. 316; *Official Records of the Union and Confederate Armies* (Washington: Government Printing Office, 1880-1904), Series I, I, p. 682.

[122] Albert Pike to Peter P. Pitchlynn, Aug. 30, 1859, Peter Pitchlynn Collection, Box 3, Folder 48, Western History Collection, University of Oklahoma; Kinneth McNeil, "Confederate Treaties With the Tribes of Indian Territory," *The Chronicles of Oklahoma* XLII (Winter, 1964-65), p. 409; Dean Trickett, "The Civil War In The Indian Territory, 1861," *The Chronicles of Oklahoma* XVII (December 1939), p. 401; *Congress of the Confederate States of America Journal* (Washington: Government Printing Office, 1904-05), I, p. 105; *Journal*, Series IV, I, p. 785.

[123] Robert Lipscomb Duncan, *Reluctant General: The Life and Times of Albert Pike* (New York: E.P. Dutton & Co., Inc., 1961), p. 184; Kenny A. Franks, "An Analysis of the Confederate Treaties With The Five Civilized Tribes," *The Chronicles of Oklahoma* L (Winter, 1972-73), p. 470; LeRoy H. Fischer, (ed.), *The Civil War in Indian Territory* (Los Angeles: Lorrin I. Morrison, 1974), p. 132.

[124] Whit Edwards, "Butternut and Blue: Confederate Uniforms in the Trans-Mississippi," *The Chronicles of Oklahoma* LXXIII (Winter, 1995-96), p. 433; J. S. Murrow to "Bro Hornaday," Jan. 11, 1862, Grant Foreman Collection, Box 24, Vol. 97, Gilcrease Institute, Tulsa; Fairfax Downey, "The Blue, the Gray, and the Red," *Civil War Times Illustrated* I (July 1962), p. 9; Sampson Folsom to Albert Pike, Sept. 5, 1861, Peter P. Pitchlynn Collection, Box 3, Folder 95, Western History Collection, Norman.

[125] Bell I. Wiley, "The Common Soldier of the Civil War," *Civil War Times Illustrated* XII (July 1973), p. 8.

[126] Bernice Norman Crockett, "Health Conditions In Indian Territory 1830 to the Civil War," *The Chronicles of Oklahoma* XXXV (Spring, 1957), p. 90.

[127] Frank A. Balyeat, "Joseph Samuel Murrow, Apostle To The Indians," *The Chronicles of Oklahoma* XXXV (Autumn, 1957), p. 299.

[128] Dean Trickett, "The Civil War In The Indian Territory, 1861" *The Chronicles of Oklahoma* XVIII (June 1940), p. 145; *Official Records*, Ser. I, IV, p. 99; Annie Heloise Abel, *The American Indian as Participant in the Civil War* (Cleveland: Arthur H. Clarke Co., 1919), p. 173.

[129] Angie Debo, "The Site of the Battle of Round Mountain, 1861," *The Chronicles of Oklahoma* XXVII (Summer, 1949), p. 203; Angie Debo, "The Location of the Battle of Round Mountain," *The Chronicles of Oklahoma* XLI (Spring, 1963), p. 70; Muriel H. Wright, "Civil War Report on the Battle of Round Mountain," *The Chronicles of Oklahoma* XXXIX (Winter, 1961-62), p. 354; Orpha Russell, "Ekvn-Hv'Luruce: Site of Oklahoma's First Civil War Battle," *The Chronicles of Oklahoma* XXIX

(Winter, 1951-52), p. 407; Dean Trickett, "The Civil War In The Indian Territory, 1861," *The Chronicles of Oklahoma* XVIII (Sept., 1940), p. 270; Charles Bahos, "On Opothleyahola's Trail: Locating the Battle of Round Mountain," *The Chronicles of Oklahoma* LXIII (Spring, 1985), p. 80; Peter P. Pitchlynn to Peter P. Howell, Oct. 21, 1861, Peter P. Pitchlynn Collection, Box 3, Folder 96, Western History Collection, University of Oklahoma.

[130] Edward Everett Dale and Gaston Litton, *Cherokee Cavaliers* (Norman: University of Oklahoma Press, 1939), p. 111; Laurence M. Hauptman, *Between Two Fires: American Indians in the Civil War* (New York: The Free Press, 1995), p. 47.

[131] *Official Records*, Series I, VIII, p. 27; Arthur Shoemaker, "The Battle of Chustenahlah," *The Chronicles of Oklahoma* XXXVIII (Summer, 1960), p. 181.

[132] *Douglas Hale,* "Texas Units in the Civil War," *The Chronicles of Oklahoma* LXVIII (Fall, 1990), p. 253.

[133] Douglas Hale, "Rehearsal for Civil War: The Texas Cavalry in the Indian Territory, 1861" *The Chronicles of Oklahoma* LXVIII (Fall, 1990), p. 254; Rev. W. F. Dunkle, "A Choctaw Indian's Diary," *The Chronicles of Oklahoma* IV (March 1926), p. 65.

[134] Roy A. Clifford, "The Indian Regiments in the Battle of Pea Ridge," *The Chronicles of Oklahoma* XXV (Winter, 1947-48), p. 315.

[135] Harry J. Lemley, "Letters of General McCulloch and Chief Ross in 1861," *The Chronicles of Oklahoma* XL (Autumn, 1962), p. 290; *Official Records of the Union and Confederate Armies*, (Washington: Government Printing Office, 1880-1904), Series I, Vol. VIII, p. 206; Dean Trickett, "The Civil War In The Indian Territory, 1862," *The Chronicles of Oklahoma* XIX (December 1941), p. 395; Annie Heloise Abel, *The American Indian as Participant in the Civil War* (Cleveland: The Arthur H. Clark Company, 1919), p. 30.

[136] D. Alexander Brown, "Pea Ridge: Gettysburg of the West," *Civil War Times Illustrated* VI (October 1967), p. 4.

[137] James C. Milligan, "Fort McCulloch, Indian Territory," *Red River Valley Historical Review* VII (Spring 1982), p. 26; *Official Records*, Vol. XXII, Ser. I, Pt. II, p. 925; Sampson Folsom to Peter P. Pitchlynn, June 19, 1862, Pitchlynn Collection, Box 3, Folder 103, Western History Collection, University of Oklahoma, Norman; Carolyn Thomas Foreman, "Lieutenant-General Theophilus Hunter Holmes, C.S.A., Founder of Fort Holmes," *The Chronicles of Oklahoma* (XXXV) (Winter, 1957-58), p. 431; Kenny A. Franks, "The Implementation of The Confederate Treaties With the Five Civilized Tribes," *The Chronicles of Oklahoma* LI (Spring, 1973), p. 22.

[138] Gary N. Heath, "The First Federal Invasion of Indian Territory," *The Chronicles of Oklahoma* XLIV (Winter, 1966-67), p. 419; Charles R. Freeman, "The Battle of Honey Springs," *The Chronicles of Oklahoma* XIII (June 1935), p. 155; William J. Willey, "The Second Federal Invasion of Indian Territory," *The Chronicles of Oklahoma* XLIV (Winter, 1966-67), p. 27; LeRoy H. Fischer and Jerry Gill, "Confederate Indian Forces Outside of Indian Territory," *The Chronicles of Oklahoma* XLVI (Autumn, 1968), p. 266; LeRoy Fischer, "The Honey Springs National Battlefield Park Monument," *The Chronicles of Oklahoma* XLVII (Spring, 1969), p.515; Dudley Taylor Cornish, *The Sable Arm: Negro Troops in the Union Army, 1861-1865* (New York: Longmans, Green and Co., 1956), p. 78.

[139] Alfred Wade to Peter P. Pitchlynn, Sept. 4, 1863, Pitchlynn Papers, Box 3, Folder 113, Western History Collection; Muriel H. Wright, "Notes on Perryville," *The Chronicles of Oklahoma* VIII (June 1930), p. 148; Tom Franzmann, "The Battle of Devil's Backbone Mountain," *The Chronicles of Oklahoma* LXII (Winter, 1984-85), p. 427.

[140] Fred Hood, "Twilight of the Confederacy in Indian Territory," *The Chronicles of Oklahoma* XLI (Winter, 1963-1964), p. 428.

[141] Muriel H. Wright and LeRoy H. Fischer, "Civil War Sites in Oklahoma," *The Chronicles of Oklahoma* XLIV (Summer, 1966), p. 162; Ernest F. Darling, "Lincoln's Message to Indian Territory," *The Chronicles of Oklahoma* LXIII (Summer, 1985), p. 186; Tom Franzmann, "The Final Campaign: The Confederate Offensive of 1854," *The Chronicles of Oklahoma* LXIII (Fall, 1985), p. 267; Steve Cottrell, *Civil War in the Indian Territory* (Gretna, La.: Pelican Publishing Company, Inc., 1995), p. 90.

[142] Ruth Ann Overbeck, "Colbert's Ferry," *The Chronicles of Oklahoma* LVII (Summer, 1979), p. 218; LeRoy H. Fischer and Larry C. Rampp, "Quantrill's Civil War Operations," *The Chronicles of Oklahoma* XLVI (Summer, 1968), p. 178; Albert Castel, "The Guerrilla War, 1861-1865," *Civil War Times Illustrated* XIII (October 1974), p. 29.

[143] LeRoy H. Fischer and Jerry Gill, "Confederate Indian Forces Outside of Indian Territory," p. 281.

[144] Larry C. Rampp, "Negro Troop Activity In Indian Territory, 1863-65," *The Chronicles of Oklahoma* XLVII (Spring, 1969), p. 550; Keun Sang Lee, "The Capture of the J.R. Williams," *The Chronicles of Oklahoma* LX (Spring, 1982), p. 31.

[145] LeRoy H. Fischer and William L. McMurry, "Confederate Refugees From Indian Territory," *The Chronicles of Oklahoma* LVII (Winter, 1979-1980), p. 458; Allan C. Ashcraft, "Confederate Indian Department Conditions in August 1864," *The Chronicles*

of Oklahoma XLI (Autumn, 1963), p. 279; Czarina C. Conlan, "Peter P. Pitchlynn: Chief of the Choctaws," *The Chronicles of Oklahoma* VI (June 1928), p. 224; Mary Jane Warde, "Now the Wolf Has Come: The Civilian Civil War In The Indian Territory," *The Chronicles of Oklahoma* LXXI (Spring, 1993), p. 79.

[146] Martha Royce Blaine, "A Brief Excursion Into Journalism: The Choctaw and Chickasaw Observer, Formerly the Ft. Gibson Appeal or the Indian Courier," *The Chronicles of Oklahoma* LI (Winter, 1973-74), p. 411.

[147] Allan C. Ashcraft, "Confederate Indian Troop Conditions In 1864," *The Chronicles of Oklahoma* LXI (Winter, 1963-64), p. 442.

[148] James F. Morgan, "The Choctaw Warrants of 1863," *The Chronicles of Oklahoma* LVII (Spring, 1979), p. 65.

[149] George H. Shirk, "The Place of Indian Territory In The Command Structure of The Civil War," *The Chronicles of Oklahoma* XLV (Winter, 1967-68), p. 471; George H. Shirk, "Confederate Postal System in the Indian Territory," *The Chronicles of Oklahoma* XLI (Summer, 1963), p. 198; Peter P. Pitchlynn to E. Kirby Smith, May 17, 1865, Pitchlynn Papers, Box 4, Folder 19; Francis C.J. Herron to Asa G. Mathews, June 9, 1865, Pitchlynn Papers, Box 4, Folder 21; A. J. Stanton to Peter P. Pitchlynn, June 27, 1865, Pitchlynn Papers, Box 4, Folder 29.

VIII. Chapta Untuchena A Clap Of Thunder In A Clear Sky

[150] Jessie Randolph Moore, "The Five Great Indian Nations," *The Chronicles of Oklahoma* XXIX (Autumn, 1951), p. 334; Allan C. Ashcraft, "Confederate Indian Territory Conditions in 1865," *The Chronicles of Oklahoma* XLII (Winter, 1964-65), p. 426; Lewis Anthony Kensell, "Phases of Reconstruction in The Choctaw Nation, 1865-1870," *The Chronicles of Oklahoma* XLVII (Summer, 1969), p. 138; James David Morrison, "Social History of the Choctaws, 1865-1905," Doctor of Philosophy Dissertation, University of Oklahoma, Norman, Oklahoma, 1951, p. 176.

[151] David Buice, "Prelude to Fort Smith: Congress and the Five Civilized Tribes," *Red River Valley Historical Review* VII (Summer, 1982), p. 16; Annie Heloise Abel, *The American Indian Under Reconstruction* (Cleveland: The Arthur H. Clark Company, 1925), p. 173; Annie Heloise Abel, *The American Indian and the end of the Confederacy, 1863-1866* (Lincoln: University of Nebraska Press, 1993), p. 177.

[152] Baird, T*he Choctaw People*, p. 61; Muriel H. Wright, "Contributions of the Indian People to Oklahoma," *The Chronicles of Oklahoma* XIV (June 1936), p. 157; Davis D. Joyce, *An Oklahoma I Had Never Seen Before* (Norman: University of Oklahoma

Press, 1994), p. 6; Rennard Strickland, *The Indians in Oklahoma* (Norman: University of Oklahoma Press, 1980), p. 6; A. R. Durant, *Constitution and Laws of the Choctaw Nation* (Dallas: Johnson F. Worley, Printer and Publisher, 1894), p. 49.

[153] Kensell, "Phases of Reconstruction in The Choctaw Nation, 1865-1870," p. 151; Muriel H. Wright, "Old Boggy Depot," p. 11; Walt Wilson, "Freedmen in Indian Territory During Reconstruction," XLIX *The Chronicles of Oklahoma* (Summer, 1971), p. 243; Elihu B. Maytubby, "Maytubby Springs Hotel 1866 to 1907," *Bryan County Heritage Quarterly*, (November 1988), p. 9.

[154] Arrell M. Gibson, "The Cowboy in Indian Territory," *Red River Valley Historical Review* II (Spring, 1975), p. 153; Perry Case, "The Long Drive," *American Heritage* XI (April 1960), p. 73; Peter Iverson, *When Indians Became Cowboys: Native Peoples and Cattle Ranching in the American West* (Norman: University of Oklahoma Press, 1994), p. 69; Donovan L. Hofsommer, "Bawling Cattle and Barking Brakemen: An Oklahoma Railroad Memory," *The Chronicles of Oklahoma* LIV (Fall, 1976), p. 360.

[155] *Caddo Herald*, Dec. 14, 1903; The *Sherman Daily Democrat*, February 14, 1928; J. B. Wright, "Ranching in The Choctaw and Chickasaw Nations," The *Chronicles of Oklahoma* XXXIII (Autumn, 1959), p. 296; *Bishinik*, December 1995; Dorothy Arnote West, P*ushmataha County: The Early Years*, p.132.

[156] James D. Morrison, "Problems in The Industrial Progress and Development of the Choctaw Nation, 1865 to 1907," *The Chronicles of Oklahoma* XXXII (Spring, 1954), p. 75: Laura Baum Graebner, "Agriculture among the Five Civilized Tribes," p. 52; Norman Arthur Graebner, "Cattle Ranching in Eastern Oklahoma," *The Chronicles of Oklahoma* XXI (1943), p. 308.

[157] James D. Morrison, *The Social History of the Choctaw Nation: 1865-1907* Ed. by James C. Milligan and L. David Norris, (Durant: Choctaw Nation of Oklahoma, 1987), p. 93.

[158] W. B. Morrison, "Colbert Ferry on Red River, Chickasaw Nation, Indian Territory," *The Chronicles of Oklahoma* XVI (Sept., 1938), p. 310; James D. Morrison, "The Union Pacific, Southern Branch," *The Chronicles of Oklahoma* XIV (June 1936), p. 186; *Historic Denison*, Denison, Texas, Jan. 1, Feb. 15, 1929; Walter A. Johnson, "Brief History of the Missouri-Kansas-Texas Railroad Lines," *The Chronicles of Oklahoma* XXIV (Autumn, 1946*), P. 343;* Nancy Hope Self*, "The Building of the Railroads in the Cherokee Nation," The Chronicles of Oklahoma* XLIX (Summer, 1971), p. 192; David Bowden, "Toll Roads and Railroads: A Case of Economic Conflict in the Choctaw Nation, 1870-1876," *The Chronicles of Oklahoma* LXXIV (Winter, 1996-

97), p. 385; *The Sterrett Sun*, April 13, 1906; V.V. Masterson, *The Katy Railroad and The Last Fronti*er (Norman: University of Oklahoma Press, 1952), p. 166; Donovan L. Hofsommer (ed.), *Railroads in Oklahoma* (Oklahoma City: Oklahoma Historical Society, 1977), p. 5; Durant, *Footsteps of the Choctaws*, p. 1-23; Henry MacCreary, *A Story of Durant: Queen of Three Valleys* (Durant: The Democrat Printing Company, 1946), p. 9.

[159] Craig Mener, "The Struggle for An East-West Railway Into the Indian Territory, 1870-1882," *The Chronicles of Oklahoma* XLVII (Spring, 1969), p. 577; W. Edwin Derrick and James Smallwood, "Miles of Track: The Coming of Railroads to Oklahoma," *Red River Valley Historical Review* VI (Summer, 1981), p. 89.

[160] H. Wayne Morgan and Anne Hodges Morgan, *Oklahoma* (New York: W. W. Norton & Co., 1977), p. 151.

[161] Paul Nesbitt, "J. J. McAlester," *The Chronicles of Oklahoma* XI (June 1933), p. 763; Michael J. Hightower, "Cattle, Coal, and Indian Land," *The Chronicles of Oklahoma* LXII (Spring, 1984), p. 9.

[162] Lonnie E. Underhill and Daniel F. Littlefield, Jr., "Wild Turkeys in Oklahoma," *The Chronicles of Oklahoma* XLVIII (Winter, 1970-71), p. 385; *The Atoka Vindicator*, Nov. 24, 1875; Daniel F. Littlefield, Jr., "Roost Robbers" and "Netters:" Pigeoners in The Indian Territory," *The Chronicles of Oklahoma* XLVII (Summer, 1969), p.158; Morrison, *The Social History of the Choctaw Nation*, p. 59; *Bishinik*, August 1996.

[163] James Franklin Holden, "The B.I.T.: The Story of an Adventure in Railroad Building," *The Chronicles of Oklahoma* XI (March 1933), p. 656.

[164] Stanley Clark, "Immigrants in The Choctaw Coal Industry," *The Chronicles of Oklahoma* XXXIII (Winter, 1955-56), p. 450; Philip A. Kalisch, "Ordeal of the Oklahoma Coal Miners: Coal Mine Disasters in The Sooner State, 1886-1945," *The Chronicles of Oklahoma* XLVIII (Autumn, 1970), p. 340; Don F. Badinelli, "Struggle in the Choctaw Nation: The Coal Miners Strike of 1894," *The Chronicles of Oklahoma* LXXII (Fall, 1994), p. 306; Steve Sewell, "Amongst the Damp: The Dangerous Profession of Coal Mining in Oklahoma, 1870-1935," *The Chronicles of Oklahoma* 70 (Spring, 1992), p. 67.

[165] Morrison, *The Social History of the Choctaw Nation*, p. 76.

[166] Laura Baum Graebner, "Agriculture Among the Five Civilized Tribes," p. 60; Bernice Norman Crockett, "Health Conditions in The Indian Territory From the Civil War to 1890," *The Chronicles of Oklahoma XXXVI (Spring, 1958), p. 31.*

[167] James Y. Bryce, "From Reports of the Board of Indian Commissioners," *The Chronicles of Oklahoma* V (March 1927), p. 86; Kathleen Garrett, "Dartmouth Alumni in The Indian Territory," *The Chronicles of Oklahoma* XXXII (Summer, 1954), p. 137.

[168] Curtis L. Nolen, "The Okmulgee Constitution: A Step Toward Indian Self-Determination," *The Chronicles of Oklahoma* LVIII (Fall, 1980), p. 264; Francis Paul Prucha, "The Board of Indian Commissioners and The Delegates of the Five Tribes," *The Chronicles of Oklahoma* LVI (Fall, 1978), p. 261; Muriel H. Wright, "A Report to The General Council of the Indian Territory Meeting at Okmulgee in 1873," *The Chronicles of Oklahoma* XXXIV (Spring, 1956), p. 13.

[169] Mary Jane Warde, "Fight for Survival: The Indian Response to the Boomer Movement," *The Chronicles of Oklahoma* LXVII (Spring, 1989), p. 49.

[170] Baird, T*he Choctaw People*, p. 71; Baird, *Peter Pitchlynn*, p. 211.

[171] Morrison, *The Social History of the Choctaws*, p. 76.

IX. Chapta Chakkali   Progress In Religion And Education

[172] Natalie Morrison Denison, "Missions and Missionaries of the Presbyterian Church, among the Choctaws-1866-1907," *The Chronicles of Oklahoma* XXIV (Winter, 1946-47), p. 429; Coleman, *Cyrus Byington*, p. 117.

[173] *Bishinik*, January 2000; Phil D. Brewer, "Rev. Willis F. Folsom, A Biographical Sketch with Excerpts From His Diary," p. 61.

[174] Alice Hurley Mackey, "Father Murrow: Civil War Period," *The Chronicles of Oklahoma* XII (March, 1934), p. 65.

[175] J.S. Murrow to "Bro. Hornaday," Jan. 11, 1862, Grant Foreman Collection, Box 24, Vol. 97, Gilcrease Institute, Tulsa, p. 436; Raymond L. Holcomb, *Father Murrow* (Atoka: The Atoka County Historical Society, 1994), p. 20; Frank A. Balyeat, "Joseph Samuel Murrow, Apostle To The Indians," p. 300; Carolyn Thomas Foreman, *Oklahoma Imprints*, p. 137; Marie Wilson, (ed.), *Tales of Atoka County* Heritage (Atoka: The Atoka County Historical Society, 1983), p. 251.

[176] *Bishinik*, February 2001.

[177] Denison, "Missions and Missionaries," p. 446; *Bishinik*, January 1993; *Bryan County Heritage Quarterly*, (May, 1987), p. 4.

[178] *Morrison, The Social History of the Choctaws*, p. 26.

[179] Peter J. Hudson, "Temperance Meeting Among the Choctaws," *The Chronicles of Oklahoma* XII (June 1934), p. 132; Peter Hudson, "Recollections of Peter Hudson," p. 504.

[180] Todd Downing, *Cultural Traits of the Choctaws* (Durant, Oklahoma: The Choctaw Bilingual Education Program, 1973); Wilson, (ed.), *Tales of Atoka County Heritage*, p. 65.

[181] Sister Mary Urban Kehoe, "The Educational Activities of Distinguished Missionaries Among the Five Civilized Tribes," *The Chronicles of Oklahoma* XXIV (Summer, 1946), p. 179; *Muskogee Times-Democrat*, July 10, 1911; Brother John Michalicka, "First Catholic Church In Indian Territory, 1872, St. Patrick's Church at Atoka," *The Chronicles of Oklahoma* L (Winter, 1972-73), p. 485; *The Daily Oklahoman*, Feb. 24, 1946; Carolyn Thomas Foreman, "St. Agnes Academy for the Choctaws," *The Chronicles of Oklahoma* XLVIII (Autumn, 1970), p. 329; Velma Nieberding, "St. Agnes School of the Choctaws," *The Chronicles of Oklahoma* XXXIII (Summer, 1955), p.192; Rev. James D. White, "The Saga of St. Agnes," *The Kiamichi Journal* VIII (January 2002), p. 4.

[182] Morrison, *The Social History of the Choctaws*, p. 29.

[183] Joy McDougal Smith, "Alice Lee Elliott Memorial Academy: A School for Choctaw Freedmen," *The Chronicles of Oklahoma* LXXII (Fall, 1994), p. 276.

[184] Angie Debo, "Education In The Choctaw Country after the Civil War," *The Chronicles of Oklahoma* X (Sept., 1932), p. 388; R. L. Williams, "Peter James Hudson, 1861-1938," *The Chronicles of Oklahoma* XVII (March, 1939), p. 4; J. N. Kagey, "Jones Academy," *The Chronicles of Oklahoma* IV (Dec., 1926), p. 339; Lona Eaton Miller, "Wheelock Mission," p. 323; *Bishinik*, February 1992.

[185] Sammy D. Hogue, *The Goodland Indian Orphanage: A Story of Christian Missions* (Goodland, Okla.: The Goodland Indian Orphanage Publishers, 1940), p. 24; *The Daily Oklahoman*, Aug. 1, 1926; Ruby Wile, "Yakni Achukma, 'The School with a Soul,'" *The Chronicles of Oklahoma* LXXX (Winter 20002-03), p. 414.

[186] *Bishinik*, June 1993.

X. Chapta Pokkoli We Want To Preserve The Integrity Of Our Race

[187] *Bishinik*, January 1996.

[188] Benay Blend, "The Indian Rights Association, The Dawes Commission and The Five Civilized Tribes," *Red River Valley Historical Review* VI (Fall, 1981), p. 5.

[189] Gov. W. N. Jones to General Council, Oct., 1892, Dovie Jones Papers, M326, Folder 1, Western History Collection, University of Oklahoma, Norman; Loren N. Brown, "The Establishment of the Dawes Commission For Indian Territory," *The Chronicles of Oklahoma* XVIII (June 1940), p. 179; James C. Milligan and L. David Norris, "The Last Choctaw Execution," *The Chronicles of Oklahoma* LXXIII (Winter, 1995-96), p. 392; *Bishinik*, October 1996.

[190] Loren N. Brown, "The Dawes Commission," *The Chronicles of Oklahoma* IX (March 1931), p. 87.

[191] Muriel H. Wright, "A Brief Review of the Life of Doctor Eliphalet Nott Wright, 1852-1932," *The Chronicles of Oklahoma* X (June 1932), p. 280; A. D. Hefley, "A Choctaw Landmark," *The Chronicles of Oklahoma* XII (December 1934), p. 477.

[192] Kent Carter, "Tams Bixby: Doing Government Business In The Gilded Age," *The Chronicles of Oklahoma* LXXVIII (Winter, 2000-2001), p. 438.

[193] Robert L. Williams, "Tams Bixby, 1855-1922," *The Chronicles of Oklahoma* XIX (Sept., 1941), p. 211; Peter J. Hudson, "Reminiscences by Peter J. Hudson," *The Chronicles of Oklahoma* XII (Sept., 1934), p. 294; Carolyn Thomas Foreman, "The Armstrongs of Indian Territory: Part III," *The Chronicles of Oklahoma* XXXI (Spring, 1953), p. 57.

[194] Loren N. Brown, "The Appraisal of the Lands of the Choctaws and the Chickasaws By the Dawes Commission," *The Chronicles of Oklahoma* XXII (Summer, 1944), p. 191; Beard, *The Choctaw People*, p. 76; Angie Debo, *And Still the Waters Runs* (Norman: University of Oklahoma Press, 1940), p. 51.

[195] Joe C. Jackson, "Summer Normals In Indian Territory After 1898," *The Chronicles of Oklahoma* XXXVII (Autumn, 1959), p. 326.

[196] Louis Coleman, "We Are Making History: The Execution of William Going," *The Chronicles of Oklahoma* LXXVI (Spring, 1998), p. 41.

[197] James C. Milligan and L. David Norris, "A Connecticut Yankee in the Indian Territory," *The Chronicles of Oklahoma* LXVIII (Fall, 1990), p. 267; *The South McAlester News*, Dec. 24, 1903; Charles H. Sawyer, "The Choctaw Indians of Mississippi, Part I," *Twin Territories: The Indian Magazine* (June 1902), p. 160.

[198] Steven Crum, "America, Love It or Leave It: Some Native American Initiatives to Move to Mexico, 1890-1940," *The Chronicles of Oklahoma* LXXIX (Winter, 2001-02), p.416; Theda Perdue, *Nations Remembered: An Oral History of the Cherokees, Chickasaws, Choctaws, Creeks, and Seminoles in Oklahoma, 1865-1907*, p. 186.

[199] D. C. McCurtain to Editor, Feb. 8, 1900, D. C. McCurtain Collection, Box M, FF2, Western History Collection, University of Oklahoma, Norman; Milligan, "A

Connecticut Yankee in the Indian Territory," p. 270; Esther Witcher, "Territorial Magazines," *The Chronicles of Oklahoma* XXIX (Winter, 1951-51), p. 449; David I. Bushnell, Jr., The *Choctaws of Bayou Lacomb, St. Tammany Parish, Louisiana* (Washington: Government Printing Office, 1909), p. 3.

[200] Reprinted in Arrell Morgan Gibson, "The Centennial Legacy of the General Allotment Act," *The Chronicles of Oklahoma* LXV (Fall, 1987), p. 243; Lacy Pierce Bobo, "Reminiscences of Pioneer Days," *The Chronicles of Oklahoma* XXIII (Autumn, 1945), p. 282.

[201] *Report of the Select Committee to Investigate Matters Connected with Affairs in the Indian Territory* (2 vols., Washington, 1907), I, p. 962.

[202] *Indian Citizen*, Oct. 7, 1897.

[203] Mace Davis, "Chitto Harjo," *The Chronicles of Oklahoma* XIII (June 1935), p. 145; *Bishinik*, May 1979.

[204] *Caddo Herald*, January 22, 1909; Lawrence Mills, *The Lands of the Five Civilized Tribes* (St. Louis: The F. H. Thomas Law Book Company, 1919), p. 97.

[205] Amos Maxwell, "The Sequoyah Convention," *The Chronicles of Oklahoma* XXVIII (Summer, 1950), p. 187.

[206] Amos Maxwell, "The Sequoyah Convention, Part II," *The Chronicles of Oklahoma* XXVIII (Summer, 1950), p. 304.

[207] Beard, *The Choctaw People*, p. 81.

XI. Chapta Auah Achvffa The Removal Chiefs Of The Choctaw

[208] Peter J. Hudson, "A Story of Choctaw Chiefs," *Bryan County Heritage Quarterly* (May 1999), p. 6; *Bishinik*, July 1980, February 1993.

[209] W. B. Morrison, "The Saga of Skullyville," p. 236.

[210] Peter J. Hudson, "A Story of Choctaw Chiefs, Part II," *Bryan County Heritage Quarterly* (August 1999), p. 3; Foreman, "The Choctaw Academy," X, p. 106.

[211] John Bartlett Meserve, "Chief George Hudson and Chief Samuel Garland," *The Chronicles of Oklahoma* XX (1942), p. 17; *Bishinik*, March 1979; Joseph P. Folsom, *Constitution and Laws of the Choctaw Nation* (New York: William P. Lyon and Son, Printers and Publishers, 1869), p. 25.

[212] W. David Baird, *Peter Pitchlynn: Chief of the Choctaws*, p. 211; Hudson, "A Story of Choctaw Chiefs, Part II," p. 6.

[213] John Bartlett Meserve, "Chief Allen Wright," *The Chronicles of Oklahoma* XIX (Dec., 1941), p. 321; Muriel H. Wright "Contributions of the Indian People to Oklahoma," p. 156; Richard H. Harper, "The Missionary Work of the Reformed (Dutch) Church in America," *The Chronicles of Oklahoma* XVIII (Sept. 1940), p. 253; J. B. Wright, "Dedication Speech," Th*e Chronicles of Oklahoma* XXXVI (Autumn, 1958), p. 324; *The Daily Oklahoman*, January 12, 1930; Allen Wright Collection, Box W-25, Folder 26, Western History Collection, University of Oklahoma, Norman; *ibid.*, Box W-25, Folder 4; *ibid.*, Box W25, Folder 3; *The Indian Champion*, April 11, 1885; *The Sunday Oklahoman*, June 17, 2001.

[214] Allen Wright Collection, "Message of Allen Wright at Chahta Tamaha, C.N.," Nov. 17, 1866, Box W-25, Folder 1, Western History Collection, University of Oklahoma, Norman.

[215] Allen Wright Collection, "Laws Regulating Granting Permits by Allen Wright," November 20, 1867, Box W-25, Folder 6, Western History Collection, University of Oklahoma, Norman; *ibid.,* "Report of Wright, Supt. Of Schools," December 28, 1880, Box W-25, Folder 23; *ibid.*, "Inventory of Allen Wright Library," Box W-14, FF 2, Western History Collection, University of Oklahoma, Norman.

XII. Chapta Auah Tuklo No 'Count White Man Come To Our Country

[216] Peter J. Hudson, "A Story of Choctaw Chiefs," p. 6.

[217] Norman Arthur Graebner, "Provincial Indian Society in Eastern Oklahoma," *The Chronicles of Oklahoma* XXIII (Winter, 1945-46), p. 332.

[218] V. M. Locke, Jr. "Governor Cole," *The Chronicles of Oklahoma* IV (Sept., 1926), p. 230.

[219] *The Atoka Vindicator*, March 27, 1875; Coleman Cole Collection, Folder 1, September 4, 1875, Folder 4, Folder 5, Folder 9, Western History Collection, University of Oklahoma, Norman.

[220] John Bartlett Meserve, "Chief Coleman Cole," *The Chronicles of Oklahoma* XIV (March 1936), p. 21; *Bishinik*, August 1996.

[221] Peter James Hudson, "A Story of Choctaw Chiefs," *The Chronicles of Oklahoma* XVII (June 1939), p. 202; Angie Debo, *The Rise and fall of the Choctaw Republic*, p. 166.

[222] "Jackson F. McCurtain Biography," 1901, Jackson McCurtain Papers, Box M-46, FF 14, Western History Collection, University of Oklahoma, Norman; *ibid.*, *Star Vindicator*, McAlester, November 6, 1877, Box M-46, FF 2; *ibid.*, July 5, 1883, Box M-46, FF 9; Hudson, "A Story of Choctaw Chiefs," p. 203.

[223] Jackson F. McCurtain Collection, "Message of J. F. McCurtain to The Honorable Senate and House of Representatives of the Choctaw Nation in General Council Assembled," Oct. 3, 1883, Box M-46, Folder 10, Western History Collection, University of Oklahoma, Norman.

[224] W.C. Riggs, "Bits of Interesting History," p. 151.

[225] *Bishinik*, September 1995; Allen Wright, "Wheelock Seminary," p. 119.

[226] Edmund McCurtain to Editors, May 8, 1875, Edmund McCurtain Collection, Box M-45, Folder 1, Western History Collection, University of Oklahoma, Norman; *ibid.*, Edmund McCurtain to *Vindicator* June 19, 1875, Box M-45, Folder 2.

[227] Edmund McCurtain to General Council, Oct. 25, 1884, Edmund McCurtain Papers, Box M-45, Folder 8, Western History Collection, University of Oklahoma, Norman.

[228] Edmund McCurtain, "A Proclamation," April 11, 1885, Edmund McCurtain Papers, Box M-45, Folder 9, Western History Collection, University of Oklahoma, Norman.

[229] "Edmund McCurtain Biography," Edmund McCurtain Collection, Box M-45, Folder 14, Western History Collection, University of Oklahoma, Norman; *ibid.*, Box M-45, Folder 12; *The Indian Chieftain*, Vinita, Nov. 13, 1890.

[230] W. B. Morrison, "The Saga of Skullyville," p. 239; W. B. Morrison, *Military Posts and Camps in Oklahoma* (Oklahoma City: Harlow Publishing Co., 1936), p. 240.

[231] Hudson, "A Story of Choctaw Chiefs," p. 206; Muriel H. Wright, "Organization of Counties in the Choctaw and Chickasaw Nations," *The Chronicles of Oklahoma* VIII (September 1930), p. 332; *Bishinik*, June 1991.

XIII. Chapta Auah Tuchena   Gone But Not Forgotten

[232] Hudson, "A Story of Choctaw Chiefs," p. 206; Muriel H. Wright, "Organization of Counties in the Choctaw and Chickasaw Nations," *The Chronicles of Oklahoma* VIII (September 1930), p. 332; *Bishinik*, June 1991.

[233] Monty Olsen, "Wilson N. Jones," *Bryan County Heritage Quarterly* (August 1997), p. 3.

[234] James D. Morrison, "Problems in the Industrial Progress and Development of the Choctaw Nation, 1865-1907," p. 82; *The Sherman Daily Democrat*, Feb. 14, 1928; *Bishinik*, December 1995.

[235] John Bartlett Meserve, "Chief Wilson Nathaniel Jones," *The Chronicles of Oklahoma* XIV (Dec., 1936), p. 426; Monty Olsen, "Wilson N. Jones," p. 3.

[236] Basil A. Hayes, "Leroy Long-Teacher of Medicine," *The Chronicles of Oklahoma* XX (1942), p. 231.

[237] *Bishinik*, August 1993; *The Star-Vindicator*, McAlester, January 20, 1877, Edmund McCurtain Collection, Box M-45, Folder 1, Western History Collection, University of Oklahoma, Norman; Dorothy Aronote West, *Pushmataha County: The Early Years*, p. 252.

[238] *Bishinik*, February 1993, February 2,000.

[239] Olsen, "Wilson N. Jones," p. 7.

[240] John Bartlett Meserve, "Chief Benjamin Franklin Smallwood and Chief Jefferson Gardner," *The Chronicles of Oklahoma* XIX (Sept., 1941), p. 220.

[241] *The South McAlester News*, Dec. 24, 1903, D. C. McCurtain Collection, Box M46, FF 4, Western History Collection, University of Oklahoma, Norman; *ibid*., D.C. McCurtain, Feb. 8, 1900, Box M 46, FF 2; *ibid*., *The Marietta Monitor*, Jan. 5, 1911, Box 46, FF 6.

[242] John Bartlett Meserve, "The McCurtains,"p.311.

[243] John Bartlett Meserve, "Chief Gilbert Wesley Dukes," *The Chronicles of Oklahoma* XVIII (March 1940), p. 56.

[244] A.D. Hefley, "Tobucksy County Courthouse," *The Chronicles of Oklahoma* XLVIII (Spring, 1970), p. 30.

[245] John Bartlett Meserve, "Chief Gilbert Wesley Dukes," p. 59.

[246] *Bryan County Heritage Quarterly*, February, 2,000; Meserve, "The McCurtains," p. 311; Green McCurtain, "Messages of Chief to the National Council,"Green McCurtain Collection, Series II, Sub-Series A, Box 22, Western History Collection, University of Oklahoma, Norman; Duane Champagne, *Social Order and Political Change: Constitutional Governments Among the Cherokee, the Choctaw, the Chickasaw, and the Creek* (Stanford: Stanford University Press, 1992), p. 222.

XIV. <u>Chapta Auah Ushta We Must Remember The Past...</u>

[247] Carolyn Thomas Foreman, "St. Agnes Academy for the Choctaws," p. 326; *Bryan County Heritage Quarterly*, August 1999, p. 23; Dorothy Arnote West, *Pushmataha County: The Early Years*, p. 253; E. Dudley, *"Days Gone By,"* (Antlers: Pushmataha County Historical Society, 1988), p. 23.

[248] Victor M. Locke, Jr. to Semple, December 8, 1919, William F. Semple, Principal Chief to Gabe E. Parker, Feb. 1, 1919, Durant, Oklahoma William F. Semple Papers, Personal copy, Durant, Oklahoma; Hugh D. Corwin, "The Folsom Training School," *The Chronicles of Oklahoma* XLII (Spring, 1964), p. 52; West, *Pushmataha County: The Early Years*, p. 253.

[249] Beard, *The Choctaw People*, p. 82; Gabe E. Parker, July 3, 1916, Phillips Pamphlets Collection, 4738.2, Western History Collection, University of Oklahoma, Norman; Hazel B. Green, "Indian Pioneer Papers: An interview with Mrs. Edwin Dwight," *Bryan County Heritage Quarterly* (Nov., 1997), p. 4; Muriel H. Wright, "A Brief Review of the Life of Doctor Eliphalet Nott Wright, 1852-1932," p. 285; Arlene LeMaster, trans., *Eastern Oklahoma Indians and Pioneers* (3 vols. Poteau, Ok.: Family Heritage Resources, 1992-93), III, p. 52.

[250] Peter M. Wright, "John Collier and the Oklahoma Indian Welfare Act of 1936," *The Chronicles of Oklahoma* L (Autumn, 19720, p. 357; Ben Dwight to Elmer Thomas, December 3, 1935, Elmer Thomas Papers, Box 70, Western History Collection, University of Oklahoma, Norman; W. F. Semple and Winnie Lewis Gravitt, "Grady Lewis, Choctaw Attorney," *The Chronicles of Oklahoma* XXXIII (Autumn, 1955), p. 305; Marcia Haag and Henry Willis (eds.), *Choctaw Language and Culture: Chahta Anumpa*, p. 315.

[251] Beard, *The Choctaw People*, p. 84; A. D. Hefley, "A Choctaw Landmark," *The Chronicles of Oklahoma* XII (December 1934), p. 476; Jesse O. McKee and Jon A. Schlenker, *The Choctaws: Cultural Evolution of a Native American Tribe* (Jackson: University Press of Mississippi, 1980), p. 152; L. David Norris, *Southeastern Oklahoma State University Since 1909: Volume 1* (Durant, Okla.: Mesa Publishing Company, 1986), p. 7; *Bishinik*, November 1990; *The Bryan County Star*, October 21, 1971.

[252] Harry J. W. Belvin, *Choctaw Tribal Structure and Achievement, August 18, 1948 to August 25, 1975* (Durant, Okla.: SOSU Choctaw Bilingual Education Program, 1981), p. 16; *Bishinik*, June 1994; Sharon O'Brien, *American Indian Tribal Governments* (Norman: University of Oklahoma Press, 1989), p. 82; Debo, *And Still the Waters Run*, p. 13.

[253] *Bishinik*, August 1986; Milligan, (ed.), *The Indian Way: the Choctaws*, p. 188.

[254] *Hello Choctaw*, February 1, 1976, December 1, 1976.

[255] Edwin Alexander Anderson, (ed.), *Choctaw English Dictionary* (Oklahoma City: Central Choctaw Council, Inc., 1978), p. 266; John W. Morris, Charles R. Goins, and Edwin C. McReynolds, *Historical Atlas of Oklahoma* (Norman: University of Oklahoma Press, 1976), p. 30; *Hello, Choctaw*, November 1, 1977; M. B. Davis (ed.), *Native Americans in the Twentieth Century* (New York: Garland Publishing, 1994), p. 111.

[256] B*ishinik*, March 1996; James H. Howard and Victoria Lindsay Levine, *Choctaw Music and Dance* (Norman: University of Oklahoma Press, 1990), p. 61; Sandra Faiman-Silva, *Choctaws At The Crossroads: The Political Economy of Class and Culture in the Oklahoma Timber Region* (Lincoln: University of Nebraska Press, 1997), p. 211; Interview with Randle Durant, January 10, 2001.

[257] *Bishinik*, March 1996, August 1998; *The Durant Daily Democrat*, April 21, 2002.

[258] *The Durant Daily Democrat*, September 24, 2000; *Chahta Gazette*, June 25, 1987; *Bishinik*, September 1997; *The Daily Oklahoman*, June 4, 2001; Interview with Assistant Chief Mike Bailey, March 14, 2003.

XV. Chapta Auah Tahlapi The Choctaw War Cry In Foreign Lands

[259] *Bishinik*, August 1986; *Bryan County Heritage Quarterly*, February 1999; Kenny A. Franks, *Citizen Soldiers: Oklahoma's National Guard* (Norman: University of Oklahoma Press, 1983), p. 30; Thomas A. Britten, "The Creek Draft Rebellion of 1918: Wartime Hysteria and Indian-Baiting in World War I Oklahoma," *The Chronicles of Oklahoma* LXXIX (Summer, 2001), p. 209; Thomas A. Britten, *American Indians in World War I: At Home and at War* (Albuquerque: University of New Mexico Press, 1997), p. 184; Marcia Haag and Henry Willis, *Choctaw Language & Culture: Chahta Anumpa*, p. 284; *Durant Daily Democrat*, May 31, 2002.

[260] *Hello, Choctaw*, March 1, 1976; *Bishinik*, October 1992, July 1993, November 1993, September 1995, November 1997, October 1999, March 2000, September 2001; Frances Imon, *Smoke Signals from Indian Territory*, Vol. II (Wolfe City, Texas: Henington Publishing Company, 1977), p. 88; A. W. Bloor to The Commanding General 36th Division, January 23, 1919, National Archives, Washington, D.C.; Capt. Ben F. Chastaine, *The Story of the 36th* (Oklahoma City: Harlow Publishing Co., 1920), p. 266; Carter, *McCurtain County and Southeast Oklahoma*, p. 308; Interview of Bertram Bobb, KXII-TV, May 22, 2002; Louis Coleman, "Oklahoma's "Greatest" Hero? A Review of the Military Record of Joseph Oklahombi," *The Chronicles of Oklahoma* LXXX (Summer, 2002), p. 205.

[261] *Bishinik*, February 1996.

[262] *Bishinik*, February 1997.

[263] *Bishinik*, February 1995; Duane K. Hale, "Uncle Sam's Warriors: American Indians in World War II," *The Chronicles of Oklahoma* LXIX (Winter, 1991-92), p. 415; Alison R. Bernstein, *American Indians and World War II* (Norman: University of Oklahoma Press, 1991), p. 40.

[264] *Bishinik*, January 1994, May 1996; Franks, *Citizen Soldiers*, p. 30.

[265] *Bishinik*, August 1992, January 2000, March 2000.

[266] *Bishinik*, April 1996, January 2000.

[267] *Hello, Choctaw*, April 1, 1977.

[268] *Bishinik*, December 1979.

[269] *Bishinik*, May-June, 1980; *The Daily Oklahoman*, July 2, 2001.

[270] *Bishinik*, July 1991.

[271] *Bishinik*, May 1993, September 1997.

[272] *Bishinik*, June 1994, June 1998, March 2000, July 2000.

[273] *Bishinik*, September 1998.

[274] B*ishinik*, April 1992, March 2000; Kenneth William Townsend, *World War II and the American Indian* (Albuquerque: University of New Mexico Press, 2000), p. 150; War Memorial, Tvshkahomma; *Durant Daily Democrat*, Nov. 11, 2002.

[275] *Bishinik*, June 1995.

[276] *Bishinik*, August 1996; Hale, "Uncle Sam's Warriors: American Indians in World War II," p. 424; Townsend, *World War II and the American Indian*, p. 132.

[277] *Bishinik*, September 1997, November 1999; John C. Powell, "Oklahoma and the Medal of Honor," *The Chronicles of Oklahoma* LXXIV (Fall, 1996), p. 328.

[278] *Bishinik*, January 1980.

[279] *Bishinik*, February 1993.

[280] *Bishinik*, March 1995; *The Durant Daily Democrat*, August 6, 2002.

[281] *Bishinik*, July 1979, February 2001; Interview with Sue Whitfield Severn, December10, 2003.

[282] *Bishinik*, May 1999, October 1999.

[283] *Bishinik*, January 1991.

[284] *Bishinik*, January 1994.

[285] *Bishinik*, December 1986, February 1991, September 1995, June 1996.

[286] *Bishinik*, April 2001, April 2003.

XVI. Chapta Auah Hannali For The Greatest Good Of The Nation

[287] *Hello, Choctaw*, February 1, 1976, March 1, 1977, February 1978.

[288] *Tulsa World*, March 25, 1978.

[289] *Hello, Choctaw*, May 1, 1978.

[290] *Bishinik*, December 1978.

[291] *Bishinik*, April 1979.

[292] *Bishinik*, June 1979.

[293] *Bishinik*, July 1979.

[294] *Hello, Choctaw*, November 1, 1977; *Bishinik*, August 1979.

[295] *Bishinik*, October 1978, November 1978; Superintendent Donald G. Moon to Rubin L. White, Chairman, October 23, 1979, Choctaw Nation Papers, Talihina, Oklahoma.

[296] *Bishinik*, March 1979, December 1979.

[297] *Bishinik*, October 1979.

[298] *Bishinik*, November 1979.

[299] *Bishinik*, January 1986; *Chahta Gazette*, June 26, 1987.

[300] *Bishinik*, February 1981.

[301] *Bishinik*, November 1980.

[302] *Bishinik*, January 1981.

[303] *Bishinik*, July 1981.

[304] *Bishinik*, February 1981.

[305] *Bishinik*, March 1981.

[306] *Bishinik*, November 1980, July 1981, April 1986.

[307] *Bishinik*, August/September 1981, January 1983.

[308] *Bishinik*, October 1981.

[309] *Bishinik*, November 1983, February 1984.

[310] *Bishinik*, April 1979, September 1984.

[311] *Bishinik*, October 1984, November 1984, December 1984.

[312] *Bishinik*, January 1985.

[313] *Bishinik*, September 1985.

[314] *Bishinik*, October 1985.

[315] *Chahta Gazette*, June 25, 1987.

[316] *Bishinik*, July 1987.

[317] *Bishinik*, August 1987.

[318] *Bishinik*, December 1987.

[319] *Bishinik*, September 1988.

[320] *Bishinik*, March 1989.

[321] *Bishinik*, May 1989.

[322] *Bishinik*, June 1989, July 1989.

[323] *Bishinik*, September 1990.

[324] *Bishinik*, December 1990, September 1995.

[325] *Bishinik*, March 1991.

[326] *Bishinik*, May 1991.

[327] *Bishinik*, June 1991.

[328] *Bishinik*, July 1991.

[329] *Bishinik*, September 1991.

[330] *Bishinik*, May 1992.

[331] *Bishinik*, April 1992.

[332] *Bishinik*, June 1992.

[333] *Bishinik*, August 1992; *The Sunday Oklahoman*, February 16, 2003.

[334] *Bishinik*, March 1993, March 1994.

[335] *Bishinik*, May 1993.

[336] *Bishinik*, July 1993.

[337] *Bishinik*, March 1994, September 1994.

[338] B*ishinik*, June 1995, August 1995, September 1995.

[339] *Bishinik, January 1996, January 1997; The Daily Oklahoman*, Dec. 20, 2000.

[340] *Bishinik*, June 1997.

[341] *Bishinik*, July 1997, August 1997.

[342] *Bishinik*, September 1997.

[343] *Bishinik*, September 1998, October 1999.

[344] *Bishinik*, May 1999.

[345] *Bishinik*, June 1999.

[346] *Bishinik*, July 1999, September 1999, December 1999.

[347] *Bishinik*, August 1993, September 2000, May 2001; *The Daily Oklahoman*, July 16. 2001, August 6, 2001.

[348] *The Daily Oklahoman*, July 21, 2001; *The Durant Daily Democrat*, July 22, 200l; *Bishinik*, April 1987, May 1990, January 1998.

[349] *Bishinik*, July 1990, May 1993, October 1992; Interview with Charley Jones, April 4, 2000.

[350] *Bishinik*, December 1, 1977, January 1985, June 1993, April 2003; *Chahta Gazette*, June 26, 1987.

[351] *Bishinik*, June 1984, June 1993, Sept., 2001, November 2001; Interview with Delton Cox, October 4, 2001.

[352] Interview with Randle Durant, January 13, 2001; *Bishinik*, September 1985, April 1993; Randle Durant, *"Footsteps" of a Durant Choctaw* (Talihina, Ok: Private printing, 2002), p. 91.

[353] Interview with Glenn D. Johnson, June 22, 2001; interview with Jack Austin, April 21, 2003.

[354] *Chahta Gazette*, June 25, 1987; *Bishinik*, November 1997.

[355] *Bishinik*, January 1985; Interview with Ted Dosh, December 9, 2002.

[356] *Bishinik*, June 1993.

[357] *Bishinik*, September 1998; Interview with James Frazier, November 1, 2002; Interview with Bob Pate, February 12, 2003.

XVII. Chapta Auah Untuklo From A Trail Of Tears To A Road Of Progress

[358] *Bishinik*, February 1993, April 1993, June 2000.

[359] *Bishinik*, March 1996.

[360] *Bishinik*, March 1993, February 1996, June 1996, October 1996, July 2000; The *Durant Daily Democrat*, July 27, 2001.

[361] *Bishinik*, June 1995; *Arkansas Intelligencer*, April 3, 1847.

[362] *Bishinik*, June 1993, November 1998.

[363] *Bishinik*, March, 199, November 1998, December 1998, March 1999, June 1999, February 2000; *The Durant Daily Democrat*, May 8, 2002.

[364] *The Durant Daily Democrat*, October 4, 2000; *Bishinik*, October 2000.

[365] *Bishinik*, March 2000.

[366] *Bishinik, October 2000; The Durant Daily Democrat*, September 27, 2000, May 19, 2002.

[367] *Bishinik*, January 1991, December 1991, August 1997, November 1999, April 2001.

[368] *Bishinik*, March 1993, July 1993.

[369] *Bishinik*, February 1996, August 1997.

[370] *Bishinik*, December 1998, October 1999.

[371] *Bishinik*, December 1999.

[372] *The Daily Oklahoman*, August 23, 2000.

[373] *Bishinik, February 2000; The Sunday Oklahoman*, June 9, 2002.

[374] The *Sunday Oklahoman*, March 11, 2001; *Bishinik*, July 1998, November 1998; *The Durant Daily Democrat*, October 12, 2000; *The Daily Oklahoman*, July 30, 2001.

[375] *Bishinik*, November 1992, March 1993, July 1998, November 1998, March 1999, September 2000, November 2001; *The Durant Daily Democrat*, June 12, 2001; *The*

Sunday Oklahoman, June 23, 2002.
[376] *Bishinik*, February 1993, April 6, 1996, November 1998, March 1999.

[377] *Bishinik*, August 1997, December 1998, March 1999, October 1998, April 1999, January 1999, April 2001.

[378] *Bishinik*, January 2001; *The Daily Oklahoman*, July 6, 2001.

[379] *The Durant Daily Democrat*, January 15, 2001; *Bishinik*, October 1998, January, March, November 2000; Interview with Richard Lewis, March 14, 2001.

[380] George William Stevenson, "The Hymnody of the Choctaw Indians of Oklahoma," p. 88; *Bishinik*, April 2001.

[381] *Bishinik*, October 2000; Interview with Joy Culbreath, May 9, 2001.

[382] *Bishinik*, April 1999, February 2002; Interview with Chief Pyle, January 12, 2000; *The Durant Daily Democrat*, November 11, 2001; *The Sunday Oklahoman*, December 2, 2001; Daniel F. Littlefield, Jr., and James W. Parins, *American Indian and Alaska Native Newspapers and Periodicals, 1925-1970* (New York: Greenwood Press, 1986), p. 322.

[383] *The Durant Daily Democrat*, March 19, 2001.

[384] *Bishinik*, August 1997.

[385] *The Daily Oklahoman*, March 7, 2001.

[386] *Bishinik*, March 1996.

[387] *Bishinik*, April 1996.

[388] *Bishinik*, June 2000, April 2001.

[389] *Bishinik*, April 2001; The *Durant Daily Democrat*, Oct. 21, 2001, Oct. 24, 2001.

[390] *Bishinik*, April 2001.

[391] *Bishinik*, April 2000, September 2000.

[392] *The Daily Oklahoman*, October 13, 2000; *Indian Country Today Newspaper*, October 25, 2000; *The Sunday Oklahoman*, Aug. 19, 2001; *The Daily Oklahoman*, January 12, 2002; *The Daily Oklahoman*, November 22, 2002.

[393] *Bishinik*, March 1995.

[394] *Bishinik*, April 1994.

[395] *Bishinik*, August 1996.

[396] *Bishinik*, July 1998, July 2000.

[397] *Hello, Choctaw*, Feb. 1,1976; *Bishinik*, June 1, 1978, January 1981, May 1981, July 1981, January 1984, May 2001; James P. Danky (ed.), *Native American Periodicals and Newspapers 1828-1982* (Westport, Connecticut: Greenwood Press, 1984), p. 71; Interview with Judy Allen, April 12, 2003.

[398] *Bishinik*, July 1998, October 1998, December 1998; *The Daily Oklahoman*, November 8, 2001; *The Durant Daily Democrat*, June 30, 2002.

[399] *The Durant Daily Democrat*, January 8, 2001.

[400] *The Daily Oklahoman*, September 20, 2001; *The Durant Daily Democrat*, September 23, 2001, October 11, 2001.

[401] *Bishinik*, February 1998, January 2000.

[402] T*he Daily Oklahoman*, June 4, 2001; *Bishinik*, March 1999.

[403] *Bishinik*, January 1999; *Bishinik*, February 2003.

[404] *Bishinik*, December 1991, November 1998, May 2001.

[405] *Bishinik,* July 2000.

[406] *Bishinik,* March 1999.

[407] *Bishinik,* October 1998.

Endnotes

Bibliography

PERSONAL INTERVIEWS

Judy Allen, Durant, OK, 4-12-03
Jack Austin, Clayton, OK, 4-21-2003
Mike Bailey, Durant, OK, 3-14-03
Bertram Bobb, Antlers, OK, 3-23-01
Delton Cox, Durant, OK, 10-4-01
Joy Culbreath, Durant, OK, 5-09-01
Ted Dosh, Bennington OK, 12-09-02
Randle Durant, Talihina, OK, 1-13-0 1
James Frazier, Coalgate, OK, 11-01-02
Charley G. Jones, Idabel, OK
Glenn Dale Johnson, Antlers, OK, 6-22-01
Richard Lewis, Durant, OK, 3-14-01
Bob Pate, Durant, OK, 2-12-03
Greg Pyle, Durant, OK, 1-12-00; 3-5-03
Sue Whitfield, Golden, OK, 1-21-03

DOCUMENTS AND COLLECTIONS

Allen Wright Collection, Box W-25, F1-26, Western History Collection, University of Oklahoma, Norman, Oklahoma

Byington Typescripts, Research Library, Oklahoma Historical Society, Oklahoma City, Oklahoma

Byington, Cyrus. *An English and Choctaw Definer; For the Choctaw Academies and Schools*, New York: W. Benedict, 1852

Choctaw Agency, 1824-1833, Letters Received, MSS, Records of the Bureau of Indian Affairs, National Archives, Washington, D.C.

Choctaw Nation Papers, Oct. 23, 1979, Talihina, Oklahoma

Coleman Cole Collection, Folder 1-9, Western History Collection, University of Oklahoma, Norman, Oklahoma

Congress of the Confederate States of America Journal, Washington: Government Printing Office, 1904-05, Ser. I, IV.

Czarina C. Conlan Collection, "Notes on the Choctaws and Pushmataha," Box C43, Folder 3, Western History Collection, University of Oklahoma, Norman, Oklahoma.

Britt Willis, "Personal Reminiscence of the Days of Indian Territory by Britt Willis" M928, C43-F3, Western History Collection, University of Oklahoma, Norman, Oklahoma

D. C. McCurtain Collection, Box M, FF2, Western History Collection, University of Oklahoma, Norman, Oklahoma

Dovie Jones Papers, October 1892, M326, Folder 1, Western History Collection, University of Oklahoma, Norman, Oklahoma

Draper Collection, Frontier War Papers, "Indian Biography: Pushmataha," Mss. U10, 6 reels. Western History Collection, University of Oklahoma, Norman, Oklahoma

Edmund McCurtain Collection, Box M-45, Western History Collection, University of Oklahoma, Norman, Oklahoma

Elmer Thomas Papers, Box 70, Western History Collection, University of Oklahoma, Norman, Oklahoma

France, Archives des Colonies, Archives Nationales, Paris, Series C 13c, Vol. 1: folios 362-374. Memoir of Bienville, 1725

Grant Foreman Collection, Gilcrease Institute, Tulsa, Oklahoma, Box 24, Vol. 97

Green McCurtain Collection, "Messages of Chief to the National Council," Series II, Sub-Series A, Box 22, Western History Collection, University of Oklahoma, Norman, Oklahoma

Herbert Otho Boggs Collection, B-59, Folder 1, Western History Collection, University of Oklahoma, Norman, Oklahoma

Hodge, Frederick W. *Handbook of American Indians North of Mexico*, Bureau of American Ethnology, Bulletin 30 Washington: Smithsonian Institution, 1912.

Jackson F. McCurtain Papers, "Jackson F. McCurtain Biography, 1901," Box M-46, Western History Collection, University of Oklahoma, Norman, Oklahoma.

Letters to the Secretary of War-Received, 1818, Microfilm Series 271, Record Group 75, National Archives, Washington, D C

Muriel H. Wright Collection, Western History Collection, University of Oklahoma, Norman, Oklahoma

Official Records of the Union and Confederate Armies (Washington: Government Printing Office, 1880-1904), Series I, I

Papers of Panton, Leslie and Co, Western History Collection, University of Oklahoma, Norman, Oklahoma, Microfilm, 26 rolls, C-50

Peter P. Pitchlynn Collection, 1858 Box 3, Folder 33 Western History Collection, University of Oklahoma, Norman, Oklahoma

Phillips Pamphlets Collection, 4738.2, July 3, 1916, Western History Collection, University of Oklahoma, Norman, Oklahoma

Report of the Select Committee to Investigate Matters Connected with Affairs in the Indian Territory, 2 vols. Washington, 1907

Swanton, John R., *The Indians of the Southeastern United States*. Smithsonian Institution: Bureau of American Ethnology, Bulletin 137. Washington: Gantt Printing Office, 1946; *Source Material for the Social and Ceremonial Life of the Choctaw Indians*, Bureau of American Ethnology Bulletin 103. Washington: U.S. Government Printing Office, 1931

Walter Scott Ferguson Collection, "Angie Debo Papers," Box 47, Folder 4, Western History Collection, University of Oklahoma, Norman, Oklahoma.

William Hemsley Emory Papers, Western Americana Collection, Beinecke Rare Book and Manuscript Library, Yale University, New Haven, 1860-1861

William F. Semple Papers, Personal Copy, Durant, Oklahoma

WPA Indian Pioneer History Project for Oklahoma, Interview with Anna Smallwood McClendon, Jan. 26, 1938

NEWSPAPERS

Arkansas Advocate, Dec. 7, 1831.

Arkansas Intelligencer, April 3, 1847.

Arkansas Gazette, Feb. 9, 1831; Nov. 14, 1832; Nov. 21, 1832; Nov. 28, 1832; Jan. 9, 1833; May 9, 1833; May 22, 1833; July 3, 1833; Oct. 16, 1833; Nov. 13, 1833.

Bishinik, December 1, 1978-2001.

Caddo Herald, Dec. 14, 1903; January 22, 1909.

Chahta Gazette, June 25, 1987.

Hello Choctaw, February 1, 1976-May, 1978.

Historic Denison, Denison, Texas, Jan. 1, Feb. 15, 1929.

Indian Citizen, Oct. 7, 1897.

Indian Country Today Newspaper, Oct. 25, 2000.
Muskogee Times-Democrat, July 10, 1911.
The Sterrett Sun, April 13, 1906.
The Atoka Vindicator, March 27, 1875; Nov. 24, 1875.
The Bryan County Star, Caddo, OK, Oct. 21, 1971.
The Daily Oklahoman, Aug. 1, 1926; Jan. 12, 1930; Feb. 24, 1946; Dec. 29, 1999; October 13, 2000; March 7, 2001; June 4, 2001; July 2, 2001; July 16, 2001; July 21, 2001; July 30, 2001; August 6, 2001; November 22, 2002.
The Durant Daily Democrat, Sept. 27, 2000; Oct. 12, 2000; March 15, 2001; March 19, 2001; July 22, 2001; July 27, 2001.
The Indian Champion, Atoka, April 11, 1885.
The Indian Chieftain, Vinita, Nov. 13, 1890.
The Marietta Monitor, Jan. 5, 1911.
The Sherman Daily Democrat, February 14, 1928.
The South McAlester News, Dec. 24, 1903.
The Sunday Oklahoman, March 11, 2001.
The Star-Vindicator, McAlester, Jan. 20, 1877; Nov. 6, 1877.
Tulsa World, March 25, 1978.
Washington Gazette, January 22, 1825.

ARTICLES IN JOURNALS

Adams, Evelyn Crady, "Kentucky's Choctaw Academy, 1819-1842: A Commercial Enterprise," *The Filson Club History Quarterly* XXVI (1952), 28-37
Blend, Benay, "The Indian Rights Association, The Dawes Commission and The Five Civilized Tribes," *Red River Valley Historical Review* VI (Fall, 1981), 4-14
Brown, D. Alexander, "Pea Ridge: Gettysburg of the West," *Civil War Times Illustrated* VI (October, 1967), 4-12, 46-47
Brown, Thomas, "The Miscegenation of Richard Mentor Johnson as an Issue in the National Election Campaign of 1835-1836," *Civil War History* 39 (March, 1993), 5-30
Buice, David, "Prelude to Fort Smith: Congress and the Five Civilized Tribes," *Red River Valley Historical Review* VII (Summer, 1982), 4-18

Byrd, Edward L., Jr., "The Old South as A Modern Myth," *Red River Valley Historical Review* I (Spring, 1974), 55-66

Case, Perry, "The Long Drive," *American Heritage* XI (April, 1960), 65-108

Castel, Albert, "The Guerrilla War, 1861-1865," *Civil War Times Illustrated* XIII (October, 1974), 3-50

Catholic Encyclopedia, Vol. III New York: Robert Appleton Company, 1908

Conrad, David E., "Whipple's Pacific Railroad Survey In The Indian Territory," *Red River Valley Historical Review* I (Winter, 1974), 390-415

Crosby, J. H., "The Butterfield Overland and Pony Express," *Prairie Lore* 13 (July, 1976), 43-45

Derrick, W. Edwin, and James Smallwood, "Miles of Track: The Coming of Railroads To Oklahoma," *Red River Valley Historical Review* VI (Summer, 1981), 87-94

Downey, Fairfax, "The Blue, the Gray, and the Red," *Civil War Times Illustrated* I (July, 1962), 7-10

Durant, Randle, "Randle Durant Writes History of Our Region and His Family," *Bryan County Heritage Quarterly* (Nov., 1998), 28-29

Franks, Clyda Reeves, "Oklahoma's Distant Past," *Oklahoma* 4 (Fall/ Winter, 1999-00), 32-36

Franks, Kenny and Clyda, "Thomas L. McKenney's Portraits of Oklahoma Indians," *Oklahoma* 4 (Spring/Summer, 1999), 12-24

Galloway, Patricia, "Ougoula Tchetoka, Ackia, and Bienville's First Chickasaw War: Whose Strategy and Tactics?" *The Journal of Chickasaw History* Vol. 2 (1996), 3-10

Gibson, Arrell M.," The Cowboy in Indian Territory," *Red River Valley Historical Review* II (Spring, 1975), 147-162

Goldsmith, Sarah Sue, "Choctaw, Like Most Eastern Tribes, Had Little Control Over Own Destiny," *Advocate Magazine* Baton Rouge, La.: June 2, 1996

Graebner, Laura Baum, "Agriculture Among The Five Civilized Tribes," *Red River Valley Historical Review* III (Winter, 1978), 45-61

Green, Hazel B., "Indian Pioneer Papers: An interview with Mrs. Edwin Dwight," *Bryan County Heritage Quarterly* (Nov., 1997), 2-4

Halbert, Henry S., "A Choctaw Migration Legend," *The American Antiquarian and Oriental Journal* 16 (1894), 215

Halbert, Henry S., "Nanih Waiya, the Sacred Mound of the Choctaw," *Publications of the Mississippi Historical Society*, 2 (1898)

Hudson, Peter J., "A Story of Choctaw Chiefs," *Bryan County Heritage Quarterly* (May 1999); Part II (August 1999), 1-6

Jordan, H. Glenn, "Choctaw Colonization in Oklahoma," in Arrell Morgan Gibson ed., *America's Exiles: Indian Colonization in Oklahoma* (Oklahoma City: Oklahoma Historical Society, 1976), 16-24

McDonald, Archie P., "The Texas Road," *Red River Valley Historical Review* VI (Summer, 1981), 57-68

Milligan, James C., "Fort McCulloch, Indian Territory," *Red River Valley Historical Review* VII (Spring, 1982), 17-27

Olsen, Monty, "Wilson N. Jones," Bryan *County Heritage Quarterly* (August, 1997), 3-8

Peterson, Susan, "The Butterfield Overland Mail in Indian Territory, 1858-1861," *Red River Valley Historical Review* VI (Summer, 1981), 77-87

Rouse, Alice Read, "Colonel Dick Johnson's Choctaw Academy: A Forgotten Educational Experiment," *Ohio Archeological and Historical Quarterly* XXV (January, 1916), 88-117

Sawyer, Charles H., "The Choctaw Indians of Mississippi, Part I," *Twin Territories: The Indian Magazine* (June 1902), 160-164

Shoemaker, Edward C., "Fort Towson: An Early Communications Route to Oklahoma," *Red River Valley Historical Review* VII (Summer, 1982), 18-30

Silverman, Jason H., "Confederate Ambitions for the Southwest: A New Perspective," *Red River Valley Historical Review* IV (Winter, 1979), 62-71

Smith, C. Calvin, "The Oppressed Oppressors: Negro Slavery Among the Choctaw Indians of Oklahoma," *Red River Valley Historical Review* II (Summer, 1975), 240-253

Smith, David P., "Conscription and Conflict on the Texas Frontier," *Civil War History* 39 (Sept., 1990), 250-262

Stein, Gary C., "A Fearful Drunkenness: The Liquor Trade to the Western Indians as Seen by European Travelers in America, 1800-1860," *Red River Valley Historical Review* I (Summer, 1974), 109-122

The Indians: Time Life Books, 94-97

Vaughn, Courtney Ann, "Jobe's Legacy: Cyrus Byington, Missionary to the Choctaws In Indian Territory," *Red River Valley Historical Review* III (Fall, 1978), 5-18

Vernon, Walter N., "Methodist Pioneers Along the Great Bend of the Red River," *Red River Valley Historical Review VI* (Winter, 1981), 46-58

White, Rev. James D., "The Saga of St. Agnes," *The Kiamichi Journal* Vol. VIII (January 2002), 2-13

Wiley, B. I., "The Common Soldier of the Civil War," *Civil War Times Illustrated* XII (July, 1973), 2-64

Winston, James E., "The Lost Commission: A Study in Mississippi History," *The Mississippi Valley Historical Review* V (Sept., 1918), 158-189

ARTICLES IN THE CHRONICLES OF OKLAHOMA

Agnew, Brad, "The Dodge-Leavenworth Expedition of 1834," *The Chronicles of Oklahoma* LIII (Fall, 1975), 376-397

Allen, Virginia R., "Medical Practices and Health in the Choctaw Nation, 1831-1885," *The Chronicles of Oklahoma* XLVIII (Spring, 1970), 69-74

Allgood, Samuel Y., "Historic Spots and Actions in the Washita Valley Up to 1870," The *Chronicles of Oklahoma* V (June, 1927), 221-260

Ashcraft, Allan C., "Confederate Indian Department Conditions in August, 1864," The *Chronicles of Oklahoma* XLI (Autumn, 1963), 270-286; "Confederate Indian Troop Conditions In 1864," *The Chronicles of Oklahoma* LXI (Winter, 1863-64), 442-449; "Confederate Indian Territory Conditions in 1865," *The Chronicles of Oklahoma* XLII (Winter, 1964-65), 421-429

Bahos, Charles, "On Opothleyahola's Trail: Locating the Battle of Round Mountain," *The Chronicles of Oklahoma* LXIII (Spring, 1985), 58-90

Baird, W. David, "Spencer Academy, Choctaw Nation," *The Chronicles of Oklahoma* XLV (Spring, 1967), 25-44

Badinelli, Don F., "Struggle in the Choctaw Nation: The Coal Miners Strike of 1894," *The Chronicles of Oklahoma* LXXII (Fall, 1994), 292-311

Balyeat, Frank A., "Joseph Samuel Murrow, Apostle To The Indians," *The Chronicles of Oklahoma* XXXV (Autumn, 1957), 297-313

Benson, Henry C., "Life Among the Choctaw Indians," *The Chronicles of Oklahoma* IV (June, 1926), 156-161

Billington, Monroe, "Black Slavery in Indian Territory: The Ex-Slave Narratives," *The Chronicles of Oklahoma* LX (Spring, 1962), 56-65

Blaine, Martha Royce, "A Brief Excursion Into Journalism: The Choctaw and Chickasaw Observer, Formerly the Ft. Gibson Appeal or the Indian Courier," *The Chronicles of Oklahoma* LI (Winter, 1973-74), 411-420

Bobo, Lacy Pierce, "Reminiscences of Pioneer Days," *The Chronicles of Oklahoma* XXIII (Autumn, 1945), 277-290

Bowden, David, "Toll Roads and Railroads: A Case of Economic Conflict in the Choctaw Nation, 1870-1876," *The Chronicles of Oklahoma* LXXIV (Winter, 1996-97), 384-398

Brewer, Phil D., "Rev. Willis F. Folsom, A Biographical Sketch with Excerpts from his Diary," *The Chronicles of Oklahoma* IV (March, 1926), 54-69

Britten, Thomas A., "The Creek Draft Rebellion of 1918: Wartime Hysteria and Indian-Baiting in WWI Oklahoma," *The Chronicles of Oklahoma* LXXIX (Summer, 2001), 200-215

Brown, Loren N., "The Appraisal of the Lands of the Choctaws and the Chickasaws By the Dawes Commission," *The Chronicles of Oklahoma* XXII (Summer, 1944), 177-192; "The Dawes Commission," *The Chronicles of Oklahoma* IX (March, 1931), 71-105; "The Establishment of the Dawes Commission For Indian Territory," *The Chronicles of Oklahoma* XVIII (June, 1940), 171-181

Brown, Vernon H., "American Airlines along the Butterfield Mail Route," The *Chronicles of Oklahoma* XXXIII (Spring, 1955), 2-14; "Committee Report Butterfield Overland Mail," *The Chronicles of Oklahoma* XXXVI (Winter, 1958-59), 446-473

Bruce, Michael L., "Our Best Men Are Fast Leaving Us: The Life and Times of Robert M. Jones," *The Chronicles of Oklahoma* LXVI (Fall, 1988), 294-305

Bryant, Jr., Keith L., "The Choctaw Nation in 1843: A Missionary's View," The *Chronicles of Oklahoma* XLIV (Autumn, 1966), 319-322

Bryce, J. Y., "About Some of Our First Schools in Choctaw Nation," *The Chronicles of Oklahoma VI* (September, 1928), 354-394; "From Reports of the Board of Indian Commissioners," *The Chronicles of Oklahoma* V (March, 1927), 79-94

Caldwell, Norman W., "The Red River Raft," *The Chronicles of Oklahoma* XIX (September, 1941), 253-268

Carr, Susan J., "Bloomfield Academy and Its Founder," T*he Chronicles of Oklahoma* II (Dec., 1924), 366-379

Carter, Kent, "Tams Bixby: Doing Government Business in the Gilded Age," *The Chronicles of Oklahoma* LXXVIII (Winter, 2000-20001), 412-444

Christian, Emma Ervin, "Memories of My Childhood Days In The Choctaw Nation," *The Chronicles of Oklahoma* IX (June, 1931), 154-165; "Memories of My Childhood In The Choctaw Nation," *The Chronicles of Oklahoma* XI (Sept., 1933), 1034-1039

Clark, Joseph Stanley, "The Eastern Boundary of Oklahoma," *The Chronicles of Oklahoma* XI (Dec., 1933), 1084-1110

Clark, Stanley, "Immigrants In The Choctaw Coal Industry," *The Chronicles of Oklahoma* XXXIII (Winter, 1955-56), 440-456

Clifford, Roy A., "The Indian Regiments In The Battle of Pea Ridge," *The Chronicles of Oklahoma* XXV (Winter, 1947-48), 314-323

Coleman, Louis, "Cyrus Byington: Missionary to the Choctaws," *The Chronicles of Oklahoma* LXII (Winter, 1984-85), 360-388; "Twenty-five Days to the Choctaw Nation," *The Chronicles of Oklahoma* LXIX (Winter, 1986-87), 4-16; Oklahoma's Greatest Hero? A Review of the Military Record of Joseph Oklahombi," *The Chronicles of Oklahoma* LXXX (Summer, 2002), 204-215; "We Are Making History: The Execution of William Going," *The Chronicles of Oklahoma* LXXVI (Spring, 1998), 38-47

Conlan, Czarina C., "David Folsom," *The Chronicles of Oklahoma* IV (December, 1926), 340-355; "Peter P. Pitchlynn: Chief of the Choctaws, 1864-66" *The Chronicles of Oklahoma* VI (June,

1928), 215-224; "Site of Dancing Rabbit Creek Preserved," *The Chronicles of Oklahoma* VII (Sept., 1929), 323-328

Corbett, William P., "Rifles and Ruts: Army Road Builders in Indian Territory," *The Chronicles of Oklahoma* LX (Fall, 1982), 294-310

Corwin, Hugh D., "The Folsom Training School," *The Chronicles of Oklahoma* XLII (Spring, 1964), 46-53

Crockett, Bernice Norman, "Health Conditions In Indian Territory 1830 to the Civil War," *The Chronicles of Oklahoma* XXXV (Spring, 1957), 80-90; "Health Conditions In The Indian Territory From The Civil War To 1890," *The Chronicles of Oklahoma* XXXVI (Spring, 1958), 21-40

Crossett, G. A., "A Vanishing Race," *The Chronicles of Oklahoma* IV (June, 1926), 100-115

Crum, Steven, "America, Love It or Leave It: Some Native American Initiatives to Move to Mexico, 1890-1940," *The Chronicles of Oklahoma* LXXIX (Winter, 2001-2), 408-429

Darling, Ernest F., "Lincoln's Message to Indian Territory," *The Chronicles of Oklahoma* LXIII (Summer, 1985), 186-191

Davis, Carl L. and LeRoy H. Fischer, "Dragoon Life In Indian Territory, 1833-1846," *The Chronicles of Oklahoma* XLVIII (Spring, 1970), 2-25

Davis, Edward, "Early Advancement Among the Five Civilized Tribes," *The Chronicles of Oklahoma* XIV (June, 1936), 162-172; "Early Life Among the Five Civilized Tribes," *The Chronicles of Oklahoma* XV (1937), 70-101; "The Mississippi Choctaws," *The Chronicles of Oklahoma* X (June, 1932), 257-266

Davis, Mace, "Chitto Harjo," *The Chronicles of Oklahoma* XIII (June, 1935), 138-145

Debo, Angie, "Education In The Choctaw Country After The Civil War," *The Chronicles of Oklahoma* X (Sept., 1932), 383-391; "The Location of the Battle of Round Mountain," *The Chronicles of Oklahoma* XLI (Spring, 1963), 70-105; "The Site of the Battle of Round Mountain, 1861" *The Chronicles of Oklahoma* XXVII (Summer, 1949), 187-207

De Morse, Colonel Charles, "Indians for the Confederacy," *The Chronicles of Oklahoma* L (Winter, 1972-73), 479-486

Denison, Natalie Morrison, "Missions and Missionaries of the Presbyterian Church, among the Choctaws, 1866-1907," *The Chronicles of Oklahoma* XXIV (Winter, 1946-47), 426-449

DeRosier, Arthur H., Jr., "Negotiations for the Removal of the Choctaws: U.S. Policies of 1820 and 1830," *The Chronicles of Oklahoma* XXXVIII (Spring, 1960), 85-100

Doran, Michael F., "Population Statistics of Nineteenth Century Indian Territory," *The Chronicles of Oklahoma* LIII (Winter, 1975-76), 492-516

Dunkle, Rev. W. F., "A Choctaw Indian's Diary," T*he Chronicles of Oklahoma* (March, 1926), 61-69

Edwards, Whit, "Butternut and Blue: Confederate Uniforms in the Trans-Mississippi," *The Chronicles of Oklahoma* LXXIII (Winter, 1995-96), 424-438

Fessler, W. Julian, "The Work of the Early Choctaw Legislature," *The Chronicles of Oklahoma* VI (March, 1928), 60-68

Fischer, LeRoy H., "A Civil War Experience of Some Arkansas Women in Indian Territory by Francena Lavinia (Martin) Sutton," *The Chronicles of Oklahoma* LVII (Summer, 1979), 137-164; "The Honey Springs National Battlefield Park Monument," *The Chronicles of Oklahoma* XLVII (Spring, 1969), 515-531; "United States Indian Agents To The Five Civilized Tribes," *The Chronicles of Oklahoma* L (Winter, 1972-73), 410-415; and Kenny A. Franks, "Confederate Victory at Chusto-Talasah," *The Chronicles of Oklahoma* XLIX (Winter, 1971-72), 452-476; and Jerry Gill, "Confederate Indian Forces Outside of Indian Territory," *The Chronicles Of Oklahoma* XLVI (Autumn, 1968), 249-285; and William L. McMurry, "Confederate Refugees From Indian Territory," *The Chronicles of Oklahoma* LVII (Winter, 1979-80), 451-463; and Larry C. Rampp, "Quantrill's Civil War Operations," *The Chronicles of Oklahoma* XLVI (Summer, 1968), 155-183

Foreman, Carolyn Thomas, "Journal of a Tour in the Indian Territory," *The Chronicles of Oklahoma* X (June, 1932), 219-256; "Lieutenant-General Theophilus Hunter Holmes, C.S.A., Founder of Fort Holmes," *The Chronicles of Oklahoma* XXXV (Winter, 1957-58), 425-435; "New Hope Seminary, 1844-1897," *The Chronicles of Oklahoma* XXII (Autumn,

1944), 271-299; "St. Agnes Academy For The Choctaws," *The Chronicles of Oklahoma* XLVIII (Autumn, 1970), 323-331; "The Armstrongs of Indian Territory," *The Chronicles of Oklahoma* XXX (Autumn, 1952), 292-309; "The Armstrongs of Indian Territory, Part II," *The Chronicles of Oklahoma* XXX (Winter, 1952-53), 420-454; "The Armstrongs of Indian Territory: Part III," *The Chronicles of Oklahoma* XXXI (Spring, 1953), 56-66; "The Choctaw Academy," *The Chronicles of Oklahoma* VI (December, 1928), 452-480;"The Choctaw Academy," *The Chronicles of Oklahoma* IX (September, 1931), 382-411; "The Choctaw Academy," *The Chronicles of Oklahoma* X (March, 1932), 77-114; "The Foreign Mission School at Cornwall, Connecticut," *The Chronicles of Oklahoma* VII (Sept., 1929), 242-259; "The Light-Horse In The Indian Territory," *The Chronicles of Oklahoma* XXXIV (Spring, 1956), 17-43; "Report of Captain John Stuart on the Construction of the Road from Fort Smith to Horse Prairie on Red River," *The Chronicles of Oklahoma* V (September, 1927), 332-347

Foreman, Grant, "A Century of Prohibition," *The Chronicles of Oklahoma* XII (June, 1934), 133-141; "Notes from the Indian Advocate," *The Chronicles of Oklahoma* XIV (March, 1936), 67-83; "The California Overland Mail Route through Oklahoma," *The Chronicles of Oklahoma* IX (Sept., 1931), 300-317

Foster, William Omer, "The Career of Montfort Stokes in Oklahoma," *The Chronicles of Oklahoma* XVIII (March, 1940), 35-52

Franks, Kenny A., "An Analysis of the Confederate Treaties with the Five Civilized Tribes," *The Chronicles of Oklahoma* L (Winter, 1972-73), 458-474; "The Implementation of the Confederate Treaties with the Five Civilized Tribes," *The Chronicles of Oklahoma* LI (Spring, 1973), 21-33

Franzmann, Tom, "The Battle of Devil's Backbone Mountain," *The Chronicles of Oklahoma* LXII (Winter, 1984-85), 420-429; "The Final Campaign: The Confederate Offensive of 1864," *The Chronicles of Oklahoma* LXIII (Fall, 1985), 266-280

Freeman, Charles R., "The Battle of Honey Springs," *The Chronicles of Oklahoma* XIII (June, 1935), 154-168

Fritz, Henry E., "Humanitarian Rhetoric and Andrew Jackson's Indian Removal Policy," *The Chronicles of Oklahoma* LXXIX (Spring, 2001), 62-92

Gage, Duane, "Oklahoma: A Resettlement Area for Indians," *The Chronicles of Oklahoma* XLVII (Autumn, 1969), 282-298

Garrett, Kathleen, "Dartmouth Alumni In The Indian Territory," *The Chronicles of Oklahoma* XXXII (Summer, 1954), 123-142

Gettys, Marshall, "Historic Choctaw Pottery in the State Museum of History," *The Chronicles of Oklahoma* LXVII (Winter, 1989-1990), 414-425

Gibson, Arrell Morgan, "America's Exiles," *The Chronicles of Oklahoma* LIV (Spring, 1976), 3-16; "The Centennial Legacy of the General Allotment Act," *The Chronicles of Oklahoma LXV* (Fall, 1987), 228-252

Graebner, Norman Arthur, "Cattle Ranching in Eastern Oklahoma," *The Chronicles of Oklahoma* XXI (1943), 300-311; "Pioneer Indian Agriculture in Oklahoma," *The Chronicles of Oklahoma* XXIII (Autumn, 1945), 232-249; "Provincial Indian Society In Eastern Oklahoma," *The Chronicles of Oklahoma* XXIII (Winter, 1945-46), 323-338

Graham, A.M. Rev. William, "Lost Among the Choctaws during a Tour of the Indian Territory, 1845," *The Chronicles of Oklahoma* L (Summer, 1972), 226-234

Hale, Douglas, "Rehearsal for Civil War: The Texas Cavalry in the Indian Territory, 1861," *The Chronicles of Oklahoma* LXVIII (Fall, 1990), 228-265; "Texas Units in the Civil War," *The Chronicles of Oklahoma* LXVIII (Fall, 1990), 228-266

Hale, Duane K., "Uncle Sam's Warriors: American Indians in World War II," *The Chronicles of Oklahoma* LXIX (Winter, 1991-92), 408-429

Hall, Arthur H., "The Red Stick War," The *Chronicles of Oklahoma* XII (September, 1934), 264-293

Harbour, Emma Estill, "A Brief History of the Red River Country since 1803," *The Chronicles of Oklahoma* XVI (March, 1938), 58-88

Harper, Richard H., "The Missionary Work of the Reformed (Dutch) Church in America," The *Chronicles of Oklahoma* XVIII (Sept., 1940), 252-266

Hartshorne, Dr. George Ewing, "Skullyville and Its People in 1889," *The Chronicles of Oklahoma* XXVIII (Spring, 1950), 85-88

Hayes, Basil A., "Leroy Long-Teacher of Medicine," *The Chronicles of Oklahoma* XX (1942), 228-236

Hayes, Jerry G., "Ardent Spirits among the Chickasaws and Choctaws, 1816-1856," *The Chronicles of Oklahoma* LXIX (Fall, 1991), 294-307; "Liquor in the Indian Territory," *The Chronicles of Oklahoma* LXIX (Fall, 1991), 294-310

Heath, Gary N., "The First Federal Invasion of Indian Territory," *The Chronicles of Oklahoma* XLIV (Winter, 1966-67), 409-420

Hefley, A.D., "A Choctaw Landmark," *The Chronicles of Oklahoma* XII (Dec., 1934), 474-479; "Tobucksy County Courthouse," *The Chronicles of Oklahoma* XLVIII (Spring, 1970), 25-39

Heimstra, William H., "Presbyterian Mission Schools Among the Choctaws and Chickasaws, 1845-1861," *The Chronicles of Oklahoma* XXVII (Spring, 1949), 33-41

Hightower, Michael J., "Cattle, Coal, and Indian Land," *The Chronicles of Oklahoma* LXII (Spring, 1984), 4-26

Hofsommer, Donovan L., "Bawling Cattle and Barking Brakemen: An Oklahoma Railroad Memory," *The Chronicles of Oklahoma* LIV (Fall, 1976), 360-370

Holden, James Franklin, "The B.I.T.: The Story of an Adventure in Railroad Building," *The Chronicles of Oklahoma* XI (March, 1933), 637-666

Hood, Fred, "Twilight of the Confederacy in Indian Territory," *The Chronicles of Oklahoma* XLI (Winter, 1963-64), 425-442

Howell, Elmo, "President Jackson and William Faulkner's Choctaws," *The Chronicles of Oklahoma* XLV (Autumn, 1967), 252-259

Hudson, Peter James, "A Story of Choctaw Chiefs," *The Chronicles of Oklahoma* XVII (March, 1939), 7-16; "A Story of Choctaw Chiefs," *The Chronicles of Oklahoma* XVII (June, 1939), 192-211; "Choctaw Indian Dishes," *The Chronicles of Oklahoma* XVII (September, 1939), 333-35; "Recollections of Peter Hudson," *The Chronicles of Oklahoma* X (December, 1932), 503-519; "Reminiscences By Peter J. Hudson," *The Chronicles of Oklahoma* XII (Sept., 1934), 294-304; "Temperance Meeting Among the Choctaws," *The Chronicles of Oklahoma* XII (June, 1934), 130-132

Huggard, Christopher J., "Culture Mixing: Everyday Life on Missions among the Choctaws," *The Chronicles of Oklahoma* LXX (Winter, 1992-93), 432-450

Jackson, Joe C., "Summer Normals in Indian Territory after 1898," *The Chronicles of Oklahoma XXXVII* (Autumn, 1959), 307-329

Jacobson, O. B. and Jeanne d'Ucel, "Early Oklahoma Artists," *The Chronicles of Oklahoma* XXXI (Summer, 1953), 122-131

Johnson, Walter A., "Brief History of the Missouri-Kansas-Texas Railroad Lines," *The Chronicles of Oklahoma* XXIV (Autumn, 1946), 340-358

Jordan, H. Glenn, "Choctaw Colonization in Oklahoma," *The Chronicles of Oklahoma* LIV (Spring, 1976), 16-33

Kagey, J. N., "Jones Academy," Th*e Chronicles of Oklahoma* IV (December, 1926), 337-339

Kalisch, Philip A., "Ordeal of the Oklahoma Coal Miners: Coal Mine Disasters In The Sooner State, 1886-1945," *The Chronicles of Oklahoma* XLVIII (Autumn, 1970), 331-341; and Beatrice J., "Indian Territory Forts: Charnel Houses of the Frontier, 1839-1865," *The Chronicles of Oklahoma* L (Spring, 1972), 65-82

Kehoe, Sister Mary Urban, "The Educational Activities of Distinguished Missionaries among the Five Civilized Tribes," T*he Chronicles of Oklahoma* XXIV (Summer, 1946), 166-182

Kelleher, Michael, "The Removal of the Southeastern Indians: Historians Respond to the 1960s and the Trail of Tears," *The Chronicles of Oklahoma* LXXVIII (Fall, 2000), 346-353

Kensell, Lewis Anthony, "Phases of Reconstruction in the Choctaw Nation, 1865-1870," *The Chronicles of Oklahoma* XLVII (Summer, 1969), 138-154

Knight, Oliver, "Fifty Years of Choctaw Law," *The Chronicles of Oklahoma* XXXI (Spring, 1953), 76-96

Langley, Mrs. Lee J., "Malmaison, Palace In a Wilderness, Home of General LeFlore," *The Chronicles of Oklahoma* V (December, 1927), 371-380.

Lee, Keun Sang, "The Capture of the J. R. Williams," *The Chronicles of Oklahoma* LX (Spring, 1982), 22-33

Lemley, Harry J., "Letters of General McCulloch and Chief Ross in 1861," *The Chronicles of Oklahoma* XL (Autumn, 1962), 286-295

Lewis, Anna, "Diary of a Missionary to the Choctaws, 1860-1861," *The Chronicles of Oklahoma XVII* (December, 1939), 428-44; "Jane McCurtain," *The Chronicles of Oklahoma* XI (Sept. 1933), 1025-1034; ed., "Letters Regarding Choctaw Missions and Missionaries," *The Chronicles of Oklahoma* XVII (Sept., 1939), 275-285; "Nunih Waiya," *The Chronicles of Oklahoma* XVI June, 1938), 214-220

Littlefield, Daniel F., Jr., "Roost Robbers" and "Netters: Pigeoners in the Indian Territory," *The Chronicles of Oklahoma* XLVII (Summer, 1969), 154-159

Litton, Gaston L., "The Negotiations Leading To the Chickasaw-Choctaw Agreement, January 17, 1837," *The Chronicles of Oklahoma* XVII (December, 1939), 417-427

Locke, V. M., Jr., "Governor Cole," *The Chronicles of Oklahoma* IV (Sept, 1926), 228-232

Mackey, Alice Hurley, "Father Murrow: Civil War Period," *The Chronicles of Oklahoma* XII (March, 1934), 54-65

Maxwell, Amos, "The Sequoyah Convention," The *Chronicles of Oklahoma* XXVIII (Summer, 1950), 161-193; "The Sequoyah Convention, Part II," *The Chronicles of Oklahoma* XXVIII (Summer, 1950), 299-330

McMillan, Ethel, "First National Indian School: The Choctaw Academy," *The Chronicles of Oklahoma* XXVIII (Spring, 1950), 52-63; "Women Teachers In Oklahoma, 1820-1860," *The Chronicles of Oklahoma* XXVII (Spring, 1949), 33-41

McNeil, Kinneth, "Confederate Treaties with the Tribes of Indian Territory," *The Chronicles of Oklahoma* XLII (Winter, 1964-65), 408-421

Mener, Craig, "The Struggle for an East-West Railway into the Indian Territory, 1870-1882," *The Chronicles of Oklahoma* XLVII (Spring, 1969), 560-582

Meserve, John Bartlett, "Chief Allen Wright," *The Chronicles of Oklahoma* XIX (Dec., 1941), 314-322; "Chief Benjamin Franklin Smallwood and Chief Jefferson Gardner," *The Chronicles of Oklahoma* XIX (Sept. 1941), 213-220; "Chief Coleman Cole," *The Chronicles of Oklahoma* XIV (March, 1936), 9-31; "Chief George Hudson and Chief Samuel Garland,"

The Chronicles of Oklahoma XX (1942), 9-18; "Chief Gilbert Wesley Dukes," *The Chronicles of Oklahoma* XVIII (March, 1940), 52-59; "Chief Wilson Nathaniel Jones," *The Chronicles of Oklahoma* XIV (Dec., 1936), 419-433; "The Indian Removal Message of President Jackson," *The Chronicles of Oklahoma* XIII (March, 1935), 63-67; "The McCurtains," *The Chronicles of Oklahoma* XIII (Sept., 1935), 297-315.

Michalicka, Brother John, "First Catholic Church in Indian Territory, 1872, St. Patrick's Church At Atoka," *The Chronicles of Oklahoma* L (Winter, 1972-73), 479-486

Miller, Lona Eaton, "Wheelock Mission," *The Chronicles of Oklahoma* XXIX (Autumn, 1951), 314-324

Milligan, James C. and L. David Norris, "A Connecticut Yankee in the Indian Territory," *The Chronicles of Oklahoma* LXVIII (Fall, 1990), 266-275;"The Last Choctaw Execution," *The Chronicles of Oklahoma* LXXIII (Winter, 1995-96), 386-404; "William H. Emory and Fort Arbuckle," *The Chronicles of Oklahoma* LXIX (Fall, 1991), 256-282

Moore, Jessie Randolph, "The Five Great Indian Nations," *The Chronicles of Oklahoma* XXIX (Autumn, 1951), 324-337

Morgan, James F., "The Choctaw Warrants of 1863," *The Chronicles of Oklahoma* LVII (Spring, 1979), 55-67

Morris, Cheryl Haun, "Choctaw and Chickasaw Indian Agents, 1831-1874," *The Chronicles of Oklahoma* L (Winter, 1972-73), 415-437

Morrison, James D., "News for the Choctaws," *The Chronicles of Oklahoma* XXVII (Summer, 1949), 207-222; "Note on Abolitionism in the Choctaw Nation," *The Chronicles of Oklahoma* XXXVIII (Spring, 1960), 78-85; "Notes From the Northern Standard, 1842-1849," *The Chronicles of Oklahoma* XIX (Sept., 1941), 269-284; "Problems In the Industrial Progress and Development of the Choctaw Nation, 1865-1907," *The Chronicles of Oklahoma* XXXII (Spring, 1954), 70-92; "The Union Pacific, Southern Branch," *The Chronicles of Oklahoma* XIV (June, 1936), 173-188; ed., "Travis G. Wright and the Leavenworth Expedition," *The Chronicles of Oklahoma* XXV (Spring, 1947), 7-14

Morrison, W. B., "A Visit to Old Fort Washita," *The Chronicles of Oklahoma* VII (June, 1929), 174-179; "Colbert Ferry on Red River, Chickasaw Nation, Indian Territory," *The Chronicles of Oklahoma* XVI (Sept., 1938), 302-314; "Fort Towson," *The Chronicles of Oklahoma* VIII (March, 1930), 226-232; "Fort Washita," *The Chronicles of Oklahoma* V (June, 1927), 251-259; "Old Philadelphia Baptist Church," *The Chronicles of Oklahoma* XIII (Sept., 1935), 266-272; "The Choctaw Mission of the American Board of Commissioners For Foreign Missions," *The Chronicles of Oklahoma* IV (June, 1926), 166-183; "The Saga of Skullyville," *The Chronicles of Oklahoma* XVI (June, 1938), 234-240

Morton, Ohland, "Confederate Government Relations With The Five Civilized Tribes," *The Chronicles of Oklahoma* XXXI (Summer, 1953), 189-205; "Confederate Government Relations With The Five Civilized Tribes, Part II," *The Chronicles of Oklahoma* XXXI (Autumn, 1953), 299-323

Murphy, Justin D. "Wheelock Female Seminary, 1842-1861," *The Chronicles of Oklahoma* LXIX (Spring, 1991), 248-262

Nesbitt, Paul, "J. J. McAlester," *The Chronicles of Oklahoma* XI (June, 1933), 758-764

Nieberding, Velma, "St. Agnes School of the Choctaws," *The Chronicles of Oklahoma* XXXIII (Summer, 1955), 183-193

Nolen, Curtis L., "The Okmulgee Constitution: A Step toward Indian Self-Determination," *The Chronicles of Oklahoma* LVIII (Fall, 1980), 264-283

Overbeck, Ruth Ann, "Colbert's Ferry," *The Chronicles of Oklahoma* LVII (Summer, 1979), 212-224

Parke, Frank E. and J. W. LeFlore, "Some of Our Choctaw Neighborhood Schools," *The Chronicles of Oklahoma* IV (June, 1926), 149-152

Parman, Donald L., "Wholly Occupied with My Special Work: Reverend William Graham's Stay At Fort Coffee and New Hope, 1845-47," *The Chronicles of Oklahoma* LXXVI (Fall, 1998), 262-281

Perry, Mrs. A. E., "Colonel Forbis LeFlore, Pioneer and Statesman," *The Chronicles of Oklahoma* VI (March, 1928), 75-88

Pickett, Ben Collins, "William L. McClellan, Choctaw Agent, West," *The Chronicles of Oklahoma* XXXIX (Spring, 1961), 42-53

Powell, John C., "Oklahoma and the Medal of Honor," *The Chronicles of Oklahoma* LXXIV (Fall, 1996), 302-331

Prucha, Francis Paul, "The Board of Indian Commissioners and The Delegates of the Five Tribes," *The Chronicles of Oklahoma* LVI (Fall, 1978), 247-265

Rampp, Larry C., "Negro Activity in Indian Territory, 1863-65," *The Chronicles of Oklahoma* XLVII (Spring, 1969), 531-560

Riggs, W. C., "Bits of Interesting History," *The Chronicles of Oklahoma* VII (March, 1929), 148-152

Rister, C. C., "A Federal Experiment in Southern Plains Indian Relations, 1835-1845," *The Chronicles of Oklahoma* XIV (Dec., 1936), 434-455

Russell, Orpha, "Ekvn-Hv'Luruce: Site of Oklahoma's First Civil War Battle," *The Chronicles of Oklahoma* XXIX (Winter, 1951-52), 401-408

Scott, Douglas D., "Archeological and Historical Investigations at the Fort Towson Powder Magazine," *The Chronicles of Oklahoma* LIII (Winter, 1975-76), 516-528

Self, Nancy Hope, "The Building of the Railroads in the Cherokee Nation," The *Chronicles of Oklahoma* XLIX (Summer, 1971), 180-206

Semple, W. F. and Winnie Lewis Gravitt, "Grady Lewis, Choctaw Attorney," The *Chronicles of Oklahoma* XXXIII (Autumn, 1955), 301-306

Sewell, Steve, "Amongst the Damp: The Dangerous Profession of Coal Mining in Oklahoma, 1870-1935," *The Chronicles of Oklahoma* LXX (Spring, 1992), 66-83

Shawner, Lona, "Stanley Explores Oklahoma," *The Chronicles of Oklahoma* XXII (Autumn, 1944), 259-279

Shirk, George H., "Confederate Postal System in the Indian Territory," *The Chronicles of Oklahoma* XLI (Summer, 1963), 160-219; "Mail Call at Fort Washita," *The Chronicles of Oklahoma* XXXIII (Spring, 1955), 14-35; "Malmaison Today," *The Chronicles of Oklahoma* XLII (Spring, 1964), 74-81; "The Place of Indian Territory In The Command Structure of The Civil

War," *The Chronicles of Oklahoma* XLV (Winter, 1967-68), 464-472

Shoemaker, Arthur, "The Battle of Chustenahlah," *The Chronicles of Oklahoma* XXXVIII (Summer, 1960), 180-185

Smith, Joy McDougal, "Alice Lee Elliott Memorial Academy: A School for Choctaw Freedmen," *The Chronicles of Oklahoma* LXXII (Fall, 1994), 264-280

Spalding, Arminta Scott, "From the Natchez Tract to Oklahoma: Development of Christian Civilization among the Choctaws, 1800-1860," *The Chronicles of Oklahoma* XLV (Spring, 1967), 3-25

Stein, Gary C., "Indian Removal As Seen By European Travelers," *The Chronicles of Oklahoma* LI (Winter, 1973-74), 399-411 XXVIII (Autumn, 1950), 226-231

Stoddard, Francis R., "Amiel Weeks Whipple," *The Chronicles of Oklahoma* XXVIII (Autumn, 1950), 226-231

Strickland, Rex W., "Establishment of "Old" Miller County, Arkansas Territory," *The Chronicles of Oklahoma* XVIII (June, 1940), 154-170; "Miller County, Arkansas Territory: The Frontier That Men Forgot," *The Chronicles of Oklahoma* XVIII (March, 1940), 12-35; "Miller County, Arkansas Territory: The Frontier That Men Forgot, Chapter III," *The Chronicles of Oklahoma* XIX (June, 1941), 37-54

Swanton, John R., ed., "The Choctaw Indians In the Middle of the Nineteenth Century by John Edwards," *The Chronicles of Oklahoma* X (Sept., 1932), 392-425

Syndergaard, Rex, "The Final Move of the Choctaws," *The Chronicles of Oklahoma* LII (Summer, 1974), 207-220

Thoburn, Joseph B., "The Tropical and Subtropical Origin of Mound Builder Cultures," *The Chronicles of Oklahoma* XVI (March, 1938), 97-117

Trickett, Dean, "The Civil War In The Indian Territory," *The Chronicles of Oklahoma* XVII (Sept., 1939), 315-327; "The Civil War In The Indian Territory, 1861," *The Chronicles of Oklahoma* XVII (Dec., 1939), 401-412; "The Civil War In The Indian Territory, 1861," *The Chronicles of Oklahoma* XVIII (June, 1940), 142-153; "The Civil War In The Indian Territory, 1861," *The*

Chronicles of Oklahoma XVIII (Sept., 1940), 266-280; "The Civil War In The Indian Territory, 1862," *The Chronicles of Oklahoma* XIX (Dec., 1941), 381-397

Underhill, Lonnie E. and Daniel F. Littlefield, "Wild Turkeys in Oklahoma," *The Chronicles of Oklahoma* XLVIII (Winter, 1970-71), 376-389; and John H. Battle, "Classification of Oklahoma Indian Tribes: Language Stocks, Population, and Locations," *The Chronicles of Oklahoma* XLVIII (Summer, 1970), 197-209

Ward, Mary Jane, "Now the Wolf Has Come: The Civilian Civil War in the Indian Territory," *The Chronicles of Oklahoma* LXXI (Spring, 1993), 64-87

Warde, Mary Jane, "Fight For Survival: The Indian Response to the Boomer Movement," *The Chronicles of Oklahoma* LXVII (Spring, 1989), 30-51

Wells, Samuel J. "Rum, Skins, and Powder: A Choctaw Interpreter and the Treaty of Mount Dexter," *The Chronicles of Oklahoma* LXI (Winter, 1983-84), 422-429

West, Ruth Tenison, "Pushmataha's Travels," *The Chronicles of Oklahoma* XXXVII (Summer, 1959), 162-175

Wile, Ruby, "Yakni Achukma, 'The School with a Soul,'" *The Chronicles of Oklahoma* LXXX (Winter, 2003-03), 410-435

Willey, William J., "The Second Federal Invasion of Indian Territory," *The Chronicles of Oklahoma* XLIV (Winter, 1966-67), 420-431

Williams, Robert L., "Peter James Hudson, 1861-1938," *The Chronicles of Oklahoma* XVII (March, 1939), 3-6; "Tams Bixby, 1855-1922," *The Chronicles of Oklahoma* XIX (Sept., 1941), 205-213

Wilson, T. Paul, "Delegates of the Five Civilized Tribes to the Confederate Congress," *The Chronicles of Oklahoma* LIII (Fall, 1975), 353-367

Wilson, Walt, "Freedmen In Indian Territory During Reconstruction," *The Chronicles of Oklahoma* XLIX (Summer, 1971), 230-245

Witcher, Esther, "Territorial Magazines," *The Chronicles of Oklahoma* XXIX (Winter, 1952-52), 484-499

Wright, Allen, "Wheelock Seminary," *The Chronicles of Oklahoma* I (Oct., 1921), 117-121

Wright, J. B., "Dedication Speech," *The Chronicles of Oklahoma* XXXVI (Autumn, 1958), 324-326; "Ranching In The Choctaw and Chickasaw Nations," *The Chronicles of Oklahoma* XXXIII

(Autumn, 1959), 294-300

Wright, Muriel H., "A Brief Review of the Life of Doctor Eliphalet Nott Wright, 1852-1932," *The Chronicles of Oklahoma* X (June, 1932), 267-286; "American Corn Dishes," *The Chronicles of Oklahoma* XXXVI (Summer, 1958), 155-167; "A Report To The General Council of the Indian Territory Meeting at Okmulgee in 1873," *The Chronicles of Oklahoma* XXXIV (Spring, 1956), 2-7; "Brief Outline of the Choctaws and the Chickasaw Nations in the Indian Territory, 1820-1860" *The Chronicles of Oklahoma* VII (December, 1929), 388-413; "Civil War Report on the Battle of Round Mountain," *The Chronicles of Oklahoma* XXIX (Winter, 1961-62), 352-398; "Contributions of the Indian People to Oklahoma," *The Chronicles of Oklahoma* XIV (June, 1936), 156-161; "Early River Navigation in Oklahoma," *The Chronicles of Oklahoma* VIII (March, 1930), 65-88; "General Douglas H. Cooper, C.S.A.," *The Chronicles of Oklahoma* XXXII (Summer, 1954), 142-185; "Historic Places on the Old Stage Line from Fort Smith to Red River," *The Chronicles of Oklahoma* XI (June, 1933), 798-822; "Historic Spots In The Vicinity of Tuskahoma," The Chronicles of Oklahoma IX (March, 1931), 27-43; "Lee F. Harkins, Choctaw," *The Chronicles of Oklahoma* XXXVII (Autumn, 1959), 285-288; "Notes on Perryville," *The Chronicles of Oklahoma* VIII (June, 1930), 146-147; "Old Boggy Depot," *The Chronicles of Oklahoma* V (March, 1927), 4-17; "Official Seals of the Five Civilized Tribes," *The Chronicles of Oklahoma* XVIII (Sept., 1940), 357-376; "Organization of Counties in the Choctaw and Chickasaw Nations," *The Chronicles of Oklahoma* VIII (Sept., 1930), 315-334; "Seals of the Five Civilized Tribes," *The Chronicles of Oklahoma* XL (Autumn, 1962), 214-219; "Some Geographic Names of French Origin in Oklahoma," *The Chronicles of Oklahoma* VII (June, 1929), 188-193; "Tewah Hokay," *The Chronicles of Oklahoma* XXXIII (Winter, 1955-56), 434-440; "The Butterfield Overland Mail One Hundred Years Ago," *The Chronicles of Oklahoma* XXXV (Spring, 1957), 55-72; "The Great Seal of the Choctaw Nation," *The Chronicles of Oklahoma* XXXIII (Winter, 1955), 430-434; "The Removal of the Choctaws To The Indian Territory, 1830-1833" *The Chronicles of Oklahoma* VI (June, 1928), 103-128; "Tryphena," *The Chronicles of Oklahoma* IX (June, 1931), 180-194; "Wapanucka Academy, Chickasaw Nation," *The Chronicles of Oklahoma XII* (Dec., 1934), 402-431

Wright, Muriel H. and LeRoy H. Fischer, "Civil War Sites in Oklahoma," *The Chronicles of Oklahoma* XLIV (Summer, 1966), 158-215

Wright, Muriel H. and George H. Shirk, "Artist Mollhausen in Oklahoma, 1853," *The Chronicles of Oklahoma* XXXI (Winter, 1953-54), 392-441; "The Journal of Lieutenant A. W. Whipple," *The Chronicles of Oklahoma* XXVIII (Autumn, 1950), 235-283

Wright, Peter M., "John Collier and the Oklahoma Indian Welfare Act of 1936," *The Chronicles of Oklahoma* L (Autumn, 1972), 347-372

Young, Marjorie Hall, "Stars in a Dark Night: The Education of Indian Youth at Choctaw Academy," *The Chronicles of Oklahoma* LXXV (Fall, 1997), 280-306.

BOOKS

Abel, Annie Heloise. *The American Indian and the end of the Confederacy, 1863-1866* Reprint, Lincoln: University of Nebraska Press, 1993. *The American Indian as Participant in the Civil War* Cleveland: Arthur H. Clarke Co., 1919. *The American Indian Under Reconstruction* Cleveland: The Arthur H. Clark Company, 1925

Anderson, Edwin Alexander, (ed.). *Choctaw English Dictionary* Oklahoma City: Central Choctaw Council, Inc., 1978

Baird, W. David, *The Choctaw People* Phoenix: Indian Tribal Series, 1973. *Peter Pitchlynn: Chief of the Choctaw* Norman: University of Oklahoma Press, 1972

Barker, Maxine W. *The Third Arrow: A Story of Moshulatubbee, Choctaw Chief* Carrollton, Miss.: Pioneer Publishing Company, 1997

Bearss, Ed and Arrell M. Gibson. *Fort Smith* Norman: University of Oklahoma Press, 1969

Belvin, Harry J.W. *Choctaw Tribal Structure and Achievement, August*

18, 1948 to August 25, 1975 Durant, Oklahoma: SOSU Choctaw Bilingual Education Program, 1981

Benson, Henry C. *Life among the Choctaw Indians and Sketches of the Southwest* New York: Johnson Reprint Corporation, 1970

Bernstein, Alison R. *American Indians and World War II* Norman: University of Oklahoma Press, 1991.

Billard, Jules B., (ed.). *The World of the American Indian* Washington, DC: National Geographic Society, 1974

Blitz, John Howard. *Ancient Chiefdoms of the Tombigbee* Tuscaloosa: The University of Alabama Press, 1993

Bourne, Edward Gaylord, (ed.). *Narrative of the Career of Hernando de Soto* New York: Allerton, 1922 2 vols.

Britten, Thomas A. *American Indians in World War I: At Home and at War* Albuquerque: University of New Mexico Press, 1997

Brown, Charles E. and Will T. Nelson (eds.). *Choctaw Social and Ceremonial Life* Oklahoma City: Oklahoma Choctaw Council, Inc., 1983

Brown, Douglas Summers. *The Catawba Indians: The People of the River* Columbia: University of South Carolina Press, 1966

Burton, Arthur T. *Black, Red, and Deadly: Black and Indian Gunfighters of the Indian Territory* Austin: Eakin Press, 1991

Bushnell, David I., Jr. *The Choctaws of Bayou Lacomb, St. Tammany Parish, Louisiana* Washington: Government Printing Office, 1909

Carson, James Taylor. *Searching for the Bright Path: The Mississippi Choctaws from Prehistory to Removal* Lincoln: University of Nebraska Press, 1999

Carter, W.A. *McCurtain County and Southeast Oklahoma: History, Biography Statistics* Idabel, Ok: Tribune Publishing, 1923

Chambers, Henry E. *Mississippi Valley Beginnings* New York: G. P. Putnam's Sons, 1922

Champagne, Duane. *Social Order and Political Change: Constitutional Governments among the Cherokee, the Choctaw, the Chickasaw, and the Creek* Stanford: Stanford University Press, 1992

Chastaine, Capt. Ben F. *The Story of the 36th* Oklahoma City: Harlow Publishing Co., 1920

Coleman, Louis. *Cyrus Byington: Missionary and Linguist* Kearney,

Nebraska: Morris Publishing, 1996
Cornish, Dudley Taylor. *The Sable Arm: Negro Troops in the Union Army, 1861-1865* New York: Longmans, Green and Co., 1956
Cotterill, R.S. *The Southern Indians: The Story of the Civilized Tribes before Removal* Norman: University of Oklahoma Press, 1954
Cottrell, Steve. *Civil War in the Indian Territory* Gretna, La.: Pelican Publishing Company, Inc, 1995
Cushman, Horatio Bardwell. *History of the Choctaw, Chickasaw, and Natchez Indians* Reprint, Norman: University of Oklahoma Press, 1999
Dale, Edward Everett and Gaston Little. *Cherokee Cavaliers* Norman: University of Oklahoma Press, 1939.
Daniels, Jonathan. *The Devil's Backbone: The Story of the Natchez Trace* New York: McGraw-Hill Book Co., Inc., 1962.
Danky, James P. (ed.). *Native American Periodicals and Newspapers 1828-1982* Westport, Connecticut: Greenwood Press, 1984.
Davis, M.B. (ed.). *Native Americans in the Twentieth Century* New York: Garland Publishing, 1994
Debo, Angie. *And Still the Waters Run* Norman: University of Oklahoma Press, 1940. A *History of the Indians of the United States* Norman: University of Oklahoma Press, 1970. *The Rise and fall of the Choctaw Republic* Norman: University of Oklahoma Press, 1934. *The Road to Disappearance* Norman: University of Oklahoma Press, 1941
Densmore, Frances. *Choctaw Music* New York: De Capo Press, 1972
DeRosier, Arthur H., Jr. *The Removal of the Choctaw Indians* New York: Harper and Row, Publishers, 1970
Downing, Todd. *Cultural Traits of the Choctaws* Durant, Oklahoma: The Choctaw Bilingual Education Program, 1973
Dudley, C. E. *"Days Gone By"* Antlers, Ok: Pushmataha County Historical Society, 1988
Duncan, Robert Lipscomb. *Reluctant General: The Life and Times of Albert Pike* New York: E. P. Dutton & Co., Inc., 1961
Durant, A.R. *Constitution and Laws of the Choctaw Nation* Dallas: Johnson F. Worley, Printer and Publisher, 1894
Durant, Randle. *Footsteps of the Choctaws* Durant, Ok: Private Printing, 1982. *"Footsteps" of a Durant Choctaw* Talihina, Ok:

Private Printing, 2002

Edmunds, R. David. *Tecumseh and the Quest for Indian Leadership* Boston: Little, Brown and Company, 1984

Faiman-Silva, Sandra. *Choctaws At The Crossroads: The Political Economy of Class and Culture in the Oklahoma Timber Region* Lincoln: University of Nebraska Press, 1997

Farb, Peter. *Man's Rise to Civilization as Shown by the Indians of North America From Primeval Time to the Coming of the Industrial State* New York: E. P. Dutton & Co., Inc., 1968

Fischer, LeRoy H., (ed.). *The Civil War in Indian Territory* Los Angeles: Lorrin I. Morrison, 1974

Fleck-O'Keefe, Marlynn Ann. *Fort Towson Indian Territory: A Link to the West* Fort Towson: Lakeside Publications, 1997

Folsom, Joseph P. *Constitution and Laws of the Choctaw Nation* Chahta Tamaha: William P. Lyon & Son, Printers and Publishers, 1869

Foreman, Carolyn Thomas. *Oklahoma Imprints, 1835-1907* Norman: University of Oklahoma Press, 1936

Foreman, Grant. *Advancing the Frontier* Norman: University of Oklahoma Press, 1933. (ed.). *A Traveler in Indian Territory: The Journal of Ethan Allen Hitchcock, Late Major General in the United States Army* Cedar Rapids: The Torch Press, 1934. *Indians and Pioneers: The Story of the American Southwest before 1830* Norman: University of Oklahoma Press, 1936. *The Five Civilized Tribes* Norman: University of Oklahoma Press, 1934. *The Last Trek of the Indians* Chicago: The University of Chicago, 1945. *The Removal: The Emigration of the Five Civilized Tribes of Indians* Norman: University of Oklahoma Press, 1932

Franks, Kenny A. *Citizen Soldiers: Oklahoma's National Guard* Norman: University of Oklahoma Press, 1983

Galloway, Patricia. *Choctaw Genesis* Lincoln, Neb.: University of Nebraska Press, 1995

Gibson, Arrell Morgan. *America's Exiles: Indian Colonization in Oklahoma* Ok. City, Oklahoma: Oklahoma Historical Society, 1976. *The Chickasaws* Norman: University of Oklahoma Press, 1971

Gregory, Jack and Rennard Strickland. *Choctaw Spirit Tales* Muskogee,

Ok: Indian Heritage Association, 1972

Guyton, Pearl Vivian. *Our Mississippi* Austin, Texas: The Steck Company, 1952

Haag, Marcia and Henry Willis. *Choctaw Language & Culture: Chahta Anumpa* Norman: University of Oklahoma Press, 2001

Hauptman, Laurence M. *Between Two Fires: American Indians in the Civil War* New York: The Free Press, 1995

Hofsommer, Donovan L., (ed.). *Railroads in Oklahoma* Ok City: Oklahoma Historical Society, 1977

Hogue, Sammy D. *The Goodland Indian Orphanage: A Story of Christian Missions* Goodland, Oklahoma: The Goodland Indian Orphanage Publishers, 1940

Holcomb, Raymond L. *Father Murrow* Atoka, Oklahoma: The Atoka County Historical Society, 1994

Howard, James H. and Victoria Lindsay Levine. *Choctaw Music and Dance* Norman: University of Oklahoma Press, 1990

Hudson, Charles and Carmen Chaves Tesser (eds.). *The Forgotten Centuries: Indians and Europeans in the American South, 1521-1704* Athens: The University of Georgia Press, 1994

Hyde, George E. *Indians of the Woodlands* Norman: University of Oklahoma Press, 1962

Imon, Frances. *Smoke Signals from Indian Territory* Vol. II. Wolfe City, Texas: Henington Publishing Company, 1977

Iverson, Peter. *When Indians Became Cowboys: Native Peoples and Cattle Ranching in the American West* Norman: University of Oklahoma Press, 1994

Jordan, H. Glenn and Thomas H. Holm, (eds.). *Indian Leaders: Oklahoma's First Statesmen* Oklahoma City, Oklahoma: Oklahoma Historical Society, 1979

Josephy, Alvin M., Jr. *The Indian Heritage of America* Boston: Houghton Mifflin Company, 1968

Joyce, Davis D. *An Oklahoma I Had Never Seen Before* Norman: University of Oklahoma Press, 1994

Kappler, Charles J. (ed.). *Indian Treaties, 1778-1883* New York: Interland Publishing Inc., 1973

Kidwell, Clara Sue. *Choctaws and Missionaries in Mississippi, 1818-1918* Norman: University of Oklahoma Press, 1995

Kidwell, Clara Sue and Charles Roberts. *The Choctaws: A Critical*

Bibliography Bloomington: Indiana University Press, 1980

Lafferty, R. A. *Okla Hannali* New York: Doubleday & Co., Inc., 1972

La Harpe, Jean-Baptiste Benard de. *The Historical Journal of the Establishment of the French in Louisiana* trans. by Joan Cain and Virginia Koenig Lafayette, La.: University of Southwest Louisiana, 1971

La Vere, David. *Contrary Neighbors: Southern Plains and Removed Indians in Indian Territory* Norman: University of Oklahoma Press, 2000

LeMaster, Arlene. *Eastern Oklahoma Indians and Pioneers: Choctaw Nation, Indian Territory* 3 vols., Poteau, Ok: Family Heritage Resources, 1992-93

Lewis, Anna. *Chief Pushmataha: American Patriot* New York: Exposition Press, 1959

Littlefield, Jr., Daniel F., and James W. Parins. *American Indian and Alaska Native Newspapers and Periodicals, 1925-1970* New York: Greenwood Press, 1986

MacCreary, Henry. *A Story of Durant: Queen of Three Valleys* Durant: The Democrat Printing Company, 1946

Martin, Novella Goodman. *Choctaw Little Folk* San Antonio, Texas: The Naylor Company, 1970

Masterson, V.V. *The Katy Railroad and the Last Frontier*. Norman: University of Oklahoma Press, 1952

McKee, Jesse O. *The Choctaws* New York: Chelsea House Publishers, 1989

McKee, Jesse O. and Jon A. Schlenker. *The Choctaws: Cultural Evolution of a Native American Tribe* Jackson: University Press of Mississippi, 1980

Milanich, Jerald T. and Susan Milbrath. *First Encounters: Spanish Explorations in the Caribbean and the United States, 1492-1570* Gainesville: University of Florida Press, 1989

Milligan, Dorothy (ed.). *The Indian Way: The Choctaws* Durant, Ok: Title IV, Office of Indian Education, 1977

Milligan, James C., L. David Norris, and Ann Vanmeter. *Durant, 1872-1990* Durant: Bryan County Heritage Association, 1990

Mills, Lawrence. *The Lands of the Five Civilized Tribes* St. Louis: The F. H. Thomas Law Book Company, 1919

Morgan, H. Wayne and Anne Hodges Morgan. *Oklahoma* New York:

W.W. Norton & Co., 1977

Morris, John W., Charles R. Goins, and Edwin C. McReynolds. *Historical Atlas of Oklahoma* Norman: University of Oklahoma Press, 1976

Morrison, James D. *The Social History of the Choctaw Nation: 1865-1907* ed. by James C. Milligan and L. David Norris Durant, Oklahoma: Choctaw Nation of Oklahoma, 1987

Morrison, W.B. *Military Posts and Camps in Oklahoma* Ok City: Harlow Publishing Co., 1936

Nabokov, Peter. *Native American Testimony* New York: Viking Penguin, USA, Inc., 1978

Naire, Thomas. *Naire's Muskogean Journals: The 1708 Expedition to the Mississippi River* Jackson: University Press of Mississippi, 1988

Norris, L. David. *Southeastern Oklahoma State University since 1909: Vol. 1* Durant, Oklahoma: Mesa Publishing Company, 1986

Norris, L. David and James C. Milligan and Odie B. Faulk. *William H. Emory: Soldier, Scientist* Tucson: The University of Arizona Press, 1998

O'Brien, Sharon. *American Indian Tribal Governments* Norman: University of Oklahoma Press, 1989

Perdue, Theda. *Nations Remembered: An Oral History of the Chickasaws, Choctaws, Creeks, and Seminoles in Oklahoma, 1865-1907* Norman: University of Oklahoma Press, 1993

Peterson, Jr., John H. *A Choctaw Source Book* New York: Garland Publishing, Inc., 1985

Poulin, Betty Jeanne Ward. *Choctaw Heritage* Heavener, Ok: Choctaw Heritage, 1981

Prucha, Francis Paul. *American Indian Policy in the Formative Years: The Indian Trade and Intercourse Acts 1790-1834* Lincoln: University of Nebraska Press, 1962

Rafferty, Milton D. and John C. Catau. *The Ouachita Mountains* Norman: University of Oklahoma Press, 1991

Reeves, Carolyn Keller (ed.). *The Choctaw Before Removal* Jackson: University Press of Mississippi, 1985

Ross, Marvin C. *George Catlin* Norman: University of Oklahoma Press, 1979

Satz, Ronald N. *American Indian Policy in the Jacksonian Era* Lincoln:

University of Nebraska Press, 1975

Shetrone, Henry Clyde. *The Mound Builders* New York: D. Appleton and Co., 1930

Strickland, Rennard. *The Indians in Oklahoma* Norman: University of Oklahoma Press, 1980

Taylor, Colin F. and William C. Sturtevant. *The Native Americans* New York: Salamander Books Ltd., 1996

Tocqueville, Alexis de. *Democracy in America* ed. J. P. Mayers trans. George Lawrence Garden City, N.Y.: Anchor Books, 1969

Townsend, Kenneth William. *World War II and the American Indian* Albuquerque: University of New Mexico Press, 2000

Underhill, R.M. *Red Man's America* Chicago: The University of Chicago Press, 1953

Wells, Samuel J. and Roseanna Tubby. *After Removal: The Choctaw In Mississippi* Jackson: University Press of Mississippi, 1986

West, Dorothy Arnote. *Pushmataha County: The Early Years* Antlers, Ok: Dorothy Arnote West, 2002

White, Richard. *The Roots of Dependency: Subsistence, Environment, and Social Change Among the Choctaws, Pawnees, and Navajos* Lincoln: University Of Nebraska Press, 1983

Wilson, Marie, (ed.). *Tales of Atoka County Heritage* Atoka: The Atoka County Historical Society, 1983

Wiltshire, Betty C. *Register of Choctaw Emigrants to the West* Carrollton, Miss.: Olde Times Publishing Co., 1993

Wise, Lu Celia. *Indian Cultures of Oklahoma* Ok City, Ok: State Department of Education, 1978

Wissler, Clark. *Indians of the United States* Garden City: Doubleday and Co., Inc., 1941

Wright, Jr., J. Leitch. *The Only Land They Knew: The Tragic Story of the American Indians in the Old South* New York: The Free Press, 1981

Wright, Muriel H. *A Guide to The Indian Tribes of Oklahoma* Norman: University of Oklahoma Press, 1951

Young, Mary Elizabeth. *Redskins, Ruffleshirts, and Rednecks* Norman: University of Oklahoma Press, 1961

UNPUBLISHED WORKS AND DISSERTATIONS

Blackburn, Bobby L. "Oklahoma Law Enforcement Since 1803." Unpublished Ph. D. Dissertation, Oklahoma State University, Stillwater, Oklahoma, 1976

Goss, Charles Wayne. "The French and the Choctaw Indians, 1700-1763." Unpublished Ph. D. Dissertation, Texas Tech University, Lubbock, Texas, 1977

Lawless, Beth. "Choctaw Code Talkers in World War I." Unpublished research project, Rattan Elementary School, Rattan, Oklahoma, 1997

Lewis, Bessie Kate. "A History of Education Among the Choctaw and Chickasaw Indians of Oklahoma." Unpublished Master's thesis, University of Texas, Austin, 1927

Morrison, James D. "Schools for the Choctaws," Durant, Oklahoma: Choctaw Bilingual Program, 1975, "Social History of the Choctaws, 1865-1905." Unpublished Ph. D. Dissertation, University of Oklahoma, Norman, Oklahoma, 1951

Pipkin, William Philip. "Some of My Choctaw Kinfolks." Unpublished manuscript. Comp. Lila Douglas Swink. Goodland, Ok: Choctaw County Genealogical Society, 1992

Stevenson, George William. "The Hymnody of the Choctaw Indian of Oklahoma." Doctoral Dissertation to the School of Church Music, The Southern Baptist Theological Seminary, Louisville, Kentucky, 1977

Index

D

E

F

G

H

I

J

M

N

O

P

Q

R

S

U

V

W

Y

Z